The Kingdon Field Guide to
African Mammals

THE KINGDON
FIELD GUIDE TO
AFRICAN MAMMALS

Jonathan Kingdon

HELM

First published by Academic Press, 1997
Reprinted with corrections, 2001
Reprinted by Christopher Helm, 2003

Published by Christopher Helm, an imprint of A&C Black Publishers Ltd.,
37 Soho Square, London W1D 3QZ

ISBN 0-7136-6513-0

A CIP catalogue record for this book is available from the British Library.

Typeset by Selwood Systems, Midsomer Norton
Printed in Great Britain by Butler and Tanner, Frome, Somerset

10 9 8 7 6 5 4 3

PREFACE AND ACKNOWLEDGEMENTS

The motivation and impetus to prepare a guide to the mammals of a continent came from a mix of immediate and more distant influences. My parents and naturalists such as Bill Moore–Gilbert, Willoughby Lowe, Mtemi Senge Masembe and Fairfax Bell illuminated a nomadic youth in Tanganyika. This led on to a more disciplined interest in Natural History and a Darwinian outlook on life. Reg Moreau and Desmond Vesey–FitzGerald were early influences while L.S.B. Leakey, Sir Julian Huxley, Peter Miller, Leonard Beadle and Alan Walker were among those who helped and provoked me into compiling an Evolutionary Atlas of African Mammals that was an essential precursor to this book. Indeed, since its publication there has been continuous pressure, from friends and publishers alike, to condense the text and enlarge the range of that work to embrace a continental scope.

A decisive influence on this project has come from my family, especially my sons. Zachary read, processed, discussed and helped refine the entire text while Rungwe pushed me into taking the first plunge. Elena has selflessly supported a lifetime of research on mammals.

I am indebted to many institutions for their support over the years, from Makerere University in Uganda and Oxford University in England to briefer or less formal associations with Kyoto University, Japan, CSIRO Australia, various museums both within and outside Africa, Wildlife Departments, National Parks and numerous Universities. I owe some independence of mind and movement to all those who have purchased my paintings, drawings, prints, sculptures and books.

The contents of this Guide are drawn from observations made in various parts of Africa, often in the company of friends and colleagues. They are also compiled from publications, correspondence and conversation with more people than can be acknowledged by name but some have had a more direct role. Morris Gosling, Colin Groves, David Pye, Simon Bearder, Alan Root, David Macdonald, Claudio Sillero, Patrick Duncan, Steve Gartlan, Mark Stanley Price, John Phillipson, Redmond O'Hanlon, Tom Butynski, Annie Gautier, Hilary Morland and John Fanshawe have kindly vetted structure, blocks of text or illustrations. Annie and Jean–Pierre Gautier, Tom Butynski, Steve Gartlan and many others, including John Skinner, Chris Hillman, Andrew Conroy, Gerard and Ahn Galat, Caroline Tutin, Tom Struhsaker, Lysa Leland, Robert Glen, Dick Estes and Keith Eltringham have hosted me in camps or homes in Africa. Their company, ideas and hospitality have contributed in more ways than can begin to be enumerated. Likewise Wildlife and National Park authorities in many African countries have helped with permits, hospitality, transport and guidance, assistance that has been vital in building up a broad overview as well as detailed documentation of the mammals. The Welcome Trust gave vital aid (1968–78).

Among the many sources of help and encouragement over the years the following are a far from adequate sample: P. Agland, I. Aggundey, T. E. Ahmed, K. Al-Khalili, P. Anadu, L. Ambrose, M. Anderson, P. Andrews, W.F.H. Ansell, A. Archer, E. Ayensu, E. Balson, W. Banage, W.W. Bishop, F. Bourliere, A. Brosset, E. Bunengo, J. Bushara, S. Cobb, M. Coe, S. Cole, G.B. Corbet, D. Cummings, M. Delaney, B.D. Dutrillaux, T. Fison, T. Flannery, G. Frame, U. Funaioli, A. Gentry, W. Gewalt, L. Goodwin, J. Goodall, P. Grubb, A. Guillet, A. Hamilton, D. Happold, M. Happold, G. Harrington, J. Harris, D.L. Harrison, R.W.H. Hayman, H. Heim de Balsac, R.S. Hoffmann, R. Hofmann, M.E. Holden, P. Honess, K. Howell, R. Hughes, R. Hutterer, E. Huxley, J. Itani, C.J. Jolly, D. Jones, J. Karmali, F.X. Katete, T.A. Kindy, H. Klingel, S. Kondo, K.F. Koopman, A. Koortland, H. Kruuk, J. Kundaeli, R. Laws, M. Leakey, R. Leakey, J.M. Lernould, J.M. Lock, B. Loka–Arga, L. Lokwang, A. MacKay, H.S. Mahinda, G. Maloba, G. Maloiy, R. Martin, A. Mongi, P. Morin, C. Moss, G. Musser, F. Mutere, G. Mutinda, E. Neal, J. Nel, H. Ngweno, G. Ntenga, E. Nyampunjo, J. Oates, J. Obondio–Odur, W.K. Otim, I. Parker, R. Pellew, A. Pienaar, D. Pomeroy, S. Price, U. Rahm, G. Rathbun, A. Rogers, T. Rowell, S. Ruweza, J. Sabater–Pi, S. Sanford, R. Savage, G. Schaller, D.A. Schlitter, K. Schmidt–Nielsen, C. Sekintu, P. Shipman, R. Southwood, C. Spinage, P. Ssali, J. Ssenkebugye, C. Stuart, J. Sugiyama, A. Suzuki, T. Synnott, J. Thompson, E.O. Wilson, C. Thouless, N. Tinbergen, S. Tomkins, E. Vrba, S. Wainwright, R.J. Wheater, J. White, F. White, L. White, N. Winser, W.C. Wozencraft, R. Wrangham, S. Zuckerman.

My association with Academic Press, which dates back to 1966, has always been cordial and I thank Roger Farrand and Andy Richford for maintaining our long collaboration, also Maggie O'Hanlon and Shammima Cowan for their editorial talents.

Perhaps this short list of today's enthusiasts will give heart to tomorrow's warriors who must carry on the fight to save Africa's fauna and flora and the deeper realities of which they are the expression.

CHECKLIST OF SPECIES

INTRODUCTION

A field guide, like any other artefact, has an individual history and behind that a much longer generic history, in this case of books about African mammals. Such books are products of their times as well as of authors and over some 500 years they reflect a changing history of ideas as well as a growing list of species.

Acknowledging debts to previous authors is important both for the data and for the ideas they have bequeathed. They also provide juxtapositions to help define what is new about one's own time and about one's own work. A major peculiarity of this volume is its genesis within tropical Africa. Any home-grown author has frequent reminders that books on African subjects originated abroad and that visitors are still major interpreters. Field guides do not escape that legacy.

For the people who first printed books African mammals were mostly distant fable. Thus, mythological Bestiaries were the first of four main phases in the development of books about African animals.

The second phase is linked with Europe's expansion and colonialism. Animals, as in Europe, were little more than playthings of the privileged – game. Guides for this period began as hunters' 'Records of Big Game'.

In the third phase there was a change in vocabulary, 'game' became 'wildlife' as vast urbanised audiences received animal images and natural history stories in their homes and schools via books and television. The life histories of some popular species became familiar through the work of talented film-makers, naturalists and scientists. This phase coincided with the growth of mass tourism and the declaration of many magnificent national parks. Most current field guides are oriented to this period of expanding tourism and the growth of Natural History as a major form of recreation.

Now we have begun a fourth era, marked by our self-discovery as mammals that have created their own extraordinary niche. It is a niche in which consciousness and technological power have brought responsibility for the fate of our own and all other life on earth. Space travel and satellite photography have given us a new awareness of our cosmic fragility and biological limitations, while problems created by pollution and environmental degradation have led to a new concern for the health of the biosphere. As we are ever more frequently reminded of the finite nature of natural ecosystems and their fragile complexity, Africa's uniquely rich 'biodiversity' has become a by-word. That biodiversity happens to include us. These contemporary perspectives have shaped this field guide as they have my other books.

We live in a time of unprecedented accumulation of knowledge. Each year we learn more about living and extinct animals, about pre-history, human origins and processes that govern our past, present and future. From this cascade of new discovery has come the awareness that the survival of other animals is not entirely detached from our own. At the same time human penetration into previously untouched habitats has led to the spread of African primate diseases, such as HIV and Ebola virus, to cities and communities around the world, heightening our sense of proximity to, yet ignorance of, the natural world from which we have emerged so very recently. This is no aesthetic or historical conceit. Detatching ourselves from our biological past renders us less likely to understand our true nature. Dangerous repercussions follow in medicine and human ecology.

There is everything to be said for the observation of African mammals as recreation. As more people gain the ability and leisure to see African wildlife their pleasure and awe may be heightened by an awareness that what they are seeing would have been a familiar aspect of the existence of their ancestors, from ancient hominids to recent hunter-gatherers.

We call individual types of organism 'species' but, in the texts that follow, I try to give an indication of the countless structured relationships that each animal has with other species of animal and plant, and with the African landscape, its climates and a pre-history that stretches back many tens of millions of years. For a naturalist there are few greater delights than that of discovering for oneself the extraordinary fitness of animals for the niches they occupy. As observation reveals why animals are formed the way they are and how they relate to their surroundings one's sense of wondering enquiry can only increase. Curiosity may be the underlying motivation for the study of natural history but knowledge of African mammals easily leads on to more involved interests. As we come to understand how human beings have evolved within African natural communities we can gain a perspective on ourselves as an inextricable part of mammalian life on earth. This, surely, adds a new incentive to the joys of learning about African mammals.

AFRICAN MAMMALS

This field guide lists over 1,150 species of mammals from Africa. While it is certain that more species await discovery (especially among bats, insectivores and rodents) the overall scale and composition of Africa's mammal fauna is now reasonably well known. As the checklist and field guide to a continent's mammalian fauna, the pages that follow are broadly up to date. There are descriptions and illustrations of all known species of primates, small groups, such as pangolins and hares, all large mammals, carnivores and squirrels. All genera of insectivores, bats and rodents are described and illustrated but limitations of space have precluded species profiles in some genera with many species (for example, there are more than 100 species of *Crocidura*, the white-toothed shrew). The written profiles of mammals are supported by a full-colour illustration (generally of an adult male) and a map showing the animal's overall range or, in the case of better-known species, a map of its current distribution. In some cases past and present distributions are presented. Where subspecies are of special interest and their distributions are well known these are also mapped. In all cases colour-coding of distributions has enhanced clarity and helped reduce the amount of space taken up by maps.

Names

The classification and nomenclature first published by Linnaeus in 1758 provided an hierarchical system and a set of Latin names that could be applied to all organisms and be used by all nationalities. This ensured that no matter what language was used all naturalists and scientists could be sure of referring to the same animal or plant as long as it was correctly identified. The vernacular English or French names are therefore much less important than scientific names. The former often vary or have alternatives while the latter are arrived at by strict rules of priority and can only be changed when the rules are shown to have been broken by the application of a mistaken name.

Today new genetic techniques are refining the naming process, sometimes showing that long-recognised separate species should be amalgamated, or sometimes subdivided. These changes are often confusing but, in the long run, naming is becoming more stable. All changes still have to conform with well-tested Linnaean rules. Of over 20 named subspecies of red colobus several have long been recognised as full species but each authority has come up with a different permutation of species and subspecies. Until planned gene profiles of all forms of red colobus have been completed the arrangement offered here remains provisional. Many new species of primates have been discovered (or named/renamed on the basis of new information) in the last decade: a drill-mangabey in Tanzania, two guenons in central Africa and a large number of galagos (their identities first signalled by tape-recordings of their distinctive voices). Although most change has been at the species level, the grouping or revision of species by specialists can actually create or abolish higher taxons ranging from the genus to the family. These higher classifications help us to allocate individual species to their natural groupings. I have therefore included brief profiles of most tribes and families. To avoid unnecessary repetition subgroups, infra-groups and super-groups are sometimes ignored or subsumed within larger categories.

Although Linnaean systematics were originally designed to bring order to the apparent chaos of diverse species, this hierarchical system also gives us a useful indication of relationships and hence a guide to how species have diversified and lineages branched out. By way of illustration the following represents the position of human beings within its structure:

Class Mammalia
Subclass Eutheria
Order Primates
Suborder Haplorhini
Infraorder Catarrhini
Superfamily Hominoidea
Family Hominidae
Subfamily Homininae
Tribe Hominini
Genus *Homo*
Species *Homo sapiens*
Human beings

Sometimes relationships between species are so close that the cluster is called a 'superspecies' or 'species-group'. Similar clusters can be found at higher levels. For example rodent diversity is so complex and ancient it requires numerous subfamilies. Likewise, a most useful taxon for antelopes is the tribe. This lower-level clustering implies a more recent evolutionary radiation than that of the rodents. Controversies over naming still exist, especially when it comes to 'splitting' or 'lumping' species. I have followed the many authors of the Smithsonian volume on mammal species of the world (Wilson and Reeder, 1992) with special guidance from Colin Groves and Simon Bearder (world authorities on the taxonomy of primates). For bovids I have used the arrangement from my own *East African Mammals* and I have made certain small changes of my own (for example the special significance of the springbok's extinct ancestors means that it has been designated its own tribal category, the Antidorcini).

Many mammals have been given regional names, I have tried to use generally acceptable ones. In addition to English and French, German and Swahili names have been given.

USING THIS GUIDE

Correct identification of an animal depends upon the nature of the encounter. In the field the great majority of clues are indirect but, in a guide to a fauna of well over 1,000 species, an inventory of tracks, outlines of burrows, forms of excreta, etc., would be impractical. This guide is therefore limited to concise verbal descriptions and detailed full-colour illustrations (sometimes backed up by diagnostic details in the skull, teeth or pattern).

Mammal books that emulate bird books with an item-by-item enumeration of colour patches, long or short crests, etc., are not well suited to the more subtle variation and complexity of most mammals. Comparisons with familiar animals, such as dogs, cats, sheep, etc., are rendered useless by the sheer diversity of African mammals. Therefore, the colour plates in this guide aim to assist identification by illustrating something of a species' 'jizz'. Jizz is the naturalist's word for the total sum of form, colour, stance, silhouette and movement that allows an accurate assessment of a species-specific shape. Ritualised displays often serve to emphasise a species' peculiarities. Some plates illustrate these postures.

While I hope the 'once-in-a-lifetime' visitor to Africa will find this guide useful it is designed to help those with a more involved interest in African mammals. It aims to outline the ecology and evolutionary history of mammals and is intended as a celebration of the great diversity of their forms. The guide includes summary descriptions of behaviour but readers seeking more detail on the behaviour of African mammals should refer to Richard Este's excellent *Behaviour Guide to African Mammals*.

Species profiles present information under the following headings. After the scientific, English and other names are presented Measurements, then Recognition, Subspecies, Distribution, Habitat, Food, Behaviour, Adaptations and, finally, Status. An abbreviated format is used for species or genera that are poorly known or have closely related species already described in greater detail. The headings in such cases are Names, Recognition, Habitat, Food and Status. For profiles dealing with tribes, families or higher categories I have adopted a more flexible approach but information is summarised under the headings Recognition, Genealogy, Geography, Ecology, Natural history and Adaptations.

Taking these headings in sequence:

Measurements: Head and body HB, Tail T, Shoulder height SH, Weight W, Forearm FA.

Recognition: This heading deals with what makes a species (or group of related animals) easy to recognise, with a focus on those characteristics that are unique to that species or group.

Subspecies: These are listed for the majority of species with individual profiles especially when they show well-defined geographic differences (in some cases future genetic studies may well lead to reclassification of some of these as full species).

Distribution: Description of distribution is accompanied by a map and special geographic features are noted.

Habitat: Physical and climatic determinants of habitats are mentioned, with the central focus on vegetation and, for the smaller species, their micro-environment. The distribution of major vegetation zones is shown on page 450.

Food: Wherever known, dietary preferences are summarised by characteristics (rather than long species lists).

Behaviour: Most profiles describe a 'nugget' of behaviour that is typical or diagnostic of the species. Where relevant, reference is made to social structures, modes of communication, activity cycles, senses, gaits and breeding.

Adaptations: Special adaptive characteristics that help to define the species' niche or features of its anatomy or physiology.

Status: Under this heading is recorded recent assessments as published by the World Conservation Union or IUCN Species Survival Commission. The main categories used before a recent revision are Endangered, Vulnerable, Rare and Not Endangered. The full revised categories are Extinct, Extinct in the Wild, Critically Endangered, Endangered, Vulnerable, Lower Risk, Data Deficient and Not Evaluated. As few African countries have been accurately evaluated for any but the commonest 'game' animals, most assessments need to be viewed with caution. The real situation may be much better or worse than recorded and the status of those species that are most vulnerable to the destruction of their habitat or to hunting may change quite rapidly. Where IUCN assessments on status have yet to be made a consensus of contemporary views from relevant experts is offered.

WHERE TO FIND MAMMALS

The larger mammals, particularly those in well-protected national parks, are generally easy to view (sometimes on foot, but more usually from a vehicle or hide). Outside protected areas they can usually only be seen at some distance. The great majority of African mammals are small, very shy, mainly nocturnal species. Scientists employ sophisticated methods to study such species, including tailor-made traps, electronic sensors, radio- and spool-tracking, bat-detectors and hidden recorders. However, for both the amateur naturalist and scientist alike, a good pair of eyes, a pencil and notebook can be all that are required. To augment the naked senses and provide permanent records of momentary events binoculars, a tape-recorder and camera are useful adjuncts.

Anyone interested in mammals should keep notes and records. Every human/animal encounter has some significance, even apparent 'accidents', such as an otter shrew in a fishing net, a wild dog killed by a speeding lorry, or a tomb bat drowned in a school cistern. Indeed there are aspects of the biology of such animals that might never have been discovered but for such mishaps.

Most mammals are encountered indirectly, most commonly by their tracks, diggings, excreta and feeding sites. Bones and skulls are occasional finds but, sadly, some of the richest sites for animal remains, often of rare and little-known species, are on town market stalls. This plunder is a growing menace in those African countries that permit the commercial exploitation of 'bush-meat' for urban markets. A campaign against this highly damaging trade is gathering momentum and deserves the widest possible support.

We owe to amateur naturalists most of what we know about mammals in Africa, much of it collected from keen African observers. From the earliest foreign explorers to contemporary civil servants, naturalists have recorded countless interesting details. The collators of this accumulated knowledge have, for the most part, been non-Africans writing for non-African audiences. Today this is changing. Fire-side gossip is no longer the preferred medium for communicating indigenous knowledge about local animals. African naturalists and scientists increasingly publish for an international audience and this is the context for a new generation of field guides.

I began this introduction with a generic history of books about animals. I end with a more personal history. The authority for this book lies in an African childhood and lifetime of research , travel, university teaching and writing on various aspects of evolution in Africa. Most publishing projects rely on author, studio artist and graphic workshop to supply the texts, illustrations and maps for their co-operative enterprise. The dislocations are obvious to any careful analyst of the end result. This book breaks new ground in that the author is also illustrator, cartographer and designer. I trust that the results speak for themselves. My qualifications for the task lie with several previous works, most notably with *East African Mammals, An Atlas of Evolution in Africa, Island Africa* and *Self-made Man* (a Biologist's Genesis). I hope this field guide will accompany the solitary naturalist on his mammal-watching excursions through the African landscape. I also hope it will reach new potential audiences in schools and cities. Here there are new demands for a working knowledge of wildlife. Rapid growth of economically vital tourist industries (mostly founded on wildlife) ensures that the new enthusiasts and wildlife experts are teachers, rangers, couriers and drivers in schoolrooms and minicabs or on park outings. I hope that my work will help these new persuaders to convince both locals and visitors alike of the enormous value and significance of Africa's natural heritage.

MAMMALIA MAMMALS

Every user of this book is a mammal and, as doctors, drug-manufacturers and physiologists have always known, the study of human kinship with other mammals offers us many fundamental truths about ourselves. Take warm blood for example. Internally stable temperatures are central to what mammals are. A naked human freezes to death within hours in a northern winter and, likewise, quickly dies of heatstroke if exposed to a desert midsummer. This is because *biologically* we are still equatorial primates. While we have developed technical solutions to both these extremes of climate (i.e. clothes or air conditioners), other mammals have biological techniques that enable them to survive both extremes, relying on fur for insulation against extremes of temperature, and sweating or panting in order to cool down.

It is glands similar to sweat glands, mammae, which have been modified to produce the milk that give mammals both their common and their scientific name – mammals are animals whose mothers have mammary glands.

Mammal mothers are unique not only in nursing their offspring on milk but in nurturing them *before* birth through a placenta that grows into the wall of the uterus. The placenta allows the foetus to plug into its mother's circulation and so share in her respiratory and excretory systems and in the nutrients carried in her blood. It also stops the mother rejecting the foetus as an alien body.

A mammal is not only sheltered as a foetus in the womb, maternal care also shelters it after birth. Whereas emergence from an egg exposes a newly hatched invertebrate fish or reptile to predators, competitors, changes in climate and the need to find food, newborn mammals escape these rigours through maternal care. Mammals are also relatively independent of the environment for the duration of their infancy and adolescence. This trait is unique to mammals and is most prolonged in primates, especially hominid apes. Among hominids humans have extended this central mammalian characteristic furthest. Not only has our childhood been extended biologically, contemporary humans continue to extend its environmental dimension – detachment from ecological systems. Because much of our technology plays a role analogous to maternal protection we have, in a limited sense, become permanent youngsters, the most mammalian of mammals.

Mothering is also the key to social life in mammals. The physical costs of bearing and suckling offspring are so great for the ♀♀ that they go to elaborate lengths to fit the timing of reproduction to the best time of year and to ensure access to the best resources both for themselves and for their offspring. To achieve this some species share or enter the territories of prime ♂ land-holders. Others seek out the protection of dominant ♂♂ at the top of a strict hierarchy while still others choose ♂♂ that will help raise offspring.

Different patterns of ♂ competition and ♀ choice have dramatic consequences for the external appearance and anatomy of ♂♂. Weaponry, in the form of horns, tusks or antlers, has been developed to defend territories or rank. Age-graded gigantism has evolved in the ♂♂ of hierarchical species, such as gorillas, elands and giraffes. Long-term pair-bonding is usually matched by the sexes being of similar size (typified by wild dogs).

Diversity of size and form is built on those most fundamental of faculties: finding and processing food. Major groupings within the mammals are often named and defined by the shape and form of their teeth (such as ro*dents*, scan*dents*, tubuli*dents*). Furthermore, mammals as a whole have uniquely modifiable teeth and lower jaws. Although these derive from structures similar to those in other vertebrates, the jaw consists of a single mandibular bone anchored in and powerfully hinged onto the skull. Reptiles by contrast have jaws that are a weaker assemblage of bones.

Long-series of fossils of the now-extinct 'mammal-like reptiles', or synapsids, have revealed that the tooth-bearing bone (the reptilian 'dentary') first developed a hinge with the squamosal, or cheek bone, about 200 million years ago. As a consequence three of the original reptilian jaw bones (themselves derived from fish gill-arches) declined in size and became detached from the lower jaw. However, these diminutive bones did not become redundant but attached themselves to the skull base, where they became the inner components of the mammal ear capsule. Partly because of the fine tuning of these minute bones mammals have developed a much more discriminating sense of hearing than reptiles and have elaborated numerous forms of sonic communication, sonar orientation and detection systems. Thus mammals owe their good ear for the nuances of sound to their peculiar legacy from reptile anatomy.

Transformations through time. Mammal-like reptile skulls, left, *Ophiacodon* (an early form). Centre, *Probainognathus* (a later form) compared with a modern mammal, the civet, right.

The senses play a very precise role in the life of all mammals. Sight, hearing, scent and touch are balanced in permutations that are unique to each species and that balance finds a gross expression in the shape of animal heads. For example, a serval cat's huge ears, a fishing genet's moustache of face whiskers, a bushbaby's bulging eyes and an aardvark's nose tube each manifest unique techniques for finding food. All possess a full set of faculties but the serval cat must pick up sound waves from tiny mice in dense grass, the genet senses waves from small fish in water, the bushbaby receives optical wavelengths in near total darkness and the aardvark locks onto molecular traces of scent emanating from termites hidden deep in the soil. All these faculties had to be developed by stages from the less specialised conditions that preceded them.

The overall shape and proportions of a mammal are therefore the end-products of its lineage and its progressive adaptation to an exact and exacting ecological niche. Much of the fascination of observing animals lies in matching such expressions of form to function. Form is not only anatomical; mammals act, behave, occupy habitats and have habits that are all expressions of their total adaptation. Every species manifests a unique way of making a living.

(a)

(b)

(c)

(d)

Mammal heads and senses. (a) Serval cat (hearing). (b) Fishing genet (touch). (c) Galago (vision). (d) Aardvark (scent).

Much of that life is accessible to quiet observation but any serious contemplation of mammals can only be a humbling experience. In their world we are like deaf-mutes. We can neither register nor interpret the most important dimension of their existence: scent. For a few species (mostly primates like us) scent may be subordinate to vision but for the majority scent is a central regulator of their social life, a major mechanism for orienting themselves and a source of what we would call 'exquisite sensations'.

If mammals have been shaped by the way they make a living they also shape the lives of their prey and of the plants they eat. An example is my own discovery of a unique relationship between bark-eating anomalures and the awoura (*Julbernardia*) trees on which they feed (see p. 176). This interdependence between gigantic, slow-growing forest trees and small, short-lived, gliding rodents is so specific that it must go back millions of years. In keeping their flight paths to the tree trunks clear, the anomalures prune (and eventually kill) the tree's competitors, thereby compensating them for wounding their bark. Mutually beneficial relationships are known among bats and the flowering plants which they pollinate, and among primates and the tree seeds which they disperse, but many, much subtler relationships await discovery and study. The inter-relatedness of mammals and all other organisms in natural communities is a compelling reason why we should strive to conserve ecosystems intact, as well as the entire range of mammal species, not just the ones we find attractive or agreeable.

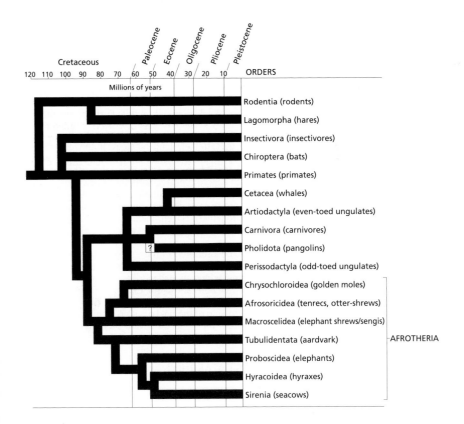

African mammal Orders. Branching pattern and timimg tentative but suggested by new molecular evidence. Uniquely African radiation of Afrotheria only recently recognised.

ORDER 1 PRIMATES PRIMATES

| Old World monkeys and apes | Catarrhini |
| Prosimians | Strepsirhini |

All primates derive from, and to some degree retain, a primitive body plan which they share with other unrelated arboreal mammals, such as squirrels, tree shrews and possums. The common arboreal condition is long-backed and short-necked, with five-fingered, clinging hands and feet. The forearms are linked to the chest by collar bones (clavicles) and the compact head has forward-oriented eyes and a short, flexible neck.

A great diversity of anatomical specialisations has developed in primates and these correspond to different climbing or locomotory techniques. Relatively slow, careful climbers have specialised in extreme mobility in their limb joints and a powerful grip in their hands and feet. Fast branch-runners have long tails to serve as balancers, long, flexible backs, limbs with narrow hands and fingers, small thumbs and well-developed bifocal vision to help them accurately assess distance and space.

Judging from tooth structures in fossils, the arboreal mammals that gave rise to primates were mainly insectivorous. The earliest extensions in diet would have been small vertebrates and ripe, soft fruits. Later some tackled unripe or hard fruits, resins, flowers, nectar, buds, young leaves and, finally, a few took on mature leaves. From very early times up to the present, omnivorous primates might have been able to eat small quantities of any of these foods and insect-eating has remained important for many species. Trends towards consuming larger quantities of abundant but more difficult foods (such as old leaves, resins, hard nuts and seeds) led to early specialisation in lineages such as colobus monkeys and gum-eating bushbabies.

The commonest, most versatile and probably earliest type of locomotion consists of running and walking on four limbs of approximately equal length. This can be modified for both tree- and ground-dwelling (with marked elongation of the limbs in the more terrestrial forms, such as patas and green monkeys). The most economic and efficient locomotion in open woodlands and forests, where there are abundant vertical stems or trunks, is fast, frog-like springs powered by extremely long hindlegs. Bushbabies show varying degrees of this trait. By contrast, lengthening of the forelimbs is typical of the great apes. Best developed in the Asiatic gibbons, which are true brachiators, this trait is correlated with shortening of the trunk into a more compact, barrel-like body.

Powerful big toes are known to have developed in fossil primates by at least 60 million years ago. Thumbs have a less certain ancestry and are less universal (some primates, notably colobus species, have lost them altogether). Naked, padded digits and palms on both hands and feet are universal and clearly represent one of the very earliest adaptations of primates.

The decline of the sense of smell seems to be associated with the superiority of touch and vision as the means of exploring and surviving in a world of three-dimensional space latticed by branches. Where muzzles are large or long, as in mandrills and some bushbabies, this seems to be linked with enlargement of the bony anchorage for powerful sets of teeth.

Fossils reveal that some primates had begun to have a more forward orientation of the eyes by about 60 million years ago. This narrowing of the field of vision seems to have been compensated for by greater ability to rotate the head on a very short neck. Efficient rotation is helped by a compact, round head.

OLD WORLD MONKEYS AND APES CATARRHINI

| Anthropoids | Hominoidea |
| Monkeys | Cercopithecoidea |

Shortening of the face seems to be linked with an ancient convergence of the nostrils into a single nose unit and an enlargement of the upper lip. This enlargement has allowed muscles to spread into the upper lip, assisting manipulation of food but also enhancing facial expressions and vocalisations. Such enhancement has proceeded furthest among anthropoids, as has brain enlargement. It is still uncertain when Old World monkeys diverged from their South American counterparts.

MAN AND APES HOMINIDAE

Chimpanzee	*Pan troglodytes*
Bonobo or 'Pygmy' chimpanzee	*Pan paniscus* (earliest name *P. marungensis*)
Gorilla	*Gorilla gorilla* (possibly two species)

Recognition: African apes are so frequently illustrated and filmed, and captive specimens are so familiar in zoos, that a formal description of apes may seem superfluous. There have been bland scientific descriptions dating back more than 200 years. All tended to suppress human resemblances and stressed the similarity of apes to one another. All failed to anticipate the extraordinary discoveries of the last few decades. Study of fossils, genes, physiology and behaviour has revealed that the common ancestry of humans and apes is much more recent than anyone thought possible. By the rules that govern the classification of other animals both have had to be united in a single group: the anthropoids or hominids. In this entirely new perspective the differences between chimpanzees and gorillas become as significant and interesting as their similarities.

Likewise, bonobo biology is being compared with that of humans, with the ultimate objective of revealing the roots of our own uniqueness. We all share compact, tail-less bodies, large, rounded, big-brained heads and long forearms with hands and strong fingers. While both hands and feet of apes share the three main functions of body support, climbing and manipulating objects, the ancestors of humans shifted all weight-bearing onto the hindlegs and freed the hands to become purely manipulative. Looking at other primates and other mammals there are innumerable other examples of physical transformation linked with similar small shifts in function. Our most obvious peculiarity, developing two-handed skills, is paralleled by clawless otters and marsh mongooses while such diverse mammals as spring hares, ground pangolins and gerenuk have all found advantages in regular two-footedness. Like us, all these species have become very different from their closest relatives simply by evolving novel ways of using their limbs.

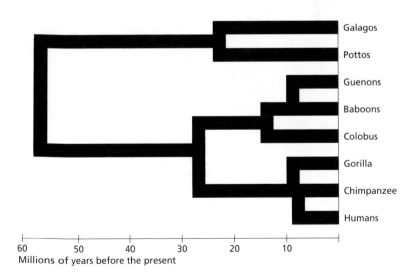

Primate tree.

Chimpanzee *Pan troglodytes*

Other names: Fr. *Chimpanzé*. Ger. *Schimpanse*. Swah. *Sokwe mtu*.

Measurements: HB 63.5–90cm. SH 100–179cm. W av. 30kg (♀), 35kg (26–40kg) (♂).

Recognition: A robust ape with long, somewhat tufted black hair, bare face, bare prominent ears and bare parts of the abdomen. The brows are rounded and the margins of the nostrils are scarcely raised. ♀♀ are slightly lighter than ♂♂ and develop pink swellings of the ano-genital skin which fluctuate in size according to the phase of their menstrual cycle.

Subspecies: *P. t. troglodytes* (R. Cross to R. Zaïre/R. Ubangi): pale, freckled face, darkening with age, and shows early balding. *P. t. verus* (Guinea, W Africa): dark mask, light muzzle, darkening with age, bearded. *P. t. schweinfurthi* (R. Ubangi/R. Zaïre to W Uganda and Tanzania): light to dark face, dense dark fur, bearded.

(a) West African chimpanzee. (b) Eastern chimpanzee. (c) Central African chimpanzee. (d) Bonobo.

Distribution: From S Senegal across the forested belt north of the R. Zaïre to W Uganda and Tanzania.

Habitat: Predominantly in rainforests and forest galleries extending into savannah woodlands. Chimpanzees also frequent lowland and mountain forests, showing a marked preference for mixed and colonising communities.

Food: Omnivorous and highly variable according to individual population and season. Fruit comprises about half the diet but leaves, bark and stems are also important. Animal foods range from termites and other insects to birds, eggs and nestlings; small mammals are taken occasionally. While preferred foods, such as figs, are fruiting, chimpanzees may spend most of their time feeding on a few species. At other times they may be forced to forage widely and have been recorded as taking up to 300 different food types and as many as 20 in a single day.

Behaviour: Chimpanzees form social communities of 15–120 animals within large territories that are defended by both sexes but mostly by ♂♂. Only ♀♀ cross community boundaries. Groups vary in composition and size according to the seasonal distribution of food. All-M parties, single mothers with offspring, and mixed groups are common but ♂♂ are frequently separate and may forage on their own for short periods.

Home ranges are smaller in mixed rainforest and larger in woodland forest mosaics and open savannah, i.e. 5–400km^2 (average 12.5km^2). Adult ♂♂ are fiercely intolerant of their counterparts in neighbouring groups and occasionally kill solitary individuals or small groups (including ♀♀ and young) close to the community's territorial boundary. ♂ associations within the group are strong.

Immigrant oestrous ♀♀ are generally accepted but their offspring may be attacked or killed. Non-breeding ♀♀ with young offspring evade other chimpanzees and tend to live within separate and contracted home ranges. This preference breaks down when ♀♀ come into oestrus (3–4 years after giving birth or following the death of their infant). At this time ♀♀ wander more widely and excite intense ♂ interest. Temporary pairs may form during the week in which ♀♀ are at their most receptive.

Chimpanzees feed most actively during the earlier part of the morning and evening and rest during the heat of the day. At dusk each adult and subadult animal builds a nest by pulling in, snapping and interweaving the branches that surround the chosen nest site. Nests are normally situated between 6 and 25m above the ground, depending on the local configuration and height of the forest. Because feeding takes place in the evening, they are normally built very close to the final feeding site. Short-term day-nests are most typical of the wet season and are more summary in construction.

Adult ♂♂ co-operate in hunting monkeys (particularly red colobus, baboons and young antelopes and pigs). The hunting is often opportunistic but can display rapid mobilisation and co-operative specialisation in the roles played by hunters, i.e. blockers, chasers and ambushers. Sticks and stems are dipped into termite, ant and bee nests, and both clubs and rocks are used to break open nuts. Chimpanzees communicate vocally using more than 30 calls. These convey information about mood, status, danger, sexual excitement, food and various social interactions. Facial expressions sometimes suggest almost human levels of subtlety but may also be part of very loud and active social displays.

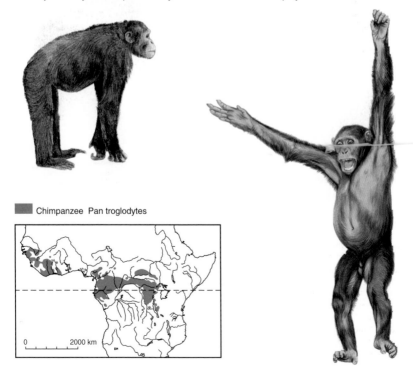

Chimpanzee *Pan troglodytes*

0   2000 km

♀♀ become fertile at about 11–12 years of age. Their sexual cycle of approximately 24 days is marked by swelling of the pink ano-genital skin. This reaches maximum extension for about a week and the swelling attracts maximum sexual interest from the ♂♂ at this time.

Although ♀♀ only give birth at about 13 years of age this has been preceded by some 4 or 5 years of sexual activity. Likewise ♂♂ are only sexually mature at about 15 years but are sexually active at least 10 years before that and ♂♂ initiate most sexual activity. A gestation of 8 months is followed by the birth of an infant that is born with open eyes and a strong clinging reflex but is otherwise completely dependent on the mother for some 6 months.

Adaptations: Chimpanzee anatomy shows a fine balance between fast quadrupedal activity on the ground and the need to manoeuvre a large, heavy body through different levels of the forest on very variably sized supports. Thus, chimpanzees can mount large tree trunks with spread-eagled, hugging movements that require a very powerful grip in both hands and feet and more subtle manipulation of fragile supports, such as stems, lianas and small branches. Fast travel on the ground is always quadrupedal, with long strides taken on the sole of the foot and the knuckles of the hand. Short distances are often covered with a bow-legged, bipedal waddle, especially when the arms are preoccupied with carrying fruits.

Status: The three subspecies have different ranges and face different threats. (They are also known to have had distinct genetic histories for more than 1 million years.) IUCN rates the western form (*P. t. verus*) as Endangered, the central chimpanzee (*P. t. troglodytes*) as Vulnerable and the eastern chimpanzee (*P. t. schweinfurthi*) as Vulnerable.

Bonobo or 'Pygmy' Chimpanzee *Pan paniscus* (earliest name *P. marungensis*)

Other names: Fr. *Bonobo, Chimpanzé nain*. Ger. *Bonobo, Zwergschimpanse*. Lingala dialect *Mokomboso*.

Measurements: HB 55–60cm. SH 90–100cm. W 30 (25–35) kg.

Recognition: A large and beautiful chimpanzee, juvenescent rather than pygmoid. The more obvious of its numerous youthful characteristics are a rounder cranium, less pronounced brow ridges and muzzle, and less tendency to go bald. Hair on the scalp is splayed and flat while that on the cheeks and chin is heart-shaped and surrounds a black face with pink-edged eyes and lips. All limbs, especially the legs, are long and fine, their slenderness emphasised by sleek, tight fur. The narrow foot opposes an enlarged 'thumb'. There is very little difference in size between the sexes. Like the unbroken voices of human youths bonobos' calls are higher and weaker equivalents of those uttered by common chimpanzees.

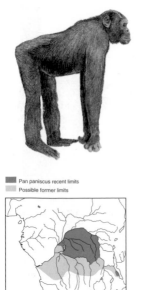

■ Pan paniscus recent limits
■ Possible former limits

Subspecies: It is possible that the south-eastern montane population could be distinct. The lowland form would then be *paniscus*, the montane form *marungensis*.

Distribution: Today the bonobo mainly occurs within the low-lying riverine basin enclosed between the R. Zaïre, R. Lualaba and R. Kasai/R. Sankuru. It is possible that this ape once inhabited most of the southern Zaïre basin but it now occupies a scatter of pockets within an increasingly settled region. It appears to have been progressively eliminated from most settled areas and from the immediate hinterlands bordering major rivers. In some areas it may be naturally absent or scarce.

Habitat: A mosaic of swamp, primary and secondary forests in a landscape of very mild relief, with a humid, stable climate. To the far east of its range the bonobo occupies montane forest but it has not been studied there. Leguminous trees, particularly Caesalpinaceae, such as *Brachystegia*, *Cynometra*, *Dialium*, *Julbernardia* and *Baibiaea*, are dominant species and important sources of food. A single bonobo community has a small core area but can range across 20–60km^2 of forest, with extensive overlaps between community ranges.

Food: More than half the diet comprises fruits and seeds. Leaves, flowers and various other plant parts provide fibre and protein, as do smaller quantities of mushrooms, invertebrates, small vertebrates, honey and eggs. Salt needs may be met by eating a swamp grass (*Ranalisma*). Some 150 foods are currently known but a few species, notably velvet tamarind (*Dialium*), a liane (*Landolphia*) and soap-berries (*Pancovia*), fruit super-abundantly and are staple foods for periods of a month or more. These foods ripen in the canopy where most feeding takes place. The main feeding bout, in the morning, is usually on fruits. In the afternoon the bonobo may switch to less energy-rich, more fibrous foods.

Behaviour: Some differences from common chimpanzees can be related to the bonobo's greater environmental affluence; for example, ♂ defences are obsolete during frequent gluts of fruits. Other differences derive directly from the extension of juvenile traits in both sexes. Thus ♂♂ remain close to their mothers up to adulthood, an attachment that delays ♂–♂ contacts. Prolonged subordination of young ♂♂ also results in general inhibition of ♂ aggression towards ♀♀. Juvenescence of the loud calls further diminishes ♂ dominance by toning down threat displays. ♂ aggression is further dampened by prolonged 'adolescent sterility' and sexual receptiveness in ♀♀.

Juvenescence of the ♀ sexual cycle (typically longer and more irregular than in adults) lengthens the average menstrual cycle to 46 days. For nearly half of this time her attractiveness is evident in her behaviour and in her distended sexual skin. ♀♀ with young are also sexually active for 3–4 years of the 5-year gap between births. They remain infertile, like adolescent ♀♀, until their offspring are weaned, whereupon they come into full oestrus. During this period their behaviour is analogous to that of adolescent common chimpanzees in their close and frequent association with both sexes. When parties converge on a rich feeding site, potential antagonisms are dissipated by very frequent sex involving every combination of age, sex and status. Mutual sexual stimulation by ♀♀ is frequent and it is quite usual for both homo- and hetero-couples to copulate face to face. This diversion of reproductive behaviour to social ends demonstrates that seduction has overtaken ♂ dominance as the main regulator in bonobo society. Either sex will initiate copulation.

Although a very rich and concentrated crop of fruits can attract all members of a regional community (up to 80 animals), they are usually dispersed in various loose and temporary combinations. These differ from those of common chimpanzees in that more fruits, greater immunity from ♂ threats and frequent sexual bonding induce ♀♀ to be more gregarious. All-♂ clusters are correspondingly impermanent, draw in fewer recruits and are less stable.

Where food is plentiful active feeding takes up no more than a third of the day. Afternoon rests and early retirement (at about 17.00h) involve the construction of flimsy day-nests and more robust night-nests. Although nests are commonly made very close to the current feeding site, the bonobo nonetheless prefers to seek out flexible, multi-branched *Leonardoxa* trees for this purpose. It draws in all reachable fronds and stamps them into a wedging fork to form a springy, globular platform. Courtship in the bonobo is gentler and more tentative but more frequent than in any other primate. In most other respects bonobo reproduction broadly resembles that of common chimpanzees.

Adaptations: A narrowed choice of abundant and highly concentrated foods has demanded adaptation to living at higher densities. More social contacts in less competitive settings have favoured many of the behavioural traits described above. Some of these can be described as neoteny, or 'retention of youth'.

Map 3. Bonobo distribution in relation to human activities in the Zaïre Basin. (Note: virtually all mammal distribution could be mapped in this way since all mammals are to a greater or lesser extent constrained by human activities.)

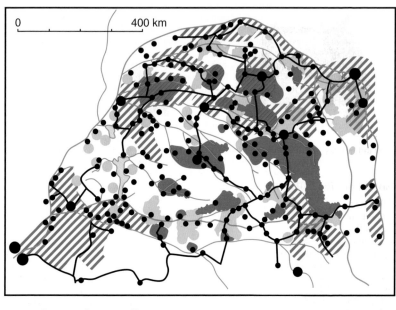

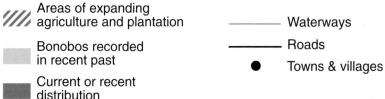

Areas of expanding agriculture and plantation

Bonobos recorded in recent past

Current or recent distribution

Waterways

Roads

● Towns & villages

Status: 'If the bonobos are there we will eat them' is an oft-repeated assertion of Mongo people in the Zaïre basin. This brief statement sums up the plight of the bonobo. Not all Mongo used to eat bonobos but tastes and taboos change and the most pervasive changes followed colonialism. The principal large-scale economic activities in central Zaïre are logging and coffee, rubber, cocoa, oil-palm and cotton plantation. For over 100 years such industries have diverted traditional hunting into a commercial trade to supply their workers with a year-round supply of meat.

Such commercialisation long ago extended to markets in virtually every town and village. As people and their transport systems have expanded, and as their hunting techniques have improved, vulnerable species have been the first to decline. The slow-breeding, conspicuous and large-bodied bonobo is easily killed and is a favourite quarry of both subsistence and commercial hunters. This progression has only been modified in the immediate vicinity of primate research stations where scientists might have influenced attitudes or coincidentally chosen study sites in culturally benign regions.

The bonobo's rapid decline can only be slowed if commercial hunting is arrested and local industries are persuaded actively to support rather than subvert conservation. The dominant logging company in the region is the influential multinational Karl Danzer Furnier-Werk, with headquarters in Germany. In Salongo, the only National Park, the bonobo is relatively scarce. There are no other formal refuges. The bonobo breeds well in captivity but there are less than 100 registered in 11 zoos. Numbers in experimental laboratories and irregular collections are unknown.

Listed as Class A (African Convention), Appendix 1 (CITES), Highly Vulnerable (IUCN).

Lowland gorillas: adult female and adult male.

Gorilla *Gorilla gorilla*

Other names: Fr. *Gorille*. Ger. *Gorilla*. Swah. *Makaku, Gorila*.

Measurements: SH 130–150cm (♀), 140–185cm (♂). W 68–114kg (♀), 160–210kg (♂).

Recognition: Very large, barrel-chested ape with relatively even hair, a bare black face and chest, and small ears. The bar-shaped brows are joined and the nostril margins are raised. ♀♀ are much smaller than ♂♂. The belly of wild gorillas is very much more massive than in captive specimens. The long blue-black coat of the mountain gorilla contrasts with the shorter and sparser brownish coat of the lowland forms. The small of the back, or 'saddle', of mature ♂♂ becomes grey or white with age, hence the name 'silverback' for old ♂♂.

Subspecies: Western lowland gorilla, *G. g. gorilla* (W Nigeria to R. Zaïre/R. Sangha): brownish with a broad face but relatively small jaws. (It is possibly a species, distinct from the eastern form.) Mountain gorilla, *G. g. beringei* (volcanic slopes of Rwanda and Zaïre): very black and densely furred, with a broad face and massive jaws. Eastern lowland gorilla, *G. g. graueri* (Impenetrable forest, Uganda, rift wall and lowlands of E Zaïre): short black fur, narrow face and very large body size. (Uganda gorillas could be a fourth race.)

Distribution: Discontinuous. The western population extends from the R. Cross to R. Zaïre/R. Sangha while the eastern population occupies a triangular wedge between the R. Lualaba (R. Zaïre), L. Edward and L. Tanganyika. A relict western population survived until the turn of the century at Bondo on the R. Uelle.

Habitat: Discontinuous. Both lowland populations are found in lowland tropical rainforest; over part of their range in W Africa they inhabit mixed tropical rainforest where fruits play a larger part in the diet and the animals frequently climb trees to feed. The mountain gorilla is confined to mountain and subalpine environments. In most areas gorillas prefer old clearings, valley bottoms, landslides, etc., where there is a dense tangle of ground-level herbaceous growth.

Male mountain gorilla.

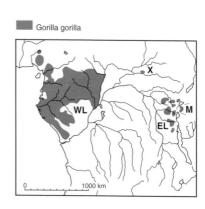

Gorilla gorilla

Food: Compared with the lowland gorillas, the mountain gorilla eats fewer plant species and feeds mainly on leaves, shoots and stems; *Galium* vines, wild celery and three or four other species make up a high proportion of the diet. The western lowland gorilla eats more fruits but also relies on wild ginger (*Afromomum*) for a high proportion of its diet.

Behaviour: Gorillas form small, non-territorial harems dominated by a single, mature ♂. ♂ offspring are driven out and ♀♀ not infrequently change groups. ♀♀ gravitate to solitary adult ♂♂ and such primary pairs display the strongest bonds (adult ♀♀ do not bond with other ♀♀). Whenever established pairs are joined by other adult ♀♀ the sequence of arrival determines ♀ rank order. The western lowland gorilla seldom forms groups with more than three adult ♀♀ (average 5 in all; maximum 12). The mountain gorilla has less exclusive groups, with dominant 'silverback' ♂♂ tolerating a few younger adult 'blackback' ♂♂ and these larger groups attract more ♀♀. Such groups number 10 on average (maximum 37).

The abundance of fast-growing food permits such large groups to forage together (something physically impossible in most W African habitats). There is no defence of the home range and the ranges of all groups overlap those of their neighbours quite extensively; avoiding action is normally taken during encounters. More than half the day is spent foraging, either on the move or temporarily static. Gorillas tend to behave like ruminants, with very long rest periods. Mutual evasion is facilitated by frequent advertising signals emitted by dominant ♂♂. The commonest call bears some structural resemblance to chimpanzee hooting. It is a crescendo of deep, booming hoots, culminating in a tattoo of chest-beating (this can be heard over 2km away on a clear day). Various degrees and conditions of alarm are signified by barks, roars or screams, almost all made only by the ♂.

On rare occasions when neighbouring ♂♂ fail to evade one another, there are displays of roaring, chest-beating, plant-bashing and charging. Very occasionally these culminate in a fight. Similar displays greet human intruders, predators and competing herbivores (such as giant hogs or buffaloes). In contrast to dominant ♂♂, ♀♀ and young are quiet and retiring. They have a modest repertoire of grunts, burps, growls and whines.

Gorillas reproduce at a very slow rate, on average one young every 4 years (a maximum of about 10 in a ♀'s lifetime). Mothers give continuous care and attention to their young and the dominant ♂ is always alert to the safety and well-being of all members of his group, willing to defend the young against all-comers. Gorillas live for 50–60 years.

Adaptations: While ♀♀ bear some superficial resemblance to chimpanzees, ♂♂ are by far the largest living primate and their bulk is reflected in their architecture. ♂ defence against predators permits gorillas to live more safely on the ground than any other primate. Their mass is less apparent in captive specimens, which eat much less bulk food. Wild ♂♂ often have paunches that hang almost to the ground and the rib-cage and pelvis are correspondingly splayed. Because they spend less time in the trees and more on the ground, their hands and feet are correspondingly broad and stub-fingered.

Status: In areas where agriculture is expanding, gorillas are killed in retaliation for crop-raiding. The commercial bush-meat trade is also expanding rapidly and gorilla meat is sold in markets and restaurants in several central African towns. As a result gorillas are declining fast in parts of their range. In less accessible areas the secondary growth that follows large-scale logging may temporarily favour them.

The western lowland gorilla is listed as Vulnerable while both eastern lowland and mountain gorillas are Endangered (IUCN).

MONKEYS CERCOPITHECOIDEA

| Colobid monkeys | Colobidae |
| Cheek-pouch monkeys | Cercopithecidae |

Recognition: With the exception of nocturnal bushbabies and their allies, and the great apes, all African primates are cercopithecoid monkeys. There are two main groupings: the colobids, or 'thumbless monkeys', with long limbs, large bodies and small heads; and the 'cheek-pouch' monkeys, which are a more diverse group. Cheek-pouch monkeys range from the miniature talapoin monkey and numerous colourful guenon monkeys to the stocky, large-headed baboons.

Phyletic tree of African monkeys.

(a) Cheek-pouch monkeys–baboon.
(b) Thumbless monkey-redcolobus.

Genealogy: All African monkeys derive from a common ancestral group, probably the extinct 'Victoria monkeys' (*Victoriapithecus* and allies). Fossils dating from a long hot period between 20 million and 15 million years ago have been found at sites associated with arid-adapted fauna. In all moister habitats apes were the dominant primates of that period.

By 10 million years ago colobids appear in the fossil record in Africa, Asia and Europe. By extrapolation from modern species and tooth structure, it appears that their first specialisation centred on diet. They could safely extract nutrients from indigestible parts of plants (stems, unripe fruits and leaves). Semi-terrestrial, arid-adapted Victoria monkeys had long abandoned the moist arboreal environments of all early primates but some of their descendants, whose lines eventually gave rise to the colobids, led a return into true forest. This niche probably opened to them because apes could only digest the easier types of plant material, such as shoots and ripe fruits.

Those descendants of Victoria monkeys that remained omnivorous heightened their adaptations to a dry, open-country realm; they developed cheek pouches, substantial differences in the sizes of ♀♀ and ♂♂, and polygynous social groups. Large numbers of primates foraging for sparse resources in open terrain must compete intensively for all but the most abundant foods. With danger from both predators and other monkeys, cheek pouches provide an ingenious solution. Holding as much as a full stomach, they serve the same function as a shopping basket at a bargain sale. They can be crammed rapidly and the contents dealt with later. For adult ♂♂ foraging in large, exposed groups, winners are the biggest, best-armed and most impressive fighters. ♂♂ with enlarged canines and body sizes are typical of all open-country cheek-pouch monkeys. Differences between the sexes relate both to ♂ competition and group defence.

Geography: Cheek-pouch monkeys occupy all habitats except the Sahara but are most diverse in forested areas. Thumbless monkeys occur only within the tropical forested belt.

Ecology: The evolutionary shift from arid environments back into forests occurred earlier in thumbless monkeys than in cheek-pouch monkeys. Some of the latter are still savannah species but many, notably drills, mangabeys and guenons, have become true forest species.

Natural history: Activity patterns of thumbless and cheek-pouch monkeys differ radically, with the former, like ruminants, spending the middle of the day totally inactive or asleep.

Adaptations: Terrestrial and arboreal monkeys have different limb proportions: hindlimbs are longer in the latter and more evenly balanced in the former. Early monkeys, colobids and apes all have broad faces and bold, well-separated orbits. Cheek-pouch monkeys have the eyes closer together in a narrowed, more singular structure. Stomach structures differ in that colobids have developed sacculations analagous to the rumen of ruminants.

COLOBID MONKEYS COLOBIDAE

Olive colobus	*Procolobus verus*
Red colobus	*Piliocolobus*
Pied colobus	*Colobus*

Recognition: Colobids are medium-sized, variously coloured monkeys with big bodies and small heads. Some are black, or black and white; some have red tints, some have dull olive colouring. At close quarters their most distinctive peculiarity is a lack of a thumb. Amputation of the thumbs is a mutilation for humans, hence the monkeys' anthropocentric name, from the Greek *colobe*, meaning 'cripple'.

Genealogy: A resemblance between colobus and gibbon faces is frequently noted and is best explained by a common *lack* of specialisation in their skulls and heads. It is also a resemblance that shows how conservative Old World higher primates can be in one feature while developing specialisations in another. The main colobus specialisation is hidden in the chemistry and anatomy of their digestive tracts.

Nonetheless, their thumblessness does disclose two primary adaptations that would have separated colobids from other Old World monkeys by at least 11 million years ago and probably earlier. Only in monkeys that had become wholly committed to living in dense forest would the hands become modified into flexible hooks. This involved the alignment of the long fingers into a single, narrow, curved arc (where a thumb would actually obstruct its branch-gripping function). Because their hands have lost the ability to manipulate isolated 'droppable' objects or living prey, colobus prefer to take material off a plant directly into the mouth. Thus thumblessness confirms that colobids became wholly arboreal and wholly vegetarian at an early date.

Living Asian species and African fossils (one a giant ape-sized form) are more diverse than the living African colobids, which represent a single adaptive array. The small olive colobus is a relatively primitive species that has a less demanding diet of easily digested buds, flowers and soft, young leaves. Red colobus are also conservative, requiring about half of their intake to be young digestible growth. The pied colobus are less constrained by the quality of their diet because they survive periods of shortage on drier, more mature herbage. They are the most recently evolved, having taken plant processing that much further than the other species.

Geography: Dietary limitations in the different colobus species are reflected in their distribution and their status. The olive colobus is a relict species confined to the forests of W Africa. A much wider scatter of populations shows that red colobus once ranged all over the forested parts of Africa. However, much regional differentiation shows that their present, very scattered distribution is of long standing while wide gaps prove that they have been poor dispersers. Pied colobus, on the other hand, are a widely distributed and successful group. Among them the guereza has made the most recent expansions in range and had colonised the cool montane forests of E Africa by at least 2 million years ago.

Although some Asian colobids spend much time on the ground, African species rarely leave the trees and no contemporary species occurs beyond the main outliers of Africa's tropical and montane forest belt.

Ecology: A prominent part of most colobid diets consists of leguminous plants, the leaves and fruits of which are exceptionally well protected by chemicals. Because of this peculiar chemistry, and because legumes have dominated African forests, the processing of legume toxins must have been an important factor in the evolution of colobid digestion. Difficulties in breeding captive specimens could therefore be influenced by this history of co-evolution between African colobids and leguminous trees.

Natural history: Simplistically portrayed as leaf-eaters, colobus monkeys are more accurately described as processors of difficult plant materials. These include fruits, seeds and petioles, as well as leaves, but colobus avoid ripe, soft and colourful fruits, preferring unripe, green or brown fruits, seeds or seed pods. All species include the latter in their diet but there are significant differences between species in the proportions of fruits and seeds that they eat.

The olive colobus takes the least (about 15%), followed by red colobus (about 30%). For the West African and Angolan pied colobus, fruits and seeds make up about a third of the diet while the proportion exceeds a half for the black colobus. Reasons for this reliance on seeds may lie in a consistent scarcity of nutrients in the foliage within the black colobus's ancestral range. It has developed a specific preference for the seeds for which its incisor teeth are appropriately enlarged.

Guerezas, instead, have small incisors; they do not need to rely on seeds because their digestion can extract nutrients from hard, old leaves. This enables guerezas to survive the long dry seasons typical of NE Africa.

Adaptations: That colobids have abandoned an omnivorous diet is further confirmed by the structure and chemistry of their complex, sacculated stomach which holds one-third of their body weight in food and requires long rests to allow digestion. This involves a process of bacterial fermentation that is similar to that of ruminants and other herbivorous mammals.

This form of digestion has developed to break down the cellulose that strengthens plants and to detoxify the compounds that protect leaves and seeds. Deep jaws, powered by heavy cheek muscles, and large salivary glands are further colobid adaptations. The most external manifestation of colobid adaptations are disproportionately large, heavy abdomens, long limbs, small heads with square faces, and long, 'acrobatic balancer' tails.

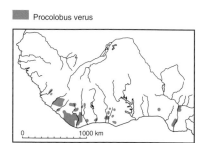

Procolobus verus

0   1000 km

Olive Colobus *Procolobus verus*

Other names: Fr. *Colobe de Van Beneden.* Ger. *Grüner stummelaffe.*
Measurements: HB 43–50cm (♀ and ♂). T 57–64cm. W 3–4.5kg (♀), 3.3–5.7kg (♂).
Recognition: The smallest colobus, cryptically coloured, with a dull grey underside and greenish olive upperside, graduating to brown on the back. The small, rounded head is distinguished by a short crest running down the crown with a light grey whorl on each side of the forehead. The hairless, dark grey face is framed by a dull-white ruff.
Distribution: Discontinuous from S Sierra Leone and Guinea to SE Nigeria. In a few localities, e.g. the Tai forest, the Ivory Coast, it is only locally distributed but numerous.
Habitat: Secondary growth within high forest; also along the margins of the forest zone, as well as in swamp and palm forests. The olive colobus prefers to move and seek refuge in dense growth below 10m but may ascend to 30m, or even the canopy, when feeding in the company of other species.
Food: About 70% young leaves, buds and flowers, and only 10% mature leaves. The quantities of fruits and seeds vary seasonally but there is a strong preference for unripe fruits. As with other colobus, food is taken into the mouth directly off the plant and not picked by hand.
Behaviour: Groups of 5–15 animals tend to contain one adult ♂ with several ♀♀ and their young. Larger groups (of up to 20 animals) may have more than one adult ♂ and could be aggregates of smaller units. The olive colobus is almost exclusively arboreal and extremely shy. The main response to any disturbance is to move into dense foliage and freeze in a hunched or crouched position in which the khaki colouring renders it very difficult to see. This behaviour is slightly modified when it is moving in mixed groups with guenons or mangabeys; it may then move temporarily into more open parts of the forest.

♀♀ have perineal swellings and appear not to breed seasonally. During the first month after birth the very small young are carried in the mouth while the mother is moving. Later the infant may wrap itself around her neck or cling to her body.

The olive colobus communicates only infrequently, with very quiet chirping or burring calls.
Adaptations: This species appears to be close to the lower size limits for a folivore.
Status: The olive colobus has never been successfully raised in zoos and captive breeding is not an option. It is declining due to loss of forest habitats and hunting. Listed as Class A (African Convention), Appendix 2 (CITES), Endangered (IUCN).

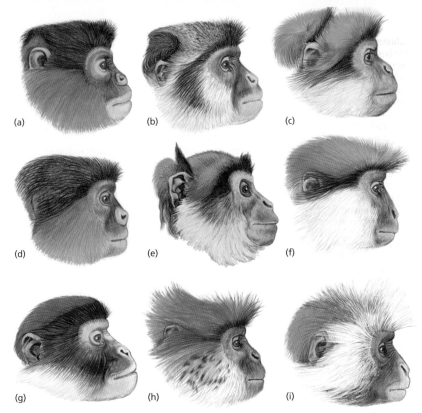

(a) Western red colobus. (b) Pennant's red colobus. (c) Tana River red colobus.
(d) Preuss's red colobus. (e) Central African red colobus. (f) Iringa red colobus.
(g) Tshuapa red colobus. (h) Montane race of Central African red colobus (*foai*).
(i) Zanzibar red colobus.

Red Colobus *Piliocolobus*

Zanzibar red colobus	*Piliocolobus kirkii*
Iringa red colobus	*Piliocolobus gordonorum*
Tana River red colobus	*Piliocolobus rufomitratus*
Tshuapa red colobus	*Piliocolobus tholloni*
Central African red colobus	*Piliocolobus oustaleti*
Pennant's red colobus	*Piliocolobus pennanti*
Preuss's red colobus	*Piliocolobus preussi*
Western red colobus	*Piliocolobus badius*

Other names: Fr. *Colobe bai*. Ger. *Roter Stummelaffe*.
Measurements: HB 45–62cm (♀), 45–70cm (♂). T 42–80cm. W 7–9kg (♀), 9–13kg (♂).
Recognition: Red colobus occur in numerous populations and species, some of which show much variation at the individual level while others are more uniform. All tend to be some permutation of red, white, black, brown and grey but build is the surest guide to recognition. They have exceptionally small heads on long-backed, pot-bellied bodies. The limbs are very long, with the legs slightly exceeding the arms in length. While the thumb is atrophied to a mere bump, the other fingers are aligned in a long, very powerful hook. All species tend to have dark or black faces, and some have pink lips and nose. Young ♂♂ have peri-anal swellings which appear to mimic the genital swellings of ♀♀.
Distribution: Equatorial forests from the Atlantic to the Indian Ocean but populations are extremely localised and always found near permanent water. In E Zaïre they occur up to 1,500m.

Habitat: Only in moist, evergreen forest close to permanent water. Although most red colobus are found in lowland forest, some occur in montane areas up to 1,500m. Their distribution may be determined by past climatic events and human hunting habits (both past and present) rather than by current vegetation patterns.

Food: Red colobus are very selective of the plant types and parts that form the principal components of their diet but they eat many species in the course of a single day. The proportions of fruits, seeds and young or old leaves are strongly influenced by local availability and by the feeding habits of other primates. Groups scatter to feed and can have a massive impact on the foliage of their food trees.

Behaviour: Although small family groups are ocasionally seen, red colobus typically form large troops, numbering up to 100 animals.These form a territorial unit which remains strictly resident within a 25–150ha territory. Densities can approach 300 per km². The territory is vigorously defended against intruders and advertised by all group members calling with a variety of barks and chirps. The composition of territorial units includes many ♂♂ that remain in the territory throughout their lives but ♀♀ may move between groups. Feeding is concentrated in two main sessions during the morning and evening, with a period of inactivity during the middle of the day. Red colobus follow routines of movement and have preferred sites for sun-bathing or sleeping in.

Movement through the canopy is very characteristic, with animals crossing relatively wide gaps by leaping and catching slender supports with hooked hands or by setting up a catapult effect by rocking back and forth on a vertical stem. Some populations are more exclusively arboreal than others. Although some populations may be relatively shy, nearly all colobus are extremely vulnerable to hunting as they are noisy, conspicuous and relatively slow.

Young are carried, clinging to the belly of the mother for 3 months. Weaned at 1 year, ♀♀ mature by 2 years of age and ♂♂ at 3–3½ years.

Adaptations: Red colobus have a long digestive tract with a sacculated stomach that shows adaptations comparable with those of folivorous ungulates but is less specialised than those of pied colobus.

Status: See individual entries below.

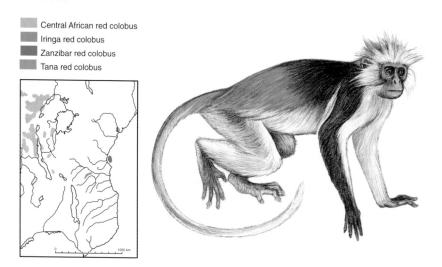

Central African red colobus
Iringa red colobus
Zanzibar red colobus
Tana red colobus

1000 km

Zanzibar Red Colobus *Piliocolobus kirkii*

Other names: Fr. *Colobe de Zanzibar*. Ger. *Zanzibar Stummelaffe*.
Measurements: See red colobus (lower range of measurements).
Recognition: Colobus with a ragged, tesselated coat of three colours: red, black and white, individually very variable. The pink lips and nose form a strong contrast with the bare black skin on the rest of the face. The long, limp hair on the crown of the head is particularly characteristic. The vocalisations of this species are different from any other species.

Habitat: Occurring in relict patches throughout Zanzibar I., but found mainly in the southern part of the island and also in scrub forest growing on waterless coral rag on the eastern side of the island. A small population has been translocated to Pemba I.

Food: Some groups feed almost exclusively on mangrove leaves and the populations on coral rag appear to subsist on a drier, coarser diet than any recorded for red colobus. In the absence of any other colobus competitor, these populations show no disproportionate preference for leaf stems but fruits and seeds comprise one-third of the diet while mature leaves are scarcely eaten at all. Young leaves, buds and flowers are the preferred parts. *Bridelia*, figs and Alexandrian laurel (*Calophyllum*) are the preferred species from a total of over 60 food plants.

Status: In 1981 the total population was estimated at 1,500 animals distributed in 75 groups. Some groups show evidence of decline while others, notably those on Jozani, Muyuni and Uzi Is. appear to be healthy, stable groups. The Zanzibar colobus is nominally protected and the formation of national parks on Zanzibar I. is currently under discussion. Listed as Class A (African Convention); Appendix 1 (CITES), Highly Endangered (IUCN).

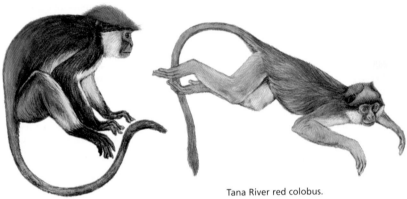

Tana River red colobus.

Iringa red colobus.

Iringa Red Colobus *Piliocolobus gordonorum*

Other names: Fr. *Colobe bai de Gordon*. Ger. *Uhehe Stummelaffe*.

Measurements: See red colobus (lower range of measurements).

Recognition: A dark, tricoloured species (red, black and white) with a thin, shaggy coat, less tesselated than the Zanzibar species and with a tendency to darker tones.

Habitat: Restricted to a few small forests on the Uzungwa Mts, where it survives in riverine and montane forest patches between 550 and 6,000m. The range is shared by Angola pied colobus and other monkeys.

Food: About two-thirds leaf stems (petioles) from some 35 tree species. Both ripe and unripe fruits make up nearly 20% of the diet, with buds, flowers, new leaves and very small quantities of older leaves making up the balance. Competition with other monkeys may explain why this species is a leaf-stem specialist. Selective clearance, reducing the colobus's food choice, will severely affect this species.

Status: Now thought to number no more than 450 individuals, this species suffered a major catastrophe as a result of the construction of a railway, combined with extensive logging and agricultural expansion, in the 1970s. Although nominally protected by law, the animal is frequently hunted as a delicacy. Listed as Class A (African Convention), Appendix 2 (CITES), Endangered (IUCN).

Tana River Red Colobus *Piliocolobus rufomitratus*

Other names: Fr. *Colobe bai de la Tana*. Ger. *Tana Stummelaffe*.

Measurements: See red colobus (lower range of measurements).

Recognition: Colobus with a dull, greyish brown back, paler greyish limbs and a grey-white underside. The russet cap with cow-licks above each ear are the only prominent feature. In spite of resembling some *P. tephrosceles* in colour, it differs in size and skull shape.

Habitat: Frequenting riverine and gallery forest, only on the levees of the R. Tana between Kipendi village and the mouth of the river, notably the Mnazini and Kinyadu forests. These forests are dominated by *Pachystela* and *Barringtonia*.

Food: On the R. Tana only 22 food trees are used by red colobus, fewer than in any other area where this monkey has been studied. In spite of such a narrow choice, it maintains a similar range of food types to other populations. Diet comprises a quarter fruits and seeds, two-thirds buds, flowers and young leaves, and just over 10% of old mature leaves. This species is peculiarly dependent on the leaves and fruit of *Ficus sycomorus*.

Status: Living in a dispersal group of 4–25, a 1972 census estimated a population of 1,860 individuals. By 1995 this had dropped to 1,200. This decline appears to have several causes: (a) drastic changes in vegetation due to dam construction and water diversion which changed the water-table; (b) forest clearance for agriculture; (c) fires eroding levee forests; (d) degradation due to livestock and wood collection; (e) selective felling of *Ficus* trees for canoes; (e) hunting. Nominally protected by law and listed as Class A (African Convention); Appendix 1 (CITES), Endangered (IUCN). Now probably Highly Endangered.

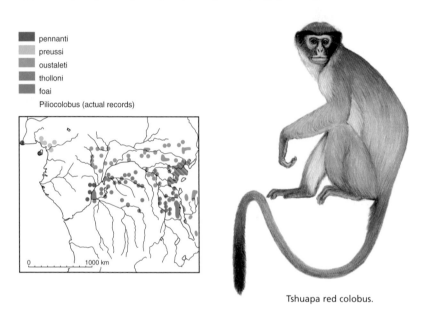

pennanti
preussi
oustaleti
tholloni
foai

Piliocolobus (actual records)

0   1000 km

Tshuapa red colobus.

Tshuapa Red Colobus *Piliocolobus tholloni*

Other names: Fr. *Colobe bai de Thollon*. Ger. *Tshuapa Stummelaffe*.

Measurements: See red colobus (upper range of measurements).

Recognition: Of almost uniform foxy-red colouring, darkening to a deep brown on the shoulders and lighter on the underside. This colobus has a longer face, with a prominent square muzzle and an overshot lower jaw. The coat is short and sleek.

Subspecies: This species has an uncertain relationship with two populations which may represent the product of long-term mixing between *P. tholloni* and colobus from the north-east of its range, *P. oustaleti langi* and *P. o. lulindicus*.

Habitat: Ranges intermittently through the forested areas south of the R. Zaïre and west of the R. Lomami in widely separated localities along rivers draining from the south into the R. Zaïre.

Food: Not yet studied.

Status: Largely unknown but extensive expansion of human populations and cultivation from Kasai northwards and uncontrolled hunting are sure to have affected its status. Classified as Insufficiently Known (IUCN), it is listed with others of the red colobus group as Class B (African Convention), Appendix 2 (CITES).

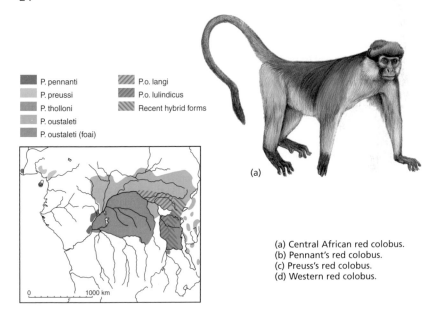

P. pennanti
P. preussi
P. tholloni
P. oustaleti
P. oustaleti (foai)
P.o. langi
P.o. lulindicus
Recent hybrid forms

0   1000 km

(a)

(a) Central African red colobus.
(b) Pennant's red colobus.
(c) Preuss's red colobus.
(d) Western red colobus.

Central African Red Colobus *Piliocolobus oustaleti*

Other names: Fr. *Colobe bai d'Ouganda*. Ger. *Uganda Stummelaffe*.
Measurements: See red colobus (upper range of measurements).
Recognition: Some populations are relatively uniform and others are highly variable at the individual level. Most have dark extremities to the limbs (often black hands and feet), with red markings especially on the cap. Body sizes are among the largest of the red colobus radiation and montane populations tend to have thick coats, with the shoulder fur lengthened into a heavy cape in mature ♂♂.
Subspecies: 20 subspecies have been described of this highly variable species. Provisionally eight subspecies with definable ranges can be recognised (after M. Colyn): *P. o. oustaleti* (north of R. Zaire and R. Aruwimi), *P. o. parmentierorum* (R. Lualaba/R. Lomani junction); *P. o. foai* (Itombwe massif – very distinctive montane form), *P. o. langi* (between R. Aruwimi and R. Maiko – some *tholloni* traits), *P. o. lulindicius* between R. Lowa and R. Lualaba – some *tholloni* traits), *P. o. semlikiensis* (R. Semliki valley – localised isolate), *P. o. elliotti* (Lubero Mts, west of L. George – hybrid?), *P. o. tephrosceles* (east of Rift Valley).
Distribution: Central Africa north and east of R. Zaïre to W Uganda and W Tanzania.
Habitat: Ranges between 300 and 2,500m, spanning a wide range of forest types from levee, swamp, lowland and mixed to montane forests.
Food: The easternmost race, *P. o. tephrosceles*, has been studied in considerable detail. In Kibale (Uganda) young leaves and buds comprise nearly half and mature leaves a quarter of the annual diet. At Gombe, in Tanzania (a more markedly seasonal forest), these proportions are inverted. At both sites intense competition from frugivorous primates probably helps to explain their very minor consumption of fruits and seeds. Leaf stalks are also important at Kibale.
Status: With a very wide scatter of populations, most in remote, seldom-visited areas, conservation status is insufficiently known. Some of the distinctive races or varieties included here are of very restricted distribution.

Pennant's Red Colobus *Piliocolobus pennanti*

Other names: Fr. *Colobe bai de Bouvier*. Ger. *Bioko Stummelaffe*.
Measurements: See red colobus.
Recognition: Reddish above and paler red below, with forequarters and crown verging towards black, and a white ruff. A radial parting of hair on the forehead is distinctive. Overall tints are paler in the mainland form.

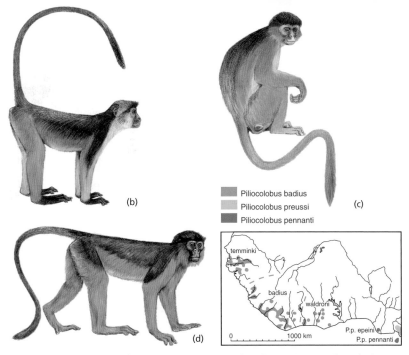

(b)

Piliocolobus badius
Piliocolobus preussi
Piliocolobus pennanti

(c)

temminki

badius

waldroni

0   1000 km

P.p. epeini

P.p. pennanti

(d)

Subspecies: *P. p. pennanti* (Bioko I., formerly Fernando Po), *P. p. bouvieri* (R. Lefini), *P. p. epieni* (R. Niger delta). (Note: "epieni" is a *nomen nudum*.)

Habitat: This species poses a major biogeographical puzzle. Apart from the vestigial populations in Bioko and R. Lefini there are virtually no red colobus over most of central W Africa, which is otherwise a region of exceptional floristic and faunal richness. This near-elimination does not seem to be recent. Climatic changes, competition with other primates and past hunting by humans are possible, but less likely, explanations than some major species-specific disease pandemic. The effects of such a catastrophe could have been long lasting because all red colobus are poor dispersers. Neither the habitat nor the availability of food offer any clue to the relict status of these populations.

Food: Not yet studied.

Status: It is uncertain which populations survive. Nominally protected; listed as Class B (African Convention), Appendix 2 (CITES), Endangered (IUCN).

Preuss's Red Colobus *Piliocolobus preussi*

Other names: Fr. *Colobe bai de Preuss*. Ger. *Preuss Stummelaffe*.

Measurements: See red colobus.

Recognition: Tentatively treated as a distinct species this colobus shares some features (colour) with *P. pennanti* while others (such as hair-growth patterns on the head and nose shape) are typical of the western *P. badius* group.

Habitat: A vestigial population now restricted to an interface between the low-lying R. Cross and the formerly forested uplands of Cameroon.

Food: Not yet studied.

Status: Now restricted to forests within a strip 120 by 60km, it is estimated that less than 8,000 survive, most in Korup National Park and Ejagham Forest Reserve. Listed as Class B (African Convention), Appendix 2 (CITES), Endangered (IUCN).

Western Red Colobus *Piliocolobus badius*

Other names: Fr. *Colobe bai d'Afrique Occidentale*. Ger. *Westafrikanischer Stummelaffe*.

Measurements: HB 47–63cm. T 52–75cm. W 5.5–10kg.

Recognition: Black or dark grey upperparts with lower limbs and underparts ranging from rich red to light orange. The face is characterised by a very flat profile but with the nostrils forming a peculiar swollen structure arising from a saucer-like depression (less marked in *waldronae*).

Subspecies: *P. b. badius* (Sierra Leone, Liberia, Guinea, Ivory Coast), *P. b. temminckii* (Senegambia, Guinea Bissau, NW Guinea), *P. b. waldronae* (Ghana and Ivory Coast east of R. Bandama).

Habitat: Various forest types, including mangrove swamps, woodland and cultivation mosaics, especially in the north-western part of the range.

Food: In Senegal, where there are fewer primates, less competition may explain why over a third of the diet is fruits and seeds (another peculiarity here is occasional consumption of bark). Young leaves, buds and flowers are the main food while mature leaves are very rarely eaten. Only 40 food plants have been recorded in Senegal. In Sierra Leone fewer fruits and seeds and more old leaves are eaten, reflecting the much higher levels of competition from other monkeys.

Status: The range of this species is declining rapidly due to logging and increasing cultivation but it is nominally protected in several national parks or protected areas. Listed as Class B (African Convention); Appendix 2 (CITES), Vulnerable (IUCN).

Pied Colobus *Colobus*

Black colobus	*Colobus satanus*
Western pied colobus	*Colobus polykomos*
Angola pied colobus	*Colobus angolensis*
Geoffroy's pied colobus	*Colobus vellerosus*
Guereza colobus	*Colobus guereza* (syn. *C. abyssinicus*)

Recognition: Pied colobus are long-fingered, agile monkeys. Each species has a distinctively shaped face but they are best distinguished by their colouring. Except for the all-black *C. satanus*, all species sport patches of white fur which contrast strongly with the predominantly black body. These flashes appear on the chin, cheeks, shoulders, rump, thighs or tail. Their heavy bodies, long backs and limbs impart a bouncy gait that differs strikingly from the more fluent movements of guenon monkeys.

Genealogy: Pied colobus radiation is exclusively African and predominantly tropical. In their ability to digest coarse, older material they are more specialised than red colobus. This has allowed them to expand into drier, colder and more seasonal environments.

Geography: Guereza colobus, restricted to northern and eastern forests, appear to be the most cold-adapted form and may be the most recently evolved. They are likely to have colonised much of their eastern range during a cool dry period. North of the R. Zaïre, overlaps in range between common guerezas and the scarcer Angola colobus might reflect the pre-eminence of guerezas in recent cooler times superimposed upon Angola colobus, which represent older colobus stock.

Ecology: Pied colobus occupy a broad swathe of tropical and subtropical forests across the whole of Africa. Montane forests have been colonised by Angola colobus in more southerly and central regions and by guerezas in the north-east.

Natural history: Pied colobus territories are smaller than those of red colobus. They can subsist on material that is older and less palatable to the red colobus. They also tend to feed from fewer tree species.

Adaptations: The colouring of pied colobus is most conspicuous during daily chorusing around dawn and dusk, at which times animals climb into a prominent tree or onto the roof of the forest. Each group advertises its strength and numbers by joining together in very loud tattoos of croaking, with much jumping, branch-shaking and flouncing of tails and tassels, in a prolonged, ritualised threat display. The most extravagant movements, loudest calls and most aggressive postures are exhibited by dominant ♂♂.

Black Colobus *Colobus satanus*

Other names: Eng. Satanic colobus. Fr. *Colobe noir*. Ger. *Satananaffe*.

Measurements: HB 50–77cm. W 9–15kg.

Recognition: All-black, without tassels or a tufted tail, and most like the Angola colobus in general morphology. It has a shorter nose, thicker incisors and lacks the loud, reverberating calls heard in other species.

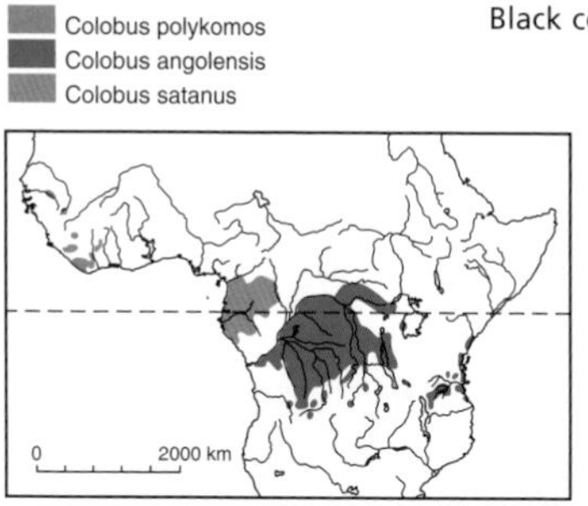

Colobus polykomos
Colobus angolensis
Colobus satanus

Black colobus.

Western pied colobus.

Black colobus.

Habitat: Limited to high-canopy forests between SW Cameroon, Bioko I. (formerly Fernando Po) and the R. Zaïre. The black colobus has been found to exist at about one-tenth the density of pied colobus in Uganda. Part of its mainland range is dominated by coastal sand-dune forests with an impoverished flora. Many of the local tree species, especially legumes, have been found to be protected by distasteful, or even toxic, compounds.

Food: A very high proportion of seeds and unripe fruits. The black colobus shows a marked preference for the leaves of lianas. In sand-dune forest young and old leaves are eaten equally. In the Ogooué basin it scarcely eats old leaves at all but takes a larger proportion of fruits and seeds.

Status: A low density and a poorer diet might have reduced the value of energetic territorial behaviour. This could help explain why this species is duller in colouring and has a quieter vocal repertoire. Widely hunted, it is a popular and vulnerable quarry for hunters armed with shotguns or bows and arrows. It appears to be a weak colonist of secondary growth after logging and is currently declining in number in most parts of its range. Listed as Class B (African Convention), Appendix 2 (CITES), Endangered (IUCN).

Western Pied Colobus *Colobus polykomos*

Other names: Eng. Ursine colobus. Fr. *Colobe blanc et noir d'Afrique Occidentale*. Ger. *Weissbart Stummelaffe*.

Measurements: HB 50–61cm (♀), 50–67cm (♂). T 63–90cm. W 6.6–10kg (♀), 8–11.7kg (♂).

Recognition: Long-limbed and long-fingered, with an intensely black body and legs, a wholly white tail, a peculiar bonnet of straggly silver hair around the face and a long epaulette of white fur on each shoulder and forearm. The callosities on the rump are fringed with a narrow margin of white hairs.

Subspecies: *C. p. polykomos* (west of R. Sassandra to Sierra Leone and S Guinea). '*C. p. dollmani*' (from east of the R. Sassandra) is probably a hybrid with *C. vellerosus* in this very narrow contact zone.

Habitat: Rainforest and forest galleries are preferred.

Food: Selective in their feeding habits, taking only about one-third of their total diet from the 20 dominant species of trees and lianes available. Fruits and seeds comprise more than a third of the diet; buds, flowers and other foliage form another third and mature foliage makes up the balance. Unripe seeds are frequently eaten but the diet varies both regionally and seasonally. Of foliage there is a strong preference for lianes, leguminous trees and *Strychnos* leaves.

Status: This species was until recently common and widespread. While the total range is still extensive, habitat loss and hunting have confined the remaining animals to a decreasing scatter of vestigial populations. Currently listed as Vulnerable with a threat rating of 3 (IUCN.)

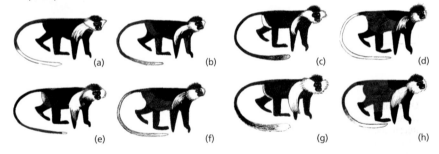

Angola Pied Colobus *Colobus angolensis*

Other names: Fr. *Colobe d'Angola*. Ger. *Angola Stummelaffe*. Swah. *Mbega*.

Measurements: HB 50–61cm (♀), 50–67cm (♂). T 63–90cm. W 9–20kg.

Recognition: A black-bodied colobus with a white ruff and long shoulder epaulettes. The tail varies from all-white to nearly all-black. The coat is short and thin in lowland forms but long and coarse in highland populations.

Subspecies: *C. a. angolensis* (Zaïre basin south of river), *C. a. cottoni* (NE Zaïre basin, north of river), *C. a. palliatus* (Eastern Arc forests and Kenya/Tanzania coastal forests), *C. a. ruwenzori* (Ruwenzori to Burundi). Further subdivision is possible (see black and white illustrations above).

Habitat: Montane and lowland forests. In E Tanzania, Angola pied colobus are most concentrated at elevations between 400 and 1,000m.

Food: Diet is similar to that of *C. polykomos* in combining about two-thirds of leaves with one-third fruits and seeds. In E Tanzania mainly ripe fruits are eaten and nearly a third of the diet is mature leaf growth. This capacity to subsist on old leaves could explain why Angola colobus have the most extensive range of any pied colobus. Significantly they are either outnumbered or encircled by guerezas on the margins of their range in parts of central Africa. This could imply that their original range in E Africa might have been eroded by the guerezas because of the latter's better ability to digest cellulose and mature leaves.

Status: Angola colobus are not especially rare but isolated populations on the E African coast and highlands are locally vulnerable.

Opposite (above). Angola pied colobus, southern highlands form ("*sharpei*").
Right. Geoffroy's pied colobus.
Opposite (below). Colour/regional morphs of Angola pied colobus.
(a) *angolensis* (S. Zaire basin).
(b) *cottoni* (N.E. Zaire)
(c) "*adolphi frederici*" (Kagera valley).
(d) "*prigoginei*" (Mt Kabobo).
(e) *ruwenzori* (Central highlands).
(f) "*cordieri*" (Uzimba).
(g) "*sharpei*" (Southern highlands).
(h) *palliatus* (Eastern Arc forests).

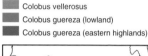

■ Colobus vellerosus
■ Colobus guereza (lowland)
■ Colobus guereza (eastern highlands)

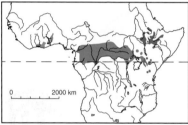

0   2000 km

Geoffroy's Pied Colobus *Colobus vellerosus*

Other names: Fr. *Colobe de Geoffroy*. Ger. *Geoffroy Stummelaffe*.
Measurements: HB 50–67cm. T 63–90cm. W 8–15kg.
Recognition: A black monkey distinguished by a broad white ruff which completely encircles the face and is reminiscent of a nun's wimple. There is a white patch on the thigh, a white tail and vestigial epaulettes of sparse white hairs. The facial profile and skull bear more resemblance to *C. guereza* than to *C. polykomos*.
Habitat: Ranges between the R. Bandama to Dahomey and Togo in lowland rainforest and gallery forests. Voice and social structure resemble those of *C. guereza*, with only one ♂ in the smaller groups and only a few mature ♂♂ in the larger groups (which may number up to 50 animals).
Food: Tends to feed in more shaded, middle layers of the forest when mixed with red colobus (which prefer rapid regrowth canopy foliage near the forest roof). The diet is thought to resemble that of *C. guereza*, but the exact composition may vary according to the presence or absence of other monkeys.
Status: Currently listed as Vulnerable (IUCN) but likely to become Endangered if present rates of habitat change and hunting continue.

Guereza Colobus *Colobus guereza* (syn. *C. abyssinicus*)

Other names: Fr. *Colobe guereza*. Ger. *Guereza Mantelaffe*. Swah. *Mbega*.
Measurements: HB 48–65cm (♀); 54–75cm (♂). T 65–90. W 10–23kg.
Recognition: A black and white monkey with shorter, thinner fur in lowland forests but very long and thicker fur in mountain areas. The white on the tail and mantle is most extensive in easternmost populations. In the west, the black shoulders and tail root are more extensive.
Subspecies: *C. g. caudatus* (E African mountains), *C. g. guereza* (Ethiopia), *C. g. occidentalis* (E Nigeria to W Kenya).

Guereza colobus. (a) Highland East African form. (b) Central African lowland form.

Habitat: Wide ranging, from lowland tropical rainforest to the upper reaches of montane forest, as well as in *Acacia*-dominated riverine galleries and evergreen thicket forests. Where the range of guerezas overlaps with that of red colobus, they feed from fewer tree species (usually less than half the usual number) and choose different plant parts. A less varied diet allows them to occupy forests or thickets with impoverished or specialised floras. They can survive in drier, more degraded forests.

Food: In all areas where they have been studied, guerezas have been found to be the most folivorous colobus species except for the olive colobus, which takes almost identical ratios of plant parts (the lack of any overlap with these two species suggests that they may be competitively exclusive). About three-quarters or more of the diet consists of leaves but the proportion of old leaves varies with the locality and season and is influenced by the presence of other monkeys. For example, where guerezas and red colobus feed on *Markhamia*, the former eat leaf blades and the latter strip out and consume petioles alone.

Behaviour: Guerezas live in small territories where several related offspring live with one or more hierarchically ranked ♂♂. Mutual ♂ intolerance forces ♂♂ to disperse and promotes ♀ cohesion.

Status: Guerezas are abundant in most parts of their lowland range, although they are declining in many localities. In Ethiopia continuous habitat loss and hunting over centuries has reduced a formerly very extensive range to a wide scatter of relict populations. They are still abundant in E African forest reserves and parks but are declining elsewhere. As guerezas are not considered to be endangered, IUCN gives them a low conservation rating. However, unrestricted trade in their skins could lead to extinction of eastern montane populations which have the most desirable pelts and the most restricted distribution.

CHEEK-POUCH MONKEYS CERCOPITHECIDAE

Baboons	*Papio*
Gelada	*Theropithecus gelada*
Mandrill and drill	*Mandrillus*
Drill-mangabeys	*Cercocebus*
Baboon-mangabeys	*Lophocebus*
Barbary macaque	*Macaca sylvanus*
Guenons and allies	*Certhopithecinae*

Recognition: This family embraces all the non-colobine African monkeys. They vary greatly in size, colour and shape, ranging from the miniature, round-headed talapoins to heavily built, long-faced baboons and drills. The more arboreal lowland species tend to have longer tails; terrestrial and montane species have shorter tails. As their popular name indicates, all these monkeys have voluminous sacs behind each cheek.

Genealogy: This family is thought to derive from the main-line branch of 'Victoria monkeys', which continued as omnivores in drier habitats after colobines had split off to become primate 'pseudo-ruminants'.

There are two main subfamilies of cheek-pouch monkeys: 'baboon-macaques', or Papioninae, and guenons, or Cercopithecinae. Once proto-baboons and proto-macaques had differentiated, the latter spread into Eurasia (where they speciated into many forms) while the baboon group radiation continued within Africa.

Among the earliest 'baboons' were at least seven species of grass-eating geladas (including a gorilla-sized one). They flourished from one end of the continent to the other but are now reduced to relict populations of a single species in the Ethiopian mountains. True baboons also radiated into numerous forms and one branch, the drills, colonised the equatorial forests of central-west Africa. These early drills and baboons in turn gave rise to smaller more arboreal forms which survive as 'mangabeys'. In spite of their resemblances, molecular evidence suggests that 'drill-mangabeys' and 'baboon-mangabeys' are parallel derivatives from separate, more terrestrial ancestors. The failure of baboons to get beyond Africa, and the success of early macaques in crossing extensive arid barriers, is explained by the latter's ability to tolerate extremes of temperature and live off the poorest, most difficult land. Well illustrated by several living macaques this is no recent development because fossils show that the Barbary macaque has lived along the edges of the Sahara for over 6 million years.

Temperature tolerance, relatively small size, cheek pouches and a sophisticated social system allow macaques to exploit mangrove swamps, seashores, floodplains and other habitats with harsh seasonal or daily changes. That early macaques succeeded in colonising these difficult environments is suggested by the existence of Allen's swamp monkey, which is a relict tropical African macaque.

Talapoin monkeys appear to be the culmination of a trend toward miniaturisation in an early stock of 'tropical macaques'. Talapoins and Allen's swamp monkey retain macaque-like characteristics (e.g. sexual swellings of the F) but also point to the emergence of the second subfamily of cheek-pouch monkeys: the guenons, or Cercopithecinae. The guenon radiation, a late but highly successful offshoot of the Papioninae, is outlined later (see p. 50).

Geography: Living cheek-pouch monkeys include representatives from many geographical and climatic extremes. The Barbary macaque inhabits the N African littoral and mountains. Baboons range through many habitats, both dry and humid, from the Cape of Good Hope to Cape Verde. Within equatorial Africa both subfamilies are represented from the two extremes of climate. Desert baboons and the Sahelian patas inhabit dry environments whereas drills and putty-nosed guenons live in moist forest habitats.

Ecology: Almost all species are dependent on water or relatively moist foods but the cheek-pouch monkeys remain the most arid adapted of all primates. Secondary re-invasion of moist habitats is thought to be most recent in the guenons, less recent for the mangabeys, and earliest in the case of the drills.

Natural history: African cheek-pouch monkeys are the epitome of agility, speed and ingenuity. Bright colours, ritualised swaggering, head-bobbing and emphatic facial expressions bear witness to highly specific and elaborate systems of visual communication.

Mixed groups of monkeys are common, especially among the smaller, most arboreal species, a strategy which helps increase vigilance against predators as well as reveal more food.

As the most numerous and widespread primates in Africa, cheek-pouch monkeys represent a major disease reservoir and the natural history of monkey diseases has special importance for human AIDS. Many African monkeys are resistant to AIDS. The monkey retrovirus, SIV, is genetically closer to human HIV2 than either of them are to the main human aids virus, HIV1. If it could be understood how and why wild African monkeys are naturally resistant to AIDS, better ways of protecting humans might be developed.

Adaptations: The diagnostic cheek pouches of these monkeys clearly evolved after their ancestors split away from the colobines, which lack them. The most likely context for their evolution would have been competitive feeding on sparse foods in dangerous, exposed environments. This is evidently an effective strategy for the semi-terrestrial, open-country species. Because conditions are rather different in richer, arboreal habitats; tree-dwelling in closed forests is evidently a more recent adaptation.

Grey-cheeked baboon–mangabey, showing cheek pouches.

Baboons *Papio*

Sacred baboon	*Papio hamadryas*
Guinea baboon	*Papio papio*
Olive baboon	*Papio anubis*
Yellow baboon	*Papio cynocephalus*
Chacma baboon	*Papio ursinus*

Recognition: Baboons are predominantly quadrupedal, brownish, grizzled terrestrial monkeys among which adult ♂♂ are both bigger and longer muzzled than ♀♀. Resemblance of ♀♀ from all regions has encouraged the view that ♂ differences are merely racial. However, there are many anatomical and behavioural differences that distinguish five major populations, treated as species here.

Genealogy: Fossil baboons from S and E Africa go back at least 3 million years but the timing of regional separation or differentiation is still not known. A mosaic of resemblances and differences implies that relationships between baboon types are not simple. Nonetheless the mosaic pattern suggests a possible sequence of events. Following an initial dispersal over all sub-Sahara savannahs, northern and southern populations emerged. The smaller Guinea and sacred baboons (which have several features in common) are northern derivatives. The other, bigger baboons derive from a single southern group which first split along the Rift Valley fracture line. Strong resemblances between the Chacma and olive baboons suggest that southerners then channelled through a Gaboon savannah corridor to colonise Cameroon during a period of dry climate. These originally southern baboons bisected the former northern population and expanded both eastwards and westwards. Guinea baboons appear to be the westernmost relict of this retreat (but electrophoretic studies suggest that olive baboons have assimilated Guinea baboon genes along the way). Sacred baboons, which are now restricted to mountains bordering the Red Sea, are also hybridising with olive baboons and are probably in the course of retreating from a once pan-Ethiopian range. The East African yellow baboon also seems to have bisected a formally continuous range by interposing itself between the olive and Chacma baboons (another closely related pair).

Ecology: The ecological implications of this interpretation are that yellow baboons have become particularly well adapted to fire-climax woodlands. Their expansion westwards could be very recent if this type of vegetation has spread through human use of fire.

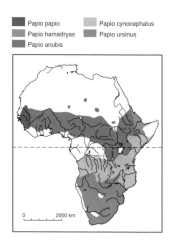

Papio papio
Papio hamadryas
Papio anubis
Papio cynocephalus
Papio ursinus

0   2000 km

If the northern baboons were originally adapted to drier and colder conditions than the southerners it is possible that olive baboons owe their present vast range to quite recent changes in climate. It is known that the last and penultimate Ice Ages were followed by warmer, wetter weather and more wooded environments. This would have suited olive baboons better than either Guinea or sacred baboons. Present distributions are best explained by some such sequence of events but the timing remains highly speculative.

Natural history: A primary north/south division prior to the evolution of olive baboons is consistent with behaviour. Both Guinea and sacred baboons live in minimal social units consisting of a ♂ and up to five ♀♀ with their offspring. These harems allow the animals to be more dispersed than is the case with the large multi-M groups typical of other species. Large groups are more destructive but the impact is offset in richer habitats.

Adaptations: The baboons' heavy canine teeth and whole tooth row are cantilevered out from the skull as far as is mechanically feasible. This extreme projection of the muzzle allows baboons to make visually emphatic signals, such as ritualised yawns (as well as providing very long, seed-grinding molar surfaces). This kind of signalling is especially important for regulating ♂ relationships. The ♂'s muzzle is enhanced by a bare face surrounded by a big, circular ruff or cape of hair. Social display of these features, punctuated with loud, explosive barks, deters both potential rivals and predators.

Gross sexual dimorphism in this large, open-country monkey allows ♂♂ to be scouts and protectors for the group as a whole. It is also a factor which enables the principle of 'armoured truce' to bring order to aggregations at sleeping, feeding or drinking sites.

Sacred Baboon *Papio hamadryas*

Other names: Eng. Hamadryas baboon. Fr. *Hamadryas*. Ger. *Mantelpavian, Hamadrayas*.
Measurements: HB 50–65cm (♀), 70–95cm (♂). T 40–60cm. SH 40–50cm (♀), 50–65cm (♂). W. 10–15kg (♀), 15–20kg (♂).
Recognition: A grizzled, greenish brown monkey, except for sexually active harem ♂♂ which are grizzled dove-grey, with lighter cheek ruffs, tail tip and callosity margins, and darker hands and feet. The face and callosities are flesh coloured. Callosities are largest and brightest in dominant ♂♂ and apparently mimic ♀ sexual skin.
Habitat: Arid subdesert, steppe, hillsides, escarpments and mountains bordering the Red Sea. Ranges through E Ethiopia from Suakin (Sudan) to Somali border; also in SW Arabia. The basic social unit consists of a single ♂ with one or more ♀♀ (a harem), who are abducted while still immature or 'inherited' from an aged ♂. ♀♀ are coerced by harem masters who initiate all the group's movements. Harems whose members are related by blood frequently sleep together or gather when foods are concentrated. These associations, called 'clans', occasionally converge to form 'bands' on a single resource, especially sleeping-cliffs. Very occasionally several hundred animals may come together at common feeding or sleeping sites to form a regional 'troop'.

(a) Guinea baboon. (b) Yellow baboon. (c) Olive baboon.

Food: Opportunistic omnivore. Grass, buds, invertebrates and the fruits of desert plants, notably heglig (*Balanites*) and buffalo thorn (*Ziziphus*), are of great seasonal importance.
Status: Agricultural expansion and irrigation projects lead to conflict. The fine, long-haired capes of adult ♂♂ are used to embellish ceremonial cloaks in Ethiopia. Large numbers of these baboons were formerly trapped for medical research in the former USSR.

The former range of this baboon extended into Egypt where it was held sacred to the Ancient Egyptian god Thoth. Free-living baboons in the temple of Thoth were regarded as priests to the god of Learning and Lord of Time. They were also used by Ancient Egyptian 'police' to arrest malefactors.

Listed as Vermin (African Convention), Appendix 2 (CITES).

Guinea Baboon *Papio papio*

Other names: Fr. *Babouin de Guinée*. Ger. *Sphynx-pavian*.
Measurements: HB 55cm (♀), 75cm (♂). T 35–60cm. SH 45cm (♀), 60cm (♂). W est. 12kg (♀), est. 19kg (♂).
Recognition: A grizzled, reddish brown baboon with a sharply defined cape on adult ♂♂. There are prominent nostrils above the mouth and dark pink skin on the face and callosities. The tail is smooth and 'unbroken'.
Habitat: Woodlands, savannah and Sahelian steppe within reach of water; gallery forests in south of range. Ranges from S Mauritania to Sierra Leone. Along its eastern limits the Guinea baboon may be hybridising with the larger olive baboon. Richer food resources and protection in Niokolo Koba National Park, Senegal, allow large aggregations of harem groups, numbering 10–200 (sometimes exceeding 500) individuals, to forage together.
Food: Seeds, shoots, roots, fruits, fungi, invertebrates, small vertebrates and eggs. Where agriculture has expanded, rice, maize, yams, groundnuts and other cultivated crops are also taken.
Status: Protected in Niokolo Koba National Park where densities of 2–15 per km² have been estimated. Agricultural expansion, tree-felling and direct hunting for laboratory specimens or crop protection have caused widespread decline elsewhere. It is not known whether the olive baboon is currently expanding westwards. Listed as Not Threatened (IUCN).

Olive Baboon *Papio anubis*

Other names: Fr. *Babouin doguera*. Ger. *Anubis-pavian*. Swah. *Nyani*.
Measurements: HB 50–114cm; est. 75cm (♀), est. 100cm (♂). T 45–71cm. SH est. 55cm (♀), est. 70cm (♂). W 11–30kg (♀), 22–50kg (♂).
Recognition: A large, grizzled, olive-brown or khaki monkey. Adult ♂♂ have a thick cape over the neck and shoulders and shell-shaped greyish cheek ruffs. The face is naked and dark grey, with the nostrils projecting beyond the lips. Fused tail bones cause a sharp angle to form in the tail as if it were broken.
Habitat: The most extensively distributed of all baboons, ranging throughout Sahelian woodland and forest-mosaic habitats from S Mauritania and Mali to the Sudan and southwards to Zaïre and Tanzania. Outlying populations inhabit the Tibesti and Aïr massifs

(c)

in the Sahara. In E Africa distribution is bounded by changes in vegetation rather than well-defined geographic barriers. Wherever the large olive baboon's range encounters that of other species there are hybrid zones and a strong implication that this species is still in a phase of active expansion.

Food: Grass is a principal food in open areas, and fruits in forests. Resin or gum act as buffers in dry seasons and locusts provide the occasional glut. As an omnivorous opportunist the olive baboon changes its diet depending on the region, the season and even the time of day. Differences in social organisation and behaviour follow from its varied feeding strategies and habits. ♂♂ may form associations. These 'cabals' represent ♂ co-operation in some situations and have elements of hierarchy in others. ♂-♀ alliances are also formed (but seldom to the point of becoming permanent harems). ♀ hierarchies generate family hierarchies; thus juveniles from high-ranking families can coerce or threaten older animals from lower-ranking ones. In competition over food, groups with more ♂♂ prevail. This is the incentive for the large troops that form in all baboon species.

Status: The overall distribution of the olive baboon suggests that it has caused the ranges of neighbouring, smaller baboons to contract.

It seems likely that the olive baboon has been the main beneficiary of recent climatic changes. In other situations it can be a loser. Along its ragged frontiers with the equatorial lowland rainforests there is no clear, permanent ecological boundary. Here and there olive baboon populations range deep into the rainforest. These expansions may be temporary because these forests, with their dense and diverse communities of monkeys and apes, are hot-beds of disease. In the long term, the olive baboon is probably excluded from closed forests by competition and disease.

The olive baboon remains widespread and common in spite of vigorous trapping, shooting and poisoning campaigns. Listed as Vermin (African Convention).

Yellow Baboon *Papio cynocephalus*

Other names: Fr. *Babouin cynocéphale*. Ger. *Steppen-pavian, Barenpavian*. Swah. *Nyani*.
Measurements: HB est. 65cm (♀), est. 98cm (♂). T 45–68cm. SH est. 50cm (♀), est. 66cm (♂). W 11–15kg (♀), 22–30kg (♂).
Recognition: A slender baboon with brindled yellow-brown upperparts, tail and outer limb surfaces. Pale off-white below, it lacks cape or mane. There are prominent patches of white hair on the bare-skinned, dark grey muzzle and the nostrils are set back from lips. Baboons from west of Lake Tanganyika are of smaller 'Kinda' type.
Habitat: Ranges from Somalia to the Zambezi valley and across south-central Africa to Benguela (Angola). Over a great part of this area it is specific to fire-climax Miombo (*Brachystegia*) woodland. Both within this zone and especially to the north-east the yellow baboon also occupies dry bushland, thickets, steppes and the coastal littoral (including mangroves). The predominantly leguminous trees produce abundant seeds, many of which are eaten. A preference for foods with an unusual chemistry implies that this baboon has acquired special adaptations in its digestion. This may help to explain why the boundaries of its distribution do not follow any geographic discontinuities but coincide very closely with the distribution of a plant community.

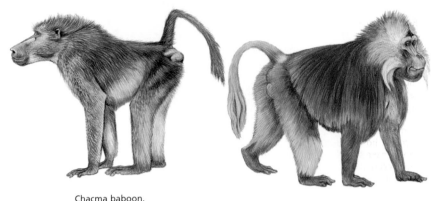

Chacma baboon.

Gelada.

Food: The seeds, flesh and pods of leguminous trees, such as *Acacia*, *Albizia*, mopane (*Colophospermum*) and tamarind, are seasonal staples but Miombo fauna, such as mopane worms and various other insects, are equally important at times. An opportunistic omnivore, like all baboons, it also eats grasses, shoots, fungi, lichens and many invertebrates. The yellow baboon typically forages in extended, well-spaced troops which can occasionally number up to 300 animals, with an average of between 30 and 80. During the calving season many young antelopes and hares are caught.

Status: Commonly exported from E Africa for biomedical research, this species has been heavily trapped in several areas. It is still widespread and common, in spite of being locally displaced by agriculture and tree clearance in many areas. Listed as Vermin (African Convention).

Chacma Baboon *Papio ursinus*

Other names: Fr. *Chacma*. Ger. *Tchakma*. Swah. *Nyani*.
Measurements: HB 50–80cm (♀), 80–110cm (♂). T 50–85cm. SH 40–60cm (♀), 50–75cm (♂). W 12–30kg (♀), 25–45kg (♂).
Recognition: Colour varies from grizzled khaki or grey to very dark brown and black. The underside is paler. ♂♂ have very long, narrow muzzles, black and bare, with paler patches between eyes and nostrils. The pointed nostril septum rises directly above the lips. The sharply angled or 'broken' tail is reinforced by fused vertebrae at its base. Adult ♂♂ may have recurved hair on neck hackles. Sizes vary locally. A cline exists between paler, grey-footed type in north-east and darker black footed chacmas in south west.
Habitat: Ranges all over S Africa up to the Zambezi valley, Caprivi to Angola littoral. Within this range the Chacma baboon occupies all types of woodland, savannah, steppes and subdesert, montane, Cape and Karoo flora. Cliffs, koppies or large trees are necessary night-time retreats. Water also limits its overall range in Namibia. Regional populations may be distinct subspecies.

Densities can rise from 3 or 4 up to 43 per km² in protected localities. Troops average between 20 and 50 animals but may total up to 100. Multi-♂ hierarchies are normal.
Food: An opportunistic omnivore, showing local preferences for bulbs, roots, shoots, seeds or fruits. Invertebrates, small vertebrates, seashore life, fungi and lichen are eaten as and when available. Crops (maize, tomatoes, citrus and root crops) are raided in settled areas. Lambs and small stock are taken in some ranching areas.
Status: Common and widespread; this baboon is totally dependent on drinking daily and in drier localities artificial water supplies have allowed substantial expansion of territory. Classed as vermin by most countries.

Gelada *Theropithecus gelada*

Other names: Fr. *Gelada*. Ger. *Dschelada*, *Blutbrust Pavian*.
Measurements: HB 50–65cm (♀), 68–75cm (♂). T 32–50cm (♀), 45–55cm (♂). SH 40–50cm (♀), 55–65cm (♂). W 13kg (10–15kg) (♀), 20kg (15–22kg) (♂).

Recognition: Brown terrestrial monkey with thick fur, giving the impression of a heavy body on short limbs. Outer fur tassels of adult ♂♂ often have a bleached appearance, especially on the head, chest, tufted tail and lower hindlimbs. Shoulders, hands and feet are very dark brown. Adult ♂♂ develop a cape that envelops them to below the elbows and to the root of the tail. A deep prognathous lower jaw, retracted nostrils and concave muzzle give the face a dished look. This shortened upper muzzle allows the pink-lined upper lip to be retracted and everted, covering the entire upper muzzle in the brief 'gelada grin' display (see p. 37).

♀♀ are smaller than ♂♂, more uniform in colour and coat length. Vesicles of pink sexual skin frame the genital area during oestrus. Similar vesicles (which also swell during oestrus) form an hourglass-shaped necklace framing the naked pink breasts of ♀♀. ♂♂ have a similar naked patch on the chest but without vesicles.

Subspecies: A boundary between so-called '*T. g. gelada*' in the drier north and the darker '*T. g. obscurus*' in the moister south is probably impossible to draw. Another population in the Wabe Shebelle gorges might represent a distinct subspecies.

Distribution: Central Ethiopian plateau with the Blue Nile Gorge and the upper Wabe Shebelle valley (east of the Bale massif) marking respectively the western and south-eastern boundaries of their range. They inhabit escarpments between 2,000 and 4,000m altitude.

Habitat: Feeds mainly on the flat margins of high grass plateaus (known locally as high Wurch or Puna grassland steppe), with *Agrostis* and *Festuca* grasses and giant *Lobelia* groves. Bands keep within 2km of the escarpment edges, where they retreat at night or at the least alarm. Ranges are therefore linear, encompassing as little as 1–3km² for a band's core area, although their year-long range may cover up to 70km². Steep cliffs provide sleeping-roosts.

Food: Almost all the food comprises the leaves of grasses, which are plucked blade by blade with strong, neatly opposable thumb and fingers. Virtually all feeding is conducted seated and animals often shuffle from clump to clump without getting up (saving energy and conserving warmth is important for an animal that exists on an energy-poor diet in a cold climate). During dry seasons when there is heavy overgrazing by livestock, or when gelada bands are very concentrated, subterranean stems and rhizomes are excavated, causing temporary devastations locally described as 'gelada fields'. Fruits and invertebrates are eaten opportunistically but are not a significant part of the diet. Where agriculture encroaches on the gelada's habitat, cereal crops may be taken.

Behaviour: Gelada bands are social units, numbering between 50 and 250 animals, which consist of 2–30 harems (each led and controlled by a single adult ♂) and one or more bachelor groups. Bands cluster together on sleeping-cliffs and often feed and move in a single, dispersed scatter. They join up with other bands from time to time and may aggregate into herds of up to 600 individuals. Members of a harem or band keep in touch with low-contact grunts and signal alarm with a high-pitched bark. Occasional violent outbursts among ♂♂ elicit loud screams and distressed juveniles utter a prolonged wail. Breeding is seasonal with most births falling between February and April. Gestation is about 6 months; the young are weaned at 2 years and mature sexually at 5 years (♀♀) or 6–7 years (♂♂).

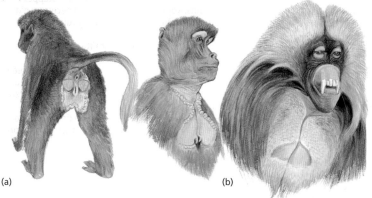

(a) Gelada female, showing sexual swellings. (b) gelada female from the front, and gelada male, also showing the lip flip.

Adaptations: In spite of their long teeth, thick manes, ruffs and large size, ♂ geladas only display obvious aggression during contests over ♀♀. Nonetheless, intimidation or warning displays help regulate gelada society. As with other baboons, ritualised yawning combines warning with appeasement but their unique 'lip-flip' constitutes an everyday greeting; a species-specific 'gelada-grin'.

Because harems are founded on force there would be a serious potential for disruptive aggression among the formidable-looking ♂♂. This danger is offset by an attractive, non-threatening signal. As with sacred baboons, ♂ geladas have evolved areas of naked skin that mimic ♀ sexual skin. Unlike sacred baboons, however, this bare skin is not on the buttocks but on the chest, an area better suited to an animal that spends more time sitting down than standing. This vivid hourglass-shaped patch on the throat and breast of both sexes has earned the gelada the English name 'bleeding-heart monkey'. The evolution of such complex mimicry suggests that sexual signs are important not only in reproductive behaviour but also in the regulation of social life. Chest patches make 'presentation' of the rear a redundant gesture and apparently represent a benign and attractive signal. The gelada is a poor tree-climber and is almost entirely terrestrial.

Status: The fossil record indicates that six species of geladas became extinct during the last 3 million years. A combination of human predation, climatic change and bovid competition might account for their disappearance. Geladas were estimated to number 0.5 million in the early 1970s. They are still widespread but continuous agricultural expansion into their habitat is steadily eroding their overall range. They are shot as crop-pests and have been trapped as laboratory animals in the past (for example 1,200 were imported into the USA between 1968 and 1973). Selective shooting of adult ♂♂ for their capes (as fur hats for sale to tourists or for local ceremonial costumes) has been shown to have reduced adult ♂♂ in one locality from 9% to 2% of the total population. A few gelada bands range within the minuscule Simen National Park but there are proposals for a new Blue Nile Gorges National Park and Indeltu (Shebelle) gorges Reserve that would protect larger numbers.

Listed as Vulnerable, Class A (African Convention), Appendix 2 (CITES), Vulnerable (IUCN).

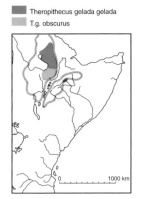

■ Theropithecus gelada gelada
■ T.g. obscurus

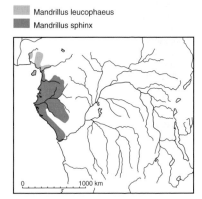

■ Mandrillus leucophaeus
■ Mandrillus sphinx

Mandrill *Mandrillus sphinx*

Other names: Fr. *Mandrill*. Ger. *Mandrill*.
Measurements: HB 55–70cm (♀), 70–95cm (♂). T 7–10cm. SH 45–50cm (♀), 55–60cm (♂). W 10–15kg (♀), 19–30kg (♂).
Recognition: A heavily built baboon with a grizzled olive-brown coat, pointed orange beard, crested crown and dull white to grey underside. In ♂♂ the bare face and posterior are bright red, white and blue. ♂♂ have two swollen nasal ridges which are electric blue and grooved, giving the impression of a permanent snarl. White fur surrounds the red-lipped mouth and forms leaf-shaped flashes behind the flesh-coloured ears. A red midline runs between the nasal arches, culminating in a circular scarlet nose patch. Other scarlet areas include the penis and the circle around the anus. Adult ♂♂ are stocky and the great

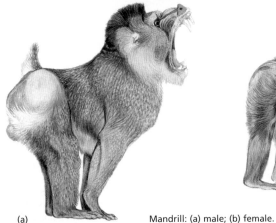

(a) Mandrill: (a) male; (b) female. (b)

width and muscularity of their buttocks is emphasised by their being naked and coloured pink above and blue below (graduating through mauve). ♀♀ are half the size and weight of ♂♂; their faces are flatter and shorter with grooved, pale blue ridges on the muzzle and a pink mouth and nose.

Distribution: Central W Africa from R. Sanaga to R. Zaïre inland to R. Ivindo and R. Ogooué. Mandrill distribution follows moist evergreen forest where this high-density, social animal can find bulk forage throughout the year. Its primary need appears to be abundant herbaceous growth to buffer it while fruits are scarce.

Habitat: Primary evergreen rainforest, stretching between 100 and 300km inland from the Atlantic coast. In this forest the fruiting of trees and lianes is irregular, resulting in periodic shortages of fruits. Undergrowth is typified by extensive patches of perennial herbs, such as gingers (Zingiberidae)and arrowroots (Acanthaceae), notably *Brillantaisia* and *Phaulopsis*. Within this zone the secondary growth that follows logging, settlement and shifting cultivation is also used by the mandrill.

Food: Omnivorous, with fruits preferred whenever they are available. In the course of a year groups of mandrills are thought to range over an area of about 50km². They forage very intensively in a succession of small subsections, exhausting local resources over variable amounts of time (but on average moving on about once a month). The size of foraging groups depends on the extent to which food resources are scattered within an area. During seasons in which many trees are fruiting, the mandrill disperses in its smallest social units. When fruits become scarce it turns to leaves and herbaceous growth as the staple. At such times a less nutritious but ubiquitous food supply permits temporary mega-groups, numbering over 600 animals, to form. These hordes supplement their main diet with herb stems and leaves, roots, fungi, invertebrates, including crabs and snails, and occasionally vertebrates – frogs, lizards, rodents, even young duikers. Foraging in large congregations is mostly terrestrial but fruits are sought wherever they can be found, including the canopy.

Behaviour: The smallest social unit is the extended harem led by a single dominant ♂. In groups with two or more ♂♂ subordinate individuals establish size hierarchies. Their subordinate status is revealed in their slimmer proportions and duller colouring. About half the total membership of a harem consists of juveniles and infants with up to 20 adult ♀♀. The average total for a harem is about 30 animals. Harems readily join up with other harems within their home range. Aggregated harems resemble sacred baboon and gelada bands and it is thought that these may incorporate ten or more harems. The mandrill can walk 5–15km in the course of a day and densities in undisturbed areas have been estimated at five to seven animals per km². Single animals are uncommon, often old ♂♂ presumably displaced by fighting. Adult ♂♂ have been estimated at only 7% of the total population, a figure which suggests heavy casualties sustained during fights for control of harems.

Small groups of mandrills may forage silently but bands or clans are very noisy and emit a continuous chorus of two-phase barks, frequent 'crowing', grunts and squeals. The mandrill sleeps in trees but always travels on the ground.

Gestation lasts about 25 weeks and sexual maturity is reached in about 5 years. Full maturation in subordinate ♂♂ appears to be inhibited by the harem-master's presence. Captive specimens have lived for up to 47 years. Some breeding continues all year round but there appear to be peak breeding times with births 1 or 2 years apart. Harem masters monopolise mating of oestrus ♀♀, identifiable by their pink- and violet-mottled sexual swellings.

Adaptations: As with other monkeys ritualised yawns express tension and can be a form of appeasement. Among mandrills the most frequent greeting is a low-intensity 'yawn' which consists of opening the corners of the mouth and wagging the head. The mandrill's facial features accentuate the impact of such gestures, especially the nasal folds, which appear to mimic a snarl with their enlarged and brilliantly enhanced creases. The size and brilliance of the nasal folds accurately reflect the age and condition of a ♂ mandrill, thus allowing other individuals to make an instant assessment of his rank. In a densely obstructed, poorly lit forest environment this signal is unambiguous and highly specific.

The mandrill's ancestral stock and its competitive, multi-♂ social organisation originated in savannah environments. Because the potential for ♂ conflict is increased in more closed environments, a visual device that facilitates group cohesion and reduces ♂ conflict suggests obvious benefits for the mandrill.

Status: Destruction and degradation of evergreen forests in many areas reduces the capacity of environments to support mandrill populations. However, human hunting poses the most immediate threat. In Gabon mandrill meat is more highly prized than imported beef or mutton. Commercial bush-meat hunters pose a real threat to all populations close to main roads and towns. This rapidly expanding and lucrative trade employs dogs, guns, spotlights, deep-freezers and trucks to harvest mandrills and many other forest animals. Researchers have recorded far fewer contacts with mandrills in recent years. It appears to be most seriously endangered in Congo (Brazzaville). There are several reserves within the mandrill's range, one of the most important being Lopé-Okanda, Gabon, which awaits National Park status (while logging is still permitted within its boundaries). Listed as Class B (African Convention), Appendix 1 (CITES).

Drill *Mandrillus leucophaeus*

Other names: Fr. *Drill*. Ger. *Drill*.

Measurements: HB 45–60cm (♀), 75–90cm (♂). T 6–12cm. SH 45–50cm (♀), 55–60cm (♂). W 10–15kg (♀), 15–20kg (♂).

Recognition: A stocky, large-headed olive-brown baboon with an off-white underside and a broad, leaf-shaped white ruff surrounding a naked black face. A dense neck-cape serves to greatly enlarge the visual impact of the adult ♂'s head and chest. Below the stumpy tail the broad, bare buttocks resemble those of the mandrill, especially in the adult ♂. Pink, graduating to blue with extensive metallic mauve, they top a scarlet scrotum. Hands and feet resemble those of the mandrill in being broad and strong. The hind big toe or 'foot thumb' is particularly well developed.

Subspecies: *M. l. leucophaeus* (mainland), *M. l. poensis* (Bioko I., formerly Fernando Po).

Distribution: Moist evergreen forest on Bioko I. and between the R. Cross and R. Sanaga valleys. Limitations to the drills' range are likely to be similar to those that affect the mandrill.

Mandrill grimace.   Drill head tilt.

Habitat: Evergreen forest on littoral and in Cameroun mountains up to 1,000m; also forest-savannah mosaics. Drills have also been noted in rocky areas within the forest.

Food: Omnivorous with reliance on fruit staple; also much herbaceous growth, roots, mushrooms, invertebrates (notably worms, termites, ants and spiders) and small vertebrates. Seasonal changes in diet are unlikely to differ greatly from those of the mandrill. Giant land snails, coconuts and sea turtle eggs have been recorded. Disabled duikers may be infrequently eaten.

Behaviour: Social structure resembles that of the mandrill. The basic units are harems of up to 25 drills that periodically come together to form bands which have been recorded as numbering up to 200 animals. It is likely that the smaller size of these units reflects the drills' lower densities. ♂♂ remain in harems, except for a few presumed expellees who wander alone. Groups travel on the ground but forage and sleep in the trees. Like baboons, drills utter a sharp alarm bark and grunt while foraging. They also have a distinctive crowing call that typifies contact between harems. Distressed juveniles make a croaking call. Dominant ♂♂ make threat displays involving much branch-shaking and head-bobbing. Breeding is continuous but births are spaced at up to 6 years apart. Reproductive tempos and maturation rates are similar to those of the mandrill.

Adaptations: Adult ♂♂ of both drills and mandrill have chest glands which are regularly rubbed on branches or tree trunks. This scent-marking increases the 'ambience' of a harem-master's presence among other harem members and thus reinforces his role as a physical, visual, auditory and olfactory beacon in a highly mobile, non-territorial but easily dispersed social unit. Because the dominant ♂ initiates all movements and his own actions elicit a strong 'follow' response in his harem members, his rump has a role as a beacon. Its brilliance and breadth is a clear sign of status while atrophy of the tail probably eliminates ambiguous or distracting signals (the same is probably true of the mandrill).

A ritualised 'smile' that displays the teeth is often combined with tilting of the head. A vivid crimson lower lip accentuates this gesture, which functions as a greeting or appeasement. Whereas the facial features of the mandrill draw attention mainly to the muzzle, the signal given by drills emphasises the lower jaw and overall enlargement of the head. Head-tilting makes the open lips and teeth more prominent and visible.

Status: Drills are in danger of becoming extinct. In the heart of their range, between Douala and Edea, they have been totally displaced by clear-felling for chipboard factories and settlement. They are hunted everywhere for their meat and it is common for all the members of a harem who have taken refuge in the trees to be shot *en masse*. As cultivation expands, drills are frequently killed in defence of crops such as bananas, cocoa or manioc. The main remaining populations centre on SW Cameroon, the Korup National Park and the southern corner of Bioko I. Listed as Class B (African Convention), Appendix 1 (CITES).

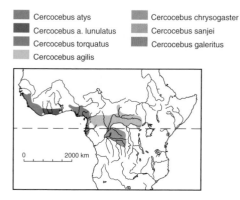

Cercocebus atys
Cercocebus a. lunulatus
Cercocebus torquatus
Cercocebus agilis
Cercocebus chrysogaster
Cercocebus sanjei
Cercocebus galeritus

0   2000 km

Drill-Mangabeys *Cercocebus*

Red-capped mangabey	*Cercocebus torquatus*
Sooty mangabey	*Cercocebus atys*
Agile mangabey	*Cercocebus agilis*
Tana mangabey	*Cercocebus galeritus*
Sanje mangabey	*Cercocebus sanjei*
Golden-bellied mangabey	*Cercocebus chrysogaster*

Recognition: Sometimes known as 'eyelid monkeys', because of their white upper eyelids, these longer-muzzled monkeys were formerly classified together with the black mangabeys, which are more arboreal, longer tailed and shorter muzzled. The W African species have the longest muzzles and are smoky-grey in colour. Those from central and E Africa are smaller, with shorter muzzles and browner, more grizzled coats. Pockets, or fossae, between the eyes and corners of the mouth are distinctive in both types of mangabey.

Genealogy: Fossils from S and E Africa show that mangabeys were commoner and more widespread between 4 million and 2 million years ago. They are now exclusively equatorial. Studies of their anatomy, blood proteins and chromosomes suggest that their closest affinities are with mandrills. A retracted position for the muzzle in relation to the rest of the skull suggests that they derive from a larger, longer-faced ancestor.

Geography: The contracted and fragmented distribution of drill-mangabeys suggests that their present status is but a vestige of what it was in former times. This decline is unlikely to be the result of human interference and may be the consequence of a long period of subtle competition with, and displacement by, guenon monkeys and baboons, which they most closely resemble.

Ecology: Rivers and swamps often represent vestigial islands of water-dependent vegetation remaining in the wake of climatic changes that have brought drier communities elsewhere. Both within and outside the forest belt drill-mangabeys are consistently riverine species but might be considered more of a 'vestigial' group in comparison to other swamp-forest specialists.

Natural history: All drill-mangabeys live in multi-♂, multi-♀ groups where competition among members of both sexes may be sharper between neighbouring bands than within the immediate group. Differences between the sexes in size and morphology are therefore much less extreme than in drills and baboons. A reduction in overall size (especially in the canine teeth) would help explain the facial pockets, or fossae, which may be the result of buckling in the plane of junction as a once extended muzzle contracted (over a relatively short period of evolutionary time).

Adaptations: Both drills and drill-mangabeys derive from lineages that moved into moister galleries and forests from drier, more open habitats. In spite of this they remain relatively terrestrial, a conservative habit that may render them less able to compete with the guenons. The robust molar teeth of drill-mangabeys enable them to cope well with nuts and hard fruits typical of their riverine ecotype. In addition, drill-mangabeys show an ability and a willingness to swim.

Red-capped mangabey.   Sooty mangabey.

Red-Capped Mangabey *Cercocebus torquatus*

Other names: Fr. *Cercocèbe à collier blanc.* Ger. *Rotkopf Mangabe.*
Measurements: HB 45–60cm (♀), 47–67cm (♂). T 60–75cm. SH 38–42cm (♀), 40–45cm (♂). W 5–8kg (♀), 7–12.5kg (♂).
Recognition: A large slate-grey monkey with white underside and inner limb surfaces. The dark grey tail is frequently held so that its white tip hovers over the head, which is bisected laterally by a boldly outlined ridge of fur running from cheek to neck. Large blackish ears project from the white collar that surrounds a bright russet cap. White eyelids are particularly conspicuous in the long-muzzled, dark face.

The metallic-sounding cackles and alarm barks of this species are very loud and are accompanied by much branch-shaking and grimacing by the adult ♂♂. Several adult ♂♂ are present in the larger groups, which number between 12 and 23 animals, but subgroups readily form. Rolling calls preceded by a whoop signal the positions of neighbouring groups and individuals.
Habitat: Seldom far from swamp or valley forest but the dry-season range may expand as fruits become scarcer and less concentrated. Occupies region between Cross R to Ubangui/Zaïre rivers.
Food: Mainly fruits and nuts, supplemented by the stems and roots of undergrowth plants. Seasonal fluctuations in foraging behaviour ensure substantial overlaps between neighbouring groups.
Status: Once a successful and widespread species the red-capped mangabey is nonetheless incompatible with intensive cultivation and is disappearing from all areas where agricultural expansion is being consolidated. It is intensively hunted, especially in Cameroon and Nigeria. Listed as Class B (African Convention), Appendix 2 (CITES), Vulnerable (IUCN)

Sooty Mangabey *Cercocebus atys*

Other names: Fr. *Cercocèbe fuligineux.* Ger. *Mohren Mangabe.*
Measurements: HB 45–60cm (♀), 47–67cm (♂). T 40–80cm. SH 38–42cm (♀), 40–45cm (♂). W 4.5–7kg (♀), 7–12kg (♂).
Recognition: A smoky- or slate-grey monkey with a lighter underside and facial whiskers (white collared with greater contrast in eastern race) and slightly darker hands and feet. The bare facial skin is dark grey or mottled, the upper eyelids are white and the orbits and muzzle are 'rectangular' in outline. The sooty mangabey is often more easily heard than seen. The commonest calls are a staccato bark, a rapid succession of grunts and a whoop followed by a many-syllabled rumble; a rattling scream signifies alarm. Facial expressions are varied and eyelids are flashed a lot, especially in threat.
Subspecies *C. a. atys* (S Guinea to R. Sassandra), *C. a. lunulatus* (between R. Sassandra and R.Volta).
Habitat: Restricted to Upper Guinea, ranging along valleys within primary and secondary forests out into gallery forest and mosaic zones. Sooty mangabeys are commonest close to swamp and palm forests, which provide a refuge to which they retreat at any alarm.
Food: Fruits, including the flesh and kernels of very hard fruits and nuts, are the main staple.

(a) Agile manabey. (b) Tana mangabey. (c) Sanje mangabey.

Sooty mangabeys also eat the leaves, stems, shoots and roots of many swamp plants and the seeds of grasses. They frequently raid farms, including rice paddies, where damage can be extensive.

Status: Sooty mangabeys are still widespread in W Africa partly because they are difficult to hunt in their dense, swampy refuges. However, they are easy to trap because of their ground-foraging habits. Currently not threatened, they are treated as vermin in many pioneer agricultural areas.

Agile Mangabey *Cercocebus agilis*

Other names: Fr. *Cercocèbe agile*. Ger. *Olivmangabe*.

Measurements: HB 44–55cm (♀), 51–65cm (♂). T 45–79cm. SH 37–42cm (♀), 40–45cm (♂). W 5–7kg (♀), 7–13kg (♂).

Recognition: A drab, speckled olive monkey with short, fine fur. The underside and inner limbs are pale and very thinly furred. The tail is tapered. The darker, grizzled crown has a parting at the front which often exposes a naked pale-coloured forehead behind a projecting brow tuft. The upper eyelids are scarcely paler than the pale grey face. The agile mangabey is more often heard than seen; its loud call is a whoop followed by a rumble which is made by the ♂. Groups numbering up to 18 are led and defended by a single adult ♂. Single ♂♂ are common. Group encounters are often amicable with occasional exchange of members.

Habitat: Endemic to regions north of the R. Zaïre, especially to the extensive swamp forests that follow the equator from the Atlantic to eastern Zaïre. In areas where this type of vegetation follows narrow creeks and rivulets the habitat is essentially linear because the agile mangabey seldom moves out of seasonally flooded swamp forest. During dry seasons more time is spent on the ground but most activity is restricted to within some 5m from the ground, only adult ♂♂ climbing to higher levels.

Food: Almost entirely certain dominant swamp-forest trees (notably dika nuts or Gabon chocolate, *Irvingia*, and sugar plums, *Uapaca*) for the period in which they are fruiting. Another dominant, the raffia palm, provides fresh leaf shoots that can buffer any shortage of fruits. Some 42 species of fruits have been recorded in the diet, with grasses, mushrooms and animals making up more marginal foods.

Status: There are substantial overlaps between the diet of the agile mangabey and that of other monkeys, especially the de Brazza's monkey. The agile mangabey is only half as numerous as any of the guenon species with which it shares its habitat, but its larger size and ability to fall back on raffia shoots or harder foods in times of shortage may make it competitive within the swamp ecotype. Dense vegetation and treacherous ground protect the agile mangabey from predators, including humans. IUCN regards this species as Not Threatened and it is unlikely that its status will change in the immediate future.

(c)

■ Cercocebus sanjei
■ Cercocebus galeritus

Tana Mangabey *Cercocebus galeritus*

Other names: Fr. *Cercocèbe de la Tana*. Ger. *Tana Mangabe*.
Measurements: HB est. 42–53cm (♀), est. 50–63cm (♂). T 45–77cm. SH est. 35–41cm (♀), est. 40–44cm (♂). W est. 5–6.5kg (♀), est. 8–10kg (♂).
Recognition: A grizzled ash-coloured monkey with limp, shaggy fur, prominent white eyelids, a flash of paler fur on the temples and white borders to the black face. Hair on the crown is particularly long and limp. The hands and feet are dark brown and the tail has an off-white tip that is somewhat tufted in adult ♂♂. ♂♂ vocalise with the whoop-rumble typical of all drill-mangabeys. Unlike the agile mangabey, groups of 13–36 contain up to six adult ♂♂. Two or more of these units occasionally aggregate to form temporary bands of up to 60 monkeys. It is semi-terrestrial, especially during the dry season.
Habitat: Restricted to gallery forests along the floodplain of the R. Tana in Kenya, a zone only 60km long and nowhere more than a few kilometres wide. The preferred vegetation type is levee forest dominated by *Pachystela* but the Tana managabey also ranges into drier *Acacia/Mimusops* riverine strips. Surrounded by open grassland, which is regularly fired, it occupies a strictly finite environment centred on the Nkanjonja forest.
Food: Mainly fruits, of which figs are especially important. However, the restricted nature of the habitat may mean that a larger proportion of seeds and animal foods are taken, including insects, frogs and lizards.
Status: This species was estimated to number about 2,000 in 1972. In 1995 the estimate was 1,100 or less. The main threats are forest clearance (especially the felling of figs and other food trees for canoes), forest fires and degradation due to livestock and an artificially lowered water-table. Gazetting of the Tana River Primate Reserve may have been insufficient to reverse the overall contraction and degradation of this mangabey's habitat. The Tana River Development Authority, responsible for changing the water regime through damming and irrigation projects, continues to aggravate the critical situation which it has precipitated. Listed as Class A (African Convention), Appendix 1 (CITES), Endangered (IUCN).

Sanje Mangabey *Cercocebus sanjei*

Other names: Fr. *Cercocèbe de Sanje*. Ger. *Sanje Mangabe*.
Measurements: HB est. 50–65cm. T est. 55–65cm. SH est. 40–50cm. W est. 7–9kg.
Recognition: Crown, back, limbs and tail are a fine ash-grey grizzle. Hands and feet are darker. Belly and chest pale apricot and there is a tufted off-white tip to the tail. The crown is swept into a bouffant with two 'horns' above semi-concealed ears and a very narrow black margin separates brow and cheeks from the paler face. The outer cheek skin is pale blue-grey and the orbits and upper muzzle are pink (eyelids not strikingly white). The lower muzzle is grey. Bare buttocks are bluish grey with narrow pink callosities. The penis and anus are vividly scarlet and the scrotum is pink and blue. Vocalisations include slow, deep, paired hoots followed by more rapid and croaking hoots, sudden very deep groans and sharp, shrill cries when excited.

Habitat: Valley forests on the wetter eastern flanks and below the Uzungwa (African Ghats) massif from 400–1,230m altitude. Although the Sanje managabey ranges through several forest and woodland types, it prefers the lower understorey in riverine galleries.

Food: Fruits, mostly ripe, comprise 70% of the diet while foliage makes up most of the balance. In an item-by-item comparison the diet shows very little difference from that of the guenons that share their habitat (e.g. *Cercopithecus mitis*). The guenons have the advantage of superior arboreal skills and larger numbers. The Angola pied colobus (*Colobus angolensis*) also shows some overlap with foods favoured by the Sanje mangabey.

Status: The likelihood that long-term competition from guenons and colobus have reduced this mangabey to its present relict distribution makes it imperative that the ecological richness that allowed its survival at Sanje and Mwanihana be fully studied and conserved.

Current proposals for an Uzungwa National Park may ensure this objective but widespread pit-sawing and charcoal burning is continuing to degrade these forests. Hunting with dogs (to which this monkey is particularly vulnerable) is also spreading as the area becomes more densely settled. In 1981 the mangabeys were estimated to number between 1,800 and 3,000 animals. Listed as Endangered (IUCN). Other conservation ratings await the formal description and naming of this monkey. In the absence of specimens 'sanjei' is a *nomen nudum* used for convenience.

Golden-Bellied Mangabey *Cercocebus chrysogaster*

Other names: Fr. *Cercocèbe à ventre doré.* Ger. *Goldbauch Mangabe.*

Measurements: HB 45–55cm (♀), 52–66cm (♂). T est. 50–75cm. SH 38–42cm (♀), 42–46cm (♂). W 6–8kg (♀), 10–14kg (♂).

Recognition: The most drill-like of drill-mangabeys in having a naked violet rump, bright-coloured fur and relatively robust build (including the muzzle of adult ♂♂). The crown, back and outer limbs are a rich, dark, grizzled olive. The underside is cream, turning to bright orange on the belly. The cheek whiskers are swept out into a prominent ridge that begins near the corner of the mouth and ends behind the ears. Below the temples the whiskers form a golden-yellow furrow that frames the upper face like a high collar. The tapered tail is carried in a backward arch (unlike other mangabeys).

Habitat: Restricted to the southern (lower) section of the Zaïre depression swamp complex, the golden-bellied mangabey's environment resembles that of the agile mangabey living immediately north of the R. Zaïre. Nonetheless, their separation could be quite ancient not only because of the sheer width and speed of the river in its lower reaches. It could date back to times when the basin was a lake.

Food: Presumed to be mainly fruits, such as figs, sugar plums, dika nuts, raphia and dwarf date palms.

Status: Least known of the mangabeys, this species occupies an area where hunting is quite intensive. Nonetheless, its swampy habitat is likely to protect satisfactory numbers for the time being. It occurs in Salonga National Park. (Currently classed in conservation inventories as a subspecies of *Cercocebus galeritus*.)

Baboon-Mangabeys *Lophocebus*

Grey-cheeked mangabey	*Lophocebus albigena*
Black mangabey	*Lophocebus aterrimus*

Other names: Fr. *Lophocèbes*. Ger. *Mantelmangabe*.

Recognition: Black or brown monkeys with very long tails and rather 'ragged', tesselated fur with tufts on the crown or brows. Their all-black faces display large, baboon-like incisors in a short, pointed muzzle above a receding chin. Deep suborbital pockets throw the very muscular cheeks (which are not hidden by fur) into strong relief. Their oblique eye sockets give them a somewhat mournful expression. Their deliberate movements, exaggerated postures, general demeanour and choruses of grunting are reminiscent of baboons.

Genealogy: Baboon-mangabeys differ from drill-mangabeys in being almost wholly arboreal, living at high densities and in the vocal repertoires of ♂♂. There are no fossils to indicate early origins.

Geography: Primarily central African, their absence from Upper Guinea suggests that the Zaïre basin is where they evolved. They are rainforest monkeys but a preference for swamp forest becomes most obvious when many other monkeys are present.

Ecology: Although all mangabeys are dependent on being close to water, baboon-mangabeys are less riverine specialists (as *Cercocebus* seems to be) than nut and hard fruit specialists (a distinction blurred by the prevalence of these fruits in swamps). Such fruits are picked at all levels, as, or before, they ripen, rather than on the ground or at lower levels only.

Natural history: Baboon-mangabeys live at higher densities than drill-mangabeys (18–77 per km^2 as opposed to 6–12 per km^2). Less direct competition with guenons may influence this but their social system has shifted from small units to larger groups that depend on ♂♂ as vocal (and often unseen) beacons for their orientation. The principle expression of ♂-♂ competition is through very loud calls. By advertising their whereabouts in this way adult ♂♂ are able to conserve energy which might otherwise have to be used in defence of territories or harems. This strategy also reduces the need for physical expressions of dominance in ♂♂ and, likewise, life in the tree tops reduces the need for a protective role for ♂♂.

Adaptations: Baboon-mangabeys are relatively small monkeys well suited to safe movement on smaller branches and efficient harvests of fruits and foliage. They show little difference in size between the sexes and no marked differences in the size of ♂♂ or their muzzles. These characteristics have evolved without their having lost the big incisors and nut-cracking skills of their more terrestrial, larger, long-muzzled ancestors. The specialised air sacs that ♂♂ have evolved to amplify their loud calls would appear to have replaced big muzzles as a primary feature of ♂ self-advertisement.

Grey-Cheeked Mangabey *Lophocebus albigena*

Other names: Fr. *Mangabey à joues grises*. Ger. *Grauwangen Mangabe*.

Measurements: HB 43–61cm (♀), 54–73cm (♂). T 73–100cm. SH 38–43cm (♀), 40–45cm (♂). W 4–7kg (♀), 6–11kg (♂).

Recognition: A dark brown monkey with a long, ragged tail and tufted crown. A shoulder cape of longer paler fur in ♂♂ varies in colour, both from individual to individual and regionally. The black face is naked and the cheeks only very thinly haired. The ♂'s loud call is a very distinctive 'whoop gobble'. It is uttered several times a day and provides a clear indication of the presence of this mangabey. ♀♀ are more slenderly built than ♂♂ and develop very conspicuous pink swellings while in oestrus.

Subspecies: *L. a. albigena* (central Africa): fawn cape. *L. a. zenkeri* (S Cameroon): grey cape. *L. a. johnstoni* (E Zaïre, Uganda): brown- to straw-coloured cape. *L. a. osmani* (R. Cross): russet cape, pale underside. Individual variation and intermediate forms make precise delimitation of races difficult.)

Distribution: From the R. Cross to the R. Nile north of the R. Zaïre/R. Lualaba. Mainly lowland but recorded up to 1,600m in strictly equatorial zone.

Habitat: Rainforest, both primary and secondary but with a strong preference for swamp forest (especially where many other monkey species are present). In one Uganda gallery forest, with only two marginally sympatric species, densities of 77 grey-cheeked mangabeys

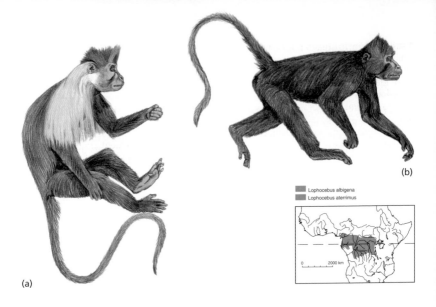

(a) Grey-cheeked mangabey. (b) Black mangabey.

per km² have been recorded. In the mixed primate communities of Cameroon and Gabon densities of 10–20 animals per km² are more usual.

Food: Mainly fruits and nuts, notably false nutmeg (*Pycnanthus*), breadfruit (*Treculia*), dwarf dates (*Phoenix*) and oil palm (*Elaeis*). Shoots may be taken and roots dug for when fruits are scarce. Grey-cheeked mangabeys feed for 3–4 hours after dawn and before dusk, with a short bout at midday, and rest in the late morning and afternoon.

Behaviour: Social units consist of five to six ♀♀ and their offspring with several adult ♂♂, one of which is dominant. The dominant ♂ is the most frequent caller and marks the position of his group relative to other neighbouring groups. Home ranges of about 4km² are non-territorial, with extensive overlaps between groups. Groups rest and sleep in a tight formation in a single tree or clump of dense foliage. Breeding is not seasonal and gestation lasts about 24 weeks. ♂♂ take an active interest in young. Longevity is markedly affected by local variations in diet. Those consistently feeding on hard nuts wear out their teeth much faster than those with a softer, less restricted diet. The former tend to live in multi-species primate communities and show a faster turnover of population, including ♂♂.

Adaptations: The air sacs and enlarged vocal tracts of ♂ grey-cheeked mangabeys serve their special reliance on sound. As every ♂ matures he elaborates an individual call-signature or 'gobble'. When a ♂ becomes dominant within his group his call becomes the beacon for his entire group's movements and orientation.

Status: Although this species is very widely distributed and common within much of its very extensive range, agricultural expansion, hunting and tree-poisoning by foresters has caused local disappearances. Loud calls increase vulnerability but this is offset by its agility and arboreal skills. Listed as Not Threatened (IUCN).

Black Mangabey *Lophocebus aterrimus*

Other names: Fr. *Mangabey noir*. Ger. *Schopf Mangabe*.
Measurements: HB 45–65cm. T 80–85cm. SH 40–45cm. W 4–7kg (♀), 6–11kg (♂).
Recognition: A long-limbed, all-black monkey with a ragged, slightly prehensile tail, a pointed crest, and cheek whiskers. ♀♀ are smaller and more slender than ♂♂, with pink sexual swellings during oestrus. Very closely related to grey-cheeked mangabeys, the black mangabey makes similar vocalisations which probably serve similar social functions.
Subspecies: *L. a. aterimus* (central Zaïre basin): upswept sepia cheek whiskers, conical crest. *L. a. opdenboschi* (NE Angola and W Zaïre): sideswept black cheek whiskers, ridged crest.

Distribution: Low-lying parts of the SW Zaïre basin.

Habitat: Moist rainforest, both primary and secondary but especially swamp forests and their margins. Black mangabeys utilise all levels but seldom descend to the ground.

Food: Mainly fruits – similar to grey-cheeked mangabeys.

Behaviour: Multi-M groups numbering 14–20 animals break down into smaller units while feeding. In some localities densities of nearly 70 animals per km² have been recorded. The variety of grunts suggests a complex web of social relations. Home ranges may be smaller than those of grey-cheeked mangabeys but most parameters are very similar.

Adaptations: The absence of any colour markings, deliberate movement and exaggerated postures suggests that the black silhouette of the animal is its most important visual signal. This relatively poor capacity for visual communication is offset by a very rich vocal repertoire.

Status: The current status of these monkeys is insufficiently known. It is thought to be present in Salonga National Park and is known from the proposed Lomako conservation area. They are hunted for meat in most parts of their range. Currently listed as Class B (African Convention) and Appendix 2 (CITES).

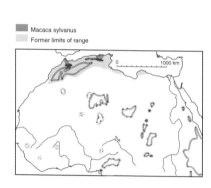

Macaca sylvanus
Former limits of range

Barbary Macaque *Macaca sylvanus*

Other names: Fr. *Magot*. Ger. *Berberaffe*.

Measurements: HB 55–65cm (♀), 65–75cm (♂). SH 45cm (♀), 50cm (♂). W 4–7kg (♀), 7–10kg (♂).

Recognition: A dull ochre-grey monkey with variable intensities of orange tinting the crown, hands and feet. Darker flushes of brown or black surround the bare face, which is pink or mottled. Hands are short and broad, with a small thumb. Limbs are of equal length and appear to be thick because of the dense, woolly hair (especially in winter). Oestrus ♀♀ have prominent swellings of sexual skin on their buttocks.

Distribution: Formerly ranging from Libya to Morocco (and in SW Europe in prehistoric times), the Barbary macaque is now restricted to the Middle Atlas Mts and a scatter of localities in Morocco and Algeria. It ranges from sea-level up to 2,000m altitude.

Habitat: Cedar forests at higher altitudes are presently preferred but this is likely to be the result of contraction of the range due to the expansion of human settlement and persecution in more favourable areas. The Barbary macaque also occurs in oak forests, coastal scrub and overgrazed rocky slopes with vestigial vegetation. Home ranges vary from 25 to 1,200ha.

Food: In cedar forests, grass and cedar leaves are the winter and spring staple, with acorns, caterpillars and daffodil (*Asphodelus*) bulbs the main summer and autumn foods. In deciduous oak forests, seed and acorn staples last from June to November while grass, lichens and bark see the macaque through the winter. A brief flush of caterpillars between April and May is important, as may be scarcer invertebrates, roots, bulbs and fungi.

Behaviour: Groups of 7–40 individuals (more usually 10–30), comprising adults and young of both sexes, maintain contact with one another by means of a wide range of vocalisations.

Births occur from February to June after a 7-month gestation. ♂♂ pay much attention to infants. Adult ♂♂ co-operate in defending the group and will even attack dogs. The macaques are sexually mature at about 4 years of age and have a life-span of about 20 years.

Adaptations: These tail-less, short-limbed, thick-furred monkeys are the most terrestrial of all macaques and spend more than half of their time on the ground. Their occupation of dry, cool, impoverished habitats goes back at least 6 million years and represents a primary adaptation of cheek-pouch monkeys, not the late and marginal offshoot of an arboreal, tropical monkey, as is often suggested. These primary adaptive characteristics make conservation and further study of this species especially important.

Status: Three-quarters of all surviving Barbary macaques are found in the Middle Atlas Mts in Morocco. Others persist in numerous pockets of declining size in N Morocco and Algeria. The main threat to their survival is intensive logging, charcoal-burning, firewood-collecting and land clearance for agriculture at lower altitudes. Degradation of the remaining areas by livestock also affects the macaque's long-term future. In Morocco it occurs in the Toubkal National Park and Thassem Reserve. In Algeria it survives in the Djurdjura, Taza, Chrea and Gouraya National Parks. There have been proposals to reintroduce it to the Kouf National Park in Libya. Listed as Class A (African Convention), Appendix 2 (CITES), Vulnerable (IUCN).

Guenons and allies *Cercopithecinae*

Allen's swamp monkey	*Allenopithecus nigroviridis*
Talapoins	*Miopithecus*
Patas monkey	*Cercopithecus (Erythrocebus) patas*
Savannah monkeys	*Cercopithecus (aethiops) superspecies*
l'Hoest's monkeys	*Cercopithecus (l'hoesti) superspecies*
Salonga monkey	*Cercopithecus dryas*
Diana monkey	*Cercopithecus diana*
De Brazza's monkey	*Cercopithecus neglectus*
Mona monkeys	*Cercopithecus (mona) superspecies*
Owl-faced monkey	*Cercopithecus hamlyni*
Gentle monkeys	*Cercopithecus (nictitans) superspecies*
Cephus monkeys	*Cercopithecus (cephus) superspecies*

Recognition: Guenons are medium-sized to small monkeys with long tails and grizzled fur on the back or limbs. Their colouring, particularly on the face, sometimes rivals that of birds for its brilliance and complexity of pattern. Although ♂♂ of some of the more terrestrial species have relatively long muzzles and canine teeth, most have short faces and reduced molars. Two forms, *Allenopithecus* and *Miopithecus*, retain some prominent ancestral features more typical of macaques (such as 'pinched' molar cusps and enlarged sexual swellings in oestrus ♀♀) but are otherwise like guenons. The convention of associating Allen's swamp monkey and the talapoins with guenons is a convenience. They could equally well be treated as equatorial macaques.

Genealogy: Guenons share a common ancestry with other cheek-pouch monkeys, baboons and macaques which diverged from the colobines over 10 million years ago. An absence of guenon fossils suggests that their earliest forebears inhabited minor regional niches for a long period before exploding into the largest and most recent of all known primate radiations. Genetic studies directed by Professor B. Dutrillaux have charted the course of this radiation. These studies indicate that patas, talapoin, savannah and forest-floor monkeys of the l'hoesti or 'mountain monkey' lineage form a distinct terrestrial branch while a second branch comprises four single species and three superspecies, embracing a total of 14 species and 46 subspecies. Guenons vary greatly in the number of genetic changes which they have accumulated. Thus, gametes of the recently evolved crowned guenons (with 72 chromosomes) are much more diverse than those of Allen's swamp monkey (with 48 chromosomes). Species with very diverse face patterns (such as the red-tailed, or cephus, group) all have sets of 66 chromosomes while the mona group, with 66–72 chromosomes, are genetically diverse in spite of their close resemblances. This implies that the cephus monkeys have diverged very recently while the mona group's evolution has been protracted over a longer period.

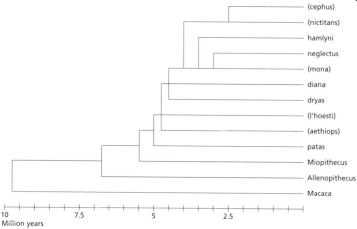

Guenon family tree (tentative, with best fit approximation of time scale).

Dutrillaux's studies also show that Allen's swamp monkey is genetically conservative while several other species (notably de Brazza's and Hamlyn's monkeys) have long histories of genetic change. Both captive and wild guenons of different species hybridise easily. Early hybridisations between ancestors of living species offer one explanation for the complex permutations of the genomes of various modern guenons. Guenons are therefore of great interest to geneticists, an interest that has been intensified by the implication of savannah monkeys in the epidemiology of AIDS.

Geography: The fact that guenons are exclusively African is consistent with their apparently recent evolution and also their probable origination from a small, equatorial focus. Both the patas and savannah monkeys are clearly secondarily adapted to arid conditions so that the basic characteristics of guenon biogeography can be represented diagrammatically as a series of concentric rings centred on the central African forests where the radiation began. The most conservative forms, Allen's swamp monkey and the talapoins, are strictly equatorial, riverine species. By contrast their closest relative, the patas, is likely to have been 'displaced' outward to the margins of habitable territory by more recently evolved species (notably the savannah monkeys).

Between these extremes, making up a complex mosaic, lie the other guenon species. Diana monkeys (whose ancestors were probably pioneers in colonising the forest canopy) survive in a few W African High Forests. Mona and cephus monkeys, also arboreal, only occupy the main forest blocks while a larger, less exclusively arboreal group, the gentle monkeys, are more successful in outlying peripheral forests.

Ecology: Conventional division of guenons into mainly terrestrial and mainly arboreal groups obscures the more complex patterns of ecological adaptation that emerge if, for example, gait is related to foraging strategy. Thus, the swamp monkey and talapoins can be described as versatile branch-walker/climbers restricted to dense cover. The much larger, so-called 'mountain monkeys', or l'hoesti group, are combined ground-walker/climbers restricted to dense forest undergrowth. Savannah monkeys are riverine ground-walker/climbers with a foraging strategy which demands fast, short-distance running. The patas monkey is a longer-distance loper-runner (and a marginal, yet still competent climber).

In the 'arboreal' division, de Brazza's monkey is a slow-climber/walker restricted to relatively dense cover. The Diana monkey is a fast-climber/big branch-runner adapted to a relatively open canopy. Mona monkeys are fast-climber/small branch-runners. Cephus monkeys are fast, small branch-climbers and leapers while the larger, closely related gentle monkeys are versatile, wide-spectrum climbers and leapers. Hamlyn's monkey is a climber/walker apparently combining gentle and mountain monkey foraging strategies with a special aptitude for slow, vertical climbing.

In addition to their different foraging techniques each guenon species has a different diet, which would seem to explain how multi-species communities of up to six species of guenons are able to live at high densities in most riverine or forest vegetation types.

Natural history: The success of guenons can partly be attributed to their species-specific foraging techniques, which reduce interspecies competition, and partly to their relatively egalitarian social systems, which place few constraints on ♀♀ and young (unlike baboons among which dominant ♂♂ are long-term members of the group who have priority access to food and initiate all movements).

Guenon territories are permanently occupied only by ♀♀ while individual territorial ♂♂ may come and go. The territorial ♂ of a guenon group advertises and defends his tenancy of the territory and serves as its audio-visual marker. ♀♀ are not permanently dependent on him and they actively participate in defending the territory against other groups of ♀♀.

Guenons are very vocal and most have evolved species-specific loud calls. However, Allen's swamp monkey, patas and talapoin monkeys appear to have retained many macaque-like vocalisations. Gautier (1988) has compared the loud calls of guenon ♂♂ and has shown that they conform to a pattern consistent with Dutrillaux's proposed evolutionary radiation. ♀ guenons utter high-pitched bleats or barks which may serve to regulate distances between animals. Like other cheek-pouch monkeys they also make a variety of grunts which help to keep the group together and these are augmented by more specific moans or quavers in certain species. Warning calls are less specific and consist variously of whistles, chirps and barks. Guenon calls are typically modulated and may identify the caller. In certain cases they also appear to be able to convey the identity of a disturbance or predator and the status of the caller.

Adaptations: In all guenon species the ♂ is larger than the ♀ but the difference is small (particularly in the case of the smaller more arboreal species) compared with the gross sexual dimorphism typical of baboons. ♂ guenons are also more brightly coloured than ♀♀ and more emphatic in their visual signalling but the differences are of degree not kind. At

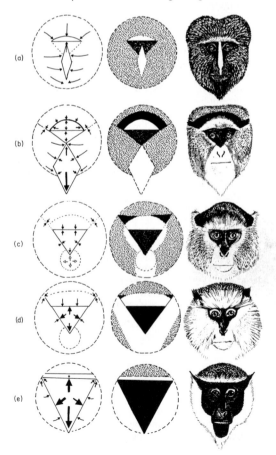

Schematic diagram of tonal distribution on the faces of *Cercopithecus* species. (a) *C. hamlyni*. (b) *C. neglectus*. (c) *C. (mona) lowei*. (d) *C. (mona) campbelli*. (e) *C. diana*. C represents least differentiated pattern. Arrows on disks suggest intensifications of tonal contrast or extensions of tonal area.

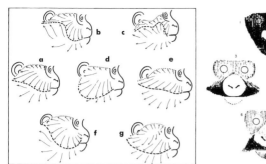

Cheek-hair arrangement (left a–g) and tonal contrasts on facial masks (right 1–7) of Cephus monkeys. Sclater's (b, 4), Lesser spot-nose (*buttikoferi*, c, 2) (*petaurista*, 1), Moustached (d, 6), Red eared (e, 3), Red tailed (*schmidti*, f, 5), Red tailed (*atrinasus*, g, 7), generalised guenon (a).

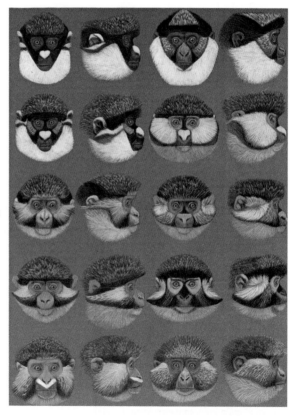

L. Lesser spot-nose (*petaurista*)
R. Nigerian white-throated

L. Lesser spot-nose (*buttikoferi*)
R. Red tailed (*schmidti*)

L. Sclaters
R. Red tailed (*whitesidei*)

L. Red eared
R. Red tailed (*atrinasus*)

L. Moustached
R. Generalised guenon

first sight the extraordinary diversity of guenon facial patterns betrays little sense of a relationship between the different species. However, comparable elements can be established (see the diagrams at the top of this page). The diagram on the opposite page illustrates the underlying geometry of facial signals in more primitive members of the forest-monkey radiation. Thus for species that rely on being cryptic, grizzled areas expand while species that have developed facial signals an elaborate set of light and dark patches expands or contracts to generate an extraordinary diversity of signal patterns (as above).

Guenon species have evolved a range of specialised foraging strategies and must tolerate continuous side-by-side foraging by other specialists. In such a situation distinct species run the risk, through wholesale hybridisation, of losing the advantages conferred by their specialisations. The evolution of distinctive vocal repertoires, coat coloration and facial patterns would appear to reduce the risk of excessive hybridisation between guenon species.

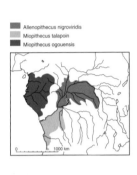

Allenopithecus nigroviridis
Miopithecus talapoin
Miopithecus ogouensis

♂ Allens swamp monkey.

Allen's Swamp Monkey *Allenopithecus nigroviridis*

Other names: Fr. *Singe des marais, Cercopithèque noir et vert*. Ger. *Sumpf Meerkatze*.
Measurements: HB 40–45cm (♀), 45–50cm (♂). T 45–55cm. SH est. 30cm (♀), est. 35cm (♂). W 3.6kg (♀), 6.2kg (♂).
Recognition: Stocky khaki-coloured monkey with off-white underparts and a shortish tail which appears to be a survival of an archaic lineage in that it possesses anatomical features characteristic of macaques as well as guenons. Its intermediate status is confirmed by chromosome analysis. Allen's swamp monkey resembles guenons in the shape of its skull and in many details of its internal anatomy. It resembles macaques or baboons in its gait, limb proportions, pointed ears, the loud rumbling calls and large testes of ♂♂ and in the sexual swellings of ♀♀. The fur is soft and dense and especially long on the cheeks, where it forms a circular, grizzled facial disc. The darkened margins of this disc describe a sinuous curve over each cheek. Eyes are set deep beneath a broad, flattened cap. The muzzle is dark grey and the chin clear white. A strongly scented chest gland is marked by white bristles. First digits on the feet are long and powerful while the hand is shorter and broader than in any guenon. Adult ♂♂ have a brilliant red margin to the anus above an orange perineal tuft and large, pale blue scrotum.
Distribution: Limited to the borders of the main R. Zaïre and its lower tributaries; also minor rivers and lake borders in the region and the borders of the R. Ubangi, R. Uelle, R. Kasai, R. Fini and R. Lukenyi. At the time when L. Zaïre existed, the swamp monkey's predecessors were probably lake-shore monkeys.
Habitat: Swamp and levee forest bordering rivers and lakes. These forests are regularly and deeply flooded so that the swamp monkey is arboreal during flood seasons and more terrestrial when water subsides. It makes forays into drier, more open habitats, including agricultural fields. Groups often sleep 8–20m above the ground in large trees close to or overhanging the river. Such sites are probably cool and safe and may serve to help space groups along a predominantly linear habitat.
Food: Omnivorous, taking fruits, leaves and invertebrates (including crabs). Allen's swamp monkey may also take fish but its feeding ecology awaits detailed study.
Behaviour: Small groups of two to eight individuals feed together. Single ♂♂ have also been recorded but they congregate with others in sleeping-trees, which suggests a harem, clan or band that can number over 40 individuals. Group members utter short baboon-like grunts but also have a guenon-like, single, high-pitched warning chirp. ♂♂ make a rumbling loud call.

Adaptations: ♂ swamp monkeys have air sacs that serve to amplify their loud rumbling call. Similar calls uttered by some baboons, macaques and colobids suggest that this may have been a vocalisation common to many early African monkeys. A slightly sacculated stomach implies some capacity to digest plant materials that are indigestible to most other cheek-pouch monkeys.

The swamp monkey's mixture of macaque- and guenon-like features is shared with patas and talapoin monkeys but, unlike them, it shows no obvious specialisation. Its evident versatility is likely to be a conservative characteristic typical of early cheek-pouch monkeys. Thus, in spite of the fact that it inhabits a limited ecotype, Allen's swamp monkey would appear to represent a profoundly conservative monkey species.

Status: The swamp monkey is easily hunted by torchlight from boats during the night and its carcasses are frequently sold on the steamers and pirogues that ply the R. Zaïre. In areas where cultivation borders the river, the swamp monkey and its habitats are progressively constricted. The great extent and remoteness of much of its habitat makes any assessment of its status very difficult. Currently listed as Class B (African Convention), Appendix 2 (CITES).

Northern Talapoin *Miopithecus ogouensis*

Other names: Fr. *Talapoin du nord*. Ger. *Ogoue Zwerg Meerkatze*.

Measurements: HB 25–37cm (♀), 30–40cm (♂). T 26–53cm. SH est. 19cm (♀), est. 22cm (♂). W 0.8–1.2kg (♀), 1.2–1.9kg (♂).

Recognition: A very small, large-headed monkey with a bright, grizzled yellow-olive crown and back, and golden-yellow outer surfaces to the limbs, hands and feet. The inner surfaces and underside are yellow tinged with off-white and the tail is dark tipped. The naked skin of the face and ears is flesh-coloured with a yellowish tint to the eyelids and lips. There are darker streaks on the nose and on the margins of elaborate 'cow-licks' that sculpt the fur on cheeks and temples. ♀♀ have a pink sexual swelling. ♂♂ have a large, pale blue scrotum.

Subspecies: This species has awaited formal description since 1969, when Dr A. de Barros Machado first pointed out the anomaly that this, the better-known form, had been assumed to be the typical talapoin. A *nomen nudum*, '*Miopithecus ogouensis*' is used here in anticipation of a formal description. (Plate pelage ex BM no. ZD 1897.7.1.1.)

Distribution: Endemic to the equatorial coastal watersheds between Cabinda and the R. Nyong. The principal river and centre of its distribution is the R. Ogooué but its range spills over into the upper reaches of some Zaïre tributaries, such as the R. Sangha, R. Alima and R. Lefini.

Habitat: Strictly equatorial, riverine species never found more than 500m from a watercourse. The northern talapoin lives in the very dense undergrowth typical of riverbanks and seldom ascends to higher levels except through foliage-covered liane tangles. It can swim and dive under water if disturbed in overhanging vegetation. Terrestrial foraging is known to be common but it is rarely seen due to dense cover. Home ranges cover 100–500ha at densities of 40–90 animals per km².

Food: In N Gabon, nearly 80% of the diet consists of fruits, notably those of plums (*Uapaca*), figs, umbrella tree (*Musanga*) and mokenjo (*Pseudospondias*), and the flesh of oil-palm nuts. 'Grains of paradise', the fruits of African ginger (*Aframomum*), which can only be gathered at ground level, are frequently eaten. Beetles, caterpillars and spiders are taken opportunistically. Riverside gardens of bananas, pawpaw, maize and cucurbits attract the northern talapoin out of the forest and manioc-washing sites are specially favoured for left-overs. Feeding is concentrated into one early morning bout, with another in late afternoon.

Behaviour: The northern talapoin lives in groups of 12–20 animals which come together with other groups at specific night-roosts (situated in dense vegetation near water) that may accommodate up to 125 animals. Adult ♂♂ are less numerous than adult ♀♀ and it is they who initiate movements and take up lookout posts, especially at night-roosts. Handling of captive ♀♀ will precipitate attacks by ♂♂, suggesting that a defensive role for ♂♂ is normal. ♂ threats are accompanied by head-bobbing, grimaces and lashing of the tail tip. Outside the mating season ♂♂ tend to move separately from the ♀♀ (generally higher in the trees). In N Gabon all ♀♀ tend to give birth annually between November and April. ♀♀ suckle their young for 4–5 months but young are very active and forage at an early age.

Adaptations: The presence of a close relative, Allen's swamp monkey, with very similar habits, is probably the major factor explaining this talapoin's restricted range. Its dependence on dense evergreen cover is evidently due to its small size, which makes it potential prey to numerous carnivores, raptors and snakes. However, there must be special advantages in being a small monkey in an equatorial forest environment, as may be evident in the evolution of the similar-sized squirrel monkey of Amazonia.

Status: It has been found that densities of the northern talapoin may double close to human settlements. Horticultural activity appears to offer at least three main benefits to these monkeys: predators are deterred by the human disturbance; clearing and land rotation generates secondary growth; and new food sources can be foraged in and around gardens. Human predation is discouraged by the talapoin's unrewarding size and its exceptional elusiveness. The northern talapoin is not threatened and has a low conservation priority of 6 (IUCN).

♂ Southern talapoin.

Southern Talapoin *Miopithecus talapoin*

Other names: Fr. *Talapoin du sud*. Ger. *Angola Zwerg Meerkatze*.

Measurements: HB est. 26–45cm. T est. 25–50cm. SH est. 25cm. W est. 1–2kg.

Recognition: A small, grizzled, yellowish olive monkey with pure white underparts and inner surfaces of limbs. The outer surfaces of the limbs are pallid chrome-yellow with less grizzling than the back. The white chin and cheek flash are separated by a black streak from the corner of the mouth. The bare skin of the face is black to the base of the nostrils, as are the ears. The tail is brown above and yellowish grey below. The legs are particularly long in relation to the arms and body. ♀♀ develop pink sexual swellings during oestrus. ♂♂ have a pale blue scrotum. They make louder calls than ♀♀ and have longer canines.

Subspecies: *M. t. ansorgei*, *M. t. melahina*, *M. t. talapoin* and *M. t. vleeschouwersi* appear to be synonyms.

Distribution: Endemic to the coastal watersheds south of the R. Zaïre, notably the R. Mebridege, R. Loge, R. Cuanza, R. Nhia and R. Cuvo (but spilling over into the upper reaches of the R. Cuango).

Habitat: A strictly riverine species limited to dense evergreen vegetation on the banks of rivers that often flow through Miombo (*Brachystegia*) woodland or, increasingly, cultivated areas.

Food: Mainly fruits but also seeds, young foliage and invertebrates.

Behaviour: Southern talapoins live in dense cover and so rely on sound more than visual markings in order to keep together. Their pigeon-like contact calls are almost continuous while they are moving or foraging. Home ranges are likely to be larger and densities lower than is the case with the equatorial species because forest strips are narrower and resources scarcer.

Adaptations: Climatic fluctuations have probably reinforced the southern talapoin's primary adaptation to 'strip-living'. Longer dry seasons and less extensive flooding under generally cooler and drier climates may have favoured more terrestrial habits than are apparent in the northern species. Consistent with such differences are the southern talapoin's longer limbs and larger body size.

Status: Very little is known about this species and still less about its current status. It is not likely to be threatened but currently has a low conservation priority rating of 3 (IUCN).

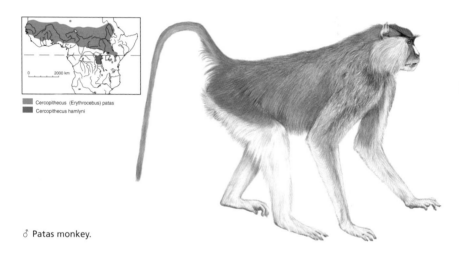

Cercopithecus (Erythrocebus) patas
Cercopithecus hamlyni

♂ Patas monkey.

Patas Monkey *Cercopithecus (Erythrocebus) patas*

Other names: Fr. *Singe rouge*. Ger. *Husarenaffe*.

Measurements: HB 48–77cm (♀), 60–87cm (♂). T 54–74cm. SH 28–45cm (♀), 34–50cm (♂). W 7–14kg (♀), 10–25kg (♂).

Recognition: A highly distinctive monkey with long limbs and slender build. ♀♀ and young are the colour of dry grass, with shades of fawn, russet and grey. ♂♂ are larger and have russet tails, hindquarters and crowns. The back and nape are sandy coloured and the shoulders are shaggy and grey streaked. Limbs are white or off-white. Western populations have pale facial skin and a dark nose; those in the east have black facial skin and a white nose. The scrotum and its surrounding skin are blue. The penis is pink and the anus of the ♂ is surrounded by bare puce-violet-pink skin.

Subspecies: *C. (E.) P. baumstarki* (pallid Serengeti isolate), *C. (E.) P. patas* (main Sahel population from Mauritania to Kordofan), *C. (E.) P. pyrrhonotus* (main Nile Valley population from Sudan to Uelle and Kenya), *C. (E.) P. villiersi* (Aïr massif isolate).

Distribution: Coincides broadly with open, wooded steppes and savannahs south of the Sahara.

Habitat: Vegetation types ranging from open grassland to dry woodland; commonest in thinly bushed *Acacia*-wooded grassland. Although the patas monkey is not a riverine species, it would appear to have retained a preference for woodland-grassland margins (which follow drainage lines in most types of *Acacia* savannahs). On floodplains, patas monkeys prefer to travel along the edges of wooded levees, moving from tree to tree with frequent stops to monitor their surroundings. All classes are vigilant but adult ♂♂ are especially so. The area travelled by a patas troop varies with the season, topography and food resources of the range (about 20–30km² in richer habitats and up to 80km² in poorer ones). Densities may decline from a known optimum of about 1.5 per km^2. A group may travel up to 12km in a day.

Food: Especially dependent on the pods, seeds, galls, young leaves, gum and flowers of *Acacia* and the fruits of common savannah trees and shrubs, such as torchwood (*Balanites*), *Euclea* and num-num (*Carissa*). Patas are poor diggers and only take grass rhizomes and leaf bases when these are in crumbly soil. Insects, small vertebrates and fungi are also taken. Visits to water are frequent in the dry season and are occasions for great vigilance.

Behaviour: In confrontations between patas groups all members of a troop display aggression towards the other troop (or solitary individual). Although troops are highly intolerant of each other their ranges may overlap by over 50%.

♂♂ often stay some distance from the main troop and social life centres on the adult ♀♀, among which pecking orders have been observed. Solitary ♂♂ and small bachelor groups have also been recorded. Patas are relatively quiet monkeys and ♂♂ do not make loud calls. A low moan or moo is the characteristic contact call. ♀♀ and young have a repertoire of chirrups, twitters, hoots and low whistles. Cohesion and precise communication would appear particularly important for small groups of monkeys living in an open, and consequently dangerous, environment.

♀♀ in oestrus do not have obvious sexual swellings but advertise their condition through their gait, by puffing up their cheeks, pursing their lips and by uttering a 'want' moan. Gestation lasts about 24 weeks and there tend to be pronounced mating peaks marked by an influx of ♂♂ into former one-M groups (July–August in Kenya). Most births occur between December and February. New babies are dark brown and ♀♀ are intensely possessive of their young. ♀♀ become mature at 3½ years. Full development may be delayed in some ♂♂ but is reached by 5 years of age. Life expectancy is thought to be at least 20 years.

Adaptations: The long limbs of the patas equip them for fast movement. Their hands and feet are narrow and the heel is long. The toes and fingers are short and have relatively weak grasping power.

Delicate digits, a long tail and many other anatomical resemblances between patas and talapoin monkeys suggest that the former may derive from much smaller, more arboreal precursors. Patas probably descend from monkeys that adapted to the driest northern margins of the Zaïre basin from whence they are likely to have been displaced by early savannah monkeys. The large size of ♂♂ relative to ♀♀ could be a relatively recent, secondary development.

Status: Recent changes in the Sahelian region have undoubtedly affected patas monkeys. In particular they have disappeared from areas in which trees have been cleared and in which cultivation and hunting have been intensified. On the other hand, they have rapidly adapted to feeding on exotic foods, from prickly pears and *Lantana* to cotton plants and food crops. Furthermore, the elimination of wild predators has undoubtedly favoured them in some localities. Patas have been declared vermin by several African countries and they are used as laboratory animals (over 14,000 were imported to the UK between 1965 and 1975). Research is currently being conducted to determine whether the simian AIDS virus, SIV, can be transmitted from savannah monkeys to patas (wild hybrids between these species have been recorded). Listed as Not Threatened, with a conservation priority rating of 3 (IUCN).

Savannah Monkeys *Cercopithecus (aethiops)* superspecies

Other names: Fr. *Grivet, Singe vert.* Ger. *Grunmeerkatze.* Swah. *Tumbili, Ngedere.*
Measurements: HB 38–61cm (♀), 45–83cm (♂). T 42–114cm. SH est. 24–40cm (♀), est. 30–54cm (♂). W 5.6kg (2.5–6kg) (♀), 7kg (3.5–9kg) (♂).
Recognition: Small, grizzled, grey, brownish or greenish monkeys with a black face mask, white ruff and a pale (or white) underside. The tail is long (except in the montane Bale monkey). There are stiff black bristles on the brow ridge in all species. The scrotum is blue or bluish in all species and both sexes have blue belly skin showing through thin white hair. The penis is red or pink and ♀♀ in oestrus have a bluish vulva around a pink clitoris.
Species: Grivet monkey, *C. (a.) aethiops* (Sudan and Ethiopia); Bale monkey, *C. (a.) djamdjamensis* (Bale massif, Ethiopia); tantalus monkey, *C. (a.) tantalus* (northern savannahs from Ghana to Uganda); vervet monkey, *C. (a.) pygerythrus* (southern savannahs and woodlands from Cape of Good Hope and Angola to Somalia); callithrix monkey, *C. (a.)*

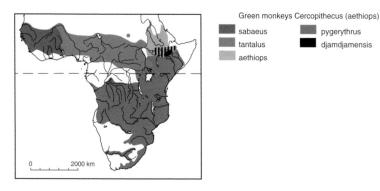

Green monkeys Cercopithecus (aethiops)

- sabaeus
- tantalus
- aethiops
- pygerythrus
- djamdjamensis

0   2000 km

sabaeus (northern savannahs from Ghana to Senegal). Because all forms are mutually fertile and have hybrid belts savannah monkeys are sometimes treated as a single species.

Distribution: By far the most numerous and widespread monkeys in Africa, ranging throughout the non-desert, non-forest areas of the continent and formerly extending along the Nile Valley.

Habitat: Savannahs, woodlands and forest-grassland mosaics. Savannah monkeys typically live along the thin but continuous belts of vegetation that follow drainage lines. The resources of these narrow belts of often deciduous trees are reduced in the dry season. Savannah monkeys therefore forage on the ground for part of the year, usually at some distance from the trees on which they depend for shelter, shade and much of their food supply. The distribution pattern of these monkeys is therefore strongly linear, following tree/grassland edges all over their wide range.

The extent of a group's home range varies from 13 to 178ha, according to habitat, food resources and the influence of neighbouring groups,. In rich environments large groups can defend small, exclusive territories. In poor habitats small groups disperse over large, undefendable ranges and population densities are consequently much lower.

Food: Fruits are the preferred and most important food, flowers and seeds become important outside fruiting seasons, and foliage and animal foods can be significant in some areas and during certain seasons. Seeds, flowers, leaves and gum of *Acacia* are important wherever this tree is dominant. The exceptionally small thumb, characteristic of these monkeys, may help to explain why they are rather inept at catching and handling active insects.

Behaviour: Savannah monkey groups may number 5–76 animals (mean 25). Both ♀♀ and ♂♂ follow a rank hierarchy but ♀ coalitions modify the pecking order and deter ♂ aggression towards the young. All young ♂♂ leave their natal group (usually joining their nearest neighbours) whereas ♀♀ habitually remain with their maternal group. ♂♂ only concert their actions during confrontations with other groups. During group challenges ♂♂ make ritualised standing 'red, white and blue' displays with erect penises. During encounters between neighbouring groups ♀♀ tend to be less aggressive.

Births tend to follow seasonal peaks but the timing is subject to much regional variation. The young mature fast, ♀♀ being able to conceive at less than 2 years of age and ♂♂ becoming fertile by 3 years. However, mature weights and development are not reached until 4 years of age in the case of ♀♀ and 5 years in the case of ♂♂.

Adaptations: Savannah monkeys are equally at home in the trees and on the ground. They are also capable of withstanding sustained solar radiation, high temperatures and dehydration. They have adapted to extreme climatic instability by high birth rates during good periods and by reducing fertility and activity during droughts and famines. They can also adjust to, and take advantage of, changes to the environment, such as the opening up of forest or woodland areas as a result of road-making, logging, cultivation, elephant damage, flooding, etc. Their alertness and acute vision is only exceeded by the patas, which they resemble in that high-ranking ♂♂ are the most continuously vigilant members of the group. High fecundity not only allows rapid response to huge fluctuations in food supply but also offsets heavy predation by eagles, leopards and other carnivores.

Status: With the single exception of the Bale monkey all populations of savannah monkeys are super-abundant, although the northern limits of their distribution are contracting as a result of tree-clearance in the Sahel.

(a) Tantalus monkey. (b) Grivet monkey.
(c) Callithrix monkey. (d) Vervet monkey.

Savannah monkeys were extensively used for medical research until the deaths of several laboratory workers from Marburg virus (transmitted by vervets) deterred what had been a substantial trade (21,779 imported to the USA in 1968–73 and 11,323 to the UK in 1965–75). Today their natural immunity to SIV (very close to the human AIDS virus, HIV), has prompted renewed interest in their biology. Listed as Not Endangered (IUCN).

Grivet Monkey *Cercopithecus (a.) aethiops*

Other names: Fr. *Grivet d'Ethiopie*. Ger. *Aethiopen Grummeerkatze*.
Measurements: HB est. 40–60cm. T est. 42–70cm. W est. 5–8kg.
Recognition: A long-tailed savannah monkey with variable, warm-olive grizzled back and crown, grey limbs and a white underside. The prominent cheek fur is laterally elongated and there is a narrow white band above the brows. The face is black (often with a fine white moustache), hands and feet are pale and there is a white tuft at the base of the white-tipped tail. In ♂♂ the scrotum is sky blue.
Subspecies: *C. (a.) a. aethiops* (east of R. Nile from Sudd to Eritrea). *C. (a.) a. matschei* (montane Ethiopia west of the Rift Valley): variable fawn to russet back. It probably hybridised extensively with the Bale monkey west of the Rift Valley, following the destruction of the latter's forest habitat over the last millennium.
Habitat: Savannahs, woodlands, riverine strips and cultivation mosaics.
Food: Heavily dependent on *Acacia* seeds, flowers, foliage and gum. Also figs and other fruiting trees.
Status: Listed as Not Threatened (IUCN).

Tantalus Monkey *Cercopithecus (a.) tantalus*

Other names: Fr. *Cercopithèque tantale*. Ger. *Tantalusmeerkatze*. Swah. *Tumbili, Ngedere*.
Measurements: HB est. 45–56cm. T est. 45–72cm. W est. 5.5–9kg.

Recognition: The largest of the savannah monkeys, with grizzled, gold to greenish back and crown, grey limbs and a white underside. The long tail has a pale tip and a white tuft at base. The face and temple bar are black and there is a sinuous, tapered white brow band. In ♂♂ the scrotum is sky blue.

Subspecies: *C. (a.) t. tantalus* (Ghana to R. Ubangi): olive-green back. *C. (a.) t. budgetti* (R. Ubangi to Uganda but with broad hybrid zone around shores of L. Victoria): olive-brown back. *C. (a.) t. marrensis* (isolate on desert mountain massif of Jebel Marra): light olive-fawn back.

It is possible that precursors of tantalus monkeys moved into the northern savannahs during a dry period through a savannah corridor cutting across the lower Zaïre River. Vervets in Angola have facial hair patterns which suggest that early pioneers may have come from this region.

Habitat: A most diverse range of woodlands, savannahs and forest mosaics.

Food: Fruits, buds, seeds, roots, bark, gum and many cultivated plants. Insects, small vertebrates and eggs are also taken.

Status: Very widespread and abundant. Listed as Not Threatened (IUCN).

Vervet Monkey *Cercopithecus (a.) pygerythrus*

Other names: Fr. *Vervet*. Ger. *Sudafrika Grunmeerkatze*. Swah. *Tumbili, Ngedere*.

Measurements: HB 38–62cm (♀), 50–65cm (♂). T 48–75cm. W 3.5–5kg (♀), 4–8kg (♂).

Recognition: A long-tailed monkey with a grizzled, grey or olive back, crown and outer limb fur. Hands and feet are darker and there is a dark tip to the tail. Tufts at the base of the tail are red. The white brow and cheeks join to frame the black face. The scrotum is turquoise or lapis blue.

Races: *Cercopithecus (a.) p. pygerythrus* (eastern-south Africa south of the R. Zambezi): ash grey coat in west graduating to olive green. *C. (a.) p. rufoviridis* (Indian Ocean to Rift lakes between R. Zambezi and L. Victoria): olive fawn back. *C. (a.) p. cynosurus* (Atlantic to Rift Lakes south of rainforests): olive-grey with pale-blotched face, lapis scrotum and cow-lick on cheeks in the north-west. *C. (a.) p. arenarius* (Somali arid zone from Horn of Africa to E Uganda and N Tanzania): brownish back and generally pallid colouring.

It hybridises with *C. (a.) tantalus* along northern shores of L. Victoria and with *C. (a) djamdjamensis* in SE Ethiopia. Dwarf forms are found on Indian Ocean islands and islands in L. Victoria, i.e. *excurbitor* (Patta I.) and *nesiotes* (Pemba I.).

Habitat: A wide variety of lightly wooded habitats across some 45 degrees of latitude, straddling the equator, ranging over half the continent and reaching altitudes of up to 3,000m. A significant part of the total range consists of Miombo (*Brachystegia*) fire-climax woodlands. Although vervets may range through these and other woodlands during fruiting or flowering seasons, *Acacia*-dominated riverine strips are primary habitat.

Food: Especially important are the seeds, flowers, foliage and gum of *Acacia* and *Albizia*, as well as the fruits of figs and buffalo thorn (*Ziziphus*). During the fruiting seasons of marula (*Sclerocarya*) or raisin bush (*Grewia*), vervets may disperse into wider fruiting zones. Animal foods are of minor significance in most habitats but may play a larger role in mangrove swamps of the east coast and islands.

Status: Common and widespread. Listed as Not Endangered (IUCN).

Callithrix Monkey *Cercopithecus (a.) sabaeus*

Other names: Fr. *Singe vert*. Ger. *Grunmeerkatze*.

Measurements: HB est. 38–60cm. T est. 42–72cm. W est. 3.8–7.7kg.

Recognition: A long-legged savannah monkey with grizzled, golden-green extending over the back, crown, down the upper arms, thighs and base of the tail. Hands and feet are pale grey and the underside is off-white. The tip of the tail is pale orange. Yellowish cheek ruffs are deflected by a cow-lick which begins below the prominent black ears and sweeps up over the temples. There is barely a trace of light brow band. The scrotum is very pale blue.

Habitat: A wide range of ecotypes, including very dry Sahelian woodlands, rainforest margins and mangrove swamps.

Food: The diets, survival and social structure of the mangrove-dwelling callithrix monkey have been extensively studied. One of its peculiarities is a reliance on crabs and other seashore foods, which are taken on mudflats at low tide.

Status: In Senegal this species is the subject of important research on the epidemiology of SIV. Evidence of infection with this virus has been found in 46% of a wild population of callithrix while only 6% of patas monkeys in the region showed evidence of infection (these differences are probably connected with the differing socio-sexual behaviour of the two species). The callithrix monkey is naturally immune to the diverse strains of AIDS-like viruses which it harbours and research is focused on a strain which might also be harmless to humans while at the same time providing immunity against HIV.

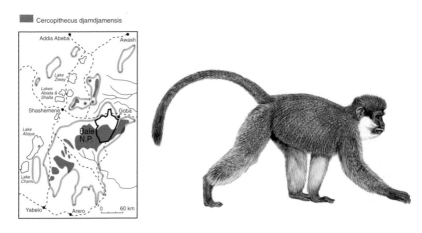

Bale Monkey *Cercopithecus (a.) djamdjamensis*

Other names: Fr. *Cercopithèque de Bale.* Ger. *Bale Grunmeerkatze.*

Measurements: HB est. 38–62cm. T est. 38–58cm. W est. 4–8kg.

Recognition: A relatively short-tailed monkey with thick, long fur. The back and crown are variably grizzled deep brown to yellowish brown, limbs and tail are grey and extremities are dark grey. The underside is off-white to grey. The black face, brows and temples show no trace of white except for a fine white moustache. The short white chin and cheek ruff leave the ears exposed and there are inconspicuous red-brown tufts at the base of the tail. ♂♂ have a blue scrotum.

Races: Numerous races of savannah monkey have been described for Ethiopia, the meeting point for three distinct forms: *aethiops, pygerythrus* and *djamdjamensis*. Most of these probably represent various permutations of hybrid, e.g. *hilgerti, ellenbecki, matschiei* and *zavattarii.*

It is possible that the Bale monkey was originally distributed all over the higher regions of the Ethiopian massif and that forest and woodland clearance over more than 2,000 years has favoured the upward spread of grivets from the lowlands. In any event, typical Bale monkeys are now restricted to a small and remote area of SE Ethiopia where it is likely that hybridisation will continue to diminish their range.

Because this population is so distinctive it seems likely that it is the montane relict of an older regional population belonging to the very earliest dispersal of savannah monkeys.

Habitat: Montane vegetation in parts of central Ethiopia is dominated by bamboo (between about 2,200 and 3,200m), juniper, koso (*Hagenia*) and St John's wort (*Hypericum*). Below this zone *Podocarpus* and various montane forest trees grow in a very patchy and fractured pattern. The Bale monkey has been recorded from the bamboo zone and is known to be a generally scarce forest-edge species.

Food: Nothing is known but *Podocarpus, Hagenia* and many other montane trees produce edible fruits. *Acacia* and *Albizia* are likely staples in the lower reaches of the Bale monkey's range.

Status: Study of this unique monkey should be made a priority, particularly in view of its much diminished range. It is possible that it occurs in a small part of the proposed Bale National Park. The cultivation mosaic that progressively replaces montane vegetation would seem to favour grivets and vervets. Thus hybridisation would appear to be the principal threat to this species, although all monkeys are hunted in reprisal for crop-raiding.

The Bale monkey deserves recognition as an endangered species. It inhabits a region of great biogeographic importance where many other unique species of fauna and flora are similarly endangered.

L'Hoest's Monkeys *Cercopithecus (l'hoesti)* superspecies

Other names: Fr. *Cercopithèques de l'Hoest.* Ger. *Vollbart Meerkatze.*
Measurements: HB 47–70cm. T 48–80cm. W 3–10kg.
Recognition: Very long-limbed dark monkeys that live on the forest floor. In contrast, however, the black muzzle stands out in sharp relief against the white fur around the chin. ♂ l'Hoest's monkeys vie with patas ♂♂ in being the largest, longest-muzzled guenons and they also show the greatest degree of sexual dimorphism. The illustrations pages 64 and 65 show the typical display postures adopted during ♂-♂ or group encounters by these remarkably quiet and otherwise cryptic monkeys; in these the tail is raised and the tip curled into a question-mark shape. Rapid about-turns also display the brilliant blue scrotum against its background of black fur. The contrast between low-key colours and behaviour on the one hand, and striking visual display on the other, is typical of l'Hoest's monkeys, which must weigh the risks of communication in a potentially dangerous environment. Unlike many forest monkeys which are easily recognised by their loud calls, l'Hoest's monkeys only rarely utter their low, two-phase boom or hoot.
Species: L'Hoest's monkey, *C. (l'h.) l'hoesti* (highland and lowland forests in E Zaïre, Uganda, Rwanda and Burundi); Preuss's monkey, *C. (l'h.) preussi* (highland and lowland forests in SW Cameroon and SE Nigeria); sun-tailed monkey, *C. (l'h.) solatus* (evergreen forest in central Gabon).
Distribution: Distribution of the three l'Hoest's monkey species cannot be understood in relation to altitude (although 'mountain monkey' has long been their misleading common name) or current vegetation patterns. The considerable divergence of l'Hoest's species and their evident conservatism help confirm their relatively ancient common ancestor and their early position in the guenon family tree (p. 51).

These monkeys live in small, tight-knit groups in well-defined home ranges and are demonstrably poor dispersers. Their dependence on continuity of experience probably makes it difficult for them to regain lost ground after disturbance to their habitat.
Habitat: Large ranges suggest that feeding strategies are expansive rather than intensive. Indeed groups of these monkeys have been observed to travel between dense mountain retreats and more exposed feeding sites down 600m of rugged escarpment, sometimes making the descent and returning twice in a single day. The fact that these monkeys regularly visit particular feeding sites during the appropriate season and are frequently seen at the same crossing points suggests that they possess intimate knowledge of their home ranges. It would appear that the composition of the vegetation is less important for them than the physical character of the undergrowth and terrain. They are known to prefer a combination of rough, steep slopes and dark, dense cover. Intimate knowledge of home ranges of this kind probably allows these highly mobile monkeys to stand up to competition from other species and to elude predators.
Food: Mainly fruits and seeds; shoots, young leaves, buds, flowers and mushrooms are also taken. L'Hoest's monkeys feed in close formation and are not known to feed from scarce, scattered sources that would force a group to disperse in order to harvest them. When cultivation expands into their home ranges they invariably become wary but persistent raiders, invading agricultural fields in tight groups. They only occasionally join other species in mixed feeding groups, probably drawn by particularly plentiful food sources.
Behaviour: Little is known about the details of l'Hoest's monkeys' behaviour. A single adult ♂ with one or more ♀♀ and their offspring form the usual social unit. Home ranges are probably too large to defend but confrontations between groups involve all members. Adult ♂♂ make frequent threats and rushes, and posture with tail raised and chin thrust forward, frequently turning to display frontal, lateral and back views. This is usually followed by a silent and sudden withdrawal.
Adaptations: These species are remarkable for their ability to run through dense undergrowth. Their limbs show minor modifications that render the relatively unspecialised hands and feet particularly flexible at the wrist and ankle.

Exceptional wariness and quietness evidently help to reduce predation (by leopards, golden cats, pythons and eagles) but low-key forms of communication mean that individuals would easily get lost and so must stay close together. A poor ability to disperse inhibits the colonisation or recolonisation of territory and gives rise to a patchy distribution at both micro- and macro-level.

The common ancestors of l'Hoest's and savannah monkeys could not have been as specialised as any of the living species. Divergence would have been influenced by major climatic fluctuations during which l'Hoest's monkeys adapted to wetter conditions and savannah monkeys to drier conditions. In habitats rich enough to supply a year-round abundance of fruits, these monkeys are well able to compete with other species. However, their ability to cope with severe seasonal shortages would seem to be reduced by the inflexibility of their social system.

Status: These monkeys respond to agricultural encroachment by raiding crops and are therefore frequently snared and hunted. Because their social and foraging habits depend on continuity and stability, any major perturbation is likely to lead to decline. This may be one of the few primate groups in which captive-breeding programmes might contribute to their survival. They might be expected to respond well to carefully phased re-introduction to well-protected, florally rich areas.

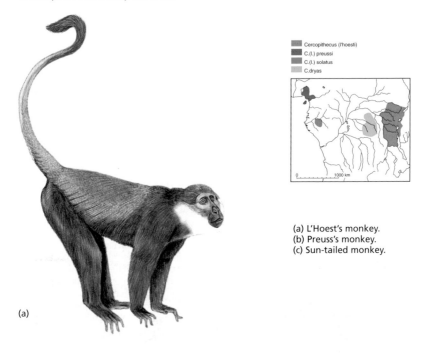

Cercopithecus (l'hoesti)
C.(l.) preussi
C.(l.) solatus
C.dryas

0   1000 km

(a) L'Hoest's monkey.
(b) Preuss's monkey.
(c) Sun-tailed monkey.

(a)

L'Hoest's Monkey *Cercopithecus (l'h.) l'hoesti*

Other names: Fr. *Cercopithèque de l'Hoest*. Ger. *Vollbartmeerkatze*.
Measurements: HB 45–55cm (♀), 54–70cm (♂). T 46–80cm. SH est. 29–36cm (♀), est. 34–46cm (♂). W 3–4.5kg (♀), 6–10kg (♂).
Recognition: A long-legged, black-bodied monkey with a brilliant white ruff and a russet 'saddle' bordered with grizzled grey. The long tail is grey at its thick base and tapers to a black brush. Fully adult ♂♂ are twice the weight of ♀♀ and have a long black muzzle and brilliant blue scrotum. The orbits are bare skinned and pale violet in adult ♂♂. The deepset eyes are pale orange.
Distribution: E Zaïre, W Uganda, Rwanda and Burundi.
Habitat: Montane and intermediate forest up to 2,500m from Itombwe to the Ruwenzori Mts. L'Hoest's monkey has also colonised a wedge of lowland forest west of this region (see map above). It always travels on the ground but will climb to any level in order to feed.

Food: Fruits of yellow wood (*Podocarpus*), koso (*Hagenia*), parasol trees (*Polyscias*), wild custard apple (*Myrianthus*), *Maesa* and the young leaves and shoots of various trees, shrubs and herbs. Resins, bracken shoots and mushrooms may be incidental foods, as are invertebrates and lichen.

Behaviour: L'Hoest's monkey groups consist of a single ♂ and a very variable number of ♀♀ and their young (10 and 17 are two cited averages). Groups form a close association reinforced by much mutual grooming. Adult ♂♂ tend to stay on the periphery and take up the rear when the group is alarmed. Solitary ♂♂ are frequently found in the vicinity of larger groups. A group will usually use one of a limited number of favourite sleeping-trees (usually situated in higher locations) at night.

Newborn infants are brown and acquire adult colours over the first 2–3 months. They are frequently observed to entwine tails with their mother's.

Adaptations: The long legs of this species correlate with its frequent and extensive travel within large home ranges. While many other guenon species elude predators by hiding in the trees, l'Hoest's monkey flees over the ground, a strategy that requires thorough knowledge of the range and co-ordination among all members in order to keep together as a group.

Status: Erosion of habitats as a result of expanding cultivation, together with concomitant hunting, are probably reducing l'Hoest's monkey numbers in many areas. While light selective felling and pit-sawing are unlikely to be highly damaging, large-scale logging is known to have threatened this species in Kibale Forest, Uganda. The monkey's last major stronghold in Rwanda, the Nyungwe Forest, is threatened by a major Development Action Plan drawn up by banks and development agencies. Although its wide range and diverse habitats (some very inaccessible) ensure the immediate future of this species, long-term prospects are less secure. Listed as Class B (African Convention), Appendix 2 (CITES), Vulnerable (IUCN).

(b)

(c)

Preuss's Monkey *Cercopithecus (l'h.) preussi*

Other names: Fr. *Cercopithèque de Preuss.* Ger. *Westafrika Vollbart Meerkatze.*
Measurements: HB est. 45–66cm. T 53–61cm. W est. 3.5–7kg.
Recognition: A long-tailed, long-legged dark monkey with grizzled grey crown, cheeks, shoulder and flanks. A mahogany-red streak extends from the shoulders to the root of the tail. The vivid orange eyes are set in pale violet orbits. The muzzle, nose and forehead are black and there is a furry white bib. The adult ♂ has a blue scrotum, a long, prominent muzzle and is twice the weight of the ♀.

Subspecies: C. (l'h.) p. *insularis* (Bioko I., formerly Fernando Po), C (l'h.) p. *preussi* (mainland).

Habitat: Originally ranging from the R. Sanaga to the R. Cross but has now disappeared over the greater part of this area. Now found in the Oban hills and Obudu but mainly on the north-western flank of Mt Cameroon between 1,000 and 1,800m. Preuss's monkey also occurs in some isolated patches of forest in the Cameroon grasslands. Groups of two to twelve animals consist of a single adult ♂ and one or more ♀♀ with their young. ♂♂ utter a deep, two-part booming in the morning and early evening.

Food: Fruits, seeds, leaves and flowers. Little is known about feeding behaviour.

Status: The substantial contraction of this monkey's range is an indication of how profoundly Cameroon forests have suffered from clear-felling (for chipboard), cultivation, hunting and the penetration of forests by roads and settlement. Confiscation of guns in Bioko (in 1976) has brought some respite for the island population but its distribution there is extremely confined. Listed as Class B (African Convention), Appendix 2 (CITES), Endangered (IUCN).

Sun-Tailed Monkey *Cercopithecus (l'h.) solatus*

Other names: Fr. *Cercopithèque à queue de soleil*. Sake dialect *Kage*.

Measurements: HB est. 47–68cm. T est. 48–80cm. W est. 4–9kg.

Recognition: Limbs are long and black, the back is grizzled brown and the grey and white tail is tipped with bright orange. The crown is grizzled grey with prominent muffs over the ears. Pale grey cheek patches are poorly differentiated from a circular off-white bib. ♂♂ are much larger than ♀♀ and have a bright blue scrotum and a prominent muzzle.

Distribution: Central Gabon between the valleys of the R. Ogooué and R. Offoué (but scarcely any records east of the R. Ogooué).

Habitat: A hilly area of approximately 10,000km^2 typified by very frequent rivers and streams that dissect the terrain deeply. The moist evergreen forest is dominated by Gaboon mahogany (*Acoumea*) the leguminous awoura (*Julbernardia*), false nutmeg (*Pycnanthus*) and mubala-oil trees (*Pentaclethra*). The sun-tailed monkey prefers densely shaded, tangled areas and remains common after light logging (perhaps because dense undergrowth increases).

Food: Prefers fruits which are abundant most of the year round. Currently undergoing study.

Behaviour: Small single-♂, multi-♀ groups. The forest in the sun-tailed monkey's area is inhabited by 13 other species of simian primate. This is a measure of the abundant food resources available but also suggests that the sun-tail is not in direct competition with other species. Neighbouring areas have no sun-tails and between six and four fewer species overall.

Status: First described as late as 1988 the sun-tailed monkey has become a 'flag-ship' species for conservation in Gabon. Its limited distribution is not due to hunting, settlement or logging, although logging concessions are being exploited over most of its range in the Forêt des Abeilles. Given the importance of this area for very many organisms the proposed Lopé National Park should be enlarged to include the Forêt des Abeilles as a unique centre of endemism, or refugium. Listed as Class B (African Convention), Appendix 2 (CITES), Vulnerable to Extinction by IUCN.

Salonga Monkey *Cercopithecus dryas*

Other names: Fr. *Cercopithèque salonga*. Ngando dialect, *Ekele*.

Measurements: HB est. 37–39cm (♀), est. 38–40cm (♂). T est. 48–52cm. W est. 2–2.5kg (♀), est. 2.5–3.3kg (♂).

Recognition: A small, forest monkey with greyish brown back and upper limbs, black lower limbs, white chest, belly and inner thighs and forearms. The medium length, bicoloured, grey and white tail has a black tip and spot near base. The black face has white or cream cheeks, chin and brow. Juveniles are grey and white and develop brown and black contrasts later. The ♂ is slightly larger than the ♀ and has longer chin fur, forming a short beard. The scrotum is light blue. Calls and vocal behaviour have yet to be recorded.

Distribution: The distribution of this relict species is sandwiched between the low basin that once formed the Pliocene L. Zaïre (p. 450) and the 'Virunga volcanics' (p. 450). The precise boundaries of its range are still not known because of its secretive habits. (A single juvenile was first described in 1932 and complete adult specimens only in 1985.)

Habitat: Thickets within secondary forest and swamp forest along small rivers. The lower levels are preferred.

Food: Very little is known but the salonga monkey has been reported to feed on the fruits, young leaves and shoots of monocot gingers and arrowroots (notably *Aframomum* and *Megaphrynium*) and the fruits of low-level trees, shrubs and vines. Major fruits in its habitat are *Landolfia, Sida, Cola, Carpolobia, Allophylus* and *Cissus*. Many of these are fleshy berries enclosing edible seeds.

Behaviour: Local hunters describe groups of up to 30 animals in which more than one adult ♂ is present. Other observers have noted groups numbering 2–15 and have recorded them associating with other primate species.

Adaptations: The salonga has very large temporal muscles and large jaws. Its molars display heavy wear at the back at an early age. Upper incisors are unusual in being weak and splayed. This unique combination of dental and anatomical features suggests a peculiar separation of the jaw's functions. Possibly soft fruits are husked in the front of the mouth and seeds stored in the cheek pouches to be cracked later between vice-like hind molars.

This is one of the few guenon species whose chromosomes have not yet been studied. It appears to be a relict species sharing very ancient affinities with de Brazza's and Diana monkeys. It resembles the latter in the pattern of its coloration and the former in its occupation of a low-level habitat. However, it differs from both these larger monkeys in its small size and peculiar dentition.

Status: The salonga monkey is hunted by the Ngando people who indicate that it is not rare in the Wamba area. It seems likely that it is a relict species with very poor capacity to disperse or colonise, in which case its strictly limited geographical range may be very ancient and its effective conservation is a high priority. Listed as Class B (African Convention), Appendix 2 (CITES), Rare or Endangered with a priority of 4 (IUCN).

Diana Monkey *Cercopithecus diana*

Other names: Fr. *Cercopithèque diane*. Ger. *Dianameerkatze*.

Measurements: HB 40–48cm (♀), 50–60cm (♂). T 52–82cm. W 2.2–3.5kg (♀), 3.5–7.5kg (♂).

Recognition: An agile, long-limbed monkey with strongly contrasting colours and pattern. The dark grey of the body graduates to black down the outer legs and arms. Chest, chin and cheeks are white and there is a white stripe down the thigh. The lower back is deep russet or orange-brown. The back of the thighs and inner legs are deep russet or cream, concealing the blue scrotum in the ♂. The white brow band is conspicuous or vestigial. The face is black. The loud call of the ♂ Diana monkey is a very distinctive volley of reverberating hacks ending in an explosive 'pyow'. These may be uttered while stationary or while running a fast arboreal circuit, punctuated by leaps against branches and shaking of foliage.

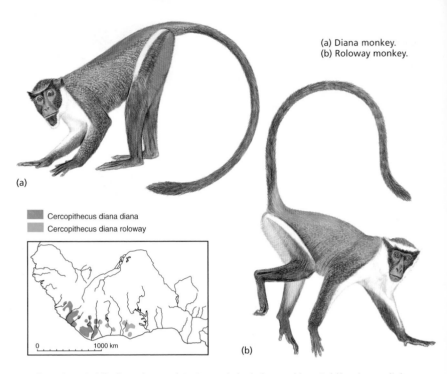

(a) Diana monkey.
(b) Roloway monkey.

Cercopithecus diana diana
Cercopithecus diana roloway

0   1000 km

Subspecies: *C. (d.) diana* (west of R. Sassandra): darker, redder. *C. (d.) roloway*: lighter, narrower face mask.

Distribution: From Sierra Leone and SW Guinea (Seredou) to W Ghana. From sea-level up to 1,400m (on north side of Mt Nimba). Now in small patches.

Habitat: An almost entirely arboreal species dependent on continuous canopy and with a strong preference for high-canopy primary rainforest. Also found in mature secondary, riverine and semi-deciduous forests and galleries. Densities vary greatly but when the river island of Tiwai (12km²) received protection between 30 and 50 Diana monkeys were recorded per km².

Food: Primarily fruits and seeds. Leaves and, incidentally, invertebrates and small vertebrates are also taken.

Behaviour: Groups of about six to eight ♀♀ and their young are accompanied by one adult territorial ♂, total 14 (10–50). Diana monkeys feed and rest in a very dispersed pattern, reinforced by ♀ hierarchies. Groups rally to ♂ loud calls, typically uttered in the morning, after resting and at any disturbance. ♀♀ frequently make a distinctive trilling contact call as well as single chirps and a barking call, uttered in appeasement. Territories of 100–200 ha are travelled over daily. These monkeys are alert and quick to flee from danger.

They have no pronounced breeding season. Young are born a light, brownish grey and acquire black and white contrasts progressively over about 6 months. They mature at 5½ years of age.

Adaptations: The particularly bright colours and linear contrasts at the hind-end of this monkey give strong visual emphasis to small changes in posture by creating contrasting, angular, geometric configurations. This 'whole-body' patterning is specifically adapted to long-range signalling in dispersed social units. Dominant animals generally stand with stiff legs and prefer to posture facing down a sloping branch.

Status: Diana monkey groups make daily reconnaissances of their relatively large territories in a characteristically noisy and conspicuous manner which renders them particularly vulnerable to hunters with shotguns. In the centre of the Diana monkeys' range in Liberia there are no constraints on large-scale 'bush-meat' hunting, using modern firearms, lights, vehicles and processing techniques. Diana monkeys are a popular prey because they are easy to find and both their meat and skins fetch high prices. In spite of all this, however, the main threat to the survival of this species comes from logging of its food trees and the trees that make up its high-canopy habitat. Described as rare in 1960, all populations have continued to decline. In parts of Sierra Leone populations of primates are thought never to have recovered from colonial extermination campaigns in which more than 250,000 primates were killed (1947–62).

Diana monkeys are nominally protected in the Ivory Coast and Ghana but vigorously hunted in practice. Without specific programmes devoted to their survival they face extinction. Listed as Class B (African Convention), Appendix 1 (CITES), Vulnerable (IUCN).

De Brazza's Monkey *Cercopithecus neglectus*

Other names: Fr. *Cercopithèque de Brazza*. Ger. *Brazzameerkatze*. Swah. *Kalasinga*.
Measurements: HB 40–50cm (♀), 50–60cm (♂). T 53–85cm. W 4–5kg (♀), 5–8kg (♂).
Recognition: A long-tailed, grey-backed guenon with orange brow and white beard. Forearms, hands, feet, belly and tail are black. The inner surfaces of the thighs and buttocks are white. There is a white stripe down the thigh. ♀♀ are smaller than adult ♂♂. The young change colour from infant brown to grey with rich russet suffusions to the head and rump. ♀♀ acquire adult colouring by the time they reach about 2.5kg but ♂♂ generally lose their russet colouring only once they have surpassed the ♀♀ in size. The ♀ shows a pink perineum while the adult ♂ has a bright blue scrotum. De Brazza's monkey habitually retreats at the least disturbance, slipping behind a branch or crouching in the foliage. When a group is disturbed the ♂ always takes up a defensive position and may threaten or give a chattering croak followed by single croaking barks. Undisturbed it is a quiet, exceptionally slow, deliberate and intensely observant monkey.
Distribution: From S Cameroon and equatorial Guinea through most of the Zaïre basin to Ruwenzori Mts, except for Virunga volcanics zone. It also occurs in the vicinity of the Elgon and Debasien Mts and in S Ethiopia (R. Omo).
Habitat: A river-oriented monkey only moving more than 200m away from the river to visit a major food source (such as fruiting fig trees). The riverine habitat spans all forest types, from lowland and swamp forests to semi-deciduous, *Acacia*-dominated and lower montane galleries. In this zone the ground is frequently flooded for long periods, which renders it an exceptionally safe refuge from terrestrial predators (the thorny undergrowth also deters eagles). De Brazza's monkey sleeps, hides and travels at low-levels (below 5m) but juveniles generally avoid descending to the ground. Home ranges frequently follow only one bank of a river. They are therefore linear and can total over 1km in length and cover up to 10ha, although in rich habitats they cover no more than 5–6ha. While the central zone of a group's range is exclusive there may be minor overlaps with the ranges of neighbouring groups.
Food: Half to three-quarters of the diet comprises fruits and seeds. However, shortfalls in fruits and seeds can be offset by taking leaves. This ability to take a significant proportion of leaves permits the monkey to remain within a small but secure home range throughout the year. It will feed on fruits in the early morning or late afternoon (and may combine this

with sun-bathing). As temperatures rise it descends to lower levels where it feeds mainly on leaves, herbs and invertebrates. The latter are mainly insect larvae and pupae uncovered by meticulous gleaning of the forest floor and overgrown tree trunks. Groups of de Brazza's monkeys travel between 300 and 500m in a day but they may remain so close to a tree throughout its fruiting season that they are effectively sedentary.

Behaviour: One or more ♀♀ are accompanied by an adult ♂. Where selective predation on ♂♂ is high (as in parts of E Africa) the total numbers in a group can rise to 35, while more equal survival rates may lead to a one-to-one sex ratio and a 'monogamous pair' social structure (recorded in Gabon). The ♂ utters a deep, humming boom most frequently in the early morning, after any disturbance and whenever there is any change in the direction of travel. Its effect is to draw the group together. Group members are observed to remain 2–100m apart and they utter a quiet croaking grunt to keep in touch. In common with Allen's swamp monkey and Hamlyn's guenon, de Brazza's monkey scent-marks its surroundings. ♂♂ are particularly active in this respect. Although temporary encounters and mixing with neighbouring groups may evoke little more than much excited grunting or croaking, adult ♂♂ are generally intolerant of other adult ♂♂. De Brazza's ♂♂ are also intolerant of other guenon species at their food trees and will force them to retreat.

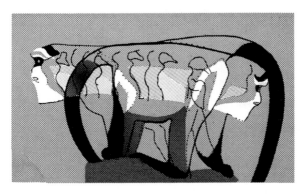

Cercopithecus neglectus. Postures of male at beginning and end of one "sweep" during loud call display with superimposed outlines of head and beard during traverse.

Adaptations: The inconspicuous, grizzled grey back and crown of de Brazza's monkey are an excellent camouflage when the animal is in hiding (a monkey can remain immobile for up to 8 hours). However, regrouping depends on visual signals as well as the M's hums and loud calls. The ♂ acts as both defender and beacon for his group and must switch from 'hider' to 'advertiser' as soon as danger has passed. Both the back and front ends of de Brazza's monkey reveal matching colours and pattern. The ♂ can therefore effectively transmit a double signal, as is evidently the case during rallying behaviour when, between violent shakings of vegetation, he will reverse his position while maintaining a similar visual beacon at both ends (either his white beard or his white buttocks). The figure above superimposes ciné frames from a typical 'sweep' of this kind.

Status: De Brazza's monkey is rare or endangered in Kenya, Ethiopia and Uganda because its habitats are being eroded by cultivation or clearance of trees. In the rest of its range it is abundant and in no danger. Listed as Not Endangered (IUCN).

Mona Monkeys *Cercopithecus (mona)* superspecies

Other names: Fr. *Mone*. Ger. *Mona meerkatze*.

Measurements: HB 40–60cm. T 54–80cm. W 2–7.5kg.

Recognition: Medium-sized to small, arboreal monkeys with a grizzled back and small dark hands and feet. The face is enlarged by pale cheek ruffs and the ears are tufted. The skin surrounding the eyes is dark grey or blue while that around the mouth is depigmented. The underside is generally light-coloured with sharp contrasts running down the forearms. The tail is long, with a dark tip and lighter midsection. Genitals are inconspicuous.

Campbell's monkey. Lowe's monkey. Mona monkey.

Crowned monkey. Wolf's monkey. Dent's monkey.

Species: Mona monkey, C. (m.) *mona*; Campbell's monkey, C. (m.) *campbelli*; Lowe's monkey, C. (m.) *lowei*; Dent's monkey, C. (m.) *denti*; Wolf's monkey, C. (m.) *wolfi*; crowned monkey, C. (m.) *pogonias*. In spite of close family resemblance, recent genetic studies have shown that chromosome numbers differ from species to species (66 in C. (m.) *campbelli*, 68 in C. (m.) *mona*, 72 in C. (m.) *wolfi* and C. (m.) *pogonias*). These differences suggest that the group has evolved over a protracted period and that C. (m.) *pogonias* and C. (m.) *wolfi* are more recently evolved than C. (m.) *campbelli* and C. (m.) *lowei*.

Distribution: Strictly limited to the main lowland rainforest blocks (although they may survive in patches that have become detached as a result of recent forest clearance). The main constraint limiting their distribution is seasonality of the climate. They are absent from forests subjected to strong seasonal fluctuations in rainfall or temperature. Similar constraints have inhibited their colonisation of forests at higher altitudes and latitudes. The more recently evolved species, C. (m.) *pogonias* and C. (m.) *wolfi*, occupy the centre of the group's range. The easternmost race of C. (m.) *wolfi* bears some resemblances to its neighbour, C. (m.) *denti*. While C. (m.) *denti* undoubtedly bears some relationship to this advanced species, it has a much older link with C. (m.) *campbelli* in the far west. This complex 'ring' of populations, in which conservative species occupy the margins, suggests that mona monkeys may be actively undergoing a group radiation.

Habitat: Almost wholly arboreal, most mona monkeys rely on dense, relatively unbroken canopy in primary, secondary or well-developed gallery forests.

Food: Fruits and up to 20% invertebrates. Foliage and other plant parts are less significant. Feeding routines begin with bulk fruit intake in the morning followed by insect-hunting in the shade during the heat of the day and a return to fruits in the afternoon.

Behaviour: Groups of 5–20 animals are accompanied (often at some distance) by a single territorial ♂ who serves as a lookout rather than a 'protector' for the rest of the group. All monas are very fast, agile monkeys that never stray far from dense vegetation in which they can hide (eagles are their main predators). Loud calls are made at the same time as highly ritualised sequences of movement and posture. Body postures alternately expose and conceal the bright face and chest patterns. Exceptionally active, curious monkeys, monas frequently interact with, and respond to, fellow group members, other primates and even squirrels, birds and insects.

F monas mature and begin breeding at 2½–4 years of age. Gestation lasts 6 months and young become independent relatively early.

Adaptations: Monas have small hands and feet with exceptionally flexible ankles and wrists well suited to their fast arboreal gymnastics. Their broad hands, with well-developed thumbs, allow them to readily catch and dismember active insects, such as grasshoppers, flies and cicadas.

Status: Fecundity, agility and an unparalleled ability to conceal themselves are among the characteristics that have enabled monas to offset depredation from a wide range of predators, including humans. Their small size makes them less attractive to hunters, although they are fairly widely hunted. Widespread forest clearance has greatly reduced numbers in some areas. All species are listed as Not Threatened (IUCN).

72

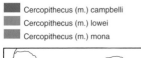

Cercopithecus (m.) campbelli
Cercopithecus (m.) lowei
Cercopithecus (m.) mona

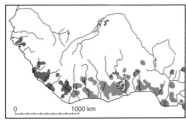

0   1000 km

(a)

Mona Monkey *Cercopithecus (m.) mona*

Other names: Fr. *Mone*. Ger. *Monameerkatze*.
Measurements: HB 40–50cm (♀), 48–60cm (♂). T 45–80cm. W 4kg (3–4.5kg) (♀), 5kg (4–6kg) (♂).
Recognition: A long-tailed monkey with a mahogany-brown back, cream-coloured underparts, chest and inner surfaces of the limbs. The rounded, furry head has an off-white brow band and pale cheek fur which contrast strongly with the blue-grey mask of bare skin surrounding the eyes. The lower limbs are black on the outer side. Two oval patches of white fur flank the tail on the hips and would appear to resemble upwardly displaced, exaggerated ischial callosities. They are unique to this species and noticeable even from a distance. The mona monkey is very vocal and utters a want call which has a metallic grating quality, harsher than equivalent calls made by Lowe's monkey. The ♂ alarm call is a two-phase 'ooé'.
Distribution: Focused on the R. Niger delta and surrounding minor rivers, from the R. Volta to the R. Sanaga.
Habitat: A lowland-forest species that inhabits all but the most degraded and upland forests within its regional range. The mona monkey is most abundant close to riversides and follows forest galleries out into much drier country in central Nigeria. It is the commonest monkey throughout the vast mangrove forests of the R. Niger delta.
Food: A true frugivore which also takes invertebrates. Invertebrates are likely to be particularly important in the diets of mangrove-dwelling populations.
Behaviour: Groups averaging 12 animals are accompanied by a single adult ♂ but larger aggregations have also been recorded. They can live at high densities when not heavily hunted. They frequently associate with other monkey species. Between the R. Cross and R. Sanaga such mixed parties include the closely related *C. (m.) pogonias*, while in the R. Volta valley they include *C. (m.) lowei*. The greater numbers of *C. (m.) pogonias* and occasional hybrids suggest that the mona monkey may be in gradual retreat in Cameroon.
Adaptations: Lowe's and mona monkeys might have first diverged because they were separated by much drier climatic phases. At such times true forest conditions would have contracted to delta mangrove swamps and narrow riverine strips, the habitat most favoured by the Nigerian mona. It would appear that the mona monkey's intrusion into the R. Volta valley system is the product of a westward expansion assisted by this species's relative tolerance of drier conditions.

If the white hip discs of the mona mimic ischial callosities then they might be interpreted as an adaptation which enables greater social cohesion. In those monkeys which possess them, ischial callosities are associated with the gesture of 'presenting', which helps to appease aggressive behaviour and makes the animal more approachable.
Status: In spite of massive destruction of their habitat and relentless hunting pressure, the mona remains a common and widespread species. Listed as Not Endangered (IUCN).

Campbell's Monkey *Cercopithecus (m.) campbelli*

Other names: Fr. *Mone de Campbell*. Ger. *Campbellmeerkatze*.
Measurements: HB est. 40–58cm. T 54–75cm. W est. 3–5.8kg.

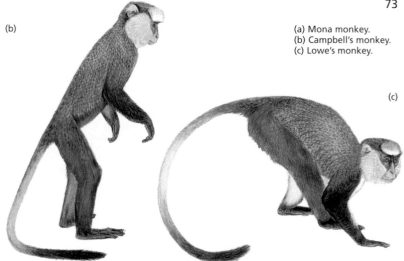

(b)

(a) Mona monkey.
(b) Campbell's monkey.
(c) Lowe's monkey.

(c)

Recognition: A long-tailed, arboreal monkey with dark grey hindquarters, belly and lower forearms, graduating into a tawny-brownish grizzle on the shoulders and crown. The pale cheek ruffs are broad and circular, with scarcely a trace of annulation or grizzling, and are separated from the broad white brow diadem by the narrowest of temporal streaks. The ear tufts are also plain white or cream. The facial pattern closely resembles that of Dent's monkey.

Distribution: From the R. Sassandra valley west to the Gambia.

Habitat: A wide range of forests, including mangroves and narrow galleries. Campbell's monkey has readily taken to secondary growth fringing gardens and fields.

Food: Mainly fruits with flowers and insects.

Behaviour: Resembles other mona species in having small, single-♂ groups and small ranges in relatively rich habitats.

Adaptations: The dull colouring of this species is probably cryptic and may reflect the more exposed and dangerous conditions under which it lives relative to other *mona* species.

Status: Although range and numbers are greatly diminished Campbell's monkey is still widespread. Listed as Not Endangered (IUCN).

Lowe's Monkey *Cercopithecus (m.) lowei*

Other names: Fr. *Mone de Lowe*. Ger. *Lowemeerkatze*.

Measurements: HB est. 40–58cm. T 54–75cm. W 3–5.8kg.

Recognition: A long-tailed, arboreal monkey with grizzled brown back, dark grey hindlegs and rump, black outer arms, tail tip, hands and feet. Underparts are white. The finely grizzled cheek fur pales to form a sharp contrast with the blue-grey eye mask that typifies all monas. A similar narrow margin edges the oval orange-yellow brow band. Ear tufts are grizzled and often yellowish. The temples are marked by a broad black band that separates the light cheeks and ears from the dark crown and orange brow. This very vocal monkey often betrays its presence with an explosive sneeze of alarm or a nasal 'ooeeoo' contact call. ♂ ♂ utter a three-phase 'ooahoo'.

Distribution: Rainforest zone between the R. Sassandra and R. Volta.

Habitat: Most forest types; primary, secondary and galleries, but not common in marshy areas or mangroves. Lowe's monkey is less exclusively arboreal than most monas and has no close association with riverbanks or water. It stays close to cover and generally avoids exposure.

Food: Mainly fruit; pulp of oil-palm seeds, figs, *Cola*, *Baphia* and garden fruits have been recorded, and flowers. Insects are frequently hunted but little interest is taken in vertebrates or leaves.

Behaviour: Groups average ten animals and comprise a single adult ♂ with about four adult ♀ ♀ and their young. Home ranges extend from about 1.5 to 3ha. Gestation lasts about 6 months and the species shows a distinct birth peak in December–January.

Adaptations: The genetic distinctness of this species from *C. (m.) mona* is evident from its co-existence in the R. Volta valley with no sign of hybridisation. However, where Lowe's and Campbell's monkeys overlap, between the R. Sassandra and R. Nzo, the former is dominant in the moister south while the latter is commoner in the marginally drier north. Hybrids do occur but a high degree of separation in the absence of any obvious barrier suggests a relatively ancient genetic divergence. It has been suggested that monas originated as a distinct group in W Africa. As the most 'generalised' of the monas, with the least well-defined coat pattern and a low chromosome count, Lowe's monkey would appear to be the most conservative of living monas. Its survival and study is important for understanding the mona radiation in particular and the adaptive trends of forest primates in general.

Status: Although habitats and numbers have been greatly reduced this species remains common and widespread. Listed as Not Endangered (IUCN).

Dent's Monkey *Cercopithecus (m.) denti*

Other names: Fr. *Mone de Dent*. Ger. *Dentmeerkatze*.

Measurements: HB 40–70cm. T 70–90cm. W 3–6kg.

Recognition: A long-tailed, arboreal monkey with a brilliant contrast between the white belly and dark back. The white inner limbs also contrast strongly with the black arms and grizzled brown legs. The back is a rich, grizzled mahogany brown; the feet are black and the tail is grey with a black tip. The face mask is blue grey with a depigmented muzzle. The circular cheek ruffs are yellowish off-white and the brow a dirty white.

Distribution: Between the R. Lualaba, R. Zaïre and R. Itimbiri and the Ruwenzori foothills.

Habitat: Lowland forests with a preference for high-canopy mixed forest. Tends to avoid swamp forest and large river margins.

Food: Fruits, flowers and invertebrates (especially caterpillars). Shoots and leaves are more marginal foods.

Behaviour: Dent's monkey lives in groups of up to 12 animals with a single adult ♂. They frequently associate with much larger groups of red-tails. When alarmed the group readily disperses in twos and threes in different directions and will freeze in knots of vegetation for long periods. The ♂'s booming loud call brings the group members together again. Dent's monkey has been implicated in the epidemiology of yellow fever and other viral diseases.

Adaptations: Resemblances between Dent's and Campbells monkeys suggests that a much more homogenous mona population was once dispersed right across the rainforest zone. There are also resemblances with *C. (m.) wolfi* (some taxonomists treat Dent's monkey as a race of *wolfi*).

Status: This successful species ranges through a very large area and is under no immediate threat. It is a particularly difficult species to hunt so that future threats are therefore likely to take the form of wholesale habitat destruction. Listed as Not Endangered (IUCN).

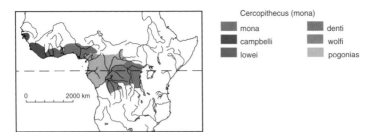

Cercopithecus (mona)

■	mona	■	denti
■	campbelli	■	wolfi
■	lowei	■	pogonias

Wolf's monkey (*C.m. wolfi wolfi*).

Wolf's Monkey *Cercopithecus (m.) wolfi*

Other names: Fr. *Mone de Meyer*. Ger. *Wolfmeerkatze*.

Measurements: HB est. 40–68cm. T 60–75cm. W est. 2–6kg.

Recognition: A long-tailed, arboreal monkey with a lighter dorsal stripe down the dark, grizzled back. Hindquarters are sharply differentiated in colour (reddish or orange) while the outer forearms are black. On each side of the eye mask, dark skin and shorter fur extend back across the upper cheeks and temples to the ears, which have brightly coloured tufts. The fur on the lower cheeks is longer and lighter. A relatively narrow and light-coloured brow diadem extends back to the ears.

Subspecies: *C. (m.) w. wolfi* (S Zaïre basin between R. Zaïre and R. Kasai): slate-grey back, white underside, orange ears, orange or reddish hindlegs and lateral stripe. *C. (m.) w. elegans* (short stretch between upper reaches of R. Lomami and R. Lualaba): dark back, white underside, grey hindlegs, white ear tufts, very narrow brow stripe. *C. (m.) w. pyrogaster* (forests south of R. Kasai): dark back, dark red hindlegs, red ear tufts and underside.

Habitat: Lowland rainforests of the S Zaïre basin, with a preference for high-canopy primary and secondary forests.

Food: Fruits, flowers and invertebrates.

Behaviour: Thought to closely resemble that of *C. (m.) pogonias*. The typical display is a stiff-legged, raised-rump posture in which the distinctively coloured hindlegs form an eye-catching angle with the tail and lowered torso.

  Whereas most guenons have broad ruffs of cheek fur that make their heads look larger, this species has flattened fur in front of the ears. As the ears are elaborated with a bright flash of colour it would appear that the ears and ear movements are important in communication. This peculiar flattening correlates with a ritualised 'head-flagging' behaviour which is typical of several guenon species and would appear to originate in avoidance of eye-contact gestures (the commonest form of mammal appeasement behaviour). In Wolf's monkey this behaviour involves an emphatic turning of the head to give more of a profile view than in most other species (a gesture that is taken a step further in the crowned monkey).

Status: A widespread and common species which has nonetheless suffered considerable reduction in numbers due to increasingly dense settlement in parts of its range. Listed as Not Endangered (IUCN).

Crowned Monkey *Cercopithecus (m.) pogonias*

Other names: Fr. *Cercopithèque pogonias*. Ger. *Kronenmeerkatze*.

Measurements: HB 45 (40–46cm) (♀), 50cm (45–58cm) (♂). T 50–87cm. W 3kg (2.8–3.6kg) (♀), 4.5kg (3.6–4.8kg) (♂).

Recognition: Relatively small, long-tailed, arboreal monkey with grizzled sides and hindlegs and black outer arms and feet. A striped crest runs along the centre of the crown and the ear tufts are very prominent and usually pointed. The underside is orange, yellow or white. The crowned monkey is exceptionally agile and vocal.

Subspecies: C. (*m.*) *p. pogonias* (R. Cross to R. Sanaga and Bioko I., formerly Fernando Po): grizzled khaki sides and thighs, black dorsal stripe, short, yellow-grizzled crown stripe, yellow undersides and ear tufts, yellow-flecked black feet. C. (*m.*) *p. grayi* (S Cameroon to central Africa north of R. Zaïre): grizzled chestnut back and thighs, medium yellow crown stripe, orange to yellow underside and ear tufts, yellow-flecked black feet. C. (*m.*) *p. nigripes* (R. Ogooué basin south to R. Zaïre): grizzled grey-olive sides and thighs, grey dorsal stripe, broad, creamy-white crown stripe, variable deep orange to white underside and ear tufts, jet-black feet.

Distribution: Central African forest zone from R. Cross to R. Zaïre and R. Itimbiri.

Habitat: Commonest in mature forests and in upper strata but also in secondary forest and gallery forests extending well into savannah regions.

Food: Fruits (80%) and invertebrates. Crowned monkeys very rarely take leaves or buds, preferring soft, pulpy, red or yellow fruits. Bulk fruits are taken in the morning and late afternoon while insects, especially beetles and caterpillars, are hunted in the middle of the day.

Behaviour: Groups of 8–20 (mean 10) animals with a single dominant ♂ occupy home ranges of 0.5–1km². Crowned monkeys are very vocal. The dominant ♂'s booming call serves to rally group members after dispersal or a disturbance and more than one ♂ may utter the territorial loud call, or hack. Both sexes make the strange miaow that is the typical cohesion call. This, and other shorter, whining calls are intragroup calls and capable of much modulation. They have a versatility of expression which would appear to range from 'inviting' and 'inquisitive' to repelling and aggressive. Group members readily disperse and reaggregate, and usually sleep huddled together in family groups.

Adaptations: The striking Mohican crest which earns this species its name is marked by strong contrasts of black and white or black and yellow that form a pattern that is most striking when viewed from the side. Like their close relative, Wolf's monkey, crowned monkeys perform a ritualised head display involving frequent jerking turns to left and right. It would seem that C. (*m.*) *pogonias* evolved from an ancestor with *wolfi*-like traits which implies that the founders of the *pogonias* lineage would have had to cross the R. Zaïre along its lower, very swift-flowing reaches. Such an origin could have resulted in a narrow genetic bottleneck but one that has clearly been followed by outstanding success. Indeed C. (*m.*) *pogonias* may yet be actively expanding and displacing C. (*m.*) *mona* in SW Cameroon.

Status: Forest clearance (especially clear-felling by chipboard companies in Cameroon) has eliminated this species in some localities but it remains abundant in others and is still widespread. Listed as Not Endangered (IUCN).

Owl-Faced Monkey *Cercopithecus hamlyni*

Other names: Fr. *Cercopithèque de Hamlyn*, *Cercopithèque à tête de hibou*. Ger. *Eulenkopfmeerkatze*. Lega dialect *Mutuba*. Kahuzi dialect *Fuya*.

Measurements: HB est. 40–55cm (♀), est. 50–65cm (♂). T 50–65cm. W est. 4.5–6kg (♀), est. 7–10kg (♂).

Recognition: A thickset, monochrome, grizzled grey monkey with black arms, feet, underside and tail tip. The face is black or marked with a white nose stripe and pale cream brow ridge. The fur is exceptionally fine, dense and long. There is bare blue skin on the buttocks and the ♂ has a large area of blue skin in the genital area covering both the scrotum and penis. The ♂ is substantially larger than ♀, with a very long, heavy muzzle. His loud call is a deep boom. This species is exceptionally wary.

Subspecies: *C. h. hamlyni* (extensive range): T-shaped face pattern and silvery thighs. *C. h. kahuziensis* (Mt Kahuzi): black face, olive-green back.

Distribution: Wedged between the mountains of the central Western Rift and a stretch of the R. Lualaba, the distribution of this species has long been interpreted as that of a mountain species that spread into lowland forest down the rivers that drain to the west. The close correspondence of this distribution with the Virunga volcanics extinction zone provides a rationale for such an extension of range. (Distribution shown on p. 57)

Habitat: Lowland forests are likely to have been recently colonised; the primary habitat is dense montane forests, especially bamboo. Owl-faced monkeys must have spread from a non-volcanic nucleus or nuclei. The most likely locality is the Itombwe Mts (north-west of L. Tanganyika), where extensive bamboo and montane forests grow on ancient basement rocks. Where revegetated habitats are populated by a very small number of founding colonists, 'genetic drift' or 'founder effects' are likely. This has occurred on one isolated volcanic massif west of L. Kivu where the melanic race, *C. h. kahuziensis*, is exclusive to bamboo forests between 2,000 and 3,300m. As few as six large mammal herbivores are common on Mt Kahuzi, of which gorillas and owl-faced monkeys are the only primates.

Food: On Mt Kahuzi the leaves of bamboos are known to be eaten (and are probably the staple in lean times) but new shoots emerge throughout the long wet seasons. The leaves, shoots, pith and stems of several other trees, shrubs and herbs are available all year, notably wild celery (*Peucedanum*) and *Vernonia*. Fruits tend to be more restricted, although blackberries (*Rubus*) are perennial. *Podocarpus*, waxberry (*Myrica*), *Schefflera*, *Dombeya* and *Cassipourea* all produce edible fruits or seeds seasonally.

Behaviour: If social groups are small, dense cover and abundant food permit very small home ranges. These diurnal monkeys are known to live in single-♂ groups numbering less than 10. Intimate knowledge of home ranges would help explain their legendary ability to evade detection. Leopards, golden cats and human hunters probably all reinforce the extreme caution of these monkeys, which must travel and feed on the ground. The massive and impressive-looking ♂♂ are intensely protective (captive ♂♂ will come forward at the slightest threat while ♀♀ and young rush off to hide in a tightly bunched huddle). Communication between these slow, deliberate and monochrome monkeys is vocal and olfactory. All ages of monkey and both sexes mark their surroundings frequently with the secretions from apocrine chest glands. In a dense and very wet environment, with rainfall of over 1,250mm, continuous herbaceous growth changes physical surroundings while the rain washes away previous markings. In such circumstances a group of monkeys must 'map' out their small, densely obstructed home range by frequent scent-marking. They also utter discrete sounds that help cohesion and orientation without alerting predators. The ♀ want call is a whimpering quaver while the ♂'s rallying call is a deep boom. Infants soon suppress the high-pitched chirps typical of other species in favour of quieter calls.

Adaptations: The hands of owl-faced monkeys are unique among guenons in the elongation of the phalanges. This is the opposite of a terrestrial trait and, combined with a relatively strong thumb, suggests a powerful grip (as would be needed for climbing among slippery bamboo). The gut of this species has yet to be studied but its diet suggests an enhanced ability to digest leaves.

Status: Extreme crypsis makes this species very difficult to study and census. Although widely distributed, it suffers loss of habitat similar to that suffered by the eastern gorilla. There has been no control of hunting in E Zaïre for many years and it is hunters with dogs who pose the main threat. Although distantly related to de Brazza's monkey, the owl-faced monkey is the sole representative of a unique guenon lineage and its preservation is of considerable importance. Listed as Class B (African Convention), Appendix 2 (CITES), Vulnerable to Extinction (IUCN).

Gentle monkeys Cercopithecus (nictitans)

mitis cluster

blue monkey cluster

white throated cluster

putty-nosed

silver monkey cluster

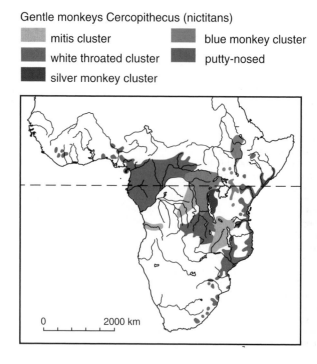

0   2000 km

Top, from left: Central African putty-nosed monkey, Pluto monkey, Moloneys monkey, Stuhlman's blue monkey, Mount Kenya Sykes monkey.
Below, from left: Martin's putty-nosed monkey, Zaïre basin gentle monkey. Mbele gentle monkey, Silver monkey, Tanganyika Sykes monkey.

Gentle Monkeys *Cercopithecus (nictitans)* superspecies

Other names: Fr. *Hocheurs*. Ger. *Fromm Meerkatze*. Swah. *Kima*.

Measurements: HB 43–70cm. T 55–109cm. W 3.5–12kg.

Recognition: Large, long-tailed, arboreal monkeys with a grizzled back and crown, black forearms, hands and feet, and dark tails. Coat patterns often have yellowish or reddish zones. Facial patterns are variable (see above). Adult ♂♂ of all species make very loud and distinctive, explosive 'pyows'.

Species: Putty-nosed monkey, C. (n.) *nictitans* (all drainage basins west of R. Zaïre and R. Itimbiri): dark species with white nose spot. Gentle monkey, C. (n.) *mitis*: similar species without a nose spot. Diverse eastern forms are sometimes treated as a third species, C. (n.) *albogularis*.

Distribution: The biogeographic name, 'greater periphery monkeys', describes the marginality of this species within the main forest blocks. The only forest guenons with a wide distribution in S and E Africa, gentle monkeys are exceptionally adaptable with respect to altitude but appear to be constrained or excluded in many areas by the presence of other primates. Their diets overlap with those of drill-mangabeys and several guenon species so that competition with these monkeys may be a factor limiting their distribution. Disease may be another.

Habitat: Evergreen forests at various altitudes with a preference for well-shaded areas 10–20m from the ground. Gentle monkeys disperse easily along narrow riverine galleries which helps to explain why the pattern of distribution corresponds with river basins.

Food: Fruits and flowers (50–60%), leaf parts (20–25%) and invertebrates (10–20%). In many marginal areas a large proportion of the annual diet may come from relatively few species. While fruits remain the preferred food at all times, leaves and insects are taken during periods of shortage. Animal foods tend to be sessile and are gathered by slow, intensive searching under bark and lichen.

Behaviour: ♀ groups with an average of between 10 and 12 breeding ♀♀ and as many offspring are accompanied by a dominant ♂. While gentle monkey ♀♀ exclude other ♀♀ from the territory (very variable but may be about 60ha) the ♂ is mainly concerned with keeping other ♂♂ away from the ♀♀. ♂ 'tenures' in a territory vary greatly and may persist for only one or a few years before being displaced by one of the solitary ♂♂ that often hover around the peripheries of gentle monkey groups. Groups are also prone to frequent fissions and fusions.

Adaptations: Gentle monkeys are generalised monkeys with two major adaptive advantages: firstly, they have highly developed arboreal skills (they are faster, more agile and better at negotiating all types of branches than either mangabeys or savannah monkeys); secondly, they are able to buffer long fruitless periods with foliage and insects. They would appear to be of optimum size for generalists but are too heavy to take full advantage of resources proffered on the more slender branches. This superspecies is excluded from consistently rich habitats where resources are efficiently partitioned among a suite of specialist primates. They are at a relative advantage in less rich, less stable forests where the specialists are unable to offset shortfalls of their staple foods.

Status: Over most of their very extensive range gentle monkeys are common but are rare in Upper Guinea and the central Zaïre basin.

(a)   (b)

(a) Martins putty-nosed monkey. (b) Moloney's monkey. (c) Golden monkey.

Putty-Nosed Monkey *Cercopithecus (n.) nictitans*

Other names: Fr. *Hocheur*. Ger. *Grosse Weissnase*.
Measurements: HB 43–53cm (♀), 55–70cm (♂). T 56–100cm. W 4.2kg (2.7–5kg) (♀), 6.6kg (5.5–8kg) (♂).
Recognition: A large, long-tailed, arboreal monkey with dark, grizzled olive fur on the back, crown, cheeks and base of the tail. The limbs and distal half of the tail are black or dark grey. A brilliant white nose spot in a dark face is this monkey's most striking peculiarity. Territorial ♂♂ utter a very loud 'pyow' call.
Subspecies: *C. (n.) n. nictitans* (Cameroon highlands and R. Sanaga to R. Zaïre and R. Itimbiri): warm greyish olive back and head, dark underside, laterally bunched fur on head. *C. (n.) n. martini* (R. Sanaga and Cameroon highlands, disjointedly west to Liberia): khaki-olive back and head, variable amounts of white and light grey on underside, white chest, more vertically bunched fur on head.
Distribution: From north of the R. Zaïre and R. Itimbiri west to Nigeria and (very sparsely and patchily) on to Liberia. The contrast between the putty-nosed monkeys' abundance east of the R. Cross and rarity to the west suggests they may have been recent and non-competitive colonists in habitats where the lesser spot-nosed monkey, Diana monkey, mangabeys and three colobus species have all been successful.
Habitat: All evergreen forests from lowland to montane, primary, secondary and narrow galleries and patches; not common in swamp or mangrove forests. Constraints from the plant community are less than those from competing primates.
Food: Fruits, seeds, flowers, foliage and invertebrates. In Gabon the limiting effects of the ♂'s larger size is evident in the fact that only 58% of its year-round diet consists of fruits while the figure is 76% in the case of ♀♀. Both sexes take a similar proportion of insects but ♂♂ take a higher proportion of foliage (30% to the F's 12%). Caterpillars, ants and spiders make up the bulk of their invertebrate foods.
Behaviour: Putty-nosed monkeys live in groups of 12–30 ♀♀ which defend a territory and are accompanied by a single adult ♂. ♂♂ utter booming rallying calls, 'pyows' and alarm hacks.
Adaptations: The French name for this species, *hocheur* or 'wagger', refers to a common appeasement gesture involving ritualised head-flagging which gives prominence to the white nose. Their greetings sometimes combine the universal 'presenting' posture with head-flagging and lip-pouting (a combination that can involve comical contortions).
Status: This species may benefit when human predation on primates is selective. Although very rare in far W Africa, it is listed as Not Endangered (IUCN).

Gentle Monkey *Cercopithecus (n.) mitis (including albogularis)*

Other names: Fr. *Cercopithèque à diadème*. Ger. *Diadem Meerkatze*. Swah. *Kima*.
Measurements: HB 43–52cm (♀), 48–70cm (♂). T 55–109cm. W 5kg (3.5–5.5kg) (♀), 7kg (5.5–12kg) (♂).

(d) Blue monkey.
(e) White-throated or Syke's monkey.

Recognition: Large, long-tailed, arboreal monkeys very similar to the putty-nosed monkey but without its distinctive nose patch. Back and thighs are grizzled while the forearms, hands, feet and terminal half of tail are black. The underside is relatively dark. The cheek fur is also grizzled but the boundary with paler chin fur is very labile from one population to another. The bristly fur on the forehead forms a pale or grizzled brow patch in some species but is undifferentiated in others. Longish muzzle in ♂.

Subspecies: The arbitrary splitting of *mitis* into two geographic divisions (*mitis* and *albogularis*) obscures a more complex pattern of distribution among various subgroups. As with the mona group, differences in chromosome number have been found within the *nictitans/mitis* superspecies which may require a revision of existing classifications. In the meantime *mitis* can be divided into four 'clusters' (each a potential species), and each embracing more than one subspecies.

Cercopithecus (n.) mitis

1. The mitis monkey cluster (*mitis, maesi, pluto, heymansi, moloneyi, francescae*). Widely separated, central African relict populations. Dark, grizzled backs, dark caps with pallid diadems, pale chins, broad and low, grizzled cheek patches. Longish muzzle in ♂.
2. The white-throated monkey cluster (*albogularis, opistostictus, samango, erythrarchus, nyassae, monoides, kibonotensis, kolbi, albotorquatus, phylax, zammaranoi*). Indian Ocean river basin distribution from Cape Province to Somalia and expansive range in upper reaches of E Zaïre basin. Grizzled back (seldom dark), grizzled cap and diadem not clearly differentiated. Boundary between white or pale chin fur and grizzled cheek fur very variable. Medium-sized muzzle in ♂.
3. The silver monkey cluster (*dogetti, kandti, schoutedeni*). Isolated populations associated with the Western Rift Valley. The golden monkey, *kandti*, is a high-altitude colonist on volcanic mountains near L. Kivu. Schouteden's monkey, *schoutedeni*, exists as a tiny population on Shushu I. in L. Kivu. Both show 'founder-effects' following a relatively recent genetic bottleneck. Silver monkey, *dogetti*, grizzled grey or golden back, black cap with a sharply defined, grizzled diadem, high, rounded, grizzled cheek patches. Long muzzle in ♂.
4. The blue monkey cluster (*stuhlmanni, elgonis, boutourlinii* – the latter an Ethiopian isolate, possibly a hybrid with the white-throated genotype; *neumanni* – similar (hybrid?) population in Tanzania). Expansive range in E Zaïre, Ethiopia and E Africa to Great Rift Valley from putative centre in Ruwenzori Mts. Very dark, grizzled back, black cap with sharply defined blue-grey grizzled diadem, high, rounded, grizzled cheek patches. Relatively short muzzle in ♂.

Distribution: South-east of R. Zaïre and R. Itimbiri, Indian Ocean coastline and Zanzibar I. From sea-level up to 3,300m.

Habitat: All types of evergreen forest from riverine, delta, gallery, secondary, primary and montane, including bamboo. Gentle monkey densities within these various habitats are very variable.

Food: Diet varies greatly by region and season and between the sexes (♂ ♂ eating less fruit). It is thought to be strongly influenced by the presence of other primates. Gentle monkeys can tolerate quantities of leaves and stems in their diet but prefer fruits wherever possible. Sources are exploited for as long as they last and are often from trees that produce gluts of fruits. They sometimes rely on smaller, more active monkey species to lead them to fruiting trees. Insects form a regular and significant part of their diet and are gathered by slow, systematic searching through bark, lichen, moss and rotten wood.

Behaviour: Social groups average ten breeding ♀ ♀ and their offspring accompanied by a single ♂. Numbers are subject to much local variation and fluctuation. Territories, averaging 60–70ha, are defended by all group members. The ♂'s loud calls primarily advertise his association with a group of breeding ♀ ♀ rather than being territorial as such. Loud calls are not regularly answered by other gentle monkeys but may evoke loud calling in red-tailed monkeys sharing the same home range.

Adaptations: In their diet, behaviour and extensive range, gentle monkeys reveal themselves to be the most versatile and generalised of all arboreal forest monkeys. Numerous subspecies could be expected across so many latitudes and different forest types. However, the complexity of distribution patterns and variations in range and population densities suggest that fluctuating numbers and frequent isolation have been a consistent feature throughout their evolutionary history. They are too arboreal to compete successfully with savannah monkeys and too generalised for long-term success in a fully diversified primate community.

Status: It is possible that the subspecies *mitis* (the Angolan or Pluto monkey) is now extinct due to its having a small range in a densely settled region. Other relict groups in Ethiopia or in the L. Kivu area could also be endangered but the species as a whole is not. The species is listed as Not Endangered (IUCN).

Cephus Monkeys *Cercopithecus (cephus)* superspecies

Other names: *Cercopithèques du groupe cephus*. Ger. *Cephusmeerkatze*.

Measurements: HB 34–58cm. T 46–92cm. W 1.8–6kg.

Recognition: Long-tailed, arboreal monkeys with grizzled brownish backs and crowns and very diverse and brightly coloured face patterns. Tails are red in several populations and bicoloured in others. Typically very lively, active monkeys, they make jerky movements of the head and forequarters. Very staccato, chirping alarm calls are made by all species. Uttered in prolonged series by several or all members of a group, these volleys of sound are often a first indication of their presence.

Species: Moustached monkey, *C. (c.) cephus* (between R. Sanaga, R. Zaïre and R. Ubangi): red or bicoloured tail, bright blue face, broad yellow cheek ruffs, black and white 'moustache'.

Sclater's monkey, *C. (c.) sclateri* (eastern margins of R. Niger delta): off-white tail, blue face, yellowish cheek fur with sinuous border, pale muzzle.

Red-eared monkey, *C. (c.) erythrotis* (between R. Cross and R. Sanaga): red tail, purplish face, cream cheek ruff with linear black border, red nose and ears.

Red-tailed monkey, *C. (c.) ascanius* (from R. Zaïre/R. Ubangi east to Uganda and W Kenya, S Sudan to Angola and N Zambia): partly or wholly red tail, dark blue face, white or grizzled cheeks and temporal region with variable margins, colour of nose spot shows regional variation.

Lesser spot-nosed monkey, *C. (c.) petaurista* (NW Sierra Leone to Benin): bicoloured khaki/white tail, black face framed by a white ruff, white nose spot.

Nigerian white-throat monkey, *C. (c.) erythrogaster* (SW Nigeria): bicoloured khaki/white tail, dark grey face, very attenuated grizzled cheek patches, broad and conspicuous white ruff framing the face, black or white nose, red or slate-grey belly.

Distribution: Equatorial forests from Sierra Leone to W Kenya and about 10° latitude north and south. Absent from colder latitudes and higher altitudes, and from strongly seasonal forests of SE Africa.

Habitat: Lowland and medium-altitude forests with high temperatures and well-distributed rainfall. Cephus monkeys traverse a very wide range of branches, lianes and tangles at all but the very lowest levels of the forest. Individuals forage in a wide scatter, covering up to 1.5km per day in a territory of about 35ha. In Uganda (where members of the mona group are absent) densities of red-tails can reach 140–175 animals per km². In Gabon, where cephus monkeys co-exist with crowned monkeys (in about equal numbers) and talapoins (locally much more numerous), they are estimated to live at less than a third of the density of red-tailed monkeys in Uganda.

Food: Mainly whole fruits and seeds (but known to include many insect-infested samples). Cephus monkeys find and arrive at fruiting trees earlier than other species (often feeding at dawn) but are more readily displaced. When not feeding at super-abundant fruit sources they are persistent and thorough foragers for scattered fruits and insects. The nutritional value of a very varied insect diet is thought to be more significant than its average volume (about 20%). Leaves, buds and stems are taken as a temporary expedient. In east-central Africa this dietary buffer helps them inhabit a larger region and more habitat types than monkeys of the mona group.

Behaviour: Groups of ♀♀ with their offspring number 10–40 and are usually attended by a single ♂ (occasionally more). ♀♀ defend their territory against other groups and even chase off solitary ♂♂. Territories often overlap those of gentle monkey groups (among which territorial ♂♂ have similar but very much louder calls). Cephus monkeys frequently duet with resident gentle monkey ♂♂, apparently in order to augment their more feeble calls. As with most guenons there are pronounced seasonal peaks in breeding, with most births occurring between November and February.

Adaptations: The cephus group appears in several respects to be a neotenous (juvenilised) form of gentle monkey (the two groups are known to be very closely related). In addition to being smaller and having a more juvenile-looking skull these monkeys have a faster metabolism and are more active for a longer day than gentle monkeys. They are also highly visually oriented and in polyspecific groups often warn other species of danger. This visual specialisation is corroborated by optical physiology (their eyes have more short-wave cones, which are especially sensitive to both space and colour perception). In contrast to gentle monkeys, which forage in groups for hidden insects, cephus monkeys are visual hunters which independently scan foliage and branches for exposed insects. This visual bias is clearly linked with greater use of visual signals. All species have evolved striking facial patterns which correlate with ritualised head-flagging displays performed during courtship and appeasement. Sharp head movements are also typical of this species and include contact and greeting gestures.

The diversity of facial patterns displayed within the cephus group suggests that this lineage must have become fragmented at an early stage in its evolution. Climate was clearly the isolating factor here. Lower temperatures and rainfall (during Ice Ages) would have affected this group more than others because insects and fruits would have become more seasonal over broad areas of central and W Africa. They would have been one of the first groups to come up against intensified competition for diminished or more seasonal resources.

In spite of their apparent diversity, all face patterns in this group are permutations and elaborations of a single facial format of the gentle monkey type. These patterns can be seen to arise through facial fur developing various pleats, deflections or tufts, through colour tinting of skin and fur, and through 'expansion' and 'contraction' of a limited number of dark or light patches (see figs on page 53). The radiation of cephus monkeys is likely to have started in W Africa (*erythrogaster* and *petaurista* as modern derivatives) with an initial eastward expansion no further than the R. Ogooué basin (*cephus* and *sclateri* as modern derivatives) and later further eastward expansion (*erythrotis* and *ascanius* as derivatives).

Status: While the group as a whole is widespread and common, several species are rare or endangered.

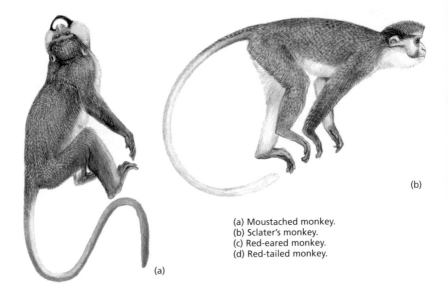

(a) Moustached monkey.
(b) Sclater's monkey.
(c) Red-eared monkey.
(d) Red-tailed monkey.

Moustached Monkey *Cercopithecus (c.) cephus*

Other names: Fr. *Moustac*. Ger. *Blaumaulkatze*.
Measurements: HB 44–50cm (♀), 50–58cm (♂). T 66–99cm. W 3kg (2–4kg) (♀), 4kg (3.8–5kg) (♂).
Recognition: Back and crown are grizzled, with a light underside and red or grey tail. The facial skin is bright blue, with broad yellow cheek ruffs and a vivid white 'moustache' of very variable shape above the jet-black lips and very bristly black fur at the corners of the mouth.
Subspecies: *C. (c.) c. cephus* (R. Sanaga to R. Zaïre and R. Ubangi): red tail. *C. (c.) c. cephode* (enclave between R. Ogooué and R. Kouilou): bicoloured grey tail.
Habitat: Lowland rainforest between the R. Sanaga and R. Zaïre/R. Ubangi. Moustached monkeys prefer dense foliage and liane tangles and will make use of all forest levels except the lowest. Their distribution between that of red-eared and yellow-nosed monkeys (very similar forms) suggests that they may have recently expanded their range out of an Ogooué basin heartland.
Food: Mainly fruits (and about 10% leaves, stems and shoots). Adult ♂♂ have been found to eat much fewer insects than ♀♀, which suggests that social monitoring may be at the expense of time spent searching for insects.
Status: Common and widespread. Listed as Not Endangered (IUCN).

Sclater's Monkey *Cercopithecus (c.) sclateri*

Other names: Fr. *Moustac de Sclater*. Ger. *Nigeria Blaumalkatze*.
Measurements: HB est. 40–45cm (♀), est. 45–55cm (♂). T est. 45–75cm. W est. 2.5–3.5kg (♀), est. 3–4.5kg (♂).
Recognition: Grizzled olive-brownish back, shoulders and crown with a warm suffusion on the lower back. Outer surfaces of limbs are grizzled grey. The tail graduates from light olive to off-white, with a deep russet suffusion on the underside close to the anus. The cap is peaked and encircled by a black margin. The facial skin is blue and there is yellowish cheek fur, with a sinuous dark-tipped border above the white throat and chin fur. Muzzle and ears are usually pallid but animals from towards R. Cross valley have varying tints of red on the nose and ears.
Habitat: Relict forests and swamps between the R. Niger delta and the Cross River south of Enugu.
Food: Likely to resemble that of other cephus group monkeys.
Status: Putative hybrids with the red-eared guenon have led to it being classified with that species. Aside from this hybrid influence, Sclater's monkey combines features characteristic of moustached, red-tailed and lesser spot-nosed monkeys, suggesting that it is a conservative species illustrative of the common origins of the cephus group radiation as a whole.

(c)

(d)

A survey in 1988 recorded small populations in the R. Niger delta, notably within the AGIP oilfield west of Oguta, Imo State. As this is one of the rarest and most interesting monkeys in Africa this puts an urgent responsibility upon AGIP and other oil companies to take practical steps towards its conservation. Currently listed as Class B (African Convention), Appendix 2 (CITES), but Endangered (IUCN).

Red-Eared Monkey *Cercopithecus (c.) erythrotis*

Other names: Fr. *Moustac à oreilles rousses*. Ger. *Rotnase*.
Measurements: HB 40-45cm (♀), 45-55cm (♂). T 53-77cm. W 2.25-3.5kg (♀), 3.5-4.5kg (♂).
Recognition: Grizzled brown back, shoulders and crown, red tail and rump, and grey forearms, hindlegs, hands and feet. Underparts and inner limbs are white. The face is purplish blue, with cream cheek fur tapered to a point below the ear and with bold black margins. Nose and ears are red.
Subspecies: *Cercopithecus (c.) e. erythrotis* (Bioko I., formerly Fernando Po): smaller, darker island race. *C. (c.) e. camerunensis* (mainland population): larger, less melanic.
Habitat: Lowland rainforests between the R. Cross and R. Sanaga and Bioko I. Today the moustached monkey inhabits the intervening country between the very small range of the red-eared monkeys and that of the yellow-nosed red-tail (some specimens of which resemble it very closely). It seems likely that the range of the red-eared monkeys has contracted. Their ecological niche resembles that of other cephus monkeys but they are reported to live mainly in lower forest strata and in regenerating secondary forest. Putty-nosed and mona monkeys frequently follow and associate with red-eared monkeys.
Food: Fruits and insects.
Status: Deforestation has destroyed a large part of this species' range and remaining populations are heavily hunted. It is common in Korup National Park and Douala Edea Reserve. Although it occurs in many smaller forest reserves it enjoys no practical protection and is in decline everywhere. Listed as Class B (African Convention), Appendix 2 (CITES), Endangered (IUCN).

Red-Tailed Monkey *Cercopithecus (c.) ascanius*

Other names: Fr. *Cercopithèque ascagne*. Ger. *Kongo-weissnase*.
Measurements: HB 34–48cm (♀), 48–52cm (♂). T 54–92cm. W 3.5kg (1.8–4kg) (♀), 4.5kg (3–6kg) (♂).

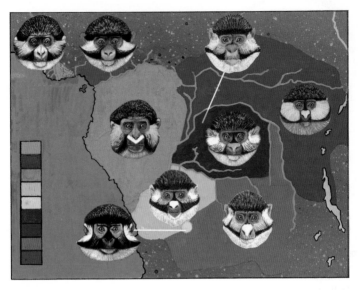

Distribution of the 'cephus' group of monkeys in the central forest block. Top left: Sclater's monkey, *Cercopithecus sclateri* and the redeared guenon, *C. erythrotis*. Top right: A newly observed and as yet unnamed type, which may be a variant of the yellow-nosed red-tail, *C. ascanius whitesidei* (centre). The moustached guenon, *C. cephus* (centre left). Far right: Uganda red-tail, *C. ascanius schmidti*. Below left: spectacled red-tail, *C. ascanius atrinasus* and Angola red-tail, *C. ascanius ascanius*. Right: Katanga red-tail *C. ascanius katangae*.

Recognition: Grizzled brown back and crown, and grizzled grey outer limbs, hands and feet. The tail is partly or wholly red and the face is dark blue. Cheeks and temporal region are white or grizzled, with variable margins above the off-white throat and chin. The nose spot varies in colour and shape by region and subspecies.

Subspecies: Angola red-tail, *Cercopithecus (c.) a. ascanius* (lower R. Zaïre and R. Kasai to R. Cuanza): broad black brow and temporal streaks, broad black boundary below white orbit-to-ear cow-licks, minuscule grizzled tawny patch below the orbits, blunt white nose patch.

Katanga red-tail, *C. (c.) a. katangae* (from N Angola and south Zaïre basin to R. Lomani and R. Lualaba): black brow and temporal streaks, black boundary below white orbit-to-ear cow-licks, grizzled tawny patch below orbit, white nose spot laterally elongated and tapering between nostrils.

Yellow-nosed red-tail *C. (c.) a. whitesidei* (south of R. Zaïre to R. Kasai): narrow black temporal streaks and narrow black boundary below white orbit-to-ear cow-licks, variable grizzled tawny patch below orbits, T-shaped nose patch varying from white to russet red, ears also white to red.

Spectacled red-tail *C. (c.) a. atrinasus* (Lunda plateau): very broad black brow and temporal streaks and very broad black boundary below white orbit-to-ear cow-licks, completely black muzzle and only a trace of grizzling in the black patch below bright blue orbits.

Uganda red-tail *C. (c.) a. schmidti* (from R. Ubangi north of R. Zaïre to Uganda and W Kenya, east of R. Lualaba to R. Lukuga): narrow black brow and temporal streaks, narrow black boundary around broad creamy-white cheek ruffs, scalloped white nose spot in narrow dark muzzle, blue facial skin.

Intermediate forms occur along all open boundaries between these forms. Intermediates between red-tails and moustached monkeys are known from the R. Ubangi region.

With respect to face pattern, the yellow-nosed red-tail is conservative (some individuals resemble red-eared monkeys very closely) while the Uganda red-tail is the most derived. This form appears to have expanded its range (both east and west) very recently.

Habitat: Lowland and submontane forests, riverine galleries and most stages of colonising, secondary or regenerating forest (except for those on poor soils). Red-tailed monkeys also occur in forest mosaics with a high preponderance of single-stand species, such as ironwood.

Food: Fruits make up half or more of the diet while insects make up a quarter. Flowers and flower buds are also important. Leaves and leaf buds become a significant part of the diet during seasons of shortage. The flowers of *Markhamia* and *Millettia* (two common colonist trees) and the fruits of false nutmeg (*Pycnanthus*), false figs (*Trilepisium*) and red milkwood (*Mimusops*) are especially favoured and are stored in the cheek pouches until the flesh and flavour has dissipated (a habit that ensures wide dispersal of the seeds). Feeding on fruits close to the sleeping-site begins at dawn (sometimes just before) and is often followed by displacement by larger monkeys. Except for the midday rest, the monkeys are often occupied hunting insects in the late morning and especially the afternoon. Feeding on fruits may then be resumed in the evening, as other monkeys retire, and continues up to nightfall. Major super-abundant food sources (especially those near the borders of two or more territories) may draw in temporary aggregations numbering more than 100 red-tails. Such groups are temporary and typically fraught with aggression.

Status: ♀♀ and their young form the stable core of red-tail society. Two or three reproducing ♀♀ can eventually give rise to a group of 20 or more adult ♀♀, all with offspring. As numbers increase, the resources of a relatively small territory (mean size 35ha but over 100ha in forest mosaics) become scarcer. Because ♀♀ do not normally leave their maternal group and oestrus tends to be synchronised (June–September), single attendant ♂♂ become unable to deter invading ♂♂, especially during the oestrus peak. Multi-♂ groups are temporary and unstable. During feeding and especially while hunting insects, red-tails typically disperse individually or in small family clusters. Antagonisms between clusters within large groups culminate in permanent fission, with new smaller groups setting out fresh territoral boundaries. ♂ 'tenancies' may last from a month to over 6 years. In addition to fathering all offspring of the group the ♂ is principal scout and sentry. He will also distract predators which threaten the group and his loud calls, threat coughs and branch-shaking help to demarcate the home range.

Status: Red-tailed monkeys have been important subjects in the epidemiology of various viral diseases, including yellow fever. They have been used as a laboratory animal and are a favourite exhibit in zoos. Currently treated as vermin and listed as Not Endangered (IUCN).

Lesser Spot-Nosed Monkey *Cercopithecus (c.) petaurista*

Other names: Fr. *Hocheur à nez blanc*. Ger. *Kleine Weissnase*.
Measurements: HB 40–44cm (♀), 44–48cm (♂). T 57–68cm. W 2–3.5kg (♀), 2.5–4kg (♂).
Recognition: Grizzled khaki-coloured back and crown, graduating to grizzled grey on outer limbs. Underparts, throat, ears and nose spot are white. The face is black and the tail is bicoloured. Adult ♂♂ utter a peculiar grating hack and a high-pitched whistle of alarm.
Subspecies: *C. (c.) p. petaurista* (Benin to R. Cavally): narrow black margins to orbits, white stripe only below ear. *C. (c.) p. buettikoferi* (R. Cavally westwards to Guinea): narrow cheek patches of grizzled fawn on orbit margins, white stripe from temple to ear (lower face).
Habitat: Lowland primary and secondary forests, riverine and gallery forests, secondary regeneration and coastal bush.
Food: Highly frugivorous and may eat less insects than other species in the cephus group. Flowers, flower buds and leaf buds are important while leaves and stems are minor items.
Status: Common and widespread. Listed as Not Endangered (IUCN).

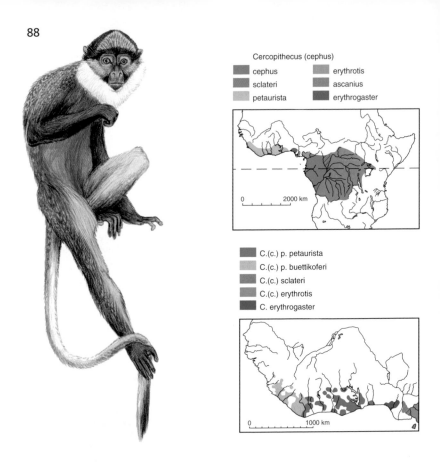

Cercopithecus (cephus)

- cephus
- sclateri
- petaurista
- erythrotis
- ascanius
- erythrogaster

0   2000 km

- C.(c.) p. petaurista
- C.(c.) p. buettikoferi
- C.(c.) sclateri
- C.(c.) erythrotis
- C. erythrogaster

0   1000 km

Nigerian White-Throat Monkey *Cercopithecus (c.) erythrogaster*

Other names: Fr. *Cercopithèque à ventre rouge*. Ger. *Rotbauchmeerkatze*.

Measurements: HB est. 40–45cm (♀), est. 45–50cm (♂). T est. 60–70cm. W est. 2–4kg (♀), est. 3.5–4.5kg (♂).

Recognition: Grizzled khaki-coloured back, shoulders and thighs, dark grey outer limbs, lighter inner limbs and a bicoloured tail. The very prominent white ruff frames the dark face, which has narrow, grizzled cheek patches. The cap is black with a broad triangle of pale grizzled fawn. The belly is grey or russet (the latter mostly towards the west of its range) and the nose is either black or white. The distinctive loud call of the ♂ most resembles the grating hack of the lesser spot-nosed monkey.

Habitat: Widespread but very scattered in remaining lowland rainforests of SW Nigeria and S. Benin. Also in secondary bush and old farmland, usually in dense vegetation between 2 and 15m. Foraging parties number about five but groups of up to 30 have been recorded. At the heart of its remaining range a spacing of one group per km^2 has been estimated.

Food: Fruits and insects.

Status: All forests in SW Nigeria are subject to intensive logging, clearance and hunting. This species is currently unprotected but a 67km^2 wildlife sanctuary has been declared in the Okomu Forest Reserve. This species also occurs in the Ifon and Omo Forest Reserves. Listed as Class B (African Convention), Appendix 2 (CITES), Endangered (IUCN).

PROSIMIANS STREPSIRHINI

Lorisids	Loridae (previously Lorisidae)
Galagos	Galagonidae (previously Galagidae)

The woolly-coated arboreal prosimians, with monkey-like hands and pointed, scent-sensitive noses, have been called both progressive insectivores and primitive primates. Their now time-honoured name (meaning 'monkey-forerunner') carries the unfortunate implication of animals frozen in a time-warp, while regrouping of the primates has saddled them with the even less fortunate name of Strepsirhini, 'twist-nosed'. In reality they are distinctive and successful members of many modern ecological communities.

Recognition: There are two major groups of lemurs in Africa (with others in Asia and Madagascar). The galagos are arboreal walkers and leapers, with long tails, elongated hindlegs and relatively large ears. The potto group (lorisids) are arboreal clingers and climbers with very short tails, limbs of equal length and relatively short ears. Both groups are wholly nocturnal, have round heads, pointed muzzles, forward-facing eyes, a moist nose and a cleft, 'tied' upper lip. They are distinct from monkeys and other primates in the structure of their placenta, retina, inner ear, blood circulation and digestion. All species have modified lower incisors which form a fur comb (in some species the incisors also form a sharp chisel). Hands, feet and fingernails have been modified in various minor ways but all have a spatulate, fur-grooming claw on the second digit of the foot. These specialisations, known to be very ancient, serve to keep the woolly fur in good condition. Fur is important as an insulator and as a scent-dispenser. Scent plays a major part in their social and territorial behaviour.

Genealogy/Geography: It had long been thought that the potto's closest relative might be the Asian slow loris. The angwantibo's nearest relative was thought to be the Asian slender loris, while the galagos were seen as a separate, uniquely African group. Recent molecular studies now indicate that all the African Loridae are more closely related to each other than to the Asian lorises. The remarkable similarities displayed between these distinct Asian and African groups suggest that the types of ecological niche available to nocturnal climbing primates are highly specific and so give rise to animals displaying similar physical characteristics.

Several galagos not only have close equivalents among Madagascan lemurs but also resemble some totally unrelated marsupials in Australia and South/Central America. Fruit-eating carnivores (olingos and kinkajous) in the South American rainforests also resemble lemurs in several respects. The New Guinea marsupial cus-cuses have several potto-like characteristics. Such resemblances across continents and Orders suggest that the generalised body form typical of the earliest arboreal mammals has remained under tight constraints in small, nocturnal species, so that phylogenetically distant animals can look superficially very similar.

Ecology: Fruit and animal foods are combined in different ratios by all lemurs. Few rely very heavily on fruits and this may be due to competition, not only from diurnal birds and mammals, but also from fruit bats, which are better adapted to seek out all major sources of ripe fruits. Most lemurs eat tree gums to a greater or lesser extent. These not only serve as a 'filler', permitting them to survive quite long periods of shortage, but may also provide them with scarce nutrients because lemurs appear to possess a special capacity to digest this low-energy resource. Buffered by gums, many lemurs are well-adapted gleaners of marginal resources (both fruit and animal) in the face of much competition.

Although predominantly an equatorial forest group, a few galago species have adapted to *Acacia-* and other dry-country woodlands. Their dependence on forests and woodlands for food and shelter has precluded them from crossing the desertic barriers that confine them to Africa.

Natural history: Lemurs are vulnerable to predation by carnivores, diurnal primates, owls and large reptiles.

Adaptations: The individual profiles (below) describe various ways in which body sizes, limb proportions and minor anatomical structures of these otherwise generalised arboreal climbers and jumpers have been modified to perform various, more specialised functions.

LORISIDS LORIDAE (PREVIOUSLY LORISIDAE)

Pottos	*Perodicticus*
Martin's potto	*Pseudopotto*
Angwantibos	*Arctocebus*

Potto *Perodicticus potto*

Other names: Fr. *Potto de Bosman*. Ger. *Potto*. Swah. *Kami*.
Measurements: HB 30–40cm. T 5–10cm. W 0.8–1.6kg.
Recognition: A slow-climbing, woolly, arboreal animal. The body and legs, disguised by thick brown fur or a hunched position, are both actually long and slender. The head is round, with small, naked ears and protuberant golden-brown eyes. Hands have a rudimentary knob for an index finger. The neck joins the back of the skull and the entire region of the shoulders, the neck and crown of the head in presenting a compact mass of muscle, bone and very thick skin under dense fur (that very often sprouts a dense clump of long vibrissae). The spines of the neck vertebrae, enclosed in sleeves of skin, project from the surrounding tissue (but are concealed in fur).

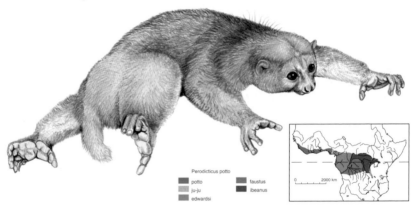

Perodicticus potto
■ potto   ■ faustus
■ ju-ju   ■ ibeanus
■ edwardsi
0   2000 km

Subspecies: *P. p. potto* (Niger to Sierra Leone), *P. p. ju-ju* (east bank of the R. Niger delta area), *P. p. edwardsi* (R. Cross to R. Ubangi), *P. p. faustus* (south of R. Zaïre/R. Lualaba), *P. p. ibeanus* (R. Ubangi east to E African Rift Valley). Some or all of these taxa may eventually prove to be distinct species.
Distribution: Sierra Leone to W Kenya.
Habitat: Lowland, swamp and lower montane forests; commonest in secondary and colonising forests and along margins.
Food: Distinct seasonal variation. Gums are dominant during drier periods, and insects, snails and fruits during the rains. Recorded fruits include figs, *Musanga*, *Parinari*, *Uapaca*, *Myrianthus*. Eggs and fungi have also been noted; ants, caterpillars, beetles and larvae are the commonest insects taken. Spiders, slugs and snails are also eaten.
Behaviour: Pottos are solitary animals which mark out territories with urine. ♀♀ range over 3–9ha while ♂♂ have a 9–40ha range overlapping that of one or more ♀♀. ♂♂ continually monitor the ♀♀, spending up to 3 hours in the immediate vicinity of each ♀ every few nights. Both sexes scent- and urine-mark. When a ♀ is in oestrus the ♂ makes a clicking want call that closely resembles the mother-infant contact call. Copulation is protracted. Gestation has been estimated at 193 days. Juvenile ♂♂ leave their territory and wander widely. Juvenile ♀♀ are accommodated by shifts in the mother's ranging pattern.
Adaptations: Both ♂♂ and ♀♀ have patches of specialised glandular skin in the genital area and anal apocrine glands. Scents play a key role in socio-sexual behaviour and the main function of the potto's neck spines appears to be stimulation of secretion flow in the genital region of a mate. Pottos spend the day hunched over a branch to which they cling. The limbs are served by vascular bundles that allow circulation to be maintained while the animal remains immobile.
Status: Pottos are widespread and common animals. Listed as Not Endangered (IUCN).

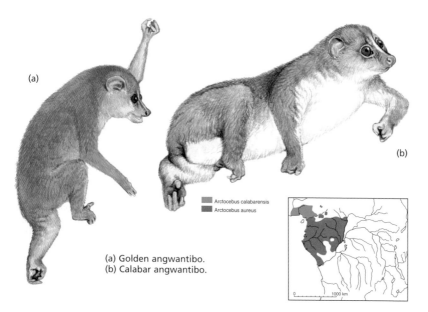

(a) Golden angwantibo.
(b) Calabar angwantibo.

Arctocebus calabarensis
Arctocebus aureus

Calabar Angwantibo *Arctocebus calabarensis*

Other names: Fr. *Potto de Calabar*. Ger. *Calabar Barenmaki*.

Measurements: HB 22.4–26.3cm. T (vestigial). W 230–465g.

Recognition: A small, almost tail-less, woolly climber with relatively short limbs (of even length), very slender wrists, and tiny hands and feet. The rounded head has short, naked ears, large eyes and a pointed muzzle. This species differs from the golden species in colour, minor teeth, skull and anatomical structures. It has soft, tan brown upperparts and a white underside. In both species the hands, in which the second finger is lost and the third is reduced to a stump, are unique. Extremely sensitive to any disturbance, this species will quickly decamp to denser vegetation or freeze into a humped ball.

Distribution: Between the R. Niger and R. Sanaga within the lowland rainforest block but very patchy and localised.

Habitat: Confined to areas of very dense, low undergrowth with abundant lianes and vines within primary, secondary and coastal rainforest. The Calabar angwantibo particularly favours the leafy growth that springs up in clearings, tree falls and along forest edges. It sleeps hunched up on a branch in dense shade, well protected from sun and rain.

Food: Mainly caterpillars; also beetles and fruits. Snails and small lizards have also been recorded. Caterpillars are found by smell in the course of carefully combing through liane tangles.

Behaviour: Solitary; young accompany their mothers for some months after weaning, keeping in touch with a high-pitched clicking call. When caught or attacked they growl. Captive ♂♂, when put together often fight, which suggests that they are territorial in the wild. After a gestation of just over 18 weeks the young are born well haired and with a strong clinging reflex. They are generally 'parked' by the mother as she hunts but they sometimes remain clinging to her body. The Calabar angwantibo is able to produce two young in a year and will drive off an offspring on the birth of the next one.

Adaptations: The large eyes of this species appear to be primarily adapted to vision at extremely low light levels. The Calabar angwantibo is most sensitive to sound and scent. It does not hunt by sight but sniffs continuously.

Status: Normal census methods (walking through the forest with torches) are impossible for the angwantibo because it hides its head and eyes at the least disturbance, depriving the observer of any clue to its presence. Wherever it is already established, small-scale clearances, selective tree-felling and road-making probably favour it. In such areas it is likely to become abundant in thickets and patches of dense secondary growth. Broader clearances, such as those made for plantations, clear-felling and agriculture are likely to eliminate it because of the its weak capacity to disperse. Listed as Class B (African Convention), Appendix 2 (CITES), Rare or At Risk but also Insufficiently Known (IUCN).

Golden Angwantibo *Arctocebus aureus*

Other names: Fr. *Potto doré*. Ger. *Goldenbärenmaki*.

Measurements: HB 22–26cm. T (vestigial). W 200–270g.

Recognition: Small, woolly climber with a golden or russet-tinted upperside and creamy underside. Fine guard hairs on the back, shoulders and haunches have glistening, crinkled tips which give a 'frosted', form-dissolving appearance to the hunched body. The pointed nose projects beyond the undershot jaws; the nostrils, sculpted and mobile, sniff continuously. Naked ears are less capable of free rotation than those of galagos and are more horizontally aligned. The fur is somewhat shorter than in the Calabar species and there are differences in the proportions of the teeth.

Distribution: Widespread all over the R. Sanaga to R. Zaïre/R. Ubangi area but very localised and patchy.

Habitat: Confined to vine tangles and areas with abundant young (or slow-growing) leafy stems in moist evergreen, lowland rainforests. Large vertical branches are never climbed because the small, narrow hands and feet of this species are adapted only to close around stems less than 6cm in diameter (the golden angwantibo never climbs spread-eagled with splayed palms).

This angwantibo is very sensitive to heat, and continuous urine-marking also makes it extremely susceptible to dehydration so that it will die very quickly if exposed to the sun or if kept without water. It is absent from all markedly seasonal areas.

Food: Caterpillars of all species, including hairy and distasteful species that are avoided by other insect-predators. Some of these caterpillars are colonial and many are abundant, especially on rank growth in clearings and on forest edges. The prey is discovered by scent (probably augmented by listening for sounds of the larvae chewing and excreting). Small caterpillars are grabbed and eaten whole, larger ones are held down and torn apart piecemeal, while hairy ones are thoroughly worked with the hands and savaged before being consumed.

The golden angwantibo avoids climbing higher than 15m (it mostly lives below 5m) due to heightened competition from birds, less consistent insect resources, more exposure to wind, sun and predators, and fewer thin-branched tangles to shelter in. It frequently descends to the forest floor for fallen fruits and invertebrates.

Behaviour: Visits to the ground expose the angwantibo to predation and its defensive reaction is unique. The animal stands on widely spaced, rigid and fully extended limbs. The head is tucked well back on the chest. This elevates the hindquarters, which become the obvious focus for attack. If touched, however, the animal lunges at its attacker from between its legs with a very quick, slashing bite (the angwantibo has very sharp canines). If on a secure site the animal simply hunches into a ball. In any exposed situation it prefers to climb rapidly up to the nearest clump of dense foliage.

Exclusively nocturnal, activity begins in the evening with a lengthy grooming session. Young animals that are 'parked' by their mothers progress from very limited movement within their 'parking lot' to more extensive explorations as they get older.

Adaptations: Food, territory and socio-sexual relations are all mediated by scent. Both sexes leave urine trails over the branches on which they travel. Both sexes also have genital glands that produce copious secretions. Captive ♀♀ have been seen to mark other ♀♀ with scent while ♂♂ also mark ♀♀. In the latter case the scrotum may contribute scents that may deter other ♂♂ or condition the ♀ to accept the ♂'s advances.

Status: This species is protected by law in Gabon but is too small and too cryptic to face much danger from human predation. Clear-felling and large-scale clearances are the only major threat to their habitat. The long-term safety of this species is of concern mainly because of its biological uniqueness and relatively restricted range. Not currently endangered but listed as Class B (African Convention), Appendix 2 (CITES).

GALAGOS OR BUSHBABIES GALAGONIDAE (PREVIOUSLY GALAGIDAE)

Greater galagos	*Otolemur*
Needle-clawed galagos	*Euoticus*
Squirrel galagos	*Galago (Sciurocheirus)*
Lesser galagos	*Galago*
Dwarf galagos	*Galagoides*

Recognition: Long-tailed, woolly, nocturnal primates with long hindlegs and elongated bases to the feet (tarsi). The head is rounded, with forward-facing eyes and large, naked ears which can retract into compact, folded structures. The moist nose is at the end of a pointed muzzle. The neck is very flexible. Lower incisors are modified to form comb-like structures and a toothed pseudo-tongue, which serves as a specialised 'comb' cleaner, is situated between the tongue and the floor of the mouth. Hands and feet have five long digits with spatulate, padded tips. Genital glands are strongly scented in both sexes. The saliva, the lips and the chest are also scented in some species. Head-and-body lengths range from 10 to 45cm (W 60–2,000g).

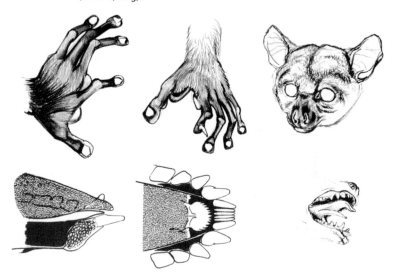

Galago hand and foot. Below: side view of tongue denticle and procumbent incisors on right with the mouth open displaying how the denticle fits in under the tongue.

The baby-like cries of the largest (*Otolemur*) have given galagos their common name but each species has one or more loud calls. Many species are best identified by such vocalisations which differ more than their relative sizes or colours.

Genealogy: Galagos have been a distinctively African lineage for an estimated 22 million years. Two extinct genera have been named and four or more genera survive. Differentiation clearly began quite early on and has given rise to dwarf 'running' forms, small 'leaping' forms, needle-clawed gum-gatherers and greater galagos. Specialised forms inhabiting regional ecotypes (which were formerly regarded as subspecies) are less likely to have derived from recent Ice Age fluctuations in climate than from older adaptations to particular regional habitats. Recent studies of galago genetic material, morphology, communication systems and biogeography have so far led to a provisional subdivision into four genera, seven subgroups and some 16–18 species.

Geography: Primarily an equatorial group that has extended into dry, seasonal woodlands in S and NE Africa. Although several morphological types range very widely, recent research has confirmed that these break down into regional or relict populations. These are now

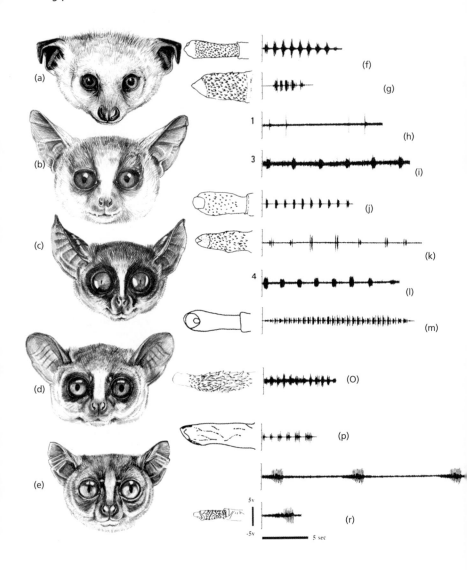

Faces, penile shapes and oscillograms of loud calls for some galagos.
(Courtesy of S. Bearder, L. Ambrose, M. J. Anderson and P. Honess.)

(a) Greater. (b) South African. (c) Spectacled. (d) Zanzibar. (e) Thomas's.

(f) Greater galago. (g) Small-eared galago. (h) Pallid needle-clawed galago.
(i) Allens galago. (j) Senegal galago. (k) South African galago. (l) Spectacled
galago. (m) Rondo galago. (o) Zanzibar galago. (p) Mozambique galago.
(q) Thomas's galago. (r) Demidoff's galago.

regarded as species because they have evolved distinct structures and unique vocal communication signals which inhibit interbreeding.

Ecology: A need for secure diurnal refuges and extreme vulnerability to predators (notably eagle owls, carnivores and nest-raiding primates) helps to explain their confinement to woodlands and forests in sub-Saharan Africa.

A link with gummiferous, leguminous trees is striking in several species. Reliance on gum as a major dietary item or as a famine-food is a partial explanation but galagos may also have adapted in more subtle ways to the ecology of leguminous communities (perhaps to the growth form of trees and lianes and a specific insect fauna).

Some species have diverged by habitat and region but equivalent rainforest species co-exist by eating different foods, moving along different arboreal pathways by different locomotor patterns and embracing different life-zones. All species forage singly.

Natural history: Matriarchal groups are the stable units in galago society, with a family defending a territory within which more mature ♀♀ have preferred home ranges. Such preferences provide the basis for a slow turnover of ♀ territories. ♂♂ are more intensely competitive and transitory, with single, very energetic and intolerant ♂♂ travelling over one to five ♀ territories every night. Subordinate ♂♂ pass through stages of behaving like juveniles within the dominant ♂'s range, becoming nomadic, and setting up small home ranges on the peripheries of a dominant ♂'s range.

Territories are advertised by loud calls and by laying down scent. Scent is laid indirectly, by urination into the palms of the hands and feet or by releasing urine directly onto the branch (and in some species by rubbing saliva or secretions from the genital glands or chest glands onto the branch). ♂♂ monitor ♀♀ very frequently. Several species make nests; others sleep in hollow trees. The more social species utter rallying calls before dawn.

Oestrous lasts for about 2 nights and excites continuous and persistent interest from the ♂♂. After a gestation of 100–150 days the young are born in a nest or hollow. Rainforest species tend to give birth to a single young once a year, while woodland species frequently give birth to twins twice a year (higher reproductive rates in woodland species probably reflect higher levels of predation). The eyes of newborn galagos are half open at birth but movements are weak and unco-ordinated. At first the young are left in the nest but they later travel with, or on, their mother. Family members exchange scent by rubbing and grooming one another. Scrotal glands, salivary scents and apocrine lip glands all play a part in the regulation of social relations. Contacts between individuals vary from frequent to almost continuous in high-density habitats (where galagos can number 500 individuals per km²). Scent is the most important social signal among galagos and, together with sound and touch, renders visual signals much less important, which helps to explain why galagos resemble each other so closely.

Adaptations: Galago fur is not only adapted to insulate the animal but also serves very effectively to hold and diffuse a range of scents secreted by the animal's various scent glands. Mutual- and self-grooming serves to bond individuals and to keep the scent-dispensing fur in prime condition, hence the complex modification of teeth and tongue structures, grooming claws and scented skin (not to mention saliva) around grooming organs. Eventually it should be possible to identify and classify galago species with reference to their distinctive scents, sounds and penis shapes. Simple visual identification of these animals has its limitations.

The limbs of some galagos are the mammalian equivalent of those of the tree frogs. Both frog and galago can move from absolute stasis on one spot to a distant, unpredictable second point and then on to a third, within seconds. The success of frogs world-wide is an indication of how difficult it is for predators to beat this mode of locomotion. The vertical clinging and leaping skills of the galagos are also well adapted to movement within stands of well-spaced, narrow, vertical stems. This form of vegetation is mostly to be found under well-shaded forest canopies and it is here that galagos are likely to have first evolved. The elongated upper foot, or tarsus, gives the galago great versatility of gait because rapid and wide flexion at the heel allows the animal to run fast with minimal involvement of the specialised thighs and shanks. It also helps the animal to accommodate to a variety of different landing sites. Long tails provide balance and a rudder for changing direction while leaping.

Heavily obstructed and densely shaded undergrowth not only demands specialised locomotion, olfaction and big, light-gathering eyes, but also favours sound as a mode of communication and involvement of hearing in hunting for active prey. All galagos therefore have large ears that resemble those of bats in their mobility and great sensitivity.

Greater Galagos *Otolemur*

Greater galago	*Otolemur crassicaudatus*
Silver galago	*Otolemur argentatus*
Small-eared galago	*Otolemur garnetti*
Mwera galago	*Otolemur* sp. nov.?

Recognition: Cat-sized, long-tailed, woolly, arboreal animals of relatively uniform brown, grey or sandy colouring. Melanistic (black) morphs are common in some areas; the tail is sometimes of a paler tint. These are the largest and among the most primitive of living galagos. They lack strong colour contrasts on the body and face. The snout is broad and dog-like, and the eyes are proportionately smaller than those of any other galagos. The ears are prominent and ribbed. Greater galagos have glands on their heels which are horny and rough.

More often heard than seen, the galagos' loud call begins as an explosive pulsing bawl or croaking which then tails off. Alarm calls (yapping, rattling or moaning cries) are often sustained for a long time.

Genealogy: Greater galagos generally move on all fours and resort to springing leaps only when alarmed or in order to get from one tree to another. Although true galagos, their more generalised gait and less specialised limb structure is indicative of an ancient common ancestry shared by pottos and bushbabies.

Geography: Range across the southern part of the continent from Angola and Namibia to the east coast from Natal to Somalia. The larger part of this extensive range is in Miombo (*Brachystegia*) fire-climax woodland but within the more severely degraded or grassy areas of the Miombo belt they are confined to riverine galleries and isolated thickets. Particularly numerous along coastal plains and on the lower slopes of mountains, they live in areas with well-defined seasons. There is virtually no overlap of range with the potto, nor are they found north of the potto's range.

Ecology: Greater galagos live at very variable densities strung out along river courses in the drier, more open savannahs but continuously in coastal thickets and forests, where they have been estimated to number up to 125 per km². Home ranges probably vary greatly but a tagged ♀ was found to live within 7ha while a ♂ was estimated to use around 20ha.

Many greater galago habitats are impoverished florally, with long dry seasons in which their main diet consists of tree exudates. When plants are fruiting and flowering, fruits and blossoms make up the main element in their diets. Invertebrates and (in some areas) vertebrates play a lesser role, although juveniles have been recorded to prefer animal foods even when fruits and gum are available. Feeding tends to be spasmodic and animals may form temporary clusters during rest periods before breaking off to seek food again.

Natural history: Ranges are shared and defended by related ♀♀. Dominant ♂♂ also permit a small number of subordinate ♂♂ within their ranges during the dry (non-breeding) season. Subordinate and peripheral individuals rely on scent-marks and loud calls to avoid face-to-face meetings with dominant animals; juveniles may accompany their mothers to form small groups.

The onset of the breeding season is marked by ♂ gargling and clucking and by physiological changes in both sexes. ♀♀ only invite copulation while they are briefly in season, but mating is phlegmatic and may go on for hours. Gestation lasts 18 weeks. The ♀ gives birth on a leaf nest or platform and up to three young remain there for about 2 weeks, after which the mother carries them with her in her mouth or on her back. By 25 days they are following her wherever she goes, only becoming wholly independent by about 300 days, at which time they tend to leave the parental range. Births peak in September on the E African coast and November in South Africa.

Adaptations: Greater galagos have bare glandular patches on their abdomen and chest (larger in ♂♂) with which they mark favourite sites. These function as land-marks along their regularly used arboreal pathways. The oily yellowish apocrine secretion has three components, of which one dissipates in about an hour while the other two remain for several days. Other galagos smell scent-markings carefully and modify their movements in relation to both olfactory and vocal signals. In this way potentially dangerous confrontations are generally avoided. Chest-gland-marking is often augmented by urine-marking and ano-genital deposits. The animal sparingly urinates on its hands and feet which it then rubs on the branch. Callosities on the palms of the feet grate on the bark, thus adding a sound signal to which other animals also pay attention. Foot-grating is also likely to spread secretions from the heel glands which, in combination with the urine-marking, may enable olfactory identification of individuals. In these ways quite dense nocturnal traffic within shared home ranges can be intricately regulated.

Greater Galago *Otolemur crassicaudatus*

Other names: Fr. *Galago à queue épaisse*. Ger. *Riesengalago*. Swah. *Komba ya Miombo*.
Measurements: HB 32cm (26–46.5cm). T 41cm (29–55cm). W 1,100g (567–2,000g).
Recognition: A large, brown or grey galago with exceptionally long ears (5–7.2cm), a broad muzzle, large canines and relatively small eyes. There is a dense covering of long guard hairs on the lower back. The greater galago walks and runs in preference to leaping. (The chromosomes and penile structure are unique.)

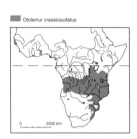
Otolemur crassicaudatus

0   2000 km

Subspecies: *O. c. crassicaudatus* (south of R. Limpopo): brownish with tail less than 40cm long. *O. c. montieri* (Angola to Tanzania): greyish with long tail and large ears. *O. c. badius* (central Tanzania): smaller reddish brown galago resembling *O. garnetti* in certain cranial features.
Habitat: Dense vegetation in Miombo (*Brachystegia*), coastal and montane areas. This is the common greater bushbaby of S and E Africa.
Food: *Acacia* gums, flowers and seeds; figs, ebony and other fruits; snails, slugs, insects, reptiles and birds.
Status: Common and widespread. Listed as Not Endangered (IUCN).

Silver Galago *Otolemur argentatus*

Other names: Swah. *Komba ya Kavirondo*.
Measurements: HB 39cm (35–40cm). T 41cm (34–43cm). W 1100g (730–1814g).
Recognition: A large galago, silvery grey (sometimes black) with a very pale tail. The face is long and broad muzzled. Ears are generally less than 6cm. May be a very distinctive subspecies of the greater galago, but the penile structure differs.
Habitat: Riverine and other woodlands and lower montane forest to the south and east of the Kavirondo Gulf.
Food: *Acacia* gum, flowers and fruits; various invertebrates and occasional vertebrates.
Status: The limited range of this species in an area of dense human settlement is mitigated by its range also falling within the Serengeti and Mara National Parks.

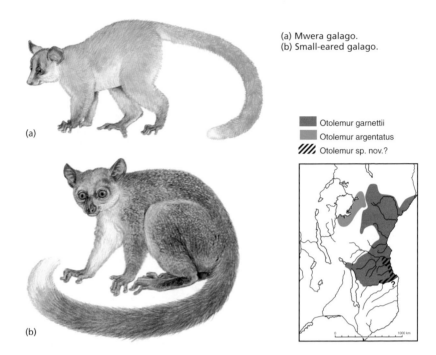

(a) Mwera galago.
(b) Small-eared galago.

Otolemur garnettii
Otolemur argentatus
Otolemur sp. nov.?

Small-Eared Galago *Otolemur garnettii*

Other names: Fr. *Galago de Garnett*. Ger. *Garnettgalago*. Swah. *Komba mkubwa ya Pwani*.
Measurements: HB 26cm (23–34cm). T 36cm (30–44cm). W 760g (550–1200g).
Recognition: A medium-sized galago with relatively short ears, a pointed muzzle and relatively larger eyes. The fingernails are unique in growing sharp, thickened points at their outer margins, which come into play when the galago climbs over large trunks. They are more active leapers. (Chromosomes and penile structure are distinctive.)
Subspecies: *O. g. garnetti* (E African coast and islands): uniform brown with dark or light tip to tail. *O. g. hindei* (Kenya highlands mainly east of Gregory Rift): dark brown. *O. g. panganiensis* (N Tanzanian montane forests and upper R. Pangani): dark brown.
Habitat: Coastal and montane forests (often dry, low-canopy and florally impoverished) but also riverine galleries with numerous *Acacia*; also various cultivation mosaics and urban suburbs.
Food: Gums, flowers and seeds of *Acacia*; fruits and invertebrates.
Status: Widespread and abundant. Listed as Not Endangered (IUCN).

Mwera Galago *Otolemur* sp. nov.?

Measurements: HB est. 21cm. T 30cm. W est. 300g.
Recognition: A small, fawnish grey galago with off-white underparts and dark brown hands and feet. Poorly defined brownish patches surround the eyes. The tail is evenly haired, somewhat gingery fawn and may have a white tip. Its calls resemble those of the greater galago but are weaker. It may be a dwarfed subspecies.
Habitat: Known from exotic plantations and secondary growth in coastal valleys close to Lindi but likely to be more widespread. This small galago may range well down into Mozambique in relict patches of coastal forest. It occurs within a few kilometres of the much larger greater galago.
Food: Recorded in mango and cashew-nut plantations but nothing known.
Status: This calls of this species have been tape-recorded and it has been observed and photographed (by Dr S. Bearder) but has yet to be formally described from specimens. It appears to be a relict form and therefore less likely to be secondarily dwarfed than to resemble an archaic precursor of the greater galago.

Needle-Clawed Galagos *Euoticus*

| Elegant needle-clawed galago | *Euoticus elegantulus* |
| Pallid needle-clawed galago | *Euoticus pallidus* |

Recognition: Long-limbed, woolly, arboreal galagos with a short, blunt muzzle and very large, pale orange eyes with rimmed brows. The hands and feet are large in proportion to the body and keels on the fingernails end in a robust, sharp point. They are unique among galagos in having mammae reduced to a single pair. The lower incisors are particularly long and form a sharp blade. Elongated second premolars have bladed tips. They are exceptionally agile runners and can race up or down slanting branches like small monkeys. When they alight on a branch all limbs touch down simultaneously. Their calls are uttered as single, short, disconnected notes with no obvious pattern. Loud calls consist of a short screech, a shrill yap or a loud click. They also make a bird-like 'kweee'.

Genealogy: These highly specialised galagos have no obvious close relatives, although the spectacled galago also has keeled nails and enlarged orbits. However, these resemblances are now thought to be convergent.

Geography: Needle-clawed galagos are restricted to forests between the R. Cross and R. Zaïre, following a distribution pattern which resembles that of many other forest organisms requiring consistently humid conditions. They range up to 1,000m on Mt Cameroun.

Ecology: The local abundance of needle-clawed galagos is determined by the distribution of their main food plants: gum-oozing trees and lianes. Up to 80% of their diet may be gums and resins produced by *Newtonia*, rain trees (*Albizia*) and *Albizia/Entada* lianes and this constitutes a year-round staple. Many *Albizia* are fast-growing colonisers and secondary forest plants. They tend to be localised but are often very abundant. They become scarcer in mature primary forest. Needle-claws have been estimated at 3–10 individuals per km^2 in Gabonese primary forest and up to 30 per km^2 in secondary forest. Up to 20% of their food is animal matter (mainly leafhoppers, caterpillars and beetles). The killing and eating of a bird has also been recorded. Fruits are an insignificant part of their diet.

Most frequently seen at between 10 and 25m, needle-claws nevertheless prefer to travel through the canopy, where they make spectacular leaps in excess of 5m. They can also drop, spread-eagled, from great heights. They are not known to make nests and sleep in huddles of up to five individuals in dense foliage or in the forks of trees. Of all forest prosimians they are the earliest to become active (18.00h) and the last to retire (05.45h).

Natural history: Small ♀ and offspring groups numbering three or four individuals are often joined at their sleeping site by one, sometimes two, adult ♂♂. Breeding appears to occur mainly between November and May. Young are 'parked' and the mothers contact call to the young is a short click.

Adaptations: A permanent diet of gums must have been adopted at an early stage in the evolution of these species because their gut shows specialisations not found in other galagos. The delicate incisor and premolar blades are only capable of minor trimming of bark wounds to keep fresh gum flowing and cannot excavate deep initial wounds. In order to harvest sufficient fresh gum, many plant types and a very large number of oozing-sites must be visited each night. The main source of gum droplets comes from bark-wounding by anomalures (see pp. 175–178) and fine bore-holes drilled by cicadas (which often have irregular life cycles). In central W Africa cicada activity appears to be continuous and on a massive scale, yet needle-claws hardly ever eat the cicadas themselves. Since several important food trees have a very wide distribution in Africa, the limited distribution of these galagos may be governed by the presence of bark-wounding animals which make the gum flow in sufficient and reliable quantities for their year-round requirements.

The sharp nails from which these galagos get their name, and the exceptionally broad span of their hands and feet, are both adaptations to getting a firm grip on the trunk while feeding. This is particularly important whenever the animals have to bite into or trim the bark but it also allows the galagos to approach gum sites from any position, however awkward.

The structure of needle-clawed galagos' limbs, their habits and their general proportions show an extraordinary degree of convergence with the Malagasy fork-crowned lemur (*Phaner*). The spectacled galago (*G. matschiei*), a less consistent gum-feeder, shows fewer signs of convergence but does have similar pointed nails.

Euoticus elegantulus
Euoticus pallidus

Elegant Needle-Clawed Galago *Euoticus elegantulus*

Other names: Fr. *Galago mignon du sud*. Ger. *Sudlicher Kielnagelgalago*.
Measurements: HB 21cm (18–33cm). T 29cm (28-31cm). W 300g (270–360g).
Recognition: Brightly coloured, very agile, long-limbed galago with white underparts sharply divided from the foxy-red back by an undulating border. Limbs are tawny, and the face and tail are ashy grey or brown. The pale eyes are very prominent. The voice is rather bird-like.
Habitat: Between the R. Sanaga and R. Zaïre in both primary and secondary forests but more common in the latter.
Food: Gum of rain trees (*Albizia*) and other Mimosaceae and insects. About 5% of the annual diet consists of fruits.
Status: Widespread and common throughout moist forest belt.

Pallid Needle-Clawed Galago *Euoticus pallidus*

Other names: Fr. *Galago mignon du nord*. Ger. *Nordlicher Kielnagelgalago*.
Measurements: HB 19 (17–20cm). T 28–33cm. W 200–260g.
Recognition: A small, very agile dull-coloured galago with yellowish grey underparts, grey shoulders, arms and tail. The back is brownish with a chocolate-brown dorsal stripe. Both needle-clawed species have similar vocal repertoires but the calls of the pallid needle-clawed galago may be slightly higher in pitch.
Habitat: Patchily distributed between the R. Cross and R. Sanaga, mainly in secondary forests; also on Bioko I. (formerly Fernando Po).
Food: Both needle-clawed species are thought to share a similar dependence on gums and insects.
Status: Rated as not endangered but fragmentation of the habitat could lead to interruptions in the food chain to which this specialised galago would be vulnerable.

Squirrel Galagos *Galago (Sciurocheirus)*

Allen's squirrel galago	*Galago alleni*

Recognition: Grey-brown galagos with various tints of russet to their limbs. The pointed muzzle has a pale medial stripe and the reddish eyes are set within well-defined mask patches. Squirrel galagos have carried frog-like vertical clinging and leaping to its extreme. They differ from most other galagos in landing 'hands first', rather than feet first or with all limbs simultaneously. At least one of the populations currently treated as races of Allen's galago may merit full species status (the loud calls of Allen's galagos north and south of the R. Sanaga, for example, are very different).

Genealogy: Squirrel galagos are a distinct group but resemble lesser galagos most in their voices and anatomical structure. It seems likely that this lineage made a secondary return to closed rainforest.

Geography: Currently only known from between the R. Niger and R. Zaïre. This distribution pattern resembles that of the drills/mandrills and other forest species with ancient but evident savannah origins.

Ecology: Almost entirely ground-feeders in primary forest with a heavily shaded, clear floor and numerous, well-spaced lianes and tree stems. Squirrel galagos avoid all areas of dense undergrowth and are effectively absent from secondary forest. Within this habitat, densities of 14–25 animals per km^2 have been estimated.

Fallen and low-level fruits account for the greater part of the diet, with the balance made up of animal foods (beetles, moths, spiders, snails and frogs). The galagos pounce on hopping or flying insects with great precision, grabbing them in the hand, like lesser bushbabies.

Natural history: Animals live in large territories with ♀♀ ranging over 8–16ha and ♂♂ over 30–50ha. Territorial ♂♂ are very energetic in defending their mating rights over up to eight ♀♀, visiting as many as five in a single night. Rendezvous are facilitated by loud croaks to which others respond (a quieter croak serves to keep mothers and their offspring in touch). Scent-marking has also been recorded. They normally shelter in hollow trees (another habit common to savannah galagos), which are sometimes shared with bats or anomalures. Within such hollows they may build rudimentary leaf nests, especially when giving birth. Gestation is 133 days and one (rarely two) infants are born at a time. Two ♀♀ and their offspring may sometimes share a shelter.

Adaptations: Fallen fruits and attendant invertebrates are major forest resources for which there is much competition. The forest floor beneath fruiting trees provides foci of activity which attract predators, and the squirrel galagos' extreme alertness and instantaneous flight responses reflect increased vulnerability. However, their frog-like escape technique depends upon the forest floor being relatively unobstructed, with adequate fine-stemmed verticals to leap onto.

■ Galago alleni
■ G.a. cameronensis
■ G.a. gabonensis
■ G.a. makande form

Gaboon Allen's galago (*G.a.gabonensis*).

Allen's Squirrel Galago *Galago alleni*

Other names: Fr. *Galago d'Allen*. Ger. *Buschwaldgalago*.

Measurements: HB 20cm (15–24cm). T 26cm (20–30cm). W 314g (200–445g).

Recognition: The three or four regional forms of Allen's galago differ in colour but are all medium-sized with narrow heads and rounded ears (3–4cm long). All have a boldly marked face mask around the eyes and pale nose stripes. The tail is long, bushy and of even thickness. All forms make a repetitive croaking loud call similar to that of the lesser galagos of the savannahs but their whistles are very distinctive.

Subspecies: *G. a. alleni* (Bioko I., formerly Fernando Po): very dark brown island form. *G. a. cameronensis* (between R. Niger and R. Sanaga): small, head and body less than 20cm, with grey back, rump and crown, raw sienna limbs and a dark grey tail; voice a whistle and kwok. *G. a. gabonensis* (between R. Sanaga and R. Ogooué): larger form with off-white underparts, brown back, orange-tinted thighs and shanks, bright orange outer surface to the arms, grey crown and dark brown tail; voice a rattle and whistle. Makande galago, *G. alleni* subsp. nov. (currently recorded from Forêt des Abeilles but probably ranges intermittently between the R. Ogooué and R. Zaïre): very dark with orange underparts and most distinctive calls. It is also possible that a squirrel galago exists in the Ivory Coast.

Habitat: Found between R. Niger and R. Zaïre but may have a wider distribution; lives in the lowest levels of mature primary forest.

Food: Mainly fruits but insects also important.

Status: The felling of primary forest destroys the habitat of this species. Listed as Not Endangered (IUCN).

Lesser Galagos *Galago*

Senegal galago	*Galago senegalensis*
South African galago	*Galago moholi*
Somali galago	*Galago gallarum*
Spectacled galago	*Galago matschiei*

Recognition: Medium-sized, mostly savannah galagos with a grey or brownish back and a round head with large eyes and a short muzzle. They have a dark eye mask and pale nose stripe. Tails are not densely furred. All utter short phrases or single cries that have a regular timing repeated many times. Their volume depends on how excited the caller is. All are agile bounders, landing feet first. A relatively arbitrary line has been drawn between lesser and dwarf galagos, which actually embrace a continuum of species.

Genealogy: With the widest distribution and the longest tarsus and shanks, the Senegal galago appears to be the most 'derived' of dry-country galagos. By contrast the Somali galago bears some resemblance to the Zanzibar galago and the Matundu to the South African galago. This suggests that *Galago* could have derived from a *Galagoides* population of the Matundu or Zanzibar type. The spectacled galago, instead, may represent a secondary return to closed forest by a woodland-adapted form.

Geography: Split between the northern and southern savannahs and the Somali arid zone, the three non-forest species of *Galago* inhabit the entire woodland and treed savannah zones of tropical Africa.

Ecology: Woodlands dominated by *Acacia*, *Brachystegia*, *Isoberlinia* and (at much lower densities) Mopane (*Colophospermum*) are the preferred habitat of the three non-forest species. The spectacled galago inhabits central African forests that share many gummiferous tree genera with these dry woodland types. Gum and insects are the main foods. Other animal foods and fruits are more marginal but can be important locally or seasonally. A single animal may travel 2km in a night and visit 500 trees but only about 6 hours are actually spent foraging. Where tree hollows are numerous they are used for shelter but tree forks and branch tangles are more generally available. Where neither hollows nor trunks are suitable lesser galagos will make a leaf shelter or take over an old bird's nest as a day-time retreat. Fires represent a major hazard, mainly because they expose lesser galagos to hawks and other predators as they flee.

Natural history: Recruitment rates tend to be very high, with ♀♀ bearing one or two young twice a year. Home ranges of both ♂♂ and ♀♀ overlap extensively. ♀♀ often share their day-shelter. They are sometimes accompanied by an adult ♂. Scent-marking with urine, genital rubbing and saliva-dribbling is most intense around sleeping-trees but is maintained at favourite posts scattered around the home range. The sizes of home ranges probably vary according to resource availability, habitat type and population density. Gestation periods are in the region of 130 days and the young develop fast, moving out of the nest or hollow at 2 weeks and becoming independent at about 2 months. ♀♀ are sexually mature at about 8 months, ♂♂ at 1 year.

Adaptations: The physiological ability to fuel an energetic life-style on gums is the main adaptation which allows these galagos to inhabit dry woodlands and thickets. Their lightning speed during escape and in hunting for prey is another key to their success.

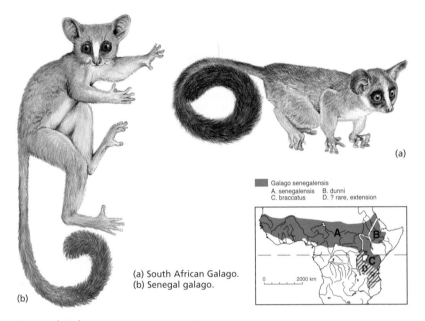

Galago senegalensis
A. senegalensis   B. dunni
C. braccatus   D. ? rare, extension

(a) South African Galago.
(b) Senegal galago.

Senegal Galago *Galago senegalensis*

Other names: Fr. *Galago du Sénégal*. Ger. *Senegalgalago*. Swah. *Komba ya Senegal*.
Measurements: HB 16.5cm (13.2–21cm). T 26cm (19.5–30)cm). W 206g (112–300g).
Recognition: A long-limbed galago with a long, short-haired tail. The back is grey or brown-grey and the underparts are yellowish (particularly where the two colours meet). Ears are 2.5–5.5cm long. The loud advertising call consists of a single, low-pitched note uttered persistently at a regular tempo. (The eye-shine is bright red.)
Races: *G. s. senegalensis* (Senegal to Sudan and W Uganda); *G. s. braccatus*, also *albipes* and *sotikae* (Uganda, Kenya and N Tanzania); *G. s. dunni* (Ethiopia). The boundaries between these populations are still uncertain.
Habitat: Woodlands dominated by *Acacia*, *Isoberlinia* and *Julbernardia* between Senegal and E Africa; montane forest margins elsewhere. Densely grassed areas are avoided. The exact boundaries of the Senegal galagos' E African range have not been determined.
Food: Gums, invertebrates and fruits (seasonally). Insects are located and caught with great speed and dexterity on the ground, in flight and on vegetation.
Status: Widespread and common. Not endangered.

South African Galago *Galago moholi*

Other names: Fr. *Galago moholi*. Ger. *Moholigalago*. Swah. *Komba ya kusini*.
Measurements: HB 15cm (8.8-20.5cm). T 23cm (11–28cm). W 160g (95–245g).
Recognition: Medium-sized to small, greyish or light brown galago with relatively large ears (2–5cm) and large orange eyes. The eye mask and tail are dark brownish grey. Legs, feet, forearms and hands have a strong yellowish suffusion. (The eye-shine is red.) The loud advertising call differs from that of the Senegal galago in being single-, double- and triple-unit cries of high pitch, mixed into series and repeated over long periods.

(a) Somali galago.
(b) Spectacled galago.

Habitat: Miombo belt from Angola to W Tanzania, Zimbabwe and the Transvaal. Within this zone the South African galago inhabits Miombo (*Brachystegia*), *Combretum*, *Acacia* and Mopane (*Colophospermum*) woodlands, riverine galleries and forest margins. Its areas of overlap with the Senegal, Zanzibar and Grant's galagos require further study.
Food: *Acacia* and other gums, invertebrates. Fruits are only occasionally taken.
Status: Common and widespread. Not endangered.

Somali Galago *Galago gallarum*

Other names: Fr. *Galago de Somalie*. Ger. *Somaligalago*. Swah. *Komba ya Somalia*.
Measurements: HB 17cm (13–20cm). T 25cm (20.5–30cm). W 250g.
Recognition: Sandy-coloured galago with a broad, round head, medium-sized ears (3–4cm), and large eyes only partially surrounded by narrow brown eye mask. The back is brownish buff and the underparts are off-white with a yellowish boundary between the two colours. The face is almost white. Scattered bush may require this galago to spend more time on the ground. Animals have been observed feeding and moving over the ground with long, high bounds. The loud call has yet to be recorded.
Habitat: *Acacia*, *Commiphora* and *Combretum* deciduous bushlands and thickets; known from between the valleys of the R. Webe Shebelle and R. Tana. The Somali galago's overlapping boundaries and interactions with the closely related Senegal and Zanzibar galagos require further study.
Food: Presumed to be mainly gum and invertebrates.
Status: General degradation of habitats in Somalia may be affecting some populations adversely. Unlikely to be endangered.

Spectacled Galago *Galago matschiei (syn. G. inustus)*

Other names: Fr. *Galago mignon sombre*. Ger. *Ostlicher Kielnagelgalago*. Swah. *Komba Miwani*.
Measurements: HB 16cm (14.7–20cm). T 25cm (19–27.9cm). W 210g (170–250g).
Recognition: A dark brown, forest-dwelling galago with very large amber eyes surrounded by almost black eye-mask patches. The brown tail is evenly furred along its length. A well-defined ridge borders the eyes, especially at the brows. The lower incisors are sharply protuberant. The nails of hands and feet are keeled and sharply pointed. Yellow secretions are absent in this species.
Distribution: Zaïre east of the R. Lualaba to interlacustrine E Africa, including very isolated mountain slopes in E Uganda.
Habitat: Primary and secondary lowland forest and lower montane forests where *Parinari excelsa* is a dominant tree. The spectacled galago can move freely between the canopy and thick tangles at lower levels but is more frequently seen at lower levels.
Food: Insects, fruits and gums with seasonal changes in preference. Fruits may be a prime choice when available. Caterpillars and beetles are taken during rainy seasons while gums appear to be a dry-season food.
Behaviour: Loud calls are repetitive barks, 'grunt-yaps' and a long, yapping screech. There appears to be a breeding peak in November/December. A pregnant ♀ has also been recorded in February.
Status: Widespread but patchy in distribution.

Dwarf Galagos *Galagoides*

Roller callers:	
Rondo galago	*Galagoides* sp. nov. "*rondoensis*"
Usambara galago	*Galagoides* sp.nov.? *orinus*?
Incremental callers:	
Zanzibar galago	*Galagoides zanzibaricus*
Mozambique galago	*Galagoides granti*
Crescendo callers:	
Demidoff's galago	*Galagoides demidoff*
Thomas's galago	*Galagoides thomasi*

Recognition: Diminutive galagos with greenish grey-brown coats, yellowish underparts and elongated, upturned noses. Until about 1980 all dwarf galagos were regularly classified as a single species because they all display similar body forms and coloration. More recently there has been extensive examination of this group across six fields of research including: (a) molecular studies; (b) anatomical re-examination – especially penile structures; (c) behaviour – especially recorded vocalisations; (d) ecology – especially locomotory patterns and life-zones; (e) biogeography – notably new forms from newly surveyed areas, revised estimates of natural variation within populations and revised assessments of distribution limits; (f) taxonomic revision – notably redefinition of generic characteristics and correction of mistakes in allocation of names.

As a consequence some previous names have been abandoned and some six or seven species are now recognised. These fall into three subgroups.

Genealogy: Dwarf galagos are so close to their derived sister-group, *Galago*, that they are frequently treated as a single genus and '*Galagoides*' remains a provisional generic name. Subgroups cluster by vocal, anatomical and biogeographic characteristics. Thus:

1. Very small galagos with long, spatulate fingers. Very sparsely distributed in a few relict E African forests. Called 'roller callers' on account of their rolling loud calls.
2. Slightly larger galagos more widely distributed in E African (mainly coastal) forests. Best identified by their 'incremental' calls.
3. The smallest (Demidoff's or dwarf galago) and its closely related ally (Thomas's galago) are distinguished by their relatively small hands and rising 'crescendo' loud calls. As equatorial forest species these are the most widely distributed and successful species (and probably the most derived in a generally conservative group).

Geography: Although found in warm, humid coastal localities as far south as 28°S, these very small-bodied animals are mainly restricted to equatorial lowlands from Guinea to the Indian Ocean.

Ecology: Primary and secondary forests including very fragmentary relict outliers in E and SE Africa. They are mainly insectivorous, rarely feeding on fruits and probably relying on gums only as a seasonal stop-gap or filler. Beetles, caterpillars, crickets and termites are known common prey.

Natural history: The preferred foods of dwarf galagos are exploited by small birds by day and by bats (notably slit-faced bats) at night. The galagos are commonly killed by owls. Predation and competition are likely to confine them to tangled evergreen vegetation and limit their capacity to colonise new areas or disperse through exposed vegetation.

Adaptations: All members of this group are primarily quadrupedal animals that make short leaps rather than long hops. Among galagos these are relatively primitive traits. Dense evergreen thickets and forests in the tropics are also primitive habitats for galagos. This combination suggests that forest-dwelling *Galagoides* are more conservative than woodland-adapted *Galago*.

Roller Callers (Relictual east coast dwarf galagos)

This group, newly recognised by Dr Simon Bearder, includes species that were formerly classified as Demidoff's galago. Initially three species were identified from recordings of their stereotyped loud calls. Two of these were then captured and their identification as distinct new species was confirmed (despite their numerous superficial resemblances to Demidoff's galago). The smaller of these new species comes from the far south of coastal

Tanzania. The larger comes from lowland forest at Ifakara, over 400km away and inland. The third voice, recorded in the Usambara Mts remains 'disembodied' but may belong to a galago first described in 1936 as *Galago demidoff orinus*.

The prospects for matching up *G. orinus* with its vocal repertoire have been reduced by the cutting down of its habitat in the Uluguru Mts since it was first collected. Hopefully further systematic tape-recording and live-trapping will allow this interesting group of relict populations to be more adequately described and classified.

Rondo Galago *Galagoides* sp. nov. (named *rondoensis* by P. Honess 1996)

Other names: Swah. *Komba ya Rondo.*
Measurements: HB 12cm. T 16cm. W 50g.
Recognition: A very small galago of warm-brown body colour, with a long, dark reddish brown tail which becomes thicker towards its tip. The pale underside has yellowish tints. The nose is long, pointed and strikingly retroussé with a pale centre line between broad black eye patches. The main vocalisation is rather insect-like: a sustained vibrating call that rises in volume and is sustained for about 10 seconds before tailing off quite suddenly.
Habitat: Known from remnant forest patches on the seward sides of low hills close to the Tanzania and, perhaps north Mozambique coast. Originally known only from Rondo plateau.
Food: Insects.
Status: Highly endangered. Logging of its known range by an overseas company has been almost total. Its known habitat and other neighbouring areas continue to suffer from relentless pit-sawing and frequent fires.

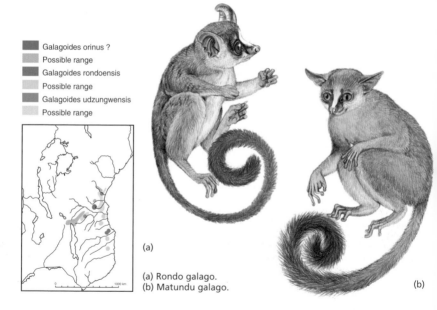

- Galagoides orinus ?
- Possible range
- Galagoides rondoensis
- Possible range
- Galagoides udzungwensis
- Possible range

(a)

(a) Rondo galago.
(b) Matundu galago.

(b)

Usambara Galago *Galagoides* sp. nov.? *orinus?*

Measurements: Not known but similar to Zanzibar galago.
Identification: A distinctive loud call of 'rolling' type has been recorded at Amani in the Usambara Mts. The galago's existence is indicated here in order to alert field naturalists and to encourage further investigation. Although there is no certainty as to whether the Usambara galago and *G. orinus* are the same species, the former is included here because it is most likely to belong to this group.

Incremental Callers (East coast small galagos)

The Zanzibar galago, which typifies members of this group, is intermediate in several respects (including size) between the other dwarf galagos and lesser galagos of the *senegalensis/moholi* group. Their calls consist of a series of staccato notes, uttered in bursts lasting 6–10 seconds, with brief crescendos near the beginning or end. Unlike the relictual east coast galagos, these species seem to have wide geographic ranges (although they remain restricted to forested or riverine environments, coastal thickets and cultivation mosaics). There are at least two well-defined species (with a possible third in Malawi).

Matundu Galago *Galagoides* sp. nov. (named *udzungwensis* by P. Honess 1996) but now considered to be a subspecies of the Zanzibar galago.

Measurements: HB 14.7cm. T 23.0cm. Ear ave. 28mm. W 110–138g.
Recognition: A small galago of greenish brown body colour, with an exceptionally long, evenly haired, dark brown tail. The ground colour graduates over the forehead into a dark sepia mask around the eyes. The lighter underparts show a rich orange flush, especially on the chest. It has a large but rather narrow head. The nose projects forward less than it does in the Rondo galago and the profile is less dished. The eyes are relatively small and the broad ears are slightly 'pinched' towards their tips. Fingers and thumbs are exceptionally long and thin, with spatulate tips.
Habitat: Presently known from low-lying secondary rainforest growing below the Uzungwa (African Ghats) mountain chain where this is the only galago species yet recorded in this ecotype.
Food: Insects, with fruits also readily taken by captive specimens.
Status: Presently known habitat borders the proposed Mwanihana National Park. It is also likely to occur in the proposed Chita National Park. Unfortunately logging interests continue to oppose recognition of this Park. The Matundu galago is highly vulnerable and its ecology requires urgent study.

(a) Zanzibar galago.
(b) Mozambique galago.

Galagoides zanzibaricus
Galagoides granti

(a)

(b)

Zanzibar Galago *Galagoides zanzibaricus*

Other names: Fr. *Galago de Zanzibar*. Ger. *Zanzibargalago*. Swah. *Komba ya Zanzibar*.
Measurements: HB 15.3cm (12–16.5cm). T 20cm (17–23cm). W 145g (104–203g).
Recognition: The dark brown body colour is suffused with warm reddish tints on the crown, shoulders, back and thighs. The tail is ashy brown with hairs of very even length. The nose is pointed but less so than in other dwarf galagos and the lower jaw is shallow and long.

The deep red-brown eyes are surrounded by broad black eye patches and there is a short and narrow strip of pale fur above the bridge of the nose. Coastal populations have relatively short but dense fur.

Distribution: Between R. Tana and R. Rufiji and Zanzibar I. It may occur in montane forest inland but confusion with relict dwarf galagos makes its inland distribution uncertain.

Habitat: Coastal lowland rainforests and thickets, riverine forests and secondary growth, including cultivation mosaics and gardens, where it normally remains below 5m. Possibly montane forests.

Food: Invertebrates, mainly insects (moths and beetles) and up to 30% fruits. Gum is readily taken by captive specimens but has not been recorded in the wild. The Zanzibar galago forages singly.

Behaviour: Individual home ranges of about 2–5ha may be wholly or partially shared with close relatives but ♀♀ are intolerant of other neighbouring ♀♀. Single adult ♂♂ associate with one or more ♀♀, sleeping by preference in tree holes. Gestation lasts 120 days and normally results in a single young. It may breed twice a year (February–March and September–October). The young reach adult size in 4 months and are sexually active by 1 year. Up to 150 galagos per km^2 have been recorded in suitable habitats.

Adaptations: The Zanzibar galago is primarily an agile, arboreal 'runner' which also makes substantial leaps but never hops bipedally nor can it land feet first. It can 'reverse-climb' backwards down vertical and near-vertical stems.

Status: The Zanzibar galago remains locally common in spite of continuous attrition of its habitats which are being cleared for cultivation. Proposed conservation areas on Zanzibar I. should ensure the preservation of viable populations there. Listed as Vulnerable (IUCN).

Mozambique Galago *Galagoides granti*

Measurements: HB 15.5cm (14–19cm). T 22cm (20–26.5cm). W 139–178g.

Recognition: The soft-brown body colour is suffused with ochre on the shoulders, back and thighs. Yellowish brown extends down the tail, the terminal third of which becomes very dark. The head is greyish with dark brown eye patches and a broad interocular stripe of white fur. Surface brushing of yellow suffuses the pale off-white fur of the underparts. Overall the fur is longer and woollier than in the Zanzibar galago.

Habitat: Forest mosaics, riverine strips and coastal forests extending along some 2,500km of the E African coast between the R. Zambezi and R. Rufiji. The Mozambique galago also extends inland into montane areas around L. Malawi. (Populations of small forest galagos north and south of this lake differ substantially but their exact identification awaits study.)

Food: Insects and fruits.

Status: Widespread and common. Not endangered.

Crescendo Callers (Equatorial dwarf galagos)

Equatorial dwarf galagos lack any distinguishing visual characteristics so successful identification of a particular species is mainly dependent on its vocalisations. Among the 'crescendo callers' only two species are currently recognised but regional populations are still poorly known.

The tiny Demidoff's galago lives at low levels while the marginally larger, more active Thomas's galago is a canopy-dweller.

Demidoff's Galago *Galagoides demidoff*

Other names: Fr. *Galago de Demidoff*. Ger. *Urwaldgalago*.

Measurements: HB 12cm (7.3–15.5cm). T 18cm (11–21.5cm). Ear ave. 24mm. W 60g (44–97g).

Recognition: The smallest primate in Africa. The body colour is brown with paler yellowish underparts. Ears are relatively short and the nose is pointed and upturned, with a prominent white stripe between the eyes and down the bridge of the nose. Loud calls are very distinctive; a series of sharp chips that gather in speed and pitch to reach a crescendo in 2–4-second bouts. They also make an insect-like buzzing alarm call.

Subspecies: *G. d. demidoff* (Senegal to R. Niger), *G. d. murinus* (R. Niger to R. Zaïre), *G. d. anomurus* (north of R. Zaïre), *G. d. phasma* (south of R. Zaïre), *G. d. poensis* (Bioko I., formerly Fernando Po).

Distribution: Equatorial W and central Africa. Less certainly N and S of Lake Victoria.

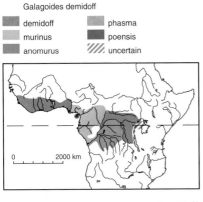

Galagoides demidoff

- ■ demidoff
- ■ murinus
- ■ anomurus
- ■ phasma
- ■ poensis
- ⧄ uncertain

0   2000 km

Demidoff's galago.

Habitat: A strong preference for dense secondary growth on forest margins, in tree-fall (chablis) zones or along road margins (where densities of over 100 animals per km² have been recorded in Gabon). Demidoff's galagos may gather in sleeping parties of up to 10 animals, huddling in dense tangles of vegetation or in rudimentary leaf nests. They live mostly within 5m of the ground.

Food: Mainly beetles, moths, caterpillars and crickets. During the dry season gum is eaten by many galagos (but only accounts for a small proportion of the year-round diet). Fruits are also eaten sporadically and may account for up to 20% of the diet. Except for a lull at about midnight, galagos forage all night and alone but utter periodic contact calls.

Behaviour: Living in overlapping home ranges of about 1ha, related ♀♀ often sleep in huddles with neighbours and their offspring. ♂ home ranges of up to 2.7ha overlap those of several ♀♀ of which one or more are monitored every night. Gestation lasts 110–114 days and new mothers avoid contact with other galagos for a week or more after giving birth. One or, less frequently, two young are born at a time. They are weaned by 2 months and are of adult size by 6 months. They can live for more than 12 years.

Adaptations: Demidoff's galagos occupy a micro-habitat occupied in similar fashion during the day by rope squirrels (*Funisciurus*). The density of the vegetation is such that it seldom necessitates long jumps and the small, deft hands and feet of the galagos are clearly best adapted to 'running' along very fine and more or less horizontal supports.

Status: Common and widespread. Not endangered.

Thomas's Galago *Galagoides thomasi*

Other names: Fr. *Galago de Thomas*. Ger. *Thomas galago*. Swah. *Komba Tomasi*.

Measurements: HB 14cm (12.3–16.6cm). T 26cm (15–24cm). Ear ave. 27mm. W 100g (55–149g).

Recognition: A small, forest galago closely resembling Demidoff's galago (until recently classed as a race of Demidoff's). The body is ashy brown with paler underparts. Fur colour is influenced by the individually variable production of yellow secretion from the skin. The face is generally paler than that of Demidoff's, the ears are somewhat larger and there are prominent eye-mask patches.

The call is a repetitive, shrill, rasping chink which increases in pitch and speed and lasts about 4 seconds. It also makes a scolding chitter reminiscent of an epauletted fruit bat (*Epomophorus*) but is not known to utter buzz calls (as Demidoff's do).

Subspecies: *G. t. thomasi* (E Zaïre, W Uganda), *G. t.* subsp. nov. (R. Niger to R. Zaïre). Distinct populations (probably new subspecies or even species) occur on the Loanda plateau in Angola, in the Shaba region of S Zaïre and possibly on Mt Marsabit in Kenya and in Togo. Central Ugandan animals are larger than those in W Uganda and have shorter tails. The W African animals differ in the pattern of their loud calls.

Distribution: Because this species has generally been lumped together with Demidoff's there is much uncertainty about its overall range. Now thought to range from Senegal and Angola to Kenya and Zambia in primary and secondary as well as seasonally dry forest.

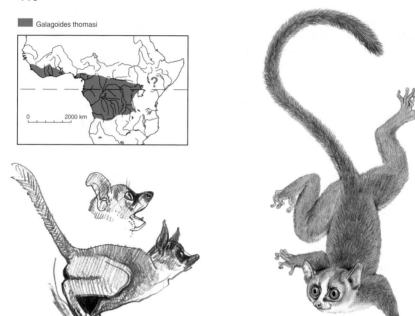

Galagoides thomasi

Habitat: A high-canopy species in primary forest in the regions shared with Demidoff's galago. Where Demidoff's is absent, as is the case in much of Uganda, Thomas's galago appears to expand its niche. In central Uganda it is found in undergrowth and in secondary forests. It is more prone to climb up and down and jump between vertical supports than *G. demidoff*. It also inhabits higher, drier and more marginal forests.

Food: Mainly insects, beetles, caterpillars, ants and termites, with some fruits and gum.

Behaviour: Thomas's galagos are thought to form localised social populations that may have little or no contact with neighbouring groups. Within an interacting group of about 12, sexes appear to be evenly balanced but the ♂♂ comprise dominant 'breeders', subordinates and peripherals. Their nests are made daily or are augmented with fresh leaves cut each morning. In Uganda they may be made at any level and the leaves cut from many tree or forest grass species. Wet-season nests (often lodged in multiple forks) tend to be larger and are used longer than dry-season nests. This is unlikely to be influenced by breeding patterns because some young are born throughout the year, although there is a pronounced peak in December–February. The newborn are heavy-headed and poorly co-ordinated but development is very rapid. The mother can make long jumps with the baby in her mouth but by 2 weeks the youngster can accompany the mother away from the nest. By the age of 1 month it urine-marks, runs about and makes clumsy jumps. Weaned at 6 weeks, it continues to harass its mother for scraps of her prey but is finding food of its own by 2 months, at which stage it begins to be repulsed by its mother. Strongly hierarchical relations between members of a local group may be mediated chemically. Bright yellow secretions emanating from bare skin on the face, ears, hands, feet and naked 'heel-spots' flow most copiously from the younger ♂♂ and from ♀♀ and their young just as they emerge from a semi-retired lactation period.

An important difference between this species and Demidoff's is its greater skill at hopping and moving through more open (and often more vertical) growth.

Status: Common in appropriate localities. Not endangered.

BATS CHIROPTERA

Over 220 million years ago the reptilian pterosaurs developed leathery webbing between their bodies and fingers and evolved powered flight. These fliers are now extinct but some living reptiles and frogs can glide.

Likewise, webs of fine skin between limbs and body have evolved independently at least seven times among living mammal groups, enabling them to glide (with variable degrees of control). Fully controllable and powered flight seems to have evolved once or twice among mammals.

Fruit bats and insect bats share a similar pattern of bare skin-webbing between elongated fingers. Both groups have also lost most of the nails of the hands but they retain nails on the toes and these have evolved into sharp hooks. In spite of the marked similarities, the two groups exhibit numerous less obvious differences which suggest that insect bats share a very ancient common ancestry with insectivores while the fruit bats may have more recent affinities with primates. Pending confirmation of separate origins (which would require two Orders) fruit bats and insect bats remain distinct Suborders.

(a) Fruit bat (Megachiroptera). Large eyes, second claw on wings, funnel-shaped ears.
(b) Insect bat (Microchiroptera). Clawless wing, complex ears and teeth.

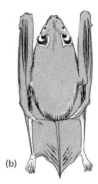

(a)   (b)

FRUIT BATS MEGACHIROPTERA, PTEROPODIDAE

Flying foxes	*Pteropus* (2 species)
Straw-coloured fruit bat	*Eidolon helvum*
Rousette bat, Egyptian fruit bat	*Rousettus aegyptiacus*
Mountain fruit bat	*Stenonycteris lanosus*
Angola fruit bat	*Lissonycteris angolensis*
Collared fruit bats	*Myonycteris* (3 species)
Epauletted fruit bats	*Epomophorus* (6 species)
Hammer bat	*Hypsignathus monstrosus*
Singing fruit bats	*Epomops* (3 species)
Dwarf epauletted fruit bats	*Micropteropus* (2 species)
Tear-drop fruit bats	*Scotonycteris* (2 species)
Golden fruit bat	*Casinycteris argynnis*
Flying calf	*Nanonycteris veldkampi*
Benguela fruit bat	*Plerotes anchietae*
Nectar bats	Macroglossinae
Nectar bat	*Megaloglossus woermanni*

Recognition: Large brown eyes in a long, lemur-like head, with funnel-shaped ears and broad, crepe-textured wings (with claws on the first and second digits) are the most notable peculiarities of fruit bats. Other features include powerful, hook-like claws on the toes, blunt, simple teeth and muscular tongues.

The repetitive chinking advertisement calls of ♂♂ are highly characteristic (but often mistaken for those of frogs). Their chattering while feeding on fruits or flowers is somewhat like that of small monkeys. Their eye-shine will reflect in torchlight but less reliably than that of carnivores or bushbabies.

Genealogy: Fossil fragments of skulls and teeth bear such a resemblance to those of lemurs that even experts have confused them. Currently the earliest fossil dates from about 30 million years ago, by which time fruit bats had achieved an essentially modern form. Long before this, tropical forests and woodlands were very extensive, probably supporting numerous species of lemuroid gliders. These would have competed to exploit scattered fruit supplies under very varied conditions and over immense periods of time. The more fragmented of woodland canopies (especially those in very windy regions) would have posed the severest challenges and would have favoured animals with greater control over their glide. It may have been under these sorts of conditions that fruit bats evolved powered flight.

Among living species, rousette bats and flying foxes are the most conservative, with a complement of 34 teeth and exceptional abilities in clambering through tangles of vegetation. Among the most derived is the nectar bat, *Megaloglossus*, which is adapted to hover and extract nectar from flowers.

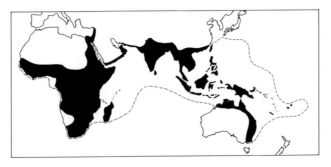

Global distribution of fruit bats.

Geography: Fruit bats probably evolved in South-East Asia where the greatest variety and range of forms still exist. In Africa there is a clear division between rainforest species (living in equatorial and mainly western regions) and savannah species preponderant in E Africa. Rousette bats, a mainly Asiatic group, span both regions, and the flying foxes, another Asiatic group, occur only on Indian Ocean islands off Africa.

Ecology: Fruit bats are entirely dependent on a year-long supply of fruits and flowers. They have large tongues, blunt, short teeth and a deeply ridged palate which, working together, crush, squeeze and rasp fruits so that only juice and pulp are swallowed. Fibres, seeds and rind are usually spat out.

Fruit bats that visit arboreal flowers for nectar sometimes act as important pollinators. Where they destroy the flowers these are usually super-abundant and adapted to such attrition. Almost all fruit bats disperse seeds by picking fruit in one tree and 'processing' or excreting its seeds in another. In cleared or open habitats fruit bats are important agents in reafforestation. Isolated trees or thickets, such as those on territaries, provide both perches for the bats and a bed protected from fire, sun and floods for the seeds which they drop.

There are several species of very common fruit bats that only live in savannah regions. This indicates how rich these habitats are in fruits but the bats are obliged to migrate or 'camp' in order to maintain a continuous fruit supply. People living in SE Africa are as familiar with the comings and goings of fruit bats as Europeans and Americans are with migrant birds.

Natural history: The need to maintain or regain contact despite seasonal shifts and nightly dispersal over wide ranges has led to the evolution of species-specific calls that carry well, even in heavily wooded country. The most audible, frequent and persistent callers are epomophorine bats (the main exclusively African radiation). In several species belonging to this group ♂ calls are synchronised with emissions of scent from the glandular pockets that contain their epaulettes. The name *Epomophorus* refers to a tuft of brilliant white fur, growing on the point of the shoulder, which opens out and dispenses scent each time the diaphragm contracts. The muscular spasms that accompany the ♂♂'s loud call evert the shoulder pouch and so allow the bat to emit simultaneous signals in each of three separate channels: sound, scent and vision.

Many African bat species form small social groups that find fruits independently; others form gigantic noisy roosts in trees or caves. Some species have developed very precise control (through prostaglandins) over the timing of their reproduction by delaying implantation of the future foetus. One species, the straw-coloured fruit bat, has now become an important research animal in the human quest for natural processes of birth control.

Sexual behaviour is initiated by ♂♂ advertising their presence and condition. The young are born blind but otherwise well developed and with disproportionately large feet. Adult ♀♀ have 'false-nipples' as well as milk-bearing teats and these form the firmest point of attachment for the infant.

Adaptations: Fruit bats have large heads which accommodate their specialised sensory organs. Because fruits are found mainly by scent and also by sight, the nasal barrel is large, as are the eyes. The bats have large brains, large tongues, extrusible lips, a wide maw and flexible cheek pouches. The ♂♂ of at least two species of singing fruit bats have even larger heads because the apparatus for amplifying sound has enlarged the nasal area and demanded resonating sacs which inflate during calling.

The cave-dwelling Egyptian rousette bat has developed an ability to fly in total darkness by clicking its tongue. The noise is only emitted to echo-locate and is unnecessary in starlight, moonlight or during the day. A rousette bat released in a blacked-out room stops clicking the instant a light is turned on and starts again the moment it is extinguished. This crude form of echo-location is the 'improvisation' of a cave-dweller and it illustrates how, through small evolutionary steps, similar solutions to similar problems could have led eventually to close resemblances between two independent mammal lineages: 'flying foxes' (Megachiroptera) and 'flying mice' (Microchiroptera).

Pemba Island flying fox.

Flying foxes *Pteropus (2 species)*

Measurements: HB 220–265mm. FA 150–161mm. W 400–650g.
Recognition: Large, dark-winged fruit bats with yellowish or red heads and 'fox-like' faces. They roost exposed in large trees, usually in large colonies and are restricted to oceanic islands.
Species: *P. comorensis* (Mafia I.), *P. voeltzkowi* (Pemba I.).
Habitat: Moist tropical islands in the Indian and Pacific Oceans.
Food: Fruits and flowers.
Status: Endangered through habitat loss.

Straw-coloured fruit bat *Eidolon helvum*

Eidolon helvum
■ Home zone
▭ Migratory range

0   2000 km

114

Measurements: HB 150–195mm. FA 110–135mm. W 250–311g.

Recognition: A large, black-winged fruit bat with pale tawny fur on the back, shoulders and underside. Roosts mainly in large groups (sometimes in tens of thousands) in open trees, often in towns or close to waterfalls or the sea. Conspicuous and high-flying, with long, tapered, but broad-based wings that carry it in strong, direct flight.

Habitat: Breeds in equatorial Africa but ranges all over sub-Saharan Africa outside the breeding season (including very dry and high montane areas). Breeding roosts are vacated 2 or 3 months after the birth season for about 3 months. Roosts are typically sited near noise (waterfalls and city streets are common choices). Noise may facilitate breeding.

Food: Fruits, flowers, nectar, pollen, buds and occasionally young leaves.

Status: Abundant and widespread. Not endangered.

Rousette bat, Egyptian fruit bat *Rousettus aegyptiacus*

Measurements: HB 1,300–1,555mm. FA 850–1,060mm. W 110–170g.

Recognition: A large, black-winged fruit bat with brownish grey fur, dark crown, rounded ears and blunt muzzle. There is only a vestige of webbing between the fifth toe and the cartilaginous heel-spur. A cave-dweller, it is often very vocal.

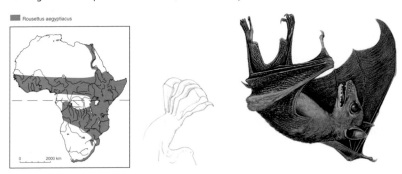

■ Rousettus aegyptiacus

Habitat: Sub-Saharan Africa, E Mediterranean and S Arabia. From its cave roosts (where it often gathers in many thousands) it flies long distances to sources of fruits in a wide range of habitats.

Food: Fruits, flowers, nectar and pollen; occasionally leaves and buds.

Status: Widespread and common. Not endangered.

Mountain fruit bat *Stenonycteris lanosus*

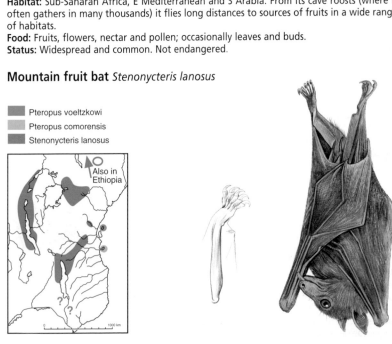

■ Pteropus voeltzkowi
■ Pteropus comorensis
■ Stenonycteris lanosus

Also in Ethiopia

Measurements: HB 1,300–1,550mm. FA 850–950mm. W 120–165g.
Recognition: A large fruit bat with black wings, shaggy, dark grey fur, pointed ears and a long but blunt-ended muzzle. A cave-dweller in montane areas. Roosts in smaller numbers than the Egyptian fruit bat.
Habitat: Montane forest areas in E Africa, Ethiopia and Madagascar.
Food: Fruits, nectar and pollen.
Status: Locally abundant but very sparsely distributed. Dependence on caves may require special protection for roosting sites.

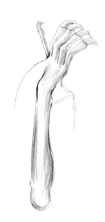

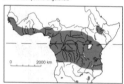
Lissonycteris angolensis

Angola fruit bat *Lissonycteris angolensis*

Measurements: HB 105–135mm. FA 65–91mm. W 65–91g.
Recognition: A plain brown fruit bat with oval ears and a pointed nose at the end of a tapered muzzle. The patagium is attached to the second toe. Adult ♂♂ have a 'collar' of sticky hair. Roosts singly or in small groups in low, thick vegetation, in hollow trees or near the mouths of caves, and is quiet and cryptic.
Habitat: Tropical Africa, mainly in forests at low and higher altitudes.
Food: Fruits and flowers.
Status: Common and widespread. Not endangered.

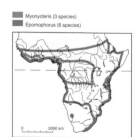
Myonycteris (3 species)
Epomophorus (6 species)

Collared fruit bats *Myonycteris* (3 species)

Measurements: FA 55–70mm. W 35–80g.
Recognition: Brown or buff fruit bat with broad shoulder ruffs, or 'collars', in ♂♂. Pointed ears resemble those of the Angolan fruit bat but are smaller. Roost singly or in small groups in dense, low vegetation.
Species: *M. torquata* (Upper Guinea to Uganda), *M. relicta* (Indian Ocean, coastal forests, Kenya, Tanzania), *M. brachycephala* (São Tomé and Principe Is.).

Habitat: In or close to rainforest, including savannah/forest mosaics where the forest has become vestigial.
Food: Fruits and nectar.
Status: Two species rare and localised.

Epauletted fruit bats *Epomophorus* (6 species)

Measurements: FA 54–90mm. W 40–120g.
Recognition: Variably tinted, brown fruit bats of differing sizes. All have tufts of white fur at the base of the ears. ♂♂ have white 'epaulettes' on their shoulders. Utter chinking, frog-like calls.

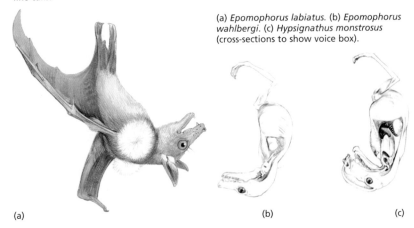

(a) *Epomophorus labiatus.* (b) *Epomophorus wahlbergi.* (c) *Hypsignathus monstrosus* (cross-sections to show voice box).

(a)   (b)   (c)

Species: *E. gambianus* (Senegal to Ethiopia and South Africa), *E. labiatus* (Nigeria to Ethiopia to Malawi), *E. minimus* (Ethiopia to Tanzania), *E. angolensis* (Namibia and Angola), *E. grandis* (Zaïre mouth region), *E. wahlbergi* (E and central Africa to Cameroon).
Habitat: Mainly savannahs, woodlands and forest mosaics. Some species occur in main forest zones.
Food: Fruits, flowers, nectar, pollen.
Status: Most species are common and widespread, but status is generally unknown.

Hammer bat *Hypsignathus monstrosus*

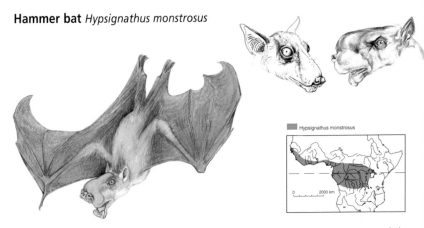

Hypsignathus monstrosus

0   2000 km

Measurements: HB 195–200mm (♀), 220–275mm (♂). FA 118–128mm (♀), 125–137mm (♂). W 250g (218–377g) (♀), 425g (228–450g) (♂).

Recognition: The largest continental African fruit bat, with brown fur and membranes and a yellowish brown skin colour on the muzzle, ears and digits. ♂♂ are almost twice the weight of ♀♀ and have inflatable sacs over the raised ridge of the nose and on each side of the neck. The ♂'s lips are also modified to control sound and form a sort of crenellated rhinarium, or 'lip-disc'. Both sexes have tubular nostrils and white tufts at the base of the ears. ♂♂ make a very loud, explosive, blaring honk that only resembles other epomophorine loud calls from a distance. The call carries several kilometres on a still night.

Distribution: Throughout the lowland forest zone from Senegal to W Uganda. Seasonal excursions take individuals or small groups far beyond these limits (both north and south) and as far afield as W Kenya.

Habitat: Roosts at low levels in heavily shaded forests of almost all types, including mangroves and swamp forest but not montane areas. Some of its preferred foods are typical of secondary growth. Seasonal movements are poorly known and are probably influenced by fruiting patterns (and perhaps also by climate as they are sensitive to drops in temperature and stop calling in cool weather).

Food: Soft fruits, especially wild figs and the fruit of cabbage trees or forest fever trees (*Anthocleista*). ♂♂ have been known to fly up to 10km in search of concentrations of ripe fruits while ♀♀ forage within a much more localised area (often on fruits of poorer quality).

Behaviour: ♀♀ and their young form temporary associations of up to 20 animals but individuals move frequently and do not appear to form lasting attachments. The loud calls of adult ♂♂s serve as acoustic beacons. Competitive assemblies of calling ♂♂, or 'leks', provide a point of reference for all hammer bats within an 8–10km radius and attract ♀♀, who make frequent visits before closing in on a particular ♂. Presumably the cumulative noise at the centre of the 'choir', as well as the volume and timbre of individual singers, influences the ♀♀'s choice. In the equatorial bimodal climate there are two mating peaks that coincide with warm dry weather, at which time both sexes converge on the 'leks'. Gestation lasts 4 months and ♀♀ often mate with an infant attached to them.

Adaptations: ♂ hammer bats might almost be described as flying loudspeakers, so extensive is the structural modification of their organs towards production and resonance of noise. The larynx has displaced heart, lungs and diaphragm to fill the entire chest with an enormous curved structure like a tuba. With the greatest mating success going to powerful singers near the centre of a 'choir', there has been strong sexual selection for large competitive singers.

Status: Locally common.

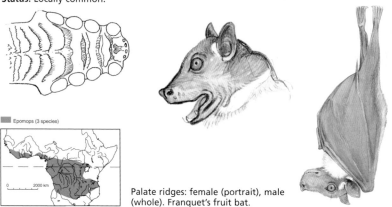

Epomops (3 species)

Palate ridges: female (portrait), male (whole). Franquet's fruit bat.

Singing fruit bats *Epomops* (3 species)

Measurements: FA 80–100mm. W 65–158g.

Recognition: Medium-sized brown fruit bats with white tufts at the base of the ears and broad, blunt muzzles. Vocalisations very loud and 'musical'.

Species: *E. franqueti* (Liberia to Uganda and Angola), *E. buettikoferi* (Guinea to Nigeria), *E. dobsoni* (Angola to Tanzania and Malawi).

Habitat: Forests and forest-woodland mosaics.

Food: Fruits and nectar.

Status: *E. franqueti* is common and widespread. Other species are insufficiently known.

118

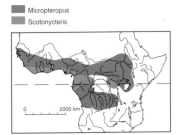
Micropteropus
Scotonycteris

(a) Dwarf epauletted fruit bat.
(b) Tear-drop fruit bat.

(a)　　　　　　　　　　　　　　　　　　　　(b)

Dwarf epauletted fruit bats *Micropteropus* (2 species)

Measurements: FA 480–600mm. W 25–40g.
Recognition: Small tawny fruit bats with white tufts at the base of the ears and white 'epaulettes' on adult ♂♂. The short muzzle has prominent nostrils. ♂♂ make a shrill, chinking call which they repeat monotonously. Roost singly or in small groups in shady vegetation.
Species: *M. pusillus* (encircles forest blocks), *M. intermedius* (Angola and Zaïre).
Habitat: Woodlands, savannahs and forest mosaics outside the main lowland forest blocks.
Food: Fruits, nectar and pollen.
Status: *M. pusillus*, common and widespread. *M. intermedius*, status not known.

Tear-drop fruit bats *Scotonycteris* (2 species)

Measurements: FA 47–78mm. W est. 35–60g.
Recognition: Prominent, tear-like white spots occur on either side of the eyes and others over the upper lip. Fur is variably tinted and wings are dark brown. Roost singly in vegetation.
Species: *S. ophiodon* (Liberia to R. Zaïre west): FA 74-78mm. *S. zenkeri* (Liberia to E Zaïre): FA 47-53mm.
Habitat: Lowland rainforests of W and C Africa; mostly found at lowest levels in undergrowth.
Food: Fruits and flowers. Fruits are possibly gathered from the forest floor.
Status: Both species are rare and little known.

Golden fruit bat *Casinycteris argynnis*

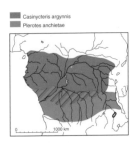
Casinycteris argynnis
Plerotes anchietae

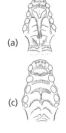

(a)　　　　　　(b)

(c)　　　　　　(d)

Palate ridges in (a) dwarf, (b) golden, (c) collared and (d) tear-drop fruit bats.

Measurements: HB 90–95mm. FA 50–63mm. W 26–33g.

Recognition: A golden-coloured fruit bat with bold white margins to the mouth, eye and ear base. The hard palate is unlike other fruit bats in not extending back behind the tooth row, implying that the fruit-squeezing action of the tongue and palate is modified in this species. Roosts singly or in pairs.
Habitat: Known from the main lowland forest block between Cameroon and E Zaïre. Recorded from low dense undergrowth.
Food: Specialised feeding habits, in which fruits are processed mainly at the front of the mouth, would seem likely.
Status: Currently one of the least known of African fruit bats.

Flying calf *Nanonycteris veldkampi*

Measurements: HB 65–75mm. FA 45–50mm. W est. 30g.
Recognition: Very small fawn-brown fruit bat with a slender muzzle and large eyes. Thick, soft fur covers the back and legs and extends onto the membranes. There is a short white 'moustache' and white tufts of fur at the base of the ears. ♂♂ have white 'epaulettes'. May congregate at feeding sites.
Habitat: Senegal to E Zaïre in lowland rainforest and forest mosaics.
Food: Nectar and pollen.
Status: Rarely seen and little known.

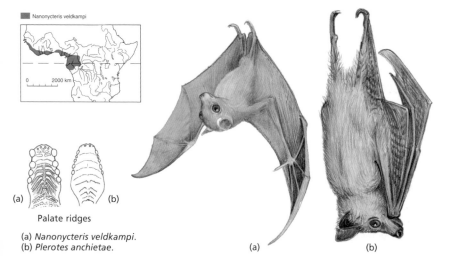

Nanonycteris veldkampi

0   2000 km

Palate ridges

(a) *Nanonycteris veldkampi*.
(b) *Plerotes anchietae*.

(a)

(b)

Benguela fruit bat *Plerotes anchietae*

Measurements: HB 87mm. FA 48–53mm. W est. 38g.
Recognition: A greyish brown fruit bat with rather long, crinkled fur on the lower back and legs. There are white spots at the base of the ears and it lacks a cartilaginous spur on the heel. The muzzle is unusually broad but flat and shallow with very rudimentary teeth. Special sound-amplifying pouches around the eyes of ♂♂ suggest an unusual loud call.
Habitat: Southern margins of the Zaïre basin between the Atlantic and L. Tanganyika. Probably forest mosaics and riverine strips.
Food: Nectar and pollen.
Status: One of the least known of African fruit bats.

NECTAR BATS MACROGLOSSINAE

Nectar bat	Megaloglossus woermanni

This subfamily is strictly limited to the tropical forest areas of the Old World. Six genera are known from Australia and South-East Asia, where the group probably originated.

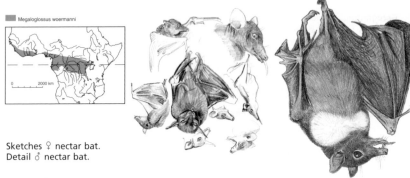

Megaloglossus woermanni

Sketches ♀ nectar bat.
Detail ♂ nectar bat.

Nectar bat *Megaloglossus woermanni*

Measurements: HB 64–82mm. FA 40–46.5mm. W 12–20g.
Recognition: A very small fruit bat with an extremely fine-pointed muzzle and a very long, thin, brush-textured tongue. The soft pale fur appears to be 'smoked' with brown or sepia. ♂ ♂ have a ruff of stiff, pure white hair, apparently growing from a glandular patch. It is apparently not very vocal. Two races have been described.
Habitat: Main forest blocks from Guinea to Uganda. Roosts in dense forest foliage and has been caught under banana fronds and in huts or houses within the forest. Has been netted flying along forest tracks bordered by flowering trees (*Spathodea*).
Food: Nectar.
Status: Very widely distributed and probably not endangered.

INSECT BATS MICROCHIROPTERA

Mouse-tailed bats	Rhinopomatidae
Sheath-tailed bats	Emballonuridae
Slit-faced bats	Nycteridae
Large-winged bats	Megadermatidae
Horseshoe bats	Rhinolophinae
Leaf-nosed bats	Hipposiderinae
Vesper bats	Vespertilionidae
Free-tailed bats	Molossidae

Recognition: The most obvious features of insect bats are their small eyes, the absence of a claw on the second digit (which is closely tied to the third) and complex ears with irregular margins. An invisible but important distinction is their use of high-frequency echo-location to navigate, hunt prey and communicate. The range of forms and global distribution is greater than any other order of mammals, a diversity that relates both to the mobility and the great age of this group. Seven or eight families occur in Africa.

As the name implies, the majority are small animals with forearm lengths (the conventional measure of relative size) ranging from 26 to 121mm. Tooth numbers vary between 26 and 38. Each family represents a different mosaic of conservative and derived characteristics; thus the slit-faced bats have relatively 'primitive' low-performance but manoeuvrable wings and very evolved (long and thin) hindlimbs whereas the free-tailed bats have 'primitive' muscular legs and very advanced, high-performance wings.

Genealogy: For arboreal insectivores the primary incentive to launch their small bodies into 'flying leaps' was likely to have been the pursuit of prey. A high proportion of living insect bats catch prey in their 'hands', or rather in the membranes stretching from or between their fingers and tails, before a quick transfer to the mouth. This is probably the original capture technique of the earliest insect bats, which evolved some 70 million to 100 million years ago. Both bats and insectivores produce ultrasound but insect bats have used it to develop complex forms of echo-location. Scientists, using bat-detecting equipment and ultrasound analysers, have identified and classified insect bat families and species according to their ultrasound signatures. Some of the most sophisticated echo-locators, such as the horseshoe bats, are already clearly recognisable in fossils dating back about 40 million years, which indicates that differentiation of specialised hunting techniques began very early on.

Geography: Insect bats have a world-wide distribution and many species (especially vesper bats) are able to hibernate, thus benefiting from the rich seasonal insect fauna of cool temperate regions. A few species migrate (but mostly within continental boundaries). Several groups have close relatives which occur in Africa, S Asia and Australia. One of these is a migrant and others, such as free-tailed bats, are also strong, long-distance fliers. Some bats, such as the strictly forest-dwelling horseshoe and leaf-nosed species appear to have diverged many millions of years ago but they occupy rather stable ecological niches and therefore resemble each other because they have remained very conservative.

Ecology: All major terrestrial habitats from desert to moist rainforest. Many species are exclusively equatorial and do not tolerate cold. Some of these are effectively limited to sea-level altitudes. Others tolerate cold montane environments. The shelters that bats exploit are very varied and range from individual roosts in vegetation or in crevices to mass roosts in caves or mines. Some species space themselves while roosting, others hang in clusters, yet others pack together in tight wedges. As they are reluctant to fly during the day insect bats are best observed while at rest in their day-roosts.

Invertebrates of various kinds (mostly insects) are caught by a variety of different techniques in different species (a bat's type of echo-location being a central aspect of its technique). Some catch fast-flying insects, others catch slow, fluttering ones, while others pluck invertebrates from vegetation or off the ground. Many species forage down valley or shoreline flyways and a few are known to ambush their prey from habitually used vantage points.

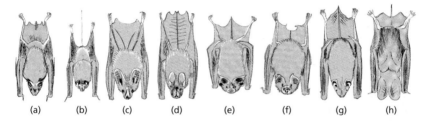

Bat families: (a) Sheath-tailed, (b) Mouse-tailed, (c) Large winged, (d) Slit-faced, (e) Horseshoe, (f) Leaf-nosed, (g) Vesper, (h) Free-tailed.

Natural history: Bat societies include many permutations of aggregations, nursery groups, age groups, all-♂, all-♀ and mixed crowds, stable pairs and solitary mothers with offspring. Most species have pungent glands which fluctuate in size and appear to play a role in reproductive behaviour in most instances. Some species smear their roost with scent but most spread it by rubbing or scratching themselves.

Courtship may involve ritualised postures, flights, chases accompanied by special calls and the production and laying of scent trails. Copulation takes place in the roost or on a perch. Births are often very seasonal and the young may be carried continuously or 'parked' in nurseries or on their own. They mature very rapidly, nourished by a rich, concentrated milk. Among insect bats various forms of delayed gestation strategies can be found which appear to help achieve optimal reproductive rates. These include sperm storage, delayed ovulation, delayed fertilisation and delayed implantation of an arrested 'foetus', or blastocyst.

Many insect bat species live for a very long time (25 years has been recorded). Their most important predator is the bat hawk (*Machaerhamphus*), while some eagle owls and snakes are less frequent and less specialised predators of bats. Hornbills, birds of prey and primates are all known to catch roosting bats

Adaptations: The precise structure of wings, teeth, nose, ears, eyes and echo-location all have a direct bearing on the detection and capture of prey. Thus beetle-eaters have massive teeth and jaws while mosquito- and moth-eaters have smaller ones. Crepuscular hunters tend to have large eyes whereas miniature gnat-eaters have the smallest, fur-blinkered eyes. Slow flyers, restricted to dense forests or swamps, have short, broad wings while fast, open-air hunters have long, narrow, 'high-ratio' wings that rely on fast air speeds and a low weight-loading. At least one family (the mouse-tailed bats) combines a long, broad membrane between body and wrist with short fingers and outer membrane (the most 'primitive' arrangement).

A most significant insect-bat division is between 'shouters' and 'hummers'. The former call through the mouth and have mouse-like faces. The latter, in contrast, possess nose-leaves of various shapes and emit 'beams' of sound through the nostrils. Nasal signals have the advantage that they do not interfere with feeding and drinking. In general nasal signallers hang passively from hooked toes on long legs with vestigial muscles whereas many simple-nosed insect bats have retained more versatile legs. The various elaborate nose and ear structures displayed by nasal signallers serve to help control emission and reception of sounds.

Two major types of sonar signals can be identified. In the first instance the major component of the signal has a constant frequency so that these are termed CF signals. In the second instance the frequency is modulated and these are called FM signals. Low frequencies and longer pulses below about 50kHz are mostly emitted by fast fliers in the open air. Low-intensity FM signals at about 100kHz allow slow-flying bats to detect slow-moving prey in an environment full of obstacles.

Insect bats display a variety of anatomical, physiological and behavioural adaptations that are independent of those required for nocturnal flying and hunting. For example, flattened skulls, folding ears and peculiar sensory hairs are typical of crevice-dwellers.

Bats often roost in houses or caves where they may come into close contact with people. The bed-bug (*Cimex*) is a bat parasite which has probably taken to humans as a secondary host. Many species of mites, ticks, flies and fleas are unique to particular bat hosts, as are many very localised viruses. Spores of fungi, such as *Histoplasma*, can proliferate in bat guano and can cause illness in humans when inhaled. Insect bats play an enormously important role in controlling insect pests. There are caves in Africa which shelter millions of bats and their denizens capture many tonnes of insects nightly. A single such cave can yield thousands of tonnes of phosphate-rich guano.

Status: Virtually unknown for most insect bats, although several species are very localised and undoubtedly rare.

MOUSE-TAILED BATS RHINOPOMATIDAE

Mouse-tailed bats	*Rhinopoma* (2 species)

Recognition: These bats have extremely slender limbs, a whip-like tail and a fat deposit at the root of the tail. In many respects this is the most primitive family of insect bats. Mouse-tails have the shortest fingers, relative to the forearm, of any bats and they are poor fliers which tire quickly. However, their modest flying abilities come with a set of physiological adaptations which allow them to live in very hot, arid, desert regions.

Mouse-tailed bats *Rhinopoma* (2 species)

Measurements: HB 50–63mm. T 48–68mm. FA 50–60mm. W est. 10–12g.

Recognition: Sandy-coloured bats with long, wispy tails and valvular nostrils set in a small, pad-like nose-leaf. A membrane joins the large, rhomboid ears above the large, prominent black eyes. There are fat deposits around the base of the tail and hindlimbs. At rest the forearm is strikingly long and thin.

Species: *R. hardwickei* (mainly deserts from Morocco to Burma), *R. microphyllum* (mainly subdeserts from Senegal to South-East Asia).

Habitat: Desert and subdesert. Has an unusual tolerance for low humidity, high temperatures and relatively unprotected shelters, such as rock walls, houses, wells, tombs and caves. Lives in small, scattered groups of mixed sexes but all-♂ and all-♀ groups are also known.

Food: The bats hunt small desert insects and beetles by flying in undulating swoops and glides at 5–10m. Fat deposits fluctuate, implying seasonal shortages of food.

Status: Widespread desert species.

SHEATH-TAILED BATS EMBALLONURIDAE

African sheath-tailed bat	*Coleura afra*
Tomb bats	*Taphozous* (5 species)
Black hawk bat	*Saccolaimus peli*

Recognition: Simple-nosed bats most easily identified by the half-sheathing of their tail within the interfemoral membrane. All species have large eyes and an alert demeanour and possess strong-smelling glands, usually enclosed in a throat sac. Throat scents are wafted at conspecifics during courtship rituals that include static wing-fanning. They are considered to be among the more primitive of insect bats but are very successful, ranging right around the world in the tropics and subtropics.

African Sheath-tailed bat *Coleura afra*
Measurements: HB 52–66mm. FA 45–55mm. W est. 6.5g.
Recognition: A small sooty-brown bat with exaggerated head-up posture and unusually vertical tail. The ear tragus has a pimple on the outer edge. The nostrils overhang the lower jaw.
Habitat: Ranges through savannahs and woodlands in Africa and Arabia. Roosts in caves, houses and on rocky outcrops, especially close to open water.
Food: Very small insects which may occasion seasonal migrations.
Status: An extremely sensitive species which dies rapidly after capture. Widespread but numbers and presence are erratic in any one locality.

Tomb bats *Taphozous* (5 species)
Measurements: HB 70–93mm. FA 58–70mm. W 20–30g.
Recognition: Typical sheath-tailed bats with a skin pocket below the wrist (which can produce a whirring sound) and a concavity behind the swollen, tubular muzzle. Tomb bats are alert while roosting but unwilling to fly if disturbed and will scurry sideways along vertical walls or trunks. They roost in spaced groupings and mark their stations with greasy smears from the throat sacs.
Species: *T. mauritianus* (sub-Saharan Africa and Indian Ocean islands), *T. perforatus* (Africa, NW India), *T. nudiventris* (Sahelian and E Africa to Burma), *T. hildegardeae* (E Africa), *T. hamiltoni* (upper Nile valley, Chad).

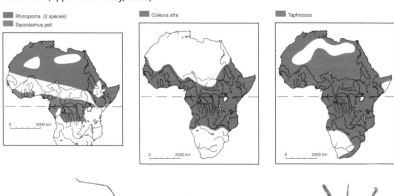

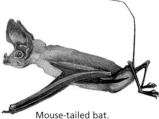
Mouse-tailed bat.

African sheath-tailed bat.

Mauritian tomb bat.

Black hawk bat.

Habitat: From arid to wooded habitats in subtropical Africa and S Asia. Tomb bats acquired their name as a result of their favouring roosting sites among the ancient monuments of Egypt. They may roost singly or in dense colonies.
Food: Mainly moths hunted along habitual flight-paths.
Status: This genus includes widely distributed and more localised species.

Black hawk bat *Saccolaimus peli*

Measurements: HB 110–157mm. FA 84–97mm. W 92–105g.
Recognition: A very large black bat with broad, flat head and shoulders, large eyes, small ears and short, greasy fur. Both sexes have a throat sac. Wings are pointed and flight is falcon-like. Often visible over forest clearings just before nightfall.
Habitat: Rainforests from Sierra Leone to W Kenya.
Food: Beetles and other high-flying insects caught above the canopy and along the margins of high forest. Very active and acrobatic while feeding, making an audible 'chuwee' call.
Status: A conspicuous rainforest species, widely distributed but apparently at low densities.

SLIT-FACED BATS NYCTERIDAE

Slit-faced bats	*Nycteris* (10 species)

Recognition: Immediately recognisable by their long ears and the foliated trench which runs from the forehead to the nostrils and upper lip. The tail terminates in a cartilaginous T- or Y-shape that is unique to this group. These bats are slow foragers, with a moth-like flight
Habitat: All but the driest and most open habitats of Africa.

Slit-faced bats *Nycteris* (10 species)

Measurements: FA 32–66mm. W 5–36g.
Recognition: Large-eared, broad-winged bats with long, silky fur and a long tail fully enclosed in membrane with a T- or Y-shaped tip. The nose trench, or slit, is surrounded by a series of lobes and flanges, which probably modulate and control their high-frequency 'whispers'. Prefer to roost in cool, dark and, ideally, moist retreats within caves, holes, hollow trees, buildings or culverts but some species will tolerate dense, dark foliage or tangled, shady thickets (notably on termitaries). Roost individually or in groups of up to many thousands. Flight is very acrobatic; if they meet an obstacle in dense vegetation they momentarily perch before taking off again.
Species: *N. arge, N. gambiensis, N. grandis, N. hispida, N. intermedia, N. macrotis, N. major, N. nana, N. thebaica, N. woodi.*
Habitat: Found in a wide range of vegetation types but forage at low levels in areas of dense undergrowth, reeds, thickets, mangroves, etc., all over Africa except open desert.
Food: Crickets, grasshoppers, moths, flies, cicadas, flying termites. Various larger insects, spiders and scorpions are plucked off vegetation, the ground, or caught in flight. Slit-faced bats emerge late and retire early.
Status: All species are widely distributed in both forest and other ecotypes.

LARGE-WINGED BATS MEGADERMATIDAE

Heart-nosed bat	*Cardioderma cor*
Yellow-winged bat	*Lavia frons*

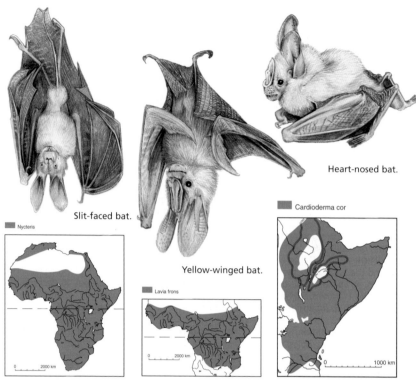

Heart-nosed bat.

Slit-faced bat.

Cardioderma cor

Nycteris

Yellow-winged bat.

Lavia frons

0 __ 2000 km

0 __ 2000 km

0 __ 1000 km

Recognition: Broad-winged, large-eared, large-headed bats with ornate nose-leaves, thin, strut-like legs and long, silky fur. Restricted to Old World tropics and Australasia, these are large-eyed bats that often emerge before dark to hunt invertebrates from perches where they may be relatively conspicuous.

Heart-nosed bat *Cardioderma cor*

Measurements: HB 70–77mm. FA 54–59mm. W 21–35g.
Recognition: Relatively large bat with long, pale fur and joined ears bearing sharp, two-pointed ear tragi. The prominent muzzle is surrounded by a heart-shaped nose-leaf.
Habitat: Restricted to NE Africa from Eritrea to central Tanzania. The Rift Valley, dry *Acacia* bush and the coastal littoral are preferred habitats. Uses houses for shelter but is shy and prefers dry caves. Roosts in groups of 3–100 or more.
Food: Invertebrates and, more occasionally, vertebrates (including other bat species), hunted from a limited number of lookout posts on the lower, outer margins of trees or bushes. After forays, prey is brought back to be eaten at the perch or even to the day-time shelter where debris collects below the roost.
Status: Although locally common this is a sparsely and irregularly distributed species that might be vulnerable to habitat change.

Yellow-winged bat *Lavia frons*

Measurements: HB 63–83mm. FA 55–64mm. W 28–36g.
Recognition: Very colourful bat with large black eyes, pale blue-grey fur and bright yellow-orange membranes and ears. The wings are exceptionally broad and the ears are long, with a spiky tragus. The elongated nose-leaf also encloses a pointed sella, or spike, that runs down its centre.Often to be seen roosting in light shade in large savannah trees (especially *Euphorbia* in the dry season). It makes a bird-like contact call.
Habitat: Low-lying savannahs, open woodlands and narrow forest galleries in tropical Africa.
Food: Invertebrates, occasionally vertebrates; known to chase other bat species.
Status: A widespread and common species, apparently able to startle potential predators with its brilliant colouring. When hanging quite still it resembles a dead leaf.

HORSESHOE BATS RHINOLOPHINAE

These bats belong to a widely distributed group in tropical and temperate regions of the Old World. Elaborate nose-leaves and broad, leaf-shaped ears are directed towards a very effective type of CF sonar. Some phalanges of the fingers are reduced and the group is unique in having a rigid ring at the top of the chest formed by the fusion of the first ribs and first dorsal vertebra. These are very ancient but highly evolved and specialised bats.

Horseshoe bats *Rhinolophus* (21 species)

Measurements: FA 38–68mm.
Recognition: The name 'horseshoe' derives from a flat leaf that loops round the front of the nostrils. Behind it and above the eyes is the 'lancet', a pointed leaf with complex folds or pockets along its sides. Emerging from the midline of the nostrils is a sella, which varies in shape from species to species and clearly serves to control the sound emitted from beneath it. The sella is supported by a thin wall in the midline plane, known as the 'connecting process'. All horseshoe bats have nose-leaves of a similar structure but the proportions and shapes of their component parts are distinctive in each species and provide a convenient aid to identification. All species hang by their hindlegs when at rest. The wings are wrapped around the body while the tail is folded back over the rump.
Species: *R. adami, R. alcyone, R. blasii, R. capensis, R. clivosus, R. darlingi, R. deckenii, R. denti, R. eloquens, R. euryale, R. ferrumequinum, R. fumigatus, R. guineensis, R. hildebrandti, R. hipposideros, R. landeri, R. maclaudi, R. mehelyi, R. silvestris, R. simulator, R. swinnyi.*
Habitat: All vegetation types. Horseshoe bats generally prefer to hunt in sheltered areas and roost in caves, holes, buildings, hollow trees. Temperate species choose warm roosts when active but retreat to cool, damp sites when torpid. Many of the species listed above are habitat-specific sibling species belonging to a few major horseshoe-bat subdivisions.
Food: Varies from species to species. Mosquitoes, moths, beetles, spiders and scorpions are caught in flight, by foraging at low levels or by ambush on the ground.
Status: The life histories of most species are virtually unknown.

LEAF-NOSED BATS HIPPOSIDERINAE

Leaf-nosed bats	*Hipposideros* (13 species)
Trident leaf-nosed bats	*Asellia* (2 species)
Percival's trident bat	*Cloeotis percivali*
Persian leaf-nosed bat	*Triaenops persicus*

Recognition: Close relatives of the horseshoe bats but with more diverse nose-leaves. The leaf structures also differ. Unlike the horseshoe bats they have remained predominantly tropical. Widely separated representatives live in South-East Asian and African forests, implying ancient connections.

Leaf-nosed bats *Hipposideros* (13 species)

Measurements: FA 28–116mm.
Recognition: A very diverse group of bats with leaf-shaped ears and less elevated nose-leaves than horseshoe bats. Many have broad, scroll-like folds and flanges above the eyes and the sides of the muzzle often bear a series of very shallow lappets 'stacked' outside the rim of the main 'horseshoe' that surrounds the nostrils. The eyes are small but functional and leaf-nosed bats in a well-lit roost will watch an intruder attentively in addition to emitting bursts of ultrasound. They prefer to hang free from the ceilings of caves or house lofts, or in tree hollows. In some species ♂♂ roost alone for much of the year; others form small parties, yet others congregate in many thousands.
Species: *H. abae, H. beatus, H. caffer, H. ruber, H. cyclops, H. camerunensis, H. commersoni, H. curtus, H. fuliginosus, H. jonesi, H. lamottei, H. marisae, H. megalotis.*
Habitat: Forests, woodlands and savannahs at low and medium altitudes. Some species (*H. cyclops, H. camerunensis, H. abae*) are strictly forest bats. *H. megalotis* is a dry upland species while *H. caffer/H. ruber* are forest-/non-forest-adapted sibling species.

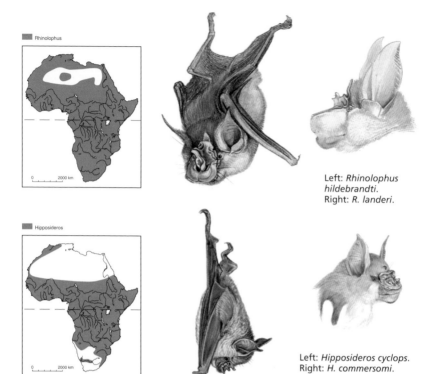

Rhinolophus

0 — 2000 km

Hipposideros

0 — 2000 km

Left: *Rhinolophus hildebrandti*.
Right: *R. landeri*.

Left: *Hipposideros cyclops*.
Right: *H. commersomi*.

Food: Diverse sizes and habitats are matched by diverse feeding habits. Beetles, cicadas, termites, moths, crickets, cockroaches, ants and woodlice have been recorded for this group. Prey is caught in flight or is snatched off leaves or litter by quartering in slow, wavering flight close to the ground.

Status: The big-eared leaf-nosed bat (*H. megalotis*) is known to be very rare and localised. Most other species have wide ranges. Intensive logging may locally eradicate some forest species by eliminating the large hollow trees in which the bats roost.

Trident leaf-nosed bats *Asellia* (2 species)

Measurements: HB 50–62mm. FA 45–60mm.

Recognition: A small pale bat with broad, pointed ears and a squat nose-leaf with three very blunt protuberances on its posterior margin. These surmount six 'cells', or pockets, that form the crenellated upper margin of the nose-leaf. The skull and back bone are also unique.

Species: *A. tridens* (Sahara to Pakistan), *A. patrizii* (S Red Sea).

Habitat: Deserts and Sahelian subdeserts, roosting in dark ruins, wells and caves, often in many hundreds.

Food: Desert insects and scorpions.

Status: Poorly known.

Percival's trident bat *Cloeotis percivali*

Measurements: HB 33–50mm. FA 30–36mm. W est. 4–6g.

Recognition: A very small, pale bat with yellowish, orange and buff morphs. Underside is pale off-white. Ears are very small and rounded. Wings are dark. The nose-leaf has three prominent points arising from the posterior margin of the nose-leaf.

Habitat: Patchily distributed in SE Africa, often coastal, mainly in low-lying woodlands and savannahs. Roosts in the darkest recesses of caves and mines. Forms dense clusters, sometimes in small groups, sometimes in colonies of several hundred.

Food: Small insects.

Status: Poorly known.

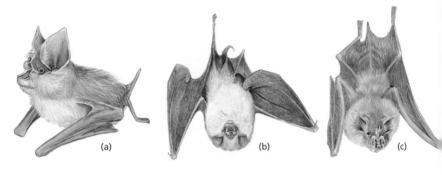

(a) Trident leaf-nosed bat. (b) Percival's trident bat. (c) Persian leaf-nosed bat.

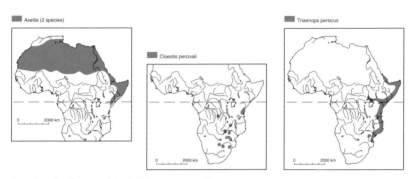

Persian leaf-nosed bat *Triaenops persicus*

Measurements: HB 50–57mm. FA 50–55mm. W 8–15g.

Recognition: A compact leaf-nosed bat with rounded ears, half buried in fur, with short projecting tips. The back of the nose-leaf has three spear-shaped leaves. A small fourth spear projects from the centre of the nose-leaf. Accessory leaflets, or 'scrolls,' surround the large, deepset nostrils. The long, narrow head is disguised by long, dense fur which may be grey, brown or a rich russet red. Wings are dark brown. Often found in large colonies where individuals hang close together but avoid actual contact.

Habitat: A mainly coastal species of NW Indian Ocean littoral but ranges up large river valleys inland to uplands.

Food: Small insects caught in slow, moth-like flight.

Status: Widely distributed and locally abundant.

VESPER BATS VESPERTILIONIDAE

Hairy bats	*Myotis* (12 species)
Woolly bats	*Kerivoula* (8 species)
Barbastelle bats	*Barbastella* (2 species)
Butterfly bats	*Chalinolobus* (syn. *Glauconycteris*) (9 species)
Serotine bats	*Eptesicus* (13 species)
Tropical long-eared bats	*Laephotis* (4 species)
Moloney's flat-headed bat	*Mimetillus moloneyi*
Noctules	*Nyctalus* (3 species)
Schlieffen's twilight bat	*Nycticeius schlieffeni*
Hempriche's long-eared bat	*Otonycteris hemprichii*
Pipistrelles	*Pipistrellus* (16 species)
Northern long-eared bat	*Plecotus austriacus*
Evening bats	*Scotoecus* (2 species)
House bats	*Scotophilus* (5 species)
Long-fingered bats	Miniopterus (4 species)

Recognition: A very large and successful family of simple-nosed bats. At a casual glance most vesper bats look bewilderingly alike. Dental patterns and skull structures must be examined in order to distinguish some genera and species. The most obvious characteristics of this family are small eyes, separate ears, with noticeable tragi, and long tails enclosed in membrane. Most species have glands on the muzzle (which may swell and shrink in size).

Primitive bat dentition is characterised by 38 teeth (2-1-3-3:3-1-3-3) set in a long, slender snout. This formula occurs in the modern hairy bats, *Myotis*. Pipistrelles and twilight bats are thought to have derived from a *Myotis*-like stem while woolly bats and long-fingered bats branched off at a very early stage. In the more advanced genera faces are shorter and the teeth have become reduced in number. The family has a world-wide distribution and occupies all but the very coldest regions and habitats.

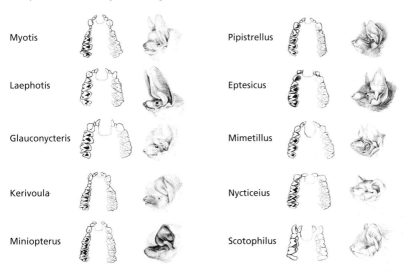

Myotis   Pipistrellus

Laephotis   Eptesicus

Glauconycteris   Mimetillus

Kerivoula   Nycticeius

Miniopterus   Scotophilus

Hairy bats *Myotis* (12 species)

Measurements: FA 31–40mm.
Recognition: Small bats with long, hairy muzzles and narrow ears with spike-shaped tragi. The numerous teeth have sharp, pointed cusps (see key for tooth formula). They seldom roost in houses, preferring hollow trees, deep caves or vegetation.
Species: *M. blythii, M. bocagei, M. capaccinii, M. emarginatus, M. lesueuri, M. morrisi, M. mystacinus, M. nattereri, M. scotti, M. seabrai, M. tricolor, M. welwitschii.*
Habitat: A wide range of vegetation types and altitudes. Some species may be scattered, roosting singly or in small groups, while others form larger colonies.
Food: Small insects caught in slow flight within 5m of the ground.
Status: Many species are very poorly known.

Myotis

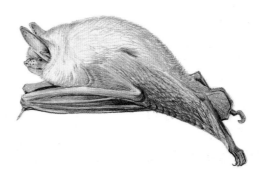

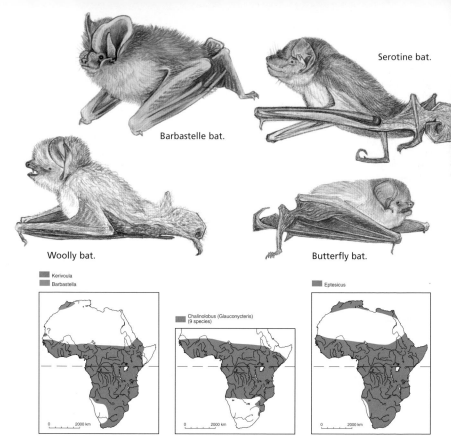

Barbastelle bat.

Serotine bat.

Woolly bat.

Butterfly bat.

Kerivoula
Barbastella

Chalinolobus (Glauconycteris)
(9 species)

Eptesicus

0   2000 km

0   2000 km

0   2000 km

Woolly bats *Kerivoula* (8 species)

Measurements: FA 36–48mm.
Recognition: The woolly fur has a frizzled, frosted or 'crinkly' appearance. The funnel-shaped ears have a long, pointed tragus. The long, sharp muzzle and domed cranium are generally concealed by dense fur, as are the minute eyes. The membrane bears a fine fringe of short hair. Roost among dead leaves, in lichen, old birds' nests, thatch or hollow branches.
Species: *K. aerosa*, *K. africana*, *K. argentata*, *K. cuprosa*, *K. eriophora*, *K. lanosa*, *K. phalaena*, *K. smithi*.
Habitat: Well-watered but otherwise diverse habitats. Woolly bats emerge late and retire early.
Food: Very small insects caught at low levels in slow, dancing flight.
Status: Poorly known.

Barbastelle bats *Barbastella* (2 species)

Measurements: FA 35–45mm.
Recognition: Very dark bats with blunt noses and upward-facing nostrils. The forward edges of the large, emarginated ears join forward of the eyes to give a very pinched, pug-nosed appearance. The tragus is triangular. All naked skin is black or deep brown. Form small summer groups of 10–100 but roost in larger numbers in winter. Utter audible chirps and hums.
Species: *B. barbastellus* (Morocco to Senegal), *B. leucomelas* (Egypt).
Habitat: Dry, open woodlands and temperate mountains. Occasional migrants; known to travel nearly 300km.
Food: Small, soft insects often caught over water or off foliage in slow but well-controlled flight.
Status: A marginal species for Africa.

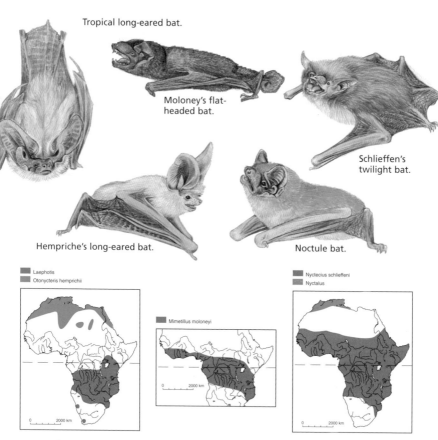

Tropical long-eared bat.

Moloney's flat-headed bat.

Schlieffen's twilight bat.

Hempriche's long-eared bat.

Noctule bat.

Laephotis
Otonycteris hemprichii

Mimetillus moloneyi

Nyctecius schlieffeni
Nyctalus

Butterfly bats *Chalinolobus* (syn. *Glauconycteris*) (9 species)

Measurements: FA 36–50mm.
Recognition: Small, furry bats with marked wings, broad, blunt faces with widely spaced nostrils, and rounded ears that flare out from the corners of the mouth and are connected by a cheek lobe below bluntly hooked tragi. Often reluctant to fly from their day perches, merely half opening their wings. Roost in trees or buildings, often attracted to lights, and make audible squeaks.
Species: *C. alboguttatus, C. argentatus, C. beatrix, C. egeria, C. gleni, C. kenyacola, C. poensis, C. superbus, C. variegatus.*
Habitat: Woodlands, forests and moist savannahs. May roost in clusters under the shelter of large leaves or in thatch.
Food: Moths and other small, soft-bodied insects caught in flight early in the evening.
Status: Poorly known.

Serotine bats *Eptesicus* (13 species)

Measurements: FA 25–55mm.
Recognition: Serotine bats are distinguished by their relatively short ears and blunt tragi and the almost flat top to their skulls. They resemble pipistrelles but have only one upper incisor. Their flight also resembles that of pipistrelles: erratic fluttering punctuated by fast swoops and dives. The wings keep relatively constant profile in flight and the tail membrane appears blunt and rounded. They may make audible clicks as they fly.
Species: *E. bottae, E. brunneus, E. capensis, E. flavescens, E. floweri, E. guineensis, E. hottentotus, E. melckorum, E. platyops, E. rendalli, E. serotinus, E. somalicus, E. tenuipinnis.*
Habitat: Both forest and non-forest species, low and high fliers, roosting in vegetation, caves and houses.
Food: Small insects caught in flight.
Status: Poorly known.

Tropical long-eared bats *Laephotis* (4 species)

Measurements: FA 35–39mm.
Recognition: The long ears have very large, curved tragi. These bats have a short face, long pale fur and a light underside. Roost in day-time under dead bark.
Species: *L. wintoni, L. angolensis, L. botswanae, L. namibensis.*
Habitat: Rare bats found in dry woodlands and savannahs of S and E Africa. *L. wintoni* has the widest distribution.
Food: Insects.
Status: Poorly known.

Moloney's flat-headed bat *Mimetillus moloneyi*

Measurements: HB 50–60mm. FA 26.5–30mm. W 6–11.5g.
Recognition: Easily recognised in the air by its fast, short-winged, whirring flight; very direct with no sharp turns. Head and body are flattened and forearms and wings are short and compact. It is dark brown all over, with short, greasy fur, and has very large glands on the frog-like muzzle.
Habitat: Forest and moist forest-savannah mosaics in equatorial Africa, roosting under bark.
Food: Flying termites and ants.
Status: Widespread and common but never in large numbers.

Noctules *Nyctalus* (3 species)

Measurements: FA 38–69mm.
Recognition: Brown pug-nosed bats with dark membranes and long, narrow wings. The fur extends from the body onto the membranes, both above and below. Flight is fast, on angled wings. The metallic calls are very audible.
Species: *N. noctula, N. lasiopterus, N. leisleri.*
Habitat: Temperate and migratory bats with marginal extensions of range into N Africa.
Food: Large insects.
Status: Marginal species; *N. lasiopterus* very rare everywhere.

Schlieffen's twilight bat *Nyctecius schlieffeni*

Measurements: HB 40–56mm. FA 29–35mm. W 6–9g.
Recognition: A variably coloured bat with dark membranes and a bare, swollen muzzle. The triangular ear has a very narrow, pointed tragus. Emerges early and has an erratic flight. Roosts alone in crevices in trees and buildings.
Habitat: Very widespread in savannahs and relatively arid habitats in Africa and Arabia.
Food: Small insects.
Status: Common and widespread.

Hempriche's long-eared bat *Otonycteris hemprichii*

Measurements: HB 70–130mm. FA 60–66mm.
Recognition: A large-eared, long-headed desert bat with long, silky pale fur and semi-translucent membranes. Flight is slow and erratic. Emits a buzz call when disturbed in roost.
Habitat: Desert and subdesert steppe environments, roosting in rock crevices, cliffs or buildings.
Food: Desert insects.
Status: Widespread but poorly known.

Pipistrelles *Pipistrellus* (16 species)

Measurements: FA 20–38mm.
Recognition: Very small bats of variable colouring. Prominent nostrils bring the nose to a sharp point behind the swollen muzzle. Dental formula is 2-1-2-3:3-1-2-3 = 34. The tragus shape is distinctive for most species. Flight is fluttering, with frequent angular turns and swoops.
Species: *P. pipistrellus, P. aegyptius, P. aero, P. anchietai, P. ariel, P. crassulus, P. eisentrauti, P. inexpectatus, P. kuhlii, P. musciculus, P. nanulus, P. nanus, P. permixtus, P. rueppelli, P. rusticus, P. savii.*

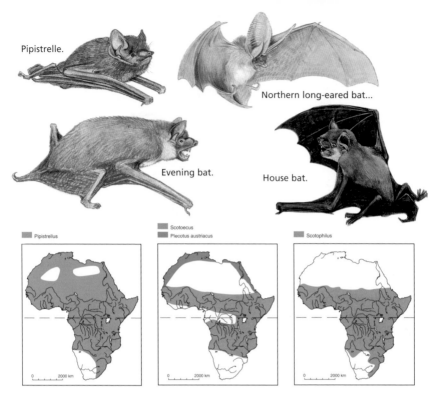

Pipistrelle.

Northern long-eared bat...

Evening bat.

House bat.

Pipistrellus

Scotoecus
Plecotus austriacus

Scotophilus

Habitat: All habitats.
Food: Insects.
Status: Unknown or poorly known.

Northern long-eared bat *Plecotus austriacus*

Measurements: HB 40–58mm. FA 37–45mm. W 7–14g.
Recognition: Very long-eared, woolly bats with large, tapered tragi and a blunt face. The long fur has a dark base and a grey-brown surface tint. Claws and feet are small. Chirps or hums if disturbed.
Habitat: Dry, open Mediterranean landscapes, especially warm valleys. Roosts alone or in twos and threes in caves, mines (winter) or buildings.
Food: Moths, beetles and other insects taken off foliage or in flight.
Status: Peripheral range in Morocco, Algeria and Egypt. Main distribution in Europe.

Evening bats *Scotoecus* (2 species)

Measurements: FA 29–39mm.
Recognition: Broad-faced brown bats with a blunt tragus in the round ears. Teeth are robust, the canines flat-fronted. ♂♂ have an exceptionally long penis. Variable in colour.
Species: *S. hirundo*: dark winged. *S. albofuscus*: pale winged.
Habitat: Tropical bats inhabiting woodlands, savannahs and dry *Acacia* country.
Food: Insects.
Status: Poorly known.

House bats *Scotophilus* (5 species)

Measurements: FA 42–80mm.
Recognition: Robust bats with blunt heads and long, tapering tragi. There are swollen glands in the corner of the mouth. Posterior teeth are greatly reduced. Colouring varies from greenish olive and yellow to dark brown and off-white. Emerge early and take fast, sweeping flights along habitual flyways.
Species: *S. nigrita, S. dinganii, S. leucogaster, S. nux, S. viridis.*

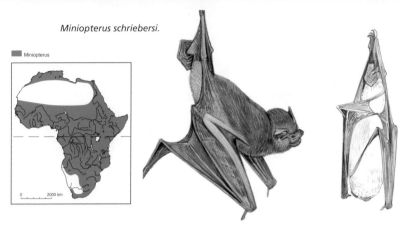

Miniopterus schriebersi.

Miniopterus

0   2000 km

Habitat: Very varied ecotypes, including uplands, forests and scrub-desert in Africa and Asia.
Food: Hard-bodied insects.
Status: Poorly known but very widespread.

Long-fingered bats *Miniopterus* (4 species)

Measurements: FA 35–50mm.
Recognition: Double folding of the wing digits (which are exceptionally long) is a very distinctive feature. These bats have a high-domed cranium, a very small, pointed muzzle and are dark in colour. Roost in large numbers deep in caves and are migratory.
Species: *M. schriebersi, M. fraterculus, M. inflatus, M. minor.*
Habitat: Very varied habitats in Africa, Eurasia and Australia.
Food: Insects.
Status: Common and widespread.

FREE-TAILED BATS MOLOSSIDAE

Guano bats	*Tadarida* (5 species)
Wrinkle-lipped bats	*Chaerophon* (10 species)
Mops free-tailed bats	*Mops* (12 species)
'Winged-rat' free-tailed bats	*Myopyterus* (2 species)
Flat-headed bats	*Mormopterus* (2 species)
East African flat-headed bat	*Platymops setiger*
Giant mastiff bat	*Otomops martiensseni*

Recognition: Bats of this family are easily identifiable by their tails, which are free beyond a narrow membrane, and by the crumpled lips, large nostrils and joined-up ears. They have short, stout feet with muscular legs and long, narrow wings. They are fast, long-distance fliers. All species are strong-smelling and possess scent-dispensing 'brushes' of specialised hairs on their outer toes. Worldwide distribution at tropical latitudes.

Guano bats *Tadarida* (5 species)

Measurements: FA 45–66mm.
Recognition: Wrinkle-lipped bats with large 'square' ears which meet but are not quite joined across the nose. They have large margins to the palate and the third molar is not reduced.
Species: *T. aegyptiaca, T. lobata, T. fulminans, T. teniotis, T. ventralis.*
Habitat: All habitats, predominantly in Africa but also in Central America and S Asia.
Food: Insects.
Status: Most species well distributed. Some very common.

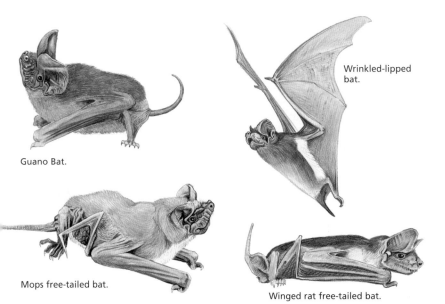

Guano Bat.

Wrinkled-lipped bat.

Mops free-tailed bat.

Winged rat free-tailed bat.

Wrinkle-lipped bats *Chaerophon* (10 species)

Measurements: FA 34–53mm.
Recognition: Wrinkle-lipped bats have large ears joined above the bridge of the nose. The tuft of fur on the forehead is very long in some species. The skull is slightly flattened. Strong-smelling bats with an audible call not unlike the screaming of swifts in muted form.
Species: *C. pumila, C. aloysiisabaudiae, C. ansorgei, C. bemmeleni, C. bivittata, C. chapini, C. gallagheri, C. major, C. nigeriae, C. russata.*
Habitat: Diverse distribution in various vegetation zones. *C. pumila* is found all over sub-Saharan Africa, Madagascar and S Arabia.
Food: Variety of small flying insects.
Status: Most species common or widespread.

Mops free-tailed bats *Mops* (12 species)

Measurements: FA 27–66mm.
Recognition: Wrinkle-lipped bats with the ears joined over the forehead (exposing the muzzle and nostrils). The third molar is reduced to a V-shape. Compact, robust and very variable in colour. The most 'derived' form of free-tailed bats. They emit sharp, audible clicks and like to fly in 'flocks'.
Species: *M. condylurus, M. brachypterus, M. congicus, M. demonstrator, M. midas, M. nanulus, M. niangarae, M. niveiventer, M. petersoni, M. spurreli, M. thersites, M. trevori.*
Habitat: Forests, woodlands and savannahs. Some species migrate. Some roost in small numbers, others in hundreds, in houses, caves, hollows and, occasionally, in shady vegetation.
Food: Small flying insects.
Status: Most species common.

'Winged-rat' free-tailed bats *Myopterus* (2 species)

Measurements: FA 33–38mm.
Recognition: Free-tailed bats with widely separated ears, large tragi, pale wings and a greatly reduced third molar. Lips are unwrinkled but bristly along their upper margins. The nose is smooth, rounded and supposedly rat-like.
Species: *M. whitleyi* (forest zone from Ghana to Uganda), *M. daubentonii* (Senegal to NE Zaïre).
Habitat: Forest and forest-savannah mosaics. Solitary, roosting in vegetation or in trunk crevices.
Food: Insects.
Status: Poorly known.

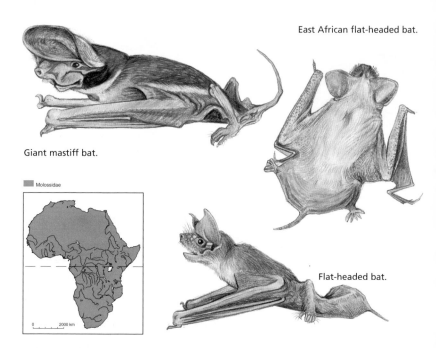

East African flat-headed bat.

Giant mastiff bat.

Molossidae

Flat-headed bat.

Flat-headed bats *Mormopterus (2 species)*

Measurements: FA 38–45mm.
Recognition: Small, free-tailed bats with 'warty' muzzles and a main 'brush' of bristles above nose. The head and body are flattened, the tail long, and ears pointed and separate. The third molar is not reduced.
Species: *M. acetabulosus, M. petrophilus.*
Habitat: Far-ranging tropical bats, commonest on Indian Ocean islands (especially Madagascar), Pacific, Caribbean and neighbouring land masses.
Food: Insects.
Status: Poorly known.

East African Flat-headed bat *Platymops setiger*

Measurements: HB 50–60mm. FA 29–36mm. W est. 10–16g.
Recognition: A very flat, free-tailed bat with a distinct, very dense 'moustache' of strong, forwardly directed bristles under the nose. Forearms are very 'warty'. Ears are blunt and laterally oriented. Small colonies roost in narrow horizontal crevices in rock outcrops and cliffs which are characteristically very strong smelling.
Habitat: Dry, rocky habitats at various altitudes in NE Africa.
Food: Small beetles and other insects.
Status: Poorly known.

Giant mastiff bat *Otomops martiensseni*

Measurements: HB 88–110mm. FA 62–72mm. W 31–39g.
Recognition: A large, free-tailed bat with very long ears attached along the whole length of the head and very long, streamlined proportions. The upper lip has flanges. Notable for a circular pocket gland on the throat. Wings are long, narrow and pointed. Flight is fast and high.
Habitat: African representative of a pan-tropical group of very successful bats hunting high above all ecotypes and at a range of altitudes. Congregates in tens of thousands in breeding caves which are vacated *en masse* on a seasonal or periodic basis.
Food: Beetles and large insects caught high above ground (or over water).
Status: Widespread and common but vulnerable as it is concentrated in a few caves.

INSECTIVORES INSECTIVORA

Otter shrews	Tenrecidae, Potamogalinae
Golden moles	Chrysochloridae
Hedgehogs	Erinaceidae
Shrews	Soricidae

The order Insectivora has been described as a 'scrap-basket' for small mammals that are generally primitive. Of the four or five groups that traditionally occupy this scrap-basket the elephant shrews are now accepted as totally separate and distinct. Golden moles, tenrecs, shrews and hedgehogs tend to remain, if only for the sake of convenience.

OTTER SHREWS TENRECIDAE, POTAMOGALINAE

Giant otter shrew	*Potamogale velox*
Mount Nimba otter shrew	*Micropotamogale lamottei*
Ruwenzori otter shrew	*Mesopotamogale ruwenzorii*

Recognition: Otter shrews are the only African survivors of a group which the fossil record indicates was once widespread. Their other contemporary representatives, the tenrecs, are restricted to Madagascar. The three species are all aquatic and of very restricted distribution. They differ from all other insectivores in lacking collar bones or clavicles. They have a flattened muzzle in which very numerous and stiff vibrissae are embedded. Each whisker is served by nerves and most food is thought to be found by touch, especially while hunting under water. Two fused toes on the hindfoot act as combs and are used in frequent and thorough grooming of their waterproof fur.

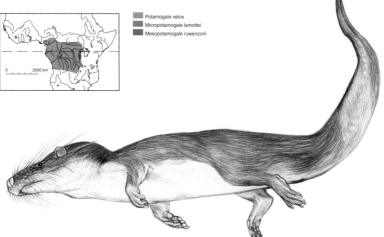

Potamogale velox
Micropotamogale lamottei
Mesopotamogale ruwenzorii

Giant otter shrew *Potamogale velox*

Other names: Fr. *Potamogale*. Ger. *Grossotterspitzmaus*.
Measurements: HB 29–35cm. T 4.5–9cm. W est. 300–950g.
Recognition: Aquatic mammal with a brown back and white underside. The broad, flat snout is covered in bristles. Flat shields cover the nostrils. The fur is generally very dense and soft but is short and silky on the bladed tail. Vertical flattening of the tail allows a fish-like, side-to-side swimming motion.
Habitat: Rivers within the main forest block from Nigeria to W Kenya. The giant otter shrew occurs in large, fast-flowing rivers, as well as streams, sluggish coastal rivers and swamps. It retreats to burrows and crevices on the riverbank to rest and breed.
Food: Freshwater crabs, fish, frogs, insects and water molluscs caught in the water at night.
Status: Widespread but sporadic distribution. Sometimes drowned in nets or fish traps.

Ruwenzori otter shrew.

Mount Nimba otter shrew.

Mount Nimba otter shrew *Micropotamogale lamottei*

Other names: Fr. *Micropotamogale de Lamotte*. Ger. *Kleinotterspitzmaus*.
Measurements: HB 12–15cm. T 10–20cm. W est. 60–90g.
Recognition: A small, soft-furred, aquatic mammal, uniformly grey-brown in colour, with a slender, rat-like tail. The feet lack any trace of webbing.
Habitat: Waters in the vicinity of Mt Nimba; montane streams, small rivers, swamps and ditches in surrounding forests, forest-savannah-cultivation mosaics.
Food: Crabs, fish and insects, mostly hunted at night in the water.
Status: Mining in Liberia and proposed mining in Guinea are major pollutants of waters. Endangered (IUCN).

Ruwenzori otter shrew *Mesopotamogale ruwenzorii*

Other names: Fr. *Potamogale du Ruwenzori*. Ger. *Mittelotterspitzmaus*.
Measurements: HB 12.3–20cm. T 10–15cm. W est. 130–150g.
Recognition: Soft-furred, aquatic mammal with a broad, whiskered nose and minuscule eyes and ears. It is dark brown above and white below. Hands and feet are partially webbed. The tail is slightly flattened vertically.
Habitat: Waters flowing off the Ruwenzori and Kivu massifs; also likely to occur in Itombwe and has been recorded from montane and lowland streams flowing through forest, savannah and cultivation. Digs burrows in riverbanks.
Food: Worms, insect larvae, small crabs, fish, frogs and tadpoles caught at night in water.
Status: Locally endangered by gold-panning in streams. Indeterminate (IUCN).

GOLDEN MOLES CHRYSOCHLORIDAE

Narrow-headed golden moles	*Amblysomus* (4 species)
Yellow golden mole	*Calcochloris obtusirostris*
Forty-toothed golden moles	*Chlorotalpa* (5 species)
Cape golden moles	*Chrysochloris* (3 species)
Giant golden moles	*Chrysospalax* (2 species)
Cryptic golden moles	*Cryptochloris* (2 species)
Desert golden mole	*Eremitalpa granti*

Recognition: A very ancient and little-known group of subterranean mammals with shiny coats of very dense fur and streamlined, formless appearance. All have a blunt, bare nose, digging forelegs, with one or more greatly enlarged claws, and less developed hindlegs. They have no visible eyes, ears or tail. They live in various habitats. Some have been seen to catch food on the surface but most species obtain the greater part of their invertebrate diet underground. They make various types of molehills and subsurface tunnels that betray their presence. They should not be confused with root-rats, or blesmols, which are rodents.

Golden mole skull shapes and proportions.

Above: *Amblysomus hottentottus.*
Middle: *Calcochloris obtusirostris.*
Below: *Chlorotalpa duthiae.*

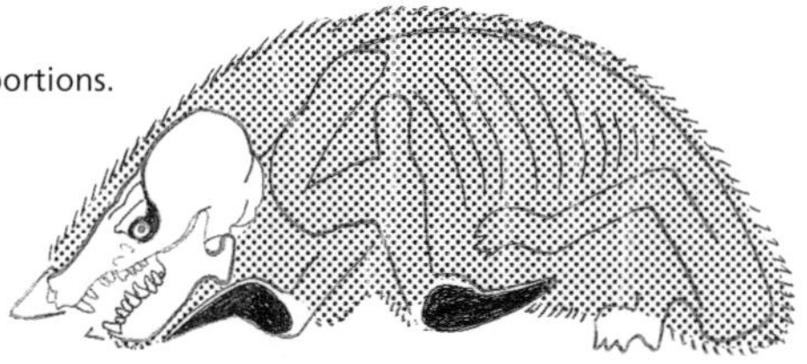

Chrysospalax villosus.

Chrysochloris asiatica.

Cryptochloris wintoni.

Eremitalpa granti.

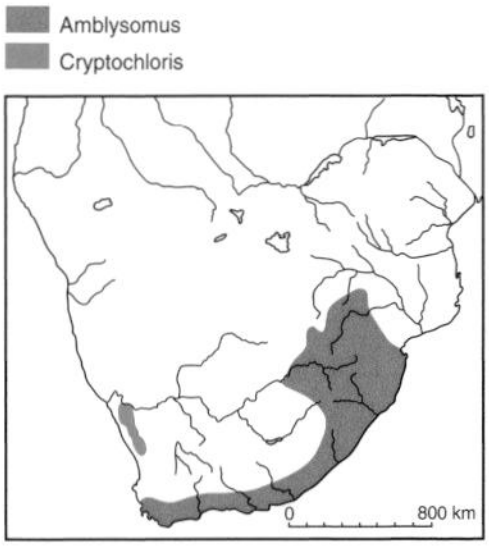

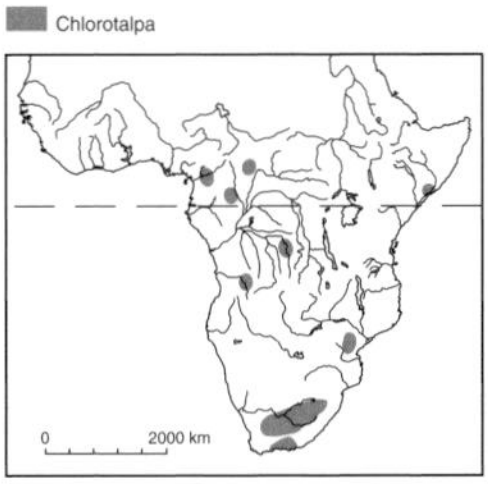

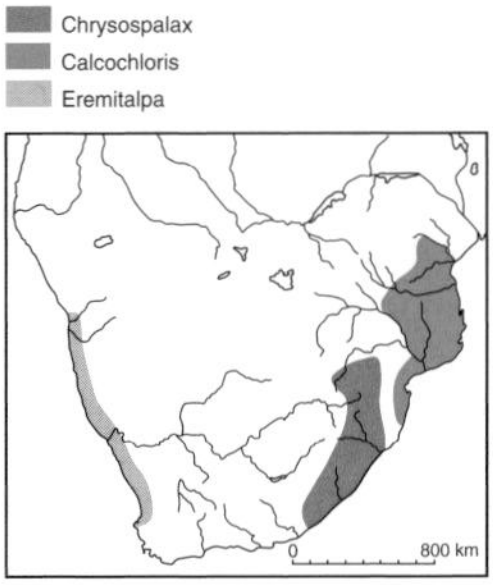

Amblysomus
Cryptochloris

Chlorotalpa

Chrysospalax
Calcochloris
Eremitalpa

Narrow-headed golden moles *Amblysomus* (4 species)
Measurements: HB 10–13cm. W21–75g.
Recognition: Dark, shiny golden moles with a long body and a small, narrow head (with 36–40 teeth). Hair bases are grey.
Species: *A. hottentotus, A. iris, A. gunningi, A. julianae.*
Habitat: Two species are widely distributed along the eastern seaboard of South Africa. *A gunningi* is only known from one montane locality. *A. julianae* is also localised in drier uplands.
Food: Invertebrates.
Status: Indeterminate (IUCN).

Yellow golden mole *Calcochloris obtusirostris*
Measurements: HB 97–108mm. W 20–30g.
Recognition: A small, long-bodied species with variably coloured upper surfaces but yellow underfur. It has 36 teeth.
Habitat: Light sandy soils and dunes in S Mozambique and vicinity.
Food: Invertebrates.
Status: Widely distributed in suitable soils but rare.

Stulmann's golden mole (*Chrysochloris stulmanni*).

Forty-toothed golden moles *Chlorotalpa* (5 species)

Measurements: HB 95–138mm. W 40–75g.
Recognition: Small, compact animals with a rounded skull. There is a metallic sheen to the generally dark fur. These golden moles have 40 teeth.
Species: *C. duthiae, C. arendsi, C. leucorhina, C. sclateri, C. tytonis.*
Habitat: Very varied, mostly dry sandy soils from Somalia and Angola to South Africa; probably more widespread than scattered records suggest.
Food: Invertebrates.
Status: Unknown.

Cape golden moles *Chrysochloris* (3 species)

Measurements: HB 98–110mm. W est. 25–35g.
Recognition: Small, metallic-coloured animals with an expanded, rounded back to the skull. They have a long second claw.
Species: *C. asiatica* (syn. *C. capensis*), *C. stuhlmanni, C. visagiei.*
Habitat: Cape Province and central and E African montane highlands.
Food: Invertebrates, mostly captured underground.
Status: Indeterminate.

Giant golden moles *Chrysospalax* (2 species)

Measurements: HB 148–230mm. W125–538g.
Recognition: Large golden moles with a 'double-hull' structure over the brain-case caused by an extensive expansion of the cheek bones into rounded bony plates (overlying the temporal muscles).
Species: *C. trevelyani, C. villosus.*
Habitat: Deep-soiled areas in forests of the E Cape (*C. trevelyani*) and borders of marshes in drier areas of SE Africa (*C. villosus*).
Food: Earthworms and other invertebrates.
Status: Rare and vulnerable.

Cryptic golden moles *Cryptochloris* (2 species)

Measurements: HB 79–90mm. W est. 20–30g.
Recognition: Small golden mole with a rounded forehead and skull. The fur has a silvery sheen with grey, white and fawn banding of hairs. Sides are yellowish or brown. The first, second and third claws are of nearly equal length, with large pads on the inner sides of the palms.
Species: *C. wintoni, C. zyli.*
Habitat: Sand dunes at Port Nolloth and Companies Drift, W Cape.
Food: Invertebrates, possibly small, sand-dwelling vertebrates.
Status: Very localised and rare.

Desert golden mole *Eremitalpa granti*

Measurements: HB 76–86mm. W16–30g.
Recognition: Very small golden mole with pale silvery fur and a disproportionately large head for a short, dumpy body. It has a short, rounded skull and three thin claws of approximately equal length.
Habitat: Sand dunes along the Namib coastline, preferring areas of dune-grass.
Food: Insects, spiders and small reptiles often dug out of dune-grass roots.
Status: Rare.

HEDGEHOGS ERINACEIDAE

African hedgehogs	*Atelerix* (4 species)
Long-eared hedgehogs	*Hemiechinus* (2 species)

Recognition: Hedgehogs are successful and widespread modern survivors of a very ancient group. The evolution of spiny armour has been a major factor in their survival. They have relatively short legs and tail, a sharply pointed face, small eyes and prominent ears. They are nocturnal insect-eaters.

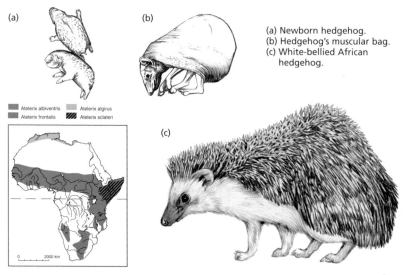

(a) Newborn hedgehog.
(b) Hedgehog's muscular bag.
(c) White-bellied African hedgehog.

Atelerix albiventris Atelerix algirus
Atelerix frontalis Atelerix sclateri

0   2000 km

African hedgehogs *Atelerix* (4 species)

Other names: Fr. *Hérissons*. Ger. *Igel*.
Measurements: HB 14–25cm. T 1.5–5cm. W 250–1600g.
Recognition: Small, spiny animals with short tails, pointed muzzles and short hairy legs with clawed, well-padded toes. Only active in evenings or at night, they make a sniffing call. They trot with fast leg movements but hunch or roll into a prickly ball at any disturbance.
Species: *A. albiventris* (sub-Saharan non-forest habitats to R. Zambezi), *A. algirus* (Libya to W Sahara), *A. frontalis* (S Africa), *A. sclateri* (Somalia).
Distribution: Very widespread but sporadic in drier regions of Africa.
Habitat: A marked preference for relatively open, dry or seasonal habitats with sparse or patchy grass cover, especially overgrazed regions with dense ungulate populations.
Food: Invertebrates, notably termites, beetles, earthworms, millepedes, small vertebrates, fungi and fallen fruits. African hedgehogs can locate hidden prey by scent and sound, and can dig in soft, loose soils.
Behaviour: Nocturnal or crepuscular animals, they are solitary except ♀♀ with young. They hibernate in temperate regions and may also aestivate in tropical dry seasons. Various vocalisations including a sniff, growl, twitter, spit, chatter and scream. They travel over a home range, sleeping in changing (but sometimes habitual) day-shelters. One to nine young are born seasonally.
Adaptions: The most striking adaptation of hedgehogs is their ability to curl up into a spiny ball. Correlated with this are short blunt ridges on the vertebrae and a wide pelvis, but the main modification is the hemispherical muscle in which the spines are embedded. When this muscle (which is anchored to the forehead) contracts it becomes a bag into which body, head and legs are withdrawn. The spines are an effective protection, although eagle owls and some hungry carnivores appear to have little difficulty in killing and eating hedgehogs.
Status: Although some hedgehog species are considered rare, most are widely distributed. The Somali hedgehog (*A. sclateri*) is of uncertain taxonomic status and may be a race of *A. albiventris*.

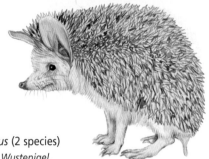

Hemiechinus aethiopicus
Hemiechinus auritus

0 __ 2000 km

Long-eared hedgehogs *Hemiechinus* (2 species)

Other names: Fr. *Hérissons du désert*. Ger. *Wustenigel*.
Measurements: HB 14–27cm. T 1.3–5cm. W est. 150–250g.
Recognition: Variably coloured desert hedgehogs with shorter spines, longer limbs and larger ears than *Atelerix*. Only active at night (or on overcast, cool mornings or evenings), they sleep in self-dug burrows during the day. ♀♀ are known to squeal in defence of their young and butt with their head spines.
Species: *H. auritus* (Egypt–Asiatic species), *H. aethiopicus* (N Africa, Sahara).
Habitat: Deserts. *H. auritus* is a moisture-dependent hibernator preferring cool deserts. *H. aethiopicus* is a drought-adapted aestivator, preferring hot, dry deserts.
Food: Invertebrates and small vertebrates.
Status: Not endangered.

SHREWS SORICIDAE

Mouse shrews	*Myosorex* (12 species)
Mole shrews	*Surdisorex* (2 species)
Congo shrew	*Congosorex polli*
Musk shrews	*Suncus* (4 species)
Climbing shrews	*Sylvisorex* (10 species)
Ruwenzori shrew	*Ruwenzorisorex suncoides*
Hero shrew	*Scutisorex somereni*
Rodent shrews	*Paracrocidura* (3 species)
White-toothed shrews	*Crocidura* (103 species)

Recognition: Shrews are small, mouse-sized mammals with a long, mobile nose and stout, cylindrical skull. They are adapted to bulldoze insects out of their retreats in plant debris. To this end their bodies are powerful and tubular. They have sensitive vibrissae to detect prey. The incisors function as pincers and the molars as fine shredders of hard insect chitin. They are a very ancient group with recognisable fossil ancestors dating back more than 40 million years.

In the evolution of the shrews there has been a progressive reduction of back molars and premolars. The nine African genera represent different phylogenetic levels with *Myosorex* (with 32 teeth) the most ancient and *Crocidura* (28 teeth) the most advanced. The former is a relict group surviving in special habitats. The latter, with over 100 species, is a highly successful advanced group. Other genera combine conservative and advanced features in various specialised permutations.

Found in most habitats, they prefer moist conditions. Some are good climbers; others burrow underground. Scent glands on their flanks probably assist the spacing of individuals as well as repelling rival shrews and some predators. Most species are solitary except while breeding and all are highly aggressive to other shrews. Their main predators are birds and snakes.

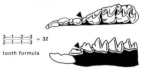

$\frac{3-1-2-3}{2-1-1-3} = 32$

tooth formula

Myosorex.

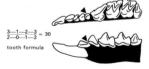

$\frac{3-1-2-3}{2-0-1-3} = 30$

tooth formula

Sylvisorex, Scutisorex
and Suncus.

$\frac{3-1-1-3}{2-0-1-3} = 28$

tooth formula

Crocidura and
Paracrocidura

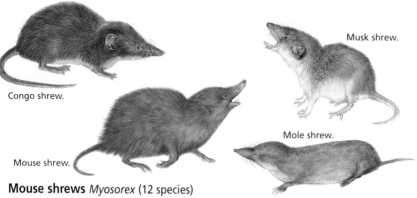

Musk shrew.

Congo shrew.

Mole shrew.

Mouse shrew.

Mouse shrews *Myosorex* (12 species)

Measurements: HB ave. 5–10cm.
Recognition: Small, dark shrews, with reduced eyes and ears, a short tail and well-clawed, slender toes. The lower canines are vestigial but the upper ones are retained and the last molars are well developed in both jaws, although they are smaller than the other two forward ones. (Dental formula: 3-1-2-3:2-1-1-3 = 32.)
Species: *M. varius, M. babaulti, M. blarina, M. caffer, M. eisentrauti, M. geata, M. longicaudatus, M. okuensis, M. rumpii, M. schalleri, M. sclateri, M. tenuis.*
Habitat: Mostly temperate or high-altitude regions, often in swampy conditions. Most species are highly localised endemics, relicts of once more-widespread populations.
Food: Small invertebrates, mainly insects and earthworms and some very small vertebrates (notably frogs).
Status: Several species are described from one or a very few specimens. All are very poorly known.

Mole shrews *Surdisorex* (2 species)

Measurements: HB 89–108mm. T 24–34mm. W est. 8–10g.
Recognition: Small brown shrews with dense, short fur and no trace of external eyes or ears. The forelegs have long, sharp claws on robust digits but with slender palms and wrists (indicating relatively recent modification).
Species: *S. norae* (Aberdare Mts), *S. polulus* (Mt Kenya).
Habitat: Surface runways and subterranean tunnels in Afro-alpine and upper montane forest zones; commonest in bamboo and grassland/sedge areas.
Food: Invertebrates 'harvested' in tunnels and runways.
Status: Not endangered.

Congo shrew *Congosorex polli*

Measurements: HB est. 90mm. T est. 60mm..
Recognition: A small brown shrew with a long tail and large ears. It lacks lower canines but otherwise resembles mouse shrews.
Habitat: Only known from Kasai, S Zaïre (fire-climax Miombo (*Brachystegia*) woodlands traversed by degraded forest galleries).
Food: Invertebrates.
Status: Unknown.

Musk shrews *Suncus* (4 species)

Measurements: HB 50–125mm. T 30–85mm. W 3.5–9.5g.
Recognition: Very small shrews of various shades of brown or grey, with a paler underside. They have large, rounded ears, a bewhiskered pink muzzle, thin limbs and a tapered tail. (Dental formula 3-1-2-3:2-0-1-3 = 30.)
Species: *S. infinitessimus, S. lixus, S. remyi, S. varilla.* (*S. murinus* introduced.)
Habitat: Very patchy distributions. Apparently more common in S Africa than tropical Africa (where *Crocidura* species might exclude them). Some species commonly associated with termitaries.
Food: Insects (up to shrew size) and other small invertebrates.
Status: Unknown (inconspicuous and rarely trapped).

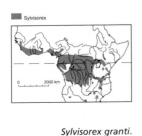

Sylvisorex granti.

Climbing shrews *Sylvisorex* (10 species)

Measurements: HB 45–85mm. T 45–90mm. W 3–12g.
Recognition: Arboreal shrews with a long tail, long, mobile digits on the hands and feet and a very extended nose. Ears vary in size, as does the colour, some species being dark all over while others are paler with off-white undersides. (Dental formula 3-1-2-3:2-0-1-3 = 30.)
Species: *S. morio, S. granti, S. howelli, S. isabellae, S. johnstoni, S. lunaris, S. megalura, S. ollula, S. oriundus, S. vulcanorum.*
Habitat: Tropical shrews predominantly of forest or riverine habitats from sea-level up to 4,000m but also from rank, grassy habitats. Some montane species (notably *S. granti*) have widely discontinuous distributions. Others are extremely localised.
Food: Invertebrates.
Status: Indeterminate but *S. vulcanorum* is thought to be threatened with extinction.

Congosorex
Ruwenzorisorex
Paracrocidura
Myosorex

(a) Rodent shrew (plus incisors).
(b) Ruwenzori shrew.

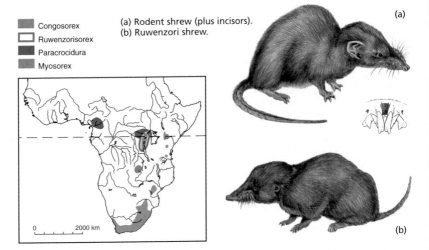

Ruwenzori shrew *Ruwenzorisorex suncoides*

Measurements: HB 92–95mm. T 61–62mm. W est. 18g.
Recognition: A small, greyish black shrew with a rounded head, short snout and small (but protruding) ears. It has short, small-toed pale forefeet and short black hindfeet with blunt pale toes. The tail is well-tapered.
Habitat: Montane forests in central Africa (E Zaïre, Rwanda, Burundi and W Uganda).
Food: Invertebrates.
Status: Indeterminate but of conservation concern.

Hero shrew *Scutisorex somereni*

Measurements: HB 105–150mm. T 70–109mm. W 70–113g.
Recognition: A large grey shrew with a long, tapered nose, shallow ears and thick woolly fur with projecting guard hairs. It is readily distinguished by its 'trotting', rather than 'crawling', gait. The name derives from its use as warrior talismans in N Zaïre. Mangbetu

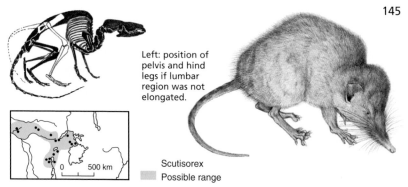

Left: position of pelvis and hind legs if lumbar region was not elongated.

Scutisorex
Possible range

tribesmen first drew the attention of scientists to this species by demonstrating that its extraordinary backbone could bear the weight of a man standing on it. The hero shrew has twice as many lumbar vertebrae as other shrews due to a shifting of the pelvis down the spine. The vertebrae of the lower back have been elaborated into components of a complex, bridge-like structure by broadening, thickening and developing interlocking spicules along their outer margins. The laterally inflexible lower back and displaced pelvis contrasts with the peculiar doubling-up of the forequarters into an S-shaped bend, which gives the shrew its peculiar 'arched' posture. The body is carried well clear of the ground on long limbs, with fingers and toes that can splay widely.

Adult animals, especially ♂♂, exude a very pungent scent and greasy yellow stains are visible on the sides and chest. They lay down substantial seasonal deposits of fat which appreciably alter the animal's appearance (fat animals seeming almost spherical in certain postures).
Habitat: Seasonally swampy forests between the R. Itimbiri, R. Lualaba and R. Nile; found only at low and medium altitudes.
Food: Invertebrates (caterpillars, earthworms, molluscs and grasshoppers) and small vertebrates (frogs). The hero shrew can swim and climb but finds most food on the forest floor. Prey appears to be immobilised by non-lethal bites, possibly due to toxins in the saliva.
Status: Not endangered.

Rodent shrews *Paracrocidura* (3 species)

Measurements: HB ave. 65mm. T ave. 34.5mm.
Recognition: Dark shrews with thin, short fur, dark skin and a short, broad muzzle. The shortish ears are nearly naked and are not hidden in the surrounding fur. Limbs are short, with minuscule claws, while the tail is shortish and finely haired. The upper incisors are laterally flattened to form cutting edges similar to those of rodents.
Species: *P. schoutedeni, P. graueri, P. maxima.*
Habitat: Montane and lowland forests from Cameroon to Uganda.
Food: Invertebrates.
Status: Unknown but localised species are of conservation concern.

White-toothed shrews *Crocidura* (103 species)

Measurements: HB 45–140mm. T 45–90mm. W 11–40g.

Crocidura

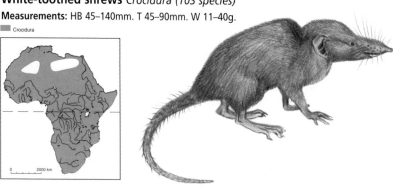

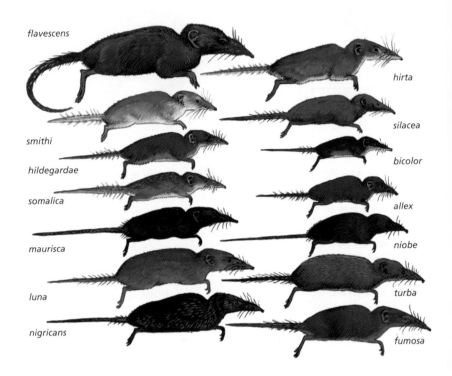

flavescens

hirta

smithi

silacea

hildegardae

bicolor

somalica

allex

maurisca

niobe

luna

turba

nigricans

fumosa

Recognition: The commonest and most diverse group of African shrews. All have a long, whiskery nose, visible ears and small eyes. Most have some long, fine hairs growing very sparsely on the tail. The group can be divided into three subdivisions on the basis of tooth reduction (especially of the last molar). Further clustering into species groups is also possible on the basis of variations in size, colour, length of the hindfeet, and length and hairing of the tail. Certain identification requires close inspection of the teeth but the above plate illustrates 14 common species which can beidentified according to external characteristics. (Dental formula 3-1-1-3:2-0-1-3 = 28.)

Species: C. aleksandrisi, C. allex, C. ansellorum*, C. attila, C. baileyi*, C. batesi, C. bottegi, C. bottegoides, C. buettikoferi, C. caliginea, C. cinderella, C. congobelgica*, C. crenata*, C. crossei, C. cyanea, C. denti, C. desperata, C. dolichura, C. douceti, C. eisentrauti*, C. elgonius, C. erica, C. fischeri, C. flavescens, C. floweri, C. foxi, C. fulvastra, C. fumosa, C. fuscomurina, C. glassi*, C. goliath, C. gracilipes, C. grandiceps, C. grassei*, C. greenwoodi, C. harenna, C. hildegardeae, C. hirta, C. jacksoni, C. kivuana*, C. lamottei, C. lanosa*, C. latona*, C. littoralis, C. longipes*, C. lucina*, C. ludia*, C. luna, C. lusitania, C. macarthuri, C. macmillani, C. macowi, C. manengubae*, C. maquassiensis*, C. mariquensis, C. maurisca, C. monax*, C. montis, C. muricauda, C. mutesae, C. nana, C. nanilla, C. nigeriae, C. nigricans, C. nigrofusca, C. nimbae*, C. niobe, C. obscurior, C. olivieri, C. parvipes, C. pasha, C. phaeura*, C. picea, C. pitmani, C. planiceps, C. poensis, C. polia*, C. raineyi*, C. religiosa, C. rooseveltii, C. selina*, C. silacea, C. smithi, C. somalica, C. stenocephala*, C. tansaniana*, C. tarella, C. tarfayensis, C. telfordi*, C. thalia*, C. theresae, C. thomensis*, C. turba, C. ultima, C. usambarae*, C. viaria, C. voi, C. whitakeri, C. wimmeri*, C. xantippe, C. yankariensis, C. zaphiri, C. zimmeri. (Several new species await names and descriptions.)

Habitat: All vegetation types at all altitudes, mainly terrestrial, but able to climb and swim. Some species are highly restricted (particularly those in the 'primitive' category); others range very widely (notably some of the 'advanced' groups).

Food: A very wide range of invertebrates and small vertebrates.

Status: Species identified by IUCN as being 'of conservation concern' have been marked with an asterisk in the list of species.

ELEPHANT SHREWS, OR SENGIS
MACROSCELIDEA

Soft-furred elephant shrews	Macroscelidinae
Giant elephant shrews	Rhynchocyoninae

Recognition: Mouse- or rat-sized animals with large eyes and ears, slender limbs and a long, bare tail. Elephant shrews have a long, tubular snout protruding from a strongly tapered skull bearing 50–60 teeth. Most species are brownish and some have bold markings on the face or back.

Modern elephant shrews are the remnants of a larger radiation that included tiny, mouse-like herbivores (*Mylomygale*) which survived until 1 million or so years ago.

Older, larger relatives appeared to resemble hyraxes closely and were therefore named '*Myohyrax*'. Like hyraxes, the earliest elephant shrews probably anticipated the more advanced herbivores that have replaced them.

All living forms of elephant shrew are specialised invertebrate-feeders (ants being particularly important) so that they were previously included in the insectivore 'scrap-basket'. Now recognised as a distinct, but equally archaic order, they are thought to have shared a common ancestry with hares some 100 million years ago. Separation of the fine-boned, soft-furred elephant shrews (Macroscelidinae) from the more robustly built giant elephant shrews (Rhynchocyoninae) dates back 25 million–35 million years. The former are superficial surface-gleaners of small invertebrates (and occasionally fruits and seeds) in shaded but dry environments while the latter favour moister habitats where they find invertebrates through an intensive turning-over of leaf litter.

SOFT-FURRED ELEPHANT SHREWS OR SENGIS MACROSCELIDINAE

Lesser elephant shrews	*Elephantulus* (10 species)
Four-toed elephant shrew	*Petrodromus tetradactylus*
Round-eared elephant shrew	*Macroscelides proboscideus*

Recognition: Characterised by long, dense, silky fur, a mass of long, fine whiskers, a fine, narrow proboscis, naked rump and large, very dark eyes with vertical pupils. They have a relatively uniform sandy colouring (except around the eyes).
Genealogy: Recognisable as fossils some 35 million years ago, the most distinct and conservative type is the narrow-headed four-toed elephant shrew, *Petrodromus*.
Geography: Exclusively African where they are mainly restricted to uplands in the east, south and (marginally) north-west. Not found in very humid habitats and their distribution is bounded by the major rivers in central Africa.
Ecology: Alert surface-foragers and pouncers, almost exclusively diurnal and mostly active while conditions are warm. The invertebrate diet is occasionally supplemented by fruits or seeds.
Natural history: Soft-furred elephant shrews mature very rapidly and have a brief but fecund adult life. Gestation may last as long as a fifth of the females life-span. Species vary in their reliance on cover, shelter or burrows but all are exceptionally fast runners and leapers. Both ♂♂ and ♀♀ defend exclusive territories from their own sexes, effectively forming permanent pairs that forage and sleep on their own.
Adaptations: The long, powerful hindlegs of soft-furred elephant shrews enable them to make vertical leaps from a standing start and to sustain their rapid, bounding locomotion, crucial defences against their numerous predators. Coat colours often match local soil types very closely. Their long, narrow tongues enable them to gather small food items with great rapidity.

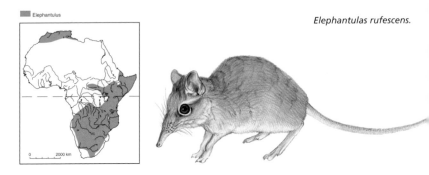

Elephantulus

Elephantulas rufescens.

Lesser elephant shrews or sengis *Elephantulus* (10 species)

Other names: Fr. *Macroscélides*. Ger. *Elefantenspitzmaus*. Swah. *Sengi*.

Measurements: Total length 210–280mm. W 25–70g.

Recognition: Mouse-sized, soft-furred, naked-tailed animals with large eyes and ears, a fine-pointed proboscis and long hindlegs. There are rings of white or paler fur around the eyes. Some species secrete from glands on the chest, soles of the feet and sites on the underside of the tail (others secrete from one or more of these areas). Coat colour often closely matches local soil colour.

Species: *E. brachyrhynchus, E. edwardii, E. fuscipes, E. fuscus, E. intufi, E. myurus, E. revoili, E. rozeti, E. rufescens, E. rupestris*. Note: defunct genus *Nasilio* now included in *Elephantulus*.

Distribution: The eastern and southern half of Africa and extreme north-west (Morocco). Species are well defined in their geographic ranges and habitat preferences, some preferring sandy areas, others rocky or densely vegetated areas.

Habitat: Relatively dry but seasonal, bushy or scrubby habitats are preferred. All species minimise exposing themselves to predation by remaining under vegetation and rocks and only crossing open ground at high speed. Some species (*E. rupestris, E.intufi*) dig burrows; others (*E. rufescens*) maintain conspicuous paths which are daily cleared of litter by scuffling with the legs; yet others (*E. brachyrhynchus*) use vacant rodent holes.

Food: A wide range of invertebrates, pounced upon in leaf litter (and near the dung piles of herbivores). Some species occasionally eat fruits and seeds. Rapid daily traverses along pathways in small, well-known territories serve to exclude trespassers and rehearse rapid escape from predators. However, the main function of such runs is to gather food.

Behaviour: Both ♂♂ and ♀♀ exclude their own sex from territories but may tolerate adult-sized offspring in home ranges of 0.25–0.6ha. Territorial displays involve fluffing out the fur and strutting on tip-toe (which displays the white or contrasting colour of the legs and underside). Very intense, rapid activity is followed by long periods of quiescence in well-concealed, shady observation posts. All species are predominantly or wholly diurnal and several sun-bathe before becoming fully active. Lesser elephant shrews communicate with squeaky calls and by drumming the hindlegs. Most species have continuous or extended breeding, with the majority of births falling in warm wet months.

Adaptations: Highly vulnerable to birds of prey and snakes, lesser elephant shrews have extremely rapid reactions. They also minimise the vulnerable period of infancy by having a long gestation (about 2 months) and giving birth to well-developed young that reach adult size in just over 1 month and become sexually mature in 2 months. Their reproductive life of about 1 year allows no more than three litters, in which one or two (rarely three) young are born. In competition with more fecund rodents and insectivores, lesser elephant shrews' intensive use of a very small, well-known area, acute observation and very fast actions compensate for a low rate of reproduction and short lives.

Status: Favoured in areas well stocked with wild or domestic herbivores (probably due to the dependence of certain invertebrates on dung and plant litter). Some species or populations may be threatened when overstocking degrades the habitat to the point where patches of shelter disappear. In general not threatened.

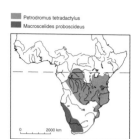

Petrodromus tetradactylus
Macroscelides proboscideus

Four-toed elephant shrew or sengi *Petrodromus tetradactylus*

Other names: Fr. *Pétrodrome.* Ger. *Russelrate.* Swah. *Isanje.*

Measurements: HB 165–220mm. T 130–180mm. W 150–280g.

Recognition: Brown, rat-sized elephant shrew with a large head and ears and conspicuous facial markings. The legs are light coloured and very slender, with only four toes. There are two pairs of mammae.

Subspecies: Five subspecies described. *P. t. sultan* (from E Kenya) has, with some justification, sometimes been regarded as a separate species; it is unique in having a profusion of knob-tipped bristles growing from a glandular tract that lines the underside of the tail (see illustration above).

Distribution: SE and central Africa with a distinct population inhabiting the Zaïre basin (south of the main river).

Habitat: Mainly in dense evergreen undergrowth in caesalpinoid forests, woodlands and thickets. The four-toed elephant shrew may depend upon a complex plant/animal community that sustains a rich leaf-litter micro-fauna. It lives without recourse to burrows or shelters on the forest or thicket floor, using habitual pathways with regularly spaced 'landing pads' of cleared, bare earth.

Food: Mainly ants and termites; also crickets, grasshoppers and other litter invertebrates.

Behaviour: This elephant shrew is most active in the early morning and evening, scuffling litter to find food. Rapping of the hindlegs is presumed to be a territorial advertisement and alarm signal. Neighbours answer with similar foot-rapping. Most young are born in the wet season at an advanced stage of development and they reach sexual maturity very rapidly. They have a wide repertoire of low-level purrs, miaows, squeaks, chirps and screams.

Status: Not endangered.

Round-eared elephant shrew *Macroscelides proboscideus*

Other names: Fr. *Macroscélide d'Afrique du Sud.* Ger. *Russelspringer.*

Measurements: HB 105–115mm. T 114–130mm. W 31–47g.

Recognition: A grizzled, mouse-sized animal with rounded, hairy ears and a short muzzle. There is no ring of white fur around the eye. The skull is characterised by crowded teeth and greatly inflated ear bullae. Colour varies from grey to buff or brown. There are three pairs of mammae.

Habitat: Areas of low Karoo scrub in SW African arid zone. Single animals or pairs live in small territories. Most births occur between September and February during warmer, wetter periods.

Food: Ants and termites.

Status: Widespread within its restricted habitat. Not endangered.

GIANT ELEPHANT SHREWS RHYNCHOCYONINAE (RHYNCHOCYON)

Chequered elephant shrew	*Rhynchocyon cirnei*
Zanj elephant shrew	*Rhynchocyon petersi*
Golden-rumped elephant shrew	*Rhynchocyon chrysopygus*

Recognition: Elegant, long-legged animals the size of a large rat with a long, naked, white-tipped tail and a very long, tapering snout. The proboscis protrudes well beyond the mouth (which is inconspicuous, as are the very rapid movements of the long, tapered tongue). The coat is short-haired and sleek. The three species differ greatly in colour but are of similar size and morphology. Their pungent smell derives from a gland behind the anus. There are no obvious differences between the sexes but ♂♂ have longer, sharper canine teeth.

Genealogy: The divergence of this group from soft-furred elephant shrews is thought to date back 35 million years or more. They mature more slowly, live longer, forage more intensively in larger territories and live a less exposed existence than their smaller relatives.

Geography: More exclusively tropical than soft-furred elephant shrews, they also live in moister, denser forests and woodlands but, like other elephant shrews, seem to have evolved in the drier, eastern half of Africa and have failed to range very far to the west. Large rivers mark their present frontiers but it seems likely that very humid habitats support a complex of competitors, predators, diseases and physical conditions that have always deterred expansion into moist, western forests.

Ecology: Feeding on relatively cryptic invertebrates (larvae, termites, ants, beetles, spiders, myriapods and earthworms), they noisily turn over litter and soil with their paws and well-reinforced but flexible nose. They require relatively well-drained soils and abundant dry leaf litter in order to construct their 1m-wide leaf-mound shelters, which are piled over shallow, body-sized scoops in the soil. Each animal makes and maintains ten or more such retreats in its territory. They serve as the night-rests of these exclusively diurnal animals, as nurseries for the young and as occasional day-time refuges. Constructed in the early morning, when leaves are damp, limp and compressible (and the sound of raking and tamping them is muffled), they provide concealment from a variety of predators. The presence of the right conditions for the building of dry, comfortable leaf mounds is probably the single most important requisite for giant elephant shrews.

Natural history: Territories average 1.7ha and are defended by each animal against others of its own sex. ♂♂ are the more frequent trespassers, provoking chases and fights in which wounds from the short, tusk-like canines are common. The entire home range is traversed daily and scent marks from the anal gland probably serve as territorial beacons. A ♂ regularly monitors the one or more ♀♀ sharing his home range but all feeding and resting is solitary. Breeding is continuous, with four or five litters (each of a single offspring) being born in a year after a gestation of 45 days. The young remain within the leaf mound for up to2 weeks before emerging and becoming independent within a few days. Young animals rapidly reach sexual maturity. Giant elephant shrews live for 4–5 years.

Large birds of prey and snakes are frequent predators of giant elephant shrews. Predation levels appear to be lower for this group than for soft-furred elephant shrews, possibly because leaf mounds are such effective refuges. The mounds are difficult to identify, even for an experienced observer, and the occupant is usually able to 'explode' out of its refuge before it can be seized. Nonetheless dogs are a serious menace for populations close to settlement.

Adaptations: Although less cryptic in their colouring and behaviour than their smaller relatives, giant elephant shrews share extremely fast reactions. Instantaneous get-aways powered by well-muscled hindlegs and fast races along very well-known trails help protect both groups from predators.

A broad, compressed skull and ground-hugging crouch allow these animals to occupy very little space within their leaf mounds, where they sleep in a posture that leaves them ready for instant action. Physiologically they appear well adapted to digest toxic or difficult foods, such as ants and myriapods. However, some millepedes may be taken less frequently or avoided. That these animals show relatively little change over some 30 million years suggests that their micro-habitats, and the niches they occupy within them, must have retained a remarkable degree of stability.

Chequered elephant shrew *Rhynchocyon cirnei*

Other names: Fr. *Rhynchocyon*. Ger. *Russelhundchen*. Swah. *Njule madoa*.
Measurements: HB 235–315mm. T 190–263mm. W 408–440g.
Recognition: The back is marked with a complex pattern of longitudinal dark bands on an agouti-grizzled background with pale (even white) spots or flecks. In the humid Zaïre basin and mountains north of L. Nyasa (formerly L. Malawi) this pattern becomes difficult to see because the overall colour becomes very dark. In SE Tanzania and Mozambique the pattern is very variable, with suffusions of orange-red and black that could suggest long-term hybridisation with the black and red Zanj elephant shrew.
Subspecies: *R. c. cirnei* (Mozambique), *R. c. macrurus* (SE Tanzania), *R. c. shirensis* (S Malawi), *R. c. hendersoni* (N Malawi mountains), *R. c. reichardi* (SW Tanzania and E Zaïre), *R. c. stuhlmanni* (NE Zaïre and Uganda).
Habitat: Forests and gallery forests at low, medium and high altitudes. *R. c. reichardi* (with colouring that closely resembles a grass-mouse) inhabits grassland during the wet season, only retreating into galleries or relict forest patches in the dry season.
Food: As other species but grasshoppers and caterpillars are important for some races.
Status: Not endangered (but declining in densely settled areas).

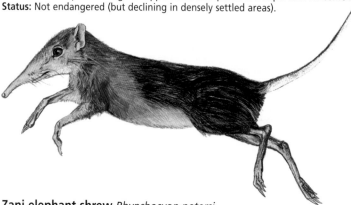

Zanj elephant shrew *Rhynchocyon petersi*

Other names: Fr. *Rhynchocyon de Zanj*. Ger. *Russelhundchen*. Swah. *Njule Kinguja*.
Measurements: HB 235–315mm. T 190–263mm. W 408–440g.
Recognition: Forequarters are orange, graduating to a deep red with a black rump. The tail is orange with a white tip.
Subspecies: *R. p. petersi* (Mombasa to R. Rufiji), *R. p. adersi* (Zanzibar I. and Mafia).
Habitat: Coastal and montane forest and thickets in E Tanzania and the Kenya coast.
Food: Cryptic invertebrates in leaf litter.
Status: Rare (IUCN). Action plan proposals are to determine: (a) current range and densities; (b) use of fallow lands; (c) effects of hunting; (d) field research priorities; (e) appropriate conservation measures.

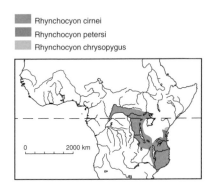

Rhynchocyon cirnei
Rhynchocyon petersi
Rhynchocyon chrysopygus

Golden-rumped elephant shrew *Rhynchocyon chrysopygus*

Other names: Fr. *Rhynchocyon à dos doré*. Ger. *Russelhundchen*. Swah. *Njule ya Gedi*.
Measurements: HB 235–315mm. T 190–263mm. W 408–440g.
Recognition: The dark body graduates to a metallic yellow rump. The neck is russet and the forehead and face are tawny agouti. Vestigial traces of a spotted pattern similar to that of the chequered elephant shrew are obvious in juveniles and just perceptible in some adults. Thickened skin under the golden rump suggests that damaging bites or slashes inflicted during territorial fights and flights may be targeted on this rump shield.
Habitat: Confined to two very small areas of the Kenya coast where it lives in dry evergreen thickets.
Food: Grasshoppers and crickets, beetles, spiders, millepedes, ants, centipedes, earthworms and termites (in order of preference).
Status: Vulnerable (IUCN). There is serious concern for the survival of this species. The IUCN Action Plan suggests *Rhynchocyon* might serve as an indicator for the health and status of forest habitats in E Africa. Domestic dogs have seriously depleted them in the Gedi National Park in recent years.

HARES LAGOMORPHA

These medium-sized herbivorous animals have an ancient but puzzling ancestry. The earliest fossils (*Eurymylus*) come from NE Asia and have been dated at 60 million years. Later fossils (38 million–20 million years) come from North America and the earliest African fossils are later still.

At an early stage hares and pikas specialised in feeding on coarse vegetation in unstable and often cold environments. The greatest diversity of lagomorphs is still found at more temperate latitudes and altitudes.

HARES LEPORIDAE

True hares	*Lepus* (3 species)
Riverine rabbit	*Bunolagus monticularis*
Common rabbit	*Oryctolagus cuniculus*
Uganda grass-hare	*Poelagus marjorita*
Rock hares	*Pronolagus* (3 species)

Recognition: Medium-sized, soft-furred animals with very short, furry tails, relatively large ears, small mouths and forelegs that are shorter and slighter than the muscular hindlegs. All African hares and rabbits belong to this family. Their teeth superficially resemble those of rodents in that the incisors are paired, chisel-like and well separated from the cheek teeth. Unlike those of rodents, however, hare incisors are wholly sheathed in enamel while the upper pair are backed by a second pair of tiny incisor 'peg teeth'.

Genealogy: A wide scatter of rare relict hares in North and Central America, the China Sea, Indonesia and Africa represents the vestiges of a radiation that is over 10 million years old. The African representatives of this vestigial group are the red rock hares of S Africa. The single most successful and widespread genus, the true hare (*Lepus*), has evolved much more recently and has probably partially displaced several earlier types (a process that is possibly still continuing).

Geography: Hares have been outstanding colonists and are widely distributed throughout North America, Eurasia and Africa.

Ecology: Hares often flourish in exposed and unstable habitats and can endure repeated population booms and busts. They can survive on a coarse plant diet and their ability to extract nutrients is enhanced by recycling excreted pellets (called caecotrophs).

Natural history: Distinctions between hares and rabbits are sometimes semantic but, as a rule, 'rabbits' live in burrows and have large litters of helpless young while hares are solitary, live in the open and bear fewer, more precocious young. Not all African hares fall into such neat categories and several are of intermediate status.

Adaptations: Hares and rabbits have various scent glands which play a role in the regulation of their social life. Anal glands scent their dung (which is often deposited in piles). The activity of orbital glands is known to be linked with sex hormones, as is the odour of urine in ♂♂ and the activity of the ♂ chin glands (both of which are used to mark objects and other animals). Inguinal, or groin, glands serve to produce a seasonal, sexual attractant.

Hares are visually alert but mainly depend on hearing and scent to detect predators. They have specialised fur which includes three distinct types of hairs and serves as an excellent insulator. The fur is kept dry and clean by shaking and frequent grooming. The fur is also regularly moulted. Populations exposed to extremes of heat (such as the desert hares) have very large, naked ears in which fine veins help cool the blood.

True hares *Lepus*

Cape hare	*Lepus capensis*
Scrub hare	*Lepus saxatilis* (syn. *L. crawshayi*)
Starck's hare	*Lepus starcki*

Other names: Fr. *Lièvres*. Ger. *Feldhase*. Swah. *Sungura*.

Measurements: W 1–5kg (strongly influenced by extremes of resources and temperature, i.e. poor/hot, rich/cool).

Recognition: Typified by their long limbs and long ears, true hares have a short black and white tail. Body colour and face patterns vary greatly, especially between regional populations of the same species.

Distribution: Found over all grassy and subdesertic areas of Africa.

Habitat: Completely open country (Cape hare); grasslands with abundant cover (scrub hare). The third African species, Starck's hare, is likely to represent a population of the European hare that became stranded in Ethiopia after the last glaciation and has subsequently adapted to the high-altitude moorlands.

Food: Grass, leaves, stems, seeds, herbs and bark. Different proportions of locally available plant parts are preferred by each species.

Behaviour: Hares are not known to be territorial but hierarchies form that include both sexes. Home ranges are well known and regularly traversed along preferred trails. Sheltered sites for sunning, sleeping or sand-bathing are also regularly used. Home ranges may vary from 5 to many tens of hectares and densities tend to fluctuate very widely with up to 10 animals per ha during boom periods.

As with all hares and rabbits, glandular scents help to regulate sexual and social behaviour. Scent, sound and movement provide important clues in detecting predators. Hares growl, grind their teeth and drum with their forelegs during aggressive or confident encounters. They scream when seized or wounded and ♀♀ utter soft bleats when approaching their young. African hares breed continuously, ♀♀ bearing about six litters a year, normally with one or two young per litter. The young are born fully haired, with eyes open, after a gestation of about 42 days. They lie up in concealed 'forms' but grow very fast so that they are fully mobile and independent by 1 month and sexually mature by 8 months. Oestrous ♀♀ attract persistent ♂ attention and frequent copulations.

Adaptations: True hares have very light skulls and skeletons, long limbs, large hearts and lungs, red muscles and enlarged air passages, all of which represent adaptations for fast, manoeuvrable and sustained running (at up to 70km/h). In contrast to their 'last resort' strategy of fleeing, hares will crouch in total immobility until a potential predator approaches too closely. Their cryptic colouring and crouching are particularly important defences against birds of prey. However, predominantly nocturnal activity provides some protection against the latter.

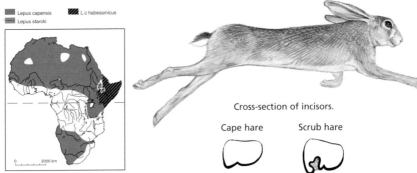

Cross-section of incisors.

Cape hare   Scrub hare

Cape hare *Lepus capensis*

Other names: Fr. *Lièvre du Cap.* Ger. *Kaphase.* Swah. *Sungura.*
Measurements: HB 40–68cm. T 7–15cm. W 1–3.5kg.
Recognition: Back is variable light shades of brown, buff or grey while the chest is normally sandy coloured. There are muted contrasts on the face and nape of the neck. The incisors are without deep grooves and a forehead spot is rare. There is enormous regional variation.
Subspecies: Over 30 subspecies have been named, included here is the small, desert-dwelling *L. c. habessinicus* (Horn of Africa).
Habitat: Prefers completely open grasslands, steppes and subdesert. The Cape hare will move into cleared or regularly fired grasslands (only to be displaced by scrub hares if there is extensive woody regrowth) but is seldom found in montane areas.
Food: A high proportion of herbs and fire-dependent grasses, cropped close to the ground.
Status: Not endangered. This species benefits from woodland clearance and overgrazing.

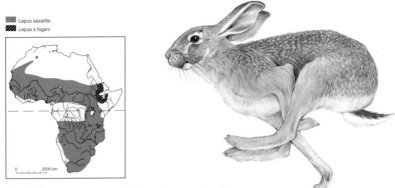

Scrub hare *Lepus saxatilis* (syn. *L. crawshayi*)

Other names: Fr. *Lièvre des rochers.*
Measurements: HB 41–58cm. T 7–17cm. W 1.5–4.5kg.
Recognition: Back is variable darker shades of brown to grey, with all-white underparts and well-defined pattern contrasts on the face. The nape of the neck is warm russet and a forehead spot is common. Incisors have deep grooves and the muzzle is more projecting than in the Cape hare. There is enormous regional variation, especially in the length of the ears.

Subspecies: Over 30 races have been named. Distinctive major populations (regarded as species by some authorities) are: *L. s. saxatilis* (S Africa), *L. s. whytei* (SE Africa), *L. s. crawshayi* (central Africa), *L. s. victoriae* (E Africa), *L. s. ansorgei* (west central Africa), *L. s. fagani* (NE Africa), *L. s. canopus*(W Africa).

Habitat: Prefers scrubby grasslands, grassy areas within woodlands, secondary growth, cultivation mosaics and stony, wooded steppes; common in upland and montane grasslands.

Food: Rank grass species, which are cropped less close to the ground. In E Africa scrub hares take fewer herbs than Cape hares.

Status: Not endangered.

Starck's hare.

Riverine rabbit.

Starck's hare *Lepus starcki*

Other names: Fr. *Lièvre éthiopien.* Ger. *Starckhase.*

Measurements: HB est. 42–60cm. T 7–12cm. W 2–3.5kg.

Recognition: Back is mottled tawny, becoming grey on the rump. Nape, sides, chest and legs are tawny and the underparts are white. The tail is all white or with black stripe. Ears have a prominent black tip.

Habitat: High-altitude moorlands (2,500–4,000m.) in Ethiopia.

Food: Common moorland grasses (*Agrostis, Eleusine, Festuca, Pennisetum* and *Poa*) are likely food plants.

Status: Common within a restricted habitat, Starck's hare is reported to fluctuate in numbers. (It may be an Ice-Age isolate of the European hare, *L. europaeus.*) Probably not threatened at present.

Riverine rabbit *Bunolagus monticularis*

Other names: Fr. *Lièvre des buissons.* Ger. *Buschhase.*

Measurements: HB 42–58cm. T 8–15cm. W 2–3kg.

Recognition: A long-eared, medium-sized hare with relatively short hindfeet, a brown tail and a very conspicuous dark line separating the white chin and bib from the darker muzzle and cheeks. There are conspicuous pale eye rings and white fringes along the upper edges of the ears.

Distribution: Restricted to a single river system in the central area of the Karoo plateau, Cape Province, South Africa.

Habitat: Dense vegetation bordering seasonal rivers in the Karoo where salt-loving plants, such as *Salsola* and *Lycium*, predominate. The riverine rabbit digs short burrows which it plugs with debris when not in use.

Food: Browses on common shrubs, i.e. *Salsola, Kochia* and the ubiquitous *Mesembryanthemum.*

Behaviour: Solitary, with ♂ home ranges of about 20ha and ♀ 13ha. Activity is nocturnal. Single young, weighing only 40g at birth, are reared in a fur- and grass-lined burrow.

Adaptations: Sharing features of both red rock hares and true hares, this species may represent the ecologically specialised relict of a once more-widespread African hare that has been displaced by the arrival of more advanced true hares from Eurasia.

Status : 60% of the riverine rabbit's habitat has been destroyed for wheat cultivation and fragmented by farms. It is protected from hunting but is currently found only on privately owned farms. Highly endangered.

Common rabbit   Uganda grass hare

Common rabbit *Oryctolagus cuniculus*

Other names: Fr. *Lapin*. Ger. *Wildkaninchen*.
Measurements: HB 30–50cm. T 3–8cm. W 0.8–3kg.
Recognition: Small, short-limbed, brown-coated rabbit or 'digging hare', with shorter ears and a rounder head than true hares. The tips of the ears are never black.
Subspecies: *O. cuniculus huxleyi* (S Spain, S France and N Africa): possibly original wild stock.
Distribution: It is uncertain whether the rabbit was endemic to NW Africa or a very early introduction from Spain. Its spread into N Europe and transportation to Australia, South America and innumerable islands has been a result of human intervention.
Habitat: Bushy and broken country in N Morocco and NW Algeria, avoiding densely wooded land and desert. Rabbits live on the surface when predators and the climate allow. The digging of dens, burrows or warrens is likely to represent a response to a combination of environmental pressures.
Food: Grass and herbs; bark in winter.
Behaviour: As with all hares, rabbits produce a variety of scents which help to regulate their social behaviour. ♂♂ mark out their home ranges with pellets, urine and chin secretions. Increasing density and social clustering generally increase the animals' intolerance of the same sex (either generally or towards strange rabbits from outside their own 'family' group). They breed all year, are fertile by 4 months and can live for up to 8 years. Gestation lasts 1 month and the young, born blind and helpless in a burrow or nest, are weaned in 3 weeks. Their potential for increase is legendary and as many as 45 young can be born to a single ♀ in 1 year.
Adaptations: The rabbit's fecundity has evolved to withstand very high levels of predation. Where predators have been destroyed, reduced or are absent (as in Europe, Australia and on islands), rabbits accommodate to their own huge numbers by forming large 'family' groups in 'warrens', or burrow clusters, and defend their group territories against other groups. Where numbers are few and shelter is ubiquitous, rabbits are spaced out more evenly, have less frequent aggressive encounters and show more resemblance to other hare species.
Status: Common and intensively hunted in NW Africa where it damages crops. Not endangered.

Uganda grass-hare *Poelagus marjorita*

Other names: Eng. Bunyoro rabbit. Fr. *Lapin sauvage d'Afrique*. Ger. *Uganda Grasshase*. Swah. *Sungura ya Bunyoro*.
Measurements: HB 44–50cm. T 4–5cm. W 2–3kg.
Recognition: Resembles the common rabbit but the fur is coarser, the nose more protuberant and the hindfeet proportionately shorter.
Subspecies: *P. m. marjorita*, (northern part of range), *P. marjorita larkeni*, (southern, Angolan, part of range).
Distribution: Uganda to central Africa, Angola.
Habitat: Moist, wooded grasslands associated with rocky or broken ground. It shelters in dense vegetation, rock clefts and self-made 'scrapes'.
Food: Grasses (preferably short), grass seeds, herbs and, occasionally, cultivated crops.

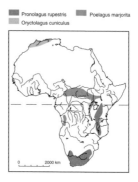

Pronolagus rupestris Poelagus marjorita
Oryctolagus cuniculus

0   2000 km

Smith's red rock hare.

Behaviour: Uganda grass-hares are continuous breeders and the helpless young are born in a nest (blocked by the mother with a vegetation barrier). Predators include serval cats, jackals, pythons and birds of prey. Mainly nocturnal and solitary or in very small groups.

Adaptations: Apparently dependent on abundant shelter from rocks, bushes or dense grass, Uganda grass-hares lack the stamina and speed of true hares. The muscles are pink (as in common rabbits) not red (as in hares).

Status : Locally declining but unlikely to be threatened overall. Occurs in several national parks.

Rock hares *Pronolagus*

Smith's red rock hare	*Pronolagus rupestris*
Natal red rock hare	*Pronolagus crassicaudatus*
Jameson's red rock hare	*Pronolagus randensis*

Other names: Fr. *Lièvre roux*. Ger. *Rothase*.
Measurements: Total length 43–67cm. W. 1.3–3kg.
Recognition: Chunky, grizzled hares with a red or dark tail, a grey head and reddish limbs.
Distribution: Very discontinuous in S Africa and the Eastern Rift Valley to Kenya.
Habitat: Broken and rocky country with abundant cover of bushes and grass. Populations of red rock hares are very scattered and patchy in distribution.
Food: Strong preference for grasses.
Behaviour: Red rock hares live close to rocky refuge areas. They are solitary and nocturnal but are occasionally also active by day. One or two young are born in a helpless condition in plant- and fur-lined nests. They are preyed on by eagle owls and sometimes also by black eagles.
Adaptations: All species are closely associated with cooler climates and rocky habitats where agility over well-known broken ground pre-empts competition from the true hares, which are adapted to more open country.
Status : All species are well represented in reserves and national parks but have been inadequately studied.

Smith's red rock hare *Pronolagus rupestris*

Other names: Fr. *Lièvre roux de Smith*. Ger. *Smith-Rothase*. Swah. *Sungura ya Mawe*.
Measurements: HB 38–53cm. T 5–12cm. W 1.3–2.5kg.
Recognition: Grey-headed hare with a bright russet rump and legs. The red tail normally has a black tip. The black colour is variable and the fur is soft and dense.
Subspecies: *P. r. rupestris* (S Africa): six subspecies possible. *P. r. nyikae* (Zambia and Malawi), *P. r. vallicola* (E Africa).
Habitat: Stony country where dense bush, grass and rocks are intermingled. Smith's red rock hares shelter in 'forms', like other hares, usually under slabs of stone or in crevices. They use habitual latrines where they are said to be readily trapped. Solitary animals, they will congregate temporarily on grassy lawns at night.

Food: Mainly grazers.
Status: Extremely discontinuous distribution and relatively small patches of suitable habitat may mean that local populations are vulnerable to extinction. Overall not endangered.

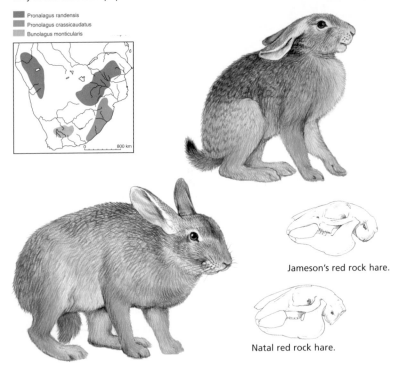

■ Pronalagus randensis
■ Pronolagus crassicaudatus
■ Bunolagus monticularis

800 km

Jameson's red rock hare.

Natal red rock hare.

Natal red rock hare *Pronolagus crassicaudatus*
Other names: Fr. *Lièvre roux du Natal.* Ger. *Natal-Rothase.*
Measurements: HB 46–56cm. T 3.5–11cm. W 2.4–3kg.
Recognition: Rock hare with a pale grey band across the cheek, russet fore- and hindlegs and rump, and an all-russet tail. The dense fur is harsher than in other rock hares.
Habitat: Steep, grassy hillsides with scattered rocks and boulders along the eastern seaboard of South Africa and S Mozambique from East London to the R. Maputo, and from sea-level up to 1,550m. The hare shelters among the rocks in tussocks or dense, low vegetation.
Food: Grasses are grazed at night. Often move to higher elevations to graze and may do so in close proximity to each other.
Status: Locally abundant. Seasonally protected as a 'game species'.

Jameson's red rock hare *Pronolagus randensis*
Other names: Fr. *Lièvre roux de Jameson.* Ger. *Rand-Rothase.*
Measurements: HB 42–50cm. T 6–13.5cm. W 1.8–3kg.
Recognition: Rock hare with a light grey head with brownish flecks and a light, warm-coloured rump and back legs. The red-brown tail has a black tip. The fur is very soft and silky.
Subspecies: *P. r. randensis* (Transvaal and Zimbabwe), *P. r. caucinus* (Namibia).
Habitat: Rocky hills, valleys and gorges in two widely separate areas of S Africa (Zimbabwe-Transvaal and Namibia). The hares shelter among rocks and tussocks during the day. They are very agile among boulders and able to run over very steep surfaces.
Food: Fresh green flushes of grasses are favoured and are usually grazed in proximity to rocks and koppies at night.
Status: Locally abundant but declining in settled areas. Not endangered.

RODENTS RODENTIA

Squirrels	Sciuridae
Anomalures	Anomaluridae
Spring hares	Pedetidae
Gundis	Ctenodactylidae
Dormice	Myoxidae (syn. Gliridae)
Blesmols	Bathyergidae
Porcupines	Hystricidae
Cane-rats	Thryonomyidae
Dassie rat	Petromuridae
Jerboas	Dipodidae
Rat-like rodents	Muroidea

Of all the mammalian orders rodents contain the largest number of species. The most obvious common feature of rodents is their prominent gnawing teeth, two incisors in each jaw with a long space, or diastema, before the cheek teeth. The body build of most rodents is that of conventional quadrupeds but evolution of burrowing, bounding, climbing and gliding has given rise to more specialised body forms in a number of groups.

The three major rodent divisions, squirrel forms (sciuromorphs), porcupine forms (hystricomorphs) and rat forms (myomorphs), have distinctly different arrangements of chewing muscles, orbits and teeth. The anomalures, spring hares and blesmols are all very ancient African groups that are so specialised that their affinities with the three main rodent groups are still uncertain.

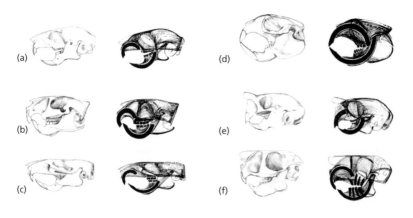

(a) Squirrel (Sciurid). (b) Cane rat (Porcupine family). (c) Giant rat (Rats or Myomorphs). (d) Blesmol (Bathyergid). (e) Flying mouse (Anomalurid). (f) Spring hare (Pedetid).

Rodent diets are diverse and include animal foods, roots, fruits and seeds. Insectivorous rodents tend to have sharp-cusped molars and a slender muzzle. True herbivores have broad incisors, mill-like grinding teeth and a stout skull, while omnivores tend to be intermediate.

While many rodents have acute sight (especially squirrels) and some are extremely sensitive to sound, all rely heavily on scent (especially in the regulation of their social behaviour). Some rodents are well-known pests and a few can present a threat to human health (notably rats). Periodic population explosions among some species are a particular hazard for rural farmers. Rodents play important structural roles in ecosystems, for example, by pruning or eliminating vegetation types, spreading seeds, competing with other animals and helping to spread diseases.

SQUIRRELS SCIURIDAE

Ground squirrels	Xerini
African pygmy squirrels	Myosciurini
Rope squirrels	*Funisciurus*
Bush squirrels	*Paraxerus*
Giant and sun squirrels	Protoxerini

The name 'squirrel' is an anglicisation of the Greek *skiouros*, meaning 'shade-tail' and their tails are, indeed, their most immediately striking feature. Some squirrels are brightly coloured, with red tints or body stripes, indicating that vision is an important sense. The eyes are relatively large, ears small and the head tends to be blunt and round, with powerful muscles for gnawing hard foods. Most are competent climbers.

Squirrels appear to be relatively late arrivals in Africa, entering the continent about 10 million years ago (probably as arid-adapted ground squirrels). They subsequently radiated into four main groups. The ground squirrels, or Xerini, retain the most widely dispersed distribution. The rope squirrels (*Funisciurus*) are small, partially terrestrial animals that often include insects in their diets. Bush squirrels (*Paraxerus*) are more consistently arboreal, while the giant and sun squirrels (Protoxerini), are highly successful, arboreal, mostly forest squirrels with a strong preference for eating nuts.

Most, if not all, squirrels build nests but many use tree or ground holes. Many species are highly vocal and sound, scent and sight are all employed in their signalling behaviour.

Squirrels tend to be conspicuous and all known species are profiled here because, like monkeys, they readily catch the attention of naturalists and can be identified by external clues alone.

GROUND SQUIRRELS XERINI

Barbary ground squirrel	*Atlantoxerus getulus*
Unstriped ground squirrel	*Xerus rutilus*
Striped ground squirrel	*Euxerus erythropus*
South African ground squirrel	*Geosciurus inauris*
Damara ground squirrel	*Geosciurus princeps*

Coarse-coated terrestrial squirrels, with claws adapted to digging rather than climbing. Ancestral ground squirrels are thought to have entered Africa about 10 million years ago. A relict population of Asian Xerini still exists in Iran. Ground squirrels have little or no pinnae to the ears and all rely on self-dug burrows to escape predators and extremes of climate. The young are born blind and helpless in secure burrows and take up to 2 months to become relatively independent.

Barbary ground squirrel *Atlantoxerus getulus*

Other names: Fr. *Ecureuil fouisseur de Barbarie*. Ger. *Barbarie-erdhornchen*.
Measurements: HB est. 30–45cm. T est. 20–25cm. W est. 50–1,100g.
Recognition: A boldly striped, ground-dwelling squirrel with a short, coarse-textured coat marked with two white stripes down each side, a prominent eye ring and a nearly naked, pale underside. The tail is bushy with bold black and white banding.
Habitat: Rocky areas with scattered trees and bushes in the Atlas Mts in Morocco and W Algeria. The Barbary ground squirrel is diurnal and shelters in burrows or among rocks during the night and during the heat of the day.
Food: Nuts and seeds, including those of the commercially valuable argan (*Argania*), which produces an oil used for cooking.
Status: Widespread within its range. Not protected.

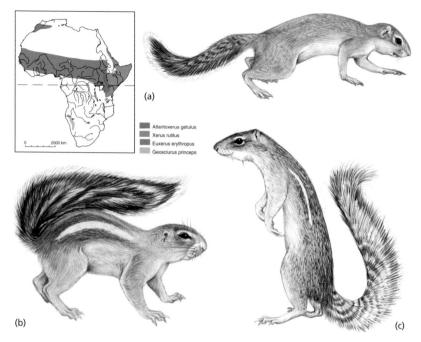

(a) Unstriped ground squirrel. (b) Barbary ground squirrel. (c) Striped ground squirrel.

Unstriped ground squirrel *Xerus rutilus*

Other names: Fr. *Ecureuil fouisseur.* Ger. *Erdhornchen.*
Measurements: HB 20–26cm. T 18–23cm. W 300–335g.
Recognition: A small, unstriped ground squirrel, ticked with white on a reddish ground, and with pale underparts. The tail is relatively sombre and often stained by earth.
Habitat: Very dry steppe, savannah and subdesert country in the Horn of Africa.
Food: Roots, pods. seeds, fruits, stems, leaves, and occasional insects.
Status: Widespread. Not endangered.

Striped ground squirrel *Euxerus erythropus*

Other names: Fr. *Ecureuil fouisseur.* Ger. *Erdhornchen.*
Measurements: HB 30–46cm. T 18.5–27cm. W 500–1,000g.
Recognition: A grizzled brown terrestrial squirrel, lighter in arid areas, darker in the more humid southern parts of its range. The long tail is lightly banded and there is a single short stripe on each side. The muzzle is long, blunt and well furred, with a projecting nose.
Habitat: Open woodlands, Sudanic savannahs and Sahelian habitats from Mauritania to E Africa. The striped ground squirrel lives in rock and tree-root crevices, in termitaria and in self-dug burrows.
Food: Roots, grass seeds, fallen fruits, seeds and nuts, *Acacia* pods, leaves and various animal foods. Nuts and seeds may be stored in burrows or crevices.
Status: Common and widespread. Not endangered.

South African ground squirrel *Geosciurus inauris*

Other names: Fr. *Ecureuil fouisseur du Cap.* Ger. *Kap-erdhornchen.*
Measurements: HB 20–30cm. T 18.25cm. W 500–1,100g.
Recognition: Tawny-yellow squirrel, bristly-haired, with a very round, blunt head and large eyes. Incisor teeth are white. The white underside is almost naked in many individuals. There is a white side-stripe on the flanks and two bands on the hairs of the tail. Diurnal and gregarious (with territorial groups based on a hierarchy of resident breeding ♀♀ and more peripatetic ♂♂). Very vocal and playful.

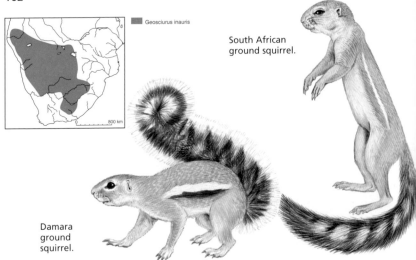

Geosciurus inauris

South African ground squirrel.

800 km

Damara ground squirrel.

Habitat: Open country in S Africa, with a strong preference for compacted sandy areas where it digs its communal burrows. Stones and shallow scrapes around the colony entrances are regularly rubbed with the face or anal region or urinated on. Sunning and sand-bathing are regular activities. Continuous excavation makes warrens very large and complex and spreads spoil heaps all around the many exit holes. Spare burrow space is often used by mongooses (yellow mongoose and suricates), which sometimes also play with the squirrels. The massive impact that the squirrel has on its immediate surroundings is also partly due to its excavation of food plants and excretion of nutrients.
Food: Leaves and stems of grasses and shrubs, seeds, bulbs, and tubers; also leaves, buds and fruits of bushes and various insects.
Status: Not endangered.

Damara ground squirrel *Geosciurus princeps*

Other names: Fr. *Ecureuil fouisseur du Damara*. Ger. *Damara-erdhornchen*.
Measurements: HB est. 20–33cm. T est. 20–34cm. W est. 500–1,200g.
Recognition: Resembles the South African ground squirrel but has a longer, bushier tail (with three black bands terminating in a long white point that forms a conspicuous white 'halo'). The incisor teeth are orange and the eye orbits are relatively large. Colouring is slightly lighter and brighter.
Habitat: Rocky hillsides and outcrops along the Kaokoveld escarpments from S Angola to S Namibia. The squirrel frequently takes refuge among rocks and crevices. It avoids flat, open land, preferring broken, hilly land.
Food: Presumed to feed on hillside equivalents of the South African ground squirrel's diet, i.e. grass leaves, stems and seeds, roots, bulbs and tubers and the fallen fruits and seeds of bushes. Insects are also taken.
Status: A long, linear but probably patchy distribution in mainly uninhabited country. Not endangered.

AFRICAN PYGMY SQUIRRELS MYOSCIURINI

African pygmy squirrel	*Myosciurus pumilio*

Pygmy squirrels in Africa, South-East Asia and South America have such close resemblances that they were formerly lumped together in a subfamily Nannosciurinae. It is now agreed that these resemblances are due to convergence and that the African species has evolved from the same stock as other African squirrels. Although its relationships remain opaque it probably shares an ancient ancestry with *Funisciurus*.

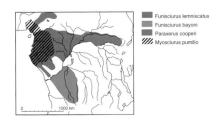

Funisciurus lemniscatus
Funisciurus bayoni
Paraxerus cooperi
Myosciurus pumilio

African Pygmy squirrel *Myosciurus pumilio*

Other names: Fr. *Écureuil nain*. Ger. *Zwerghörnchen*.

Measurements: HB 70–78mm. T 52–58mm. W 15–18g.

Recognition: Extremely small mahogany-coloured squirrel with pale underparts, cream-coloured fur around the eye and mouth, and white ears. The tail has a reddish base and a darker terminal bush. A shy species, tending to hide at any disturbance. It can move very fast.

Habitat: Only found in the wettest area of the Bight of Biafra, from the Cross R to S Gabon. It lives on the trunks and larger branches of large trees in primary forest and shows a strong preference for caesalpinoid-dominated tree communities.

Food: Mainly invertebrates (often collected from resin sites where the gums are ignored by this species). Buds and young leaves, and fruits, are also taken.

Status: Although locally abundant, probably declining due to felling of primary forests.

Rope squirrels *Funisciurus*

Ribboned rope squirrel	*Funisciurus lemniscatus*
Lunda rope squirrel	*Funisciurus bayoni*
Thomas's rope squirrel	*Funisciurus anerythrus*
Fire-footed rope squirrel	*Funisciurus pyrropus*
Red cheeked rope squirrel	*Funisciurus leucogenys*
Lady Burton's rope squirrel	*Funisciurus isabella*
Kintampo rope squirrel	*Funisciurus substriatus*
Congo rope squirrel	*Funisciurus congicus*
Carruther's mountain squirrel	*Funisciurus carruthersi*

Recognition: Small, thin, soft-furred squirrels with a fluffy, rather flimsy tail that is frequently carried curled over the back and is continuously flicked. Tail jerks are sometimes synchronised with loud territorial or warning calls. Some species have red or yellowish tints, pale side-stripes or even spots. Their coats are less agouti-grizzled and plainer than other African squirrels. In spite of loud calls and a tendency to approach disturbances, the dark colours of rope squirrels are very difficult to see and their main defence is to freeze or move behind the nearest tree.

Genealogy: Rope squirrels are relatively primitive squirrels that maintain partly terrestrial habits but have differentiated in diet and in their degree of arborealism. The most terrestrial and insectivorous is the ribboned rope squirrel, *F. lemniscatus* (the little-known Lunda squirrel, *F. bayoni*, may be its counterpart south of the R. Zaïre). Somewhat more frugivorous are the fire-footed (*F. pyrropus*), red-cheeked (*F. leucogenys*) and Thomas's (*F. anerythrus*) rope squirrels. The third group, Lady Burton's (*F. isabella*), Kintampo (*F. substriatus*) and Congo (*F. congicus*) rope squirrels are predominantly fruit- and leaf-eaters that spend more time in the trees. Primary divergences in diet may have been followed by separation in response to past changes in climate and as a result of isolation of populations. During wet phases fire-foots, true forest species, would have been dominant. During drier periods the more strictly riverine Thomas's might have been favoured. Today their ranges interdigitate or overlap.

Geography: Rope squirrels tend to live in dark, shady habitats but, in common with all squirrels, like to sun-bathe in transitory shafts of light. Their almost exclusive equatorial and mainly lowland W African distribution may reflect a compromise between sensitivity to cold and adaptation to life on the forest floor.

Ecology: Ground-dwelling is combined with a tendency to hoard (they may be important dispersers and planters for some tree species). The divergence between more and less insectivorous species reflects the need for different physiologies and strategies in exploiting the rich resources of fallen fruits and insects on the forest floor. Rope squirrels tend to use habitual feeding stations (generally a raised root with a good view of the surroundings). They are frequent prey to forest birds of prey.

Natural history: Frequent noisy contacts between squirrels constitutes an aspect of their territorial behaviour, as does their use of scent, which is strong even to the human nose. Rope squirrels mob snakes, birds and large mammals with bird-like chirps which are extremely difficult to locate and are combined with rapid advances and retreats. Oestrous ♀♀ advertise their condition with sound and scent.

Adaptations: Complex nest-making behaviour, which includes laborious daily shredding of bark, palm leaves or other fibres, appears to be necessary to maintain warm, dry resting conditions. Their large nests are concealed (usually at low levels) in buttresses, palm-frond bases or in hollow or perforated trunks. Such behaviour may have facilitated their colonisation of a dark, wet habitat.

Ribboned rope squirrel *Funisciurus lemniscatus*

Other names: Fr. *Funisciure rayé*. Ger. *Vierstreifenhornchen*.
Measurements: HB 15–18cm. T 13–19cm. W 100–150g.
Recognition: A small olive-coloured squirrel with two dark and two pale stripes restricted to the flanks. Underparts are white. The tail is banded with sombre cream and sepia.
Habitat: Ranges from R. Sanaga to R. Zaïre and R. Aruwimi; predominantly terrestrial.
Food: About 40% animal matter and 60% fruits and seeds. Leaves and mushrooms are occasionally taken. Almost all food is collected on the ground.
Status: Not endangered.

Lunda rope squirrel *Funisciurus bayoni*

Other names: Fr. *Funisciure de Bocage*. Ger. *Bocages Streifenhornchen*.
Measurements: HB 16–19.5cm. T 13–17cm. W 110–160g.
Recognition: The back is greyish olive-green, with a fine black grizzle and the underside is pale grey. There is a pale eye ring and a poorly defined pale stripe on flanks. The indistinctly barred tail has hairs broadly banded in black and white near their tips.
Habitat: Mosaic of rainforest and moist woodlands in NE Angola and SW Zaïre.
Food: Not known (if research in this area is carried out it may provide clues to this species' affinity with other rope squirrels).
Status: Insufficiently known.

Thomas's rope squirrel *Funisciurus anerythrus*

Other names: Fr. *Funisciure à dos rayé*. Ger. *Thomas-Streifenhornchen*.
Measurements: HB 16–23cm. T 13–20cm. W 200–220g.
Recognition: The back is brownish olive, with variable pale flank stripes. The underside is grey or buff. The tail has a light 'halo' over a broad band of very dark grey. The base of the tail hairs is greyish or dull orange.
Habitat: Predominantly recorded from the margins of the R. Zaïre, R. Ogooué and other rivers from Nigeria to Uganda in the north, and from Angola to S Zaïre. Lives in the lower strata of dense secondary growth along the margins of rivers and swamps, spending much of its time on the ground.
Food: In Gabon, about 80% fruits and 20% animal matter. Leaves and mushrooms are occasionally taken.
Status: Widespread and common. Considered a pest of cocoa in some areas. Not endangered.

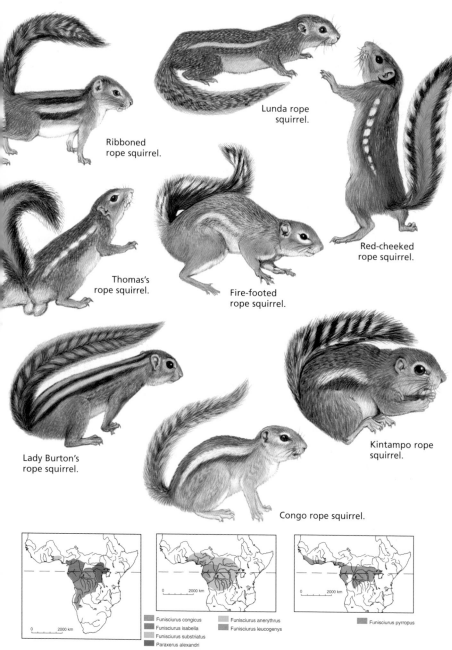

Ribboned
rope squirrel.

Lunda rope
squirrel.

Red-cheeked
rope squirrel.

Thomas's
rope squirrel.

Fire-footed
rope squirrel.

Lady Burton's
rope squirrel.

Kintampo rope
squirrel.

Congo rope squirrel.

Funisciurus congicus
Funisciurus isabella
Funisciurus substriatus
Paraxerus alexandri

Funisciurus anerythrus
Funisciurus leucogenys

Funisciurus pyrropus

Fire-footed rope squirrel *Funisciurus pyrropus*

Other names: Fr. *Funisciure à pattes rousses.* Ger. *Roteschenkelhornchen.*
Measurements: HB 13.5–26.6cm. T 10–20cm. W 160–300g.
Recognition: A velvety-furred squirrel with rich rufous limbs and face, and a dark
(sometimes almost black) back, finely flecked with pale buff to give it a greenish
appearance. The underside is white, sometimes orange. A pale side-stripe on the flanks is a
variable feature (as is the intensity of red in the tail and limbs). Tail hair bases are orange,
then black with white tips, giving a silvery 'halo'. Often heard before it is seen, this species
utters a series of strident, bird-like chirps or a loud three-syllable call.

Habitat: From Sierra Leone to the R. Nile and throughout the R. Zaïre basin at low and medium altitudes. It prefers undergrowth and especially palm groves under a closed canopy. Nests are generally made at low level, especially among buttress roots.

Food: In Gabon, about 75% fruits and about 18% animal matter (this may differ in less rich forest communities). Gums and mushrooms are also eaten regularly. Forages mostly on the ground.

Status: Common and widespread. Not endangered.

Red-cheeked rope squirrel *Funisciurus leucogenys*

Other names: Fr. *Funisciure à tête orange*. Ger. *Orangekopf Streifenhornchen*.

Measurements: HB 17–21.5cm. T 13–20cm. W 200–300g.

Recognition: A small squirrel of rather variable tints. The olive-brown back is punctuated by a line of pale or orange dashes or spots running over the flank from shoulder to haunch. The face is usually orange-red. The underside is grey or pale orange. The bases of the tail hair show as a broad orange midline from below but terminal black and white bands make a bold cross-bar pattern from above.

Habitat: Lowland and montane forests from the R. Volta eastwards to the R. Ubangi and R. Zaïre; also Bioko I. (formerly Fernando Po). Restricted to forest floor and low levels in old mature rainforest.

Food: Not known in detail. Mainly fallen fruits.

Status: A wide range suggests that this species is not endangered overall , but declining locally with felling of primary forest.

Lady Burton's rope squirrel *Funisciurus isabella*

Other names: Fr. *Funisciure de Gray*. Ger. *Gray Streifenhornchen*.

Measurements: HB 15–18cm. T 13–18cm. W 100–115g.

Recognition: A small dark squirrel with pale stripes delimiting four bold black stripes running from head to tail. The head and outer limb surfaces are olive brown and the underside pale grey. Tail hairs are relatively short and are banded in ochre and black, giving the appearance of warm flashes along its entire length.

Habitat: Occurs patchily between the R. Zaïre and R. Cross in Gabon, lower Cameroon and in montane forest in the Highlands. Woven nests, in the form of a complete globe, are sealed when occupied by the young.

Food: In Gabon, fruits (80%) and leaves (about 10%). Small amounts of animal matter and occasionally mushrooms are also taken.

Status: Patchy distribution. Presumed not endangered.

Kintampo rope squirrel *Funisciurus substriatus*

Other names: Fr. *Funisciure du Kintampo*. Ger. *Togostreifenhornchen*.

Measurements: HB 15–18cm. T 14–20cm. W est. 100–150g.

Recognition: A small olive-coloured squirrel with short, poorly defined light and dark stripes on the flanks. Tail hairs are grey at the base then dark brown with buff tips, giving a pattern of muted bands from above and a pale longitudinal strip from the side.

Habitat: Woodlands and forest edges in the 'Dahomey Gap' area between Nigeria and Ghana.

Food: Not recorded.

Status: Dense settlement and cultivation coupled with a scarcity of records from its area of distribution suggest that this is a rare or vulnerable species.

Congo rope squirrel *Funisciurus congicus*

Other names: Fr. *Funisciure de Kuhl*. Ger. *Kongo Streifenhornchen*.

Measurements: HB 14.5–15.6cm. T 16–17cm. W 108–113g.

Recognition: The back is grizzled brown, with a long white side-stripe and a narrower dark line below it. Outer surfaces of the limbs, flanks and face are buff. The underside and eye ring are white or pale. The long tail has distinct bars and a yellowish 'halo'. A very vocal species, often seen in groups numbering up to four.

Habitat: Ranges over a large part of the Zaïre basin and W Angola., occupying diverse habitats, from isolated belts of large trees growing in very dry savannahs to true rainforest.

Food: The Congo rope squirrel spends about half of its time on the ground, foraging for fallen seeds and fruit of dominant tree or shrub species, such as mopane (*Colophospermum mopane*), *Commiphora* and *Grewia*. It is also an agile climber after leaves and shoots of *Justicia* and leaf galls. Caterpillars are also eaten. In N Namibia optimal feeding may influence two birth peaks (just before and after the wet season).
Status: Widespread and common. Not endangered.

Carruther's mountain squirrel *Funisciurus carruthersi*

Other names: Fr. *Funisciure de montagne*. Ger. *Bergstreifenhornchen*.
Measurements: HB 20–26cm. T 18–20cm. W 200–336g.
Recognition: Olive-green squirrel with a cloud-grey underside and a black and yellow barred tail with a black tip. Rings of pale cream-coloured fur surround the eyes.
Habitat: Between 1,500 and 2,800m in the mountain chains of E Zaïre and W Uganda, especially in stands of African wild plums (*Prunus africanum*), a dominant tree of the area. Large, globular nests, lined with finely shredded bark, are constructed in dense tangles. This squirrel ranges through all vegetation levels and frequently spends time on the ground.
Food: Various fruits and seeds (e.g. *Bridelia* and *Strombosia*); occasionally insects.
Status: Common within several national parks. Of special interest as a morphological 'bridge' combining characteristics of *Funisciurus* and *Paraxerus*. Not endangered.

Bush squirrels *Paraxerus*

Cooper's mountain squirrel	*Paraxerus cooperi*
Tanganyika mountain squirrels	*Paraxerus lucifer*
Lushoto mountain squirrel	*Paraxerus vexillarius*
Red-bellied coast squirrel	*Paraxerus palliatus*
Smith's bush squirrel	*Paraxerus cepapi*
Ochre bush squirrel	*Paraxerus ochraceus*
Striped bush squirrel	*Paraxerus flavovittis*
Green squirrel	*Paraxerus poensis*
Boehm's squirrel	*Paraxerus boehmi*
Alexander's dwarf squirrel	*Paraxerus alexandri*

Recognition: Short, thick fur, very variable (and sometimes bright) colour patterns and a tendency to slightly longer ear pinnae are typical features of bush squirrels. Although closely related to rope squirrels, bush squirrels are a much more heterogenous group and include both very small and quite large species. Most species have three pairs of mammae.
Genealogy: The largest, most diverse and adaptable of African squirrels, some species are effectively intermediate between small, largely terrestrial rope squirrels and the larger, almost wholly arboreal sun squirrels.
Geography: Predominantly E and central African (in contrast to the rope squirrels' W African forest bias). Some species appear to be at an advantage in climatically unstable areas. As a group they span a wide range of ecotypes.
Ecology: Like rope squirrels, many species of bush squirrels show a preference for low-level vegetation and shade, spending much time on the ground. Some are clearly the eastern ecological equivalents of rope squirrel species in W Africa. The very varied diets include fruits, seeds, nuts, mushrooms, gum and invertebrates.
Natural history: Unlike sun squirrels, which are fast arboreal 'fleers', bush squirrels tend to be 'hiders' and, in the face of a potential threat, will slide or creep out of sight, hugging themselves close to a branch.
Adaptations: Bush squirrels have robust, well-cusped teeth with hard enamel, well suited to varied and omnivorous diets.

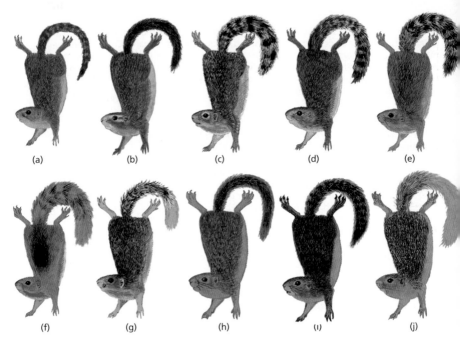

(a) Cooper's mountain squirrel (*Paraxerus cooperi*). (b) Green squirrel (*Paraxerus poensis*). (c) Carruther's mountain squirrel (*Funisciurus carruthersi*). (d, e, f) Tanganyika mountain squirrels (*Paraxerus lucifer*), byatti, laetus, lucifer. (g) Lushoto mountain squirrel (*Paraxerus vexillarius*). (h, i) Montane variants of palliatus – Selinda mountain squirrel, *Pp. vincenti*, *Pp. ornatus*. (j) Red bellied coast squirrel (*Paraxerus palliatus palliatus*)

Cooper's mountain squirrel *Paraxerus cooperi*

Other names: Fr. *Ecureuil des bois de Cooper*. Ger. *Cooper Buschhornchen*.
Measurements: HB 19–20cm. T 19cm. W est. 200–300g.
Recognition: The back is grizzled olive green and the underparts are pale grey mixed with a yellowish sheen. Cheeks are yellowish. The long, slender but bushy tail has narrow ochre stripes between broader brown bars. Hands, feet and thighs are of variable colour, sometimes deep russet.
Habitat: Montane and intermediate forests in the Cameroon highland area.
Food: Fruits and flowers of the tallow tree (*Pentadesma*) have been noted.
Status: Highly localised in habitats subject to rapid destruction. Vulnerable, although locally common.

Tanganyika mountain squirrels *Paraxerus lucifer*

Other names: Fr. *Ecureuil des bois du Tanganyika*. Ger. *Berg-Buschhornchen*.
Measurements: HB 20–33cm. T 16–27cm. W est. 650–750g.
Recognition: There are three separate populations of closely related Tanganyika mountain squirrels. All have soft fur with warm tints on the face, feet and base of the tail and silvery-tipped dove-grey undersides. In *P. l. byatti* the tints are muted, the back is grizzled olive and the tail is barred with dark brown and fine cream cross-bars. In the larger *P. l. laetus* the face, limbs and rump region are more strongly russet and the tail is more thickly haired with bold black and white bars. *P. l. lucifer*, the largest race, is richly red all over, with a black back and half-hidden black bars in the thick red tail.
Habitat: Montane forests of E Tanganyika (*P. l. byatti*), the eastern side of L. Malawi (*P. l. laetus*) and north and west of L. Malawi (*P. l. lucifer*).
Food: Fruits, nuts and invertebrates.
Status: All populations are vulnerable and totally dependent on continued protection of their now very fragmented forest relict ranges.

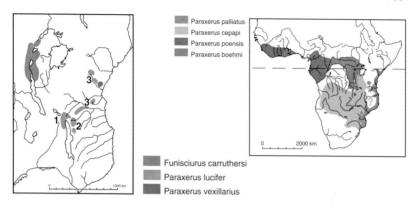

Funisciurus carruthersi
Paraxerus lucifer
Paraxerus vexillarius

Lushoto mountain squirrel *Paraxerus vexillarius*

Measurements: HB 24cm. T 21cm. W est. 650–700g.
Recognition: This squirrel has bright orange hands, feet and tail tip, with a dark olive-green back, dove-grey belly and black and white barred tail.
Habitat: Confined to the montane forests of the W Usambaras and sandwiched between two isolated mountain forests occupied by *P. l. byatti*. While the possibility of this squirrel being the result of hybridisation (with *P. palliatus*) was once considered, it now seems more likely that it derives from genetic drift in a very small founding stock. It could equally well be regarded as one more race of Tanganyika mountain squirrel.
Food: Fruits and seeds.
Status: Fragmentation of the Lushoto forests and expanding cultivation of cardamon threaten its survival. Endangered.

Red-bellied coast squirrel *Paraxerus palliatus*

Other names: Fr. *Ecureuil des bois à ventre rouge*. Ger. *Rotbauch Buschhornchen*.
Measurements: HB 17–25cm. T 10–27cm. W est. 200–550g.
Recognition: Pepper-and-salt grizzled squirrel with orange limbs, underparts and face. Tail hairs show variable degrees of red or orange tipping.
Subspecies: *P. p. palliatus* (centre of range): black and orange tail. *P. p. tanae* (north of range): orange tail. *P. p. ornatus* (south of range): dark red and black tail. *P. p. vincenti* (Namuli Mt): melanic back and tail. *Note:* It is possible that this species hybridises with *Paraxerus cepapi* in Mozambique.
Habitat: Coastal forests and evergreen thickets, lowland riverine forests; isolate (*P. p. vincenti*) in montane forest on Mt Namuli.
Food: Fruits, berries, seeds and various plant parts.
Status: Not endangered but *P. p. vincenti* and *P. p. tanae* are vulnerable.

Smith's bush squirrel *Paraxerus cepapi*

Other names: Fr. *Ecureuil des bois de Smith*. Ger. *Ockerfuss Buschhornchen*.
Measurements: HB 13–18.5cm. T 12–18cm. W 100–260g.
Recognition: Pale grizzled squirrel of very variable tints. Yellowish tints on the face, hindquarters and shoulders may be localised or more extensive. Underparts are white or yellowish. The tail is grizzled, with indistinct black bars and a broken pale-tipped 'halo'. *Note:* It is possible that this species hybridises with *Paraxerus palliatus* in Mozambique.
Habitat: Miombo (*Brachystegia*) woodlands and associated woods and thickets from Angola to W Tanzania and Mozambique.
Food: Various plant foods and insects.
Status: Not endangered.

Ochre bush squirrel *Paraxerus ochraceus*

Other names: Fr. *Ecureuil des bois ocre*. Ger. *Ocker Buschhornchen*.
Measurements: HB 13–18.5cm. T 13–19cm. W 80–100g.

Alexander's dwarf squirrel.

Striped bush squirrel.

Smith's bush squirrel.

Boehm's squirrel.

Recognition: Very variable, grizzled squirrel, with a pale off-white to yellow ochre underside. Subdesertic forms are very pallid; montane populations have darker olive backs. The tail has fine, irregular barring.
Habitat: Dry forests and thickets at various altitudes; also, wooded riverine strips in very arid country from S Sudan to E African coast as far south as R. Rufiji.
Food: Fruits, seeds, buds, flowers, roots, bulbs, *Acacia* gum. Occasionally some animal foods.
Status: Not endangered.

Striped bush squirrel *Paraxerus flavovittis*

Other names: Fr. *Ecureuil des bois rayé*. Ger. *Streifen Buschhornchen*.
Measurements: HB 16–20cm. T 14–18cm. W est. 120–200g.
Recognition: Medium-sized to small, grizzled squirrel with a white stripe down the side emphasised by dark lines above and below. The face also has indistinct 'bands' across the cheek and eye regions. The tail is indistinctly marked with irregular bars. The pale feet have large, heavily clawed toes.
Habitat: Savannah, forest, thicket and cultivated land, with a marked preference for groves of sugar plum (*Uapaca*) trees. This squirrel ranges from Zambezi east of L. Malawi to the Tanganyika coast.
Food: Fruits, seeds, buds, leaves and roots. The striped bush squirrel feeds on the ground and in trees.
Status: Probably declining in some areas but not endangered.

Green squirrel *Paraxerus poensis* (illustrated p. 168)

Other names: Fr. *Ecureuil de Fernando Po*. Ger. *Grun Buschhornchen*.
Measurements: HB 14–18cm. T 14–19cm. W 90–150g.
Recognition: A small, grizzled green squirrel with a yellow belly, grey chest and grizzled black tail.
Habitat: Forest and forest fringes with a marked preference for secondary growth, oil palms and cultivation mosaics (in the west) and for rainforest canopy (in the east). The green squirrel ranges from Sierra Leone to the R. Ubangi and R. Zaïre.
Food: In Gabon, palm husks, palm kernels and fruits (90%), animal matter (10%).
Status: Not endangered.

Boehm's squirrel *Paraxerus boehmi*

Other names: Fr. *Ecureuil des bois de Boehm.* Ger. *Bohm Buschhornchen.*
Measurements: HB 10–15cm. T 9–20cm. W 40–100g.
Recognition: A small olive-coloured squirrel with a yellowish dorsal stripe and conspicuous pale flank stripes in between bold black stripes running from shoulder to rump. The tail is distinctly barred in dark brown and cream. The underside is off-white.
Races: *P. b. boehmi* (N, E and S Zaïre): dark olive. *P. b. emini* (east of Rift, Uganda): light olive. *P. b. vulcanorum* (Ruwenzori, Kivu): russet tints.
Habitat: Undergrowth and liana tangles in mixed, swamp, lowland and montane forests. Also (marginally), in wooded savannahs from R. Zaïre eastwards to the R. Nile and L. Victoria. This species appears to be the eastern ecological equivalent of the ribboned rope squirrel (*Funisciurus lemniscatus*).
Food: Insects and resinous gums, mushrooms, fruits and seeds.
Status: Locally common. Not endangered.

Alexander's dwarf squirrel *Paraxerus alexandri*

Other names: Fr. *Ecureuil d'Alexandre.* Ger. *Alexander Buschhornchen.*
Measurements: HB 9–12cm. T 11–14.5cm. W 37–72g.
Recognition: Very small greenish squirrel with white ears and a medial tawny-yellow stripe flanked by thin dark and light stripes from shoulder to rump. The tapered tail is thinly haired, with indistinct, irregular ochre and dark brown barring.
Habitat: Strictly equatorial lowland forests (below 1,500m), from the eastern bank of the R. Lualaba to the R. Nile in Uganda. This dwarf squirrel prefers to hunt over the surfaces of the thick limbs of large trees.
Food: Insects, resin, micro-flora and plant matter.
Status: Locally common but declining due to felling of primary forest. Not endangered.

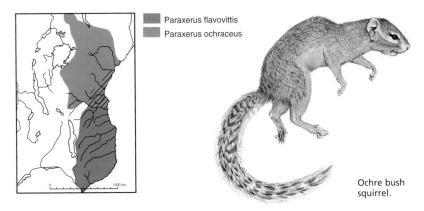

Paraxerus flavovittis
Paraxerus ochraceus

Ochre bush squirrel.

GIANT AND SUN SQUIRRELS PROTOXERINI

Ruwenzori sun squirrel	*Heliosciurus ruwenzori*
Gambian sun squirrel	*Heliosciurus gambianus* (incl. *punctatus*)
Zanj sun squirrel	*Heliosciurus undulatus*
Mutable sun squirrel	*Heliosciurus mutabilis*
Red-legged sun squirrel	*Heliosciurus rufobrachium*
Western palm squirrel	*Epixerus ebi*
Biafran Bight palm squirrel	*Epixerus wilsoni*
African giant squirrel	*Protoxerus stangeri*
Slender-tailed squirrel	*Protoxerus aubinnii*

An exclusively African group which probably derives from early populations of bush squirrels. The Ruwenzori sun squirrel appears to be a linking form with the same tooth count as bush squirrels.

(a) Ruwenzori sun squirrel. (b) Gambian sun squirrel. (c) Red-legged sun squirrel.
(d) Zanj sun squirrel. (e) Mutable sun squirrel.

Giant and sun squirrels have particularly robust jaws and teeth which enable them to feed on the hardest of nuts. They are mainly arboreal and very agile, crossing from tree to tree in the canopy.

Ruwenzori sun squirrel *Heliosciurus ruwenzori*

Other names: Fr. *Héliosciure du Ruwenzori*. Ger. *Ruwenzori Sonnenhornchen*.
Measurements: HB 20–26cm. T 22–28cm. W 205–377g.
Recognition: Thickly and densely furred squirrel with a grizzled grey upperside contrasting strongly with the white underside. The tail is boldly barred in grey and white. Vestigial teeth suggest that this may be a relict population of early sun squirrels. The Ruwenzori sun squirrel tends to carry the tail in line with the body.
Habitat: Montane forests between 1,600 and 2,700m in E Zaïre and W Uganda, Rwanda and Burundi. This species has adapted to secondary growth and cultivation mosaics.
Food: Fruits of dominant trees. Insects and lichen have also been recorded.
Status: In spite of its limited range, not endangered.

Gambian sun squirrel *Heliosciurus gambianus* (incl. *punctatus*)

Other names: Fr. *Héliosciure de Gambie*. Ger. *Gambia Sonnenhornchen*.
Measurements: HB 17–27cm. T 18–26cm. W 250–350g.
Recognition: Variably coloured squirrel with a grizzled back and head and lighter underparts. The tail is boldly barred (about 14 rings) and there is a pale surround to the eyes.
Habitat: Woodlands and savannahs and montane habitats from Senegal to Ethiopia and Kenya; south of the forest block from Angola to Tanganyika. Enclaves in forest areas are considered to be the product of 'engulfment' after changes in climate. It descends to ground to visit isolated trees but prefers branch travel.
Food: Fruits, seeds and the pods of *Acacia*; animal foods are also taken.
Status: Not endangered.

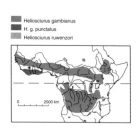

Zanj sun squirrel *Heliosciurus undulatus*

Other names: Fr. *Héliosciure de Zanj.* Ger. *Zanj Sonnenhornchen.*
Measurements: HB 20–25cm. T 21–28cm. W est. 250–380g.
Recognition: The back is tawny grizzled and underparts are cream. The tail is barred in brown and cream.
Habitat: Lowland and montane forests and thickets, and secondary growth, east of the Gregory Rift from Mt Kenya to R. Rufiji, and on Zanzibar and Mafia Is. Nests in hollow trees or branches.
Food: Fruits and seeds, palm dates, leaves and buds. Insects are of seasonal importance.
Status: Not endangered.

Mutable sun squirrel *Heliosciurus mutabilis*

Other names: Fr. *Héliosciure mutable.* Ger. *SudAfrikanische Sonnenhornchen.*
Measurements: HB 20–28cm. T 17–20cm. W 200–380g.
Recognition: Upperparts are grizzled brown or orange, with tones from pale to nearly black. Underparts also vary from white to fawn or grey. The tail has a narrow, indistinct barring in similar tints to the body.
Habitat: Lowland and montane forests and thickets, including riverine strips and cultivation mosaics, from the R. Rufiji southwards to Zimbabwe and Mozambique.
Food: Various plant foods; occasionally insects and small vertebrates.
Status: Common and not endangered.

Red-legged sun squirrel *Heliosciurus rufobrachium*

Other names: Fr. *Héliosciure à pattes rousses.* Ger. *Rotbein Sonnenhornchen.*
Measurements: HB 20–27cm. T 18–30cm. W 250–400g.
Recognition: Upperparts are grizzled, graduating to warm reddish tints on the outer surfaces of the limbs. The underside is paler cream-coloured (often with sparse fur). The long tail is barred with black and white (about 18 bands of each). Loud calls and a flicking tail are particularly noticeable.
Habitat: Very common at low and medium altitudes from Senegal eastwards across the R. Zaïre basin to Uganda to the Gregory Rift.
Food: Fruits, palm dates, leaves, buds; occasionally animal material.
Status: Not endangered.

Western palm squirrel *Epixerus ebi*

Other names: Fr. *Écureuil d'Ebi.* Ger. *Nachtbauchhornchen.*
Measurements: HB 26–29cm. T 27–31cm. W est. 450–700g.
Recognition: Large squirrel with a grizzled grey back and a warm orange to red underside. The very conspicuous black-fringed tail has black and white bars across the upperside and fine longitudinal stripes, fading into an orange brush, on the underside. The muzzle is more protuberant than in giant squirrels.
Habitat: Palm forests and mature rainforest in mainly coastal areas from Sierra Leone to Ghana.
Food: Fruits and nuts are collected on the tree or from the ground.
Status: Greatly contracted range. Rare, possibly endangered as it is intolerant of secondary growth.

(a) Western palm squirrel.
(b) Biafran Bight palm squirrel.
(c) African giant squirrel.
(d) Slender-tailed squirrel.

Epixerus wilsoni
Epixerus ebii

Biafran Bight palm squirrel *Epixerus wilsoni*

Other names: Fr. *Ecureuil du Biafra*. Ger. *Biafra Bauchhornchen*.
Measurements: HB est. 26–29cm. T 27–31cm. W 500–620g.
Recognition: Large squirrel with a grizzled grey back. The face and underparts are cream, with warmer tints on the wrists and rump. The tail has a predominantly white upperside, with bold black bars or chevrons and a warm-coloured stem on the underside. The head is broad and flat, with a long robust muzzle. (It is distinguishable from the western species mainly by cranial differences.)
Habitat: Lowland rainforests near the coast from S Cameroon to R. Zaïre. Areas with abundant palms are preferred
Food: Fruits and nuts (98% in Gabon); occasionally animal foods.
Status: Rare.

African giant squirrel *Protoxerus stangeri*

Other names: Fr. *Grand écureuil de Stanger*. Ger. *Olpalmenhornchen*.
Measurements: HB 22–40cm. T 24–36cm. W 540–1,000g.
Recognition: Large grizzled squirrel with a disproportionately large, rounded head which is predominantly grey. The back and limbs are of warm tints, very variable in colour and intensity. The yellowish underside is often semi-naked. Nose, ears and eyelids also tend to be naked. The long, black and white tail has about 18 bars. Nineteen subspecies have been described.
Habitat: Exclusively limited to well-developed equatorial rainforests, in tall swamp forest and at altitudes up to 2,000m.
Food: Mainly fruits, seeds and nut kernels of numerous rainforest trees (87.6% in Gabon, with 8.5% leaves, 3.5% mushrooms and traces of animal matter).
Status: Not endangered.

Slender-tailed squirrel *Protoxerus aubinnii*

Other names: Fr. *Ecureuil d'Aubinn*. Ger. *Dunnschwanzhornchen*.
Measurements: HB 23–27cm. T 27–33cm. W est. 300–400g.
Recognition: A largish, very dark squirrel with a long, slender, tapered tail with very fine black and olive annulations. The short, dense coat is very fine and silky and covers upper and underparts equally.
Habitat: Moist high forests from Liberia to Ghana, with a marked preference for palms.
Food: Fruits, particularly palm dates. Unlike the giant squirrel, which prefers to eat only the kernels, this species has been recorded feeding on the husks.
Status: Rare. Probably endangered over most of its range.

ANOMALURES ANOMALURIDAE

Lord Derby's anomalure	*Anomalurus derbianus*
Pel's anomalure	*Anomalurus peli*
Lesser anomalure	*Anomalurus pusillus*
Beecroft's anomalure	*Anomalurus beecrofti*
Zenker's flying mouse	*Idiurus zenkeri*
Long-eared flying mouse	*Idiurus macrotis*
Cameroon scaly-tail	*Zenkerella insignis*

Recognition: Mainly gliding rodents with slender bodies concealed by long, fine fur and (in the gliders) by the gathered membrane or 'patagium'. Anomalures have narrow hands and feet with strong bat-like claws. The tail has a short strip of two rows of spiked scales on its underside. Since these animals live on vertical surfaces, the scales help the tail to act as a rest for the body's weight and allow it to hang passively from the claws. Membranes are attached to the margins of both limbs and to a cartilaginous elbow strut. Anomalures often have a strong scent which is produced by inguinal glands that fluctuate in size.

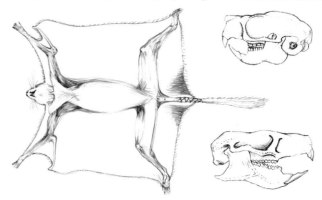

Underside and skull of Lord Derby's anomalure. R. below 30MY + old fossil anomalurid.

Genealogy: Anomalures are well represented in fossil finds dated to 30 million years ago (20 genera have been identified). These primitive rodents are thought to resemble the common stock from which rats, squirrels and porcupines would have descended.

Gliding volplanes are most likely to have first evolved in response to the problems of moving between tall, isolated trees. Relatively dry, liane-free woodlands are the habitats that are most likely to have provided the conditions necessary for this adaptation. Contemporary equivalents of such habitats are ironwood forests and Miombo (*Brachystegia*) woodlands, both of these being prime habitats for the commonest of the scaly-tails, Lord Derby's anomalure.

The success of this rodent is due to a very specific dietary staple, namely bark, gnawed from little over a dozen species of tree. It would appear that anomalures and their food plants have evolved together because mutually beneficial relationships have been observed between them.

Anomalures, like beavers, use their incisors not only to eat bark but to cut small branches. This pruning activity can be directly correlated with habitual glide-lines radiating from dens. Dens are usually holes in vertical trunks and lateral branches growing from such trunks can be obstructing. Removal of leaf-bearing branches below a closed canopy causes 'die-back' which, in some species, opens a shallow hole in the main trunk. Such cavities are easily enlarged by anomalures, which suggests that their branch-cutting behaviour may provide additional benefits. Anomalures are also known to cut the tops off young trees near the bases of food trees. In effect, this results in the death of the competitors of food trees. Persistent pruning of competitors by anomalures may provide food trees with a distinct advantage. In many forests it has been observed that known food trees are dominant or common and it is theoretically possible that the pruning behaviour of anomalures is an important factor contributing to this dominance.

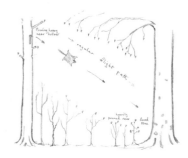

Left: diagram of pruned flight path.
Right: Lord Derby's anomalure.

Geography: At least five known food trees, miombo (*Brachystegia*), awoura (*Julbernardia*), ironwoods (*Cynometra*), owala oil trees (*Pentaclethra*) and velvet tamarinds (*Dialium*), are leguminous Caesalpinaceae. The distribution of anomalures corresponds very closely with the distribution of this group of trees, which is a major component of tropical African woodlands and forests.

Ecology: Tall trees with relatively vertical stems, a clear subcanopy layer, an abundance of den holes and trees with edible bark are all necessary conditions for Lord Derby's anomalure. Other species may not share all the same requirements but close interdependencies between animal and tree are probably vital factors in the existence of all anomalure species. This family may be more precariously dependent on a specific ecology than has previously been realised. Significantly, all the food-tree species listed above are valued for their timber. Hornbills compete for their nest holes.

Natural history: Anomalures have excellent bifocal sight, very acute (possibly ultrasonically sensitive) hearing and depend on sound and scents for communication. Up to three precocious young, with open eyes and thick fur, are born in a hollow. Fed from the ♀'s rather long pectoral nipples they grow fast. They are weaned on chewed food from the parents' cheek pouches.

Adaptations: Almost half the weight and much of the volume of a large anomalure is taken up by its digestive tract. Thus, in order to compensate for their relatively low-energy diet, the remaining tissues, such as bones, hair and skin, are models of economy in combining tensile strength with very light weight.

Lord Derby's Anomalure *Anomalurus derbianus*

Other names: Fr. *Ecureuil volant de Derby.* Ger. *Gemeines Dornschwanz-hornchen.*
Measurements: HB 27–38cm. T 22–30cm. W 450–1,100g.
Recognition: Predominantly grey or brown anomalure with a rippling silvery grizzle to the tips of the very long, fine textured fur. The membranes, which stretch between limbs and onto the root of the tail, are similarly coloured above but black bristle hairs reinforce the hem of the membrane behind the elbow strut. Colours vary greatly and 16 subspecies have been named. The main variation is in the grey or russet tints on the back and shoulders. The face is relatively short and round. The naked pinkish ears are set in a surrounding bed of dense velvet-black fur. Bristles covering the hindclaws are black.
Distribution: From Sierra Leone to W Kenya and, more inconsistently, from N Angola to Tanganyika (and probably N Mozambique). Ranges from sea-level up to 2,400m.
Habitat: Moist rainforests to relatively dry woodlands at various altitudes; probably dependent upon the presence of abundant food trees.
Food: Staple is bark (of *Strombosia*, *Klainedoxa*, *Neoboutonia* and species mentioned in the group profile). In addition, fruits, flowers, leaves, nuts and occasional insects have been recorded. Thick bark from the trunk and main branches is preferred and feeding seems to be more concentrated at lower levels during drier seasons. Bark is gnawed at numerous separate sites, each about 15cm wide, which are maintained by nightly removal of a single narrow strip immediately adjacent to the previous night's strip. Wounds to the bark, caused by falling branches, elephant tusks, growth splits, etc., very often become the focus for anomalure feeding. It would appear that anomalures exploit the physiology of bark-healing in their food-tree species. As a consequence of anomalure activity some awoura trees (*Julbernardia pellegriniana*) may, over a number of years, lose all the bark of their trunk and main branches (possibly more than once). The tree is clearly able to cope with this decortication and is able rapidly to regrow its cambium layer, suggesting that rodent and tree have co-evolved.

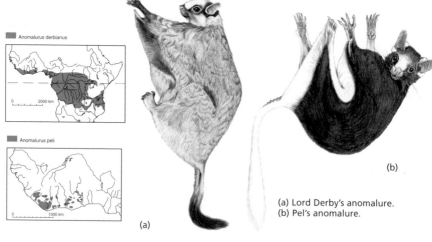

Anomalurus derbianus

0   2000 km

Anomalurus peli

0   1000 km

(a) Lord Derby's anomalure.
(b) Pel's anomalure.

(a)

(b)

Behaviour: Up to eight individuals may share a denning tree but little is known about their social behaviour. Lord Derby's anomalure is nocturnal and lives in vertical hollow tree trunks with exit holes or cracks up to 40m up (in some woodlands they may occupy empty bee-hives). Individuals retain use of their dens over very long periods, although seasonal shifts have been recorded. Breeding is likely to be seasonal in drier areas but not in the main forest block. In some areas ♀♀ are known to segregate to give birth and rear young. Apart from a threatening or defensive hiss and growl this species also purrs and twitters. The animals like to sun-bathe in the early mornings and more rarely in the evenings.
Adaptations: In closed-canopy forest the pruning described in the group profile is often less frequent or conspicuous than in more open or sun-lit areas. Where light breaks through close to a food tree intensified pruning of young trees may serve to help maintain access to a ready food supply by killing or maiming competing trees and keeping flight-paths open.
Status: Although localised populations may be at risk from logging and forest clearance this common and widespread species is not endangered.

Pel's Anomalure *Anomalurus peli*

Other names: Fr. *Ecureuil volant de Pel*. Ger. *Pel Dornschwanz-hornchen*.
Measurements: HB 40–46cm. T 32–45cm. W 1,300–1,800g.
Recognition: A large scaly-tail with a black back and face vividly outlined with pure white borders around the ears and on the muzzle. The underside and tail are also white, as are the borders to the flight membranes. Like Lord Derby's anomalure, Pel's anomalure also has six pairs of pointed scales on the underside of the tail (particularly robust in this species).
Distribution: Liberia to Ghana.
Habitat: Moist high forests with numerous tall emergents and palm trees.
Food: Bark supplemented by fruits (especially oil and other palm dates), leaves and flowers.
Behaviour: Up to six animals are known to share a den. This species is wholly nocturnal and emerges well after sunset. Contact calls have been described as deep hoots. Up to three young are born at a time and two litters a year have been recorded.
Adaptations: When disturbed in its den Pel's anomalure growls, hisses and snaps its teeth (noises that are amplified in a hole). This behaviour may deter birds of prey, primates and small carnivores, as well as hornbills (which may compete for nest-holes). Its bold colouring suggests that aggressiveness and large size may make it less vulnerable to predation than the smaller anomalure species.
Status: Endangered.

Lesser Anomalure *Anomalurus pusillus*

Other names: Fr. *Ecureuil volant pygmée*. Ger. *Zwergdornschwanz-hornchen*.
Measurements: HB 18.5–24.6cm. T 13.8–20cm. W est. 200–300g.
Recognition: A small scaly-tail with back coloration varying from near black to mottled tan. The membrane adjoining the tail is usually yellower while the lateral membranes are dark grey. The head is grey without borders around the ears. The underside has a yellowish tinge, as do the bristles covering the hindclaws.

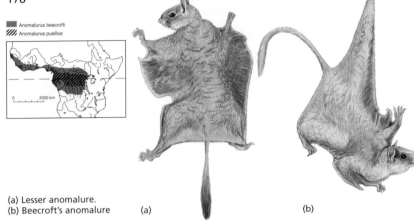

Anomalurus beecrofti
Anomalurus pusillus

0   2000 km

(a) Lesser anomalure.
(b) Beecroft's anomalure   (a)   (b)

Habitat: A rare and probably very localised species, especially west of Cameroon. Its range may just include W Uganda but it has a strictly equatorial, non-montane distribution. Has been found sheltering in hollow trees in lowland rainforest.
Food: Probably bark and fruits. The drupes of parasol trees (*Musanga*) have been recorded.
Status: Rare everywhere. Biology unknown.

Beecroft's Anomalure *Anomalurus beecrofti*

Other names: Fr. *Ecureuil volant de Beecroft.* Ger. *Beecroft Dornschwanzhornchen.*
Measurements: HB 25–31cm. T 16–24cm. W est. 640–660g.
Recognition: A very variably coloured scaly-tail with a prominent, narrow snout. The underside is always yellow-orange to some degree and similar warm tints occur on the back in some populations (notably an almost wholly orange subspecies, *A. b. fulgens*, in Gabon). Beecroft's anomalure often has a white spot on the forehead but does not have a dark 'mask' around the eyes. The tail, which is narrower than in other species, has up to nine pairs of scales on its underside.
Habitat: Tropical rainforests from Sierra Leone to E Zaïre, from sea-level up to 2,500m. Beecroft's anomalure shows a marked preference for palm groves and can withstand some cultivation and plantation in its habitat if palms and some big trees remain. It rests up in holes and will also hide in the junctions between palm fronds or cling to the sheltered underside of major tree branches close to the trunk.
Food: Fruits, especially palm dates, bark, leaves and occasional insects.
Status: Declining locally but widespread. Not endangered.

Zenker's flying mouse *Idiurus zenkeri*

Other names: Fr. *Ecureuil volant de Zenker.* Ger. *Zenker Gleitbilch.*
Measurements: HB 6.5–9cm. T 7–13cm. W 14–17.5g.
Recognition: A miniature scaly-tail resembling a very silky-furred, tawny-coloured, snub-nosed mouse, with a membrane like those of the larger anomalures. The very long tail is fringed on the underside by two rows of short stiff hairs. Zenker's flying mouse also has sparse, very long hairs on the upperside of the tail. It utters a shrill mouse-like squeak and is a very efficient, fast and agile glider.
Habitat: Very moist equatorial rainforests, from Cameroon to the R. Zaïre, and between the R. Aruwimi and R. Zaïre to the foothills of Ruwenzori and Kivu. Roosts in hollow trees (more rarely under bark), sometimes in ones or twos but more usually in groups that may number up to 100.
Food: Oil-palm pulp, occasional insects and possibly exudates or nectar. It has been suggested that Zenker's flying mouse may travel many kilometres in a night to feed. However, nothing is known of its feeding behaviour. The notched upper incisors project out of the mouth, which may mean that the food requires sharp chiselling.
Status: Clear-felling and other logging operations in the centre of their range must be eliminating them from some areas. Not endangered overall.

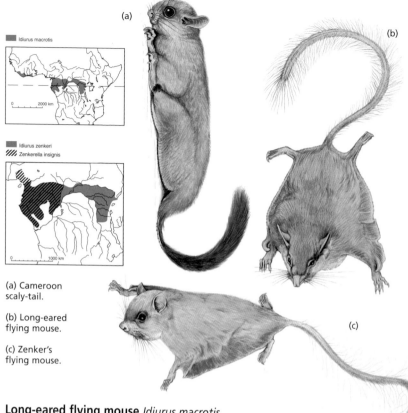

(a) Cameroon scaly-tail.

(b) Long-eared flying mouse.

(c) Zenker's flying mouse.

Long-eared flying mouse *Idiurus macrotis*
Other names: Fr. *Anomalure nain*. Ger. *Grossohrgleitbilch*.
Measurements: HB 8–11cm. T 13–19cm. W 25–35g.
Recognition: A small scaly-tail of slightly more robust build than Zenker's flying mouse and with darker fur. This species is pale grey in colour with a brownish sheen. The ears and the face are somewhat longer than Zenker's and the tail is proportionately shorter, with similar short, stiff hairs on the underside. Dense, short fur covers the rest of the tail.
Habitat: Equatorial lowlands (like Zenker's flying mouse). The overall range is similar but the long-eared flying mouse appears to be rarer than Zenker's in the eastern part of their ranges. This species sometimes shares hollow trees with Zenker's (and with bats).
Food: Not known.
Status: Rare and little known.

Cameroon scaly-tail *Zenkerella insignis*
Other names: Fr. *Anomalure aptère*. Ger. *Dornschwanzbilch*.
Measurements: HB 18–23cm. T 15–17cm. W est. 180–220g.
Recognition: Superficially resembling a large dormouse, this scaly-tail has no trace of a membrane (although its loose, woolly coat might cushion short, spread-eagled leaps). Head and body are a soft slate grey with ochre tints on the forearm, lower shin and cheeks. Underparts are very pale grey and the tail is black and bushy. The strip of paired scales on the underside of the tail resembles that of other scaly-tails and implies similar 'hanging' while at rest (see above). The ankles have a brush of highly specialised 'spoon-hairs' over a glandular area. Its function and operation are not known.
Habitat: Only known from Cameroon to Gabon. Animals thought to be scaly-tails have been seen moving among low level vines by means of very fast springy leaps. May also inhabit under-storey and canopy.
Food: Not known.
Status: Extremely rare and status unknown.

SPRING HARES PEDETIDAE

Spring hare	*Pedetes capensis*

In spite of the many obvious differences between the gliding anomalures and the kangaroo-like spring hares, both rodents probably share an ancient common ancestry. Spring hares resemble many burrow-living desert rodents in having hugely enlarged inner ears, which would seem to explain their enormous sensitivity to sound and vibration.

It is remarkable that Australian kangaroos and an African rodent, both of which live on poor resources, should have evolved a mode of hopping which combines speed with great economy of energy.

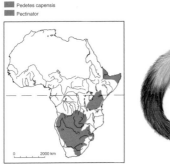

Pedetes capensis
Pectinator

Spring hare *Pedetes capensis*

Other names: Fr. *Lièvre sauteur*. Ger. *Springhase*. Swah. *Kamendegere*.

Measurements: HB 35–43cm. T 34–49cm. W 3–4kg.

Recognition: A long-tailed, hopping rodent with long, soft fur, varying from warm reddish tints to yellow-grey above and white to pale tawny underneath. The brush tip of the tail and sometimes the ear tips are black. The hindlegs have four toes (most weight is carried on the enlarged third and two flanking nails). The short forelegs, often tucked out of sight, have five closely bunched, long, sharp, curved claws.

Subspecies: *P. c. capensis* (S Africa), *P. c. surdaster* (NE Africa).

Distribution: Two distinct regions of semi-arid Africa; north-east and south. Spring hares are very localised within both these areas.

Habitat: Sandy plains, pans and lake margins with well-drained soils and an extensive seasonal cover of grasses (which dry out in the long dry season). Spring hares are fast and energetic diggers of burrows which may extend up to 50m, often twisting and turning haphazardly about 80cm down. Warren areas are marked by large spoil heaps near some entrances. Animals can number up to 10 per ha in relatively undisturbed habitats.

Food: Fresh grasses, grazed to the ground, stems, roots and storage bases of grasses, new sprouts of herbs and fruits. Very occasionally insects, such as locusts, are taken. Spring hares feed only at night and within about 400m of a burrow. Up to nine animals graze in close proximity.

Behaviour: Perennial breeders, the ♀♀ give birth about three times a year after a 77-day gestation. One or, more rarely, two well-developed young are fed from four pectoral teats. The young only emerge from the burrow when fully mobile and over half adult size. Spring hares grunt and have a piping contact call. They bleat in distress and will bite and kick if captured. They are hunted by humans, various carnivores, eagle owls and pythons. Their burrows are used by many other animals for shelter. Spring hares are able rapidly to block their burrows, and frequently do so, in order to protect themselves against attack or disturbance.

Adaptations: Quick, although not very manoeuvrable jumpers, spring hares can leap up to 4m.

Status: Widespread and locally common. Heavy grazing by livestock may cause local declines. Eradicated as a crop pest in some areas. Locally vulnerable but not endangered.

GUNDIS CTENODACTYLIDAE

Gundis	*Ctenodactylus* (2 species)
Senegal gundi	*Felovia vae*
Fringe-eared gundi	*Massouteria mzabi*
Pectinator	*Pectinator spekei*

Recognition: Compact, brown or tawny animals resembling guineapigs, gundis have short legs and blunt, padded toes with tightly curved claws and rows of stiff bristles on the hindfeet. The incisor teeth are less hard than in other rodents. Gundis are less prone to generalised gnawing.

Genealogy: Fossil gundis have been widely recorded from Eurasia where the family is represented as early as 28 million years ago. Gundis have been found only at more recent fossil sites in Africa.

Geography: Now exclusively African, gundis apper to be remnants of a once less specialised rodent group.

Ecology: Rock-dwelling herbivores in hot deserts, gundis have specialised kidneys which allow them to conserve scarce moisture obtained entirely from the plants they eat. Shortage of water helps explain the curtailed suckling period of gundis and the rapid maturation of the young. Mother gundis wean their two young on chewed plants and weaning is complete in 4 weeks. This family of rodents does not collect vegetation or make nests.

Natural history: Gundis rely on rock outcrops as refuges but face risks when emerging for food by day. As social animals in dangerous environments they have developed elaborate ways of communicating by voice, scent and tail gestures. They also thump their feet loudly in alarm.

Adaptations: Exposed to extremes of temperature, gundis have developed ultra-fine fur that insulates against both heat and cold. Stiff bristles on the feet serve as a comb for daily grooming sessions.

The food of these animals is scarce and often of poor quality but they are able to conserve energy by adopting a lizard-like strategy of sun-bathing to augment their body temperature in the early morning, followed by retreat into the shade to cool down in the heat of the afternoon. Hearing is extremely well developed. However, this involves enormous internal bullae rather than large external ears.

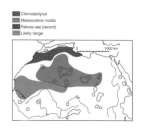

Gundis *Ctenodactylus* (2 species)

Other names: Fr. *Goundi*. Ger. *Gundi*.

Measurements: HB 15–21cm. T 3–5cm. W 175–180g.

Recognition: Reddish gundis with a minuscule tail and oval, white-fringed ear. A horny comb is present on the claw of the inner hindtoe. Diurnal, social animals, their whistling or chirping calls can be heard in the early morning.

Species: *C. gundi* (near N African coast): chirps. *C. vali* (Sahara desert outcrops): whistles.

Habitat: Rock outcrops with abundant crevices in which the gundis shelter singly or in small groups. Two to four young are born during February–April in a secure rocky den. Gundis are extremely agile at running over rocks and when captured will go into spasm.

Food: Grass, leaves, stalks and flowers, generally grazed or browsed no more than 100m from rocks during morning and evening.

Status: Not endangered.

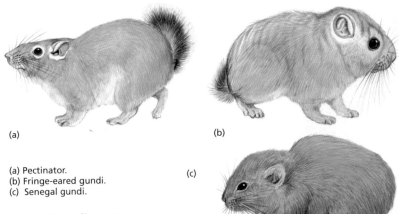

(a)

(b)

(c)

(a) Pectinator.
(b) Fringe-eared gundi.
(c) Senegal gundi.

Senegal gundi *Felovia vae*

Other names: Fr. *Goundi de Felou*. Ger. *Senegalgundi*.
Measurements: HB 15–21cm. T 3–5cm. W 200–210g.
Recognition: A long-haired, dark walnut-brown gundi with a paler reddish underside and a short but bushy tail. There is an inconspicuous white tuft behind the ears. Incisors are weakly grooved. The loud harsh screech of alarm is repeated very persistently.
Habitat: Rock outcrops in dry or semi-arid regions of Mauritania, Mali and Senegal.
Food: Various grasses, trees and herbs.
Status: Localised distribution. Status not known.

Fringe-eared gundi *Massouteria mzabi*

Other names: Fr. *Goundi du Sahara*. Ger. *Sahara Kammfinger*.
Measurements: HB 17–24cm. T 3–4cm. W est. 200–220g.
Recognition: A pale tawny gundi with massively enlarged inner ear bullae opening into a fixed immovable outer ear with complex hair border fringes. The tail is frisked conspicuously. Quieter than other gundis, it only makes occasional chirps.
Habitat: A very low-density species living among rocks in very arid areas of the W and central Sahara Desert and in the Tassili, Hoggar and other massifs. Some regional differences in pelage have been observed.
Food: Grasses, *Acacia* and other desert plants.
Status: Very widely, but sparsely and discontinuously distributed. Not endangered.

Pectinator *Pectinator spekei*

Other names: Fr. *Goundi à queue touffue*. Ger. *Speke Kammfinger*.
Measurements: HB 16–18cm. T 4–5cm. W est. 160–160g.
Recognition: A tawny gundi with a prominent, frequently flicked tail. The muzzle is longer and more pointed than in other gundis and the ears are of a more conventional form. More crepuscular than other gundis, it lives in large, very vocal colonies that emit a variety of chirps and whistles.
Habitat: Rocky outcrops in the Horn of Africa and Ethiopia where home ranges may be extensive (3km^2).
Food: A variety of grasses, *Acacia* and other desert plants.
Status: Scattered occurence over a large area of distribution. Not endangered.

DORMICE MYOXIDAE (SYN. GLIRIDAE)

African dormice	*Graphiurus* (14 species)
Eastern orchard dormouse	*Eliomys melanurus*

Recognition: Small, climbing rodents of nocturnal habits, intermediate in form between rats and squirrels. They often have a prominent black 'mask' around the eyes, a bushy tail and deft fingers with very small but needle-sharp, curved claws. Their tails detach easily and the hair may regrow as a 'brush' (see opposite, right).

Graphiurus
Eliomys melanurus

Eastern orchard dormouse.

African dormouse.

Genealogy: Dormice appear in the fossil record at 40 million years ago. They have retained a primitive, generalised gut, having no caecum for digesting cellulose. Their molar teeth are also generalised. African dormice are the least herbivorous and the most primitive of all dormice.

Geography: Seven genera in Eurasia and two in Africa.

Ecology: Most Eurasian species lay down fat and become torpid. A similar tendency is found in dormice which live in temperate regions of Africa (well-fed African dormice also lay down fat). Dormice usually exist at relatively low densities and several species are known to be territorial.

Natural history: Dormice are vocal rodents, producing audible clicks, growls and whistles, especially while mating, at which time both sexes call. An average of about four young (two to nine) are born completely blind, deaf and naked in a nest that is built by the mother (who defends it vigorously against visiting dormice). The young become independent in just over 1 month.

Adaptations: Generalised, omnivorous and predatory rodents with very high activity levels. Dormice are intensely exploratory and very agile, both on the ground and in trees and bushes, easily able to overpower animals similar in size to themselves.

African dormice *Graphiurus* (14 species)

Measurements: HB 7.5–15cm. T 5–11cm. W 18–85g.

Recognition: African dormice are usually grey with white undersides, a dark eye mask and prominent ears. They may also be brown or tawny. The tail is bushy and they are agile climbers, with sharp-clawed, dextrous fingers.

Species: *G. christyi, G. crassicaudatus, G. hueti, G. kelleni, G. lorraineus, G. microtis, G. monardi, G. murinus, G. ocularis, G. olga, G. parvus, G. platyops, G. rupicola, G. surdus.*

Distribution: Most sub-Saharan environments except open arid desert (but known as a relict in the central Saharan mountains).

Habitat: Almost all habitats but with a marked preference for dense woodlands, thickets and forests; also rocky areas (where a specialised crevice-adapted species has a flattened skull). All species make nests.

Food: Invertebrates and small vertebrates, including small birds, lizards, eggs and carrion. African dormice pounce very fast and prey may include sleeping birds, in which case deep bites are directed at the head (only the brain may be eaten).

Behaviour: Some species of dormice are territorial and intolerant, but a nest of 11 adults, including animals of both sexes, has been recorded. They are very vocal and can make a loud shriek.

Adaptations: Fat deposits and nest-building behaviour enable them to weather seasonal food shortages.

Status : Many species are common; others have very local distributions. Dormice have been partially displaced as a commensal in huts and houses by the black rat.

Eastern orchard dormouse *Eliomys melanurus*

Measurements: HB 10–17cm. T 9–15cm. W est. 45–200g.

Recognition: A handsome dormouse with a tawny forehead and a dorsal midline flanked by grey. The underparts and the base of the ear are white. Mask and jaw-line are black and there is a black brush to the tail. Often noticed because of its varied (and occasionally quite loud) vocalisations – squeaks, grunting and tooth clicking.

Habitat: All along the Mediterranean N African littoral in woodlands, date-palm oases, sand dunes and rocky country. This dormouse ranges high into treeless mountains. It may build nests in piles of natural debris or old birds' nests.
Food: Fruits, nuts, buds, invertebrates and occasional vertebrates.
Status: Not endangered.

BLESMOLS BATHYERGIDAE

Dune blesmols	*Bathyergus* (2 species)
Common blesmols	*Cryptomys* (7 species)
Cape blesmol	*Georychus capensis*
Silky blesmol	*Heliophobius argenteocinereus*
Sand-puppy (Naked mole-rat)	*Heterocephalus glaber*

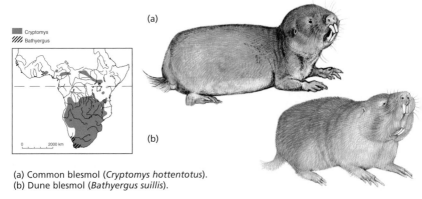

(a)

■ Cryptomys
/// Bathyergus

0   2000 km

(b)

(a) Common blesmol (*Cryptomys hottentotus*).
(b) Dune blesmol (*Bathyergus suillis*).

Recognition: Compact, subterranean rodents with minuscule eyes and concealed ears. The mouth closes *behind* the sharp white incisors. Feet are often armed with long claws. The short tail is fringed with hairs in all but the naked mole-rat. They have great sensitivity to vibrations. Spoil heaps provide the only indication of their presence.
Genealogy: The anatomy of blesmols is so radically modified and their unique adaptations so ancient that affinities with other rodents are obscure.
Geography: Exclusively sub-Saharan Africa with the greatest variety in the south. Displaced from NE Africa by Eurasian root-rats (Rhyzomyidae).
Ecology: Blesmols dig tunnels with their teeth, assisted by the forepaws, and spoil is pushed out with the rump. The velvety fur is adapted to abrasion and repeated reversals. Their sight is very poor. They display seasonal variations in activity and numbers.
Natural history: Most species are solitary or live in small groups but two species, the naked mole-rat (*Heterocephalus glaber*) and Damaraland blesmol (*Cryptomys damarensis*), are eusocial with 'queen mothers', one reproductive ♂ and a colony of workers.
Adaptations: Eusocial behaviour has evolved independently in two widely separate desert-dwelling populations (fulfilling the predictions of Dr R. Alexander, who anticipated that a bee-like social system might be found among mammals living in a closed environment, with a large, storable food supply, most likely underground, in a desert). These predictions were confirmed by Dr J. Jarvis's studies of the African blesmols.

Dune Blesmols *Bathyergus* (2 species)

Measurements: HB 17–33cm. T 3–7cm. W 500–750g.
Recognition: Large blesmols with very long, pointed claws and grooved incisors.
Species: Cape dune blesmol, *B. suillus*: large, cinnamon-coloured. Namaqua dune blesmol, *B. janetta*: slate-grey and silver.
Habitat: Restricted to sandy habitats in extreme south-west of Africa. Dune blesmols live in small groups (of about five) and are very territorial.
Food: Roots, bulbs and grass stolons.
Status: Restricted range in highly populated area. Vulnerable.

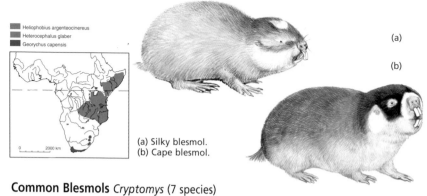

Heliophobius argenteocinereus
Heterocephalus glaber
Georychus capensis

(a)
(b)

(a) Silky blesmol.
(b) Cape blesmol.

Common Blesmols *Cryptomys* (7 species)

Measurements: HB 13–21.5cm. T 1–2.5cm. W 100–300g.
Recognition: Velvety-furred blesmols with broad palms and relatively small nails (vertically flattened at the front, laterally flattened in the rear, correlating with their respective digging and pushing functions). Eyes and ears are scarcely visible. The white incisor teeth are without grooves.
Species: *C. bocagei* (Angola to Zambia), *C. damarensis* (Angola, Namibia to Zambia, Botswana), *C. foxi* (Nigeria), *C. hottentotus* (S Africa to S Zaïre and Tanganyika), *C. mechowi* (Angola to Malawi – a large species), *C. ochraceocinereus* (Nigeria to Uganda), *C. zechi* (Ghana, Togo).
Habitat: Drier soils outside main forest blocks.
Food: Roots, bulbs, grass, leaves and occasional invertebrates.
Behaviour: Food-gathering is seasonal; burrows are extended in the rains and collected roots brought back to stores. Colonies vary in size and some species are solitary. The Damaraland blesmol colonies average 16 animals with only one reproductive ♀ and ♂. The rest of the colony collect roots in a central store, digs new galleries and feeds, grooms and warms the one to six young that are born to the 'queen' two or three times a year. If the queen dies, subordinate ♀♀ fail to take her place (as happens with naked mole-rats).
Adaptations: The adaptations of these blesmols are sufficiently similar to those of the root-rat (*Tachyoryctes*) for the two to be mutually exclusive. The blesmols' overall range is interrupted in NE Africa where they have presumably been replaced.
Status : Some species (notably *C. mechowi* and *C. foxi*) may be endangered by the spread of agriculture.

Cape Blesmol *Georychus capensis*

Measurements: HB 14–20–5cm. T 2–4cm. W 124–360g.
Recognition: Surprisingly colourful for a subterranean animal, with a cinnamon and orange back, black head and pale to white underparts. The head resembles a mask, with white surrounding the vestigial eyes, the ears and also the muzzle, with its prominent teeth. A prolific species known to have produced as many as 10 young in a single litter.
Habitat: Discontinuous distribution; the Cape littoral and scattered upland areas further to the north-east, coastal sand dunes, and valleys with sandy soils.
Food: Stores roots and bulbs harvested from very shallow burrows.
Status: Occurs in several reserves and national parks.

Silky Blesmol *Heliophobius argenteocinereus*

Measurements: HB 10–20cm. T 1.5–4cm. W 142–168g.
Recognition: A long-haired grey blesmol with prominent white incisors. The coat is grey, sandy or reddish and paler below. White markings on the head or belly are individually variable.
Habitat: Distribution corresponds approximately with the central and eastern areas of Miombo (*Brachystegia*) woodlands. Its range overlaps with that of *Cryptomys* but it prefers lower altitudes with a drier climate. It likes well-drained, sandy soils on rocky hillsides, open plains or in woodlands.
Food: Roots and tubers, including that of a lablab (*Dolichos*) and pulses (*Vigna*).
Status: Not endangered.

Sand-puppy (Naked mole-rat) *Heterocephalus glaber*

Measurements: HB 8–10cm. T 2–5cm. W 30–80g.

Recognition: A small, naked blesmol resembling a newborn, even foetal, animal. Its transparent skin goes pale or bright red depending on body heat and circulation. Within a colony of about 75 animals different castes can be distinguished by size and by their role in the 'hive'. Largest is the breeding ♀, attended by 'drones' or non-working adults, of medium size. 'Workers' (communal diggers, foragers and carriers) are the smallest animals. The usual sign of the sand-puppy's presence is little volcano-shaped spoil heaps.

Distribution: The sand-puppy is confined to the Horn of Africa where it lives in a variety of mostly hard, compacted soils in a hot, dry climate. Fossils found further south in Tanganyika suggest a wider range during past, drier periods.

Habitat: Plains, thickets, dry savannahs and open woodlands, i.e. areas with abundant plants bearing subterranean storage organs and edible roots. The micro-climate within sand-puppy burrows is very stable (about 30°C).

Food: The roots of dominant trees, such as *Acacia* and *Commiphora*, the vine (*Cissus*), lilies (*Ammocharis*) and the bulbs and tubers of other common plants. Such roots are eaten *in situ* and the plant is often not killed because only the 'store' is taken.

Behaviour: The sand-puppy is celebrated as the prime example of a highly social mammal which exhibits division of labour (as in bees and termites). As with bees the life of the colony is governed through chemical mechanisms. The dominant ♀ generates stress and produces scents (pheromones) that suppress sexual development and growth in all other ♀♀. All the colony share a single nest and are communally affected by the 'queen's' current sexual condition (for example both sexes develop teats just before she gives birth). Her young become workers on weaning.

Adaptations: The eusocial life-style appears to have evolved in order to cope with the difficulties that a single pair of animals would face gathering food, breeding, raising offspring and keeping secure from predators in the habitat occupied by the sand-puppy. The benefits of safety from predation, secured by a wholly subterranean existence, is compromised by the hardness of the ground. Soil hardness also makes foraging for scattered and patchy foods a huge labour. By specialising in digging and foraging, workers are able to supply adequate food for a colony of closely related brothers and sisters while the 'queen' ensures continuity by producing up to four litters a year each numbering about 12 babies (as many as 27 have been recorded in captive animals).

Status : Very widespread. Not endangered.

PORCUPINES HYSTRICIDAE

Crested porcupine	*Hystrix cristata*
South African porcupine	*Hystrix africaeaustralis*
Brush-tailed porcupine	*Atherurus africanus*

Recognition: Large rodents with spines.

Genealogy: The most primitive forms (rather like large prickly rats) occur in South-East Asia, where the group may have originated.

Geography: Old World from South-East Asia and India to sub-Saharan Africa and parts of the Mediterranean.

Ecology: The smaller brush-tailed porcupine is exclusively a forest-dweller. The larger species inhabit a wider spectrum of habitats.

Natural history: Porcupines are nocturnal herbivores which rely on their spines to deter predators.

Adaptations: The large size and formidable spines of crested porcupines can be correlated with movement out of the forest (with relatively few and relatively small predators) into more exposed, non-forest habitats (with many more, large carnivores). At the same time subterranean roots in drier habitats require a good sense of smell and the ability to dig in hard soil; both well-developed faculties in porcupines.

Rattle quills and rear views of:
(a) Crested porcupine, (also above)
(b) South African porcupine.

(a)

(b)

Crested porcupine *Hystrix cristata*

Other names: Fr. *Porc-épic*. Ger. *Stachelschwein*. Swah. *Nnungu*.
Measurements: HB 60–100cm. T 8–17cm. W 12–27kg.
Recognition: A very large, black-bodied, nocturnal rodent with long, black and white spines and a prominent crest of elongated, spiny hairs from forehead to shoulders. The crested porcupine can be distinguished from the southern species by its black rump and short, rattle-like quills in the tail. The forefeet have strong, digging claws. Fallen quills, tracks and burrows are often the most obvious signs of its presence.
Distribution: Most non-desert habitats from sea-level up to 3,500m mainly north of the equator. In E Africa north of the R. Rufiji or R. Ruvuma; also in NW Africa.
Habitat: Savannahs, woodlands, steppes and uplands. The crested porcupine is sometimes found along forest margins or galleries. It prefers hilly or rocky country.
Food: Roots, bulbs, bark and fallen fruits. Bones and dried animal remains are frequently gnawed. Root crops, maize and cucumbers are frequently raided.
Behaviour: Family groups often share a burrow or cave but foraging is a solitary activity during which an animal commonly travels up to 15km in a night. Natural holes or crevices are frequently exploited but the crested porcupine also digs its own burrow, especially in sandy soils. Galleries are continually expanded so that warrens occupied over many years become very extensive. Up to four young are born within the burrow, possibly twice a year. Baby porcupines are active and mobile at birth. They are suckled for 6 or 7 weeks and travel with the mother for about 1 year.
Adaptations: The hollow rattle-quills in the tail warn off potential predators but their primary role is probably in communication with other porcupines, especially during courtship, when both sexes rattle their tails before copulating.
Status : Considered an agricultural pest in many areas. Not endangered.

South African porcupine *Hystrix africaeaustralis*

Other names: Fr. *Porc-épic d'Afrique du Sud*. Ger. *Sud-afrika Stachelschwein*. Swah. *Nnungu*.
Measurements: HB 75–100cm. T 10–17cm. W 10–24kg.
Recognition: A very large, black and white rodent with a sweeping, erectile neck crest of white-tipped bristles. Back and tail are covered in black and white quills and there is a white rump area. Rattle-quills are 6cm long and conspicuous. The mouth is slightly more overhung by the nose than in the crested porcupine. This porcupine usually grunts while foraging.
Habitat: Found mainly south of the equator in most habitats from sea-level up to about 3,000m. The South African porcupine follows routines along regularly used pathways, making detours and pauses to excavate food. It is a summer breeder in South Africa. It matures by 2 years and may live for up to 20 years.
Food: Mainly roots, bulbs, tubers and bark, with occasional scavenging from carcasses or old skeletons.
Status: Not endangered (although already eliminated in some settled areas).

Atherurus africanus africanus
Atherurus africanus centralis
Atherurus africanus turneri
? Reported Tana delta form
Lophiomys imhausi

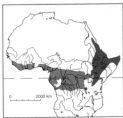

Brush-tailed porcupine *Atherurus africanus*

Other names: Fr. *Athérure africain*. Ger. *Quasenstachler*. Swah. *Njiko*.
Measurements: HB 36–60cm. T 15–23cm. W 1.5–4kg.
Recognition: A long-bodied, low-slung brown rodent with very bristly fur on the limbs and face, progressing to very sharp, thick quills on the back and shorter ones on the rump and tail. Swollen, hollow white rattle-quills are borne on the tip of the tail. Ears are large and flesh-coloured. The muzzle is swollen. Legs and feet are sturdy.
Subspecies: *A. a. africanus* (W Africa), *A. a. centralis* (Zaïre basin), *A. a. turneri* (E Africa).
Distribution: From Sierra Leone to Kenya, from sea-level up to 700m within the equatorial zone.
Habitat: Nocturnal inhabitants of rainforests, where a preference for valley bottoms may reflect their need for natural shelters (eroded rock or root systems). Warrens are used for many years and are associated with latrines, habitual, radiating trails and, occasionally, 'slides'.
Food: Fallen fruits, roots, tubers and stems. Oil-palm, crabwood and ginger fruit are especially favoured but animal foods are rarely taken. Brush-tailed porcupines are masticators rather than gnawers.
Behaviour: Groups of up to 20 animals (usually six to eight) inhabit an area of 2–5ha. They sleep in their burrows during the day and are active much of the night. Brush-tailed porcupines respond to the attentions of predators by stamping the feet, erecting the spines and thrashing the rattle-tail (the tail easily detaches and is often missing). Captive specimens are very playful.
Adaptations: These porcupines are relatively slow breeders (normally one young but four have been recorded). Young are precocious but do not mature until 2 years old. Up to three litters a year are possible (gestation lasts about 14 weeks). This suggests fairly infrequent predation but the brown (rather than black and white) colouring implies a greater vulnerability than that of larger species.
Status: Eliminated in some localities due to settlement and hunting. Not endangered overall.

CANE-RATS THRYONOMYIDAE

| Savannah cane-rat | *Thryonomys swinderianus* |
| Marsh cane-rat | *Thryonomys gregorianus* |

Recognition: Medium-sized to large, robust rodents with grizzled brown coats, prominent chisel-like orange incisors, short tails and short, strong legs with sharp digging claws.
Genealogy: Represented in the fossil record from about 20 million years ago from N Africa, the cane-rat lineage is conservative and shows some resemblance to certain living South American rodents (notably *Carterodon*).
Geography: Exclusively African, cane-rats have very wide ranges but are absent or rare over much of SW Africa, from the Sahara and from the arid Horn of Africa.
Ecology: Dependent on water and coarse valley-bottom grasses. Cane-rats can be major consumers of mature valley grasses and reeds, for which their cutting teeth and manipulative hands are well adapted.

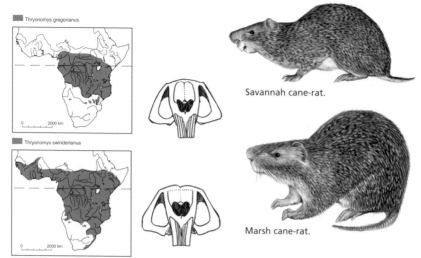

Savannah cane-rat.

Marsh cane-rat.

Natural history: Probably territorial, cane-rats are highly vocal. They grunt, whistle, hoot and thump their legs (when alarmed on *terra firma*). Fighting is highly ritualised and serious biting is inhibited. Instead, noses are engaged in weight-testing contests.

Adaptations: At least two litters a year are common, with an average of four young (two to eight) in each litter. Young are born very well developed and are sexually mature and reproductively active by 6 months. Very high levels of reproduction, fuelled by unlimited food, compensates for short life-spans and high mortality rates (cane-rats are preferred prey for many carnivores, eagles and people). The great fecundity of cane-rats is effectively exploited by people throughout tropical Africa and should be amenable to further systematic management.

Savannah cane-rat *Thryonomys gregorianus*

Measurements: HB 35–51cm. T 6.5–14cm. W 2.6–7.5kg.

Recognition: A large, grizzled rodent with a bulbous nose, short tail and very deeply grooved incisors. The savannah cane-rat is mainly nocturnal and uses habitual paths between feeding areas and shelter. These are often in termitaries or in the holes of other burrowing animals. It sometimes excavates its own shallow holes. Its coarse, stiff hair is frequently to be found in the scats of carnivores.

Habitat: Mainly areas of reliable rainfall and rank grass growth in tropical Africa east of Nigeria. There is much overlap of habitat with the marsh cane-rat but the savannah cane-rat lives on grassy hills and savannahs. It is especially common in elephant grass (*Pennisetum purpureum*).

Food: Stems of elephant grass; also *Setaria*, *Hyparrhenia*, *Exotheca* and *Melinus*. The ginger (*Aframomum*) is eaten in wet, well-wooded areas. Fruits, bark and roots are also eaten.

Status: The savannah cane-rat has a patchier distribution than the marsh cane-rat. Not endangered.

Marsh cane-rat *Thryonomys swinderianus*

Measurements: HB 43–58cm. T 17–26cm. W 4.5–8.8kg.

Recognition: Distinguished by its slightly larger size, its longer tail, less protuberant nose and restricted fine grooving of the incisors. The marsh cane-rat has a highly characteristic whistle (and foot-thumping in the dry season) and is mainly nocturnal.

Habitat: Beds of *Setaria*, *Echinochloa*, *Sorghastrum* and *Hyparrhenia* in seasonally waterlogged valley bottoms throughout the moister parts of Africa. The pidgin name 'cutting-grass' is an apt description of this cane-rat's very rapid and systematic consumption of coarse grass stems.

Food: Dominant grasses within its habitat.

Status: Unsuited to small-scale domestication. Well-suited to free-range management. Not endangered.

DASSIE RAT PETROMURIDAE

Dassie rat	*Petromus typicus*

Although the only living representative of this family is the dassie rat, the fossil record shows it to have been large and diverse, with two subfamilies and seven genera. Competition from more advanced rodents presumably eliminated them from all but the most specialised of niches in remote localities.

Dassie rat *Petromus typicus*
Measurements: HB 13.5–21cm. T 11.5–17cm. W 170–262g.
Recognition: A squat, coarse-furred rodent with a long, hairy tail and a peculiarly flattened head. Colour varies from pale grey or ochre, through shades of brown, to nearly black. The feet have rounded, naked pads on the palms and digits (an adaptation for travel on rock). The dassie rat likes to sun-bathe in pairs or small groups but it is very shy and flees for shelter at any disturbance. Urine is used to mark particular rocks and forms characteristic yellow-white streaks near the dens.
Habitat: Rocky outcrops in Namibia, N Cape and SW Angola where the dassie rat shelters in very narrow crevices. Leaf-lined retreats are used as birthing dens for the precocious young.
Food: Leaves, stems and heads of grasses. The leaves and fruits of shrubs and trees are taken less frequently.
Status: Not endangered.

JERBOAS DIPODIDAE

Desert jerboas	*Jaculus*
Four-toed jerboa	*Allactaga tetradactyla*

Jumping rodents with hindlegs four or more times the length of their forelegs. In spite of having small forelegs, they are efficient diggers (with forelegs and teeth) in sandy soil, building burrows that descend up to 2m below the surface. All species are nocturnal and live in arid environments, mostly in Asia, where they undoubtedly evolved. Fossils of the jerboa lineage in Eurasia go back at least 30 million years.

Desert jerboas *Jaculus* (2 species)
Measurements: HB 17–32cm. T 14–22cm. W 50–71g.

Right
Jaculus jaculus

Recognition: Specialised, long-legged rodents with tawny-orange upperparts, a white underside (and thigh stripe). The hindfeet are very elongated and hair-tufted, with toes reduced to three. The black eyes are night-adapted and very large. The nose is flat and is used to tamp the soil. The very long, black and white tufted tail is often held in an elegant, button-hook curl and acts as a tripod with the hindlegs. Desert jerboas are active most of the night.

Species: *J. jaculus* (mainly sand dunes in the Sahara), *J. orientalis* (mainly steppe on Mediterranean littoral).

Habitat: These sand-dwelling jerboas dig deep burrows and mainly live and forage on their own but may form temporary groups of four or five in their burrows. Both species range from Mauritania to Egypt but the three-toed jerboa (*J. jaculus*) is the more wide-ranging and common.

Food: Seeds, stems and roots of desert grasses.

Status: Not endangered.

Four-toed jerboa.

Four-toed jerboa *Allactaga tetradactyla*

Measurements: HB 24–30cm. T 15–20cm. W est. 20–40g.

Recognition: A mottled, sandy-coloured jerboa with four long toes, long ears and a rounded, snub-nosed, rounded head with large eyes. The long tail has a black brush terminating in a white tip.

Habitat: Restricted to the gravel plains that lie between Alexandria in Egypt and the Gulf of Sirte in Libya. This essentially Asiatic genus has adapted to cold deserts with fewer specialisations (such as the three toes and nose flaps of the desert jerboas).

Food: Grass seeds and roots.

Status: Localised and rare.

RAT-LIKE RODENTS MUROIDEA

Pseudo-hamsters	Mystromyinae
Maned rat	Lophiomyinae
Gerbils	Gerbillinae
Dendromurines	Dendromurinae
Pouched rats	Cricetomyinae
Pygmy rock mice	Petromyscinae
Groove-toothed rats	Otomyinae
Root-rats	Rhizomyidae
Mole-rats	Spalacinae
Murid rats and mice	Muridae

Numbering some 1,330 species, 281 genera and 17 subfamilies, the rat-like rodents were, until recently, divided into two main groups, murids and cricetids, mainly distinguished by their cusp patterns. While the subfamilies remain in the new classification, the traditional clustering of cricetids and murids has now been generally abandoned.

PSEUDO-HAMSTERS MYSTROMYINAE

White-tailed mouse	*Mystromys albicaudatus*

The white-tailed mouse has an outward resemblance to the smallest Eurasian hamsters (with which it has sometimes been grouped). With further study it has been placed in its own subfamily, the Mystromyinae. Its affinities remain obscure and the white-tailed mouse would appear to be the lone survivor of a very archaic group. *Mystromys* means 'spoon-mouse'.

White-tailed mouse *Mystromys albicaudatus*

Measurements: HB 10.5–18.4cm. T 50–97cm. W 75–111g.
Recognition: A plump, short-tailed mouse resembling a hamster, with soft grey upperparts and a white underside. The eyes are large. Incisors are yellowish and without grooves. The molar teeth are unique in their pattern of cusps and folding of enamel.
Habitat: Savannah grasslands and scrub in the South African uplands and Cape region. The white-tailed mouse lives in crevices and burrows where it makes a nest of shredded material.
Food: Seeds, green vegetable matter and insects.
Status: Poorly known.

(a) Crested rat.
(b) White-tailed mouse.

(a)

(b)

MANED RAT LOPHIOMYINAE

Crested (Maned) rat	*Lophiomys imhausi*

This singular rodent, in a subfamily of its own, is generally regarded as being distantly related to the Eurasian hamsters. Its unique skull is roofed over with granulated bone so that the form of the cranium resembles that of a turtle. The maned rat occurs on both sides of the Red Sea. It is either very rare and secretive or has been suffering a continuous decline in recent years.

Crested (Maned) rat *Lophiomys imhausi*

Measurements: HB 25.5–36cm. T 14–21.5cm. W 590–920g.
Recognition: A slow-moving, mainly nocturnal rodent with dense, woolly grey fur and bold black and white markings on the face. The muzzle and feet are the only areas of short fur. Fur on the flanks is able to part to reveal a tract of specialised hairs that resemble hemp string in texture and colour. When alarmed the animal opens this fur-tract and twists to present it to the attacker. It also hisses, growls and snaps its teeth if approached too closely. The crested rat is a skilful, but slow climber and uses its hands like a squirrel to manipulate foods while squatting on its haunches.
Habitat: Dry, rocky woodlands and montane forests, especially juniper forests in NE Africa; also known from the Arabian peninsula. The crested rat often shares its habitat with rock hyraxes.
Food: Fruits, shoots, leaves, roots and insects.
Status: Little known and rare.

GERBILS GERBILLINAE

Gerbils	*Gerbillus* (51 species)
Dwarf gerbil	*Desmodilliscus braueri*
Bushy-tailed jird	*Sekeetamys calurus*
Jirds	*Meriones* (3 species)
Fat sand-rats	*Psammomys* (2 species)
Tatera (Naked-soled) gerbils	*Tatera* (11 species)
Taterillus gerbils	*Taterillus* (8 species)
Hairy-footed gerbil	*Gerbillurus* (4 species)
Namaqua gerbil	*Desmodillus auricularis*
Fat-tailed gerbil	*Pachyuromys duprasi*
Walo	*Amodillus imbellis*

Recognition: Nocturnal desert rodents with well-muscled and longer hindlegs and more slender forelegs. They are mostly of sandy colouring and have large eyes and enlarged inner ears. External ears vary in size and shape.

Genealogy: Gerbils are probably of Eurasian origin and have only been recorded as fossils in Africa from about 7 million years ago. Older genera are essentially Eurasian immigrants. Others have evolved more recently in Africa.

Geography: Most genera are restricted to arid areas of Africa but several types have adapted to sandy soils or semi-arid corridors within the tropics.

Ecology: Their ecological success has been greatly assisted by drought-resistant physiology, the digging of extensive burrows and the storing of food.

Natural history: Secure burrows have allowed gerbils to raise litters of blind, naked young which develop relatively slowly. Principal foods are seeds and vegetable matter but many species eat invertebrates.

Adaptations: Food storage probably originated as a response to Eurasian winters. Social living contributes to collection of food, strengthens defences against other rodents (and helps to reduce heat loss during winters). Food-rich corners of the desert can support social gerbils of Asian origin (i.e. jirds and fat sand rats) while poorer areas sustain solitary gerbil types.

Gerbillus gerbillus.

Gerbils *Gerbillus* (53 species)

Measurements: HB 70–12cm. T 80–15cm. W 15–25g.

Recognition: Small gerbils with very long hindlegs and short front legs. Soles of the feet are naked in some species, hairy in others. Most species have white fur above the eyes or behind the ears. Many species are gregarious. (The inner ear bullae are very large.)

Species: *G. acticola, G. agag, G. amoenus, G. andersoni, G. bilensis, G. bonhotei, G. bottai, G. brockmani, G. burtoni, G. campestris, G. cosensis, G. dalloni, G. diminutus, G. dongolanus, G. dunni, G. floweri, G. garamantis, G. gerbillus, G. grobbeni, G. harwoodi, G. henleyi, G. hesperinus, G. hoogstraali, G. jamesi, G. juliani, G. latastei, G. lowei, G. mackillingini, G. maghrebi, G. mauritaniae, G. muriculus, G. nancillus, G. nanus, G. nigeriae, G. occiduus, G. percivali, G. perpallidus, G. peeli, G. principulus, G. pulvinatus, G. pusillus, G. pyramidum, G. quadrimaculatus, G. riggenbachi, G. rosalinda, G. ruberrimus, G. simona, G. somalicus, G. stigmonyx, G. syrticus, G. tarabuli, G. vivax, G. watersi.*

Habitat: Open dry and sandy habitats in N and NE Africa.

Food: Grass, roots, seeds and insects.

Status: Largely unknown.

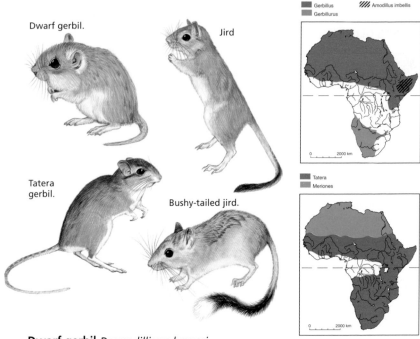

Dwarf gerbil.

Jird

Tatera gerbil.

Bushy-tailed jird.

Gerbillus
Gerbillurus
Amodillus imbellis

Tatera
Meriones

Dwarf gerbil *Desmodilliscus braueri*

Measurements: HB 5–7cm. T 3.5–5cm. W est. 8–15g.
Recognition: A very small, soft-furred fawn gerbil with white spots behind the ears, small hindfeet, and a tail shorter than the body. It has large cheek pouches. The inner ear bullae are very large.
Habitat: Sahelian steppes from Mauritania to the Sudan.
Food: Presumed to be grass seeds, which are stored in the burrow.
Status: Not known.

Bushy-tailed jird *Sekeetamys calurus*

Measurements: HB 10–12.5cm. T 11–16cm. W est. 30–60g.
Recognition: A sandy-coloured gerbil with darker forehead and a mantle of brownish streaking. The tail is long and brown or black towards the end, with a white tip.
Habitat: Broken rocky country in Egypt, where it burrows under rocks and slabs, often in hilly country or on slopes. It is an agile climber.
Food: Presumably seeds and leaves.
Status: Little known.

Jirds *Meriones* (3 species)

Measurements: HB 11–13cm. T 9–11cm. W est. 50–75g.
Recognition: Sandy-coloured, robustly built gerbils with relatively short, narrow feet and a tufted, dark-tipped tail. They are capable of climbing trees and rocks. Social behaviour is flexible (social in some areas, solitary in others). They build complex burrows.
Habitat: Various desertic and subdesertic habitats in N Africa, Niger, Chad and Sudan.
Species: *M. crassus, M. libycus, M. shawi.*
Food: Seeds, stems, leaves, roots and bulbs (often stored in burrows).
Status: Not endangered.

Fat sand-rats *Psammomys* (2 species)

Measurements: HB 13–18cm. T 11–15cm. W est. 50–75g.
Recognition: Unusually for a gerbil, these species are diurnal. They are rotund and buff, with numerous long, fine guard hairs. Ears are thick, short and oval.
Species: *P. obesus, P. vexillaris.*

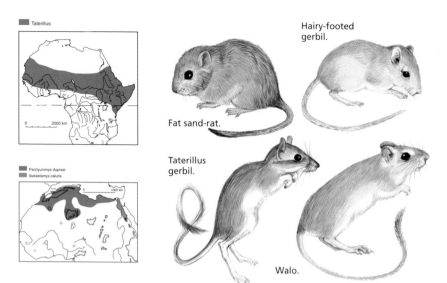

Taterillus

Pachyuromys duprasi
Sekeetamys caluris

Hairy-footed gerbil.

Fat sand-rat.

Taterillus gerbil.

Walo.

Habitat: Firm, compacted sands in valleys and on alluvial plains, salt-brush floodplains and neighbouring slopes in the Sahara Desert from Morocco to Egypt.
Food: Specialised to feed on the leaves and stems of salty succulents, notably *Suaeda*, *Traganum* and *Salsola*.
Status: Not known.

Tatera (Naked-soled) gerbils *Tatera* (11 species)

Measurements: HB 12–16cm. T 14–17cm. W est. 60–125g.
Recognition: Variously coloured gerbils with long hindlegs, naked-soled feet, large eyes and ears, and a prominent, hairy muzzle. The upper incisors are grooved. They commonly build extensive warrens.
Species: *T. afra, T. boehmi, T. brantsii, T. guineae, T. inclusa, T. kempi, T. leucogaster, T. nigricauda, T. phillipsi, T. robusta, T. valida*.
Habitat: Most of sub-Saharan Africa (except rainforest areas) and margins of Sahara. Tatera gerbils inhabit well-drained, sandy areas.
Food: Seeds, stems and roots of grasses; also roots, bulbs and insects.
Status: A successful diverse group.

Taterillus gerbils *Taterillus* (8 species)

Measurements: HB 10–14cm. T 14–17cm. W est. 50–80g.
Recognition: Smaller gerbils of tatera type. The eyes are particularly large but the internal ear bullae are relatively smaller than in most gerbils. A diagnostic feature of the skull is a very large cavity in the palate.
Species: *T. arenarius, T. congicus, T. emini, T. gracilis, T. harringtoni, T. lacustris, T. petteri, T. pygargus*.
Habitat: Mainly Sudanic and Sahelian savannahs and steppes along the southern borders of the Sahara.
Food: Various plant foods and (probably) insects.
Status: Little known.

Hairy-footed gerbil *Gerbillurus* (4 species)

Measurements: HB 8–12cm. T 10–13cm. W 22–40g.
Recognition: Small, pale-coloured gerbils with long tails and large, hairy hindfeet.
Species: *G. paeba, G. vallinus, G. tytonis, G. setzeri*.
Habitat: Arid areas of SW Africa, with a preference for sandy soils. Hairy-footed gerbils excavate warrens where they live in small groups.
Food: Seeds and probably insects.
Status: Little known.

Fat-tailed gerbil.

Namaqua gerbil.

- Desmodilliscus
- Desmodillus
- Psammomys

Namaqua gerbil *Desmodillus auricularis*

Measurements: HB 10–14cm. T 8–10cm. W 39–70g.
Recognition: Variably coloured gerbil with short hindlegs. The tail is shorter than the body and there is white fur behind the flesh-coloured ears. The inner ear bullae are vastly inflated.
Habitat: SW Africa, Kalahari, Karoo and Namibian deserts, where this gerbil is associated with open pans and compacted calcareous soils. The burrows of this species are unusual for their almost vertical exit holes.
Food: Seeds of grasses (mainly) and of shrubs and trees. These are stored in the burrows.
Status: Not endangered.

Fat-tailed gerbil *Pachyuromys duprasi*

Measurements: HB 105–135cm. T 45–61cm. W 30–65g.
Recognition: A small gerbil with a pale, soft coat, pinkish buff sides and white underparts. The short, fat-covered tail is almost naked and the forefeet are well clawed. Incisors are faintly grooved. Inner ear bullae are vastly inflated.
Habitat: Deserts in N Africa with solid substrates. Populations are thought to fluctuate.
Food: Fruits, gathered as far as 2km from the burrows, in which they are stored.
Status: Little known.

Walo *Amodillus imbellis*

Measurements: HB 10.5–11cm. T est. 13–15cm. W est. 40–60g.
Recognition: A reddish fawn gerbil with a long, hairy tail. The base of the ears and brows to the large eyes are white. The bare pads of the feet have an unusual granular texture.
Habitat: Recorded from sandy desert in Somalia.
Food: The very feeble jaw structure suggests that only soft foods are taken, possibly fruits and soft-bodied insects.
Status: Not known.

DENDROMURINES DENDROMURINAE

Climbing mice	*Dendromus*
Giant climbing mouse	*Megadendromus nicolausi*
Velvet climbing mouse	*Dendroprionomys rousseloti*
Dollman's climbing mouse	*Prionomys batesi*
Large-eared mouse	*Malacothrix typica*
Link rat	*Deomys ferugineus*
Fat mice	*Steatomys*
Togo mouse	*Leimacomys buettneri*

Although dendromurines are now exclusive to Africa, the earliest fossils, from 15 million years ago, have been found in Thailand and Pakistan. Later fossils appear in various parts of Africa where there was a radiation into many niches. The living genera probably represent relics of that radiation. Two of them, climbing mice (*Dendromus*) and fat mice (*Steatomys*) are very widespread and successful specialists while the remaining genera are all to some degree relics with small ranges or a constricted niche (*Deomys*). The principal cause of this constriction or decline was probably the invasion of Africa by modern rats and mice.

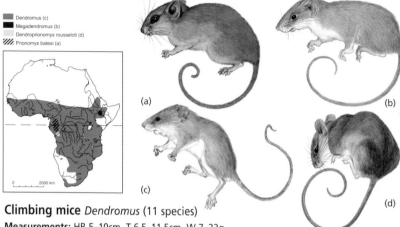

Dendromus (c)
Megadendromus (b)
Dendroprionomys rousseloti (d)
Prionomys batesi (a)

0   2000 km

(a)

(b)

(c)

(d)

Climbing mice *Dendromus* (11 species)

Measurements: HB 5–10cm. T 6.5–11.5cm. W 7–23g.
Recognition: Large-headed climbing mice with long, semi-prehensile tails, long, extremely dextrous toes and a peculiarly specialised, 'padded hook' hand structure. Coat colour varies from pale fawn to grey or a rich brown. Undersides are usually white. Ears vary in size and shape.
Species: *D. insignis, D. kahuziensis, D. kivu, D. lovati, D. melanotis, D. mesomelas, D. messorius, D. mystacalis, D. nyikae, D. oreas, D. vernayi.*
Habitat: Tall grass and shrubby secondary growth, in which these mice are rapid and adept climbers. They build large, globular nests.
Food: Specialist grass-seed-eaters.
Status: A diverse and successful group but some species have very restricted montane distributions.

Giant climbing mouse *Megadendromus nicolausi*

Measurements: HB 11–13cm. T 9–10.5cm. W 49–66g.
Recognition: A large climbing mouse with dark brown upperparts and paler underside. Digits are adapted to climbing. The tail is long, fine and flexible. (Comparison of the teeth of this species with murines, when it was discovered in 1978, suggests that dendromurines and murines may share a more recent common origin than had previously been supposed.)
Habitat: High altitudes in the Bale massif in central Ethiopia. It has been caught in everlasting sage-brush (*Helichrysum-* and *Artemesia*-dominant) among mountain grasses (*Andropogon, Festuca* and *Poa*).
Food: Probably grass seed.
Status: Extremely localised in a zone threatened by sheep grazing. Vulnerable or endangered.

Velvet climbing mouse *Dendroprionomys rousseloti*

Measurements: Unavailable.
Recognition: A velvety-furred, dark brown climbing mouse with tawny flanks and a white underside. It has a black patch of fur below the eyes and a long, prehensile tail. Features are somewhat intermediate between the common climbing mice and Dollman's mouse (*Prionomys*).
Habitat: Only known from the zoological gardens on the banks of the R. Zaïre at Brazzaville.
Food: Unknown but thought to include insects.
Status: Not known.

Dollman's climbing mouse *Prionomys batesi*

Measurements: HB est. 5.5–6.5cm. T est. 9.5–10cm. W est. 10–15g.
Recognition: A climbing mouse with shrew-like, velvety fur of a deep pink-tinged tawny-brown, blending into pinkish grey underparts. Eyes are surrounded by a narrow mask of black fur. The forefeet lack a thumb.

Habitat: Moist rainforest zone between the R. Dja and R. Zaïre; probably grass and shrub-dwelling.
Food: Not known.
Status: Not known.

Large-eared mouse *Malacothrix typica*

Measurements: HB 7–8cm. T 3.2–4cm. W 10–20g.
Recognition: A small, prettily marked mouse with ash-grey streaks on the back and flanks and a tawny face and shoulders. The underside and fur at the base of the very large ears are white. The tail is short and tapered. This species is nocturnal.
Habitat: Areas of short grass and karoo bush growing on or close to calcareous pans in dry SW Africa. This mouse digs deep burrows among low bushes.
Food: Seeds and green plant parts.
Status: Poorly known.

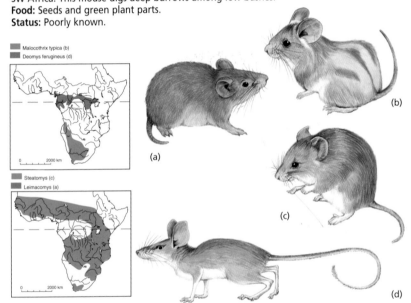

Malocothrix typica (b)
Deomys ferugineus (d)

Steatomys (c)
Leimacomys (a)

(a)

(b)

(c)

(d)

Link rat *Deomys ferugineus*

Measurements: HB 12–14.5cm. T 15–21.5cm. W 40–70g.
Recognition: The link rat is highly distinctive for its long legs and pointed, narrow head surmounted by enormous ears. It has a very long, bicoloured tail. The back and forehead are rich orange and brown and the underside is white. Rump hairs are rather stiff. It is nocturnal and crepuscular.
Habitat: Prefers seasonally flooded forest floors between Cameroon and the Victoria Nile. This strictly equatorial species ranges north of the R. Zaïre.
Food: Mainly insects, crustaceans, slugs and some fallen fruits (notably palm-nut husks).
Status: Widespread but scattered distribution. Seldom common.

Fat mice *Steatomys* (6 species)

Measurements: HB 5–14cm. T 3–75cm. W est. 15–30g.
Recognition: Small mice with large ears and short limbs and tail. Upperparts are sandy brown and underparts white. They are often very fat and lethargic.
Species: *S. caurinus, S. cuppedius, S. jacksoni, S. krebsii, S. parvus, S. pratensis.*
Habitat: Savannahs, woodlands and (marginally) semi-arid environments. Very local in distribution, fat mice are apparently absent over large intervening areas. They live in deep burrows where they store food and aestivate.
Food: Seeds, bulbs, roots, insects, grass.
Status: *S. jacksoni* in Ghana and W Nigeria is probably rare. All other species are widely distributed. Not endangered.

Togo mouse *Leimacomys buettneri*

Measurements: HB 11.8cm. T 3.7cm. W est. 50–60g.
Recognition: A medium-sized brown mouse with a very short, tapered tail and paler fawn flanks and shoulders. It has small, well-haired ears and well-developed claws on the forefeet. Teeth are grooved.
Habitat: Not known but collected within the 'Dahomey Gap', a savannah-forest-mosaic region separating the Upper Guinea and Nigerian forests.
Food: The delicate muzzle suggests that small, soft-bodied insects or unripe seeds may be the main foods.
Status: Possibly extinct. Extremely localised and little known.

Beamys (both Beamys and
C. emini live within C. gambianus range)

Cricetomys emini

Cricetomys gambianus

C. emini cosensi

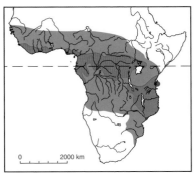

0   2000 km

Lesser pouched rat.

Pouched mouse.

Giant-pouched rat.

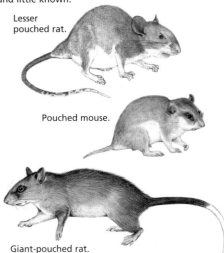

POUCHED RATS CRICETOMYINAE

Lesser pouched rat	*Beamys hindei*
Giant pouched rats	*Cricetomys* (2 species)
Pouched mice	*Saccostomus* (2 species)

All species have large cheek pouches which they fill during forays after food. All dig burrows with food-storage chambers and tend to 'camp' close to the current food source. Pouched rats are generally sluggish, grey or greyish brown animals. The group has distinctive teeth. All are strictly nocturnal.

Lesser pouched rat *Beamys hindei*

Measurements: HB 13–18.7cm. T 10–15.5cm. W 55–150g.
Recognition: Small rat with limp, soft fur, grey or brown upperparts, white underparts and a dark grey tail with a white tip and much mottling. It possesses cheek pouches. A good but slow climber, it is strictly nocturnal.
Subspecies: (sometimes treated as species) *B. h. hindei* (coastal Kenya and Tanzania), *B. h. major* (mainly montane Tanzania and Malawi).
Habitat: Sandy riverbanks in forest, thicket or dense woodland, from the Kenya coast to Malawi.
Food: Fruits and seeds; occasionally animal foods.
Status: Not endangered.

Giant pouched rats *Cricetomys* (2 species)

Measurements: HB 28–45cm. T 36–46cm. W 1–1.4kg.
Recognition: Large, brown or grey pouched rats, with large, naked ears. The terminal half of the long tail is white. Although sluggish, they are good climbers. They are strictly nocturnal.

Species: *C. gambianus*: robust, brown, with eye mask. *C. emini* (rainforests only): gracile, grey. *cosensi* (Zanzibar I.) might be a third species.
Habitat: Very varied (*C. gambianus*); exclusively lowland rainforest (*C. emini*).
Food: Fruits, seeds, nuts, roots and leaves, which are collected in the cheek pouches and taken back to the extensive burrow (where found objects, pebbles and metallic trash are also collected).
Status: Not endangered. The Zanzibar race requires further investigation.

Pouched mice *Saccostomus* (2 species)

Measurements: HB 11.5–19cm. T 3–8cm. W 40–85g.
Recognition: A grey or greyish brown mouse with short, limp fur, enormous cheek pouches, and short legs and tail. It is strictly nocturnal.
Species: *S. campestris*: (southern Africa). *S. mearns*: (NE Africa).
Habitat: Savannahs, woodlands and semi-arid habitats in S and E Africa. The pouched mouse uses the burrows of other species as well as digging its own.
Food: Seeds, fruits and occasionally insects.
Status: Not endangered.

PYGMY ROCK MICE PETROMYSCINAE

Pygmy rock mice	*Petromyscus* (4 species)
Delaney's mouse	*Delanymys brooksi*

This subfamily currently accommodates two rare, relict genera: *Petromyscus* and *Delanymys*. These rodents are dentally intermediate between Dendromurinae and Mystromyinae but are very divergent and distinctive in other respects. They are small brown mice with distinctive tooth patterns.

Pygmy rock mice *Petromyscus* (4 species)

Measurements: HB 7.5–11.5cm. T 7.5–10.5cm. W 17–25g.
Recognition: Small brown mice with broad, flattened heads and prominent ears and whiskers. The soft fur is buff or brown above, greyish below. The tail is scaly.
Species: *P. barbouri, P. collinus, P. monticularis, P. shortridgei.*
Habitat: Arid regions of SW Africa from S Angola to the Cape.
Food: Mainly seeds.
Status: Little known relict species.

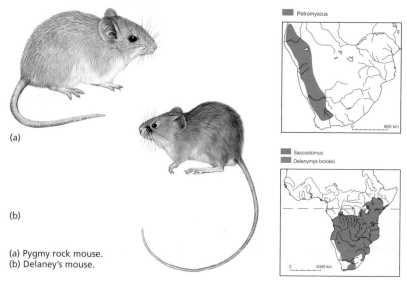

Petromyscus

Saccostomus
Delanymys brooksi

(a)

(b)

(a) Pygmy rock mouse.
(b) Delaney's mouse.

Delaney's mouse *Delanymys brooksi*
Measurements: HB 5–6cm. T 8.5–10.5cm. W 5g.
Recognition: A very small, long-tailed mouse with long hindlegs, five mobile fingers and a vestigial thumb. The dense soft hair is reddish brown interspersed with long guard hairs. There is a black spot between the eye and nostril.
Habitat: High-altitude (1,700–2, 625m) marshes in E Zaïre and W Uganda, among sedges and grasses, where it builds very small, round nests.
Food: Grass and sedge seeds (possibly unripe); perhaps also fruits.
Status: Vulnerable or endangered.

GROOVE-TOOTHED RATS OTOMYINAE

Groove-toothed rats	*Otomys* (12 species)	Normal ear bullae
Whistling rats	*Parotomys* (2 species)	Enlarged ear bullae

Stocky, shaggy, blunt-faced rats with short legs, a short tail and large ears. The skull is robust and most species have grooved upper incisors. The cheek teeth have mill-like laminations. All are vegetarian and most feed on stems and rhizomes of rank grasses.

Groove-toothed rats *Otomys* (12 species)

Measurements: HB 12–22cm. T 6–12cm. W 100–260g.
Recognition: Shaggy rats of very varied colouring (but usually dark) with a very blunt muzzle and large ears. Upper incisors are always grooved (similar *Dasymys* has plain incisors). Very placid, they give birth to precocious young.
Species: *O. anchietae, O. angoniensis, O. denti, O. irroratus, O. laminatus, O. maximus, O. occidentalis, O. saundersiae, O. sloggetti, O. tropicalis, O. typus, O. unisulcatus.*
Habitat: Grasslands, marshes, dense secondary growth, tangles and open savannah, especially at higher altitudes. Some species may have become 'relicts' because they are adapted to moist, fire-less regimes. Their distributions are therefore discontinuous and mainly eastern upland and southern temperate.
Food: Green grass, reed and herb stems and bark; occasionally roots and seeds.
Status: Some species have limited ranges.

Whistling rat.

Groove-toothed rat.

Whistling rats *Parotomys* (2 species)
Measurements: HB 12–17cm. T 8–12cm. W 90–155g.
Recognition: Shaggy, large-eyed, short legged, diurnal rats of variable colouring from fawn to grey-brown (paler than groove-toothed rats). These animals whistle loudly, often from an upright, seated position at the burrow entrance.
Species: *P. brantsii*: upper incisors ungrooved. *P. littledalei*: upper incisors grooved.
Habitat: Dry, sandy environments in SW Africa where both species excavate burrows.
Food: Grass stems and seeds. Stems and leaves of xerophytic shrubs.
Status: Locally abundant.

ROOT-RATS RHIZOMYIDAE

Root-rats	*Tachyoryctes* (11 species)

Recognition: Chunky, subterranean, tunnelling rats with diminutive ears, small eyes and prominent orange incisors. The fur is soft and thick, usually russet on the surface but with a dark grey undercoat. An immigrant group confined to upland areas closest to Ethiopia. Other genera occur in the Himalayas and South-East Asia.

Root-rats *Tachyoryctes* (provisionally 11 species)

Measurements: HB 16–28cm. T 5–10cm. W 160–600g.

Recognition: Robust, digging rodents of very variable colouring, size and skull structure. Rapid speciation in this group has probably been facilitated by extremely rapid breeding, very high densities, discontinuous distribution and periodic fluctuations in numbers. The giant root-rat (*Tachyoryctes macrocephalus*), a very large, golden brown species, is highly distinctive. It lives at densities of 20–60 animals per ha at 3,000–4,100m above sea-level and has eyes projecting above the forehead. Activity varies; most species are nocturnal but alpine populations may be partially or wholly diurnal.

Species: (provisional) *T. ankoliae, T. annecteus, T. audax, T. daemon, T. macrocephalus, T. naivashae, T. rex, T. ruandae, T. ruddi, T. spalacinus, T. splendens.*

Habitat: Uplands (including very high-altitude Afro-alpine grasslands), where the root-rats make large, composting midden-mounds as well as extensive tunnels and soil heaps. They range discontinuously from Ethiopia to E Zaïre, Burundi and N Tanzania.

Food: Varies from species to species. Roots, tubers, stems and bulbs are indiscriminately taken underground within a short radius of the hole. Material is sorted and unwanted debris is expelled onto a large midden mound.

Status: The current species list is in need of revision.

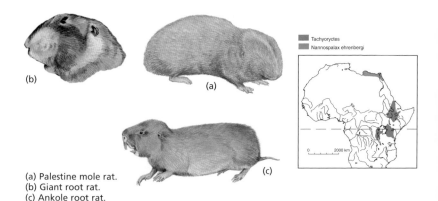

Tachyoryctes
Nannospalax ehrenbergi

(a) Palestine mole rat.
(b) Giant root rat.
(c) Ankole root rat.

MOLE-RATS SPALACINAE

Palestine mole-rat	*Nannospalax ehrenbergi*

Recognition: Cylindrical rodents with dense, dark, mole-like fur, very short legs, minute ears, blind, sealed eyes and a very broad nose. The projecting incisors and head movements are employed in digging (the forelegs merely shuffle spoil backwards). A mainly Eurasian group, mole-rats share very ancient ancestry with voles and rats. They have only a marginal presence in Africa.

Palestine mole-rat *Nannospalax ehrenbergi*

Measurements: HB 15–27cm. T 0cm. W 130–220g.

Recognition: A variably coloured mole-rat with a blunt, rounded head merging into the

body with no obvious neck region. Fore- and hindlegs are short and weakly clawed. The small nasal area is horny and reinforced. The most obvious signs of the mole-rat's presence are the mole hills. It is nocturnal.
Habitat: Areas of very low rainfall (absent from waterless desert) in N Egypt and Libya. Each mole-rat makes extensive burrows with a large winter breeding mound and small summer resting mounds.
Food: Roots, bulbs, tubers and rhizomes below ground; grass, seeds and, rarely, insects, above ground.
Status: Poorly known in Africa.

MURID RATS AND MICE MURIDAE

Spiny mice	*Acomys* (11 species)
Brush-furred mice	*Lophuromys* (9 species)
Uranomys mouse	*Uranomys ruddi*
Broad-headed stink mice	*Zelotomys* (2 species)
Velvet rat	*Colomys goslingi*
Long-footed rats	*Malacomys* (5 species)
Soft-furred rats	*Praomys* (9 species)
African wood mice	*Hylomyscus* (8 species)
De Balsac's mouse	*Heimyscus fumosus*
Multimammate rats	*Mastomys* (8 species)
Meadow rats	*Myomys* (6 species)
Ethiopian meadow rats	*Stenocephalemys* (2 species)
Wurch mouse	*Muriculus imberbis*
Common mice	*Mus* (20 species)
Long-tailed field mouse	*Apodemus sylvaticus*
Short-tailed bandicoot rat	*Nesokia indica*
Narrow-footed woodland mice	*Grammomys* (11 species)
Acacia rats	*Thallomys* (4 species)
Shaggy swamp rats	*Dasymys* (5 species)
Bush-rats	*Aethomys* (10 species)
Target rat	*Stochomys longicaudatus*
Rusty-nosed rats	*Oenomys* (2 species)
Mount Oku mouse	*Lamottemys okuensis*
Broad-footed thicket rats	*Thamnomys* (2 species)
Dephua mice	*Dephomys* (2 species)
Hump-nosed mice	*Hybomys* (6 species)
Four-striped grass mouse	*Rhabdomys pumilio*
Zebra mice	*Lemniscomys* (10 species)
Unstriped grass rats	*Arvicanthis* (5 species)
Creek rats	*Pelomys* (5 species)
Mill rat	*Mylomys dybowski*
Dega rat	*Desmomys harringtoni*

Murid rats and mice range from 2 to 170g in weight and may have a long or short tail, limbs, nose and ears. They can have fine or coarse fur, either short or long and shaggy. Some species are patterned, others are dark or plain. This diverse group numbers over 30 genera and 150 species. Their radiation is not well understood but includes distinct omnivorous and herbivorous groups, as well as specialist offshoots. Within lineages there tend to be closely related species or genera which are forest or non-forest adapted, or divide into mainly arboreal or terrestrial branches.

Murids are thought to be relatively late arrivals in Africa (about 6 million years ago). As dominant species or groups have spread they have progressively replaced earlier types of rodent and have relegated more conservative forms to relict status.

Omnivorous types tend to be rat- or mouse-like, with a soft, short coat and irregularly cusped cheek teeth, while herbivores are shaggier, with a blunter, vole-like head and more mill-like cheek teeth. The wide spread of murid genera and species conceals an important clue to their evolutionary history. A number of genera form closely related clusters, some of which are associated with particular ecological and geographic regions. The more specialised species are so well adapted to local peculiarities of ecosystems that they are very abundant there and nowhere else. It is likely that most regional ecosystems began with much more limited suites of murine rodent lineages than inhabit them today. Biogeographic regions having pronounced associations with particular rodent groups are:

E African and Ethiopian uplands (omnivore niches)	Meadow and multimammate rats (*Myomys*, *Mastomys* and *Stenocephalomys*)
Equatorial central Africa: lowland rainforests (omnivore niches)	Soft-furred, velvet and long-footed rats, African wood mice (*Praomys*, *Colomys*, *Malacomys*, *Hylomyscus*, *Heimyscus*)
South-central Africa: forest-savannah mosaics, woodlands and sumplands	Bush and shaggy swamp rats, target rat (*Aethomys*, *Dasymys*, *Stochomys*)
E Africa: forest-savannah mosaics, montane and coastal	Acacia rats and narrow-footed woodland mice (*Thallomys*, *Grammomys*)
Equatorial north-central Africa: forest-savannah mosaics and grasslands	Rusty-nosed and broad-footed thicket rats, Mount Oku mouse (*Oenomys*, *Thamnomys*, *Lamottemys*)
Equatorial lowland rainforest (herbivore niches)	Hump-nosed and Dephua mice (*Hybomys*, *Dephomys*)
E African and Ethiopian uplands (herbivore niches)	Unstriped grass, mill and Dega rats (*Arvicanthis*, *Pelomys*, *Mylomys*, *Desmomys*)
S and E Africa: 'temperate' and upland grasslands (herbivore niches)	Zebra and four-striped grass mice (*Lemniscomys* and *Rhabdomys*)

Geographic centres of endemism for 'older' genera, such as *Mus*, *Acomys* or *Zelotomys*, are no longer perceptible.

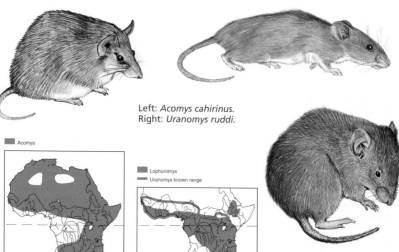

Left: *Acomys cahirinus*.
Right: *Uranomys ruddi*.

Acomys

Lophuromys
Uranomys known range

0   2000 km

0   2000 km

Lophuromys flavopunctatus.

Spiny mice *Acomys* (11 species)

Measurements: HB 7–12cm. T 4–10cm. W 10–40g.
Recognition: Mice with short limbs and tail and very spiny, coarse fur. Upperparts are rufous or fawn to grey or brown and underparts are white or tinted. They mainly inhabit drier areas.
Species: *A. cahirinus, A. cineraceus, A. ignitus, A. kempi, A. louisae, A. mullah, A. percivali, A. russatus, A. spinosissimus, A. subspinosus, A. wilsoni*.
Habitat: Deserts and dry areas from the Mediterranean to the Cape; absent from moist forest zone. Spiny mice are dependent on natural shelter beneath rocks, in gerbil or other rodent warrens, in termitaries or houses.
Food: Opportunistic; seeds, leaves, dry plant matter, invertebrates and organic debris.
Status: Considered a pest in some dry settlements. Not endangered.

Brush-furred mice *Lophuromys* (9 species)

Measurements: HB 8.5–16cm. T 5.5–15cm. W 20–100g.
Recognition: Compact mice with short legs and tails. The dark or speckled coats have a brush-like texture. Brush-furred mice have a distinctive scent and exhibit variable activity patterns, both diurnal and nocturnal.
Species: *L. cinereus, L. flavopunctatus, L. luteogaster, L. medicaudatus, L. melanonyx, L. nudicaudus, L. rahmi, L. sikapusi, L. woosnami*.
Habitat: Moist, grassy areas of tropical Africa from sea-level to about 3,000m.
Food: Invertebrates, especially ants, carrion and plant material.
Status: Successful group.

Uranomys mouse *Uranomys ruddi*

Measurements: HB 8.5–13.5cm. T 5–8cm. W est. 30–60g.
Recognition: Chunky mouse with short legs and a coarse, brush-textured coat. Coloration is very variable, ranging from near black to pale grey, fawn or russet. Underparts are white.
Habitat: Tropical species showing a preference for *Hyparrhenia* grassland with borassus palms (*Palmyra borassus*). Very disconnected records from Senegal to Uganda to Malawi.
Food: Omnivorous. Little known.
Status: Poorly known.

Broad-headed stink mice *Zelotomys* (2 species)

Measurements: HB 11.5–14cm. T 8.5–11.5cm. W 50–65g.
Recognition: Broad-headed mice with grey-brown or flecked grey upperparts and pale grey to white underparts and cheeks. Tail and limbs are off-white. Upper incisors are very protuberant. These mice have a very strong smell.
Species: *Z. hildegardeae* (E Africa and S Zaïre basin, in woodlands), *Z. woosnami* (central Kalahari).
Habitat: S and E Africa., in arid and semi-arid (*Z. woosnami*) or grassy savannahs and scrub dominated by sword grass, *Imperata*.
Food: Invertebrates, notably myriapods (*Z. hildegardeae*). *Z. woosnami* takes more seeds.
Status: Poorly known. Records very scattered.

Velvet rat *Colomys goslingi*

Measurements: HB 11.5–14cm. T 14.5–18cm. W 50–75g.
Recognition: A long-limbed, long-tailed rat with a very swollen rhinarium and very profuse whiskers. The dense, velvet-textured fur is chocolate brown above, pure white below. There is a white flash at the base of the ear. The chest glands of sexually active ♂♂ exude a yellowish secretion.
Habitat: Margins of forest streams and swamp forests among palms, gingers and arrowroots; may follow narrow permanent river courses out of forest. Ranges from Cameroon to W Uganda, Angola to L. Tanganyika, and is found along montane forest streams in Kenya and Ethiopia.
Food: Aquatic insects, worms, slugs and crustaceans; occasionally vegetable matter.
Status: Very localised in Kenya and Ethiopia. Not endangered.

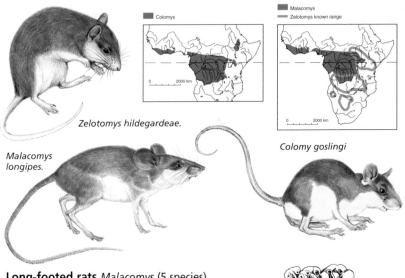

Zelotomys hildegardeae.

Malacomys longipes.

Colomy goslingi

Long-footed rats *Malacomys* (5 species)

Measurements: HB 12–18cm. T 14–21cm. W 50–150g.
Recognition: Long-legged, short-furred rats with large ears and a conical muzzle. Eyes are surrounded by a black 'mask'. The colour of the upperside varies from deep brown to grey, graduating to a lighter underside.
Species: *M. cansdalei, M. edwardsi, M. longipes, M. lukolelae, M. verschureni.*
Habitat: Very moist forest floor close to streams and swamps under a closed canopy; prefers ginger and arrowroot undergrowth. Long-footed rats have a tropical range from Guinea to Uganda and L. Tanganyika.
Food: Invertebrates and vegetable matter (fruits, seeds and roots); occasional small vertebrates.
Status: Poorly known but *M. longipes* is widespread and common.

Soft-furred rats *Praomys* (9 species)

Measurements: HB 9–15cm. T 10–17cm. W 30–50g.
Recognition: Generalised rats with short, soft fur, a long tail and large, round ears. They have brown or grey upperparts and paler underparts.
Species: *P. delectorum, P. hartwigi, P. jacksoni, P. minor, P. misonnei, P. morio, P. mutoni, P. rostratus, P. tullbergi.*
Habitat: Tropical forests, woodlands, moist savannah-forest mosaics and montane areas from Gambia to the Indian Ocean. Humid, heavily shaded forest floor or secondary scrub is preferred.
Food: Omnivorous: invertebrates, fruits, seeds and leaves.
Status: Poorly known but *P. jacksoni* and *P. tullbergi* are widespread and common.

African wood mice *Hylomyscus* (8 species)

Measurements: HB 7–12cm. T 10–17.5cm. W 8–42g.
Recognition: Small arboreal mice with large, round ears, a long, thin tail and slender hands and feet. The grey-based fur has warmer-coloured tips in some species. These mice have a bright russet or orange back, a pale grey or white underside and a dark mask around eyes. They are strictly nocturnal.
Species: *H. aeta, H. alleni, H. baeri, H. carillus, H. denniae, H. grandis, H. parvus, H. stella.*
Habitat: Lowland and montane rainforests, Afro-alpine and subalpine moorlands (*H. denniae*) and secondary growth. Nests are made in holes and crevices and in the frond axils of palms and banana trees. African wood mice have an equatorial distribution from Guinea to the E African mountains.
Food: Omnivorous: fruits, seeds and insects.
Status: Some species, i.e. *H. carillus, H. baeri, H. grandis*, are highly localised.

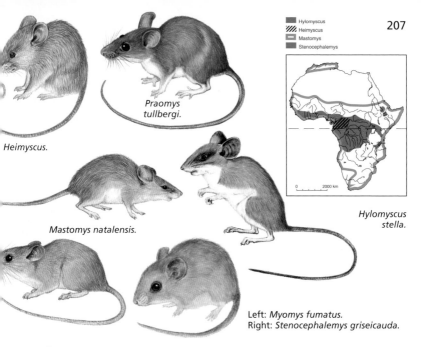

Hylomyscus
Heimyscus
Mastomys
Stenocephalemys

Praomys tullbergi.

Heimyscus.

Mastomys natalensis.

Hylomyscus stella.

Left: *Myomys fumatus.*
Right: *Stenocephalemys griseicauda.*

De Balsac's mouse *Heimyscus fumosus*

Measurements: Unavailable.
Recognition: A long-tailed, soft-furred mouse resembling *Hylomyscus* (originally described under that name). More detailed study of chromosomes and morphology has revealed it as distinct.
Habitat: Caught in rainforest in Gabon, S Cameroon and Central African Republic.
Food: Not recorded.
Status: Currently known from only three localities.

Multimammate rats *Mastomys* (8 species)

Measurements: HB 6–16cm. T 5–15cm. W 12–70g.
Recognition: Typical unspecialised rats with short, soft fur, a grey, brown or yellow upperside and a pale grey underside. The tail is usually shorter than the body. ♀♀ have 8–12 pairs of mammae. They are exceptionally fecund (6–22 young have been recorded).
Species: *M. angolensis, M. coucha, M. erythroleucus, M. hildebrandtii, M. natalensis, M. pernanus, M. shortridgei, M. verheyeni.*
Habitat: Savannahs, woodlands, secondary growth, forest clearings, houses and fields in all but the driest areas of sub-Saharan Africa.
Food: Fruits, seeds, invertebrates and household debris.
Status: The classic 'multimammates' (*M. coucha* and *M. natalensis*) are well known (especially as dangerous disease vectors), the remainder less so.

Meadow rats *Myomys* (6 species)

Measurements: (*M. fumatus*) HB 7.5–10.5cm. T 9.5–15cm. W 24–35g.
Recognition: Similar to multimammate rats but some species have a longer tail, paler underparts and fewer mammae. The main differences are the form of the skull, the teeth and the chromosomes.
Species: *M. albipes, M. daltoni, M. derooi, M. fumatus, M. ruppi, M. verreauxii.*
Habitat: Very varied; scrubby growth and fellings on forest margins, riverine habitats, rocky broken ground and grasslands. The main range is north of the forests, from Senegal to the Horn of Africa and all the drier parts of E Africa. One very isolated species (*M. verreauxii*) is found in the Cape of Good Hope.
Food: Omnivorous. Food is collected on the ground at night.
Status: *M. albipes* and *M. ruppi* are Ethiopian endemics.

Ethiopian meadow rats *Stenocephalemys* (2 species)

Measurements: HB17cm. T 14cm. W est. 100g.
Recognition: Very large-headed rats with flimsy limbs and long, soft fur, dark grey at the base and tipped with orange. (A specialised montane isolate of *Myomys* stock.)
Species: *S. albocaudata, S. griseicauda.*
Habitat: Ethiopian high-altitude endemics. These rats inhabit the Afro-alpine meadows and moorlands at 2,400–4,050m above sea-level. They make burrows in short grass, everlasting (*Helichrysum*) and *Alchemilla* meadows (*S. albocaudata*). Also *Hypericum* scrub growing at slightly lower altitudes (*S. griseicauda*).
Food: Omnivorous.
Status: Abundant within a restricted range.

Wurch mouse *Muriculus imberbis*

Measurements: HB 7–9.5cm. T 4.5–6cm. W est. 12–25g.
Recognition: A small, short-faced mouse with crisp, dense fur, blue-grey with yellow-brown tips. The lower back is marked by a black dorsal stripe. Underparts are yellowish to creamy white.
Habitat: Known from Ethiopian mountains between 1,900 and 3,400m in subalpine heather and *Hypericum* moorlands. The wurch mouse lives in holes in which it has been reported associating with grass rats (*Arvicanthis*).
Food: Diet not known but narrow, forward-pointing incisors imply mainly soft insects.
Status: Not known.

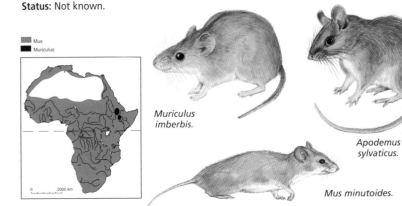

Mus
Muriculus

Muriculus imberbis.

Apodemus sylvaticus.

Mus minutoides.

0   2000 km

Common mice *Mus* (20 species)

Measurements: HB 4.5–11cm. T 3.5–10cm. W 2.5–18g.
Recognition: A very variable group of mice, all bearing some resemblance to the common house mouse. Proportions of visible features, i.e. tail, ears, muzzle, hands and feet, as well as skull form and teeth, serve to distinguish different species.
Species: *M. baoulei, M. bufo, M. callewaerti, M. goundae, M. haussa, M. indutus, M. kasaicus, M. mahomet, M. mattheyi, M. minutoides, M. musculoides, M. neavei, M. orangiae, M. oubanguii, M. setulosus, M. setzeri, M. sorella, M. spretus, M. tenellus, M. triton.*
Habitat: Almost all vegetation types and all altitudes. Mice conceal themselves in every type of nook and cranny, dig burrows in various types of soil and gnaw holes in vegetation and buildings. They shred material to make substantial nests.
Food: Omnivorous but individual species are likely to be dietary specialists to some extent.
Status: Mostly little known or not known.

Long-tailed field mouse *Apodemus sylvaticus*

Measurements: HB 8–10.5cm. T 7–11.5cm. W 13–30g.
Recognition: A mouse with large ears and eyes, and long hindlegs. Upperparts are brown

with sandy flanks. Underparts are greyish white. It is normally absent from open areas.
Habitat: Restricted to the Mediterranean zone in N Africa where it is common in all wooded and bushy areas, from sand dunes by the sea to high-altitude cedar forests.
Food: Omnivorous: seeds, fruits, fungi, invertebrates.
Status: Widespread along the Mediterranean littoral.

Short-tailed bandicoot rat *Nesokia indica* see p. 467.

Narrow-footed woodland mice *Grammomys* (11 species)

Measurements: HB 8–14cm. T 12–22cm. W est. 28–65g.
Recognition: Slender, arboreal rats with prominent, oval ears and a very long, finely haired tail. They have a brown, tan or grey back and pure white or creamy belly (variation by species and habitat). Guard hairs are present on the rump.
Species: (provisional) *G. aridulus, G. buntingi, G. caniceps, G. cometes, G. dolichurus, G. dryas, G. gigas, G. ibeanus, G. macmillani, G. minnae, G. rutilans.*
Habitat: Mainly moister vegetation types from Guinea to the Indian Ocean coast. It is convergent with thicket rats.
Food: Fruits, seeds, stems and other vegetable matter; occasionally insects.
Status: The genus is in need of revision in order to clarify status of the various species.

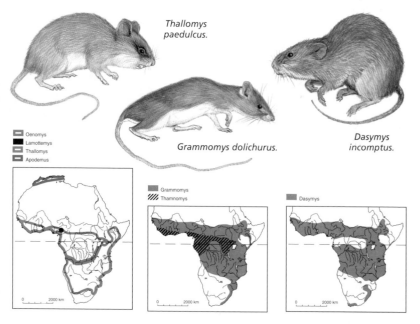

Thallomys paedulcus.

Oenomys
Lamottemys
Thallomys
Apodemus

Grammomys dolichurus.

Dasymys incomptus.

Grammomys
Thamnomys

Dasymys

0   2000 km

0   2000 km

0   2000 km

Acacia rats *Thallomys* (4 species)

Measurements: HB 12–17cm. T 13–21cm. W est. 63-100g.
Recognition: Arboreal rats with a long, slightly hairy tail, large, round ears and sharp, curved claws on short feet. The back is brown or grey and the underside is white. There is a bold black mask around the eyes. Acacia rats frequently build twig structures along branches and trunks (presumably to provide cover in an exposed and very dangerous savannah environment).
Species: *T. loringi, T. nigricauda, T. paedulcus, T. shortridgei.*
Habitat: Dry *Acacia*-dominated woodlands and savannahs from South Africa to the Horn of Africa and Ethiopia. Acacia rats construct twig nests in hollows or forks, as well as twig 'runways'.
Food: Buds, leaves, seeds, gum; occasionally roots and insects.
Status: Poorly known.

Shaggy swamp rats *Dasymys* (5 species)

Measurements: HB 12–19cm. T 10–18cm. W 80–165g.
Recognition: A robust, shaggy rat with a somewhat flattened, disc-like face, small eyes and rounded pink ears, almost lost in the dark brown fur. Underparts are pale brown-grey. The tail is shorter than the body. Incisors are plain orange.
Species: (provisional) *D. foxi, D. incomptus, D. montanus, D. nudipes, D. rufulus.*
Habitat: Wetter grassy areas of sub-Saharan Africa in marshes, especially at higher altitudes where they may be common in moss and sedge bogs.
Food: Stems, roots, shoots and flowers of plants in waterlogged habitats, including moss, rushes and everlasting (*Helichrysum*).
Status: The genus requires revision of species.

Bush-rats *Aethomys* (10 species)

Measurements: HB 12–19cm. T 12–21cm. W est. 50–150g.
Recognition: Generalised rats with streaky-looking, soft fur of very variable colour (by species and region). The underside is paler and the ears are large and rounded. Body and tail are about equal in length.
Species: (provisional) *A. bocagei, A. chrysophilus, A. granti, A. hindei, A. kaiseri, A. namaquensis, A. nyikae, A. silindensis, A. stannarius, A. thomasi.*
Habitat: Strong preference for rocky habitats in S and E Africa, with an outlying population in Nigeria (*A. stannarius*). Common on cultivated land and close to termitaries, as well as on rough slopes.
Food: Grass, stems, leaves and seeds.
Status: Successful group. The species need revision.

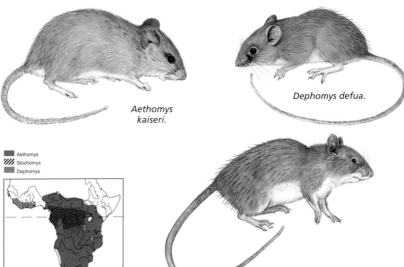

Aethomys kaiseri.

Dephomys defua.

Aethomys
///// Stochomys
Dephomys

0   2000 km

Stochomys longicaudatus.

Target rat *Stochomys longicaudatus*

Measurements: HB 12–17.5cm. T 18.5–25cm. W 50–104g.
Recognition: A dark reddish forest rat that gets its name from the long black bristles on its rump, which have been likened to arrows. The pale-tipped belly hairs form a deep brown fur closer to the skin. The feet are off-white and the tail is long and finely tapered.
Habitat: Equatorial lowland forests from the R. Cross to W Uganda. Riversides and swampy areas; also in secondary growth around villages. Although very patchily distributed, aggregations have been found in oil-palm plantations. Target rats make round nests of shredded material.
Food: Fruits, seeds and possibly some insects.
Status: Wide distribution. The reasons for its irregular occurrence are not known.

Rusty-nosed rats *Oenomys* (2 species)

Measurements: HB 13–18cm. T 14–21cm. W 50–121g.
Recognition: Shaggy brown rats with a bright red or orange nose and rump. The fur is soft, with long guard hairs. The belly is white or pinkish, with a warm tinge to the margin with the darker fur. Semi-arboreal and nocturnal.
Species: *O. hypoxanthus, O. ornatus.*
Habitat: Forest belt from Guinea to central Kenya. Not a true forest species but they favour secondary growth in clearings – road verges, chablis, clearings and margins of marshes, where they are commonest in elephant grass (*Pennisetum*) and sedge beds. They commonly nest in exotic billy-goat weed (*Ageratum conyzoides*).
Food: Green leaves, stems, shoots, buds and green seeds; also insects.
Status: Common.

Mount Oku mouse *Lamottemys okuensis*

Measurements: Unavailable.
Recognition: A shaggy brown, semi-arboreal mouse related to the rusty-nosed rats and thicket rats.
Habitat: Secondary growth in montane habitats surrounding Mt Oku, Cameroon uplands. This mouse is possibly the relict of a formerly widespread form.
Food: Not known.
Status: Very rare and little known.

Broad-footed thicket rats *Thamnomys* (2 species)

Measurements: HB 12–16cm. T 18–22cm. W est. 50–100g.
Recognition: Montane arboreal rats with longish, broad feet and a long, lightly haired tail. The back is brown with soft grey underfur of a very dense, even texture. The underside is white but soft and grey under the white hair tips. The structure of the teeth suggests that thicket rats are arboreal relatives of the rusty-nosed rats.
Species: *T. kempi, T. venustus.*
Habitat: Montane forests in E Zaïre, Uganda, Rwanda and Burundi.
Food: Plant material, including leaves and seeds.
Status: Rare relict species.

Oenomys hypoxanthus.

Lamottemys okuensis.

Thamnomys venustus.

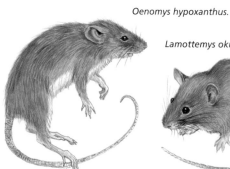

Dephua mice *Dephomys* (2 species)

Measurements: HB 11.5–13.5cm. T 18–20.5cm. W est. 40–65g.
Recognition: Arboreal mice with broad hindfeet, a very long tail and a long conical head with medium-sized oval ears. Back and flanks are reddish brown, sharply demarcated from the white belly. The fur is somewhat stiff in texture and has fine guard hairs projecting from the rump. Dephua mice are nocturnal.
Species: *D. defua, D. eburnea.*
Habitat: Secondary and swampy palm forests and secondary scrub in Upper Guinea forests, Sierra Leone to Ghana.
Food: Not recorded.
Status: Little known.

Rhabdomys pumilio.

Hybomys univittatus.

Hybomys
Rhabdomys

Hump-nosed mice *Hybomys* (6 species)

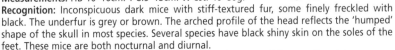

Measurements: HB 10–16cm. T 8.5–13cm. W est. 40–80g.
Recognition: Inconspicuous dark mice with stiff-textured fur, some finely freckled with black. The underfur is grey or brown. The arched profile of the head reflects the 'humped' shape of the skull in most species. Several species have black shiny skin on the soles of the feet. These mice are both nocturnal and diurnal.
Species: *H. basilii, H. eisentrauti, H. lunaris, H. planifrons, H. trivirgatus, H. univittatus.*
Habitat: Equatorial forests between Sierra Leone and the Nile valley. Strictly terrestrial, preferring areas with abundant leaf litter and heavy shade, hump-nosed mice are known to shelter in rotting logs.
Food: Mainly fallen fruits.
Status: The genus is in need of revision.

Four-striped grass mouse *Rhabdomys pumilio*

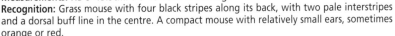

Measurements: HB 9–13.5cm. T 8–13.5cm. W 30–40g.
Recognition: Grass mouse with four black stripes along its back, with two pale interstripes and a dorsal buff line in the centre. A compact mouse with relatively small ears, sometimes orange or red.
Habitat: Limited to cooler grasslands in S Africa and in the E African mountains; very discontinuous distribution.
Food: Vegetarian: stems, leaves and seeds of grass.
Status: Common.

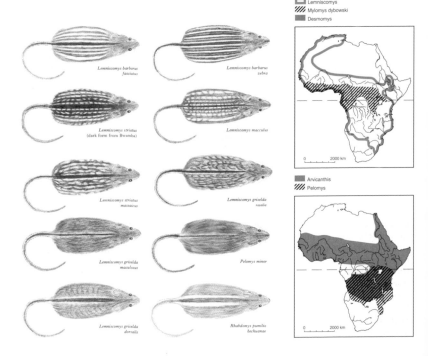

Lemniscomys barbarus fasciatus

Lemniscomys barbarus zebra

Lemniscomys striatus (dark form from Bwamba)

Lemniscomys macculus

Lemniscomys striatus massaicus

Lemniscomys griselda ruasia

Lemniscomys griselda maculosus

Pelomys minor

Lemniscomys griselda dorsalis

Rhabdomys pumilio bechuanae

Lemniscomys
Mylomys dybowski
Desmomys

Arvicanthis
Pelomys

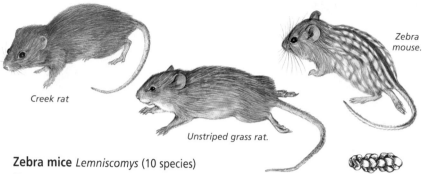

Creek rat

Unstriped grass rat.

Zebra mouse.

Zebra mice *Lemniscomys* (10 species)

Measurements: HB 9–14cm. T 9.5–15cm. W est. 18–70g.
Recognition: Grass mice with variable numbers of dorsal stripes, some with light unbroken lines, others fragmented into dashes. All have a near-black dorsal midline. Thought to be an actively speciating genus.
Species: *L. barbarus, L. bellieri, L. griselda, L. hoogstraali, L. linulus, L. macculus, L. mittendorfi, L. rosalia, L. roseveari, L. striatus.*
Habitat: African grasslands south of the Sahara (and one species, *L. barbarus*, in Morocco). The ranges of several species overlap and they partition the habitat in such areas but broaden their niches when free of competition. Very fecund, a single pair can produce four litters of up to 12 (usually four or five) young in less than 4 months.
Food: Grass stems, leaves and seeds. Insects are periodically taken.
Status: This group awaits a comprehensive revision of species.

Unstriped grass rats *Arvicanthis* (5 species)

Measurements: HB 9–21cm. T 22–32cm. W 48–130g.
Recognition: Robust grizzled grass rats with a harsh brown, ochraceous or greyish coat. They have smooth incisors and distinctive, mill-like molars.
Species: *A. abyssinicus, A. blicki, A. nairobae, A. niloticus, A. somalicus.*
Habitat: Grasslands, steppe, moorland, all types of savannah and derived grasslands within forest belts. Ethiopia appears to be their evolutionary centre but these grass rats have now spread throughout the northern savannahs and Nile valley. They are diurnal.
Food: Seeds, leaves and shoots of grasses.
Status: A highly successful genus.

Creek rats *Pelomys* (5 species)

Measurements: HB 10–16cm. T 10–17cm. W 50–100g.
Recognition: Creek rats resemble grass rats but have grooved incisors and a blunt face, with body and tail of similar length. They have a glossy brown coat of longish, coarse fur on which the ears are partly hidden. Mainly nocturnal.
Species: *P. campanae, P. fallax, P. hopkinsi, P. isseli, P. minor.*
Habitat: Associated with marshes, reed beds, damp valley bottoms, lakeshores and mountain bogs in central and E Africa. Creek rats excavate burrows.
Food: Grass and reed shoots, stems, leaves and seeds.
Status: Locally common within appropriate habitats or region.

Mill rat *Mylomys dybowski*

Measurements: HB 12–19cm. T 10–18cm. W 46–165g.
Recognition: Named after its mill-like grinding molars, this species is externally very similar to creek rats and grass rats. It has three functional digits on the forefeet, grooved incisors, shiny, streaked brown upperparts and a white underside. The tail is conspicuously bicoloured.
Habitat: Tropical northern savannahs from Guinea to W Kenya. Found in a variety of moist grasslands at altitudes of up to 2,500m, it is locally and discontinuously distributed. It is sometimes dominant in stands of sword grass (*Imperata*) and other mono-dominant grass types.
Food: Green grass stems and leaves.
Status: Locally abundant.

Mill rat.

Dega rat.

Dega rat *Desmomys harringtoni*

Measurements: H 14.5cm. T 10.5cm. W 90g.
Recognition: A shaggy, blunt-faced rat which closely resembles the creek rat, *Pelomys*, but with bold ochraceous flanks and a pure white belly. The molar teeth are also mill-like but have their own pattern of lophs and cusps.
Habitat: Ethiopian mountains between 1,500 and 3,000m (a zone locally known as Dega). It lives among grasses in degraded juniper, Podo and *Hagenia* forests and in upland *Acacia* savannahs.
Food: Grass stems and leaves.
Status: Locally abundant.

CARNIVOR

Habitat	Fruits	Sessil or cryptic invertebrates and eggs	Active invertebrates	Aquatic or semi aquatic fauna
Forest		←———— *Nandinia* ————→		
		←——————— *Crossarchus* ———————→		←
	←——————— *Bdeogale nigripes* ———————→			
	←———— *Genetta servalina* ————→			
	Genetta victoriae			←
Secondary growth		*Dologale*		
	←——————— *Ichneumia** ———————————→			
	←——————— *Genetta tigrina** ———————→			
	←———— *Civettictis** ————————→			
	←———— *Rhynchogale* ————→			
Moist savannas and Woodlands		←———— *Bdeogale crassicauda* ————→		
	←——————— *Mellivora** ———————→			
	←———— *Canis adustus** ————————————→			
	←———— *Herpestes sanguineus** ————————→			
Marshes and aquatic			←———————— *Atilax** ————————→	
		←———— *Aonyx* (*Paraonyx*)(forest swamps and rive		
		←———— *Aonyx* (*Aonyx*) (swamps and riv		
		←———— *Lutra* (rivers and lal		
Thickets dry savannas and woodlands		←———— *Helogale** ————→		
	←———— *Hyaena* ————→			
	←———— *Otocyon* ————————→			
	←———— *Genetta genetta* ————→			
	←———— *Canis mesomelas* ————→			
(Interzones)		←———— *Ictonyx** ————————→		
	←———— *Proteles** ——→			
Grasslands		←———— *Mungos** ————————→		
	←———— *H. ichneumon** ——→			
	←———— *Canis aureus* ————→			

Species marked * occupy a wider range of habitats than can be suggested in a simplifie

CARNIVORES CARNIVORA

Dogs and allies	Canidae
Mustelids	Mustelidae
Mongooses	Herpestidae
Hyaenids	Hyaenidae
Genets and civets	Viverridae
Cats	Felidae

Recognition: The carnivores are a group of mainly 'animal-eaters', ranging from the weasel (75g) to the lion (200kg). All share 'carnassial', or slicing, teeth (fourth upper and fifth lower cheek teeth), although these are modified in some species.

Genealogy: All modern carnivores derive from a well-known fossil group, the miacids, which flourished 60–50 million years ago. Some of these generalised carnivores resembled modern types, such as the civet. Mongooses, Herpestidae, evolved in Africa, as did the hyaenas. Mustelids are carnivores adapted to northern temperate climates but a few specialised forms have become established in Africa. The dog family originated in North America and has become very widespread and successful. The origins of the cat family are less certain but are unlikely to have been in Africa.

Ecology: Carnivores are well distributed throughout the many ecosystems of Africa and the chart below summarises the separation of species according to habitat and diet.

HES

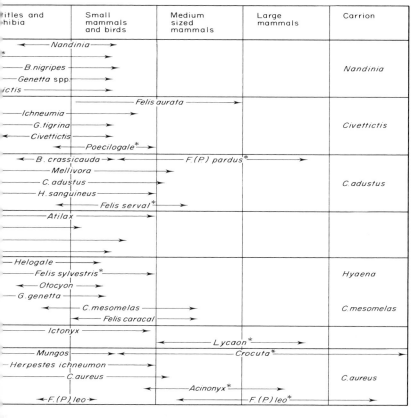

Natural history: The number and diversity of carnivores is one of the surest signs of ecological richness because each species sits at the top of a different food chain belonging to a different cycle of organic matter. Each type of carnivore therefore implies a much larger ecological community. Most carnivores are solitary hunters and foragers but certain otters, mongooses, wild dogs, hyaenas and lions are social. The mechanisms whereby originally solitary species became social are of the greatest interest.

Adaptations: Limb proportions, body size, gait and colouring all manifest specific adaptations but one of the clearest expressions of adaptive diversity in carnivores is the shape of the head and the relative sizes of ears, eyes and muzzle. Differences in the shape of the head closely relate to the importance of different sense organs and hunting strategies in the different carnivore species. We can therefore readily appreciate the remarkable transformations wrought by evolution simply by comparing the shapes of carnivore heads. The serval cat, with its big ears, hunts largely by sound, the otter relies mainly on vision and whisker-touch, and the jackal, with its long, sensitive nose, depends on scent. The jackal's long tooth rows snap at prey while the short, vice-like jaws of the cheetah serve as clamps. The hyaena's skull is built around its bone-cracking teeth and huge chewing muscles.

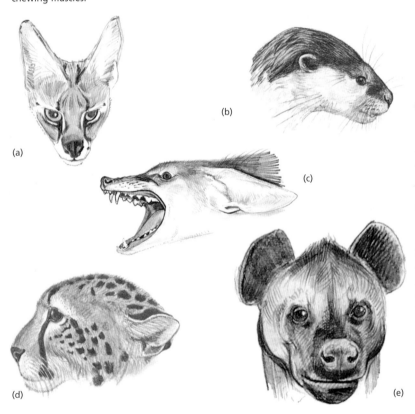

(a) Serval cat. (b) Otter. (c) Jackal. (d) Cheetah. (e) Hyaena.

Conservation: Apart from direct persecution and destruction of habitats by humans, domestic and feral dogs are a major threat to very many species of wild carnivores. Dogs harass most wildlife within one or more kilometres of their home bases. Sustained over years this persecution drives all but the most agile or arboreal species away. As settlement spreads, the baneful influence of dogs (and their diseases) affects an ever larger part of Africa's natural ecosystems. Domestic and feral cats have similar but only very localised effects.

DOGS AND ALLIES CANIDAE

Common (Golden) jackal	*Canis aureus*
Side-striped jackal	*Canis adustus*
Black-backed jackal	*Canis mesomelas*
Ethiopian wolf	*Canis simensis*
Red fox	*Vulpes vulpes*
Ruppell's fox	*Vulpes rueppelli*
Cape fox	*Vulpes chama*
Sand fox (Pale fox)	*Vulpes pallida*
Royal (Hoary) fox	*Vulpes cana*
Fennec fox	*Vulpes zerda*
Bat-eared fox	*Otocyon megalotis*
Wild dog	*Lycaon pictus*

Recognition: These relatively long-legged, long-muzzled carnivores are adapted to running down prey in relatively open and dry environments. Most have a bushy tail and compact feet with four functional toes.

Genealogy: Separation into fox, wolf/jackal and wild dog lineages began outside Africa. However, the bat-eared 'fox' clearly evolved at an early stage as an African termite-eating specialist. True foxes have been unable to maintain a hold in tropical Africa, in spite of having traversed the continent in the past. Nevertheless, one species survives in temperate South Africa. Dogs and their diseases threaten these and all other canids.

Geography: The difficulties that non-African immigrant fauna has in sustaining a foothold in Africa may be illustrated by the Ethiopian wolf. Although well adapted to a specialised diet of highland rodents, this species almost certainly originated as a consequence of a southward expansion (probably during the Ice-Ages) of a Eurasian wolf population. Although persecuted by humans it is a naturally rare and localised species (now the rarest canid in Africa).

Ecology: The distribution of the three jackal species, each with an individual range, but with substantial overlaps, illustrates their different origins. The common jackal is a Eurasian, desert-adapted form that has colonised the Sahara and arid E Africa. Fossils reveal that the black-backed jackal is known to be a very stable species, present in S and E Africa for several million years. It is exclusive to the arid north-east/south-west axis and is split into two populations. By contrast the side-striped jackal, the most versatile species in both diet and behaviour, currently has the widest range south of the Sahara. However, if the climate was to get drier, the range of this species would almost certainly contract. Similar matching of moist and arid-adapted 'species pairs' is a common feature of African fauna.

Natural history: Canids have evolved special patterns, markings and hair tracts to communicate with one another. In some instances canids can transform their appearance to intimidate other species. Thus the tiny-toothed bat-eared fox can chase off much larger animals by fluffing out its crest and tail and snapping fearlessly and ferociously. Its black markings help neatly to outline and emphasise every gesture. Many canids rely on older siblings to help feed and guard nursing mothers and pups.

Adaptations: Groups of jackals and wolves co-operate to flush, bring to bay and kill large prey. Prehistoric humans clearly learnt to manipulate this behaviour at an early date when they domesticated the ancestors of dogs.

Bat-eared fox, mobbing postures.

Canis aureus

Common (golden) jackal *Canis aureus*

Other names: Fr. *Chacal commun*. Ger. *Goldschakal*. Swah. *Bweha wa mbuga*.

Measurements: HB 65–105cm. T 18–27cm. W 6–15kg.

Recognition: Sand-coloured jackal with a black-tipped tail. The back has streaks of black and white hair scattered irregularly through the fawn body colour. Active at night, in the early morning and evening.

Subspecies: Twelve races have been named but individual variation conceals any regional pattern.

Distribution: Patchily across the Sahara and Horn of Africa south to open plains in N Tanzania; also S Asia as far as Burma.

Habitat: Dry, open country from sea-level to over 3,000m. Flourishes around villages and small towns. Depends on secure burrows or dens (self-dug or modified), especially on open plains.

Food: Omnivorous. Invertebrates and small vertebrates (up to the size of a small gazelle) are taken. Bulbs, berries, fallen fruits and cucurbits are also eaten when available.

Behaviour: Territorial pairs with their offspring may hunt socially. Several families may form group territories where there is access to super-abundant resources (i.e. rubbish tips). Grown offspring frequently help their parents rear young siblings. Its Arabic name *ibn awee* is onomatopoeic for the high-pitched howling which allows individuals or groups to locate one another. The barks and yelps resemble those of dogs.

Adaptations: Drought resistance and the ability to subsist without water is the principal determinant of its extensive range.

Status: Not endangered (but has been exterminated in some localities by poisoning). (IUCN status: not listed.)

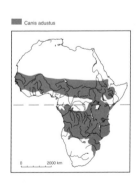

Canis adustus

Side-striped jackal *Canis adustus*

Other names: Fr. *Chacal à flancs rayés*. Ger. *Streifenschakal*. Swah. *Bweha*.

Measurements: HB 70–80cm. T 35–45cm. W 7.3–12kg.

Recognition: Drabber, shorter legged and shorter eared than other jackals, this species can generally be distinguished by the white tip to its tail and by the poorly defined black and white stripes along the flanks. Mainly nocturnal but also active at dawn and dusk.

Subspecies: (differences may be a consequence of individual variation) *C. a. adustus* (S Africa), *C. a. lateralis* (equatorial Africa), *C. a. kaffensis* (Ethiopia).

Distribution: Ranges in a broad band both north and south of the main forest belt (which it has penetrated in the wake of settlement). Absent from the drier parts of S, N and NE Africa.

Habitat: Various savannah and thicket types to the edges of forest. Common in various montane habitats up to 2,700m, especially in disturbed vegetation and cultivation, and also in swamps and moist flood-plains (where it replaces the common jackal). Side-striped jackals mark their territories with scats and urine. They use natural dens where possible and often modify termitaries for their own use.

Food: Omnivorous. The diet is very responsive to local resources. Invertebrates and small vertebrates (including fish, stranded or in shallows, and gazelle fawns) are taken, as well as fallen fruits, unripe maize, carrion and organic rubbish.

Behaviour: Pairs defend territories. They may travel as a family group but more frequently move individually. The Swahili name *bweha* derives from the characteristic explosive bark of this species but it has a wide repertoire of growls, yaps, cackles, whines and screams. A croaking distress call elicits intense interest in other members of a family group. 'Howling' is more like hooting in this species.

Adaptations: Shorter proportions, more skulking habits and great flexibility of diet in diverse habitats suggests that these jackals occupy the 'tropical fox' niche and suggests that they may be a factor contributing to the absence of foxes from central Africa.

Status: Not endangered. (IUCN status: not listed.)

Canis mesomelas

0   2000 km

Black-backed jackal *Canis mesomelas*

Other names: Fr. *Chacal à chabraque*. Ger. *Schabrackenschakal*. Swah. *Bweha nyekundu*.

Measurements: HB 70–100cm. T 30–35cm. W 6.5–13.5kg.

Recognition: Slender, long-legged jackal with large ears and a black back (streaked with white). Limbs and flanks are variously fawn to rufous. The tail is black tipped.

Subspecies: *C. m. mesomelas* (S Africa), *C. m. schmidti* (NE Africa).

Distribution: Horn of Africa, E Africa and S Africa.

Habitat: The black-backed jackal could be called the acacia jackal because of its close association with dry *Acacia* savannahs. However, in the southern part of its range it occupies most habitat types, from upland veld and mountains to coastal desert. (It may be more constrained in the north-east where there are other jackals.)

Food: Omnivorous but small and medium-sized mammals and carrion are frequently taken. Co-operative hunting by parents rearing young is often assisted by older offspring and improves the survival chances of the pups. Food is bolted and regurgitated in response to the pups' begging.

Behaviour: Black-backed jackals form more hierarchical family groups than the golden jackal, in which subadult or young adult 'helpers' are less co-operative in assisting their parents to raise pups. Parents and siblings are very protective of pups and may attack other predators, such as hyaenas, near the den. Vocal communication in South Africa (where they are the only jackal) includes howling. In areas of overlap, only the golden jackal howls. Other calls are a loud explosive yelp followed by shorter, shriller yelps. Loud yelps signal alarm. Black-backed jackals also utter a clattering distress call and a dog-like 'woof' when startled.

Adaptations: Intensive guarding behaviour of the young may reflect high risks from larger predators in areas where both predators and prey are at high densities. Their brighter, more contrasting colour pattern is also consistent with less cryptic behaviour. Black-backed jackals harass prey and some competitors and are generally more aggressive than other jackal species.

Status: Treated as vermin in pastoral farmlands. Not endangered. (IUCN status: not listed.)

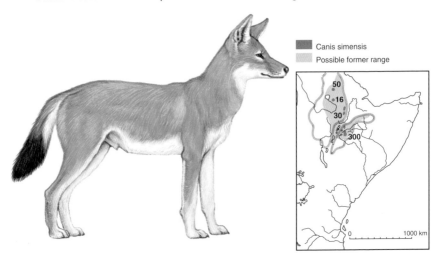

Canis simensis
Possible former range

Ethiopian wolf (formerly "Simien fox") *Canis simensis*

Other names: Fr. *Loup d'Abyssinie*. Ger. *Aethiopienfuchs*.

Measurements: HB 90–100cm. T 25–34cm. W (♀) 11.5, (♂) 14–18.5kg.

Recognition: A tall, large-eared, dog-like animal, rich russet-red above, with white underparts and a black tip to the tail. The long muzzle ends with a somewhat 'squared-off' nose and upper lip. It has splayed, well-reinforced canine teeth. Highly vocal, its calls include group yip-howls, a yelping bark, a two-phase bleating and an explosive scream.

Subspecies: *C. s. simensis* (north-west of the Rift), *C. s. citernii* (south-east of the Rift).

Distribution: Once widespread over Ethiopian uplands, but now restricted to relict populations in Simen, Mt Guna, NE Shoa, Bale and Arsi massifs.

Habitat: Mainly Afro-alpine meadows and *Helichrysum* moorlands in areas of high rodent density. Packs regularly patrol the boundaries of their territories, marking them with urine and faeces as well as by frequent howling. They scrape shallow hollows or rest on the midden mounds of giant mole-rats (which generate warmth and provide ambush sites for their favourite prey).

Food: Giant mole-rats (*Tachyoryctes macrocephalus*) comprise nearly 40% of the prey captures (and the main mass of the diet) on the Bale massif. Smaller rodents (mainly murids), hares and carrion make up the balance. Ethiopian wolves are solitary foragers but, very occasionally, a pack will hunt antelope or small livestock. Mole-rats and rodents are ambushed, stalked, pounced on or excavated. Less frequently they are also snatched in wild scampers across rodent warrens. Foraging is mainly diurnal (as is rodent activity) at higher altitudes but human interference probably explains crepuscular or wholly nocturnal activity in the declining northern populations. (In undisturbed habitats rodent biomass may periodically reach 3,000kg per km^2.)

Behaviour: Cohesive, highly hierarchical packs live in regularly demarcated territories of 5–15km². A typical pack includes two or more adult ♀♀ and about five closely related adult ♂♂, together with the current offspring of the dominant pair (subordinate ♀♀ occasionally have pups but tend to desert them in favour of staying with the pack). Pack members forage individually but meet up several times a day to rest, play or sleep together (or to feed pups and the mother by regurgitation). They also meet up to boundary-mark and, while breeding is in progress, they rest up close to the mother's den. The texture and colour of the F's coat changes during breeding, becoming woollier and yellower.

Adaptations: DNA analysis suggests that Ethiopian wolves share a recent common ancestry with the Eurasian wolf (*Canis lupus*). In spite of the restricted range, small habitat and rodent-catching behaviour of the Ethiopian species, its specialisations appear to be relatively recent modifications of typically flexible and generalised canine behaviour. As Ethiopian ecosystems degraded and cooler habitats retreated higher, the wolves may have shrunk back into an ever-smaller range and refined their skills at exploiting a very numerous but untypical prey. With a longer history as tropical species, African jackals and wild dogs have probably always inhibited the expansion of Ethiopian wolves out of their cool, Eurasian-like enclave.

Status: Highly Endangered (IUCN). Unless the last retreat of this species (the Bale Mts) is given its promised national park status the Ethiopian wolf and many other animals will become extinct. Domestic and feral dogs brought into this formerly uninhabited region by recent settlers have introduced disease, competition and genetic contamination to wolf populations. The habitat is being degraded by an invasion of people and livestock into a very fragile ecosystem and direct killing of wolves is accelerating. Less than 550 animals are thought to remain in the Bale/Arsi massif. Northern populations are unlikely to survive under current conditions.

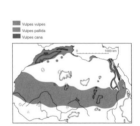

Red fox *Vulpes vulpes*

Other names: Fr. *Renard roux*. Ger. *Rotfuchs*.

Measurements: HB 50–55cm. T 33–40cm. W 4–8kg.

Recognition: Externally indistinguishable from populations living on the northern side of the Mediterranean, N African red foxes vary individually and by season (they moult into a short summer coat). The back may be sandy red or greyish, surrounded by red or yellowish flanks, limbs, neck, face and tail. Tail tip, throat and chin are white. Ears, nose, whisker patch, forepaws, and sometimes the belly, are black. The most frequently heard call is a loud, multiple wow-bark.

Subspecies: *V. v. barbarus* (NW African coast), *V. v. atlanticus* (Atlas Mts), *V. v. niloticus* (Egypt, Libya, N Sudan). All are probably invalid.

Distribution: N African Mediterranean and Moroccan littoral and Nile valley.

Habitat: Cultivated and urban land, settlements, desertic steppe, scrub, woodlands and hillsides up to 4,500m. Red foxes dig or modify burrows. Territories have bolt-holes, scent posts on paths, boundaries, and food stores. They vary in size from 30 to 4,000ha.

Food: Omnivorous: vertebrates and carrion, invertebrates, fruits and household debris.

Behaviour: Social grouping varies but pairs occupy large territories in impoverished habitats. Where there is more than one adult ♀ she may be a 'helper'. Tails lashed in greeting dispense scent from the 'violet gland' near the base of the tail. Other scent glands are situated on the lips and between the toes.

Adaptations: Scent marks, urine, faeces and a wide variety of gestures and postures, together with 28 recorded categories of vocalisation, all play a part in the red foxes' complex social behaviour which helps to explain their status as the most successful small carnivores in W Eurasia. However, they remain subordinate to the common jackal in N Africa, and are less numerous.

Status: Not endangered. (IUCN status: not listed.)

(a)

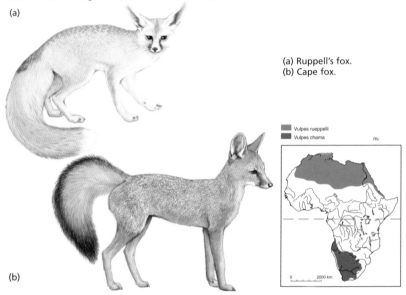

(a) Ruppell's fox.
(b) Cape fox.

Vulpes rueppelli
Vulpes chama

mi

(b)

Ruppell's fox *Vulpes rueppelli*

Other names: Fr. *Renard du désert*. Ger. *Ruppelfuchs*.

Measurements: HB 40–48cm. T 25–38cm. W 2–4.5kg.

Recognition: A very large-eared, slender fox with a soft, thick coat and rich, bushy tail. The grizzled fur tends to be greyish on the sides, with a sandy-yellow or brown flush on the midline (from forehead to tail), elbows and heel. Apart from black whisker patches, the ears and face are very pale, as are the underside and limbs. The tip of the tawny tail is white and above its 'violet gland' (near the root) is dark brown. The loud call is a harsh, yelping bark. This is a strictly nocturnal, cool-adapted fox.

Subspecies: *V. r. rueppellii* (Egypt and Sudan), *V. r. somaliae* (Eritrea and the Horn), *V. r. cufrana* (Libyan desert and Kufra).

Distribution: Central Sahara, Libya, Egypt and the Red Sea coast to NW Somalia. Probably of Asiatic origin.

Habitat: Sand and stone deserts where burrows are commonly excavated under slabs of stone or the roots of bushes.

Food: Rodents, reptiles, insects and occasional fruits (dates). Ruppel's foxes can tolerate a total absence of water.

Behaviour: Commonly solitary or in pairs, this very vocal species has brittle hacking calls, a high-pitched whistle, trilling (when tense) and hissing (in warning). There is also a barking loud call. Breeding is thought to be seasonal, with three or four blind helpless young born in late winter after a gestation of just under 2 months.

Adaptations: The most striking adaptation is the skunk-like ability to squirt noxious anal secretions at potential predators.

Status: Common in all non-dune areas of the Sahara. However, this species is known to retreat wherever red foxes, feral dogs, and cats have become established in desert settlements. Insufficiently known. (IUCN status: not listed.)

Cape fox *Vulpes chama*

Other names: Fr. *Renard du Cap*. Ger. *Kapfuchs*.
Measurements: HB 54–62cm. T 29–39.5cm. W 2.5–3.5kg.
Recognition: A lightly built, slender fox, with bushy tail, medium to large ears and a fine-tapered muzzle. It has a grizzled grey back and russet ear backs and limbs. The face, underside and base of tail are tawny cream. The tip and margins to the tail, and the muzzle stripe, are sepia to black. The loud call is a high-pitched 'wow', ending in two or three yaps. It is a nocturnal animal.
Distribution: Drier parts of SW Africa from S Angola to the Cape and outer margins of the Kalahari region.
Habitat: Open *Acacia* grasslands, steppe, subdesert scrub and open grassy areas within bushland. The Cape fox digs burrows or lies up in dense vegetation during the day.
Food: Predominantly invertebrates and mice; also other small vertebrates, carrion, fallen fruits and grass.
Behaviour: The Cape fox forages alone but ♀♀ have been observed out with subadult young. There are one to five young per litter. ♂♂ are not seen to associate with ♀♀ except at mating. Limited records suggest that most births take place during the warm, wet summer period.
Adaptations: The dietary versatility of the Cape fox and its adaptation to cooler temperate climates would appear to have facilitated its colonisation of SW Africa. However, it is not as abundant as jackals and bat-eared foxes.
Status: Officially persecuted for 100 years, many Cape foxes were killed without research to justify their supposed vermin status. Not endangered, although locally depleted.

Sand fox (Pale fox) *Vulpes pallida*

Other names: Fr. *Renard pâle*. Ger. *Blassfuchs*.
Measurements: HB 38–45cm. T 23–28cm. W 2–3.6kg.
Recognition: A small, very pale fox with large ears, long legs and a relatively thin coat. It has sandy-fawn upperparts and a pale to white underside. There is some variation in the intensity of the colour. The tail is black-tipped and there is black above the weakly scented 'violet gland'.
Subspecies: *V. p. pallida* (Sudan), *V. p. oertzeni* (Chad basin), *V. p. edwardsi* (W Africa).
Habitat: S Sahara and Sahel from Mauritania to the Red Sea, in steppe country, sandy and stony deserts. Sand foxes dig extensive burrows and tolerate heat well. They are active from dusk till dawn. They are unable to tolerate totally waterless conditions, although they can survive very protracted hot, dry seasons (presumably on the residual moisture in their prey).
Food: Small vertebrates (mainly rodents and lizards) and invertebrates.
Status: A little-known African endemic fox with a very extensive distribution within an unstable and fluctuating ecological band lying between true desert and the sub-Saharan savannahs. Conservation status inadequately known.

(a)

(a) Sand fox.
(b) Royal fox.

(b)

Royal (Hoary) fox *Vulpes cana*

Other names: Fr. *Renard royal*. Ger. *Königlich Fuchs*.
Measurements: HB 40–60cm. T 29–41.5cm. W 2–3kg.

Recognition: A densely furred, sandy-coloured fox with 'frosted' grey sides, white underparts and a furry, sandy tail that has densely packed, very long, dark guard hairs. Large, funnel-like ears are scantily haired on their inner surfaces and the eyes are set in a narrow brown 'mask' that extends to the corners of the mouth. The general demeanour is very cat-like and animals are invariably very evasive and timid.

Distribution: Recently discovered in NE Egypt, this fox ranges from Pakistan to Sinai but is only known from a few localities.

Habitat: Marked preference for rocky mountainous regions up to 2,000m. Possibly the relic of an Ice Age fauna. Thought to prefer natural crevices and rock shelters.

Food: Insects, supplemented by fruits and small vertebrates.

Behaviour: The royal fox is extremely sensitive to sound and very shy, escaping notice with a fast ground-hugging run.

Adaptations: The exceptionally dense fur implies adaptation to very cold conditions and Iranian furriers call the pelt *Siah Rubah* or 'Royal Fox' because of its luxurious texture. The volume of the tail almost matches that of the body (a possible decoy against larger predators). The muzzle is short and delicately tapered but molars are exceptionally deep, sharp and narrow.

Status: Very rarely seen, this fox may range down the entire Red Sea Ranges, possibly as far as Ethiopia. Status unknown. (IUCN status: not listed.)

Fennec fox *Vulpes zerda*

Other names: Fr. *Fennec*. Ger. *Fennek*.

Measurements: HB 37–41cm. T 18–21cm. W 0.8–1.5kg.

Recognition: A very small, rather short-legged fox with huge ears and a very small, pointed muzzle. Upperparts are tawny (with a very fine grizzle on the back). The underside, legs, face and ear linings are white. Both the extreme tip of the tail and the fur over the 'violet gland' are black or dark brown. The fur is very fine, soft and dense. The loud call is a brief shuddering howl, descending in pitch and repeated serially. It is strictly nocturnal.

Distribution: Central Sahara to N Red Sea; also N Arabia.

Habitat: Sand-dune deserts and steppes with light, sandy soils. Self-dug burrows are extensive and dry grass is brought in to line the resting chamber.

Food: Favours desert grasshoppers and other desert invertebrates. Lizards, rodents and birds, and occasionally fruits and roots, are also taken. The fennec fox is an extremely fast and efficient digger in sand, both to catch prey and to escape detection. It can survive without surface water.

Behaviour: The fennec fox is most frequently seen in pairs but up to ten animals have been recorded in a group. Up to five blind and helpless young are born in a burrow after about 50 days gestation. They are suckled for 2 months and are mature by 6 months. Captive groups are very vocal and sociable, uttering chattering, whimpering and wailing calls as well as growls, chirps and screams. It puts up a spirited defence against dogs or captors.

Adaptations: The huge external ears are matched by greatly enlarged inner ear bullae and most subterranean food is found by hearing.

Status: Common in the central Sahara, the fennec fox is in decline wherever settlement and domestic or feral dogs and cats are present. Insufficiently known. (IUCN status: not listed.)

Bat-eared fox *Otocyon megalotis*

Other names: Fr. *Otocyon*. Ger. *Löffelhund*. Swah. *Bweha masigio*.

Measurements: HB 47–66cm. T 23–34cm. W 3–5.3kg.

Recognition: Long-limbed, large-eared 'foxes' with a thickly furred, black-tipped tail and black-tipped ears, feet and muzzle. The eyes are contained within a dark 'mask'. The lightly grizzled upperparts are grey, with an ochraceous undercolour. Relatively quiet, they occasionally utter a series of thin, wailing howls. Contact calls among bat-eared foxes are bird-like mewings.

Subspecies: *O. m. megalotis* (SW Africa), *O. m. virgatus* (E Africa), *O. m. canescens* (Horn and Ethiopia).

Distribution: Restricted to arid areas of the Kalahari region and NE Africa, from sea-level to dry plateaus and uplands inland.

Habitat: Dry, open country, especially *Acacia* savannahs and associated plains, grasslands and steppes.

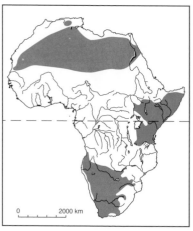

Otocyon megalotis
Vulpes zerda

Fennec.

0   2000 km

Food: Termites, especially harvester termites (*Hodotermes*), beetles and other invertebrates; also, marginally, small vertebrates and fruits. Subterranean insects are located by sound, with the ears pitched horizontally to get a fix before rapid excavation. The very dense fur helps protect against the bites of soldier termites.

Behaviour: A permanent pair is the basic social unit, often accompanied by up to six recent offspring. The young are born blind and helpless after a 60-day gestation in a burrow dug (or modified) by the parents.

Adaptations: Bat-eared foxes have between 46 and 50 sharp, cusped teeth, the largest number known for any non-marsupial land mammal. This extraordinary dentition is adapted for slicing-up hard-shelled and pincered insects. Live insects are macerated almost instantaneously because the mandible can chop up and down at least five times a second (because of a special muscle arrangement at the back of the jaw). The enlarged ears, both external and internal, allow bat-eared foxes to pick up the sounds of underground prey, while the strongly clawed forepaws allow rapid excavation.

Status: The magnificent thick fur of this species fetches high prices under its commercial name of 'Macloutsie'. Bat-eared foxes are extensively trapped for their pelts in Botswana and may be absent or rare in the vicinity of some towns. Not endangered. (IUCN status: not listed.)

Special muscle arrangement at the back of the jaw on bat-eared fox.

Wild dog *Lycaon pictus*

Other names: Fr. *Lycaon*. Ger. *Hyanenhund*. Swah. *Mbwa mwitu*.

Measurements: HB 76–112cm. T 30–41cm. W 18–36kg.

Recognition: A large, blotchy dog with prominent, round ears and a tufted tail. The tail tip is almost always white and the broad, powerful muzzle always black. Each individual's pattern of blotches is unique but there are family and regional resemblances. Although generally silent, a repetitive bell-like hoot, low but penetrating, serves as a contact call while staccato twittering accompanies any reunion or social excitement. The wild dog has a very pungent and distinctive body odour. It also has a capacious stomach so that the silhouette of a replete dog differs from that of one which has not eaten for a while.

Subspecies: *L. p. pictus* (S Africa, Angola to Mozambique), *L. p. lupinus* (E Africa), *L. p. somalicus* (Horn of Africa), *L. p. saharicus* (S Sahara), *L. p. manguensis* (W African savannahs).

Distribution: Formerly throughout non-forested, non-desert areas of Africa. The range is now fragmented.

Habitat: Woodlands, savannahs, grasslands and steppes at all altitudes. Wild dogs formerly existed wherever there was sufficient prey susceptible to their 'visual-chase' hunting techniques.

Food: Exclusively mammals. Wild dogs prefer to feed on the commonest medium-sized antelopes not more than twice their own weight. Larger animals are also taken, but less regularly. Small animals are eaten entirely but, with larger ones only the meat and viscera are stripped off and rapidly bolted. As specialised pack-hunters, wild dogs rely on an unconcealed fast chase of up to 5km at a steady 48km/h pace. During short spurts (usually less than 2km) they can exceed 60km/h. Their strategy is to snap and tear at the rear and sides of running prey until it tires.

Behaviour: The social behaviour of a pack centres on a breeding pair, with non-breeding adults assisting in the feeding (by regurgitation) of litters that can number up to 16 puppies. All pack members are subordinate to the breeding pair (which can be distinguished by their tendency to urine-mark). Every pack member is part of a same-sex hierarchy but ♀♀ are more mobile between packs than the ♂♂ (♂♂ tend to expel or kill intruding ♂♂). Packs travel over home ranges of 200–2,000km². Smaller packs always give way to larger ones and the young are known to have a higher survival rate in large packs. Today, an average wild-dog pack includes about six adult ♂♂ and four adult ♀♀ but, in the past, aggregations of many hundreds of wild dogs were recorded.

Wild dogs have a slight breeding peak during the late rains. Puppies are born blind and helpless in a burrow (usually dug by an aardvark). They emerge from the burrow after 1 month and are weaned off their mother's milk, onto meat regurgitated by the pack, by 5 weeks. They are able to follow the adults by about 9 weeks and are adult at about 1 year. Wild dogs are relatively short lived and few survive to 10 years.

Wild-dog society appears to be based on the seamless extension of infantile behaviour into adult life. Infantile begging becomes a tactic to coerce others. Its immediate effect may be to precipitate regurgitation of meat but its social benefit is to initiate 'carer responses' in potential aggressors. Any animal can switch from juvenile to adult role according to circumstances. Often both parties try to outdo each other in the intensity of their begging behaviour, all twittering and mouth-tugging from exaggerated prostrate positions.

Each morning, or after a long rest, awakening youngsters (and adults) will circulate, mobbing others as if trying to force them to regurgitate food in a unique 'meet' ceremony. To avoid being mobbed, each individual seeks out a partner (preferably a gang) with which to form a temporary alliance, and switches role to that of mobber. In rare instances mobbing can turn into serious threats, suggesting that the evolutionary beginnings and original purpose of ganging up against individuals might have been to test fitness. However, in its present form the main purpose of the 'meet' appears to be social coercion and mobilisation of individual animals into a hunting pack.

Adaptations: The tight clustering of wild dogs at the daily 'meet' ceremony, with its emphasis on inclusion and avoidance of isolation, would appear to have a bearing on their unusual colouring. An early explanation described the wild dog's marbled colouring as a form of camouflage that served to break up the body's outline. However, because the markings consist of strong contrasts, they are hardly likely to conceal the dogs from potential prey. A more likely explanation may be that the marbled markings help to create a visual experience of inclusion and merging in the circling, clustering dogs during their 'meet' ceremonies.

Status: Of all African carnivores wild dogs have suffered the greatest contraction of range in the shortest time. The take-over of land for livestock, direct persecution and diseases from a burgeoning population of domestic dogs are partly responsible. This short-lived species, dependent on frequent and large litters to replenish numbers and on unimpeded access to fluctuating prey populations, may need a spread of populations and minimum numbers to sustain itself. If wild dogs decline too much with populations too far apart their extinction could be quite swift. Wild dogs are endangered in many countries and listed as Vulnerable (IUCN) everywhere.

Lycaon pictus
Former range

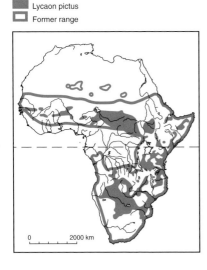

MUSTELIDS MUSTELIDAE

'Weasels'	Mustelinae
Otters	Lutrinae

Recognition: Medium-sized to small carnivores, generally with a long body and neck, a tubular skull (with a big brain) and shortish legs with five digits. Many species are boldly patterned in black and white, a feature which correlates with anal glands that secrete noxious scents. Short ears indicate limited sensitivity to sound and the eyes too are most sensitive at short range. Scent is the main vehicle for finding prey and communicating with others. All have well-developed canines while tooth rows have a reduced number of teeth. The jaws and jaw muscles are specialized for killing prey with the canines. All species have very sensitive whiskers and vibrissae.

Genealogy: Mustelids are of non-African, northern temperate origin and are predominantly fish-, mammal- and bird-predators which brought their specialisations with them. The earliest African mustelid fossils date from 5 million years ago.

Geography: Zorillas are a distinctively African group but the clawless otters also appear to have a long African history. N African mustelids are very recent immigrants from Eurasia. Ratels are also Asiatic but are now commoner in Africa.

Ecology: Deriving from cooler habitats, African mustelids are commonest in wet, nocturnal, upland or temperate conditions (see individual profiles).

Natural history: Mustelids are predominantly solitary, with sexes living in separate but overlapping territories. Most species use few vocal and visual signals but have elaborated scent as a means to help regulate reproduction and demarcate territories. All ♀ mustelids depend upon stimulation from a protracted copulation in order to induce ovulation. Sustained mating, lasting an hour or more, is assisted by a rigid bone, or baculum, in the penis of the ♂.

Adaptations: Many mustelids are well adapted to a micro-habitat that includes holes, hollows and tunnels in which they pursue their prey and also find shelter. They are highly exploratory and show good co-ordination and dexterity. Otters are particularly dextrous.

Musteline (striped weasel).

Lutrine (clawless otter).

'WEASELS' MUSTELINAE

Weasel	*Mustela nivalis*
Polecat	*Mustela putorius*
Libyan striped weasel	*Ictonyx libyca*
Zorilla	*Ictonyx striatus*
Striped (White-naped) weasel	*Poecilogale albinucha*
Ratel (Honey badger)	*Mellivora capensis*

A grouping of all the non-amphibious African mustelids. Heavy-weight diggers or 'badgers' have evolved independently in Eurasia, America and Africa. The more distinctive of these are regarded as subfamilies of their own and the ratel has sometimes been separated in this way. However, the ratel has much in common with polecats, weasels and zorillas and would appear to qualify as a giant weasel.

Weasel *Mustela nivalis*

Other names: Fr. *Belette*. Ger. *Mauswiesel*.
Measurements: HB 20–29cm. T 7–13cm. W 124–250g.
Recognition: A very small, elongated carnivore with brown upperparts and a white underside. The skull is long and tubular, with mouth, nose and eyes surprisingly small and closely placed. It leaves very small but strongly scented faeces as territorial markers. It utters a sharp alarm call.
Subspecies: *M. n. numidica* (Morocco, Algeria and Libya), *M. nivalis subpalmata* (Egypt).
Habitat: Mediterranean littoral and Atlas Mts, mainly in farmland. In Egypt they also live in urban gardens and wastelands (even entering buildings).
Food: Rats, mice and cockroaches, in semi-urban environments; frogs, lizards, small birds, rabbits and insects in more rural areas. Prey is hunted by smell in concealed drains, verges, hedges and crevices.
Status: Common. Not endangered. (IUCN status: not listed.)

Weasel.

Polecat.

Polecat *Mustela putorius*

Other names: Fr. *Putois*. Ger. *Iltis*.
Measurements: HB 35–45cm. T 12–16cm. W 700–1,500g.
Recognition: A long-bodied, furry carnivore with white ears, and face marked with a black eye mask and hood. On the body black guard hairs lie over a dense, woolly coat of ochre or sandy yellow. Legs and tail are black or deep brown. If disturbed or attacked, the polecat chatters or screams and discharges a strong, disagreeable odour.
Subspecies: *M. p. furo.* Strabo (58 BC–AD 24) wrote that domestic ferrets originated in N Africa. It is therefore possible that Moroccan polecats are either ancestral to ferrets or that they are ferrets that have been feral for 2,000 years or more.
Habitat: From sea-level up to 2,000m in the Atlas Mts west of the Riff. Polecats are found under dense cover in woodlands, secondary scrub and in farmland, and often around barns and outhouses near villages.
Food: Small mammals, reptiles, frogs, birds and insects; very occasionally fish and fruits.
Status: Inadequately known.

Libyan striped weasel *Ictonyx libyca*

Other names: Fr. *Zorille de Lybie*. Ger. *Streifenwiesel*.
Measurements: HB 22–30cm. T 12–19cm. W 500–750g.
Recognition: A conspicuous, small carnivore with long, erectile hair, mainly white upperparts and narrow black stripes down the back. Underparts, eye mask and forehead band are black. The tail is white. Black and white markings vary individually and regionally. This weasel wanders openly at night, usually with the tail carried vertically above the back. If approached it growls, fluffs its fur and presents its anus. A spray of choking, nauseous anal secretion deters a closer approach.
Subspecies: Six forms have been described but without clear geographic ranges. A highly polymorphic species.
Habitat: Sahara desert, mainly on its margins and mountains. A nocturnal species, it lives in dry stony country and sandy subdeserts. Although it has been observed in wooded country, it prefers more open steppes with sparse bush. It digs burrows at the base of dunes and can hide in rock crevices or in the burrows of other animals.
Food: Rodents and other small mammals, reptiles, invertebrates, birds and their eggs. Prey is mostly dug out of the ground after being trailed by scent. In spite of its deliberate, often slow, movements the Libyan striped weasel can pounce and kill prey very rapidly.
Status: Widespread. Little known.

Libyan striped weasel.

Zorilla.

Mustela putorius
Mustela nivalis
Ictonyx libyca

Zorilla *Ictonyx striatus*

Other names: Fr. *Zorille commun*. Ger. *Zorilla*. Swah. *Kicheche*.

Measurements: HB 30–38cm. T 22–30cm. W 700–1,400g.

Recognition: A small carnivore with strong claws on the forelegs, black underparts and a well-furred white tail. The back is boldly striped in black and white and the face is piebald in a variety of permutations. The short ears have white margins. The zorilla squirts noxious anal secretions at any attacking predator but may also sham death by lying limp (always with the pattern of black dorsal 'diamond' with two white stripes facing the aggressor).

Subspecies: Twenty-two have been described with three regional groupings as follows: *I. s. striatus* (S Africa), *I. s. erythrae* (NE and E Africa), *I. s. senegalensis* (W Africa).

Distribution: Sub-Saharan Africa, except for forest and moist woodland zone; also rare or absent in part of Somalia.

Habitat: Very patchily distributed, being scarce or absent in most heavily wooded areas. Zorillas are commonest in cool, well-grazed upland grasslands and in steppe country. Where well established they use habitual paths and appear to know their home range well.

Food: Invertebrates are the main staple but rodents form the bulk of the diet in some localities during certain seasons. Snakes and other reptiles are also commonly taken in some localities. Hares are a recorded prey animal.

Food is found during the cooler part of the night, with most hunting carried out between 22.00h and dawn. Zorillas have a springy, fast trot but can stalk and pounce on prey in spite of their striking coloration. Much prey, notably mice, dung beetles, larvae and lizards, is found by smell and dug out of shallow burrows. Dangerous snakes or large rats are wounded by sudden deep bites and may be shaken or wrenched. Bites are repeated until the prey is no longer able to bite back.

Behaviour: Several zorilla families have been kept together in captivity, where mutual grooming appears common. Normally encountered as solitary foragers, their peaceful cohabitation in captivity suggests that they may not have exclusive territories. However, exclusive core areas are likely as adult ♂♂ are mutually intolerant and ♀♀ avoid them except while in oestrus. Pups are born blind, naked and immobile after a 36-day gestation. The eyes only become functional by about 40 days but development thereafter is rapid. Young zorillas accompany their mothers for several months after leaving the breeding den at about 2 months. ♀♀ are fertile by 9 months and can be out with their first litter of two to four young before they are 1 year old.

Adaptations: Zorilla anal secretions are nauseating and also highly irritating to the eyes. The squirting of noxious anal secretions is common to many other mustelids, to some mongooses and a few species of fox. It evidently evolved to deter predators and it also appears to play a role in the regulation of social life. In situations of conflict subordinate zorillas scrape their forequarters on the ground while keeping their backsides raised and ready to squirt.

Status: Late-night activity means that zorillas are rarely seen and they remain little-known. Very widespread, although localized. Not endangered. (IUCN status: not listed.)

Ictonyx striatus

Poecilogale albinucha

Striped (White-naped) weasel *Poecilogale albinucha*

Other names: Fr. *Poecilogale à nuque blanche*. Ger. *Weissnachenwiesel*. Swah. *Chororo*.

Measurements: HB 25–36cm. T 13–24cm. W 230–350g.

Recognition: A small, very elongated carnivore with very short legs but powerfully clawed paws and a conspicuous black and white striped back. The crown and tail are white and the underside black. In spite of regular grooming, local earth colours may stain the animal's fur so that it appears red, yellow or grey (especially during the rains). The gape is very wide and the canines are proportionately as long and sharp as those of a leopard. The gait is distinctive. While walking slowly with the nose to the ground the body is arched or extended. Periodic halts are marked by rising from the haunches to sniff or peer around. Often it will swing the forequarters from side to side as if to get a visual 'fix'. Both halt movements give a remarkably snake-like impression.

Subspecies: Six subspecies have been named but these are probably not valid.

Distribution: SE Africa from E Zaïre and Uganda to the Indian Ocean as far south as Cape Province; also westwards through central Africa to Angola. Known up to at least 2,200m altitude.

Habitat: The striped weasel occurs in numerous widely separate localities which suggests that the present climate of Africa may be less favourable to it than in the past. The main centres of distribution are uplands with extensive grasslands or high veld with perennial, dense rodent populations. At higher altitudes it may be seen at dawn or dusk but is otherwise strictly nocturnal. It digs burrows but is often associated with termitaries. It is not known whether individual weasels circulate between well-spaced out burrows or are tied to smaller areas but rotational movements seem likely.

Food: Almost exclusively rodents, with occasional birds and eggs. The striped weasel is a specialized rodent-catcher and can eat three or four in a night. The mouse or rat is simultaneously seized in the jaws and paws while the weasel rolls over and over, yanking the prey with vigorous kicks. This dislocates the neck and renders the prey immobile. In this state it may be eaten, carried or stored in the home burrow.

Behaviour: The striped weasel is normally seen singly or, less often, in pairs. Larger groups (up to four) include pairs as well as single ♀♀ with young. Home ranges are marked with smeared faeces and urine at regularly used sites. Weasels purr in greeting but scream loudly when fighting. ♀♀ give birth to up to four very undeveloped young (weighing only 4g) after a 1-month gestation. They remain blind for more than 7 weeks and are only fully mobile at 11 weeks, at which time they are weaned and begin to follow the mother (a weasel family travelling in file greatly resembles a disarticulated snake). Young pups are carried by the nape, which has a white mane and very thick skin.

Adaptations: The elongated body and small proportions of the striped weasel are characteristics which allow it to hunt out prey in the prey's domain. The weasel not only digs out rodents but can also follow them down their burrows. Its technique of immobilising prey allows for the temporary storage of live mice, which may be critical for a predator with a super-active metabolism.

Status: Isolated populations might be vulnerable to land clearance and habitat change. In general, not endangered. (IUCN status: not listed.)

Mellivora capensis

0   2000 km

Ratel (Honey badger) *Mellivora capensis*

Other names: Fr. *Ratel*. Ger. *Honigdachs*. Swah. *Nyegere*.

Measurements: HB 60–77cm. T 16–30cm. W 7–16kg.

Recognition: A chunky, lumbering carnivore with a white forehead and variably coloured mantle. In some individuals the entire upperside is white or near white; in others the white forms a narrow boundary between the dark grey back and black underparts. Other permutations extend to an occasional all-black animal. The neck and shoulders are very muscular and the broad forepaws are armed with massive claws. By contrast the hindlegs are lightly built, with small claws. The skin is very thick and loose, with coarse, hog-like bristles above and sparse, finer fur below. The ears resemble oblique crevices on the sides of a big, blunt-muzzled head. For its size, the ratel has one of the largest brains of any carnivore and this is contained within a very hard and heavily constructed skull. If disturbed it utters a very intimidating, rattling roar that finds onomatopoeic expression in a number of its local names (e.g. *Entahurra* in Luganda and *Nkarungurungi* in Kimasai).

Subspecies: At least 11 subspecies have been named but these are mainly based on variations in melanism of the mantle. Colour morphs appear to lack regional consistency.

Distribution: The whole of Africa except for the driest centre of the Sahara and the Mediterranean littoral. Absent from the Nile valley and Orange Free State, possibly due to human agency. Distribution is patchy everywhere and densities are thought to fluctuate considerably.

Habitat: The ratel is commonest in open woodland but occurs in forest, in waterless desert steppe (with stunted acacias), on high mountains in Afro-alpine moorland and in coastal scrub.

Food: Opportunistic omnivore, specialising in the excavation of social insects, mice, trap-door spiders, dung beetles, larvae, scorpions, etc. from hard, subterranean hiding places. The ratel also excavates the softer parts of well-protected animals, such as tortoises and turtles. Whenever possible it will take reptiles, birds and even fish. It also occasionally takes larger animals if they are young or otherwise vulnerable. It finds most of its food by broad-spectrum, opportunistic foraging over a wide area (with its sustained bouncy gait it can cover up to 37km in a night). When feeding on bees, termites and army ants the ratel usually releases anal secretions which, among other functions, may serve to fumigate the insects, thus facilitating the robbery of their nests. The ratel readily scavenges carrion and will even appropriate the kills of other carnivores (including, on occasion, those of lions). In spite of its power, it can be very dainty and precise when feeding on larvae, insects or viscera, picking out individual items one by one. It also caches surplus food, including honeycombs.

Behaviour: Ratels have very large, overlapping ranges, and normally forage singly but two animals are very often seen together. Larger groups may be aggregations at common resources (for example 12 animals have been seen at a cattle 'boma' where concentrations of dung beetles and their larvae are very high).

It has been suggested that pairs might represent bonded, long-term mates, but it would seem more likely that the ratel, like most other mustelids, conducts brief liaisons. ♂♂ have quite exceptionally large testes in proportion to their size, implying a superproduction of sperm. The social implications of this endowment are unknown. Up to four young are born after a gestation dubiously quoted as lasting 6 months. ♀♀ give birth in a lined burrow which is usually self-dug but which may be excavated from a termitary. Once weaned, offspring accompany their mother for an unknown period before becoming independent. The ratel may live for 26 years in captivity.

Adaptations: Social insects have a number of effective defences against most predators. However, the ratel is well equipped to breach these. With its spade-like foreclaws, it is able to tear open insect nests while its thick skin and stink glands help to protect it from stings and bites. Honeybees inside their hive are immobilised by the anal secretion. It is able to locate terrestrial insects by smell and is well known to follow honeyguide birds to arboreal bees' nests.

Status: Areas in which the ratel is rare or totally absent are increasing. The reasons for this are not fully understood but may include susceptibility to cat and dog diseases. As modern apiculture displaces the more fatalistic and tolerant practices of traditional bee-keepers, the ratel is beginning to suffer serious persecution. It is also readily trapped and poisoned in retaliation for occasional raids on small livestock.

OTTERS LUTRINAE

Swamp otter	*Aonyx congica*
African clawless otter	*Aonyx capensis*
Common otter	*Lutra lutra*
Spot-necked otter	*Lutra maculicollis*

Recognition: Long-bodied, long-tailed, amphibious carnivores with dense waterproof fur, a blunt, short face and a prominent moustache of whiskers. The hindlegs (the main means of propulsion in the water) are more or less webbed. The hands may also be webbed or have dextrous, clawless fingers. Within a species there can be very considerable differences in size and clawless otters, in particular, can grow to gigantic proportions.

Genealogy: The clawless otters share certain characteristics with other large species in the Pacific and South America. All may derive from a common ancient stock. Eurasia is their most likely continent of origin but the two *Aonyx* species probably diverged within Africa. *Lutra* is likely to be a more recent arrival.

Geography: All otters are patchily distributed. They are absent in areas without permanent water, appropriate food or adequate feeding conditions. In the past high densities of crocodiles may have been a local deterrent.

Ecology: Otters have a high metabolic rate and require regular, frequent feeding on high-energy foods. Members of the clawless otter group find their food in muddy, turbid waters and have more flexible diets and hunting ecologies. The fish otters are more specialised, active hunters.

Natural history: Otters typically follow cycles of more or less tolerance toward their own species. They show some social flexibility. They are normally dispersed as solitary foragers or small family groups but form larger groups where resources permit. Otters are vocal and all species make loud attention calls as well as penetrating whistles. All use natural riverside retreats or 'holts' to raise their young and can, if necessary, dig or modify holes to this end.

Adaptations: African clawless otters and swamp otters are externally so similar that they are difficult to tell apart. Their teeth, however, are so different that taxonomists have treated them as separate genera or subgenera. The huge, plate-like molars of the African clawless otter are clearly adapted to crushing the shells of crabs, molluscs, turtles and catfish heads, but their shallow rooting in the skull suggests that this was a relatively late development.

Status: All otters are hunted for their fur. They are susceptible to trapping, hunting with dogs and drowning in fishnets. In some W African countries otter fur can still be found in open commercial markets. Elsewhere, local markets often provide sufficient incentive for hunting. Fish-farming is the primary cause of conflict in many areas. Nylon-net fishing is depleting otter populations in many inland waters.

Swamp otter *Aonyx congica*

Other names: Fr. *Loutre du Congo*. Ger. *Kleinzahn Fingerotter*.
Measurements: HB 78–97cm. T 40–59cm. W 15–25kg.
Recognition: A very large otter with a white bib, nose and ears and a prominent black patch between the eyes and nostrils. The body colour is rich sepia with some frosting on head and neck. The back of the head and neck are appreciably more slender than in the African clawless otter. The molar teeth are smaller and deeply cusped.
Subspecies: *A. c. congica* (Zaïre basin to Gabon), *A. c. microdon* (rivers off Cameroon highlands), *A. c. philippsi* (mountains of E Zaïre and Uganda to Burundi), *A. c. poensis* (Bioko I. form).
Distribution: Main forest block from E Nigeria to Uganda.
Habitat: Rivers, swamps and ponds close to or surrounded by rainforest. Sightings in papyrus swamps in the highland valleys of W Uganda have been reported. In undisturbed areas swamp otters are active during the day as well as at night.
Food: Fish, frogs, earthworms, crabs, molluscs and other vertebrates and invertebrates caught in the water, on muddy shores and in backwaters of permanent river courses and swamps.
Behaviour: Excellent swimmers, swamp otters are deft and thorough explorers of the shores of forest rivers and swamps. Animals forage singly but family parties have been observed in Cameroon rivers.
Adaptations: The powerful build of the swamp otters provides them with the physical strength necessary for foraging in tangled and muddy riversides. It may also allow them to escape the attentions of most predators as crocodiles, pythons, eagles and leopards are less likely to tackle large otters. The development of sensitive, clawless fingers is a tropical adaptation best suited to feeling about in mud and cloudy water.
Status: Swamp otters are much hunted for their beautiful coats. They are only common in very limited localities, rare elsewhere. Vulnerable.

African clawless otter *Aonyx capensis*

Other names: Fr. *Loutre à joues blanches*. Ger. *Fingerotter*. Swah. *Fisi maji kubwa*.
Measurements: HB 72–92cm. T 40–71cm. W 12–34kg.
Note: ♂♂ are larger than ♀♀ but a 20kg maximum for ♀♀ may be too light. Average weights and sizes are well below that of the occasional 'giant'.
Recognition: A large, sometimes very large otter, with blunt, unwebbed fingers and toes, and almost vestigial fingernails. The head is broad and the massive neck and crown are visibly modelled by the well-developed neck and jaw muscles. The thick fur and loose skin of the body and upper limbs contrasts with the tight, short fur on the hands and feet. The upperparts vary in colour from very dark chocolate brown to greyish brown or pale tan. Underparts are of a similar colour, except for the chest, chin and cheeks, which are white or off-white. Colour on the face is variable but the dark area between eye and nostril is never sharply isolated (as it is in the swamp otter). The mantle may be frosted in some individuals.

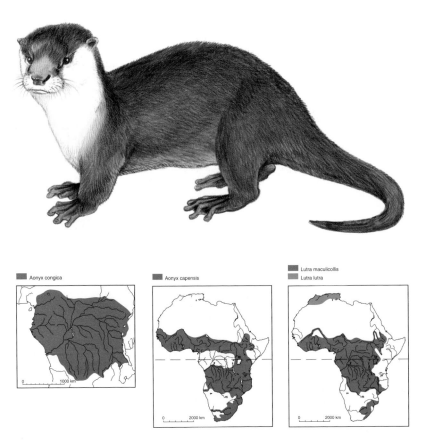

Aonyx congica

Aonyx capensis

Lutra maculicollis
Lutra lutra

0   1000 km

0   2000 km

0   2000 km

The most frequent signs of the African clawless otter are single or multiple dung deposits full of crushed crabshells or catfish bones. Waterside resting places, slides or 'holts' (as well as scented retreats in crevices, root and reed tangles or self-dug burrows) are other signs of its presence. Like other otters it utters a loud, attention-catching 'aah'.

Subspecies: Eleven races have been described. Three are in provisional use: *A. c. capensis* (S and W Africa), *A. c. hindei* (E Africa, E Zaïre and N Zambia), *A. c. meneleki* (Ethiopia).

Distribution: Very patchy distribution over most of sub-Saharan Africa from sea-level to 3,000m; absent from the central Zaïre basin. They are dependent on permanent water (even if only residual dry-season pools).

Habitat: Rivers, streams, marshes, lakes and dams with adequate cover or concealment; also estuaries and inshore sea close to mangroves or tall cliffs (in SE Africa). African clawless otters forage in swamps and the intertidal zone along southern temperate coasts. They are absent from several large rivers and many lakes where a combination of factors exclude them, including parasites, predators (crocodiles are easily evaded in some habitats, less so in others) and, particularly, waters that are too fast or otherwise unsuited to their prey or hunting techniques. They are dependent on some form of shelter, especially when breeding. They can laboriously excavate burrows in soft, sandy and wet soils but usually scrape a form in some naturally sheltered place.

Food: Freshwater crabs consistently form the major part of the diet. Seasonal changes in crab activity are offset by the otter's ability to excavate aestivating crabs from their dry-season retreats in soft, sandy soil. Crabs are extremely abundant in both permanent and many seasonal river courses. Frogs comprise a lesser, more seasonal, part of the otter's diet, as do fish, small mammals, birds and molluscs. The latter may be smashed at chosen rocks (leaving small shell middens) but mussels are usually only a fall-back resource. Food is found by thorough exploration of both above and underwater surfaces, most often by touch in turbid water.

Behaviour: African clawless otters normally forage singly or as a mother with young. However, adults may be quite tolerant and spend time together. It is possible that related animals along a stretch of 3–20km of river or coast may share a group or clan territory. These very vocal animals have a vocabulary of whistles and squeals (contact), a chirping bark (greeting) and moans, mews and sniffles (young coercing adults). Up to three young are born after about 2 months' gestation. Mothers are very fierce in defence of their young and can inflict deep, damaging bites on dogs or people.

Adaptations: African clawless otters share all primary adaptations with the more generalised swamp otter. Specialisation in eating crabs and other hard-shelled foods are secondary adaptations that have enabled them to widen their range in a rather dry continent.

Status: These otters are widely hunted for their fur and in retaliation for raiding fish farms. Dogs are an increasing hazard. African clawless otters are becoming extinct or scarcer in many localities but are still very widely distributed.

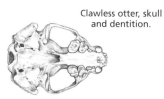

Clawless otter, skull and dentition.

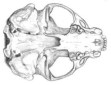

Swamp otter skull.

Common otter.

Common otter *Lutra lutra*

Other names: Fr. *Loutre d'Europe*. Ger. *Fischotter*.

Measurements: HB 60–90cm. T 35–47cm. W 6–18kg (rarely up to 27kg).

Recognition: A brown, amphibious mammal with strong, well-clawed, webbed toes. The short face has prominent eyes and a brush of stiff whiskers on the muzzle. The coat can vary from light tan or grey tints to deep dark brown. The common otter makes chirping contact calls and a soft whistle of alarm. It is now forced to be largely nocturnal. Dung left on prominent waterside sites (with oily scent smears nearby) betray its presence.

Subspecies: *L. l. lutra*.

Distribution: Formerly from Morocco to Tunisia.

Habitat: Formerly on inland rivers and lakes as well as along the Mediterranean coastline; now found only in a very few localities. Common otters need dense vegetation for cover and safe retreats in holes, hollow trees, hulks and culvert drains for breeding.

Food: Mainly fish but also frogs, crabs and many small vertebrates and invertebrates associated with fresh- or saltwater. They are known to travel 3–10km in a single night's foraging.

Behaviour: Solitary individuals, pairs or families range over 12–24km of shoreline (and some up to 60km) on which they use up to 40 habitual resting spots (each well spaced from the next). ♀♀ bear up to five young after a 2-month gestation. The mother depends on a secure, undisturbed shelter and adequate food to raise her young.

Adaptations: Common otters are mainly visual hunters of active fish which they catch in open pursuit. They require consistent and frequent sources of food.

Status: Almost extinct in Africa. This species has suffered the effects of water pollution, tree clearance, diversion and drying out of rivers and direct persecution. Endangered.

Spot-necked otter *Lutra maculicollis*

Other names: Fr. *Loutre à cou tacheté*. Ger. *Fleckenhalsotter*. Swah. *Fisi maji mdogo*.

Measurements: HB 60–65cm. T 35–40cm. W 4–6.5kg.

Recognition: A sleek, slender otter with a long tail and well-webbed, clawed toes. Apart from the brown and white blotching of the throat and underparts, which is very variable, the colour is a uniform, deep chocolate brown. Older individuals or regional populations may show paler, more ochre or grey tints. It leaves dung deposits on prominences and midstream rocks. A thin, high whistle is the most characteristic call.

Subspecies: Seven races have been described (one from a 20km^2 lake). All are probably invalid.

Distribution: Scattered thinly over the wetter parts of sub-Saharan Africa but may be locally common in the Great Lakes and in some wet montane regions. Absent from the far west, SW and NE and E Africa.

Habitat: Clear water seems to be an important determinant in the spot-necked otter's distribution (it is mainly a diurnal fisher). In many lakes and rivers it shows a preference for rocky, undisturbed areas without turbid inflow. It is present in mountain streams (where fish appear not to be abundant) but absent from many fish-rich but turbid rivers in E Africa. It is also absent from all shallow alkaline lakes of the Eastern Rift. It is a poor colonist (or recolonist) perhaps because it requires permanent and continuous waterways for dispersal.

Food: Fish and frogs; also crabs, molluscs, aquatic insects and larvae, and various other vertebrates and invertebrates. Conspicuous, slow-moving fish up to 60cm long (preferred size 10–20cm) and frogs are favoured. In undisturbed areas the most intensive feeding periods are the 2 or 3 hours after dawn and before dusk, but midday and moonlight hunting have also been observed.

Behaviour: Usually solitary, the spot-necked otter may form small family parties. It forms groups of up to 20 animals in L. Victoria. Some of these groups include both sexes while others are apparently aggregations of young ♂♂. ♀♀ give birth to up to three blind, helpless cubs in a sheltered burrow or crevice after a gestation period of 2 months. Offspring stay with their mother for nearly a year. The spot-necked otter can be very vocal and utters an aggressive trilling, a long, mewing contact call, shrill chattering and various spluttering snorts.

Adaptations: This species relies on clear water and visual hunting. Although dextrous, this is a 'mouth-oriented' otter rather than a 'finger otter', like members of the *Aonyx* group.

Status: Soil erosion near the sources of major rivers may be a more insidious threat than nylon nets and direct destruction by fur-trappers or fish-farmers. This otter is still locally abundant but is in retreat in many areas.

Newborn spot-necked otter.

MONGOOSES HERPESTIDAE

Ichneumon (Egyptian) mongoose	*Herpestes ichneumon*
Long-snouted mongoose	*Herpestes naso*
Slender mongoose	*Herpestes sanguinea*
Small grey mongoose	*Herpestes pulverulenta*
Dwarf mongoose	*Helogale parvula*
Somali dwarf mongoose	*Helogale hirtula*
Savannah mongoose	*Dologale dybowski*
Selous's mongoose	*Paracynictis selousi*
Yellow mongoose	*Cynictis pencillata*
Suricate (Meerkat)	*Suricata suricata*
Banded mongoose	*Mungos mungo*
Gambian mongoose	*Mungos gambianus*
Cusimanse	*Crossarchus obscurus*
Flat-headed cusimanse	*Crossarchus platycephalus*
Alexander's cusimanse	*Crossarchus alexandri*
Ansorge's cusimanse	*Crossarchus ansorgei*
Liberian mongoose	*Liberiictis kuhni*
Marsh mongoose	*Atilax paludinosus*
White-tailed mongoose	*Ichneumia albicauda*
Meller's mongoose	*Rhynchogale melleri*
Bushy-tailed mongoose	*Bdeogale crassicauda*
Sokoke dog mongoose	*Bdeogale omnivora*
Black-legged mongoose	*Bdeogale nigripes*
Jackson's mongoose	*Bdeogale jacksoni*

Recognition: Small to medium-sized carnivores with long bodies and tails and shortish legs. Primarily terrestrial, mongooses have coarse, grizzled coats (never blotched or spotted). A few have striped rumps. All have inconspicuous ears, small eyes and a more or less pointed muzzle. They have well-developed anal sacs but lack perineal civetone glands. Some have cheek glands. Teeth, numbering 34–40, are distinctive for each genus.

Genealogy: Living mongooses have diversified in Africa into 23 species belonging to 12 or 13 genera. In Asia eight species are all ichneumons of the conservative genus *Herpestes*. Recorded from Eurasian deposits about 30 million years old, *Herpestes* dentition has provided the prototype from which all other modern mongoose tooth rows can be derived and, apart from *Herpestes*, all other genera clearly evolved within Africa.

Geography: The South African small grey mongoose, *Herpestes pulverulenta*, has its closest relative in the Asian *Herpestes auropunctatus*. This wide separation of conservative species implies that mongooses have so diversified in tropical and SW Africa that older, more generalised types have been progressively excluded. The main centres of mongoose evolution are the equatorial forests (mainly cusimanses and their allies), east-central African woodlands (dog mongooses and dwarf mongooses) and the Kalahari region (suricates and yellow mongooses). Only in Africa are mongooses the commonest carnivores with the greatest number of species.

Ecology: Ground-dwelling predators of invertebrates and small vertebrates. Some mongooses include fruits in their diets. Although some are able to do without water for some time, most species are water-dependent inhabitants of forests, woodlands, savannahs and marshes (see page 215). Many species adapt to changed conditions or resources by enlarging their range, intensifying activity or by diversifying their diet.

Natural history: A majority of species are solitary and many of these are nocturnal. A few form pairs for variable lengths of time. At least eight species are social and most of these are diurnal. The vulnerability of small mongooses to predation may be one factor encouraging communal living. Periodic food bonanzas may be another. If the frequency of litters increases as well as the overall population density the rate of dispersal through the young is also slowed. This forces young from previous litters to become helpers in their parental family. This sort of subordination seems to be the main basis for mongoose sociality.

Herpestes		$\dfrac{3.1.4.2}{3.1.(3\text{–}4).2} = 38\text{–}40$
Mungos		$\dfrac{3.1.3.2}{3.1.3.2} = 36$
Crossarchus		$\dfrac{3.1.3.2}{3.1.3.2} = 36$
Helogale		$\dfrac{3.1.3.2}{3.1.3.2} = 36$
Atilax		$\dfrac{3.1.3.2}{3.1.3.2} = 36$
Icheumia		$\dfrac{3.1.4.2}{3.1.4.2} = 40$
Bdeogale		$\dfrac{3.1.4.2}{3.1.4.2} = 40$
Rhynchogale		$\dfrac{3.1.4.2}{3.1.4.2} = 40$

All mongooses depend on scent to communicate and to mark territories. Although little is known about most species, it is likely that, as in the case of the dwarf mongoose, anal secretions constitute long-lasting, individual signatures, while cheek-gland secretions produce a short-term, status-related signal that can easily trigger immediate aggression. Cheek glands appear never to be rubbed without the accompanying anal signature, a precaution which may protect known individuals from attack while heightening aggression against unattractive aliens.

The ability of several species to roll and crash-crack eggs and to kill dangerous snakes is well known. Both are instances of the manipulative skills, speed and versatility of many mongooses in their hunting techniques.

Adaptations: The radiation of mongooses in Africa has involved numerous and subtle specialisations in diet and niche that are expressed particularly in their differently shaped noses, ears, jaws, muzzles and whiskers.

Ichneumon (Egyptian) mongoose *Herpestes ichneumon*

Other names: Fr. *Mangouste ichneumon*. Ger. *Ichneumon*. Swah. *Nguchiro*.

Measurements: HB 45–60cm. T 33–54cm. W 2.2–4.1kg.

Recognition: A long-bodied, low-slung mongoose with a slender, almost snake-like head. The long, markedly tapered tail ends in a conspicuous black tassel. In most postures the legs are largely concealed by long fur, increasing its reptile-like form. The grizzled coat varies in shade or tint.

Subspecies: 25 subspecies have been described but there is so much variation between individuals and regions that a thorough revision of subspecies is needed.

Distribution: Africa, S Spain and Israel. Very widely distributed in Africa but absent from the Sahara, Horn of Africa, Namib Desert and other waterless regions; also absent from true forest.

Habitat: Commonest in flat, grassy areas on floodplains, coastal littorals, lakeshores and broad river valleys; also on rolling moist savannahs and in extensive forest clearings where grass has become dominant. It appears to be a speedy colonist of disturbed or seasonally flooded areas. It is water-dependent and a good swimmer.

Food: Rodents, reptiles, frogs, birds and various invertebrates. The broad range of prey is matched by the mongoose's exceptional ingenuity and versatility in hunting and catching techniques (most ending in a fast, snapping lunge). Subterranean food items (larvae, crabs, eggs, and insects) are rapidly dug out with well-clawed forepaws.

Behaviour: While this mongoose is normally seen singly or in small family parties, larger associations may form around two or more ♀♀, their immediate young and some previous young. Larger groups, seldom seen in Africa, may be a response to high population densities supported by abundant resources and an absence of competition from other carnivores. These enlarged ♀ units are associated with a single ♂ which drives ♂ offspring away and only joins the ♀♀ sporadically. After a 2-month gestation up to four young are born, blind and helpless, in a den or thicket. Only able to see at 3 weeks and taking their first solid food at 1 month, they are self-sufficient by 4 months. Some only become wholly independent after 1 year. This prolonged immaturity is linked with exceptional playfulness and much exploratory behaviour which helps to turn up more food of a wide variety. ♀♀ normally only produce one litter per year but rich resources may encourage both biannual breeding and more social behaviour, with older offspring helping to feed and care for their younger siblings. This mongoose has a wide vocabulary of chatters (excitement), hoots and clucks (contact), spits, screams and growls (threat and defence).

Adaptations: 'Ichneumon', from the Greek word for 'tracker', describes this mongoose's most conspicuous characteristic, which is to be seen trotting along with its head down. This is thought to be scent-tracking along well-established trails (laid by the mongoose itself or by other members of its family). Recent observations have revealed that a single family or group of families share a well-known home range and a single anal-scent beacon, consisting of a stone, soil or plants. All family members frequently mark this beacon by rubbing their glands all over it. In the process their long fringe of abdominal hair becomes impregnated with scent (this probably being its primary function). Deviations from regular trail-tracking are mostly carried out in pursuit of food and are followed by a return to the nearest trail point to resume 'tracking'. The snake-like appearance of the ichneumon mongoose, created by its fringe, sometimes results in the animal being mobbed by birds. With its lightning strike it may then be able to catch birds which would otherwise be impossible to hunt.

Status: Very widespread but commonest in areas with few other mongoose species. Strong scenting of trails may make them vulnerable to dogs. Not endangered. (IUCN status: not listed.)

Herpestes ichneumon
Herpestes naso

Long-snouted mongoose *Herpestes naso*

Other names: Fr. *Mangouste à long museau*. Ger. *Langnasenichneumon*.
Measurements: HB 52–59cm. T 36–43cm. W 3–4.2kg.
Recognition: A large, dark, shaggy mongoose with relatively long legs, a thick tail and pointed muzzle. The head is greyer than the deep sepia-black grizzled body and tail. The pale, sparsely haired mouth region is well-demarcated from the dark, almost black upper muzzle and bridge of the nose.
Subspecies: *H.s n. naso* (R. Cross to R. Sanaga), *H. n. almodovari* (R. Sanaga to R. Zaïre), *H. n. microdon* (NE Zaïre basin).
Habitat: Main forest block north of the R. Zaïre where they live close to clear forest streams. The restricted range, rarity, unspecialised dentition and resemblance to the marsh mongoose, suggest that this is a relict species. Originally thought to be restricted to the main forest block north of the R Zaire where they live close to clear forest streams. Now known to range extensively south of the river.
Food: Known to eat snails (a rare prey for carnivores), reputed to take carrion and likely to feed on rodents.
Status: Rare. (IUCN status: not listed.)

Herpestes sanguinea

Slender mongoose *Herpestes sanguinea*

Other names: Fr. *Mangouste rouge*. Ger. *Rotichneumon*.
Measurements: HB 26–34cm. T 23–31cm. W 350–800 g.
Recognition: Long-bodied, short-legged, partly arboreal mongooses, extremely variable in colour. The digits of the hands and feet splay readily and are armed with small but sharp, hooked claws. The tip of the tail is usually black tipped. Young have olive-green eyes up to 6 months, reddish amber thereafter.
Subspecies: Great variation is evident among 70 named subspecies. Four subgroups can be distinguished which may be incipient or actual species:

1. *sanguinea* group (W, central and south-central Africa): short coat, wholly grizzled, polymorphic in colour.
2. *ochracea* group (eastern seaboard from Eritrea to South Africa, overlapping with *sanguinea* in E Africa): shaggy, partly plain-coloured ochre or reddish.
3. *flavescens* group (Kaokoveld, Namibia and S Angola): polymorphic, partly plain coloured.
4. *swalius* (S and central Namibia): grizzled grey with yellowish hands, feet and rump; very long tail; often nocturnal.

Distribution: South of Sahara and Aïr massif to Orange R., from sea-level up to 2,500m.

Habitat: All wooded, savannah, thicket and forest habitats (including the driest *Acacia* and the wettest forests); also occurs in extensive papyrus and forest swamps. Slender mongooses use termitaries, hollow and creviced trees, burrows and holes for shelter.

Food: Rodents, insects, reptiles, frogs, birds (including nestlings and eggs). Insect larvae (notably blowfly larvae at carcasses) have been frequently recorded. Slender mongooses are mainly diurnal foragers, with a characteristic gliding, horizontal gait punctuated by pauses in which they stand up, periscope-like, to scan the environment.

Behaviour: Both sexes hold exclusive territories of variable size. Adult ♂♂ may tolerate smaller ♂♂ but confrontations within and between sexes are common. Loose associations between pairs are long-lasting. Marking posts are inconspicuous and may be close to sleeping places. Latrine sites are used but ostentatious marking appears rare.

Up to three young are born after just under 2 months' gestation. The blind and helpless young open their eyes at 3 weeks and begin eating solid foods at 4 weeks. They can become independent at 10 weeks but may stay longer with the mother if she has no second litter. Two litters a year are common.

Slender mongooses utter a faint purr (contentment), a soft hiss (playful), a bird-like whistle or hoot (contact) and a harsh, scolding caterwaul (alarm/aggression).

Adaptations: Slender mongooses resemble squirrels in their ability to climb trees at speed. This greatly increases their ability to reach certain resources and may explain their abundance and widespread distribution.

Status: Not endangered. However, *swalius* is rare and localised. (IUCN status: not listed.)

Herpestes pulverulenta

Small grey mongoose *Herpestes pulverulenta*

Other names: Fr. *Mangouste grise du Cap*. Ger. *Kleinichneumon*.

Measurements: HB 28–37cm. T 23–36cm. W 370–800g.

Recognition: A rather uniformly grizzled, grey mongoose with a thickly furred tail (without a black tip). Face and feet are slightly darker and very finely vermiculated. It is seen singly, in twos, or in small family groups.

Habitat: Mainly overgrown bushy country in all habitat types south of the Orange R. (where it replaces the slender mongoose). It prefers dry rocky ground and hillsides and is particularly common on the coastal plain.

Food: Mainly invertebrates (insects, crabs, larvae, earthworms, snails) and shellfish in estuaries; also rodents, reptiles and birds.

Status: Not endangered. (IUCN status: not listed.)

Dwarf mongoose *Helogale parvula*

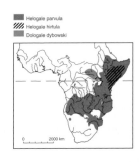

Helogale parvula
Helogale hirtula
Dologale dybowski

Other names: Fr. *Mangouste naine*. Ger. *Zwergichneumon*. Swah. *Kitafe*.

Measurements: HB 18–28cm. T 14–19cm. W 210–350g.

Recognition: The dwarf mongoose is easily distinguished by its small size, rather infantile features, smooth, finely grizzled coat and its diurnal and social habits. The colouring is extremely varied, ranging from tan, yellowish and orangey red to dark brown and black. However, most individuals within a locality and a family party tend to have similar colouring.

Subspecies: Variation among the dwarf mongoose has led to 17 subspecies being described. This classification is in need of revision but three major divisions can be recognised: *H. p. parvula* (S Africa), *H. p. varia* (central Africa), *H. p. undulata* (NE and E Africa).

Distribution: Warmer areas of E and central Africa below 2,000m; from Eritrea to Transvaal, west to Angola and Namibia. They avoid highlands and forests.

Habitat: Savannahs, thickets and woodlands, typically with numerous termitaries for shelter. Although they survive seasonally waterless periods, they avoid very arid, open country. They leave their marks in the form of communal latrines (generally a corner or crevice near the sleeping den). The site is periodically changed.

Food: Invertebrates, notably crickets and grasshoppers, termites, scorpions and spiders. Vertebrates comprise rodents (especially nests of young), lizards, snakes and birds. Dwarf mongooses forage as a group, with a spread of some 50–60m, catching their prey by 'open' chasing and pouncing (not by stalking). They are able to follow some rodents down their burrows and have a substantial impact on rodent populations within their foraging area.

Behaviour: This social species forms packs averaging over eight individuals (range 2–20), with more ♀♀ than ♂♂ and fluctuating numbers of young. Packs are strongly hierarchical, with a single dominant breeding pair. The pack is highly structured and led by the matriarch. The dominant ♂ is particularly vigilant and is generally joined by immature ♂♂ in continuous scanning from elevated posts (this exposure leads to greater casualties among the ♂♂).

Infants are suckled by their matriarch mother or by other ♀♀ that abort or lose their own offspring. The young are cared for by non-breeding adults of both sexes and there is intense competition to groom and carry infants. Litters are spaced 9–26 weeks apart and the privileged status of former infants is lost instantly on the arrival of new ones. After about 3 days of distress after being rejected, the initial generation become vigilant sentries, alert and nervous to everything around them. Older siblings help to bring food to infants, guard and retrieve them and huddle up to them at night or in cool weather.

Packs have territories that range from a very few hectares up to about 160ha (averaging about 35ha in the Serengeti). The major landmarks in these territories are termitaries, to which all members flee if seriously disturbed. There may be small overlaps in territory and confrontations between packs are generally settled in favour of the larger group. While foraging, the group keeps in touch with a tinkling, vibrating chirrup. The most urgent warning cry is a shrill, explosive double note or shriek. A grating churr is directed at dogs, snakes or other dangerous animals at some distance away. Anal marking or a plentiful cache of food elicits an outburst of shrill twittering. Distressed infants utter a twitter ending with a prolonged cheep, 'ti-ti-teee'. Group movements are begun with initiators making a scolding churr.

A matriarch can have up to three litters in succession, each of up to six young, spaced by a gestation period of about 53 days. Young emerge from the termitary or den at about 4 weeks. At this time they are extremely playful and adults join them in wrestling, mock fighting and pouncing. This phase comes to an abrupt end with the arrival of the next litter, whereon marking and adult behaviour is acquired.

Adaptations: As the smallest of the mongooses the dwarf mongoose has the most predators and must rely on termitaries for refuge and on a class of 'sentries' for early warning. Dens are often strategically sited near to bee or wasp nests, or even close to farm buildings (if there are no dogs present). Like monkeys, dwarf mongooses form mutually beneficial associations with hornbills. The hornbills catch disturbed insects and alert the mongooses to danger. Both species wait for one another and the birds are known to try and wake late risers by calling down their termitary chimneys. More one-sided relationships can form with larger mammals. Thus, dwarf mongooses have been seen to catch insects disturbed by a domestic bull and to use the bull as a perch and as a deterrent against potential predators. It is a mark of dwarf mongooses' versatility that they find such diverse sources of protection.

Status: Not endangered. (IUCN status: not listed.)

Somali dwarf mongoose *Helogale hirtula*

Other names: Fr. *Mangouste velue.* Ger. *Somali Zwergichneumon.*
Measurements: HB est. 20–27cm. T est. 15–18cm. W est. 220-330 g.
Recognition: A very small mongoose with longer, shaggier fur than the common dwarf mongoose. It also has more robust teeth. Colouring varies but is typically an overall grizzled grey with warmer-coloured underparts and face. The feet are dark brown. This is a social diurnal species.
Subspecies: *H. h. hirtula* (Somalia, Ethiopia, N Kenya), *H. h. percivali* (central and W Kenya).
Habitat: The Horn of Africa, mainly limited to a zone of bush, thicket and shrubby, deciduous woodlands dominated by *Acacia, Commiphora, Grewia* and *Cordia.* This species is able to live without water. Its habitat has been much modified by humans and their livestock and would have been more densely wooded in the past.
Food: Invertebrates and vertebrates of a similar range (but probably more arid adapted) to that taken by the common dwarf mongoose.
Status: The entire range of the Somali dwarf mongoose overlaps that of the common dwarf mongoose. The nature of their ecological separation or competitive exclusion awaits study.

Somali dwarf mongoose.

Savannah mongoose.

Savannah mongoose *Dologale dybowski*

Other names: Fr. *Mangouste de Dybowski.* Ger. *Listige Manguste.*
Measurements: HB 22–33cm. T 16–23cm. W est. 250–400g.
Recognition: A very small, grizzled mongoose with powerful claws on the forefeet and a thick, bushy tail. Body, tail and limbs are brown, the underparts are a warm, pale grey and the face is a darker grey. The throat displays a prominent reverse 'cow-lick' of fur. The savannah mongoose differs from the dwarf mongoose in having an undivided upper lip, a shorter palate and weaker teeth. It bears some resemblance to the Gambian mongoose (*Mungos*) and to the cusimanses (*Crossarchus*) in the structure of the teeth and skull.
Habitat: Currently only known from moist savannahs and margins of rainforest in NE Zaïre, S Sudan and NW Uganda. It may possibly range as far west as the Congo. It is thought to be diurnal and is associated with territories.
Food: Unknown, but the digging claws and unspecialised teeth of this species suggests fossorial invertebrates and small burrowing vertebrates.
Status: The distribution of the very common banded mongoose is likely to considerably narrow the niche of this rare mongoose and study of its biology is an urgent precondition to understanding its status and how to conserve it.

Selous's mongoose *Paracynictis selousi*

Other names: Fr. *Mangouste de Selous.* Ger. *Trugmanguste.*
Measurements: HB 35–48cm. T 28–43cm. W 1.3–2.2kg.
Recognition: A delicate-looking, long-bodied, long-legged mongoose with a bushy, white-tipped tail and a grizzled grey coat with dense underfur that shows through to give ochre tints (especially on the flanks, thighs and chest). The ears are widely spaced, rounded and fairly prominent. The feet are dark brown, have four toes and longish hard nails. It is almost wholly nocturnal.
Subspecies: Four subspecies have been named (on somewhat dubious grounds).

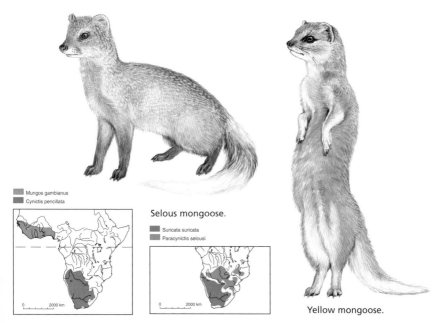

Mungos gambianus
Cynictis pencillata

Selous mongoose.

Suricata suricata
Paracynictis selousi

0   2000 km

0   2000 km

Yellow mongoose.

Distribution: Upper Zambezi basin and peripheral uplands of the northern Kalahari basin with extensions towards Malawi and Swaziland. Although it lives mainly in regions of summer rainfall (with periodic frosts from May to August), it appears to be absent from the coldest South African uplands, as well as from the surrounding warmer lowlands.

Habitat: Areas of open, short grass; well-drained, sandy country with open Mopane (*Colophospermum*) scrub, *Baikiaea* teak woodland and fire-climax Miombo (*Brachystegia*) woodland with open floors. It is also found on cultivated land and ranches. It frequently makes use of ready-made burrows in harder soils but generally digs its own two-tiered labyrinths in the loose, well-drained, sandy soils of the region.

Food: Invertebrates, with a strong preference for beetles and their larvae, termites and grasshoppers. Numerous other species are taken opportunistically. Mice, reptiles and frogs are commonly eaten; birds only rarely. Most foods are found by smell and excavated from shallow retreats. Selous's mongoose often visits cattle pens to dig for dung-beetle larvae.

Behaviour: Life histories are likely to revolve around burrows, which are dug slowly and laboriously but which retain lasting importance as key landmarks and refuges. As many as four animals have been taken from a burrow but these were thought to be a family. Animals are normally seen singly out in the open. Most births occur during the rainy season (August–March). Litters of up to four young have been recorded.

Adaptations: The slender, long-legged build of Selous's mongoose suggests that rapid digging ability is of less importance than speedy escape. An abundance of bolt-holes is provided by numerous other burrowing animals which favour the same sandy habitat (notably aardvarks, porcupines and springhares, as well as various other carnivores). Probably a relict species of generalised habits, this mongoose may overcome competitive exclusion by other herpestids (such as the white-tailed mongoose) as a result of its unique strategy of rapid flight above ground and ready refuge underground.

Status: Widely distributed and favoured by current pastoral economy. It is vulnerable to dogs. Not endangered. (IUCN status: not listed.)

Yellow mongoose *Cynictis penicillata*

Other names: Fr. *Mangouste fauve*. Ger. *Fuchsmanguste*.
Measurements: HB 25–40cm. T 18–30cm. W 440–800g.
Recognition: A small, alert mongoose with dainty, rather weak-looking limbs and a sharply tapered face, with forward-facing eyes over a short muzzle. The tail is bushy, usually with a tapered white tip. In the southern part of its range it is very yellow, whereas in the north it is grey. The coat is dense and woolly and usually conceals the long, lithe form of the body. Animals frequently sun-bathe for an hour or more in the early morning, especially in winter.

Distribution: S Africa, Karoo, Cape and Kalahari to S Angola.

Habitat: Favours open sandy areas, often valley bottoms, pans or clearings within more heavily overgrown or wooded country. The warren complexes are often of great age and their slight elevation may be the result of sustained excavation over long periods. Often shared with ground squirrels and suricates (which also dig), warrens can have over 80 entrance holes.

Food: Invertebrates, especially beetles, their larvae and harvester termites. Food preferences vary with locality and from season to season so that rodents or other vertebrates may be important in certain areas. Fruits may be taken *in extremis*. Concerted attacks on snakes may culminate in feeding but have the character of attack against a potential predator because most foods are found and dispached by individual foragers.

Behaviour: Markedly hierarchical packs numbering up to 50 animals are dominated by a breeding pair. Social structure is diffuse in that the lowest ranking members are forced to spend most of their time away from the pack or on its margins. Such 'hangers on' are often elderly or infirm animals. Up to five young are born in the burrow between October and March. They join their older siblings for their first excursions at 2 months and are adult-sized by 10 months. As with other social mongooses the dominant ♀ provides the reproductive continuity in a pack and all members help to raise her young. However, it is the dominant ♂ who is the central beacon and it is his activity and individual scent that defines the pack's identity. The most energetic individual in the pack, he marks the boundaries of the territory and the body of every pack member. He is also the principal digger of holes.

Status: Widespread and common. Not endangered. (IUCN status: not listed.)

Suricate (Meerkat) *Suricata suricata*

Other names: Fr. *Suricate*. Ger. *Scharrtier*.

Measurements: HB 24.5–31cm. T 19–24cm. W 620–970g.

Recognition: An ochre-grey mongoose with a rotund body, muscular, well-clawed forearms, a round head and a tubular muzzle. The tail is thinly haired, tapered and shorter than the body. The eyes are surrounded by 'masks' of black skin and fur, thrown into strong contrast by white brows and cheeks. The large snout-nose is also black and conspicuous. The upperparts are well furred and the rump is banded with about eight stripes. By contrast the greyish skin of the abdomen shows through the sparse white fur of the underside. The pale underside is prominently displayed when the animal stands upright on its hindlegs. In order to help regulate its body temperature the suricate often sprawls on its belly on damp ground or warm rocks, stands up with belly forwards, or lolls on its back in the morning sun.

Subspecies: *S. s. suricata* (South Africa and Kalahari), *S. s. marjoriae* (Namib Desert).

Distribution: South Africa, Namib Desert and Botswana in the Kalahari, Karoo and Highveld, in open, periodically cold upland country.

Habitat: Kalahari *Acacia* bush, Karoo scrub and Highveld rangelands. Suricates favour dry, open, often stony, country with short or sparse woody growth, mainly short grasses and extensive open pans or 'vloere'. They are commonest in rangeland grazed by large herds of wild or domestic stock. Their warrens are most frequently dug in hard, compacted soil close to water-holes or pans in areas of high ungulate concentrations. Five or six warrens, sometimes of very long standing, form clusters in favoured areas and may be shared with ground squirrels which also extend them. Clusters lie within the territory of a single territorial suricate pack which rotates its tenancy of the warrens. Warrens vary in size and extent, the largest having up to 90 entry holes, the smallest less than 10. They may have up to three depth levels with the deepest 3m below the surface. Suricates usually stay within easy reach of a warren. All nights, and part of the coldest winter days and hottest summer days, are spent in their shelter.

Food: Mainly insects associated with grassland and large herbivore herds: harvester termites, larvae and pupae of dung beetles, flies, butterflies and moths. Insect-predators, such as spiders and scorpions, are taken incidentally, as are mice and reptiles. Foraging is individual but carried out in close formation. Suricates are very thorough and different foraging patches are visited every day. When food resources in the vicinity of a warren have been exhausted, the pack decamps to another warren. In this way an irregular circuit of warrens is maintained. In dry weather tsamma melons, succulents, tubers or fruits may be chewed, probably for the moisture they contain.

Behaviour: Packs of about 10 (up to 30) animals may include several breeding pairs. Aggression is seldom obvious (although adults may squabble over food). No consistant hierarchies have been observed within an established group but both ♀♀ and ♂♂ occasionally change packs (the latter not without conflict). ♂♂ are the principal markers of territories, using anal glands, and all pack members fiercely threaten and attack trespassing neighbours.

Up to five young are born, after an 11-week gestation, in a grass-lined chamber in the warren. Breeding can be continuous but most births occur in the warmer, wetter months (October–April). Young become largely independent at 10 weeks and reach adult size by about 6 months.

The main contact call is a soft murmur. Only infants chirp and trill. Scolding clucks or cheeps signify alarm, as does a sharp bark. A growling bark is uttered in threat.

Adaptations: Living in very exposed and relatively cool habitats, suricates avoid predators (mainly birds of prey) by staying close to their warrens and being highly alert. Smaller terrestrial predators are threatened *en masse* by all animals fluffing up their coats, snapping and spitting at once. The animals also all jump up and down, giving the illusion of advance. Sun-bathing, group-nesting and retreat into warrens are all strategies to help maintain viable body temperatures.

Status: The decline of large herbivores and the spread of cultivation, rabies control, dogs and diseases have been the causes of local decline. Overall, not endangered. (IUCN status: not listed.)

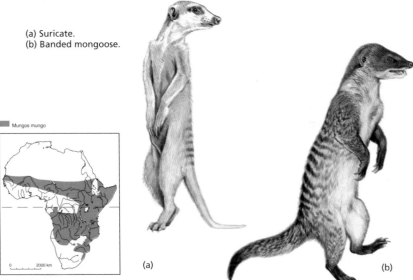

(a) Suricate.
(b) Banded mongoose.

Mungos mungo

0   2000 km

(a)

(b)

Banded mongoose *Mungos mungo*

Other names: Fr. *Mangue rayée*. Ger. *Zebramanguste*. Swah. *Nkuchiro*.

Measurements: HB 30–45cm. T 15–30cm. W 1.5–2.25kg.

Recognition: A chunky, coarse-haired mongoose with short, muscular, well-clawed legs. It has a prominently banded rump, grizzled upperparts, darker limbs and muzzle, and a pale, thinly haired underside. Colour and size varies such that animals are large and dark in moist habitats and small and pale in drier habitats. It is strictly diurnal.

Subspecies: Twenty subspecies have been described but these are in need of revision. Four distinctive regional types can be distinguished: *M. m. mungo* (W Africa), *M. m. zebra* (Horn of Africa), *M. m. taenianotus* (South Africa), *M. m. colonus* (E Africa).

Distribution: Woodlands, savannahs and grasslands of E and central Africa. Also in a broad belt between the Sahara desert and rainforests (where they have been successful colonists of cultivation and large-scale clearances).

Habitat: Various habitats ranging from forest/cultivation mosaics to arid *Acacia* scrub and open, short grasslands. They are closely associated with termitaries (which are readily modified into burrows or warrens.

Food: Termites and beetle larvae (especially in rangelands); cryptic litter fauna in more forested areas, supplemented by small vertebrates. Banded mongooses forage in a loose formation, maintaining contact by frequent chirps, twitters or churrs.

Behaviour: Banded mongooses live in packs that can reach about 40 members before dividing into smaller groups with an average of between 15 and 20 members. Packs typically include three or four breeding ♀♀ and a dominant ♂. The hierarchy appears to be based more on age, size and individual assertiveness than on sex. Packs range over exclusive territories of up to 130ha but neighbouring groups compete for refuge termitaries close to their shared boundaries. Pack membership is stable but young ♂♂ may emigrate and splits are normal when numbers increase. When newborn young are in a den any lactating ♀ will suckle them. Pack members are reluctant to leave the warren *en masse* so that foraging trips by subgroups tend to be short. Up to four young are born after a 2-month gestation. Adults will play with young.

Adaptations: Anal-gland scent-marking is very frequent, especially among high-ranking ♂♂. Landmarks in the territory (stones, stumps, termitaries, etc.) are marked daily. Every member of the group is also marked, mainly on the rump. When presented to another mongoose the striped area elicits a strong marking response, especially during periods of excitement (e.g. encounters, arrivals, departures). All pack members therefore share a strong communal odour. Marking is most intense when the writhing pack of snapping, snarling animals is threatening a medium-sized to small predator.

Status: Not endangered. (IUCN status: not listed.)

Gambian mongoose.

Gambian mongoose *Mungos gambianus*

Other names: Fr. *Mangue de Gambie*. Ger. *Gambiamanguste*.

Measurements: HB est. 33–36cm. T est. 18–22cm. W est. 1–2kg.

Recognition: A compact, coarse-haired mongoose with plain grey upperparts, ochraceous underparts and dark outer surfaces to the limbs. The white chest is separated from the grey nape by a bold black stripe on the side of the neck. The tail is bushy and tapered. The forefeet are well-clawed.

Habitat: Moist savannahs, forest/cultivation mosaics, grasslands and woodlands from Senegal to the R. Niger. This diurnal colonial species lives in packs of up to 25 animals.

Food: Invertebrates with some vertebrates. The Gambian mongoose twitters continuously while foraging in long grass.

Status: Little known, but apparently widespread and common.

Cusimanses *Crossarchus*

Cusimanse	*Crossarchus obscurus*
Flat-headed cusimanse	*Crossarchus platycephalus*
Alexander's cusimanse	*Crossarchus alexandri*
Ansorge's cusimanse	*Crossarchus ansorgei*

Recognition: Dark, shaggy mongooses with a snout-like nose and a tubular muzzle. The claws of the forefeet are very well developed. The face and limbs have very short, tight fur but the body appears to be fat due to a dense underfur overlain by darker guard hairs.

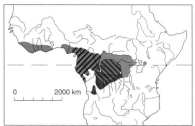

- Crossarchus obscurus
- Crossarchus (o?) platycephalus
- Crossarchus ansorgei
- Crossarchus alexandri

0   2000 km

Common cusimanse (*Crossarchus obscurus*).

Genealogy: Cusimanses have radiated into three (possibly four) distinct regional species. The most generalised of these, Ansorge's cusimanse, bears some resemblance to the Gambian mongoose. It occupies drier forest types in the south of the R. Zaïre basin and has a short, blunt muzzle. The most specialised species with the longest muzzle is Alexander's cusimanse, which also inhabits the Zaïre basin but is commonest north of the river. In many respects Alexander's cusimanse resembles the Liberian mongoose and the two probably share a common ancestry.

Geography: Strictly equatorial and, for the most part, lowland rainforest species.

Ecology: Specialists in feeding on the cryptic fauna of the forest floor and in rotting logs, both on invertebrates and vertebrates. Beetle larvae, snails and earthworms are prominent in the diets of several species. Fruits and mushrooms are only eaten by some species.

Natural history: Cusimanses are diurnal, social mongooses that form family parties numbering up to 20 animals. It is thought that their social structure might resemble that of the banded mongoose. Both sexes perform frequent anal-marking (the ♂ particularly so before mating). Up to four young are born after a 10-week gestation and reach maturity at 9 months. Captive specimens breed three times a year.

Adaptations: The long guard hairs over a warm and relatively waterproof undercoat suggest adaptation to frequent drenchings. The short-furred extremities are also well suited to a muddy existence and slimy foods in that they are easily rubbed or licked clean. Home bases are unlikely to play as important a role in the survival of cusimanses as they do in the case of non-forest, social mongooses (except during the breeding season, when the blind, helpless young must be secure). As yet there are no indications of attachment to burrows, nor have elaborate warrens been recorded. They commonly shelter under or in fallen logs or in dense tangles of lianes. Packs appear to be 'campers' that keep moving in regular circuits over their territory.

Cusimanse *Crossarchus obscurus*

Other names: Fr. *Mangue brune*. Ger. *Dunkelkusimanse*.

Measurements: HB 30–37cm. T 15–25cm. W 1–1.5kg.

Recognition: A tubby, long-nosed, strongly clawed mongoose. The paler underfur of the body is dense and fine, with shaggy, very dark outer fur that gives it a rather unkempt appearance. The legs and tail have shorter fur while the head has a very short, sleek fur that is paler around the mouth. The nape is without whorls. It is noisy when disturbed. Small parties keep in touch with frequent chirps, churrs and twitters.

Habitat: Rainforest zone between Sierra Leone and Nigeria where it inhabits the floor of the rainforest, notably in areas of dense undergrowth. It sleeps in burrows, in or under fallen logs, or in dense tangles.

Food: Insects, earthworms, snails, myriapods, crabs and invertebrates generally; also mice, lizards, frogs, and other vertebrates and their eggs. The cusimanse is said to kill rodents as large as the giant rat co-operatively. Most food is found by excavating leaf litter, dead wood and bark. A very quick and energetic forager, the cusimanse also kills and chews its prey with great rapidity. It sometimes climbs in low trees and bushy tangles.

Status: Common within its range, the cusimanse is vigorously hunted. It is especially vulnerable to hunting with dogs, which may pose a threat in some localities. Overall, not endangered. (IUCN status: not listed.)

Flat-headed cusimanse *Crossarchus platycephalus*

Other names: Fr. *Mangue à crâne plat.* Ger. *Kamerunkusimanse.*
Measurements: HB est. 30–36cm. T est. 15–25cm. W est. 1–1.5kg.
Recognition: A shaggy, forest mongoose, not easily distinguishable from the western cusimanse but with black guard hairs over a thick brown undercoat. It is distinguished by flattening of the skull and by a crest arising between the ears and upper neck. It is usually treated as a subspecies of *C. obscurus*.
Habitat: Tropical rainforest between the R. Cross and R. Zaïre. Very patchily distributed.
Food: Forest floor invertebrates and small vertebrates.
Status: Widely distributed but poorly known.

Alexander's cusimanse *Crossarchus alexandri*

Other names: Fr. *Mangue d'Alexandre.* Ger. *Kongokusimanse.*
Measurements: HB 35–44cm. T 22–32cm. W 1–2kg.
Recognition: A forest mongoose with a continuous crest running from crown to tail, thick, shaggy fur and a long-muzzled, short-furred face. The fur on the nape is conspicuously whorled in a curly cow-lick. This mongoose is a social animal that commonly grunts and twitters while foraging. It is diurnal (but reputed to be at least partly nocturnal in Kivu). There are up to 20 animals in a pack.
Subspecies: There are local variations in adult dimensions. Populations immediately south-west and east of Kisangani are substantially smaller in size. This difference is tentatively recognised as subspecific: *C. a. alexandri* (Zaïre basin), *C. a. minor* (Poke, Kivu and Uganda).
Habitat: Rainforest in Zaïre basin and W Uganda where they favour damp valley bottoms and seasonally flooded swamp forest. A relict population lives between 1,500 and 2,900m on Mt Elgon.
Food: Earthworms, snails, slugs, beetles and other invertebrates; also small vertebrates and fallen fruits. Alexander's cusimanse mainly forages in leaf litter but will climb low trees and logs to dislodge insects, which it catches with great speed.
Status: Mt Elgon population may be threatened by hunting. Overall, not endangered. (IUCN status: not listed.)

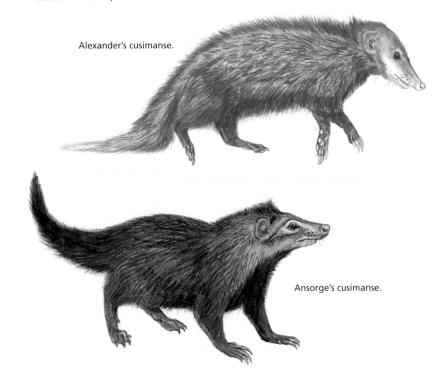

Alexander's cusimanse.

Ansorge's cusimanse.

Ansorge's cusimanse *Crossarchus ansorgei*

Other names: Fr. *Mangue d'Ansorge*. Ger. *Angolakusimanse*.
Measurements: HB est. 32–36cm. T est. 20–22cm. W est. 0.6–1.5kg.
Recognition: A dark, forest mongoose with thick brown fur on the body and dark brown or black limbs and tail. The muzzle is flat-fronted, blunt and shorter than in other cusimanses. The very dark Zaïre-basin form has conspicuous white flashes on the cheeks.
Subspecies: *C. a. ansorgei* (Angola, northern escarpment zone), *C. a. nigricolor* (Zaïre basin, south of the river).
Habitat: Known only from high deciduous rainforest and said to avoid disturbed and cultivated land. Widespread and locally abundant in the central area of the Zaïre basin. In Angola, Ansorge's cusimanse is known only from one specimen.
Food: Insect larvae, eggs and small vertebrates. Ansorge's cusimanses are apparently less omnivorous than Alexander's cusimanse (with which they co-exist) as newly captured animals absolutely refuse to take fruits, mushrooms or berries.
Status: IUCN has recommended a survey of the Angolan population's status and the establishment of a protected area to conserve this and other N Angolan local endemics. Frequently found in Zaïrian bush-meat markets.

Liberian mongoose *Liberiictis kuhni*

Other names: Fr. *Mangue du Liberia*. Ger. *Liberia-kusimanse*.
Measurements: HB 40–45cm. T est. 18–22cm. W 2–2.3kg.
Recognition: A long-clawed, long-nosed, forest mongoose with a thick dark coat and bushy tail. The very undershot mouth parts, chin and chest are off-white. There is a prominent black stripe on the neck. This species has very reduced cheek teeth but long, sharp canines and is reputed to put on a fierce display when trapped.
Habitat: Currently known only from the upper reaches of the Cess R. valley in Liberia and Tai National Park in the Ivory Coast. Its present range (probably much reduced) is thought to be bounded by the valleys of the R. St John and R. Sassandra. It is known only from low-lying areas and stream banks in overgrown, old secondary forest and in deciduous rainforest growing on sandy soils. Lack of earthworms may be the main factor excluding it from areas with hard lateritic soils.
Food: Earthworms and insect larvae are found in streambeds and sump areas by energetic digging with the claws, followed by sniffing and grubbing with the snout. Entire areas of soft soil can be ploughed up in this manner, possibly by family parties. The Liberian mongoose is also reputed to dig larvae out of dead palm trunks and it is a competent climber.
Status: Named in 1958, the first live specimen was caught and photographed in 1989. Rare and localised, this species is seriously threatened with extinction by forest clearance and intensive and uncontrolled hunting for bush meat. It occurs in the Tai National Park. Listed as Threatened (IUCN).

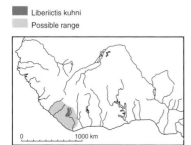

Liberiictis kuhni
Possible range

0   1000 km

Atilax paludinosus

Marsh mongoose *Atilax paludinosus*

Other names: Fr. *Mangouste des marais*. Ger. *Sumfichneumon*. Swah. *Nguchiro wa maji*.
Measurements: HB 46–64cm. T 32–53cm. W 2.2–5.0kg.
Recognition: Large, dark brown mongoose with thick, shaggy fur on the neck, body and tail but short, sleek fur on the fingered hands and feet. The hands have soft, naked palms and sensitive, flexible fingers. The blunt, slightly upturned muzzle is distinctive and the entire tooth row is well developed and powerful.
Subspecies: 16 subspecies have been described and three regional types (with ill-defined borders). These are: *A. p. paludinosus* (South Africa): brown-black. *A. p. pluto* (W Africa): black. *A. p. robustus* (E Africa): grizzled.
Distribution: All well-watered regions of sub-Saharan Africa. Absent from the Somali and Namib-Kalahari arid and semi-arid regions. Marsh mongooses range from sea-level up to about 2,500m.
Habitat: Marsh mongooses inhabit river courses and lake-shore areas in otherwise inhospitable regions. They are more generally distributed in forested or humid areas and are one of a small community of animals living in *Papyrus* swamps. Shelter is required for breeding and may be excavated in termitaries. Alternatively the burrows of aardvarks or other animals may be used (in more extensive marshes a floating nest may be constructed in a dense reed thicket).
Food: Freshwater crabs, snails, mussels, frogs, lungfish (*Protopterus*) and catfish (*Clarias*); insect larvae, reptiles, small mammals, birds and their eggs, fruits.
Behaviour: Marsh mongooses are territorial and forage individually or in pairs with young. During droughts territories appear to be used more intensively and activity (which is predominantly nocturnal) may continue well into the day. Both latrines and scent deposits are used to mark territories and regulate social contacts. Loud bark-growls are uttered as a threat against intruding mongooses or dogs. Moans and purrs (contact?) and bleats (excitement) are also uttered on occasion. Little is known about the reproductive behaviour of this shy and retiring species. However, up to three smaller animals often accompany one or sometimes two adults.
Adaptations: Marsh mongooses use their long, sensitive fingers to find food in turbid water or soft mud. They take their weight on their hindlegs while rapidly sifting back and forth through the water. Large or hard prey, such as crabs and mussels, is broken against a rock by hurling it down from a standing position.
Status: Widespread and common. Not endangered. (IUCN status: not listed.)

White-tailed mongoose *Ichneumia albicauda*

Other names: *Mangouste à queue blanche*. Ger. *Weisschwanzichneumon*. Swah. *Karambago*.
Measurements: HB 47–71cm. T 35–50cm. W 2.0–5.2kg.
Recognition: A slender, long-legged mongoose, delicate and somewhat fox-like, with a thick, silver-tinted coat. It usually has a white tail but coat coloration is very variable. Unlike the dog mongoose (which has four toes), this species has five toes. Very dark morphs with black tails are common in Uganda. It is normally wholly nocturnal.
Subspecies: Twelve subspecies have been named but individual variation obscures regional groupings.

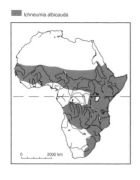

Ichneumia albicauda

Distribution: Widespread in sub-Saharan Africa except for the rainforests and the southwest. In spite of being common in the Somali arid zone it is totally absent from equivalent habitats in the Kalahari and Namibia.

Habitat: This very versatile mongoose flourishes in grassy savannahs, tropical woodlands, grassy clearings in former forest areas, cultivation, suburbia and ranchlands.

Food: Mainly invertebrates, with termites, beetles and their larvae being the preferred foods. Mice, frogs and reptiles are also taken very frequently, but fruits very infrequently.

Behaviour: Although normally solitary, adult ♀♀ are known to share home ranges amicably with adult offspring and as many as nine individuals have been seen foraging together. Localised food and delayed dispersal may explain these temporary aggregations. Home ranges are probably only a few hectares in the richest habitats, but are estimated at up to 8km² on the plains of Kenya (in Serengeti they range from 40 to 123ha). Animals have been seen to scent-mark the boundaries of their ranges and to repel unwelcome intruders with raised, fluffed-out tails and ritualised postures and displays. They utter a loud, fox-like bark and scream very loudly when fighting or attacked by dogs. Up to four young are born in a burrow.

Adaptations: The white-tailed mongoose is a good long-distance walker and trotter but a poor digger. Its dependence on unoccupied burrows or easily modified natural denning sites probably limits it severely in some areas. Its generalised habits are an advantage in unstable ecological conditions but exclude it from areas with large and diverse carnivore populations, where dietary specialists can out compete it (this may explain its absence in SW Africa).

Status: Prone to rapid fluctuations in numbers. Not endangered. (IUCN status: not listed.)

Rhynchogale melleri

Meller's mongoose *Rhynchogale melleri*

Other names: Fr. *Mangouste de Meller*. Ger. *Maushund*.

Measurements: HB 44–50cm. T 28–40cm. W 1.7–3.1kg.

Recognition: A dark, muddy-coloured mongoose with long legs and tail, shaggy, coarsely grizzled fur and a blunt, broad and rather retroussé nose. Meller's mongoose has a somewhat domed forehead and a wide, swollen upper lip, well furred and without a slit up the midline. The tail can be black, white or with lighter underfur beneath black guard hairs. The toes are arranged symmetrically in pairs (fifth toes are vestigial). A distinctive feature is the prominent 'reverse cow-licks' of long fur on each side of the throat. Where these meet the cheek fur there is something of a ruff. The rounded ears are partially concealed by long fur on the temples and forehead.

Distribution: Very rarely seen; patchily distributed over a wide area of SE Africa from sea-level to 1,500m.

Habitat: Moist areas with thick grass and abundant termitaries, particularly in wide, shallow and well-watered valleys. Meller's mongoose appears to require dense cover throughout the year and most records are from the eastern, moister region of Miombo (*Brachystegia*) woodlands. It is rarely seen in areas where fires are extensive and frequent.

Food: Termites, particularly harvester termites (*Hodotermes*) and the larger *Macrotermes*. (These insects only come to the surface after dark to forage for dead grass and the dung of large herbivores.) Meller's mongoose also takes termite-eating snakes and centipedes, and grasshoppers, beetles and frogs have also been recorded. Fallen fruits may be locally or seasonally important. Termites can only be taken in small numbers at a time because this mongoose is not a digger. Its foraging range may be limited during the dry season wherever the dry grass provides inadequate cover. The combination of a specialised diet and the need to avoid exposure would seem to confine Meller's mongoose to a rather narrow feeding niche.

Behaviour: Solitary and little-known, this extremely shy and reclusive animal is likely to range over fairly extensive but well-known home ranges. Although it is apparently rather silent, hollow sinuses on the forehead may act as resonators, in which case long-distance contact calls could be of special significance. Up to three young are born in a burrow or rock crevice.

Adaptations: Blunt, broad lips and shaggy fur may be minor adaptations to a termite diet in this species but the blunt teeth suggest a softer, less carnivorous diet than other mongooses. The digestive physiology of Meller's mongoose has not been studied but must be moderately specialised in order to cope with a termite diet (the peculiar cow-lick on the throat may allow biting soldier termites to be scratched away more easily). These minor modifications to the generalised mongoose frame suggest late and marginal adaptation to a niche that is dominated by the aardvark, pangolin, aardwolf and bat-eared fox in drier, more exposed habitats.

Status: Very poorly known. Habitat change and exposure to domestic or feral dogs are possible dangers. Indeterminate. (IUCN status: not listed.)

Four-toed or dog mongooses *Bdeogale*

Bushy-tailed mongoose	*Bdeogale crassicauda*
Sokoke dog mongoose	*Bdeogale omnivora*
Black-legged mongoose	*Bdeogale nigripes*
Jackson's mongoose	*Bdeogale jacksoni*

Recognition: Long-bodied, long-tailed, moderately tall mongooses with rounded ears, a blunt muzzle and very symmetrical four-toed feet. They have a dense, woolly fur and guard hairs of variable length and colour. All have black or dark brown limbs. The bare rhinarium around the nostrils is broad and rounded. There is a shallow groove down the midline of the upper lip. All species have peculiarly straight upper canines with bladed ridges fore and aft. They generally move slowly and deliberately but can lope along at a trot when not foraging and can run fast when chased. They may be active during the day as well as at night, especially during the wet season.

Genealogy: Most closely related to Meller's mongoose, species in this group include the less specialised bushy-tailed mongoose, which lives in drier forests and woodlands, and the more specialised, ant-eating black-legged mongoose, which lives in equatorial moist rainforests. Like other mongooses no species has entirely abandoned omnivory (perhaps because they remain marginal specialists compared to pangolins and elephant shrews).

Their four symmetrical toes have lost versatility in digging and handling food but the more compact feet are better suited to walking and trotting.

Geography: Like Meller's mongoose, dog mongooses appear to originate in the drier forests and woodlands of E Africa where they are associated with valley bottoms and soft soils.

Ecology: In strongly seasonal environments moisture and dense vegetation last longest in valleys. Dog mongooses appear to be more restricted to such valleys in the dry season. In spite of being very common in their preferred habitat, alert, fast-moving animals, such as frogs and birds, are not typical prey. They are very quiet and careful foragers with a preference for larger prey that is vulnerable to a slow, stealthy approach, such as grazing rodents, inactive but larger invertebrates (e.g. caterpillars or spiders), or very small fauna that are both surface-dwellers and abundant (e.g. ants and termites).

Natural history: Dog mongooses are seldom seen, due to their extreme caution and the dense, difficult vegetation that they favour. They are solitary, although temporary family groups may form. Evidence from crowned eagle kills suggests that the bushy-tailed mongoose may be commoner (and more diurnal) in Tanzanian forest areas than is generally supposed. This may also be true of other species.

Adaptations: The blunt, rounded molars of these species are similar to those of Meller's mongoose and imply good ability to grind soft foods and little cutting or slicing ability on tougher, harder items. The dog mongooses have a less restricted diet than Meller's mongoose but are likely to need an extensive year-round range because resources are gathered along a rather narrow, linear habitat and their food, while common, tends to come in small helpings.

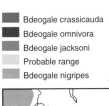

- Bdeogale crassicauda
- Bdeogale omnivora
- Bdeogale jacksoni
- Probable range
- Bdeogale nigripes

Bushy-tailed mongoose *Bdeogale crassicauda*

Other names: Fr. *Mangouste à queue touffue*. Ger. *Buschschwanzichneumon*. Swah. *Kitu*.

Measurements: HB 40–50cm. T 20–30cm. W 1.3–2.1kg.

Recognition: A brown or black mongoose with a bushy, tapered tail, relatively prominent ears and a blunt dog-like muzzle. The teeth are the least rounded, with the sharpest cusps of any *Bdeogale* species. Colouring varies locally but is relatively uniform, with long black guard hairs over a paler, dense underfur. Limbs are black or deep brown.

Subspecies: *B. c. crassicauda* (SE Africa), *B. c. puisa* (E Tanganyika and N Mozambique), *B. c. tenuis* (Zanzibar), *B. c. nigrescens* (Kenya highlands). Note: *puisa* and *nigrescens* are provisional.

Habitat: Coastal thickets, dry forests and well-vegetated valleys in the moister eastern Miombo (*Brachystegia*) woodlands; also dense vegetation around rocky outcrops and escarpments. Distribution is fairly continuous along the coast, but more patchy inland.

Food: Ants and termites; also caterpillars, crickets, grasshoppers, beetles, their larvae and other invertebrates, mostly picked off the ground or vegetation. Snakes and lizards, burrowing toads and rodents are more rarely eaten. Very active prey appears to confuse bushy-tailed mongooses but more acquiescent prey is dealt with deliberately by means of deep, forceful bites.

Status: Widely distributed but nowhere common. They are eaten in some areas and vulnerable to dogs. Not endangered.

Dog-mongoose upper tooth rows.

Bushy-tailed.

Sokoke.

Black-legged.

Sokoke dog mongoose *Bdeogale omnivora*

Other names: Fr. *Mangouste de Sokoke*. Ger. *Sokokeichneumon*. Swah. *Kitu (ya) Sokoke*.

Measurements: HB 34–45cm. T 18–24cm. W est. 0.7–1.6kg.

Recognition: A small mongoose with a pale cream-coloured body and dark brown limbs and tail. There are longer, black-tipped guard hairs in the tail, on the rump and more sparsely on the back. Head and shoulders are palest, almost white. Teeth are distinctive (oval and very wide with an enlarged last molar) This species is predominantly nocturnal.

Habitat: Only known with certainty from coastal forests between the R. Galana and Mombasa. However, it could possibly occur as far north as the R. Juba in Somalia. The lowlands immediately below the Usambara Mts are inhabited by the bushy-tailed mongoose. If supposed sightings of the Sokoke mongoose in the Usambara Mts are confirmed there should be a sharp altitude boundary between the two forms.

The Sokoke forest consists of very old Miombo (*Brachystegia*) woodland growing on white marine sands. The animals shelter in small riverine patches of evergreen thicket but forage more widely. They range through a mosaic of forest, savannah and cultivation.

Food: The first specimens collected contained insects, birds and fruits (hence the name *Bdeogale omnivora*).

Status: Only 4,332ha of Sokoke forest are nominally protected (illegal pit-sawing continues there). Cleared forest can even revert to sterile sand in this area. Hunting with dogs is widespread. Highly endangered with extinction. A captive breeding programme has been suggested.

Black-legged mongoose.

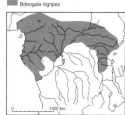

Bdeogale nigripes

Black-legged mongoose *Bdeogale nigripes*

Other names: Fr. *Mangouste à pattes noires*. Ger. *Schwarzfuss ichneumon*.
Measurements: HB 55–65cm. T 35–40cm W est. 2–3.5kg.
Recognition: A large pale mongoose with black limbs and a white tail (face and rump are also white in some individuals). The tail is long but only moderately bushy. Fur on the body is dense and thick but relatively short. Shoulders may be grey or show an upward extension of the black or sepia forelimb colour. Molars are small and rounded while the upper canines are particularly straight and long, with sharp-bladed ridges fore and aft. Although the precise function of the canines is not known, they are evidently capable of delivering a deep cutting stab.
Habitat: Lowland rainforests between the R. Cross in Nigeria to the Western Rift Valley. Within this extensive range it is localised but nowhere very common. It is apparently absent from low-lying areas south of the R. Zaïre.
Food: Mainly ants, notably army ants (*Dorylus* and *Myrmecaria*), and other insects; also a variety of invertebrates, including snails and crabs. Vertebrates, including rodents and frogs, have been recorded. Fallen fruits are taken occasionally.
Status: Widely distributed but poorly known. Not endangered.

Jackson's mongoose *Bdeogale jacksoni*

Other names: Fr. *Mangouste de Jackson*. Ger. *Jackson ichneumon*.
Measurements: HB 52–57cm. T 27–36cm. W 2–3kg.
Recognition: Often regarded as a montane isolate of the black-legged mongoose, this species is distinguished by its much longer fur, especially on the tail, and very yellowish tints on the neck and throat. Young but breeding animals may be well below average adult size. It is a mainly nocturnal and crepuscular species.
Habitat: Montane forests and bamboo zones on the Kenya mountains; also recorded from lowland forest immediately south of Mt Elgon.
Food: Analysis of about 40 boluses revealed that 40% (by volume) of the adult diet consists of insects, mostly army ants of the genus *Anona*; remains of caterpillars, beetles, millepedes, snails, lizards and snake eggs were also found. About 80% of the juvenile's diet is rodents (compared with over 5% in adults), with the rest mostly lizards, beetles and birds. Coping with well-defended columns of army ants may therefore depend on maturity and learning, which suggests that adaptation to this diet is relatively recent. This is also likely to apply to other *Bdeogale* species.
Status: The very limited range, local rarity and low density of this rare species suggests that it is very vulnerable. Some of its range is in currently well-protected areas.

HYAENIDS HYAENIDAE

Striped hyaena	*Hyaena hyaena*
Brown hyaena	*Hyaena brunnea*
Spotted hyaena	*Crocuta crocuta*
Aardwolf	*Proteles cristata*

Recognition: Hyaenids are long-legged, long-necked carnivores with large eyes and ears and a blunt muzzle. They have a shaggy, striped or spotted coat and a short, hairy tail. The feet are large, with five heavily padded toes. Shoulders are higher than the hindquarters.

Genealogy: The earliest hyaenids emerged from a civet-like viverrid stock over 25 million years ago in Africa or Eurasia. They possibly began as an Old World parallel to the earlier emergence of canids in America. In both cases short-legged woodland or forest animals adapted to more open country and to more alert, mobile prey or more dispersed food. Canids have remained the pre-eminent open-country coursers and competition with them probably forced early hyaenids into more specialised niches. The first likely fossil hyaenids (still very civet-like) date from about 25 million years ago. The earliest bone-crushers to appear as fossils are aged at about 10 million years (which would be well after the aardwolf lineage's divergence). Of living hyaenas the spotted hyaena represents the relatively small survivor (some were as big as bears) of a diverse, very successful and advanced carnivore/scavenger that ranged from Europe to Indonesia. The striped hyaena is more conservative but both spotted and striped species are recognisable in their modern forms in the fossil record of 7 million years ago. The brown hyaena is an ancient southern isolate (the intervening woodlands would appear to have remained sufficiently dense and inimical to both hyaenas as to present a permanent barrier). Fossil hyaena dung (coprolites) and calcium nodules in some African plains habitats are so numerous as to suggest that a high proportion of all mammal bones passed through the hyaena's digestive system in the past.

Geography: Once widespread in Eurasia and Africa, hyaenids are now reduced to four rapidly declining species one of which just survives outside Africa. No species occurs in forest and they are very rare in well-wooded country.

Ecology: Hyaenids require a consistent, year-round supply of prey (carrion or, in the case of the aardwolf, harvester termites) in their relatively open environments. Large anal glands exude two distinct scent marks (one long lasting and the other ephemeral). These serve as long-term territorial 'keep-out' markers or as short-term 'overlap-avoidance' markers.

Natural history: Hyaenids have complex social relationships in which use of the home range and contacts with others are regulated by scent signals, loud calls and elaborate behaviour.

Adaptations: Animals that have long legs also tend to evolve long necks, if only to reach the ground without kneeling. Gaits are strongly influenced by this extension and sloping hindquarters develop mainly because of the need for very tall spinal processes at the shoulder (the main pivot for all gaits, especially the gallop).

It has been suggested that the aardwolf is a mimic of the striped hyaena but differences in size, colour, gait and general demeanour mean that the two species are hard to confuse in the field. Their resemblances are due to the retention of similar features from an ancient common ancestry. Crests are devices for increasing apparent size and are common to many mammals. Striping of the legs may be associated with ritualised fighting and display postures that are common to both species.

The principal distinctions between hyaenas and aardwolves are related to their diets, dentitions and digestions. Hyaena skulls are short, deep and wide to accommodate bulky chewing and neck muscles. The carnassial teeth are large in all species but the spotted hyaena's are primarily adapted to slice and shear through large bones and thick hides. Carcasses of elephants and other giants would have been a major resource for the much larger Pleistocene spotted hyaenas.

Hyaenids share with civets an unusual digestive physiology and it is possible that an ability to break down complex organic materials, such as bone, chitin and semi-poisonous compounds, was evolved very early on in their common ancestral stock. Today it is the ability to shatter, swallow and digest large mammal bones and teeth (bone is digested in a few hours, teeth take rather longer) that most distinguishes true hyaenas from both aardwolves and all other carnivores. Hyaenas regurgitate matted hair, bits of horn and other indigestible fragments but, unlike many other carnivores, they never regurgitate meat and always carry cadavers in their jaws. Jaws, necks, shoulders and forelegs are adapted for sustained weight-carrying.

Striped hyaena *Hyèna hyaena*

Other names: Fr. *Hyène rayée*. Ger. *Streifenhyane*. Swah. *Fisi*.

Measurements: HB 100–120cm. T 25–35cm. W 25–55kg.

Recognition: A tall, slender hyaena with a long, thick neck, pointed ears, large eyes and a blunt black muzzle with a pointed, dog-like nose. The legs and body are striped while the throat is sometimes all black, sometimes densely banded. The fur is long and shaggy, except on the face and lower limbs, and there is a crest that runs from crown to tail. Measurements indicate that an excited hyaena with a raised crest looks 38% larger than a calm hyaena with a flattened-down one!

Subspecies: No subspecies are recognised due to overall variability (there are 22 synonyms for the striped hyaena).

Distribution: Once distributed from Britain to China, but now found only in N and NE Africa, the Middle East, Turkey, the Caucasus, through Uzbekistan to all India, from sea-level to 3,000m. The most southerly records are from central Tanzania.

Habitat: Arid steppes and subdesert, *Acacia* scrub and dry savannahs, open montane habitats and rocky escarpments. The striped hyaena can tolerate high and very cold climates if they are also dry. Home ranges are very large and individuals leave anal scent marks on boulders or plants along habitually used paths. They lie up in natural caves or in burrows that are preferably dug by other animals but can be self-dug. Dens are used over extended periods while breeding and subadult animals from a previous litter are known to help feed young siblings. Solitary individuals are less attached to a single den.

Food: Omnivorous and opportunistic but primarily adapted to coping with bones and carrion. Single hyaenas are known to kill prey up to the size of an adult donkey but they are seldom fast enough to catch alert, free-living animals. Nonetheless, hares, foxes and rodents may be stalked or snapped up. Various well-protected vertebrates, such as tortoises, are easily killed and eaten, and invertebrates, including grasshoppers and termites, are taken. Palm dates, heglig (*Balanites*) and other fruits, including cucurbits (which may be taken primarily for the moisture they contain) are also eaten and, in some areas, scraps from garbage dumps make up the main diet.

Behaviour: Striped hyaena behaviour differs according to whether or not the spotted hyaena is present. Where the two species co-exist the striped hyaena is quieter, more retiring and perhaps more solitary and cryptic with regard to dens and raising young. Mature adults of both sexes are intolerant of other members of their own sex. The very protracted dependence of offspring on their mother or parents is partly due to their need to learn foraging routines appropriate to the locality. Adult tolerance declines as the young grow up and appeasement displays therefore become more conspicuous. Averting the

head, grimacing, eye-rolling and salivating are all rather dog-like gestures of subordination. A bristling mane, extended neck and nipping lunges are signs of dominance. Meetings between neighbours are accompanied by maximum fluffing out of fur and crests and attempts at mutual intimidation. The anal glands are everted and there are ritualised fights in which the antagonists aim at the sides of each other's thick-skinned necks with 'incisor-nips' made with half-clenched jaws. Such fights, intended to inhibit bone-cracking bites, are often conducted on bent knees, which would appear to keep the slender legs out of harm's way.

All social contacts are abbreviated by the need to forage alone over very large ranges (at least 50km^2 in rich habitats, probably many times larger in poor ones).

The loudest call is a rarely heard, cackling howl. Staccato whinnies or cackles signify excitement. Threats begin with a growl, rising to a roar and low, snapping lunge. The juvenile want call is a bleat. The adult stress call is more of a moan and hoarse exclamations, 'aah, aah', are uttered when bitten.

Adaptations: The ability of the striped hyaena to break up and digest dry bones is undoubtedly its major peculiarity. The skull, teeth and neck bones are appropriately massive. By contrast the slender body and limbs look weak and flimsy. This sparse frame seems to be built for maximum economy of energy. The striped hyaena can trot for long periods at 8km/h, moving for 5–8 hours and covering up to 30km in a night, sometimes with very poor nutritional rewards.

Status: Once very abundant, especially on the margins of the Sahara desert, the striped hyaena has declined over most of its range. It has disappeared from some areas but is still widespread. It is vulnerable to poisoning. Overall, Not Endangered(IUCN).

Hyaena hyaena
Hyaena brunnea

0   2000 km

Brown hyaena *Hyaena brunnea*

Other names: Fr. *Hyène brune*. Ger. *Braune hyäne*.
Measurements: HB 110–125cm. T 25–30cm. W 40–55kg.
Recognition: This species resembles a dark, heavily caped striped hyaena but with a vivid cream-coloured throat, dark brown or slate body and shorter black tail. The pale neck fur forms a distinct mane in healthy adults. The head is like that of the striped hyaena but darker.
Subspecies: Five named but none recognised.
Distribution: Originally most of Africa south of the R. Cunene and R. Zambezi. Now exterminated over wide areas.

Habitat: Currently limited to the Kalahari Desert, the Namibian coastal littoral and less inhabited borderlands in South Africa and Zimbabwe. Formerly the brown hyaena ranged throughout the Highveld and most Cape and south-western arid habitats. In spite of its very large territories, the brown hyaena uses its range so intensively and leaves anal scent marks so systematically that it has been calculated that a strange, intruding hyaena will encounter a scent mark within 250m of entering another 'clan's' territory. In the course of a year the members of a single clan may deposit as many as 145,000 scented tokens of their presence. In addition to anal-gland deposits, the brown hyaena tends to leave dung in 'latrines' close to visual land-marks and close to clan boundaries. The deposits not only demarcate land and identify clan members, but progressive deterioration of the odour allows individual foragers to assess how long the deposit has been there, to avoid recently foraged areas and thus to concentrate their energies on less recently foraged areas.

Food: Primarily carrion, especially during the dry season or when nomadic herds pass through. Surplus food may be hidden nearby or carried back to the den, which may be many kilometres away. The brown hyaena also feeds on small mammals, invertebrates and fruits when larger carcasses are not to be found. Beach-combing for dead sea-lions, whales and ocean debris is common along the Namibian seashore. Although larger numbers may visit, no more than three hyaenas are commonly seen on one carcass at a time. The brown hyaena forages over distances of 1–54km in a night. It is almost entirely nocturnal.

Behaviour: Home ranges are occupied by a small number of closely related adults (up to three ♂♂ and five ♀♀), their immediate young and some subadults, numbering up to 14 in total. A consistent supply of carcasses encourages slower dispersal. The range varies from about 240 to 480km² and is defended against strange hyaenas. Resources tend to be sparsest in the larger ranges. Vocalisations, visual displays and dominance/subordination behaviour closely resemble those of the striped hyaena.

Mating is opportunistic; ♀♀ have a brief oestrus attracting bouts of multiple copulations, sometimes with several ♂♂. After a 3-month gestation, up to three young are born blind and deaf. The ♀ secludes herself for the birth and first few months.

Adaptations: Home ranges are so large and resources commonly so dispersed that single foraging trips may last several days. For lactating ♀♀ this puts the young at risk and it is common for ♀♀ to rejoin a central clan den a few months after giving birth. Here lactating ♀♀ suckle any cub and all ages and sexes bring home food and share it. Young may suck for up to 15 months and do not mature until they are 2½ years old. Communal clan dens may represent the response of solitary foragers to the problems of slow maturation in an environment in which resources are very thinly and widely scattered.

Status: In spite of being represented in several national parks the overall range of this species continues to decline. It currently occupies about a half of its original range. The brown hyaena is especially susceptible to trapping and poisoning. Rare and Vulnerable (IUCN).

Spotted hyaena *Crocuta crocuta*

Other names: Fr. *Hyène tachetée*. Ger. *Flecken hyäne*. Swah. *Nyangao* (also *Fisi*).
Measurements: HB 100–180cm. T 25–36cm. W 40–90kg.
Recognition: A powerfully built, dog-like hyaena with a black muzzle and black tip to the short, brushy tail. The body colour may be various tints of brown and slate in young animals but is pale tawny in old animals. Neck, body and legs are splattered with irregular spots and blotches which become fainter with age. ♀♀ average 12% heavier than ♂♂. The species' best-known peculiarity is 'hermaphroditic' sex organs. The ♀ clitoris mimics the ♂ penis, can elongate and has a foreskin. Paired swellings in the position of the scrotum consist of non-functional fibrous tissue.

The spotted hyaena is more often heard than seen. Its loud, long-distance call, a repetitive and reverberating hoot 'whoo-up', carries for up to 5km (and is most frequently made while walking with the head hanging). Less frequent is its famous 'laugh', a shrill, social-appeasement call that sounds like a maniacal human giggle. Its sloping back and long, thick neck are highly characteristic. A raised tail signifies aggression and the plate overleaf illustrates a large ♀ (witnessed defending her cub).

Subspecies: Great individual variation invalidates all of nearly 30 synonyms.

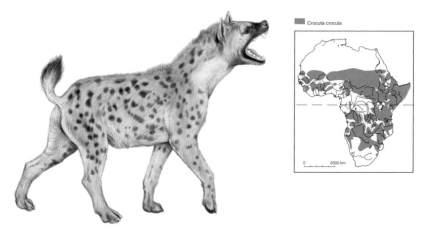

Crocuta crocuta

0 2000 km

Distribution: Formerly most of non-forested Africa (but always rare in densely wooded country). Although present in N Africa for at least 6 million years, it was not recorded in historic times. Similar early extinctions eliminated *Crocuta* populations across Eurasia. In South Africa the spotted hyaena was trapped and poisoned out of settled areas before this century. Active and rapid eradication is currently in progress over large areas of Africa. This renders any distribution map of rather ephemeral value.

Habitat: Open savannahs, all *Acacia* communities, montane moors and grasslands, various dry steppes and plains with abundant herbivores are preferred. Although the spotted hyaena digs its own burrows, communal dens are often in caves or crevices in rocky country. Large clans circulate among a few communal dens which are used over many generations (some caves may have been used for centuries). Mounds of excavated and trampled earth, radiating paths and an absence of herbivores modify the immediate surroundings to a den. Very large dens are often surrounded by a scatter of scrapes and shelters that are used by peripheral hyaenas.

Food: An opportunistic carnivore and scavenger wherever animal waste, from the feeding of other carnivores or humans, or the vicissitudes of nature, is available. The spotted hyaena is a scavenger in relation to the amount of animal waste available and absorbs a high proportion of it when no easier and fresher alternative is available (e.g. newborn calves during the calving season). Hyaena kills tend to correspond with the vulnerability of prey species rather than their relative abundance. Thus, the fast, well-protected and abundant zebra tends to be under-represented in the hyaena's diet whereas the slower, less common waterbuck is more frequently killed. Foods taken range from invertebrates, mudfish, reptiles (such as tortoises) to large mammals. Today, household or town garbage is a major resource.

The spotted hyaena forages singly (especially in low-density areas) or may live and hunt in groups. Distances covered vary from a kilometre or so to 80km and foraging may take up 1 or 2 hours to a greater part of the night. Some social hunts begin as a group activity, with a direct target, but many build momentum on the initiative of a single hunter. Hunts and kills attract followers, as does the noisy gorging at a carcass. Sometimes an entire clan of over 50 adults may feed together and, with every animal competing to swallow as much food as fast as possible, the carcass does not take long to demolish. Carrion is frequently cached in bushes, scrapes or under water, but not until hunger is sated, which may involve bolting up to 13kg at a go.

Behaviour: Where food is super-abundant a single clan can number over 100 (with a range of 35–80 adults). Territories average about 30km^2 in well-stocked wildlife parks but home ranges are much larger in subdeserts or faunally impoverished areas. Clans build up around a hierarchy of related ♀♀ and their offspring. ♂♂ tend to disperse, ♀♀ remain. Adult ♂♂ are essentially peripheral to the clan and only the imperatives of mating (at the hight of oestrus) overcomes the ♂♂'s fear of the larger ♀♀.

Up to four cubs are born after a 4-month gestation. In spite of being temporarily blind, the young are precocious and grow fast. Suckled only by their mother, who very seldom carries food, they are sufficiently large to join in at a kill at about 8 months but continue to suckle until they are 18 months old.

The spotted hyaena utters begging calls (whines and chatters) and growls or screams in a variety of social situations. Hunting clans tend to socialise intensively in the evening before setting off on a hunt or foraging expedition.

Adaptations: ♀ mimicry of ♂ genital organs has been found to derive from testosterone levels that are sometimes higher than in the ♂♂ and begin in the foetus. Testosterone may also fuel their dominant role. ♀ aggression may ensure that lactating mothers have unimpeded access to all types of food, as well as deterring ♂♂ from attacking their cubs. Social relations among spotted hyaenas centre on avoidance or appeasement of the larger, dominant ♀♀. Adult ♂♂ take the first option but younger ♂♂ and ♀♀, which could scarcely survive outside the clan, appease by lifting a leg and proffering their genitalia for inspection. Although pseudo-penises and scrotums may be a by-product of high testosterone levels, they play a part in appeasement or greeting rituals because a display of masculine attributes is a sign of subordination. Unlike other hyaenas, the spotted hyaena keeps its anal sacs closed during greetings lest it send a contradictory, aggressive signal.

The primary adaptation of the spotted hyaena is its massive teeth, which are able to cut through the bones and skin of all contemporary fauna, including elephants and rhinos. As contemporary body sizes are smaller than those of many Pleistocene spotted hyaenas, its body size has probably declined along with its dietary options (which have become more limited due to the extinction of so many mega-herbivores).

Status: Decline is accelerating in all areas due to increase in livestock and the expansion of farming. The spotted hyaena is frequently regarded as vermin and although still widespread, its long-term future outside wildlife conservation areas is not hopeful.

AARDWOLVES PROTELINAE

Aardwolf	*Proteles cristata*

Represented by a single species, the aardwolf superficially resembles its larger, heavier cousin, the striped hyaena, in having slender limbs, a long neck, stripes and a dorsal crest.

Like hyaenas its primary specialisation is in digestion. Instead of detoxifying a diet of decomposing bodies, it is adapted to digesting noxious harvester termites. These surface-feeding, colonial insects are so well protected that few other termite- or ant-eating animals can overcome the barrage of terpene chemicals squirted at them by the soldiers.

The more generalised common ancestors of hyaenas and aardwolves were likely to have tolerated many toxic and difficult foods (just as civets do today). In the aardwolf lineage cheek teeth were reduced to mere pegs while hyaenas developed vice-like, reinforced jaws capable of cracking bones.

Although the aardwolf can tolerate a proportion of noxious soldier termites it is adept at rapidly lapping up non-soldiers before they go underground. Walking up to 10km, feeding for about 6 hours, a single aardwolf is estimated to consume over 0.25 million termites in one night.

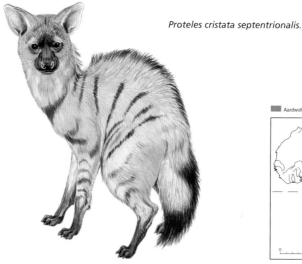

Proteles cristata septentrionalis.

Aardwolf

Aardwolf *Proteles cristata*

Other names: Fr. *Protèle*. Ger. *Erdwolf*. Swah. *Fisi ya nkole*.
Measurements: HB 55–80cm. T 20–30cm. H 40–50cm. W 8–12kg.
Recognition: A slender, cream or tawny animal with narrow, well-spaced stripes and dark brown feet, tail tip and muzzle. A long crest on the neck and back is normally inconspicuous but can stand up and bristle when the animal is alarmed or excited, greatly enlarging its apparent size. The dark skin of the muzzle is without fur and very tough and inflexible, giving the animal a rather fixed expression. Although incisors and canines are well developed, the cheek teeth are mere pegs. The light creamy fur is often stained with local soil colour from the den.

The most conspicuous signs of the presence of the aardwolf are its 'latrines', either uncovered or imperfectly covered by scrapings. Faeces contain termite remains and often include much soil or sand. Scented brown or orange marks are smeared onto bent grass stalks and twigs with the anal glands. These are not conspicuous but are very frequent near 'latrines.'
Subspecies: *P. c. cristatus* (S Africa), *P. c. septentrionalis* (E and NE Africa).
Distribution: S and NE Africa but absent in intervening Miombo (*Brachystegia*) woodlands.

Habitat: Presence is entirely dependent upon two genera of harvester termites (*Trinervitermes* and *Hodotermes*). These termites flourish best in heavily grazed and trampled grasslands and savannahs, especially on sandy plains and plateaus. Although aardwolves frequently use or modify aarvark holes or natural shelters, they can dig their own short burrows in sandy soil.

Food: The availability of the nocturnal *Trinervitermes* and the more diurnal *Hodotermes* may partly determine the times at which aardwolves are active. In temperate S Africa the former termite tends to form the summer diet while the latter is favoured in winter. Small numbers of scarab and tok-tockie beetles, grasshoppers, moths and a few small vertebrates are also eaten. Harvester termites forage for dead grass on the surface in small swarms. Aardwolves locate them by listening for the sound of them cutting up leaves and stems. The insects are lapped up and swallowed with minimal chewing, helped down by copious, somewhat glutinous, saliva. All foraging is solitary and follows an eccentric, zigzag course.

Behaviour: Defended territories vary in extent (1–2km² in habitats with a high density of termite mounds). In S Africa a single territory has been calculated to enclose about 3,000 termite mounds (about 165 million termites). Territories are vigorously defended while conditions are good but less so during periods of shortage (when all animals save energy and spend many hours underground). Territories are saturated with anal scent markings, especially along boundaries, where the holder may paste grass stems every 50m or so. Territorial fights and defensive aggression against jackals (notably near dens in the wet-season breeding period) involve a growling roar and barks, with much chasing and fluffing out of the fur, mane and long dorsal crest. Gestation is variously estimated at 2 and 3 months; young are born in a burrow during the rains. The young, miniatures of the adults, emerge to play above ground at about 6 weeks, at which time they are vulnerable to various medium-sized carnivores. By 4 months they are foraging for termites on their own. A single ♂ and ♀ share a common territory, normally feeding and sleeping apart but both care for the young during their vulnerable period. Both parents may combine to drive off jackals.

Adaptations: Frequently confused with jackals (indeed the Afrikaner name is 'maned jackal'), their overall proportions are those of many generalised but agile small carnivores. Because the very ancient termite-eaters, the aardvark and pangolins, avoid taking large numbers of harvester termites, it would seem that the aardwolf became an extreme dietary specialist at a relatively much later date (there are as yet no relevant fossils).

Status: In spite of nominal protection in most African countries, and recognition of its useful role, aardwolves are often killed for their furs (eight or more pelts are commonly incorporated in Tswana karosses). Dogs represent the greatest threat to their survival in settled and pastoral areas. Easily dazzled, they are frequent victims of vehicles at night.

GENETS AND CIVETS VIVERRIDAE

Genets and civets	Viverrinae
Genets	*Genetta*
Linsangs	*Poiana*
African civet	*Civettictis*
Aquatic genet	*Osbornictis*
African palm civets	Nandininae
African palm civet	*Nandinia*

Recognition: Viverrids are to carnivores what lemurs are to the higher primates. Civets in particular are modern approximations of the carnivores' common ancestral stock. The predominantly arboreal genets have soft fur, retractile claws, a spotted or blotched coat pattern and may be the precursors of the cats. Civets are almost wholly terrestrial; they are larger, coarse-furred animals, with blunt claws fixed in short, dog-like pads.

Genealogy: Arboreal viverrids belonging to the palm civet group are mainly South-East Asian. The genets and civets are common to both Eurasia and Africa. Genet ancestors may have entered Africa some 25 million years ago.

Geography: The viverrid radiation in Africa is mainly tropical, with a bias towards rainforests.

Ecology: Viverrids span most major habitats. The palm civet is exclusively a forest species. Ecological plasticity is evident in the occupation of both forest and non-forest habitats by genets and the civet.

Natural history: Genets, civets and palm civets are solitary foragers but some form short-lived family associations.

Adaptations: Scent is their most fundamental mode of communication and all species employ glandular secretions to regulate contacts and behaviour. The civet's perineal glands are the best known. This species' secretions are so copious and durable that they once provided the perfume trade with a valuable fixative for floral scents.

Facial expressions,
servaline genet.

Genets *Genetta*

True genets	*Genetta (Genetta)*
Common genet	*Genetta genetta* (and allies)
Blotched genet	*Genetta tigrina* (incl. *maculata* and allies)
Miombo genet	*Genetta angolensis*
Servaline genet	*Genetta servalina*
Giant servaline genet	*Genetta victoriae*
"Pseudogenets"	*Genetta (Pseudogenetta)*
Ethiopian genet	*Genetta abyssinica*
Hausa genet	*Genetta thierryi*
"Altergenet"	*Genetta (Paragenetta)*
Johnston's genet	*Genetta johnstoni*

Other names: Fr. *Genette*. Ger. *Ginsterkatze*. Swah. *Kanu*.

Measurements: HB 45–58cm. T 40–48cm. W 1–3.5kg.

Recognition: Slender, long-bodied, cat-like carnivores, described as 'rat-like leopards' in one part of Africa. They have cat-like semi-retractible claws, a long, banded tail, soft fur, large ears and a pointed muzzle. They are spotted or blotched (occasional black morphs are also known). They have anal sacs and civet-like perineal musk glands. Normally silent, they spit, hiss, growl, purr and miaow like cats but also cough, whine and scream. They are mainly nocturnal.

Distribution: Sub-Saharan Africa. (One species extends to Morocco to Tunisia, Spain, SW France, Arabia.)

Habitat: Forests and all wooded habitats, including very thinly bushed valleys in desert.

Food: Omnivorous, with marked specific preferences for either more or less vertebrates, invertebrates or plant matter. Small animals are ambushed or caught after a short stalk or fast pounce. Genets are fast but clumsy killers, relying on speed and agility and cryptic colouring to catch food (and also to evade larger predators).

Behaviour: Solitary animals except during brief courtship and for about 6 months while the young are with the mother. Ranges of ♂♂ are up to 5km^2, those of ♀♀ are much smaller. ♂ ranges overlap those of several ♀♀, and also other ♂♂. They have a well-developed spatial sense (artificially displaced genets have been recorded homing over 35km). Latrines and marking sites are used by more than one animal, with ♂♂ mainly using their urine and ♀♀ their perineal glands.

Up to five young are born, blind and helpless, in a hollow or a vine tangle after about 70 days' gestation. They become independent after about 6 months and are mature and able to breed at about 1 year.

Adaptations: Genets bear an extraordinary resemblance to the totally unrelated spotted marsupial, *Dasyurus* and to the cacomistle, *Bassariscus* (a racoon). They also resemble the Madagascan *Fossa* and Oriental linsang, *Prionodon*, in spite of their common ancestry being more than 20 million years old. This suggests that the requirements for success in the arboreal niche is as exacting for small carnivores as it is for some primates (which are also convergent on different continents).

Status: Several species are extremely rare and localised. Most are widespread and successful.

Genetta genetta

0   2000 km

Common genet *Genetta genetta* (and allies)

Other names: Fr. *Genette commune*. Ger. *Gemeine Ginsterkatze*. Swah. *Kanu*.

Measurements: HB 40–55cm. T 40–51cm. W 1.3–2.25kg.

Recognition: A genet with rather coarse fur and a short crest of longer fur along the spine. The ringed tail is nearly as long as the body and strongly tapered. The dark brown spots are small, numerous and linear on a sandy background. Hindfeet are pale (some regional types have black heels, others are pale).

Subspecies: Over 30 have been described. Regional groups are provisional. *G. g. genetta* (Mediterranean), *G. g. senegalensis* (W Africa), *G. g. felina* (S Africa), *G. g. dongolana* (E Africa). The common genet is the only genet to occur outside Africa and is also the most widely distributed species within Africa.

Habitat: A wide range of drier habitats, from seasonally arid woodlands to sparsely bushed near-desert, especially rocky, hilly country where they are able to live without water.

Food: Varies by region, with a different spectrum of local vertebrates (rodents, birds or reptiles), invertebrates and fruits.

Status: The European population originated from Morocco (possibly as a result of ancient introduction by people). Not endangered. (IUCN status: not listed.)

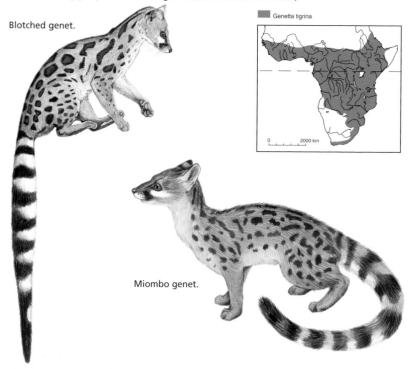

Blotched genet.

Genetta tigrina

0   2000 km

Miombo genet.

Blotched genet *Genetta tigrina* (incl. *maculata* and allies)

Other names: Fr. *Genette tigrine*. Ger. *Grossfleck Ginsterkatze*. Swah. *Kanu*.

Measurements: HB 40–55cm. T 40–54cm. W 1.2–3.1kg.

Recognition: A soft-furred, short-legged genet without a well-defined dorsal crest. The ears are broad based and slightly rounded. The tail is soft furred and has a black or smudged tip. The colours and patterns of the blotchy coat are extremely variable. Furthermore, differently coloured morphs (red or grey-black) co-exist in the same area. This has led to a great proliferation of species and subspecies names.

Subspecies: (in need of revision) *G. t. maculata*, *G. t. poensis*, *G. t. pardina*, *G. t. bini*, *G. t.aequatorialis*, *G. t. stuhlmanni*, *G. t. mossambica*, *G. t. schraderi*. (At least 20 other races named.)

Habitat: Most of sub-Saharan Africa except the Horn of Africa and SW Africa. Rainforest, riverine vegetation, secondary growth, moist woodlands and all moist forest and woodland mosaics. Blotched genets are well adapted to cultivation and suburbia; also to reedbeds, swamp forest and grassy savannahs.

Food: In comparison with the common genet, blotched genets take fewer vertebrates, more invertebrates and more fruits. However, both these species rely on rodents as their main staple.

Status: Not endangered. (IUCN status: not listed.)

Miombo genet *Genetta angolensis*

Other names: Fr. *Genette d'Angola*. Ger. *Bürstenginsterkatze*.
Measurements: HB 44–48cm. T 38–43cm. W 1.3–2kg.
Recognition: A dark grey or brownish genet with a dorsal crest and irregularly spotted coat. The underside of the paws and the feet are blackish. The tail is darker ochre above and white below, with about eight black rings. The face is dark with strongly contrasting white flashes below the eyes and muzzle. Wholly or partly melanistic morphs known.
Habitat: Miombo (*Brachystegia*) woodlands from Angola to Tanzania, with a preference for the moister woodlands, riverine vegetation and forest galleries.
Food: Rodents are likely to be the main staple; also invertebrates.
Status: Widely distributed but little known.

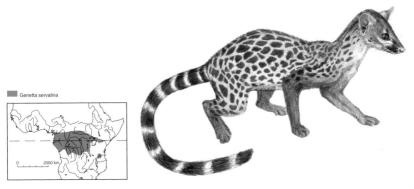

Genetta servalina

Servaline genet *Genetta servalina*

Other names: Fr. *Genette servaline*. Ger. *Waldginsterkatze*. Swah. *Kanu*.
Measurements: HB 41–50cm. T 35–44cm. W 1–2kg.
Recognition: A small, slender genet with a narrow face, rather long legs, very soft, dense, short fur and no dorsal crest (a short crest on the back of the neck may sometimes extend to the shoulders). Black spots are densely distributed over the body and limbs on a tan or orangey background. The tail is not tapered and its 8–12 black bands are often broader than the pale ones. It is exclusively nocturnal.
Subspecies: *G. s. servalina* (R. Zaïre, R. Ogooué basins, main lowland forest block), *G. s. cristata* (R. Cross to R. Sanaga, west of R. Cross?), *G. s. bettoni* (montane E and central Africa), *G. s. lowei* (Uzungwa Mts).
Habitat: A rainforest species, apparently absent from the Upper Guinea forests. Servaline genets occur in both lowland and montane forests. They are often encountered on the ground.
Food: Ground-dwelling rodents, tree hyraxes, birds, insects and fruits have been recorded. It is possible that birds are located from the ground and then stalked while sleeping in the trees but other foods suggest ground-foraging.
Status: Widely distributed but poorly known (*G. s. lowei* is known from one incomplete specimen).

Giant servaline genet
Genetta victoriae

Genetta angolensis
Genetta victoriae
Genetta abyssinica
Genetta thierryi

Other names: Fr. *Genette géante*. Ger. *Riesenginsterkatze*.
Measurements: HB 55–60cm. T 45–50cm. W 2.5–3.5kg.
Recognition: A large genet with dense soft fur, long legs and a fine, narrow muzzle. Black spots are very numerous (but subject to individual variation) and well distributed over the tan upperparts, off-white neck and undersides and sepia lower limbs. The tail is boldly banded in black and white and tapers near the tip.
Habitat: NE Zaïre and extreme W Uganda. Very patchily distributed in rainforests at low and medium altitudes.
Food: Not known from the wild but a captive specimen ate rats and bananas (mixed with milk and rice).
Status: It is likely to occur in Maiko National Park but while the reasons for its discontinuous distribution remain unknown it should be considered at risk.

Ethiopian genet *Genetta abyssinica*

Other names: Fr. *Genette d'Ethiopie*. Ger. *Streifenginsterkatze*.
Measurements: HB 40–50cm. T 40–45cm. W 1.3–2kg.
Recognition: A pale sandy genet with five black stripes running down the back. The fur is short, fairly coarse and of a uniform length. The black-tipped tail has seven or eight relatively narrow black rings. Forefeet are distinguished by the absence of fur between the digit pads and the 'palm'.
Habitat: Eritrea, Somalia and Ethiopia. It has been recorded from the Red Sea coast to the Ethiopian highlands in dry woodlands and may occur in forest but its precise range and preferred habitats are not yet known.
Food: Presumed to resemble other genets. Captive specimens have thrived on a generalised small-carnivore diet.
Status: Unknown (IUCN).

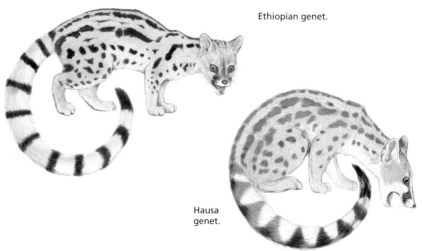

Ethiopian genet.

Hausa genet.

Hausa genet *Genetta thierryi*

Other names: Fr. *Genette de Villiers*. Ger. *Haussa-Ginsterkatze*. Swah. *Kanu*.
Measurements: HB 38–45cm. T 37–45cm. W 1.3–1.5kg.
Recognition: A small tan genet with blotchy spots following linear patterns down the back, often rich reddish orange. There is no crest and spotting is generally sparse on the face and forequarters. The long tail is black tipped, tapered and marked by incomplete dark rings which have a rich orange suffusion near the body but become darker towards the tip.
Subspecies: *G. t. thierryi*, *G. t. villiersi*.
Habitat: Sparsely distributed in drier savannahs from Guinea to Cameroon. Eastern limits uncertain.
Food: Not known.
Status: A rare species, poorly known.

Genetta johnstoni
possible range

Johnston's genet *Genetta johnstoni*

Other names: Fr. *Genette de Johnston.* Ger. *Liberia Ginsterkatze.*
Measurements: HB 40–52cm. T 40–54cm. W est. 1–3kg.
Recognition: A thickly soft-coated genet with large eyes and a fine muzzle. The upperparts are tawny with rows of spots down the flanks and back (which become larger and more regular as they approach the midline). There is a short dorsal crest. The tail is densely furred and has about 16 evenly spaced, black and white bands. This species has a feebler dentition than other genets.
Habitat: Known from rainforest in Liberia and Guinea (but may also occur in W Ivory Coast).
Food: Not recorded but likely to include soft-bodied insects.
Status: Known from only eight museum specimens, the limits of its range and ecological niche remain unknown. Rare (IUCN).

Poiana richardsoni
Poiana leightoni

Central African linsang *Poiana richardsoni*

Other names: Fr. *Poiane centrafricaine.* Ger. *Centrum Afrika-linsang.*
Measurements: HB 33–38cm. T 35–40cm. W 500–700g.
Recognition: This linsang resembles a very slender, small-muzzled, small-eared, long-tailed genet but differs in its dentition and skull. Round, brown spots are scattered over reddish brown upperparts. The spine is marked by a long line of spots or dashes. The off-white underparts are unspotted. The tail, longer than the body, is encircled by 12–14 parallel-sided black rings.
Subspecies: *P. r. richardsoni* (Bioko I., formerly Fernando Po), *P. r. ochracea* (Cameroon to E Zaïre).
Habitat: Rainforests. These nocturnal, highly arboreal linsangs are thought to move every few days, presumably on regular circuits, sleeping in nests during the day and rarely coming to the ground. Their precise habitat needs are unknown.
Food: Arboreal vertebrates, invertebrates and fruits.
Status: Capable of raising two litters a year, each of up to three young, linsangs are nonetheless rarely seen and little known. Sharing features with the Oriental linsang and African genets, they may share a very ancient common ancestry with both lineages. Widely distributed and poorly known.

West African linsang *Poiana leightoni*

Other names: Fr. *Poiane d'Afrique occidentale*. Ger. *West Afrika-linsang*.
Measurements: HB 30–38cm. T 35–40cm. W est. 500–700g.
Recognition: Notable for its very long, soft-furred tail, marked with dark asymmetrical chevrons (not parallel rings), this plush-coated, pale-coloured linsang has small, sometimes irregular spots that are well spaced but a continuous black-brown line runs down the spine. The underside is unspotted and pure white.
Habitat: Only known from rainforest in E Liberia and W Ivory Coast, where it is reputed to live in tree crowns above 30m. Several animals may share a single, globular nest constructed of fresh green material. It is thought that these are made by the linsang and not appropriated from squirrels.
Food: Young birds, insects and plant material, including kola fruits.
Status: Differences between the western and central African relict populations of a conservative viverid are likely to be very ancient. This rare and interesting species shares its small and shrinking range with many other endemic animals and plants. Rare and vulnerable. (IUCN: Status Uncertain.)

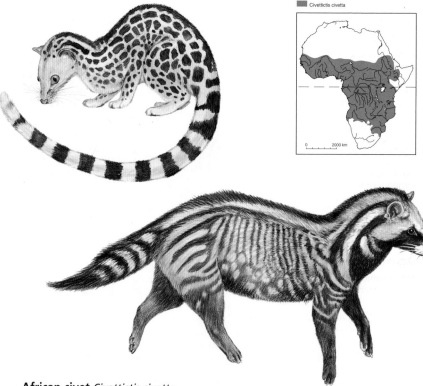

Civettictis civetta

African civet *Civettictis civetta*

Other names: Fr. *Civette d'Afrique*. Ger. *Afrika Zibetkatze*. Swah. *Fungo*.
Measurements: HB 68–95cm. T 40–53cm. W 7–20kg.
Recognition: A shaggy, low-slung, dog-like animal with an ornate pattern of bands and blotches on body and tail, black limbs and a boldly marked face mask with pale forehead, white muzzle and black eye patches. The hair is coarse and loose and a crest extends from forehead to tail tip. The African civet is mainly nocturnal. Its normal gaits are either a slow, tentative, low-headed walk or a more directed, steady trot. It makes very conspicuous dung middens called 'civettries', strongly scented with anal gland secretions. Quite independently, it scents landmarks in territories with large perineal glands. It is normally silent but growls very deeply and coughs explosively if harrassed or cornered by dogs or people.

Subspecies: Eight named. There are some regionally consistent characteristics but no clear boundaries.

Distribution: Sub-Saharan Africa but absent from South Africa (except Transvaal) most of Namibia, Eritrea and drier areas of the Horn.

Habitat: Most abundant in forested or partly forested mosaics, in cultivated and marshy areas. It occurs only in dry, open country where dense cover grows along watercourses, around stone outcrops and in broken gullied land. In spite of its dependence on thick cover, the African civet is most often seen trotting along established roads and pathways.

Food: Omnivorous: vertebrates and plants (mainly roots, shoots and fruits). The African civet is able to eat poisonous fruits, such as *Strychnos*, distasteful insects, such as stink locust (*Zonoceras*), millepedes and dangerous snakes. It is also able to feed irregularly and can fast for up to 2 weeks. Prey encountered during regular circuits is either approached slowly and cautiously or disabled in a sudden, rushing lunge. Vertebrates are bitten deeply, shaken very violently, then dropped or tossed. The civet is known to kill prey up to the size of a hare or mongoose. Large prey is torn into pieces and bolted.

Behaviour: The African civet is a solitary, very intolerant animal except while breeding. It is probably territorial. Up to four young are born after 60–72 days' gestation in a burrow, crevice, termitary or in dense vegetation. The young develop very fast, beginning to take solid food at 1 month and adopting adult behaviour at 5 months. Young normally 'freeze' until detected but hiss and spit when threatened. They make a soft, clucking contact note which persists into adulthood as a three-note 'duff, duff, duff' contact call or ♂ courtship signal. Infantile miaows of distress also resemble adult ♀ oestrus calls.

Adaptations: The copious flow of secretions from the perineal glands was once harvested from captive specimens as 'civetone', a floral-scent fixative. It is smeared on landmarks throughout the home range, especially rocks and stumps at path intersections and on the tree trunks of favourite fruiting trees. This civet circulates regularly over a large home range or territory but does not have regular dens, being essentially a 'camper' that will lie up during the day in any thick vegetation or natural hollow. Frequent and copious scent marks provide a necessary orientation and spacing system. Adult ♂♂ augment civetone and dung signals with urine that is squirted backwards, like a cat. Although most contacts are kept indirect and at a distance by means of scent marks, direct encounters elicit a variety of postures that are enhanced by raising or depressing the crest and body fur, thus exposing strongly contrasting patterns. The throat is frequently rubbed on objects and is boldly marked. Even as young cubs siblings fight readily. Presumably such intolerance is broken down by appropriate olfactory and visual signals during courtship.

Status: Widely distributed and common in spite of very frequent road kills. Not endangered. (IUCN status: not listed.)

Aquatic genet *Osbornictis piscivora*

Other names: Fr. *Genette aquatique*. Ger. *Wasserschleichkatze*.
Measurements: HB 45–50cm. T 35–42cm. W est. 1.2–2.5kg.

Osbornictis piscivora
Probable limits of range

Recognition: A very lightly built, but densely furred 'genet' with large, protuberant eyes, relatively small ears and a 'moustache' of conspicuous, downwardly deflected white whiskers. The body is a deep dark red (more ochraceous on the temples) while the thickly furred tail and limbs are black/brown. Throat, chin, upper lip and forecheek are white, contrasting strongly with the black/brown muzzle. The teeth resemble those of genets but are narrower and more sharply pointed. The hands and feet also resemble those of genets but their undersides are largely naked and they are disproportionately small (implying less arboreal habits).

Distribution: Low-lying north-eastern section of the Zaïre basin bounded by the R. Zaïre and mountainous margins of the Gregory Rift.

Habitat: Shallow headwaters of streams (preferably clear and flowing over red clays and sands) within a forest type dominated by limbali trees (*Gilbertiodendron*). It shelters in fallen hollow trunks and riverside debris and is crepuscular and nocturnal.

Food: Fish (captive specimens show no interest in small mammals, birds, lizards, frogs, insects or crabs), which are caught in the mouth with a very rapid strike. The aquatic genet approaches a quiet pool very slowly and gently pats the water surface. Fish are detected by sight or by the tips of the vibrissae, which are splayed in the surface layer of the water. These apparently pick up the vibrations made by fish. As the preferred prey is barbels (*Barbus*), catfish (*Clarias*) and 'talking fish' (*Synodontis*), all of which feed on insects and their larvae, it is possible that the technique not only detects fish but also attracts them.

Behaviour: In spite of being able to make extremely fast strikes and to flee at speed, the aquatic genet's normal gait and demeanour is slow and deliberate. This is in striking contrast to the marsh mongoose's hunting technique (which is busy and churns up mud and water). The tracks of these two amphibious species are often found in the same places (the mongoose is generally commoner). A captive pair exchanged very cat-like miaows and also a clucking or chuffing serial call.

Adaptations: The 'light-touch' fishing technique used by the aquatic genet correlates with its extremely nimble and flexible movements. Its very gracile, slender build presumably assists speed of movement but restricts it to fish of less than 25cm in length. Its teeth are mainly suited to gripping and slicing skin, flesh and hard, bony heads. Both the fishing technique and the prey are so specific that, within its very restricted habitat, the genet is clearly able to compete with both marsh mongooses and piscivorous birds. The very slow rate of colonisation that is typical of Limbali forest implies that this genet may require very stable conditions. Limbali also grow by preference in sandy red clays in river valleys of the NE Zaïre basin.

Status: The aquatic genet's close link with Limbali forest (thought to be an ancient and relatively stable forest type) suggests that it may also be dependent on a year-round supply of accessible small-fry fish of the right species. The genet's survival is likely to depend on this forest type and on the rivers not being overly disturbed. Bakumu hunters in the heart of its range claim that it is locally common. Rare and likely to become vulnerable as land-use practices change. (IUCN status: Uncertain.)

AFRICAN PALM CIVETS NANDININAE

African palm civet	*Nandinia binotata*

Recognition: Arboreal, nocturnal carnivores with cat-like claws, long tails, and dense, curly fur that half conceals their ears. Palm civets have very well-developed perineal and other skin glands.

Genealogy: It is uncertain how the single African species relates to the many species of Oriental palm civets. It is thought to be more conservative in some respects than the more specialised Asian species.

Geography: Predominantly equatorial and montane forests with scattered, patchy distribution to the east.

Ecology: Highly arboreal omnivores that live an exposed life, mainly in dense forest.

Natural history: Palm civets depend upon scent to regulate their social contacts and upon a very cryptic coat to escape detection during the day.

Adaptations: Although some Asian palm civets occupy similar niches to African genets, they are generally more muscular and acrobatic, with exceptional flexibility in all their joints. They can sustain the strains of hanging or cantilevered postures, retaining a firm grip with the hindlimbs while manipulating difficult foods with the forelimbs.

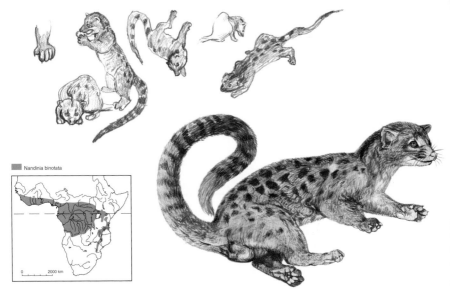

Nandinia binotata

African palm civet *Nandinia binotata*

Other names: Fr. *Nandinie*. Ger. *Pardelroller*.

Measurements: HB 45–58cm. T 50–62cm. W 2–3.2kg.

Recognition: A very inconspicuous, mottled brown, arboreal carnivore with long body and tail, well-clawed feet and distinctively textured soles to the hindlegs. The inner toes on all feet are somewhat separated from the other digits and function rather like thumbs during manipulation of foods or tangled twigs. The strong, flexible limbs allow it to descend vertical tree trunks head down. They also drop spread-eagled from considerable heights. Two pale spots on the shoulders become prominent during the hunched appeasement gesture. The olive-green eyes have a conspicuously vertical pupil.

Subspecies: *N. b. binotata* (main forest blocks), *N. b. arborea* (E African isolates).

Distribution: Tropical forested Africa and moist, montane areas as far south as Zimbabwe. They range from sea-level up to 2,000m.

Habitat: Mainly rainforest but palm civets also flourish in the cultivation mosaic that follows partial, or even extensive, clearance of the forest. This may be due to their partiality for the fruits of colonising trees, such as the umbrella tree (*Musanga*), sugar plums (*Uapaca*), corkwood (*Myrianthus*) and wild figs.

Food: The above-mentioned fruits, the fleshy pulp of oil palms and numerous other fruits (including cultivated varieties) form seasonal staples. However, palm civets are omnivorous and highly opportunistic, catching roosting birds, nestlings, rodents, lizards, fruit bats and insects. They also take carrion. Prey is stalked and pounced on, bitten repeatedly and bolted whole or in very large pieces. Animals become active shortly after nightfall, forage for about 4 hours, rest up and then forage again for 3–4 hours before dawn. They hide in a crevice or hole, where available, but more usually in a vine tangle, or even curled up in an exposed tree fork.

Behaviour: Mainly solitary but home ranges overlap extensively, with a dozen or more animals using a common resource, such as a grove of fruiting trees. Up to four young are born in a hollow tree after a 2-month gestation. There may be two breeding peaks in the late rains. Young accompany their mothers while foraging until they are near adult size.

Adaptations: Cryptic colouring limits modes of communication to scent and sound. Contact calls between family members are piping mews and a louder clucking call; they also purr. Aggression is signified by growls, spitting and a burst of screaming, and alarm by a gruff bark. However, scent represents the most important mode of signalling. The primary source of scent is a large sac on the lower abdomen which secretes a copious brown musk. Other scents are produced from the palms of the feet, the chin area and from the belly of lactating ♀♀ (the latter has a brilliant yellow colour that stains the offspring). These secretions are augmented by anal and urinary scents similar to those of genets. The exact role of this battery of scents in regulating social contacts awaits further study.

Status: A widespread and locally abundant species. It may be rare in isolated E African forests. Not endangered. (IUCN status: not listed.)

CATS FELIDAE

Wild cat	*Felis sylvestris*
Black-footed cat	*Felis nigripes*
Sand cat	*Felis margarita*
Swamp cat	*Felis chaus*
Serval cat	*Felis serval*
Caracal	*Felis caracal*
Golden cat	*Felis aurata*
Leopard	*Panthera pardus*
Lion	*Panthera leo*
Cheetah	*Acinonyx jubatus*

Recognition: Ranging from lions, at well over 200kg, to little desert cats (not much more than 1kg) all cats are built on a very similar body plan. They have a long body, a short, rounded head, with large canines and reduced molars, bifocal vision, acute hearing and an expressive face. All have curved claws and relatively soft fur with some degree of blotching or banding. Found all over the world, cats are almost exclusively meat-eaters, at the top of their respective food chains, and each species is highly dependent on an abundance of appropriate types and sizes of prey. They are therefore excellent indicators of the relative ecological health of an area.

Cats mark their home ranges with scent and scratch marks and all species are highly observant, their vigilance being directed at their own species as well as prey and enemies. Because social interactions are potentially dangerous, all species have elaborate appeasement behaviour, including body postures, rubs, lickings, purrs, miaows and tail signals. Scent is a primary mode of regulating contact, augmented by contact calls and scouting from regularly used observation posts. Of all carnivores they are the most efficient killers, clawing into their prey and directing a fast, accurate bite to whichever part of the body will lead to a rapid death. All species are in decline.

Felis sylvestris

Wild cat *Felis sylvestris*

Other names: Fr. *Chat ganté*. Ger. *Wildkatze*. Swah. *Paka mwitu*.
Measurements: HB 45–73cm. T 20–38cm. W 3–6.5kg.
Recognition: This species closely resembles a domestic cat (of which it is the direct and recent ancestor), with a grey or buff ground colour and warmer tints on the face, back of the ears and on the belly. Darker types are found in more humid areas. Tracks, typical cat faeces and fine scratch marks are indirect signs. Plain gingery backs to the ears and long legs distinguish the wild cat from domestic cats.
Subspecies: Individual variation (especially lighter and darker morphs) superimposed on regional differences makes definition of races difficult. *F. s. libyca* (N Africa), *F. s. caffra* (S Africa), *F. s. brockmani* (Horn of Africa), *F. s. ocreata* (Ethiopia) and *F. s. griselda* (SW Africa)

occupy the outer extremities of the range. Other recognised subspecies are: *F. s. sarda*, *F. s. ugandae*, *F. s. rubida*, *F. s. haussa*, *F. s. foxi* and *F. s. mellandi*.

Distribution: Most of Africa except the more extensive areas of desert and rainforest.

Habitat: Woodlands, savannahs, grasslands and steppes. In more exposed areas wild cats may shelter in and even share the dens of other animals. Litters are born in such retreats under dense grass, in hollow trees or in crevices or tangles.

Food: Mainly rats, mice and small mammals up to the size of a hare or very small antelope. Birds (especially gallinacaeous ones) and, less frequently, reptiles, frogs and insects are also taken. Wild cats traverse known hunting grounds slowly and silently, alerted to prey by hearing or sight. Prey is approached with a gliding, ground-hugging run, after which they inch forward until they can strike (within about 1m). Most hunting takes place in the early morning or evening. Sometimes a cat may hunt within sight of another and drift in the same direction as its mother, mate or sibling (but most hunting is solitary).

Behaviour: 'Rodent seasons' or periods of prey abundance (in the rains) may provide the basis for breeding peaks in wild cats. A single ♂ range tends to overlap those of several ♀♀. The latter defend the core of their range, especially when with kittens. ♂♂ spray posts with urine and leave less obvious claw scratch marks and cheek rubbings. Gestation is 56–69 days. Two to six young are born helpless and blind. Mobile by 1 month they are independent by 5 months and sexually mature by 1 year.

Adaptations: The wide ecological and geographic range of this species is due to the fact that it is small enough to subsist on insects for periods, yet strong enough to take prey of its own size.

Status: Widespread and common, the wild cat is prone to hybridising with domestic cats and is a frequently victim to dogs. In more exposed areas it is commonly taken by eagles and larger cats.

Black-footed cat *Felis nigripes*

Other names: Fr. *Chat à pieds noirs*. Ger. *Schwartzfusskatze*.

Measurements: HB 27–43cm. T 13–20cm. W 1–2kg.

Recognition: A small, pale tawny cat with very bold dark spots and prominent rings on the limbs, and a rather short tail. The margins of the eyes, ears and mouth are white, as is the underside. The nose is very small and the pointed ears are widely spaced.

Subspecies: *F. n. nigripes* (Kalahari): paler spots. *F. n. thomasi* (S Karoo): black spots.

Distribution: Arid regions of the Kalahari, Karoo and W Cape.

Habitat: Hunt in open, sandy country but keeps close to thickets, termitaries or clumps of grass where they can make a rapid retreat.

Food: Mainly gerbils and bush rats (elephant shrews also recorded). Birds, spiders, insects and reptiles are probably more marginal foods. Black-footed cats can live without water.

Behaviour: Extreme caution and strictly nocturnal habits have ensured that these cats are very seldom seen. Furthermore, they are intractable and ill-suited to captivity or zoo-breeding. They emerge 2–3 hours after dark. Records suggest summer (November–December) breeding. Up to three young are born after 67–68 days' gestation.

Adaptations: Probably a specialised gerbil-hunter. A southern relative of the sand cat.

Status: Little-known. Generally acknowledged as rare.

Felis margarita
Felis nigripes

0   2000 km

Sand cat *Felis margarita*

Other names: Fr. *Chat des marais*. Ger. *Sandkatze*.
Measurements: HB 40–57cm. T 23–35cm. W 1.5–3.4kg.
Recognition: A very small sandy-yellow cat with greyish freckling on the flanks, shoulders and forehead. Brown stripes on very young cats become faint gingery markings on adults but all have bolder markings around the elbows and tail tip. The ears are very widely spaced and can be deflected into a horizontal, downward orientation. The fur is dense, fine and woolly. The canines are exceptionally long for the animal's size.
Subspecies: Three, no longer recognised.
Distribution: Sahara Desert; also from Arabia to S Turkmenistan, Uzbekistan and Baluchistan.
Habitat: Desert areas with gerbil colonies, both sandy and rocky. It digs dens in deep sand beneath desert bushes.
Food: Mainly gerbils and lizards, which are skilfully caught at night. However, attempts at catching birds appear inept. The sand cat gains most of the moisture it needs from prey and becomes torpid during the day in its deep burrow, probably in order to conserve water.
Behaviour: By following the contours of the ground the sand cat escapes the attention of both prey and predators. Early winter births in Arabia suggest the three or four kittens may benefit from cooler, moister conditions in winter and spring.
Adaptations: Dense fur on the soles of the feet probably improves purchase on soft sand. The horizontal setting of the ears may help the cat to pick up the subterranean sounds of its prey.
Status: Very widespread range but may be locally extirpated by feral cats and dogs and by introduced deseases and parasites. Although apparently rare, unlikely to be endangered.

Sand cat.

Swamp cat.

Swamp cat *Felis chaus*

Other names: Fr. *Chat des marais*. Ger. *Rohrkatze*.
Measurements: HB 60–90cm. T 20–35cm. W 7–13.5kg.
Recognition: A large-bodied, long-legged cat with a shortish, banded tail and large, pointed ears. The colour is pale ochre, with grey tints and indistinct striping on the hindlimbs and darker bands below the elbow.
Subspecies: *F. c. nilotica* (lower Nile Valley).
Distribution: An Asiatic species just intruding into Africa (former Saharan records are due to mistaken identification).

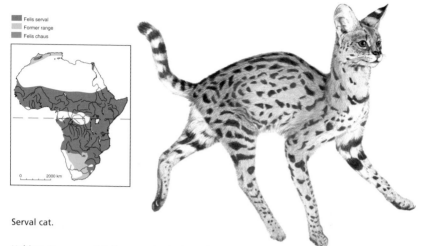

Serval cat.

Habitat: Known mainly from wetlands throughout its South-East Asian and Indian range. In Egypt they live in reedbeds and low grassy valleys, mainly near settlements.

Food: Migratory birds and waterfowl, rodents, reptiles and frogs. They are dependent on water.

Behaviour: An exceptionally hardy species that can breed and survive exposure in open marshlands. Two to five young are born after a 66-day gestation, suckle for 2 months, are independent by 5 months and sexually mature by 18 months.

Adaptations: A less specialised but close relative of the serval cat.

Status: Uncertain but evidently precarious. Very restricted habitat, wholly enclosed by dense human settlement.

Serval cat *Felis serval*

Other names: Fr. *Serval*. Ger. *Servalkatze*. Swah. *Mondo*.

Measurements: HB 67–100cm. T 24–35cm. W 11kg (6–12.5kg) (♀), 13kg (10–18kg) (♂).

Recognition: A tall, spotted cat with very large ears, a small muzzle and shortish tail. In SW Uganda and E Zaïre finely freckled servals can be nearly as common as the more widespread, bold-spotted morph (both occur in the same litter). Various forms of melanic serval through to all-black animals also occur, especially in or near mountainous areas.

Subspecies: None, but freckled morphs have been mistakenly assigned to distinct species *F. brachyura* and *F. servalina*.

Distribution: Once widespread in all savannah areas of Africa, including the N African coast, but now exterminated from most densely populated areas. Naturally absent from the rainforest blocks and open desert.

Habitat: Grass savannahs, subalpine and montane mosaics of moorland, forest and glades. Abundant along the margins of forest galleries, reedbeds and marshes, also in fallows of cultivation mosaics.

Food: Wide range of small mammals, birds, reptiles and insects; occasionally fruits. Grass-dwelling rodents are the main prey and times when local rodents are active strongly influence serval hunting patterns. Where diurnal species, such as Nile rats (*Arvicanthis*), are dominant the serval hunts during the day; nocturnal rats, such as *Otomys* and *Dasymys*, require more crepuscular or night hunting. High leaps or springs, with a powerful downward strike by the claws, are employed against larger prey, such as young antelopes and snakes as well as rodents. Loose, well-splayed toes with sharply curved claws also assist the long, slender forearms in reaching down burrows or tree hollows to extract rodents or nestlings. Fish and frogs are commonly caught by similar vertical strikes or by scooping and catching in mid-air. The serval plucks birds and hares, and typical 'play' or tossing often changes imperceptibly into deliberate plucking. It will cache parts of a larger prey, returning later to uncover and consume it. Prey is sometimes disembowelled and the viscera left uneaten.

Behaviour: The serval has small, defended core territories but shares much larger areas (from 2 to 30km²) with other servals. Both sexes mark the home range with urine squirts and employ a high-bounding display during rare territorial encounters. ♀♀ advertise their oestrus with loud, yowling cries, urine squirts, flank-rubbing and vertical tail quivers. Gestation lasts 67–77 days and the one to four young are born, blind and helpless, with very short tail and ears (growth of the ears is astonishingly rapid). The kittens are hidden in long grass, thickets or rock crevices and may be moved frequently. Although young may begin to eat prey brought to them by the mother after they are 4 or 5 weeks old, she suckles them up to 6 months. Young become independent at 1 year, by which time ♂ offspring are driven off but ♀♀ may be tolerated. Sexual maturity is reached at 2 years and animals live for between 13 and 20 years.

Adaptations: The serval, relatively, has the longest legs of all cats. These are not for fast running but to gain elevation for hunting in tall grass. Although the serval can walk up to 6km a night when prey is scarce, it normally remains in a small area and travels an average of 2km. It is capable of fast, agile dashes into dense cover if disturbed by a larger carnivore but is unable to sustain flight, preferring to hide and crouch. Its tall-grass habitat not only demands vertical leaping and striking at prey, but has shaped its typical greeting and threat displays. The head is repeatedly raised and lowered on the long neck and animals may stand on tip-toe, with highly arched back and tail. In aggression barks and growls are interspersed with forward strokes or a long-reaching, downward slash with extended claws. The primary function of the tall, vertically set ears is to act as sound funnels which allow an accurate fix on prey. For this the detector must gain maximum elevation and the serval is an efficient hunter in tall grass (very high ratios of kills to strikes have been observed). Unlike the larger cats, where one large prey may be the outcome of several attempts, the serval catches many small animals with less effort wasted.

Status: Although still widespread and common, the serval's disappearance from very large areas of its former range in N and S Africa and its known vulnerability to dogs suggests that its decline may be rapid in areas of dense settlement.

Caracal *Felis caracal*

Other names: Fr. *Caracal*. Ger. *Wüstenluchs*. Swah. *Simba mangu*.
Measurements: HB 62–91cm. T 18–34cm. W 8–13kg (♀), 12–19kg (♂).
Recognition: A large cat whose colour varies by region, age, stage of moult and wear and tear, but generally with a reddish fawn coat variably frosted with a fine grey freckle. It is sometimes melanistic. The muzzle is exceptionally short and small for such a tall cat but powerful jaw muscles underly the broad cheeks and rounded face.

Distribution: All the drier woodlands, savannahs and steppes of Africa and Arabia to NW India. Well distributed around the margins of the Sahara, common in Somali and Kalahari regions and scattered in pockets of drier country across central and E Africa.

Habitat: Plains and rocky hills in country with a short wet season and limited grass cover. *Acacia* and *Commiphora* woodlands, thickets and Karoo scrub are preferred. The Arabic name, 'rock cat', reflects the animal's preference for jebels and stony outcroppings.

Food: Depending on the locality, hyraxes, hares, small monkeys, antelopes and rodents make up the bulk of the diet. Birds such as partridges and doves are locally and seasonally important. Reptiles and fruits may also be occasional foods. The caracal stalks its prey to within range of its prodigiously long and fast bounds or spring, which is powered by disproportionately long and muscular hindlegs. This can take it several metres up into a tree or over rocks. Even eagles and ostriches have been recorded as quarry. Difficult prey may be repeatedly raked with the hindlegs until subdued.

Behaviour: Mostly solitary, the caracal forms pairs or small mother-young groups for the period of mating and rearing. It has a typical cat repertoire of growls, spits, hisses and miaows but also a highly distinctive coughing call during breeding seasons.

The breeding season may be during the spring in temperate Asia and forms an extended peak during the South African summer. Up to four young are born in a burrow, cave or thicket after a 62–81-day gestation. Eyes open by 9 days, meat is being taken by 1 month and lactation ceases by 4 months. The young mature fast and are wholly independent at 1 year of age.

Adaptations: The strongly patterned face and ears of the caracal stand out from an otherwise well-camouflaged body. The ears are a highly mobile signalling device. The long tufts on the ear tips may help to enhance hearing but also serve to emphasise the direction and movement of the ears and head. When meeting, and while still at some distance from each other, caracals make ritualised head and ear movements, or 'flagging', that is thought to semaphore information on status, identity and intentions.

Status: The caracal has proved better able to withstand persecution than many other cats and carnivores. It is known to survive in many areas of N and S Africa in spite of being rare and seldom seen. Not endangered.

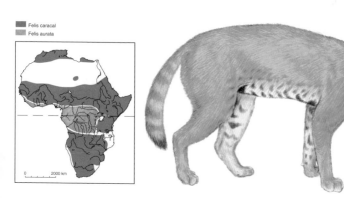

Felis caracal
Felis aurata

0   2000 km

Golden cat *Felis aurata*

Other names: Fr. *Chat doré*. Ger. *Goldkatze*.

Measurements: HB 61–101.5cm. T 16–46cm. W 5.5–18kg (♂♂ heaviest).

Recognition: A powerful cat with even limb proportions, a heavy muzzle and small, black-backed ears. Adult sizes are very variable, as is the proportion of the tail. Colour and pattern are also varied, the background colour from red or yellow to smoky grey. All animals have boldly spotted bellies and inner limb fur, but those from E Africa and Senegal are otherwise unspotted, while those from Sierra Leone to Ghana are always spotted. In central Africa both spotted and unspotted ones occur. Spots range from fine freckles to large rosettes, from faint to bold, and from partial to overall. Before all this variation was understood, many races and species were described. Captive specimens are known to have changed from grey to red and vice-versa and this may also occur in the wild.

Distribution: Forested regions of tropical Africa with a related species in S Asia, *F. temmincki*.

Habitat: Mostly in lowland forest zone; also in secondary vegetation along rivers in outlying areas. Also at high altitudes in several mountainous areas in moorland, bamboo and montane forest.

Food: The remains of duikers, monkeys, rodents and birds are commonly found in golden-cat faeces. In the Ruwenzori Mts, the golden cat feeds mainly on rats, hyraxes and red duikers. Francolins and guinea fowl are also commonly taken.

Behaviour: The Asiatic species has been observed repeatedly dashing up trees and down again which suggests that it may rely less upon leopard-like ambushes and more upon exceptional alertness and quick dashes. Nothing has been published on its social life but frequent sightings in restricted localites imply regular routines and smallish home ranges. ♀♀ may mature sexually while still of very small size. The young are well concealed. Nothing has been published on breeding.

Adaptations: The longer, heavier jaw of the golden cat implies larger, stronger prey than that of the caracals and serval cat. Duikers in particular are very strong powerfully built antelopes and are known to be regular golden-cat prey.

Status: Little known but habitat and prey populations are known to be contracting. Cat skins appear regularly in markets all over the forest zone. Rare and/or vulnerable.

Opposite: (a) Ethiopian morph. (b) Somali morph. (c) Zanzibar leopard.

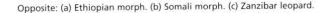

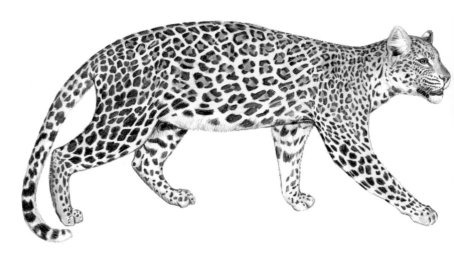

Leopard *Panthera pardus*

Other names: Fr. *Panthère*. Ger. *Leopard*. Swah. *Chui*.

Measurements: HB 104–140cm (♀), 130–190cm (♂). T 60–110cm. W 50kg (28–60kg) (♀), 60kg (35–90kg) (♂).

Recognition: A large cat with numerous, black and brown rosettes on back and upper limbs but single, solid spots on face, lower limbs and underside. Ground colour varies from pale cream (and widely spaced rosettes) in the dry Somali region to deep orange or tawny brown with variably sized and spaced rosettes. The darkest forms come from upland Ethiopia and Ruwenzori. Commonest indications are tracks, faeces and a rasping call (over a dozen inhaling-exhaling sawings repeated around dusk and dawn or at night).

Subspecies: In spite of very distinct regional morphs (26 subspecies have been named), all continental populations show intermediate intergrades. The only exception is Zanzibar I. where the 'founder effect' has established a unique population with very numerous, very small rosettes. *P. p. pardus* (continental Africa), *P. p. adersi* (Zanzibar I.).

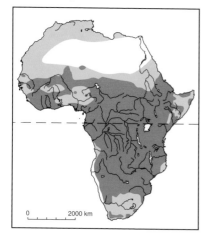

- ■ Panthera pardus
- ■ Former range

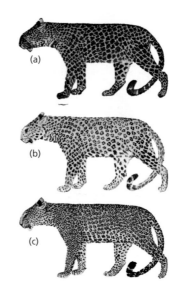

(a)

(b)

(c)

0   2000 km

Distribution: Most of Africa (excluding the Sahara desert) with former distribution beyond including much of S Eurasia. Now exterminated from N Africa and the greater part of South Africa.

Habitat: Leopards depend on broken terrain and heavy vegetation as stalking cover and as refuge from lions, hyaenas and people. They are rare or absent from wholly arid areas.

Food: Mainly small to medium-large mammals, but very diverse foods are taken. Even in an area with numerous antelopes of all ages and sizes a high proportion of leopard scats contain rodents, birds and arthropods (in one sample only 12% contained the remains of large antelopes). Overall, leopard diets reflect what can be most easily caught close to the margins of thick cover. Local and individual tastes also develop, with individual leopards regularly targeting a particular prey species, such as hyraxes, ostriches, jackals, dogs or porcupines. Although well able to kill large antelopes, leopards prefer prey no heavier than themselves. The weight of food taken at a time ranges between 8 and 17kg.

Behaviour: The ranges traversed by leopards vary from 9 to over 63km^2, but defended core areas are much smaller. They visit most of their home range very regularly, walking about 25km a night (up to 75km if disturbed). At various land-marks, especially path intersections, they may drop faeces, spray urine or scratch tree trunks with their claws. Vocal advertisement by rasping is also frequent in areas with many leopards. ♀ ranges may overlap parts of those of several ♂♂ and vice versa. Pairings are ephemeral and ♀♀ raise their young alone. Gestation is 90–112 days. Up to six young are born in a cave, burrow or dense thicket where they remain hidden for about 6 weeks. Eyes open at 1 week of age and they suckle for 3 months, gradually taking more and more of the meat brought to them by their mother. They become independent before 2 years, at which time they mature sexually. They are known to live for over 20 years.

Adaptations: The leopards' coat is supreme camouflage. The larger the animal the less easy it becomes for it to imitate a specific background. The leopards' pattern therefore must average out the light and shade in their immediate settings. Tropical leopards not only need shade, they must anticipate prey, intruders and enemies, as well as escape mobbing by birds or monkeys. The leopards' coat is a geometric abstraction that breaks up the tones of dappled shade into broad averages of area and contrast.

Status: In spite of intense persecution leopards survive in many parts of tropical Africa and they are sometimes even able to recolonise lost ground. Nonetheless, leopards have disappeared from many regions, especially in N, S and W Africa. In spite of leopards being on Appendix I (CITES) (which prohibits exploitation), the demand for their skins in the 1970s was estimated to fuel an annual off-take of some 50,000 leopards in Africa. At present, skins continue to be illicitly traded for high prices and the practice of poisoning all predators is spreading wherever there is livestock. While the leopard is unlikely to become extinct as a species in Africa as a whole, several unique morphs (notably those in Somalia, Ruwenzori and Zanzibar) are currently endangered. Until very recently, the Zanzibar Government paid a bounty on leopards to encourage their extermination.

Lion *Panthera leo*

Other names: Fr. *Lion*. Ger. *Löwe*. Swah. *Simba*.

Measurements: HB 158–192cm (♀), 172–250cm (♂). T 60–100cm. SH 100–128cm. W 122–182kg (♀), 150–260kg (♂).

Recognition: The largest of cats, ranging in colour from nearly white to deep ochre-brown. The commonest colour is a tawny yellow but ash grey is not uncommon as a body colour, especially in ♂♂. The face has subtle tints and markings around eyes, mouth and ears that enhance facial expressions. ♂♂ develop thick woolly manes that vary individually in colour, length and extent. In populations living in Africa today manes seldom extend far over the shoulders nor hang in a fringe under the belly (as they did in extinct forms in N Africa and in the Cape). A bold pattern of leopard-like rosettes is characteristic of the young but this fades and disappears as the animals mature. Both sexes roar (the ♂ more loudly). Roaring starts with a few moans followed by about a dozen full roars that then die away into grunts. On a still night roars will carry for 8km. The roar advertises the presence and position of a lion and may also denote status. Group roaring has the immediate function of reinforcing a pride's identity and solidarity. Discouraging intrusion by nomads and other prides is one of its effects.

Subspecies: The extinct Barbary and Cape lions were once treated as subspecies (*P. l. leo* and *P. l. melanochaita*). All lions are currently considered monotypic.

Distribution: Formerly most of Africa; now patchily in reserves and national parks. The lion also extended through the Middle East to Arabia, Persia and India.

Habitat: Formerly at most altitudes and in all vegetation types, except the most extensive forests and driest deserts.

Food: Most prey are mammals weighing between 50 and 300kg. When prey of this size cannot be readily caught, any animal between 15 and 1,000kg may be attacked. The smaller are eaten by individual lions, the heavier killed and eaten by groups. Prey species and their sexes, numbers and condition vary according to season and locality, but the commonest mammals (usually less than ten species) make up most of their diet. During famines, or when the lion is disabled, rats, reptiles, fish or even groundnuts may be taken. Most prey is caught after a skilled stalk (taking advantage of any type of cover, including dust, vehicles or cloud over the moon) and a fast run or charge. Larger animals are strangled; smaller ones are bitten deeply in the head, neck or chest. In many localities a high proportion of prey is pulled down by lionesses but ♂♂ are also very competent killers.

Behaviour: Lion social groups, commonly called prides, typically contain about five (two to twenty) adult ♀♀, two (one to eight) adult ♂♂ and their young and subadult offspring. Individuals spend much time on their own or with one or more companions but a kill, bouts of roaring or more subtle signals periodically reunite dispersed animals. Reunions are marked by much rubbing, leaning, purring, licking and other signs of appeasement by subordinate members. ♀ to ♀ bonds within a pride are persistent and involve vigorous allied defence of the pride's territory against intruding ♀♀ (occasionally reinforced by help from the ♂♂). ♂♂ form similar associations but their membership of a pride is more

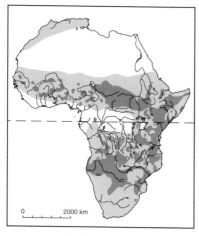

Panthera leo
Former range

0   2000 km

transitory and seldom lasts more than 3–4 years. Frequent challenges from nomadic groups ensures that ♂ lions enjoy a brief prime (while they are aged 5–10 years) and a short life thereafter. ♀♀ are longer-lived, more numerous and provide the continuity in a pride (which is therefore commonly described as matriarchal) but there is a similar, although slower, turnover of ♀ pride members. Both ♂ and ♀ membership of resident groups of pride lions is periodically augmented by immigrants drawn from highly mobile, unstable nomadic groups. Nomads wander very widely and provide the means of recolonising empty territories and account for most killers of livestock.

It is common for the ♀♀ in a pride to come into oestrus simultaneously, resulting in a large number of similarly aged cubs. Although ♀♀ will suckle one another's cubs, stragglers or weaklings are often left to their own devices and mortality among cubs is very high. Deaths include killings by newly arrived ♂♂. Gestation is around 100 days with two to six young born in a thicket, long grass or among rocks. The rate at which cubs develop and grow varies greatly and 'runts' are frequent. Eyes open between 3 and 11 days, the cubs become mobile at about 1 month, they begin to accompany adults by 2 months, are weaned by 8 months and are independent by 18 months. The young make a sharp yip contact call while mothers grunt at their young. A low, hooting 'woof' (often uttered down at the ground) signifies alarm and can send cubs scurrying into cover. Lions are fully mature by 5 years old.

Adaptations: Because lionesses reject strangers with great ferocity, the mane, as an imposing 'enlargement' of the lion's head and shoulders probably serves to intimidate ♀♀ and may assist relatively mobile ♂♂ to impose themselves on groups of more stable resident ♀♀. A lion in his prime, at about 6 years, has a luxuriant mane that comes into prominence during the 'lion strut', an artificial tip-toeing gait directed at both ♀♀ and subordinate ♂♂. Intimidation is most effective when two or more ♂♂ gang up against others. ♂ associations can be almost as close and lasting as those between ♀♀. However, it is only possible for many ♂♂ to join up with many ♀♀ in areas where a rich year-round crop of meat can sustain them all. Such conditions, once very widespread, were a likely precondition for the evolution of lioness prides and of big-maned ♂ gangs.

Status: Because lions could only evolve prides and manes where there was space and the herds of large animals to support them, it makes an appropriate symbol for conservation in Africa. It is also an indicator of a self-sustaining community of large grazers.

With wild grazers progressively being replaced by domesticated ones, the lion has had to be eliminated. This was achieved in both N and S Africa 100 years ago. This century has seen continuous extermination across tropical Africa, with rapidly accelerating decline in the last two decades. The tsetse belt, a vast area once closed to livestock because of trypanosomiasis, was formerly the main refuge for the lion and antelopes outside the national parks. New prophylactics now permit growing herds of cattle to enter this region. This expansion by livestock has been so rapid and on such a scale (often without formal sanction or recognition) that its impact on the lion is largely unknown. Its overall outcome can hardly be in doubt. Before long the lion will only survive in large national parks and reserves.

Cheetah *Acinonyx jubatus*

Other names: Fr. *Guépard*. Ger. *Gepard*. Swah. *Duma*.

Measurements: HB 110–150cm. T 65–90cm. W 50kg (35–65kg).

Recognition: A very tall, slender cat with evenly spaced, circular spots all over a tawny-cream background. The face is notable for its rounded verticality, a structural peculiarity emphasised by prominent black 'tear stripes' that link eyes and mouth. Although the small ears have black and white markings behind, they are less conspicuous than the expressive eyes and mouth. Very young cheetahs have extraordinary colouring: dirty white above, near black below. Underparts lighten and the spots emerge before they are 2 months old but the mantle of pale fur disappears more slowly and traces of the mantle are still present after animals are 1 year old.

Subspecies: All cheetahs have been shown to be very similar genetically. This confirms that there are probably no identifiable subspecies, even in Asia. As with other spotted cats, there are occasional mutants without spots, melanistic ones, white ones with bluish spots and blotched or marbled morphs which were once described as 'King cheetahs' and given the name *Acinonyx rex*. This morph is commonest in south-central Africa.

Distribution: The cheetah once ranged through Africa and the Middle East across to Tadjikistan in the north and India in the south-east. Throughout its range outside Africa it has been exterminated or is on the point of extinction.

Habitat: Any large population of small or medium-small ungulates can support the cheetah if the vegetation is not too dense or the ground too broken. Patchy cover is most favourable but the cheetah can also survive on dry, open plains. It formerly penetrated deep into the Sahara from refuge areas to the north and south. Although extinct in the Mediterranean N Africa, it is still recorded occasionally in the Tassili and Hoggar Mts.

Food: The 'staple' species taken are impala, springbok, gazelles, kob and, in Asia, blackbuck. Many other smaller mammals are also taken but only occasionally. Single cheetahs, notably ♀♀ (and the minority of solitary ♂♂) hunt smaller prey and kill less frequently than ♂ groups. Two or more ♂♂ have been known to tackle much larger animals, up to the size of a zebra or young buffalo, but this is rare. The cheetah prefers to stalk to within less than 50m before racing out at about 60km/h. At its fastest, however, a cheetah may reach 112km/h but is quickly exhausted. An individual can consume 14kg at one sitting and groups of four have been seen to finish an impala carcass in just over 15 minutes. Many groups kill daily. The cheetah is a fast, frequent and efficient killer, and a speedy swallower; such adaptations help to counter loss to a host of scavengers and thieves, from vultures and hyaenas to humans.

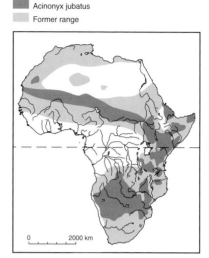

Acinonyx jubatus

Former range

0   2000 km

Cheetahs
strangling prey.

Behaviour: While two or three ♂ ♂ often form lasting associations that jointly defend cores of shared territory (40–80km²) the majority of adult cheetahs (all ♀ ♀ and some ♂ ♂) live in home ranges that are much larger (50–1,000km²).

♀ ♀ are mated by ♂ ♂ that live within their own range or by wanderers. After a 3-month gestation, the blind, helpless cubs are born in long grass, in thickets or in a temporary 'borrowed' burrow. The young open their eyes at 4–14 days and are frequently carried to fresh hiding places by the mother. The cubs' first meat is eaten before they are 1 month old. Cubs vary a great deal in the length of time they remain dependent on the mother; some stay with her for 2 years, others are on their own at just over 1 year. Territories and preferred routes are marked with sprays of urine, faeces and, occasionally, by claw-raking. These markings are most often made near regularly used observation points (termitaries, rocks, leaning trees) or at path junctions. The cheetah purrs in greeting known individuals but the most striking contact call is an explosive yelp that can carry for 2km. Juveniles make a 'whirr', or fast growl, which may rise to a squeal or subside to a rasp during fights over a kill. Chirps, hums, purrs and yelps are unique to this cat which can be very vocal in its rare social encounters. Animals mature sexually and can have cubs of their own at about 2 years. Captive specimens have lived for up to 16 years.

Adaptations: The cheetah's skull is extensively modified to allow the jaws to serve as a clamp capable of maintaining a tight throttle hold for up to 20 minutes until the prey has died of suffocation. The nasal passages are exceptionally large to let the cheetah 'pant' through the nose while maintaining its vice-like grip. The clamping action is helped by a steepened angle to the face that has raised the top of the skull and eyes. Unlike the elongated, flat head of the leopard, the cheetah's head is wide nosed and well rounded.

Status: Nominally protected by CITES and the African Convention. Almost all African countries outlaw the killing of the cheetah and trade in its skins. The cheetah is represented in many very scattered national parks. In spite of improved legal protection its overall range has shrunk and continues to shrink as livestock replaces wildlife. In spite of legislation outlawing trade in cheetah skins, which is thought to have slowed direct destruction of the cheetah, a single furrier in New York was found with nearly 2,000 skins in 1972. Fears have also been expressed that a loss of genetic diversity could render the cheetah vulnerable to pandemics.

SCALY ANT-EATERS PHOLIDOTA

Highly specialised scaly ant-eaters, pangolins are typified by long, very muscular tails and horny scales that have similar origins to those on the tails of anomalures (African flying squirrels). The scales are cornified extrusions of the outer skin (or enlargements of the miniature scales that cover many rodent and insectivore tails). Since no other mammal has more than the 47 tail vertebrae found in the long-tailed tree pangolin, it is likely that an abrasion-resistant 'fifth limb' was the primary adaptation of some arboreal proto-insectivore over 70 million years ago. Extending these scales to cover the rest of the body would have come later, after the protective function of a muscular, armoured tail was well established. Descent from the trees and further dietary specialisation would have occurred later still. All of the tail and every outer surface of pangolins is protected but the face, throat, belly and inner limbs are naked or covered in conventional mammalian hair.

Pangolin is a Malay name meaning 'one that rolls up' and, for defence, all species depend upon presenting a continuous sphere of overlapping armour when curled up into a tight ball. The top of the head is scaled but the tubular skull gains extra protection by being constructed of thick, dense bone. Pangolin heads are relatively small; mostly nose, with beady black eyes under swollen eyelids. Similar borders of thick skin surround open ear cavities (vestiges of ear cartilage under the skin indicate that pangolin ancestors had normal mammalian ears).

The small mouth is tucked in under the nose. Pangolins are toothless and have lost all capacity to chew, the lower mandible being no more than a hinged strut. The tongue is as long as the head and body and, when not extended, folds back into a throat pocket that visibly bulges and empties when the animal feeds. The tongue is very sticky and is served by enormous salivary glands so that forest species especially must drink frequently. The remarkable extensibility of the tongue is made possible through muscular action and its attachment to a very flexible prong that extends to the back of the abdominal cavity. This prong consists of the last pair of cartilaginous ribs, which, in pangolins, have become separated from their vertebral attachments and have joined up to form a free-floating extension of the sternum. The tongue's muscular extension runs the full length of this springy prong, allowing the worm-like tongue to travel right down termite holes and then whip back into the mouth smothered in insects.

In spite of their superficial resemblances to South American armadillos, pangolins evolved in the Old World along a separate evolutionary route, to arrive at parallel ant-eating specialisations.

PANGOLINS MANIDAE

Long-tailed pangolin	*Uromanis tetradactyla*
Tree pangolin	*Phataginus tricuspis*
Giant pangolin	*Smutsia gigantea*
Ground pangolin	*Smutsia temmincki*

Recognition: In spite of a similar armour of scales, pangolins are a very diverse group that range from 2kg arboreal species to the terrestrial giant pangolin weighing in at well over 30kg (fossil species were bigger still). All species have sharp claws on the forefeet. These are used to open termite mounds and tear open hollow branches and trunks. They are also employed to some extent in ♂ fighting and in defence. By contrast the hindlegs of light climbers and heavy walkers are much more divergent. In ♂♂, the testes are contained in a superficial skinfold in the groin rather than in a true scrotum.

Genealogy: Fossils show that divergence into various small/large, arboreal/terrestrial niches had taken place before pangolins spread from their place of origin. Whether this was tropical Asia or Africa currently remains unknown.

Geography: The four African and three Asiatic pangolins are the remnants of a larger radiation. European fossil genera about 40 million years old include *Leptomanis*, *Necromanis* and *Teutomanis*. Other fossils include a more recent Indian form similar to the giant pangolin.

Ecology: The two arboreal species and the giant pangolin are strictly water-dependent and only occur in the moist forest belt in regions with very abundant ants and termites. The ground pangolin is more arid-adapted but only penetrates dry areas on the margins of its range in the Kalahari, Sudanic and Somali arid regions. All pangolins are almost exclusively feeders on ants and termites. These are consumed by attachment to the sticky surface of the tongue, swallowed and ground up with sand in the hardened gizzard-like stomach. All species can travel on the ground but the two arboreal species feed and sleep in rainforest trees. Both their bodies and their scales are appropriately light in weight. The much heavier terrestrial forms have dense massive scales, reflecting more exposure to strong, well-armed predators.

Natural history: Pangolins have discrete home ranges and ♂♂ apparently defend well-marked territories that enclose the home ranges of several ♀♀. Anal scent-gland marks, squirts of urine and faeces are deposited along well-used pathways and ♂♂ commonly track ♀♀ down by scent. More than one sleeping-place and several territaries or ants' nests may be visited in a single night. The young are born in burrows or arboreal hollows and subsequently travel on their mother's tail. African pangolins normally have only one offspring at a time (Asiatic species are known to have up to three). All species can make hissing or puffing noises but they are mostly silent.

Adaptations: In spite of huge differences in size and structure, all species depend upon rapid scissor movements of the tail during defence. In the smaller species this action cuts like a sharp-toothed saw while the larger species use the heavy blades of individual scales to wound an aggressor. In the case of the giant pangolin the entire tail may encircle an attacker's limb or it may lash out like a club. In the ground pangolin the tail acts as a counter-weight to the forequarters during bipedal walking or running.

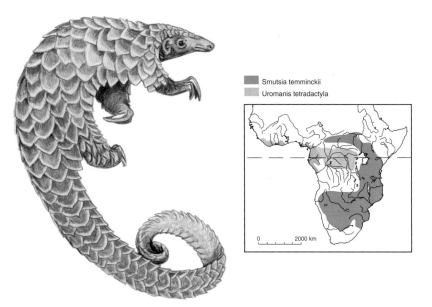

Smutsia temminckii
Uromanis tetradactyla

0   2000 km

Long-tailed pangolin *Uromanis tetradactyla*

Other names: Fr. *Pangolin à longue queue*. Ger. *Schwarzbauchschuppentier*.
Measurements: HB 30–40cm. T 55–80cm. W 2.2–3.25kg.
Recognition: A small, arboreal pangolin with a very long tail and black face and underparts. The muzzle is naked and pointed. The scales, which are relatively broad and only reveal the faintest of striations, have brown bases with light yellow margins. The long-tailed pangolin is active by day but very wary and difficult to spot.
Distribution: All permanent rivers on the Atlantic coast from Senegal to W Angola, especially the R. Zaïre throughout its lowland basin.

Habitat: Very localised; never far from permanent water and watercourses, preferring riverine and swamp forests. The long-tailed pangolin sleeps in tree hollows or in hollowed-out insect nests.

Food: Tree ants (*Crematogaster* and *Cataulacus*), which occur in swampy areas, are the favoured food. These are eaten on branches or broken out of their arboreal nests and hollows.

Behaviour: This species uses habitual routes and sleeping-holes in a well-known home range. It follows urine and anal scent-gland trails (urine and anal secretions are also expelled in order to discourage predators). Breeding is non-seasonal and almost continuous as the ♀ conceives again within 2 weeks of birth. Gestation is estimated at about 140 days. The single young is born in a hole where it may be left during its first week while the mother forages. Thereafter it clings to the mother's rump or tail and begins to glean ants at about 2 weeks. It departs at the birth of a new infant and wanders for 4 or 5 months before settling down into its own home range.

Adaptations: A long, prehensile tail is likely to have been one of the primary adaptations of proto-pangolins. Its use as a versatile third limb is demonstrated when the pangolin descends large tree trunks in a shallow, tail-clinging spiral and during copulation, when both animals entwine. This species is markedly shyer than other pangolins and shows faster responses in enclosing itself within its tightly wound tail at the least alarm. The tip of the tail has a naked, finger-like pad which is highly sensitive.

Status: Because it is small and shy and inhabits a type of forest that is forbidding (full of biting ants and frequently very thorny), it is seldom seen. Such habitats are currently the least at risk and arboreal pangolins are more secure than the two terrestrial species.

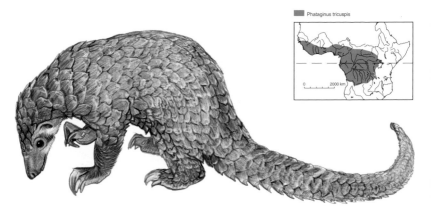

Phataginus tricuspis

Tree pangolin *Phataginus tricuspis*

Other names: Fr. *Pangolin commun*. Ger. *Weissbauchschuppentier*. Swah. *Kakakuona ya miti*.
Measurements: HB 25–43cm. T 35–62cm. W 1.6–3kg.
Recognition: A small, arboreal pangolin with very numerous, thin scales, resembling fir-cone scales in texture but with serrated ('three-cusped') points. Old animals have elongated, less striated scales with abraded ends. The muzzle is thicker and shorter than that of the long-tailed pangolin and the skin is much paler, with sparse white fur on the belly and browner hair on the limbs and neck. The tail is tipped with a sensitive, thumb-like pad.
Subspecies: None named but animals from Upper Guinea are smaller.
Distribution: Senegal to W Kenya and the R. Zaïre basin to N Angola and Zambia.
Habitat: All through the lowland rainforest block (and many outliers) but especially favours secondary growth, surviving quite well in cultivation, fallow and forest mosaics.
Food: Mainly termites, notably *Nasutitermes* and *Microcerotermes*, which are mostly found on the ground; also ants (*Dorylus* and *Myrmecaria*). Although the tree pangolin opens up decayed bark and small termite mounds, most foraging is on the surface and in leaf litter. The tail sometimes helps sweep insects within range of the flickering tongue. In keeping with the termites' activity cycle, this pangolin is predominantly nocturnal, ♀♀ feeding in bouts of 3 or 4 hours while ♂♂ travel further and only rest after 5 or 6 hours. Scent trails help ♀♀ to avoid contact with one another while foraging.

Behaviour: Adult ♀♀ are highly sedentary and sleep in self-dug holes that are used for long periods. They forage over a few hundred metres within overlapping home ranges of some 3 or 4ha. Adult ♂♂ are more nomadic, moving about a kilometre or more within territories of up to 30ha. They tolerate and regularly monitor all the adult ♀♀ within their range but expel offspring as they mature. Although some sleeping-holes are excavated in arboreal termitaries and hollow trunks, most are dug at or near ground level. Gestation is estimated at about 150 days and a single infant is born in the mother's hole (where it is only left for very short periods). The baby begins to travel perched on its mother's tail at 2 weeks and mother and young forage together for up to 5 months. Adult size is not reached before 15 months. Animals are sexually mature by 8 months.

Adaptations: Equally at home in trees and on the ground, this species is the most versatile and therefore the most common and widespread of the forest pangolins.

Status: High fecundity and a mixed diet of termites and ants allows the tree pangolin to offset heavy predation in some areas (including high levels of both internal and external parasites).

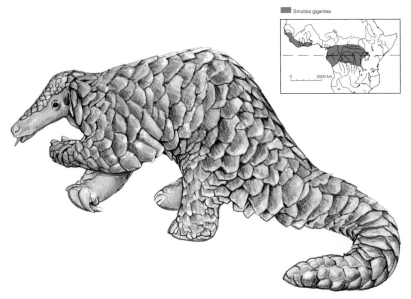

Smutsia gigantea

Giant pangolin *Smutsia gigantea*

Other names: Fr. *Pangolin géant*. Ger. *Riesenschuppentier*. Swah. *Kakakuona mkubwa*.

Measurements: HB 75–100cm. T 50–70cm. W 30–35kg.

Recognition: The largest and heaviest of living pangolins, this powerfully built scaly ant-eater has a highly precise and geometric pattern of brunette scales which darken and change both texture and shape with age. With wear and tear, the regular symmetry of scaling is also obscured in old individuals. The hindlegs leave prints that resemble those of a small elephant. At the front, weight is taken on the wrist, with long sharp claws folded inwards and facing to the rear. The tail, unlike that of the ground pangolin, often leaves a heavy drag mark. The tubular snout is appreciably longer and less tapered than that of the ground pangolin.

Distribution: From Senegal to Togo and Cameroon to W Kenya (north of the R. Kasai and R. Tshuapa). Sightings reported from Angola and the Uzungwa Mts in Tanzania might be misidentified ground pangolins.

Habitat: Mainly forest and forest mosaics but survives in high-rainfall secondary grasslands where it can shelter in thicket-covered termitaries. It is totally water dependent. It may use the burrows of other animals but also digs long deep burrows, up to 40m long and 1.5m deep. Entrances are usually plugged from within. It also rests up under fallen tree roots, thicket tangles and piles of plant debris.

Food: Termites, notably *Macrotermes, Cubitermes, Apicotermes, Protermes*, and ants, such as *Palthothyreus* and *Anomma*. Other insects and larvae are also taken. Even water-beetles (Dytiscidae) are licked off the surface of pools (the giant pangolin is an able swimmer). Most feeding takes place between midnight and dawn but seasonal differences are likely. Frequent periods of inactivity, sometimes very prolonged, suggest that this large ant-eater can survive periods of acute shortage by a form of aestivation but makes up for this with periods of glut and storage of body fat.

Behaviour: Solitary and well-spaced, the enlarged anal glands and greater marking activity of the heavier ♂♂ suggests that they are intolerant of other ♂♂. Individuals have been known to inhabit a very limited locality for up to 2 years but their seasonal and overall ranges are poorly known. Gestation has been estimated at about 5 months and a single open-eyed young is born with soft, amber-coloured scales which harden rapidly. Beginning to feed on ants by 3 months, the young accompanies its mother until the next infant is born.

Adaptations: The spread-eagled agility, strongly prehensile tail and strong clinging reflexes of the newborn are clear indications of the arboreal origins of this heavy terrestrial pangolin. A highly localised distribution implies the need for a large and sustained biomass of ants and termites. It has been recorded as taking up to 2 litres of insects a night.

Status: The use of scales as love-charms and a widespread taste for their meat (a special delicacy in Gabon) has led to much local depletion or extinction. Formerly protected in some areas as a totemic species (i.e. for the Olugave clan in Buganda), the breakdown of such taboos now sanctions interference. Mostly rare and widely vulnerable.

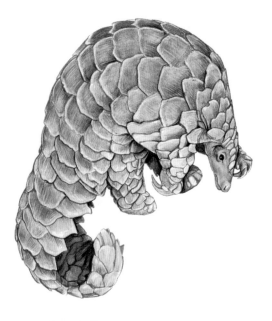

Ground pangolin *Smutsia temminckii*

Other names: Fr. *Pangolin de Temminck*. Ger. *Steppenschuppentier*. Swah. *Kakakuona*.
Measurements: HB 34–61cm. T 31–50cm. W 7–18kg. (♂♂ up to 50% heavier than ♀♀).
Recognition: A rotund pangolin with broad, rounded scales and heavy, graviportal hindlegs. The forelegs, although strong, are proportionally less massive than those of the giant pangolin. The tail is very broad, with a concave lower surface, and is shorter than that of other pangolins.
Distribution: From L. Chad, north of the R. Ubangi to S Kordofan and the upper Nile Valley (but absent from Ethiopia and Somalia). Also east of the Victoria Nile and L. Victoria to L. Nyasa (formerly L. Malawi). In subtropical S Africa, it is found in Angola and there is an undetermined distribution in Mozambique (possibly separated into southern and northern populations).

Habitat: Occurs in both high- and low-rainfall areas with both sandy and rocky soils, in woodlands, savannahs and grasslands. The main determinant of this species' range is an abundance of ants and termites of a few specific types. A scarcity or absence of these explains its absence from Ethiopia and may also account for its absence west of L. Chad (other ant-eating animals are also absent from W Africa).

Food: Mainly ants, including the genera *Anoplepis*, *Paltothyreus*, *Camponotus* and *Crematogaster*. Some of the most commonly eaten ants are tiny, colony-living species. Less frequently taken are certain termite genera: *Odontotermes*, *Microcerotermes*, *Ancistrotermes*, *Amitermes* and *Microtermes*. The ground pangolin forages very slowly, often 'freezing' and only making shallow, cup-like excavations, moving the soil slowly and carefully so that the tongue can flick in and out of the ants' passages. It tends to feed intensively for about 15 seconds and then depart abruptly. A sucking sound is made by the rapid extrusion and return of the sticky tongue. Other small insects, such as dung-beetle larvae, are also eaten. It sometimes takes loose pieces of termitary, broken wood or dry elephant dung in its forepaws and, rolling onto its back, licks the insects off as the object is manipulated or broken up. Activity is determined by whether prey species are on or near the surface; thus most feeding is nocturnal during the dry season, but may become diurnal in other seasons. Young animals tend to forage for a longer period than adults.

Behaviour: Although capable of digging a burrow, the ground pangolin prefers to use natural shelters or disused holes of other species. It is a slow but capable climber, using sharp points along the margins of the tail to gain purchase on bark or soil. During the rains it can create a shallow wallow by gyrating backwards in a tight circle so that water collects.

Only one young is born at a time after a gestation estimated at 130–150 days. After about 1 month of limited activity the young travels on its mother's back or on the root of her tail (slipping onto her belly at the least alarm). By 3 months it has begun to feed on ants but continues to be carried until it weighs about 3kg. ♀♀ breed continuously and become pregnant again while still with a small offspring.

Adaptations: The ground pangolin is very frequently bipedal and this is reflected in the structure of its pelvis, broad hips, relatively short heavy tail and kangaroo-style carriage of the forepaws (tucked in close to the chest).

Status: The ground pangolin has been exterminated in many parts of its overall range by hunting for both its flesh and scales, which are used as love-charms. It is attacked by lions and hyaenas, frequently burnt in bush fires, and faces a new danger in the form of electrocution in places where electric fences are employed. In spite of all these hazards, however, it is still widespread and locally common. Not endangered overall.

UNGULATES grandorder UNGULATA

Aardvark	Tubulidentata
Hyraxes	Hyracoidea
Proboscids	Proboscidea
Odd-toed ungulates	Perissodactyla
Even-toed ungulates	Artiodactyla

Fossils suggest a common origin for the six orders of ungulates some 65–70 million years ago. Although all are found in Africa today, their earliest separations may have spanned different continents. Hyraxes, elephants and sea-cows are of undoubted African origin. The aardvarks are Afro-Eurasian, and even-toed ungulates may be Eurasian. Odd-toed ungulates are more likely to have become distinct in North America. While only a handful of hyracoids, rhinoceroses and elephants survive today, all were much more diverse and successful groups before the rise of the artiodactyls. The latter now number over 200 species and include all the most important livestock species, such as cattle, sheep, camels, pigs and deer.

AARDVARK TUBULIDENTATA

The modern aardvark is distinguished by many peculiarities, notably in the teeth, which lack enamel and are composed of densely packed tubules surrounded by columns of dentine, the whole tooth being contained in a sleeve of dental cement. These peg-like molar teeth are at the back of a slender, toothless snout (although embryos and infants have a full complement of vestigial milk teeth, including canines). Although aardvarks probably evolved in Africa, various fossil forms also occurred in Eurasia and on the island of Madagascar.

AARDVARK ORYCTEROPODIDAE

If one disregards the aardvark's more obvious ant-eating specialisations (peculiar nose and teeth, digging claws and musculature) then its skeleton reveals numerous similarities with a 50-million-year-old fossil, *Phenacodus*. This carnivore-like animal (apparently partly herbivorous) was a proto-ungulate, close to the common ancestral stem of all modern ungulates. The aardvark's importance, therefore, includes the clues it may offer to the common genetic origins of tapirs, rhinos, horses, hyraxes, elephants and artiodactyls.

Aardvark, Orycteropus *Orycteropus afer*

Other names: Fr. *Oryctérope*. Ger. *Erdferkel*. Swah. *Muhanga, Kukukifuku*.
Measurements: HB 100–158cm. T 44–63cm. H 58–66cm. W 40–82kg.
Recognition: The aardvark's long nose, squared-off head and tapered tail are rather delicately built extensions in comparison with the massive body and the muscular limbs, which are armed with great, nailed digits. The fur on many old individuals can become heavily abraded but young animals are well furred (short on the head, nape and tail, longer and darker on the body, especially on the limbs). The aardvark is a shy nocturnal animal and rarely seen. Its burrows, spade-like scratchings and tracks are more commonly seen than the animal itself.
Subspecies: 18 subspecies have been named but most, if not all, are invalid due to substantial yet little-studied variation. The snout in particular is subject to differences in proportions and angle. The ardvark is normally rare or absent in rainforest.
Distribution: A large part of sub-Saharan Africa with past extensions down the Nile valley and Hoggar/Tassili Mts.
Habitat: Patchily distributed in areas with a year-round abundance of ants and termites and beetle larvae. The earth which is preferred for digging warrens may be at some distance from foraging areas so nightly walks between the two are normal in some localities. Very

Orycteropus afer
Former range

0   2000 km

Detail of aardvark nose.

hard or stony soils and regularly flooded areas are avoided. In highly stratified hills the aardvarks may select a particular stratum for its more regularly used warrens. These may be occupied mainly by ♀♀ and their young as ♂♂ are thought to be less sedentary. Temporary 'camping' holes of only a few metres in length are more frequent than the much longer warren complexes, which can have eight or more entrances and descend as deep as 6m. Entrances are normally plugged, sometimes with a 'vent' left open at the top of the plug. With its spade-like claws the aardvark can dig with great force and speed in suitable soils.

Food: Termites, ants and larvae are foraged for at night, beginning an hour or two after dusk. Most food is found on or very close to the surface but subterranean termitaries, ants' nests and beetle caches may be extensively excavated. However, the colonies of social insects are seldom entirely destroyed (the deterrent is probably a critical concentration of defending soldiers). Termites that live on or very near the surface are *Hodotermes, Odontotermes, Microtermes, Pseudacanthotermes, Trinervitermes* and *Macrotermes*. During periods and in localities where ant colonies outnumber or are more available than termite colonies, these may become the principal diet. Recorded ant prey are *Anoplepis, Camponotus, Crematogaster* and *Dorylus* but very many more genera are also taken. Scarabeid pupae or larvae are likely to come in similar seasonal or local bonanzas. It is gluts of termites, mainly in the wet season, that are likely to fuel seasonal deposits of fat in the aardvark. Insects are swept into the small mouth by the long, sticky tongue and are swallowed with little or no chewing. As at least one fossil aardvark species appears to have had no teeth, their function in living species may be quite marginal. Insects are processed in the pyloric region of the muscular, gizzard-like stomach.

Behaviour: Normally solitary, ♀ aardvarks are accompanied by one, occasionally two, young (of different ages). Where aardvarks are very common and large warrens well established, they may be used by more than two or three animals. ♂ genitals secrete a powerful musk and both sexes have glandular areas on the elbows and hips. These presumably help with the spacing of individuals and with mating but ostentatious scent-marking has not been observed. The only recorded sounds made by an aardvark are a grunt and, in extreme fear, a bleat. One, rarely two, young are born after a gestation estimated at 7 months. Born naked but with open eyes, they begin to follow the mother after 2 weeks and start eating insects at 3 months, becoming independent at 6 months and sexually active at about 2 years. The aardvark lives for up to 18 years.

Adaptations: The sense of smell is greatly refined by a structure that vastly increases the turbinal surfaces (which help to process olfactory signals). These are minutely convoluted bones and tissue that radiate from the olfactory lobes of the forebrain, visibly swelling the middle profile of the skull. Also linked with locating hidden food are thick, fleshy tentacles on the septum of the nose (which may function like the appendages of the North American star-nosed mole). The snout itself is not at all pig-like, being soft, mobile, rounded and furry, with dense hair around the nostrils (detail above). Swollen upper lips completely conceal the small mouth below. The sides of the face and the tail are pale-coloured or white in ♀♀, darker in ♂♂, colour differences that may help young to locate or follow their mothers.

Status: The aardvark is still widespread but has been widely exterminated in many agricultural areas. This is mainly because of hunting but many farmers and ranchers destroy the animals because their holes are inconvenient or dangerous to vehicles, stock and water dams. Cultivation tends to eliminate their food supply. Extermination has extensive side-effects because aardvark holes are extremely important as refuges for many species of small mammals, including bats and carnivores, reptiles and birds. The aardvark is vulnerable in all settled areas and endangered or extinct in many other localities.

HYRAXES HYRACOIDEA

Hyraxes are small, woolly animals with no visible tail and blunt 'hoofed' digits. They were once grouped with rodents (due to a purely superficial resemblance) and then with rhinoceroses and elephants (to which they are somewhat more closely related because they are ungulates). Thomas Huxley was the first to put them into an order of their own and this has been followed up to the present. At least 11 genera of hyracoids existed 30–25 million years ago (only in Africa), of which some were among the dominant herbivores of their time. They have been almost totally replaced by modern ruminants but the reasons for the hyraxes' decline probably has less to do with their digestion (which, judging from modern hyraxes, was probably hardly less efficient than that of ungulates) than in a poor ability to regulate body temperature, a lack of stamina, short legs and a primitive brain that still show resemblances to those of 50-million-year-old 'near ungulates'. Other limitations could be slow reproduction (a gestation of over 7 months) and their cumbersome, though fast, way of cropping vegetation. The tusk-like incisors of hyraxes are given over to defence and grooming, which has forced the molars and rear of the mouth to combine the functions of food-gathering and chewing.

The classification of hyraxes originally became associated with elephants because early fossils of both lineages were similar. More recently the antibodies, placenta, mammae and genitalia of hyraxes have been found to share features with those of odd-toed ungulates. Ancestors with much larger body sizes could be one explanation for their 7-month gestation and the very advanced state of development of the newborn.

More immediate ancestors of modern hyraxes are likely to have escaped competition by adapting to the rocky thickets that are scattered over a large part of Africa. If rock-dwelling was the initial innovation of the ancestors of all living hyraxes, the two specialisations that have developed since are arboreal skills at one extreme and grass-eating at the other. Bush hyraxes have the most generalised dentition.

All three genera are successful and they flourish in two environments that hoofed ungulates cannot cope with: trees and rock piles.

HYRAXES PROCAVIDAE

Rock hyraxes	*Procavia* (5 species)
Bush hyraxes	*Heterohyrax* (3 species)
Tree hyraxes	*Dendrohyrax* (3 species)

The three genera of hyraxes show few easily observable external differences: all are rabbit-sized, woolly and brown, with a large-mouthed, deep-jawed head and rubbery, blunt-fingered hands and feet. Their loud voices are highly distinctive but their calls still await systematic analysis.

Although the skull and teeth remain the most reliable guide to genera, each occupies a different niche with a distinct diet. Rock hyraxes are mainly diurnal, arid-adapted grazers, living in colonies among rocks. Tree hyraxes are mainly nocturnal browsers, scattered singly or in small groups among moist forest trees. Bush hyraxes are browsers that feed in trees but live in colonies among rocks.

All species have very long bodies that are concealed by a hunched posture and long fur. All have long, tactile hairs, especially on the muzzle, throat, brows, cheeks, rump and limb joints. All species have skin glands that run down the spine and most have differently coloured hair patches that can be erected or fanned open as scent-dispensers. Both identity and status are signalled by scent. Disproportionately large jaws and an ability to draw the lips right back allow them to bite off and chew large mouthfuls of vegetation at a time. This means that two or more short feeding bouts are sufficient to fill the stomach.

Long periods of inactivity (in carefully chosen sites and sometimes lasting several days) both conserve energy and also help digestion. Hyraxes can weather extended droughts in the absence of water and on diets of very low nutritive value. Both gut and kidneys are highly efficient at extracting nutrients and saving water. Urine is copious and dilute in the wet season but very concentrated and syrupy in the dry season. Several species urinate at communal 'latrines' that may be centuries (or millennia) old. All species drop their dung at specific spots. Dung, urine and very loud calls (amplified by guttural pouches) are used to define territories. These may be effectively group territories but are primarily defended by single adult ♂♂. The M's home range is shared by one or more ♀♀ and their offspring. The age at which young ♂♂ are expelled varies. They disperse into peripheral ranges, there to develop or await tenancy of their own territories in a very vulnerable situation.

Low-level aggression underpins much of the hyrax's social life. Dominance is indicated by bristling fur, an exposed dorsal gland, tooth-grinding, snapping and growling. Upper incisors are very sharp and can inflict deep and damaging bites. Appeasement gestures are therefore pervasive, especially 'presenting' of the rump with fur and body as flat as possible. This may explain why hyraxes typically enter holes, group huddles, and even fights, backwards.

The genera differ substantially in their mating calls and genital structures. Most species are seasonal breeders; in ♂♂ the weight of the testes increases by up to 20 times, with corresponding surges in testosterone and ♂ aggression. A gestation of 7 or 8 months is almost without precedent in such a small animal but the infant is born fully developed and takes its first nibble of plants within 4 days. Young are weaned by 3 months and are sexually mature by 16 months. Hyraxes suffer predation from numerous carnivores and raptors, especially cats, jackals, eagles and eagle owls.

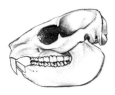
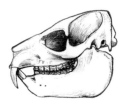

| Rock hyrax
(*Procavia johnstoni*) | Bush hyrax
(*Heterohyrax brucei*) | Tree hyrax
(*Dendrohyrax dorsalis*) |

KEY

Rock hyraxes (*Procavia*): Tooth row tapered and bowed, with broad and deep teeth. Row of four front teeth shorter than that of three back teeth. Attachments for temporal chewing muscles converge on midline of domed brain-case. Advertising call is a long series of ascending yelps descending to grunts.

Bush hyraxes (*Heterohyrax*): Cheek teeth intermediate but sharply cusped. Row of four front teeth about equal to that of the three back teeth. Attachments for temporal muscles meet or nearly meet on top of curved brain-case. Advertising call is a penetrating series of whining mews.

Tree hyraxes (*Dendrohyrax*): Cheek teeth narrow, relatively shallow, sharply cusped. Row of four front teeth longer than that of the three back teeth. Attachments for temporal muscles widely separate on sides of flat brain-case. Advertising calls are very variable but all have ascending cries and very loud crescendo.

Rock hyraxes *Procavia* (5 species)

Other names: Fr. *Daman de rocher*. Ger. *Klippschliefer*. Swah. *Pimbe*.
Measurements: HB 38–60cm. W 1.8–5.5kg.
Recognition: These blunt-faced hyraxes vary in colour both regionally and individually but are generally brown with a paler underside. Sometimes treated as a single species, *Procavia* is more usually divided into five species, most of which have been still further subdivided into subspecies. Dorsal patches can be yellow, black or piebald in the two most central populations but outlying species are more consistent in the colour of their patches.
Species: Cape rock hyrax, *P. capensis* (S and SW Africa): black dorsal patch. Ethiopian rock hyrax, *P. habessinica* (NE Africa and Arabia): variable dorsal patch. Black-necked rock hyrax, *P. johnstoni* (central and E Africa): variable dorsal patch. Kaokoveld rock hyrax, *P. welwitchii* (Kaokoveld): pale cream dorsal patch. Red-headed rock hyrax, *P. ruficeps* (S. Sahara): orange dorsal patch.

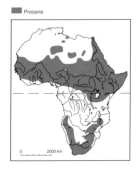
Procavia

Procavia johnstoni mackinderi.

Distribution: Drier rocky areas of Africa and Arabia.

Habitat: Mainly rock outcroppings, often in areas where the rocks themselves assist the growth of vegetation by trapping moisture or nutrients. Rocks also create micro-climates that can be cooler, warmer, drier, moister, more shady, sunnier or less windy than the surroundings. Hyraxes can therefore counter-act climatic extremes to some extent by finding surfaces or crevices that suit their physiological needs at any particular time. Crevices also provide shelter from predators.

Food: Mainly grasses and herbs grazed within easy reach of shelter. Common grasses taken are species of *Aristida*, *Chrysopogon*, *Tetrapogon* and *Latipes*. In the alpine region of Mt Kenya *Festuca* is a staple. Shrubs and trees are also climbed and browsed, sometimes only seasonally. Feeding is limited to about 1 hour in the early morning and a longer session in late afternoon. Rock hyraxes may feed at night during desert summers.

Behaviour: Rock hyraxes are territorial, with single ♂ territories containing various numbers of ♀♀ and their offspring up to a total of about 25 animals. In an outcrop the number of territories depends partly on their individual defendability but mainly on their year-round resources of food and shelter. ♀♀ are generally closely related and frequently come into close physical contact with other ♀♀ and young within their unit. However, adult ♀♀ have their own exclusive core areas, albeit ones that are very close to their fellows. There is no very marked hierarchy other than the territorial M's position of dominance. His intolerance of maturing ♂ offspring leads to an emigration and selective exposure of young ♂♂ which leads to an imbalance of the sexes, especially among adults.

All members of a single territorial group or colony share a number of latrines. These appear to be of two types. Urine is dribbled down very exposed, outward-facing rocks where calcium carbonates dissolve and are deposited as very conspicuous white or light-coloured streaks. These may serve as external olfactory and visual markers for specific colonies. The second type of latrine is situated in more shaded, protected sites. Both dung and urine are dropped in the same place, preferably on a flat or nearly flat surface. Here liquids and solids congeal slowly, there is less evaporation and the smell can be very strong indeed. These latrines appear to function as scenting parlours where all members of the group come to share a common smell that scents their feet and fur.

Breeding seasons are often very local and can differ from the top to the bottom of an escarpment. The ♂ is very vocal during the mating season and shakes his head while approaching the ♀, his dorsal gland open and actively exuding scent. Up to six young are born after a gestation of 214–240 days. Almost immediately active, and soon eating plants, young frequently climb onto their mother's back where they may become scented by her dorsal gland and warmed by her body. They mature at 16 months and are known to live for up to 12 years.

Adaptations: The main speciality of rock hyraxes is their ability to live off coarse desert grasses and both their teeth and digestion differ substantially from the arboreal, folivorous species. However, they are more conservative in being weaker and less agile climbers.

Status: Although subject to periodic epidemics, heavy natural predation and very localised depletion or extermination all species of *Procavia* are still numerous. Not endangered.

Heterohyrax

Heterohyrak brucei.

Bush hyraxes *Heterohyrax* (3 species)

Other names: Fr. *Daman de steppe*. Ger. *Buschschliefer*. Swah. *Perere mawe*.

Measurements: HB 32–57cm. W 2–3.5kg.

Recognition: A relatively small hyrax with conspicuous pale 'eyebrows', a white or off-white underside and a greyish, pepper-and-salt agouti body colour. The snout is more pointed than that of the rock hyrax and the animal is altogether more lightly built. Commonly treated as a single species, bush hyraxes comprise a very widespread form with two highly distinctive isolates, one on a Sahara massif, the other on the banks of the R. Zaïre near its mouth.

Species: Yellow-spotted hyrax, *H. brucei* (S, E and NE Africa and the Sinai): yellow dorsal spot. Hoggar hyrax, *H. antinae* (Hoggar massif): small, with mane but no spot. Matadi hyrax, *H. chapini* (mouth of the R. Zaïre): a large muzzle and brows.

Distribution: Eastern half of Africa with two western outliers. Recorded from higher altitudes (notably north-west of L. Malawi).

Habitat: Wooded localities on riverbanks, escarpments and rock outcrops. Normally shelters in rocks but may resort to trees, termitaries or old burrows. Often found in joint colonies with rock hyraxes.

Food: Leaves, fruits, stems, twigs and bark. On Serengeti outcrops virtually the entire diet comes from two trees, *Acacia tortilis* and *Allophylus*. Acacias are a major food over most of the bush-hyrax's range.

Behaviour: Single colonies can number up to 34 individuals with ♀♀ mixing very readily with each other and also, where present, with ♀ rock hyraxes. They utter sustained 5-minute bouts of loud call, a whining croak that is much less resonant and deep than that of other hyraxes. Their very bird-like alarm whistle alerts other species, including rock hyraxes and klipspringers. They flag their heads with a pronounced shiver.

Adaptations: Bush hyraxes appear to illustrate the earliest steps in the colonisation of trees by an animal apparently ill-equipped to do so. Their primary asset in this niche is probably their exceptionally efficient gut, capable of digesting difficult plant foods.

Status: The yellow-spotted hyrax is widespread and extremely abundant in many localities. Both the Matadi and Hoggar hyraxes are little known, isolated and probably rare.

300

Tree hyraxes *Dendrohyrax* (3 species)

Other names: Fr. *Daman d'arbre*. Ger. *Waldschliefer*. Swah. *Perere*.
Measurements: HB 32–60cm. W 1.5–4.5kg.
Recognition: Densely furred, arboreal hyraxes with elongated hands and feet, mostly dark (although pale, cream-coloured morphs are known). The three species are normally separable on the length of their naked dorsal patch. The western tree hyrax has very coarse, thick hair (but is softer furred in Uganda where it has probably hybridised with the southern species).

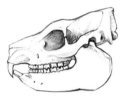

Dendrohyrox validus
Pemba Is.

Species: Eastern tree hyrax, *D. validus* (eastern mountains, islands, coast): naked patch 20–40mm long and dorsal fur russet-coloured.

Dendrohyrox arboreus
Ruwenzori

Southern tree hyrax, *D. arboreus* (S, E and central Africa): naked patch 23–30mm long and dorsal fur cream-coloured.
Western tree hyrax, *D. dorsalis* (W and central Africa): naked patch 42–72mm long and dorsal fur white.

Dendrohyrox dorsalis
Cameroon

Dendrohyrax validus
Dendrohyrax arboreus
Dendrohyrax dorsalis

Distribution: Equatorial Africa and scattered down the east coast to the E Cape; also Zanzibar and Pemba Is. Ranges from sea-level to 4,500m. Species and races occupy distinct lowland and upland zones in a very complex pattern, suggesting the expansion and contraction and hybridisation of closely related populations. The western tree hyrax is a lowland form that has reached the Nile by-passing the southern species in the central African mountains. Further east, in Tanzania, the eastern tree hyrax remains in the mountains while the southern tree hyrax dominates the lowlands.

Habitat: Forests, moist savannahs, evergreen thickets and mosaics (derived from forest) and all montane habitats. *D. arboreus ruwenzorii* and related forms are (or were) abundant throughout the Afro-alpine and forest zones of W Uganda and E Zaïre. On the higher reaches of these cold, wet mountains the hyraxes live among rocks, are partly diurnal and have colonial habits. In montane forest they are arboreal, nocturnal and tend to be more solitary.

Food: Leaves, fruits and twigs in the canopy, grasses and sedges on screes. Giant groundsel and numerous aromatic leaves and herbs are regularly eaten. Rapid feeders, tree hyraxes can eat a third of their own body weight of food in a day.

Behaviour: Tree hyraxes often live at very high densities, especially in the mountains. They are territorial and very aggressive during the mating season. Both ♂♂ and ♀♀ exude secretion from their dorsal glands at this time. ♂ courtship involves following the ♀, calling and gland-fanning with penile erection. Gestation is about 8 months with the precocious 400g newborn able to climb on its first day. Tree hyraxes are known to live for 12 years.

Adaptations: The most obvious speciality of tree hyraxes is contortionist mobility in their relatively long limbs and body. Mainly nocturnal habits may have stimulated the extraordinary volume, variety and frequency of their calls. Loud advertising or territorial calls are particularly variable, even within one species and from one side of a big river to another. All loud calls involve long series of cries that gradually grow louder, climaxing in barks, shrieks or choking screams. The eastern tree hyrax has an apparent contact call in the timbre of a man's voice asking 'whotsit?' Other calls resemble baboon grunts. Extreme volubility in tree hyraxes is mainly seasonal and can begin well before dark and continue all night during peak periods and in areas of high density.

Status: Tree hyraxes could be at risk from clear-felling in some localities, from snaring in others. Felling and firing forests on Tanzanian islands and mountains is the most immediate threat to the eastern tree hyrax. Snaring for meat and skins is also severe in many central African mountains. A lack of research into the basic biology and ecological needs of tree hyraxes is regrettable because their uneven abundance and patchy distribution will need to be understood before practical conservation plans can be attempted. Overall, the western tree hyrax is not endangered but the state of local and distinctive populations of the southern and eastern species gives cause for concern.

PROBOSCIDS PROBOSCIDEA

The proboscis or trunk is thought to have been the primary structure that made possible the evolution of the elephants' great size, height and long tusks. Trunks are capable of powerful twisting and coiling while gathering food or wrestling with other elephants but can also perform delicate movements, such as picking berries, rubbing eyes or exploring orifices. Trunks can draw up columns of water or dust and their great length can reach up to 7m or burrow down into sand, soil or crevices to reach deeply hidden water. While the development of a trunk relieved the incisor teeth of most of their feeding functions the incisors' potential as weapons developed rapidly as the elephants' ancestors increased in size. As they evolved bigger and bigger bodies, elephants lost versatility in their limbs

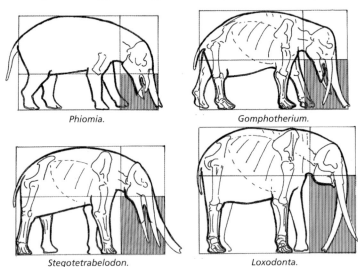

Phiomia. *Gomphotherium.*

Stegotetrabelodon. *Loxodonta.*

which, first and foremost, had to bear great weight. Physical contacts with fellow elephants and with the environment became focused on the head. The trunk handled food and gentler forms of social contact. Tusks became both tools and weapons of defence used in ritualised fighting with their own species.

Elephants fossilise well so that an ever more detailed picture of later elephant evolution continues to unfold from a wealth of fossils (the earlier stages are less well documented). Before 65 million years ago elephants had shared a common ancestry with odd-toed ungulates (rhinoceroses and horses) and with hyraxes but they only emerged as a distinctly African group after the continent has become isolated. Both early elephants and early sea-cows began as wallowing herbivorous cousins but one remained terrestrial while the sea-cows became wholly aquatic.

The earliest fossil, *Phiomia*, dates from about 35 million years ago and appears to have been a swamp-dwelling equivalent of the modern tapir. *Gomphotherium* (25 million years old) shows that, as size and weight increased, limbs had to become more like columns. Both tusks and trunk became progressively elongated.

By 7 million years ago *Stegotetrabelodon* had become tall, heavy and long-trunked but retained tusks in both upper and lower jaws. Improvement in the mechanics of chewing led to a rapid decline and elimination of the lower tusks but vestiges of their bony sleeves can still be traced in the lower jaws of living elephants (particularly in the forest race, *Loxodonta africana cyclotis*).

The direct ancestors of the African and Asian elephants and the mammoths split into three lines about 5 million years ago but reached their greatest diversity (at least ten species) by less than 1 million years ago. Just as elephants were reaching the peak of their evolutionary and ecological success they became prey to a new predator – humans. Directly or indirectly as a result of human activity eight species of elephant have become extinct within less than half a million years. Such a record places efforts to conserve the remaining elephants in a rather gloomy light.

ELEPHANTS ELEPHANTIDAE

Modern elephants evolved in Africa with startling rapidity and seem to owe their later success to an adaptive shift out of very wet, marshy environments into drier, more open and difficult habitats where they became the prime specialist in bulk-feeding on coarse vegetation. To cope with rougher diets their teeth became heavy-duty 'rasp-grinders': single molars set in very short jaws. In the course of a lifetime six cheek teeth succeed one another, travelling very slowly along the jaw at an angle that wears them away from front to back. Each in turn drops out once its grinding surface is used up. After the sixth tooth the sequence has run its course and the toothless elephant dies. Elephants are thought to live longest where wear of the teeth is slowest and their life-spans may range from about 50 to 65 years.

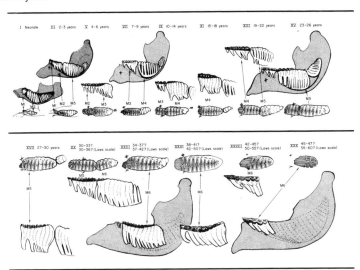

Tooth succession in the African elephant.

Linked with long life and very large size are slow growth and many years of slow maturation. This in turn demands tightly knit social groups that are both durable and reliable, not least because of the dangers to youngsters from large predators. Adult elephants are invulnerable to all living predators, except humans, but young calves are not. Maintaining complex social bonds with dozens of 'clan' members and many hundreds of regular acquaintances demands memory and intelligence of a high order. Because of a long learning period within a stable (and often very mobile) social group elephants build up a highly flexible, multi-faceted relationship with the environment, its changing resources and the other animals that inhabit it. Learnt skills help them to weather substantial fluctuations in climate and vegetation. Similar advantages were clearly shared by mammoths, *Mammuthus*, in Ice-Age Eurasia and North America and by the Indian elephant, *Elephas indicus*, in S Asia.

Throughout some 4 million years of climatic instability *Elephas* was a highly successful species in Africa as well as Eurasia, becoming extinct in Africa as late as about 20,000 years ago. By contrast, today's African elephant, *Loxodonta*, is absent or rare as a fossil. The most likely explanation for this is that its ancestors became specialised for life in the moist forests (where bones seldom fossilise). Here the very distinctive forest elephant, *Loxodonta africanus cyclotis* still exists. It is now well known that mammal populations can change their body size over very short periods of time, so the forest elephant's emergence has probably been followed by just such a secondary enlargement. The bush elephants have been the beneficiaries of the *Elephas* extinction. However, the human hunting skills that probably helped to destroy *Elephas* in Africa have now been honed on *Loxodonta* and may well bring about its extinction as well. Only a collective human will to preserve elephants and their habitats can save them now.

Forest elephant.

Bush elephant.

Loxodonta africana (1975)

Former range

///. Forest range

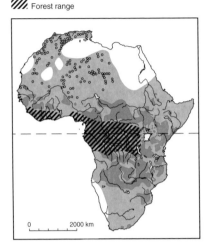

Loxodonta africana

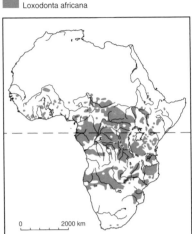

0 ____ 2000 km

0 ____ 2000 km

African elephant *Loxodonta africana*

Other names: Fr. *Elephant d'Afrique*. Ger. *Afrikanischer Elefant*. Swah. *Ndovu, Tembo*.

Measurements: Bush elephant, *L. a. africana*: HB (unstable measure). T 1–1.5m. SH 2.4–3.4m. (♀), 3–4m. (♂). W 2,200–3,500kg (♀), 4,000–6,300kg (♂).
Forest (Pygmy) elephant, *L. a. cyclotis*: HB (unstable measure). T 0.5–1.2 m. SH 1.6–2.4m. (♀), 1.7–2.8m. (♂). W 900–3,000kg (♀),1,200–3,500kg (♂).

Recognition: The largest land animals, elephants are easily identifiable in having a trunk, tusks, large ears and pillar-like legs. Their thick skin is only superficially pigmented and the intensity of the melanin layer varies from a dense black to pale grey, brown or, in rare instances, depigmented pink (in patches or overall). Newborn elephants are often very hairy and adults retain coarse, short bristles on the trunk, chin and, as abraded remnants, in the crevices over much of the rest of the body. The large, round ears are not only sound-catching dishes and flagging devices but also a cooling mechanism. The backs of the ears are laced with blood vessels which help to reduce the elephant's overall body temperature when the ears are fanned. The tusks are modified incisors composed of layered dentine and their presence or absence, size, shape, orientation and microstructure are subject to much variation.

The feet are columnar with the original five toes bound into a hoop of tissue, skin and nail above a cushion of elastic tissue. Nails vary from five on both fore- and hindfeet to four on the forefeet and three on the hindfeet, the latter being the norm in bush elephants. The smooth but cracked foot pads leave individually recognisable tracks, circular for the forefeet, smaller and more elongated for the hindfeet. Tracks, frequent boluses, occasional urine puddles and extensive harvesting of plants are the most commonly seen signs of elephants. Elephants of both sexes and all ages have temporal glands behind the eye which periodically secrete a liquid called temporin.

Subspecies: Bush elephant, *L. a. africana*; forest (pygmy) elephant, *L. a. cyclotis*. Note: Because successful adaptation to peculiar ecological conditions depends upon long-maintained family traditions, elephants readily evolve subpopulations. These can show consistent characteristics in size, ear shape, limb proportions, skull and tusk shape, number of nails, skin texture and colour. As a result 25 subspecies have been proposed. The 'forest' *cyclotis* and 'pygmy' *pumilio* have even been given full species status by some taxonomists and field-guide authors (however, see Adaptations below).

Distribution: Formerly most of Africa except the driest regions of the Sahara. Even so their ability to forage as far as 80km from water greatly augmented their overall range in otherwise marginal areas. Conflict with farmers increases as the latter continue to expand into the elephants' remaining pockets of range. Further attrition from ivory-poaching has lessened from its 1970s' and 1980s' peaks but is still substantial in some localities.

CLIMATE	ECOLOGICAL CONDITIONS	ELEPHANTS
DRY	Fires and destruction of grass	Move towards refuge areas Avoid fires and human activity
	Flood plains dry but grass still growing	Move on to flood plains Temporary concentrations in borassus groves
	Surface water finished	Move to hills, forests or rivers for permanent shade Less feeding. More resting Barking trees
Early rain	Flushes of green growth	Major movement initally by males Concentration on localized pastures, followed by dispersal
WET	Rapid growth everywhere	Longer feeding. More active
	Somer valley soils gluey	Avoid slippery, sticky soils
End of rain	Grassa long	Well dispersed in grasslands and savanna

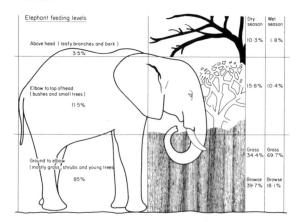

Dry season refuge areas with wet season dispersals suggested by arrows.
The map summarizes knowledge of seasonal movements.
Elephants have now been eliminated in a number of areas shown here. (Data from Brooks and Buss, 1962a; Lamprey, 1963; Cobb, 1976; Uganda, Kenya and Tanzania Game Dept. records; and personal research.)

Habitat: All major vegetation types, usually more than one being included within the annual cycle. The bush elephant's dependence on shade and water is well illustrated by the pattern of dry-season retreat into forests and swamps (shown for East Africa). This could be influenced by the short time (about 10,000–20,000 years ago) since they expanded into drier regimes.

Although elephants mainly eat the plants that are available they have preferences and dislikes which result in the local disappearance, selective survival and dispersal of particular plants and plant communities. In this way elephants have been a major influence on most vegetation communities for many millennia. The physical impact of elephants is also evident in browse lines, broad pathways, sunken waterholes, 'ploughed' soil and caves excavated for salt.

Elephant feeding levels

Above head (leafy branches and bark) 3·5%

Elbow to top of head (bushes and small trees) 11·5%

Ground to elbow (mostly grass, shrubs and young trees) 85%

	Dry season	Wet season
	10·3%	1·8%
	15·8%	10·4%
Grass	34·4%	69·7%
Browse	39·7%	18·1%

Food: Grass and browse are taken in different and changing proportions by season (see above). Elephants consume about 5% of their body weight (i.e. up to 300kg) in 24 hours and vegetation takes about 12 hours to pass through the animal. The bush-bashing that is typical of many ♂ ungulates has a nutritional by-product for the elephants. Trees are most frequently felled by young or solitary ♂♂ so that obtaining out-of-reach fruits, leaves, pith or branches may not be the only reason for such behaviour. The crash of a felled tree sometimes attracts families or other solitary ♂♂ and the arrival of the latter may precipitate chases and contests.

Sketches of young elephants.

Behaviour: The central social unit in elephant society is the mother and her offspring. In forests such families may include no more than one or two offspring. ♀ elephants are not able to conceive until 8 years of age (20 at latest) but once they become mothers they soon become unit leaders, or 'matriarchs'. Bush elephants find it easier to forage, find one another and travel in larger groups but even here the nuclear family tends to split by the time there are ten daughters and grandparents. Nonetheless, closely related 'matriarchal' groups in the same vicinity maintain frequent and friendly meetings for many years. These and larger associations have been variously labelled 'bond-groups' or 'clans'. ♂♂ are driven out of these associations at about 10–14 years of age. Thereafter, they may join up with other ♂♂ but tend to choose partners that are either substantially younger or older than themselves in an informal, linear hierarchy. Dominance is less a feature of ♀ groups but age, size and health determine the 'matriarch' in large family groups. Very aged or permanently disabled ♀♀ are forced to drop out of their groups.

♀ elephants are frequent 'talkers', using rumbles, growls, roars, snorts, squeals and trumpets to convey a variety of signals, conditions and emotions. The most remarkable part of their repertoire, infrasound, was only discovered in 1987.

♀♀ come into oestrus for 2–6 days after an interval of anything between 3 and 9 years. Their advertisement of this rare and vital condition depends on a unique sequence of sounds emitted at below the threshold of human hearing but perceptible at least 4km away and, depending on the weather and topography, sometimes much further. ♀♀ routinely use infrasound to keep in touch with and monitor other groups in their clan or regional population. ♂♂ are more silent but passively eavesdrop until the unmistakable mating song is heard. In such an event all ♂♂ within range immediately hasten towards the singer, the fastest and most urgent suitors being those that are in 'musth', periodic rutting behaviour marked by a continuous flow of secretion from the swollen temporal gland lasting 1–103 days. Rutting ♂♂ also develop a swollen, semi-erect penis that dribbles urine and a greenish fluid. Tests have shown that the aggressiveness of musth bulls is linked with high levels of testosterone. ♂♂ in this condition appear to intimidate all other classes of elephant but are the preferred partners for oestrous ♀♀, who benefit from their close (but not continuous) attention because they discourage the attentions of numerous other ♂♂.

Gestation lasts 650–660 days and one, very rarely two, young are born, with a slight peak of births in the rains. Although they rise to their feet within hours, newborn elephants are visibly unsteady for several weeks (a feebleness that attracts lions and hyaenas). Mothers are alert to all their infant's needs, helping it over all manner of obstacles with trunk and feet. They are particularly sensitive to any signs of dehydration and, in the absence of other sources, will regurgitate water from their own stomachs. Mothers will pump water directly into their infants' mouth and will squirt and massage it while playing in shallow water. Although calves can survive on solid food before they are 2 years old, mothers tend to remain in milk for about 4 years (some lactate continuously throughout their reproductive life). Offspring become independent at varying rates; some scarcely leave their mother's side until they are nearly 10 years old (an age at which some will already have calves of their own). Body size and the development of tusks are also very variable, making overall estimates of ages by height or tusk length difficult. In the case of dead elephants, jaws provide a reliable measure of age (see page 303). Elephants are thought to live no longer than 65 years.

Adaptations: Elephants are an amalgam of many extraordinary specialisations but all species were originally ecological variants on the main adaptive theme of mega-herbivore. Before widespread and recent extinction (presumably at the hands of prehistoric human hunters), elephants were diverse, abundant, highly successful and actively evolving new forms in special habitats and on many offshore islands. On a much smaller and shorter scale, modern African elephants had begun to diverge along similar lines: desert specialists in Namibia, dwarfs in the Atlas Mts. In the swamps of the R. Rufiji delta a trend towards particularly large ears, a smooth skin and tuskless jaws shows that families and subpopulations can maintain peculiar, possibly adaptive, traits even in the absence of complete isolation.

 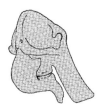

Skulls of a million-year-old *Loxodonta adaurora* and contemporary forest elephant *L.a. cyclotis*.

Recent studies of the genetics of forest elephants in central W Africa have corroborated my suggestion (1976) that these could be dwarfed ecological isolates descended from the extinct *Loxodonta adaurora* (last fossils 2 million years old). If so, forest elephant populations could represent a particularly ancient lineage at the centre of their distribution. Less conservative populations may traverse the same region (between Cameroon and the R. Zaïre) and certainly occur in other parts of the *L. a. cyclotis* range. If bush elephants have derived from these small forest animals their enormous size must be a very recent and secondary development. Contrasts in size and habitat could inhibit mixing but there are undoubted periods and areas where 'hybridisation' takes place between bush and forest elephants. There are also places where they co-exist as separate entities without genetic mixing.

Numerous features of the bush elephant's biology, especially its sensitivity to dehydration and heat, suggest that adaptation to arid environments is a recent and ongoing process.

The surviving populations of elephants, small and scattered as they are, still exemplify great diversity and continuous adaptation to climate and the new challenges posed by human control of their environment. Nonetheless, African elephants would appear to represent a single, highly dynamic species.

Status: The decline of elephants in Africa is not new. They were first eliminated from North Africa by about the fourth century AD through a combination of ivory-hunting and increasing aridity. Then they were exterminated by the settlement of South Africa during the eighteenth and nineteenth centuries and over much of W Africa in the present century. Low ivory prices and extensive legal protection between 1920 and 1970 allowed an extensive recovery in much of tropical Africa, only to be followed by massive decline in the 1980s as new business interests, as well as a few corrupt politicians and soldiers, organised the wholesale killing of elephants for ivory. From between 5 million and 10 million in the 1930s and 1940s, African elephants have declined to between half and three-quarters of a million at the present time.

Numerous bodies exist to protect elephants, both nationally and internationally. The ultimate success of all these initiatives depends upon long-term, sound education and sustained, honest management at the most local level. Among the more promising initiatives has been the production of an Action Plan and other resources, including a document on how to study elephants.

Due to the precipitous recent decline of the African elephant, IUCN has listed it as an Endangered Species, Appendix 1 (CITES).

ODD-TOED UNGULATES
PERISSODACTYLA

Horses	Equidae
Rhinoceroses	Rhinocerotidae

Perissodactyls emerged from a primitive ungulate group about 65 million years ago. The earliest forms had five toes on both fore- and hindfeet. These have been progressively reduced through time to three in rhinoceroses and one in horses (equids). Excellent fossil series document the progression and show that this evolution took place outside Africa. The fossil evidence suggests that this group diversified in America and Eurasia to become the most abundant of herbivores between 55 million and 25 million years ago. They retain a superior ability to digest coarse fibrous vegetation.

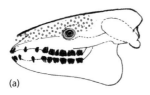

(a)

(b)

(a) The head of an archaic perissodactyl.
(b) Modern horse, light skull carried high, prominent grazing incisors, deep molars. Good vision. Fast.
(c) Rhino, heavy skull and horns swing low. Fore-mouth compressed. Poor vision strong.

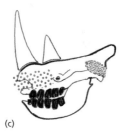

(c)

HORSES EQUIDAE

Horses evolved in North America where well-dated and well-preserved fossils record their evolution from a small, duiker-like forest animal called the 'dawn horse', or *Eohippus*. Many of the early forms were browsers but one lineage adapted to a diet of tougher vegetation and to drier, harder soils under foot.

Modern horses and zebras mostly differentiated in North America but were so successful that they spread over Eurasia and Africa during the last 3 million years.

   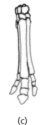

(a)   (b)   (c)   (c)

(a) Protoungulate (*Phenacodus*).
(b) Primitive perissodactyl (*Hyracotherium*).
(c) Early horse (*Miohippus*).
(d) Modern horse (*Equus*).

African horses *Equus*

Wild ass	*Equus africanus*
Common zebra	*Equus quagga*
Mountain zebra	*Equus zebra*
Grevy's zebra	*Equus grevyi*

Recognition: The African horses are all partially or wholly striped and all have a short, sleek coat. All have a big, long head, with large, flat chewing muscles over deeply rooted tooth rows. The neck is muscular and maned and the body is compact with a deep chest and very muscular haunches. The legs are strong and bony, with hard, single hooves. Horses can be very vocal, with a variety of neighs, barks or brays, squeals and whinnies.

Genealogy: Only the most successful of horses, those able to compete with ruminants, found their way to Africa from North America.

Geography: Both the common and Grevy's zebra evolved their basic adaptive specialisation outside Africa. The present distributions of all horses are only vestiges of their past ranges.

Ecology: Zebras are high-density, tropical grassland horses. Asses are low-density, desert-adapted forms. Their ability to digest tough, unpalatable grasses and move quickly between pastures is not matched by any bovid. Nor is the speed of their digestion.

Natural history: Horses are extremely flexible, easily dispersing as small units or joining up in very large aggregations. The basic unit of a ♀ and her young may acquire a permanent attendant ♂ that is equally mobile or they may move in or out of ♂ territories. All horses keep their coat in condition by dust-bathing, rolling, rubbing and some mutual nibbling.

Adaptations: The stripes of zebras appear to serve as a visual bonding device. It is known that evenly spaced, black and white bars stimulate visual neurones very strongly and the zebras' stripes appear to make them super-attractive to one another. The aggressively anti-social behaviour of territorial animals would thus appear to be counter-acted to some extent by visual attractiveness. Notwithstanding this, both ♂♂ and ♀♀ are mutually antagonistic and even young foals (the most social class) prefer members of the opposite sex.

A short, sleek coat is required in order to produce the crisp edges necessary for a striking visual pattern such as the zebra's stripes. Thick, shaggy coats required in cold climates subvert this. Striping was therefore absent or vestigial in temperate horses and in the quagga (now extinct), a population that lived on the temperate wastes of the Karoo. Likewise the value of striping as a visual bonding system is greatly reduced when an equid is at low densities with infrequent gatherings. Thus, although African asses show vestigial patterns on legs and neck, they otherwise match their tawny-grey surroundings.

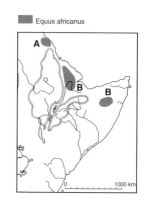

Equus africanus

Wild ass *Equus africanus*

Other names: Fr. *Ane sauvage*. Ger. *Wildesel*. Swah. *Punda*.

Measurements: HB est. 195–205cm. T 40–45cm. SH 115–125cm. W 270–280kg.

Recognition: The wild ancestor of domestic donkeys, the wild ass is lean and muscular, fawn or grey, with a near-white belly and legs. It has a short, hairy black brush to the tail, a black mane and black margins to the long leaf-shaped ears. Hooves are exceptionally narrow.

Subspecies: Nubian wild ass, *E. a. africanus*: grey with only shoulder striped. Somali wild ass, *E. a. somalicus*: fawn, with only legs striped. Note: Algerian asses depicted in rock-paintings and Roman mosaics show a form with both leg stripes and a long, bold shoulder stripe. (Invalid NW African '*atlanticus*' identification was based on zebra bones!)

Distribution: Formerly Saharan region to Red Sea and Somalia (possibly in S Arabia in prehistoric times), in regions with a brief annual rainfall of 100–200mm. Now found in relict pockets on the Red Sea littoral, Danakil, Ogaden and Nogal valley.

Habitat: Semi-desert grasslands and dwarf shrublands (typified by aloes and euphorbias) where the asses tend to retreat into rocky hills and seek shade during the day. They are most active when the weather is cooler: at dusk, dawn and during the night. They are always within a 30km walk to water (but will tolerate brackish sources). They are able to go without water for about 3 days.

Food: Grasses, notably *Eragrostis*, *Dactyloctenium* and *Chrysopogon*. Wild asses are well adapted to graze the hardest of desert grasses, such as *Panicum* and *Lasiurus* species. They use their incisors and hooves to break open tussocks.

Behaviour: Very small mother-offspring units are independent of each other but gather opportunistically in search of good grazing. Their preferred range is often within vast territories held by mature ♂♂. These may exceed 20km² and their boundaries with those of adjacent ♂♂ are marked by dung piles. Other ♂♂ are tolerated within the territory but all access to ♀♀ is monopolised by the territory-holder. Oestrous ♀♀ stimulate frequent loud braying in ♂♂. One foal is born after a 330–365-day gestation. Initially the foal is passive and fearless and will remain alone for long periods while the mother seeks water to maintain her lactation. The foal can start grazing within weeks of birth but may suckle for as long as 6 months. Animals are known to live for 40 years in captivity

Adaptations: The small narrow and very hard hooves of wild asses are specifically adapted to firm and rocky ground. Wild asses avoid sandy areas and have always been absent from all the sandy dune regions of the Sahara.

Status: Asses occupy the last vestiges of a formerly vast range. Intolerance by herders and degradation of the range by their livestock have been the principal causes of their long decline. Their only immediate salvation lies in captive breeding (notably at Basel zoo and Hai Bar reserve in the Negev Desert). Listed as Endangered on Appendix I (CITES).

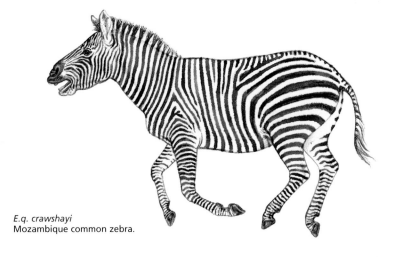

E.q. crawshayi
Mozambique common zebra.

Common zebra *Equus quagga*

Other names: Fr. *Zèbre de steppe*. Ger. *Steppenzebra*. Swah. *Punda milia*.

Measurements: HB 217–246cm. T 47–57cm. SH 127–140cm. W 175–250kg (♀), 220–322kg (♂).

Recognition: A muscular horse with relatively short neck and sturdy legs. The stripes are subject to much regional and individual variation. Patterns are better illustrated than described (see fig. above and overleaf).

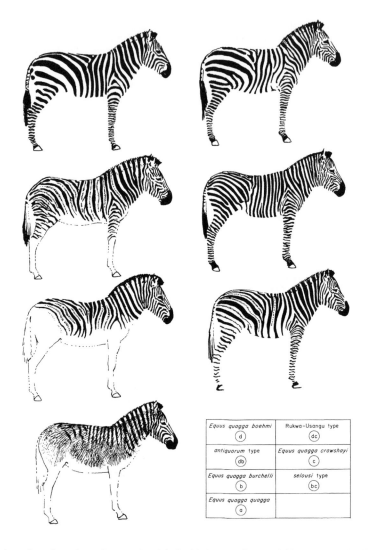

Equus quagga boehmi (d)	Rukwa–Usangu type (dc)
antiquorum type (db)	Equus quagga crawshayi (c)
Equus quagga burchelli (b)	selousi type (bc)
Equus quagga quagga (a)	

Subspecies: These form three regional foci with intermediate variable types coming from very extensive interzones. A fourth type, the quagga, is extinct (possibly a distinct species). There are four major populations: (a) *E. q. quagga* (Cape, Karoo), extinct; (b) *E. q. burchelli* (NE Cape); (c) *E. q. crawshayi* (SE Africa), tropical; (d) *E. q. boehmi* (central and E Africa). Intermediate or variable populations: (bd) *E. q. antiquorum* (subtropical SW Africa); (bc) *E. q. selousi* (SE Africa), subtropical. Intermediates between c and d occur in Rukwa/Usangu area.

Distribution: Formerly inhabited all of non-forest, non-desertic Africa (e.g. it appears to have occupied Algeria for 2 million years). In historic times limited to S and E Africa east of the Nile and south of the R. Zaïre basin.

Habitat: Grasslands, steppes, savannahs and woodlands. These zebras are totally dependent on frequent drinking. They prefer firm ground underfoot so may move off sumplands in the wet season or during flooding.

Food: Grass of the most available species. Adaptable grazers, they mow short lawns close to the roots but are equally able to take taller flowering grasses. Water shortage may concentrate zebra populations around available water-holes during the dry season. Daily activity is dominated by shifts from open night-time resting areas to pastures, to water and back to sleep or rest.

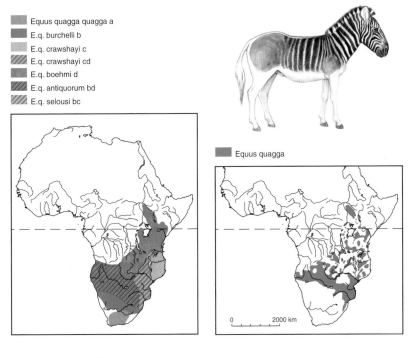

Equus quagga quagga a
E.q. burchelli b
E.q. crawshayi c
E.q. crawshayi cd
E.q. boehmi d
E.q. antiquorum bd
E.q. selousi bc

Equus quagga

0   2000 km

Behaviour: Up to six ♀♀ and their young live in very stable 'harems' where they are subject to low-key but continuous coercion by the harem stallion. He herds the ♀♀ in his group whenever they stray and threatens ♂♂ that come too close. The number of ♀♀ appears to be limited by the intolerance of established ♀♀ against incomers.

Common zebras are extremely vocal, the adult ♂♂ being particularly noisy during any nocturnal movement. For each social unit the stallion's individual 'song' (a glottal, barking bray) becomes the focal point for all harem members. Individuals which become separated from their group seek it with every sign of distress while the stallion too calls and searches until the group is reunited. Normally only harem stallions mate with harem mares but neighbours and bachelor groups show intense interest in any oestrous ♀♀. One foal (rarely 2) is born after a 12-month gestation. Foals suck milk for up to 6 months but begin to graze in the first month. They are sexually mature by 1½–3 years but ♀♀ cycle without conceiving for a year or two and ♂♂ seldom acquire harems before 5 years of age. Common zebras are known to live for 40 years.

Adaptations: Mutual nibbling of the legs, shoulders and neck is the main form of social contact within common zebra families. It is most conspicuous and frequent between mothers and their young and between similarly aged foals. This direct contact tends to diminish with age.

The movements of champing the jaws and nodding the head frequently become detached gestures that are made close to a potential grooming partner but without actually touching. Unstriped horses retain nibbling as a mode of bonding between adults. The difference may concern stripes, which are thought to facilitate bonding in adult zebra (see above). One-to-one physical bonding may develop into multi-partner 'visual bonding' through a form of conditioning or habituation. By experiencing very strong optical stimulation in the context of close contact and security the foal thereafter seeks to maintain that security by remaining close to stripes.

Status: While the causes of decline in prehistory are not known, the incompatibility of zebras with modern agriculture and ranching has led to their extermination over many areas. It is a process that continues unabated outside national parks. Given the uncertain future of small, isolated populations, some forms of common zebras may well become vulnerable or endangered in the near future.

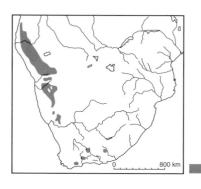

Equus zebra

Equus africanus (former range)
Equus zebra (former range)

Mountain zebra *Equus zebra*

Other names: Fr. *Zèbre de montagne*. Ger. *Bergzebra*.

Measurements: HB 220–260cm. T 40–55cm. SH 146cm (115–150cm). W 275kg (230–320kg) (♀), 300kg (250-386kg) (♂).

Recognition: Evenly spaced, vertical, black and white stripes on neck and body with a sudden 'change of scale' to three or four very bold, horizontal stripes on hindquarters. The body stripes extend into an enclosed 'grid-iron' pattern on the rump and upper tail. The legs have fine, even, black and white striping. Black stripes on the face graduate to orange-brown on the bridge of the nose and around the mouth and nostrils (which are dark brown). The ears are moderately long and broad, their backs marked with bold black and white patches. Striping in the tall mane and over a dewlap enlarges the visual impact of the neck, especially in adult ♂♂ (making them look 'front-heavy'). Hooves grow exceptionally fast, leaving a characteristic hard-edged, rounded spoor.

Subspecies: Cape mountain zebra, *E. z. zebra* (Cape and Karoo); Hartmann's mountain zebra, *E. z. hartmanni* (S Angola to Orange R.). (The smaller Cape race averages 50kg lighter.)

Distribution: Arid mountains and escarpments sufficiently close to the ocean to catch mist and cloud (and thus have springs and water sources) in a long band running from SW Angola to the mountains of the Cape and Karoo.

Habitat: Formerly widespread in bushy Karoo shrubland in uplands where extreme day-time drought in summer is offset by nocturnal dew and mist. Here the animals often occupied separate summer and winter ranges (up to 120km apart). They moved between pastures and water sources on well-worn traditional paths.

Where grazing permits, individual herds are seasonally residential (i.e. live within a 3–5km² range). Some local populations are less water-dependent than others; most prefer to drink daily and can dig into river beds with their hooves.

Food: Almost exclusively grazers (but will browse acacias on occasion). Grasses tend to be either patchy or sparse throughout their range (except for seasonal desert flushes). Recorded preferences are for *Themeda*, *Heteropogon*, *Cymbopogon* and *Aristida* species. *Stipagrostis* and *Hyparhennia* are other common grasses growing on deeply drained sites. Both individual grazers and social units tend to disperse more widely under these conditions. (They may also be less constrained by large carnivores, which are generally rare in such habitats.) The timing and intensity of grazing is strongly influenced by temperature and season, with animals taking shelter and becoming inactive during the middle of the day in summer.

Behaviour: Breeding-age ♀♀ are coerced by the largest, most active ♂♂ into 'harems' of several mothers accompanied by their latest offspring. Such harem groups average five animals and seldom exceed 12. Both harem structure and home ranges can become very stable and enduring. Elsewhere harems may be less permanent and highly mobile, with long daily or seasonal movements. Aggregations are temporary and seldom exceed 30. They rarely associate with other grazers. Non-breeding ♂♂, and occasionally young ♀♀, form small, unstable 'bachelor' groups.

Mountain zebras are less vocal than other zebras. Subordinate animals appease superiors with a high, whistling whinny. A two-phase barking bray, most often made by the ♂, both alerts and draws his harem together. When dominant ♂♂ meet, they circle and strut broadside.

Cape mountain zebra.

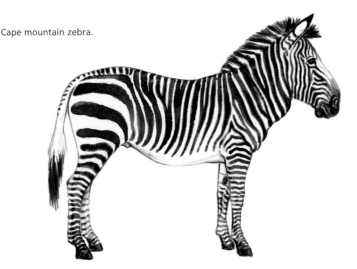

One foal is born after a 1-year gestation. The spacing of births varies. Nursing foals coerce their mothers to permit suckling by blocking her path and leaning against her chest. Most offspring have left or are chased out of the parental group by the time they are 2 years old. They live for at least 25 years.

Adaptations: The enlarged stripe pattern on the rump is visible from a greater distance than the vertical body stripes. This may help the zebras to maintain visual contact over wider distances on sparse grazing. The 'grid-iron' of smaller stripes above the root of the tail appears to be the target for 'chinning'. This is a form of ritual social behaviour in which the zebra (usually a ♂, but of any age) approaches another and presses the chin very forcefully on the 'grid-iron'. Actual grooming is very rare among adults but such rubbing, leaning and circling (especially among adult ♂♂) may be accompanied by mouth-champing. This behaviour suggests an uneasy mix of social and anti-social impulses. Inhibited forms of nibble-grooming can be seen in the context of dampened aggression. The powerful optical stimuli involved in their encounters would appear to form part of a compelling socialising mechanism among adult mountain zebras.

Status: The hunting of the Cape mountain zebra was officially prohibited in 1742 because it was already seen as rare and endangered at that time. However, the ban was ignored and the Cape mountain zebra were only saved from extinction by a single farmer, Henry Lombard, who kept 11 animals on his farm. There are now over 700 in six reserves, all descended from the 1950 nadir of seven ♀♀. Hartmann's mountain zebra is at lower risk but populations suffer continued attrition as fenced ranches interrupt free movement and turn grazing over to livestock.

Hartmanns mountain zebras, adult male and juvenile.

Grevy's zebra *Equus grevyi*

Other names: Fr. *Zèbre de Grévy*. Ger. *Grevyzebra*. Swah. *Punda milia Somali*.
Measurements: HB 250–300cm. T 40–75cm. SH 140–160cm. W 385kg (350-400kg) (♀), 430kg (380-450kg) (♂).
Recognition: A long-legged, long-faced zebra with broad, rather ovoid ears, a stripeless white belly and a white-margined spinal stripe. The stripes are very uniformly distributed over the body, head and limbs but overall widths vary so that there are lighter and darker individuals among the 'even' majority. Grevy's zebra was the 'Hippotigris' that was paraded in Roman circuses in 211–217AD pulling carts.
Distribution: The immediate historically known distribution of Grevy's zebra included a large part of the Somali arid zone, the Ethiopian Rift Valley, the Awash Valley and Danakil depression. However, a 2-million-year-old fossil in S Africa, and more recent fossils in China and Uzbekistan, of similar equids suggest that ancestral forms, or proto-Grevy's zebras, were once successful and widespread in Eurasia and Africa. At the present time (1996) they occur in a few reserves and parks in Ethiopia and Kenya. They are no longer found in Somalia, Djibouti, Eritrea or S Sudan.
Habitat: Bush/grass mosaics with a preference for tracts of grassland growing on deep sand, hard-pans, sumplands and in areas where fire and elephants have degraded the dominant *Acacia/Commiphora* woodlands. Seasonally waterlogged plains are extensive in parts of its range and gatherings of thousands of zebras were seen on such grasslands in the past. It associates with giraffe, oryx, eland and, in the southern part of their range, with common zebra, impala and buffalo. An individual's long-term range covers many thousands of kilometres.
Food: Grevy's zebra benefits from the spread of a grassland type dominated by *Pennisetum schimperi*, a tough grass incompletely exploited by other grazers. Other important grasses in the diet are species of *Chrysopogon*, *Cenchrus* and *Enteropogon* but it grazes many other genera as well.
Behaviour: Grevy's zebra has an open society in which ♀♀ with their young and ♂♂ on established territories (of up to 12km²) are the stable foci. ♀♀ associate in nursing groups, ♂♂ in bachelor groups and all classes may join up in large, mixed herds. Aggression is inconspicuous except that territorial ♂♂ assert their mating prerogatives. The most successful ♂♂ win grassy territories close to water. Grass and water are major attractions, especially for lactating ♀♀.

Resident stallions actively seek the company of visiting ♂♂. Dominance is asserted by a proud posture, with arched neck and high-stepping gait. Submission is signalled by a lowered head and raised tail. While courting and copulating the ♂ utters a very loud bray

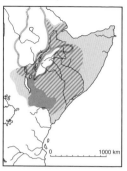

1000 km

followed by a long, strangulated squeak. Both ♂♂ and ♀♀ tend to appease the caller. A single foal is born after a variable but exceptionally long gestation of about 400 days. Mothers return to very localised birthing areas that appear to be traditional. The new foal has a mane running from forehead to tail and another hairy tract along the centre of its belly. Both are shed as the foal grows up but the dorsal mane elicits direct contact from the mother. The brown and white baby colouring darkens first on the neck and ears and a woolly coat then gives way to sleek black and white. Foals follow every detail of their mother's course and often suckle from behind. Rapid tail-lashing precedes threat and brings a foal close to its mother's side. Mothers can be in milk for up to 12 months but the young take their first water at 3 months and some cease suckling after 6 months. In spite of remaining with their mothers for up to 3 years, colts can be relatively independent at 7 months. Wild zebras mature and breed later than in zoos where births at 3–5 years are not uncommon. ♂♂ and ♀♀ tend to breed in the wild closer to 6 years. They live for at least 24 years.

Adaptations: The wide scatter of Grevy-like fossils and lack of any obvious specialisation suggests that this is the relict of a generalised and formerly widespread species. If competition from other equines has been an influence it may be significant that the distribution of Grevy's zebra is wedged between the ranges of arid-adapted wild ass and water-loving common zebra. There are superficially similar habitats south of the Sahara and the Kalahari where competition from semi-arid adapted grazers (such as hartebeest, roan antelope and other zebra species) appears to be the most likely explanation for naturally contracting ranges. A slow birth rate, limited ability to go without water (about 5 days), as well as the attachment of ♂♂ to territories, could all work against this species.

Status: This species has seen one of the fastest contractions in range and numbers of any large African mammal. Known to have declined over most of its range throughout the present century, a 1977 estimate of 13,700 animals in Kenya was followed by an estimate of 4,276 in 1988, a decline of 70% in 11 years. This decline is known to be continuing. The primary threat has come from increased livestock farming leading to their exclusion from traditional watering places. Formerly nomadic people have settled around these sources of water or above new bore-holes within good grazing areas. Limited sources of grazing are put under increasing pastoral use, especially by sheep and goats. Up-stream irrigation is causing reduced flows in the lowlands with further reductions in the water available to the zebras. About 550 animals are held in zoos and most are managed in a species survival programme. Listed as Endangered (IUCN).

Ear signals in Grevy's zebra.

RHINOCEROSES RHINOCEROTIDAE

Browse (Black) rhinoceros	*Diceros bicornis*
Grass (White) rhinoceros	*Ceratotherium simum*

When animals have become as scarce as rhinoceroses have today it is difficult to describe them as successful. Yet living African rhinos were, until very recently, the widespread, abundant, advanced and successful representatives of a family that had seen a very wide range of types in the past (i.e. 30 fossil genera).

Recognition: Rhinos are the second largest land animals only surpassed by elephants in bulk and weight. They have relatively short, powerfully muscled legs, a short neck and a massive head, armed with a nasal horn or horns. Contrary to popular belief rhinos are not ponderous and slow but are capable of running or galloping fast. Their long, heavy bodies are densely bound masses of reinforced bone and muscle enclosed in very thick skin. Most of the rhino's great weight is taken on the broad central toe but two smaller hooved toes on each foot spread the load and enhance stability. Other characteristics include backward-facing genitalia which fire powerful horizontal squirts of urine. ♂ ♂ lack a scrotum and have undescended testes.

Genealogy: The earliest rhinos were small, agile animals, something between a tapir and a horse in appearance. Large, horned forms came later (about 30 million years ago) and originated in Asia. Among the several lines that entered Africa was a close relative of the living Sumatran rhino (*Dicerorhinus*). This genus survived from at least 20 million years ago to less than 1 million years ago. Of the two surviving African species, the browse rhino has the longer fossil history. The grass rhino appears to have split from *Diceros* ancestors some 8 million years ago and has shown continuous adaptation towards grazing ever since.

Geography: Browse and grass rhinos are exclusive to Africa. Various species of the more primitive Sumatran type were also common in Africa and Europe and fossil deposits show that rhinos were conspicuous and common inhabitants of most Old World ecosystems until relatively recent times.

Ecology: The main rhino speciality is an ability to feed on coarse plant material. Rhinos are more selective than elephants but less so than most antelopes. Temperature control, digestion and scent communication all depend upon water and rhinos are unable to survive extreme droughts. Nonetheless, rhinos formerly suffered very low levels of natural mortality, a trait that goes with long life (up to 50 years) and a slow breeding rate.

Natural history: Rhinos display territorial behaviour yet can tolerate high densities and may even live in small herds. The tolerance of dominant individuals, particularly ♂ ♂, appears to vary by species, by region and in response to changes in density. Home ranges are marked with dung and urine.

Adaptations: Rhinoceros horns are solid keratin (like toenails or cows' horns). They are not set over a core but on a well-buttressed pediment that transfers all the stresses and strains of stabs, swipes and tosses to skull and forequarters (a rhino has been known to toss an adult horse into the air). Occasionally the rudiments of a third or fourth horn may grow on the muzzle and forehead of rhinos and there was a tendency towards clusters of horns on the heads of various extinct species.

The teeth can withstand a long life of chewing on tough vegetation and are deeply embedded in bony mandibles. Their food is gathered in by very muscular lips. An envelope of thick, wrinkled skin partially disguises their magnificent heads. Rhino heads are almost architectural models of form and fuction. Enclosing the vital sense organs and articulated by huge jaw and neck muscles, the skull is reinforced against its own weight. Often dubbed 'prehistoric', rhinos are no more bizarre or 'primitive' than a pig or a cockerel and should be endowed with a future, not just a past.

Status: The extreme vulnerability of rhinos under genuinely wild conditions (due to the great price paid for their horns) has reduced almost all species to something close to domestication. Until cultural and environmental attitudes have changed, rhino survival will continue to depend upon captive or closely managed populations.

Browse (Black) rhinoceros *Diceros bicornis*

Other names: Fr. *Rhinocéros noir*. Ger. *Spitzmaulnashorn*. Swah. *Faru*.

Measurements: HB 290–375cm. T 60–70cm. SH 137–180cm. W 700–1,400kg.

Recognition: A very large mammal, its thickest skin forming inflexible plates over the shoulders, haunches, sides, forehead and cheeks. Skin around the muzzle, eyes, ears, undersides and legs is thinner and more flexible The grey skin colour is most evident during the rains. Mud-wallowing and rolling in dust or ash discolours most hides during the dry season. Behind the shoulder, the dorsal silhouette swings down and back to raised haunches. The head has a short forehead and a very muscular, mobile mouth ending in a sharply pointed upper lip.

The three toes leave characteristic tracks. Other signs of the rhino's presence include rubbed trees, rocks and termitaries, well-scattered dung middens and habitually sprayed urine-posts.

Subspecies: Browse rhinos are highly variable and 23 subspecies have been named. Six regional populations correspond very approximately with named subspecies. *D. b. bicornis* (Cape): the largest, now extinct. *D. b. minor* (south and south-east, to Tanzania). *D. b. michaeli* (upland E Africa). *D. b. chobiensis* (SW Africa). *D. b. brucii* (NE Africa): the smallest, now extinct. *D. b. longipes* (W and central Africa).

Distribution: At one time a large part of sub-Saharan Africa in all but the wettest and driest areas (maximum dry-season range within 25km of water). Contemporary populations are on the brink of extinction and only hold out in a wide scatter of minuscule pockets (see map).

Habitat: Browse rhinos favour edges of thickets and savannahs with areas of short woody regrowth and numerous shrubs and herbs. They are naturally scarce or absent in closed-canopy forests and woodlands and the more extensive areas of grassland. Where woody and leafy forage could support them, rhinos were formerly found at very high densities (i.e. up to 23 animals, 17 wholly sedentary, in 2.6km^2). Where they were very common, smooth rhino pathways, dung piles, urine spray sites and rubbing posts were much in evidence.

Food: Low-level browse (leaves, twigs and branches), typically in *Acacia*, thicket, hard-pan and riverine plant communities. Some 200 species from 50 families recorded. Browse rhinos have special seasonal preferences for legumes and certain other plants are always avoided. Salt is a major attraction and their taste for salt is exploited by many tourist lodges. Animals can go for up to 5 days without water if their food is moist; otherwise they are always found within daily walking distance of water. Horns are occasionally used to loosen soil around roots or to break branches above the lips' reach.

Behaviour: A ♀ with her young is the basic social unit. Adult ♀♀ may form temporary associations and animals that share a part or all of their range have an easy-going familiarity with one another instead of the aggression that is elicited by total strangers. Home ranges can cover over 130km², but some are as small as 2.6km². Overtly territorial behaviour is also very variable. ♂♂ in high-density areas are well acquainted with, and generally tolerant of, their neighbours (except in the presence of an oestrous ♀). ♂♂ in low-density areas meet less frequently and are more likely to be aggressive. Decline can be accelerated in an already thinned population because a few very aggressive ♂♂ not only miss encounters with ♀♀ in heat but their intolerance of other ♂♂ further lessens the frequency of matings. Displays between ♂♂ resemble those of stallions: there is much strutting, broadside with lowered head, flattened ears and rolling eyes. Various snorts during encounters seem to have different shades of meaning. Rhinos utter series of snorts interspersed with pauses and very loud grunts and screams which punctuate serious fighting.

One young is born after a gestation of 15–16 months. It is soon mobile and begins browsing vegetation before it is 1 month old. It sucks milk for up to 1 year and only begins to drink water after 4 or 5 months. A mother generally drives off her previous offspring before a new birth and the interval between births ranges from 2 to 5 years. Both sexes are capable of reproduction at 4 or 5 years old but ♂♂ can seldom compete with established ♂♂ before the age of 10 years. In spite of a life spanning more than 40 years, this is one of the slowest recruitment rates of any large mammal.

Adaptations: Although all-out frontal charges occur in high-intensity fighting, browse rhinos tend to use their horns more like clubs or staves than rapiers. Mild jousting may be accompanied by shoulder-to-shoulder pushing and leaning. Weight and horn size are easily tested this way but scent and behaviour generally reveal the dominant individual. Avoidance or submission follow.

Status: Human pride, superstition and greed have combined to ensure astronomical prices for horns in the form of dagger handles, cups, supposed medicines and aphrodisiacs. In the late 1960s some 70,000 browse rhinos were estimated to survive in Africa. This was a fraction of the numbers existing at the turn of the century. By 1990 the total number of browse rhinos living within 38 officially protected conservation areas (ranging in size from 55,000 to 62km²) was about 3,300. This accounted for most of the rhinos that survived in Africa in 1990. If these areas were secured and managed for the animals benefit, their potential stock could be as high as 80,000. Listed as Appendix 1 (CITES), Endangered (IUCN).

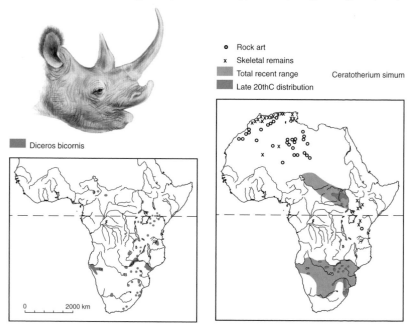

o   Rock art
x   Skeletal remains
▨   Total recent range   Ceratotherium simum
▨   Late 20thC distribution

Diceros bicornis

0   2000 km

Grass (White) rhinoceros *Ceratotherium simum*

Other names: Fr. *Rhinocéros blanc.* Ger. *Witrenoster.* Swah. *Kiaru ya majani.*
Measurements: HB 360–420cm. T 80–100cm. SH 170–185cm. W 1,400–2,000kg (♀), 2,000–3,600kg (♂).
Recognition: Although formerly called 'white', this very large rhino is of similar skin colour to the browse rhino. The highest point behind the shoulder is midback (due to tall dorsal and lumbar vertebrae) rather than the haunches. The head is long (especially the forehead). The mouth is very wide, flat fronted and set low over the chin. The flexible neck forms a prominent hump when the head is raised. Spoor are more elongate than those of the browse rhino, with greater separation of toes and a prominent cleft at the back.
Subspecies: Southern grass rhino, *C. s. simum* (southern savannahs); northern grass rhino, *C. s. cottoni* (northern savannahs).
Distribution: Fossils, bones and rock art suggest that this species was formerly abundant all over the better-watered grasslands of Africa (including much of the present Sahara). In historic times it ranged to the shores of L. Chad but reached its nadir at the turn of this century with minuscule populations in two widely separated localities: Zululand and the Zaïre-Sudan-Uganda borderlands.
Habitat: A preference for short-grass areas and seasonal movements to avoid waterlogged long grass confirm that this species evolved within a larger ungulate community that maintained short swards. In areas of high density the rhinos themselves maintain grazing lawns. Where territories are maintained by resident bulls their border-patrolling and scent-marking leave foot-scuffs, dung middens, urine sprays, rubbing posts and horned vegetation along boundaries. Linear pathways may form between grazing and waterpoints.

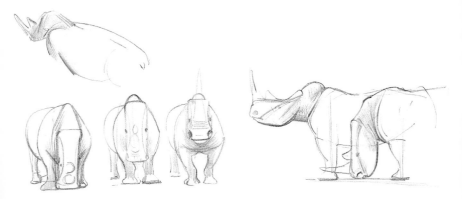

322

Food: Short grasses, typically *Cynodon, Digitaria, Heteropogon* and *Chloris* species in well-trampled, well-drained, wet-season concentration areas, are preferred. After dry-season fires, grass rhinos may move into regrowth dominated by *Themeda, Hyparrhenia* and *Setaria*. Biting flies and direct sun may influence seasonal movements by restricting the rhinos to ridges or shaded areas for a time. Frequent alternation between grazing and resting changes to long midday rests at the height of the dry season.

Behaviour: ♀♀ and their immediate offspring occupy large (4–12km²) overlapping home ranges where they frequently graze alongside one or more ♀ neighbours. ♂♂ defend territories but their size and their owners' tolerance is related to population density. In crowded Zululand parks ♂ territories can be as small as 0.75–2.6km². Grass rhinos are extremely vocal, with a wide repertoire of utterances. Infantile squeaks and pantings in adults become loud chirps, gasps and puffings (contact) or snarls and squeals of distress. Dominant ♂♂ grunt and bellow challenges at other ♂♂ or court ♀♀ with a low, pulsing cry. One well-developed but hornless young is born after a 16-month gestation. It first grazes at about 2 months and is driven away by its mother at about 2–3 years of age. ♀♀ do not usually breed until they are about 5 years old, dropping their first calf at 6½–7 years of age.

Adaptations: This species evolved from a common ancestor that was very similar to the living browse rhino; modifications in the proportions of the mouth, skull and neck enabled it to become a more efficient, short-grass grazer. Thus the neck has become short but has to crank up a heavier, longer head. This is achieved by the tall vertebral spines, web of tendons and bunched muscles that give the animal its neck 'hump'. Broad, flat-edged lips enable short grass to be cropped efficiently. Long grass is grazed more clumsily.

Status: After millennia of decline the southern form of the grass rhino was brought back from the brink of extinction through the efforts of one man, B. Vaughan-Kirby. From 10–20 animals in the earliest years of this century, the present population now approaches 5,000. The northern form was formerly more widespread and abundant but is now reduced to a few dozen animals in one or a very few localities. It is listed as Critically Endangered (IUCN). The southern form is at lower risk but is dependent on rigorous protection and maintainance of its CITES Appendix 1 status, which prohibits trade in its horns.

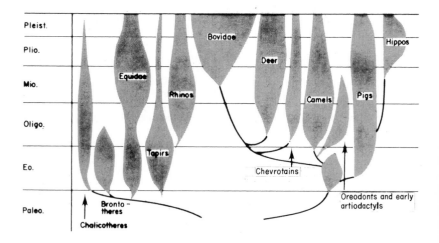

Possible scheme for radiation of artiodactyls.

EVEN-TOED UNGULATES
ARTIODACTYLA

The artiodactyls embrace all the horned antelopes and cattle, deer, giraffes, camels, chevrotains, pigs and hippopotamuses. They are one of the most important and successful of mammal lineages. The earliest types were not very different from carnivores, had prominent canine teeth and an omnivorous diet. They are distinguished by their even toes with the axis passing between the third and 4th digits which bear the body's weight in all members of the family.

The most significant feature of this group is the progressive improvement of their digestion through a system of storing, rechewing and sifting of the food and a symbiosis with bacteria and protozoans living within the chambers of the stomach. These break down cellulose and release nutrients.

The skulls of living artiodactyls have been adapted to specific modes of combat requiring elaboration of canines, incisors, horns or antlers. Artiodactyls also show very diverse social and ecological adaptations.

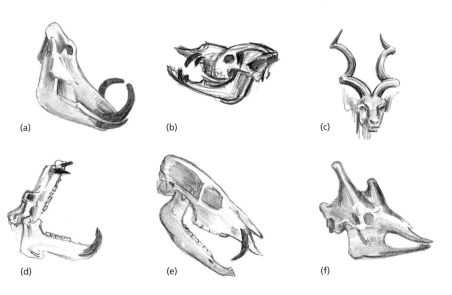

(a) (b) (c)

(d) (e) (f)

Artiodactyl skulls. (a) Warthog. (b) Camel. (c) Kudu antelope. (d) Hippo.
(e) Chevrotain. (f) Giraffe.

The principal threat to African artiodactyls is their continuing replacement by a few exotic domesticates. An ever-expanding livestock industry is eroding and exterminating natural communities of animals and plants on a huge scale. The latter are among Africa's most valuable assets because of their greater diversity, complexity, productivity and sustainability. The livestock industry operates within a kind of conceptual Dark Age in which promoters, consumers and practitioners pursue exploitation of domestic animals in ignorance of the ecological matrix from which their meat mountains and milk quotas derive. Their activities expand at inordinate cost to the long-term health of African environments and natural resources.

HIPPOPOTAMUSES HIPPOPOTAMIDAE

Recognition: Hippos resemble gigantic, amphibious pigs with enlarged lower jaw and canines, four large, blunt toes on each foot and a very rotund body build. Their shiny, naked skin is densely perforated by minute skin-conditioning mucus glands.

Genealogy: Hippos evolved from a pig-like ancestor and the two lines probably diverged about 40 million years ago. The living pygmy hippo clearly represents the more conservative type. In most respects it appears to be more primitive than any known fossil. As recently as 1 million years ago there were at least eight species of hippo in Africa and four of these are known to have co-existed in the L. Turkana basin. These differed in size, diet and aquatic niche. Other hippos have disappeared from India and at least three species have disappeared in historical times from Madagascar.

Geography: Hippos of different species survived in India until recent prehistoric times. The group's origins are probably African but could be Asiatic.

Ecology: Hippos' use of swamps and waters as day-time refuges has allowed them to develop a particularly successful ecological strategy. Great economies in energy are made possible by secure resting places, a slow but efficient digestion, a modest appetite for their size and broad, lawn-mowing lips that can gather enough food in a short period of the night.

Natural history: Although hippos inhabit very secure refuges in swamps or water, these tend to be overcrowded and the focus for much competition and fighting, especially among ♂♂. Bulky animals fighting in mud or water engage one another's teeth, after which the contest becomes a trial of weight and strength.

Hippos have evolved a number of ingenious solutions to the problems of their amphibious existence. The young can suckle under water, through their hard, grass-cropping lips, by folding their extruded tongue around the nipple. Their need to disperse scent-marks has led to the evolution of a muscular, flat-bladed tail which wags like a fan or propeller to disperse the faeces.

Adaptations: Among the most extensive modifications are a reorganisation of the skull and jaws to allow the lower mandible, its canines and incisors to take the brunt of fighting. This makes the lower jaw more massively reinforced than the upper. Its hinging is also organised to jackknife the skull upwards and transfer the main force of impact from the lower jaw almost directly back to the neck and shoulders. While the skin is well adapted to continuous immersion it also renders hippos vulnerable to dehydration. They cannot survive long away from water and only graze at night or during rain.

Status: Both hippo species are serious candidates for domestication or semi-domestic ranching beside waterways and in association with pisciculture. No living domestic animal can compete with them for the economy with which they convert vegetation into animal protein. Both species have been eliminated over much of their former range.

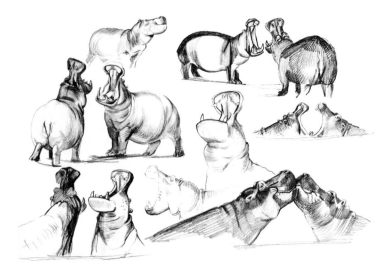

Hippopotamus *Hippopotamus amphibius*

Other names: Fr. *Hippopotame*. Ger. *Grossflusspferd*. Swah. *Kiboko*.

Measurements: HB 280–350cm. T 35–50cm. SH 130–165cm. W 510–2,500kg (♀), 650–3,200kg (♂).

Recognition: Hippos have stumpy legs and splayed toes that are just adequate for carrying their vast rotund body on land and fold neatly away while resting or swimming. Eyes, ears and nostrils have migrated to the top of the head in this species. The main colour of the smooth, shiny hide is a deep purplish grey to blue-black. The underside, eye rims, ears and mouth show very variable expanses of pink. The hide is peppered with glands that exude a blood-like fluid that spreads to form a flexible varnish (antiseptic, sunburn cream, water-loss sealant and social perfume are among the suggested functions for this secretion). The sexes are strikingly different in proportions, ♂♂ have larger canines and incisor teeth set in massive jaws and skull. They have a correspondingly huge jowl and greatly thickened neck.

Subspecies: Substantial regional variations in size but no subspecies recognised.

Distribution: Originally from the Nile delta to the Cape wherever the two requirements of permanent water and open grazing were met. Their upper altitude limit is about 2000m. Present distribution is shrinking rapidly. Hippos aggregate in permanent water sources or wallows during the dry season and disperse very widely in the rains.

Habitat: A silent, solitary grazer on land by night, a vocal, densely social and sedentary wallower by day. The foreshore or bed of lakes and rivers influence hippos, as does the depth and flow of water. Larger groups favour firm, gently sloping beaches and quiet waters, where they can stand or kneel on the bottom close to the surface. Large populations of hippos alter grass composition and inhibit fires by removing potential fuel. It is possible that such populations cause long-term vegetation cycles because their progressive degradation of the grazing increasingly encourages regeneration of thickets. Closely cropped lawns, paths radiating from the water and great accumulations of dung are characteristic signs of intensive use by hippos.

Food: Both creeping and tussock grasses are taken, notably *Cynodon* and *Panicum* species. *Brachiara, Themeda, Chloris* and *Setaria* are other important sources of grazing. The hippo crops grass entirely by means of its leathery (not muscular) lips. It walks slowly, closing its lips over mouthfuls of grass and wrenching them away with a regular swinging of the head. A hippo can ingest up to 60kg in a night's grazing and seldom needs more than 5 hours out of the water.

Behaviour: Hippos have a very hierarchical society in which individuals must advertise their status and condition, especially to superiors. Voiding urine or dung and prostration in the face of a dominant individual are the normal modes of appeasement.

♀♀ accompanied by up to four successive offspring are the only stable social unit. Individuals periodically change their resting sites but degrees of sedentariness or nomadism are highly variable. The largest ♂♂ occupy narrow strips of water and land along the foreshore, the exact size of which can be quite variable. Here they defend exclusive mating rights but tolerate most subordinate ♂♂. Both ♀ and bachelor associations are unstable in composition and vary a great deal in numbers. Aggregations range between 2 and 150.

Female.   Male.

Large groups are very vocal, the main call being a reverberating nasal wheeze followed by a series of guttural honks. In the early morning this is associated with the return to water. It is the response to all disturbances, particularly in the evenings as the hippos begin to move. ♂♂ also wheeze-honk while copulating (the ♀ lies prostrate).

One (very rarely two) young is born after an 8-month gestation. The mother segregates herself for up to 2 weeks after a birth, during which time she is very alert and aggressive. The young begins to graze after some weeks but is suckled for 8 months or more. Calves are quite playful during this period. They continue to grow over 5 or 6 years and ♀♀ become sexually mature between 7 and 15 years of age (♂♂ rather younger but they tend to be excluded from breeding for much longer by heavy dominant ♂♂). Births are spaced at about 2-year intervals. Hippos can live for up to 50 years in captivity, but probably do not survive as long in the wild.

Adaptations: The body size and weight of adult ♀♀ tends to stabilise at a regional norm, but ♂♂ continue to grow, albeit very slowly, throughout life. This favours the oldest, heaviest ♂♂ in their efforts to monopolise mating. A willingness to fight is advertised by yawning displays that are unique to the hippo and contests are settled by clashing lower jaws together (which leads to much chipping of teeth). The incisors are modified to act like the antler tines of deer, allowing contestants to parry or get a purchase for a pushing contest. It is with the pushing contest that weight and jaw span are decisive. Younger ♂♂ actively seek contests with frequent yawn displays which are preceded by a scooping up and violent tossing of waterweeds. Such rituals may be drawn out to last an hour or more, jaw to jaw, with occasional straining and weight-testing.

Status: In spite of an extensive overall range, hippos are very vulnerable to determined hunting. They are well represented in many national parks but suffer continuing local extinction. Hippos are mainly hunted for their meat and for the damage they cause to agriculture. They are readily re-introduced and can be controlled with fences and ditches. They have outstanding potential for domestication or ranching and make popular zoo exhibits.

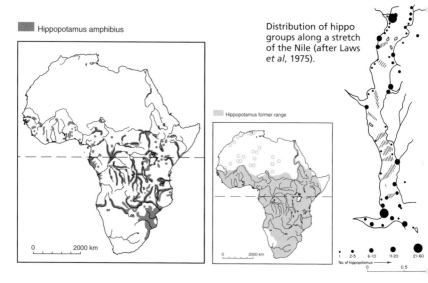

Hippopotamus amphibius

Distribution of hippo groups along a stretch of the Nile (after Laws et al, 1975).

Hippopotamus former range

0   2000 km

0   2000 km

No. of hippopotamus →

1   2-5   6-10   11-20   21-60

0   0.5

Pygmy hippopotamus *Hexaprotodon liberiensis*

Other names: Fr. *Hippopotame nain*. Ger. *Zwergflusspferd*.

Measurements: HB 150–177cm. T 15–21cm. SH 70–92cm. W 180–275kg (sexes are of similar size).

Recognition: Rotund-bodied, thick-necked hippo with a similar rounded, toothy muzzle (but proportionally much smaller head) to the common hippo. Eyes, ears and nostrils do not protrude as much as in the common hippo. The body is naked, sepia-brown with lighter more fleshy colouring on the throat and belly. The thin, sun-sensitive skin resembles that of the common hippo in its physiology and the secretions that give the animal's entire surface a glossy sheen. The toes, less webbed and more widely splayed than those of the common hippo, leave a distinctive 4-pronged spoor.

Subspecies: *H. l. liberiensis* (Upper Guinea), *H. l. heslopi* (R. Niger and R. Cross deltas).

Distribution: In geologically recent times very similar species occurred in India, Madagascar, S Europe and E Africa. Now a single species divided into two separate populations is fragmented into minuscule relics. Within the last few decades the pygmy hippo has been restricted to forests between the R. Corubal and R. Bandama, and the R. Cross and R. Niger deltas.

Habitat: Pygmy hippos inhabit forested watercourses where they shelter by day in ponds, rivers and swamps. At night they follow tunnel-like paths through dense riverine vegetation to graze in glades, clearings, chablis or along grassy margins of swamps and trails.

Food: Graze consists of various green grasses and herbs, notably the main broad-leaf forest type, *Leptaspis*, species of *Andropogon*, *Hyparrhenia* and *Imperata*, various sedges, herbaceous shoots and fallen fruits. Food is cropped by tearing the plant between the firm clamp of rounded upper and shovel-shaped lower lips.

Behaviour: Pygmy hippos have only been recorded singly, in twos or, rarely, a mother and her offspring in temporary association with a ♂. They are normally very silent but captive specimens have been recorded snorting, grunting, squeaking and hissing. They also make a much quieter groaning equivalent of the common hippo's honking call. They bear one young after a 6–7-month gestation. The young is guarded by its mother who suckles it for up to 6 months, during which time it grows rapidly. The mother may have a second calf after 2 years, at which time previous young are likely to be repelled. The young are feeding on vegetation by 3 months and mature by 3 years. Captive specimens have lived for 30 years.

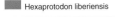
Hexaprotodon liberiensis

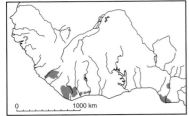

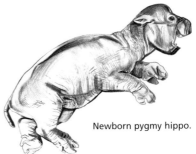

Newborn pygmy hippo.

Status: In spite of formal protection since 1933, pygmy hippos have declined drastically. This is partly due to extensive deforestation and partly to hunting.

Although there are currently 350 animals held in 131 collections, they are mainly kept as pairs or singles for 'display' and mortality is high. Captive breeding is probably the only realistic hope for their survival in the short term because none of the relict populations are adequately protected.

The western form is currently listed as Vulnerable and the Nigerian subspecies as Critically Endangered (IUCN). Both are on Appendix 2 (CITES).

PIGS SUIDAE

Wild boar	*Sus scrofa*
Bush pigs	*Potamochoerus*
Giant hog	*Hylochoerus meinertzhageni*
Warthogs	*Phacochoerus*

Recognition: Pigs are robust, large-headed animals with relatively short legs and a compact body build. They have wedge-shaped skulls, out-turned canine tusks and a barrel-like snout that is tipped with a very tough, mobile disc mounted on a well-reinforced prenasal bone. All have leathery, sparsely haired skin. Weight is taken on the two central toes of each foot but the side hooves splay out in soft ground. The skulls of African pigs show striking adaptations to their preferred foods and to modes of tusk- or snout-fighting that are unique to each species.

Genealogy: Pig skulls are among the best preserved and most abundant of fossils in African deposits. They first appear about 10 million years ago but become particularly diverse from about 5 million years ago. Bush pigs have some ancient connection with the wild pigs of Eurasia where the family may have originated. Giant hogs are an African offshoot from the bush pig lineage, while warthogs only share an unknown and much earlier common ancestry.

Geography: An Old World group, pigs do best in moist areas with dense cover and soft soils but the warthogs have adapted to arid Africa.

Ecology: Rootling is a primary adaptation in pigs. Wild boar and bushpigs, the former in Eurasia and N Africa, the latter in Africa, are the most conservative in this respect. The bushpigs have branched into true forest and savannah-adapted species while the giant hog has become a forest glade grazer. The warthogs have also become mainly grazers but have diverged into a mainline savannah species and a more specialised, arid-adapted form. The universal suid dependence on secure shelter or dens is met by self-dug or appropriated earth burrows.

Natural history: Mainly social animals, pigs communicate mainly through scent and sound. They are highly vocal and well supplied with glands around the genitalia and mouth. Competition, especially among ♂♂, is very intense and has led to elaborate threat and appeasement behaviour. They have short gestation periods, large litters, fast maturation rates and very high mortality in the young.

Adaptations: The primacy of scent and ability to dig with the nose disc is manifested in well-reinforced skulls with long, tubular muzzles. The disproportionately large head is used as a lever for food and as a weapon in trials of power and weight during contests. Short, sharp tusks are typical of primitive lateral fighters and 'snout-boxers' while more elaborate 'antler tusks' have been developed by warthogs and giant hogs. Both these latter species derive from ancient stock that included near hippo-sized animals.

Bush pig.   Giant hog.   Warthog.

Wild boar *Sus scrofa*

Other names: Fr. *Sanglier*. Ger. *Wildschwein*. Swah. *Nguruwe mwitu*.

Measurements: HB 85–130cm (♀), 100–160cm (♂). T 15–21cm. SH 60–90cm. W 30–80kg (♀), 33–130kg (♂).

Recognition: A flat-sided, shaggy pig with a long snout, large, leaf-shaped ears and a short dorsal mane. Colour varies between dark grey-brown and dirty tawny colour. Tracks reveal two oval hoof-marks (with side hooves only imprinting in mud).

Subspecies: *S. s. algira* (often regarded as no more than a small, long tusked variety of the European wild boar). Hybridises readily with bush-pigs.

Distribution: Found over most of Eurasia. Originally the entire N African littoral but extinct in Egypt by 1902 and in Libya by 1890. Still occurs from the Atlas region to N Tunisia. In a feral state (derived from early domestic stock) in South Africa, Sudan, Pemba and Mafia and most recently introduced into Gabon and Burkina Faso.

Habitat: In N Africa mainly oakwoods and scrub; also in tamarisk groves on desert margins. Wild boars make nests of gathered grass and branches or scrape a shallow depression in dense vegetation.

Food: Omnivorous, with acorns the main seasonal staple in N Africa (at which time animals put on weight rapidly); also bulbs, roots, fallen fruits, snails, insect larvae and other invertebrates. Wild boars occasionally scavenge and eat small vertebrates. The availability of food is the main determinant of its population cycles but climate, predation (in the past) and diseases such as hog cholera periodically kill large numbers of these pigs.

Behaviour: ♀♀ and their young form associations with one or more other mother families. These have loose, temporary associations with adult ♂♂ in the vicinity. The animals tend to be sedentary but are quick to respond to disturbance or hunting with rapid movement and changes in behaviour. Thus mainly diurnal habits can change to nocturnal habits and distances of 20–30km may be covered. Home ranges are very variable, from 2 to 20km². Tusk glands, salivary secretions, certain calls and genital scents are all thought to facilitate courtship and mating. 3–10 piglets are born after a gestation of 115 days. The mother gives birth in a nest of leaves, branches and grass, where she stays put for about a week before emerging, sometimes to rejoin other families in 'nursery groups'. The young grow rapidly and are sexually mature by about 1 year. They are annual breeders and have winter mating peaks. They live for up to 20 years in captivity, less in the wild.

Adaptations: Wild boar ♂♂ are unique in having dense dermal shields of protective tissue under the skin of the shoulders and on the barrel of the chest. This limits the damage from lacerating blows suffered during frequent fights between ♂♂ during the winter rut. The side-curving tusks are very sharp and are wielded with a very fast and powerful sideways swipe of the head.

Status: Wild boars fluctuate in numbers but are common and widespread in Morocco and Algeria where they are not eaten and seldom hunted. Their recent introduction into hunting reserves in Gabon and elsewhere is highly irresponsible.

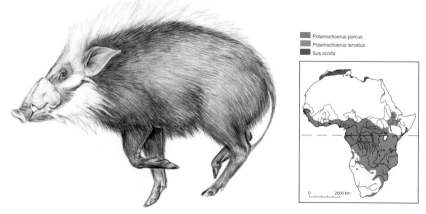

Potamochoerus porcus
Potamochoerus larvatus
Sus scrofa

0   2000 km

Bush pig *Potamochoerus larvatus*

Other names: Fr. *Potamochère*. Ger. *Buschschwein*. Swah. *Nguruwe*.

Measurements: HB 100–177cm. T 30–45cm. H 55–100cm. W 45–150kg.

Recognition: Compact, with a slab-like, short-legged body, tapering into the head and snout with little indication of a neck. Extremely variable in colour it is always covered in coarse, shaggy hair.The dorsal crest and face are often white or grey. The body colour varies from blonde or red to grey, brown or black. Colour varies with sex, age, region or individual; as a result 17 subspecies have been named.

Subspecies: Eastern bushpig, *P. l. hassama* (uplands and eastern littoral); southern bushpig, *P. l. koiropotamus* (South and SE Africa). (Note: Small pigs from the Horn of Africa have been called *P. l. somaliensis* but they appear to intergrade over a very broad front.)

Distribution: From the moister parts of S Africa to the R. Zaïre and R. Kasai in the west. Likewise, the moister parts of E and NE Africa to the mountains of the central African Rift Valley. Bush pigs range up to 4,000m on Mt Kilimanjaro. They are thought to have been so recently introduced to Madagascar that early semi-domestication by Afro-Indonesian settlers on the mainland has been suggested as an explanation for their arrival on that island.

Habitat: A wide range of forested and woodland habitats, with a distinct preference for valley bottoms with dense vegetation and soft soils. Nest-making for raising young and in cold seasons is most prominent in the cooler parts of their range. More diurnal activity in the winter suggests that low temperatures are poorly tolerated.

Food: Omnivorous and highly adaptive to local and seasonal conditions. Roots, tubers, bulbs and corms are the principal foods; also fallen fruits and herbage. In addition to fungi, bush pigs take various animals, rooting for larvae and beetles, snails, amphibians and reptiles. They occasionally scavenge and a party has been seen to drive a leopard off its kill. Seasonal changes in diet have been widely observed.

Behaviour: A ♀ and her young are often accompanied by an adult ♂ within a restricted area where trunk-slashing along paths, rubbing posts and latrines suggest that ♂♂, and perhaps ♀♀ too, are territorial, if only seasonally.

Larger associations are seen but only rarely. Home ranges of up to 10km² have been estimated and nightly foraging walks of up to 6km. Contact grunts are common. Threats, assembly and alarm are all signalled by various grunts. Squeals and roars accompany fights in which contestants are sometimes lethally wounded or killed. Brow-to-brow pushing may be a preliminary to mating. Gestation (120 days) is followed by the ♀ retiring into a nest or hollow to give birth to up to ten young. Piglets grow rapidly and slowly lose their brown and buff stripes over a period of months. They are sexually mature by about 18 months. Breeding is annual and seasonal, with most births at the end of the dry season (spring, i.e. September–November, in South Africa).

Adaptations: Bush pigs occupy a wider range of habitats than the more specialised forest-dwelling riverhog. The relationship between these two species and the possibility of hybrid populations in Uganda and Zaïre await further study.

Status: Bush pigs are a major pest for gardeners and farmers and are widely hunted for both control and meat. Without their natural predators they can become very abundant. They have been deliberately crossed with domestic pigs and wild bush pigs are reported to have hybridised with feral pigs in South Africa.

Red river hog *Potamochoerus porcus*

Other names: Fr. *Potamochère*. Ger. *Flusschschwein*.

Measurements: HB 100–145cm. T 30–45cm. SH 55–80cm. W 45–115kg.

Recognition: A bright russet pig with a narrow white dorsal crest, white 'brows', cheek tufts and jaw-line. The leaf-shaped ears end in a long white tassel. Muzzle and forehead are black and the fur is sleek and short over most of the body (except jaws and flanks which have longer hair).

Subspecies: Subject to differences and gradients in size, six named subspecies but these are generally judged invalid.

Distribution: The main rainforest belt from Gambia to E Zaïre and south to the R. Zaïre/R. Kasai. Also in galleries wherever permanent water and soft soils are maintained in valley bottoms.

Habitat: Rarely outside rainforest with a marked preference for river courses and swamp-forest margins. Here it ploughs up extensive areas while excavating roots and invertebrates. The narrow extent and linearity of its habitat in some areas may force semi-nomadic circuits of movement.

Food: Omnivorous but with underground roots and tubers the main staple. Fallen fruits are of great importance locally and seasonally, as are invertebrates. Finding fruit supplies is assisted by the noise made by primates, hornbills and other fruit-eaters.

Behaviour: Often found in small groups of up to 15 animals, the red river hog occasionally gathers in very large but temporary assocations of up to 60 animals. During confrontations between ♂♂ both animals strut broadside, with bristling fur and erect crests. They champ jaws, grunt, paw the soil and whip their slender tails back and forth. Champing clearly releases pheromones from the tusk and salivary glands while other secretions exude from the corners of the eyes, genitals and nape of the neck. Nothing is currently known of the nature of the information encoded in this barrage of scents. Litters of very variable size are born after a 4-month gestation in a hollow tree or dense nest of gathered vegetation. For about 3 months the young are very prettily coloured in stripes of pale yellow and dark brown. At this time they crouch and 'play possum' when disturbed. As they age and their stripes fade, flight becomes the more normal response. Births have been recorded in February and March in Nigeria. Full grown at 2 years, captive specimens have lived for 20 years.

Adaptations: Although the tusks of the ♂ are short, they are very sharp and snout-boxing would tend to cut the large tendons and blood vessels that serve the rooting snout and its nostril disc. The red river hog has evolved knobbed, bony excrescences on the sides of the muzzle that appear to reduce the risk of such damage. The pocket behind this maxillary flange oozes a scented secretion.

The facial pattern is well adapted for communicating contrasting signals relating to status. For example, horizontal ears signal aggression while vertically clamped ones indicate submission (see above).

Status: The red river hog is one of the staple species pursued by commercial bush-meat hunters. Although its fecundity allows it to keep up with this attrition in some areas, many rarer mammals are soon eliminated. Wherever forests have disappeared this species becomes scarce and it is now rare outside protected areas in the most westerly parts of its range.

Giant hog *Hylochoerus meinertzhageni*

Other names: Fr. *Hylochère*. Ger. *Reisenwaldschwein*. Swah. *Senge, Nguruwe nyeusi*.
Measurements: HB 130–210cm. T 25–45cm. SH 80–100cm. W 100–200kg (♀), 140–275kg (♂).
Recognition: Heavily built pig covered in long black hair. Mature ♂♂ are about 50kg heavier than ♀♀ and have enormous, naked cheeks, a broad, flat muzzle and thick tusks of moderate length. The rhinarium, or snout disc, may be over 50cm across and is very broad and swollen. Over the forehead is a dish-like depression surrounded by a circle of raised bone, tissue and bare skin. Mature ♂♂ also have grotesquely swollen preorbital glands which can exude copious secretions which spread over the face. Very young piglets are brown- or straw-coloured with side-striping most developed in the western parts of the range and mainly absent in the east.
Subspecies: Eastern giant hog, *H. m. meinertzhageni* (east of Great Rift Valley); Congo giant hog, *H. m. rimator* (W Nigeria to E Zaïre); western giant hog, *H. m. ivoriensis* (Upper Guinea).
Distribution: Scattered across tropical Africa in localised populations and in various vegetation types from sea-level to 3,800m. They live in cold uplands as well as hot lowlands but do not tolerate low humidity or prolonged solar radiation. Their range resembles that of the bongo antelope which also exploits unstable forest-edge mosaics.
Habitat: Mainly forest/grassland mosaics but range from subalpine areas and bamboo groves through montane to lowland and swamp forests, galleries, wooded savannahs and post-cultivation thickets. A year-round and plentiful supply of green fodder and dense cover are found wherever these hogs occur. Their habitat is punctuated by sleeping sites, latrines, wallows, water holes, salt-licks and grazing meadows and is laced with a tracery of habitually used pathways.
Food: Many species of grasses, sedges and herbs, which are cropped at various stages of growth. In some montane areas herbaceous growth may also be very important. Giant hogs rootle very much less than other pigs and prefer to graze on mats of relatively short green grass. They masticate less thoroughly than warthogs (having lower-crowned molars) and differ in not selecting old or dry grasses. They seek salty earth which they excavate mainly using their lower incisors. After visits to salt-licks, their dung may be mainly composed of earth. Latrines, usually sited very close to the temporary sleeping sites, are large and communally used.
Behaviour: The basic social group is a mother and her offspring of up to three generations, but this unit may associate with a variety of neighbouring families. As sleeping-sites change frequently and are used by different permutations of neighbouring families, latrines may both advertise occupancy and help familiarise the changing sleeping partners with one anothers' scent. In Kenya the home ranges of families probably comprise a series of overlapping foci but with each family having its own core area. In Zaïre ♂♂ are thought to form more permanent bonds with particular families and core areas may have more of the character of defended territories. ♂♂ defend the ♀♀ and young in their current family against other ♂♂ and against predators (mainly lions, leopards and hyaenas).

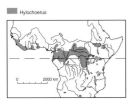
Hylochoerus

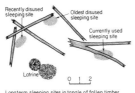
Recently disused sleeping site · Oldest disused sleeping site · Currently used sleeping site
Latrine
0 1 2
Longterm sleeping sites in tangle of fallen timber

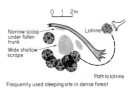
0 1 2m
Narrow scoop under fallen trunk · Latrine
Wide shallow scrape
Path to latrine
Frequently used sleeping site in dense forest

They are often very vocal, using close-contact quiet grunts in thick cover and a louder barking call to establish contact over a distance. ♂♂ make an extended grunting call that builds up to a trumpeting crescendo and then dies away. Mating peaks are prominent but do not form a regular seasonal pattern in Kenya. In Zaïre mating peaks in March and in September, with births some 5 months later in August and February. Up to 11 piglets are born at a time and they remain in dense cover with their mother for about a week. The young are intensely playful and competitive, grow rapidly and are weaned at 9 weeks and sexually mature by 18 months. In spite of very low survival rates they can live for up to 18 years.

Adaptations: Long sequences of fossil pigs that are immediate antecedents of *Hylochoerus* show that grazing was a relatively late development in this species. Grass-eating has involved the need for powerful lateral chewing. Developing the muscles and anchorage to support this has caused massive realignments in the skull and has led to unique forms of head-butting. The commonest contest, practiced from an early age, is head-on snout-ramming. This form of contest is facilitated by the slightly bulbous, flat-fronted nasal disc which is not important for rootling. Most confrontations end in one ♂ withdrawing but stalemate among larger, more evenly matched, mature ♂♂ culminates in both backing-off and charging from about 30m distance. When their massively reinforced foreheads meet in such clashes the impact rocks one or the other back on its haunches. If the concave foreheads meet in exact opposition a loud rifle-like report is produced by the escape of compressed air. Repeat charges may continue for up to half-an-hour with jaws champing, spittle flying and urine squirting every time. When the victorious ♂ rejoins his group, preorbital secretions pour over his face, expressed from his grotesquely swollen glands. Submissive ♀♀ gather to sniff him while adult ♂♂ avoid him. Skulls are not infrequently broken but the 'false hull' structure of the skull (common to all pigs) protects the brain inside a well-insulated bony capsule. Broken skulls heal and their owners live to fight another day.

Status: An easy target for hunters, especially those with dogs, which quickly bring them to bay, giant hogs are threatened by commercial meat-hunting for urban markets. Unless such markets are prohibited it can be predicted that giant hogs and many other species will disappear over most of their fragmented and declining range.

All populations are listed as Rare and the most westerly ones (*H. m. ivoriensis*) as Endangered (IUCN). They are nominally protected and are present in most forest parks and reserves within their ranges but are even vulnerable there because the grasslands and glades on which they depend are highly unstable. As a tractable grazing animal this species is a serious candidate for domestication or semi-domestication in equatorial Africa. Its potential needs investigation. Veterinary restrictions to protect domestic pigs from disease inhibit such initiatives and prohibit trade in any part of this animal.

Common warthog.

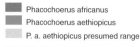

Phacochoerus africanus
Phacochoerus aethiopicus
P. a. aethiopicus presumed range

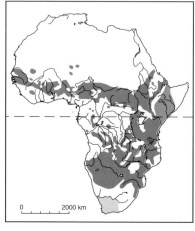

0   2000 km

Desert warthog.

Desert warthog *Phacochoerus aethiopicus*

Other names: Fr. *Phacochère du Cap*. Ger. *Desert Warzenschwein*. Swah. *Ngiri ya Somalia*.
Measurements: HB est. 100–150cm. T est. 35–45cm. SH est. 50–75cm. W 45–100kg.
Recognition: Closely resembles the common warthog in size and general morphology but the dentition and the associated leverage for chewing have been modified and specialised, apparently toward more thorough mastication. The incisor teeth usually found at the front of both jaws are either totally absent or have become rudimentary and non-functional. The enlarged third molar is rootless and muscle attachments at the back of the palate are reorganised to allow greater lateral play. The head is relatively shorter and broader.
Subspecies: *P. a. aethiopicus* (Cape and Karoo): extinct. *P. a. delamerei* (Horn of Africa).
Habitat: The now widely separate subspecies are known from recent fossils outside their present range. They are so similar it is likely that an 'arid corridor' linked them, perhaps during the last Ice Age (20,000 years ago). The extinct Cape warthog would have had to tolerate exceptionally cold and arid climates on the Karoo, conditions that were much more extensive during glacial periods.

In modern Somalia this species survives under conditions that are drier than any currently tolerated by the common warthog. Physiological adaptations are therefore likely to distinguish the two species.
Food: Desert warthogs must graze and ingest excavated roots and rhizomes with their hard, sharp-edged lips. Common warthogs only employ their incisors to wrench long tough grass or to excavate mineral-rich earth. Neither activity is possible for the desert species, which has possibly exchanged some minor dietary versatility for more thorough chewing and longer-lived molars.
Status: After decimation by settlers and hunters in the Cape the remnant appears to have succumbed to the severe rinderpest epidemic of the 1890s. The Somali population is listed as Vulnerable (IUCN). Its physiology and biology merits further study.

Common warthog *Phacochoerus africanus*

Other names: Fr. *Phacochère*. Ger. *Warzenschwein*. Swah. *Ngiri*, *Mbango*.

Measurements: HB 105–152cm. T 35–50cm. SH 55–85cm. W 45–75kg (♀), 60–150kg (♂).

Recognition: A relatively long-legged but short-necked pig with prominent, curved tusks. The nearly naked skin is grey. Lank black hair forms a dorsal crest that is longest over the neck and shoulders. Paler, often white bristles grow on the jaw-line callosity. The facial callosities, or 'warts', consist of three paired masses of thickened skin and connective tissue protecting the jaws, eyes and muzzle. Warthogs run at a high, jaunty trot, with back straight and the very narrow tail held vertically. The head, with its very protuberant eyes and ears, is held high. Feeding animals drop to their knees and commonly proceed to graze in this position, with their hindquarters raised.

Subspecies: *P. a. africanus* (Senegal to Ethiopia), *P. a. aeliani* (Eritrea), *P. a. massaicus* (E and central Africa), *P. a. sundevallii* (SW to SE Africa).

Distribution: Warthogs are unusual pigs in that they are able to live in arid and open areas. In spite of greater tolerance of heat and drought animals depend upon natural or self-dug shelters to escape extremes of heat and cold. They range up to 3,000m in Ethiopia and on Mt Kilimanjaro.

Habitat: Commonest on alluvial soils in lightly wooded country with a mosaic of vegetation types but well distributed throughout savannah and open-woodland areas of tropical Africa. High densities are assisted by abundant aardvark holes; deep burrows are essential to escape fluctuating temperatures and for protection from predators. Warthogs lack fur and surface fat and will insulate their burrows with grass, huddle together and bask in the sun to conserve heat.

Food: Grazing throughout the rains, warthogs favour mats of short species, such as *Sporobolus*, *Cynodon*, *Panicum* and *Brachiaria*. They also strip growing grasses of their seedheads. In the dry season they turn to leaf bases and rhizomes that store nutrients over that period. They unearth these with the sharp edge of the nose disc. In Zimbabwe preferred rhizomes are from species of *Digitaria* and *Tristachys*. Warthogs occasionally eat fallen fruits, faeces and animal foods. Soil is regularly eaten, presumably for minerals. Although they generally stay within walking distance of water, warthogs can subsist for a while on succulents and other water-conserving plants.

Behaviour: There are several social levels. Mothers and their ♀ offspring retain the most enduring bonds. Thus a new family unit joins others that are probably also close relatives. These loose groupings live within 'clan areas' averaging about 4km². Any one family occupies one-eighth to the whole of this area, circulating between favourite burrows that are well spaced out among 100 or more (any one of which may serve as a refuge). Any one hole is never exclusive to an individual or group, and families seldom share holes, simply avoiding occupied ones. The size of the families varies with the number and fortunes of offspring (litters average two or three but can number up to eight).

Young ♂♂ remain with their mothers until driven off or associate together very loosely while they slowly reach full size. ♂ mortality can be high and by the time adults mature at 4 years they are solitary; as few as one survives for every four ♀♀. Mature ♂♂ circulate among ♀♀ and fights are probably in defence of mating rights rather than clan 'territory'. Courtship is initiated by the ♂ when he finds an oestrous ♀. He pursues her, champing, salivating and mumbling in an engine-like 'chug, chug, chug'. The ♀ slows her flight and eventually acquiesces. The young are born in a burrow after a gestation of 160–170 days. They grow rapidly and begin to graze within 3 weeks and can be weaned at between 2 and 6 months. Piglets squeak and churr and tend to run for the nearest burrow at any disturbance. Warthogs are known to live for up to 18 years.

Adaptations: A grass and grass-root diet has involved many dental adaptations centring on the elaboration of a 'heel' on the back molar that has tripled its length. The last molars are long, very deep and durable. The rest of the tooth row is more shallow rooted and wears away. This contraction is linked with warthogs having a more downwardly depressed muzzle compared to other pigs. They employ their tusks in 'tusk-wrestling' and pushing duels. Pushing is interrupted by lightning disengagements to thump at the side of each other's faces. Both deaths and fractures are frequent and it is the hammering that their heads can expect which has selected for the huge 'warts' (that play a role comparable to the pads worn for American football).

Status: Warthogs have been eliminated from all intensively farmed areas, both as a nuisance and as a reservoir of livestock diseases. They are well represented in numerous national parks. Listed in category 1 as Widespread and Abundant (IUCN).

Individual and sexual differences in the flare of tusks and the shape of the warthog's warts.

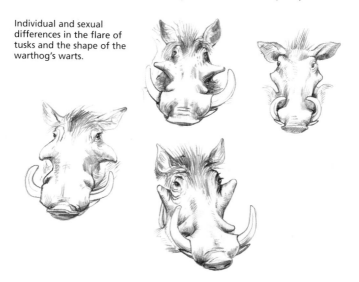

CHEVROTAINS TRAGULIDAE

Chevrotains are small, spotted ungulates that superficially resemble duikers. They are the last relic of a family that was widespread in the Old World from 40–25 million years ago and are the most primitive of all ruminants. They share some features with pigs but, unlike them, have remained relatively unspecialised. The more recent evolution of bovids is thought to have blocked most avenues of specialisation. However, chevrotains had a head-start in adapting to the heavily shaded floor of equatorial forests. This appears to have favoured a versatile animal with a varied diet living at very low densities.

Details of chevrotain anatomy, physiology and behaviour illuminate the progress of evolution, especially by illustrating many features of the generalised ancestral stock of deer, giraffes and bovids.

There are other species of chevrotain in Asia where the smallest are known as 'mouse-deer'.

Water chevrotain *Hyemoschus aquaticus*

Other names: Fr. *Chevrotain aquatique*. Ger. *Hirschferkel*.
Measurements: HB 60–102cm. T 7.5–15cm. SH 30–40cm. W 7-16kg (av. 9.7kg (♂), 12kg (♀)).
Recognition: A compactly built ungulate with a short, thick neck, small, narrow head, leathery nose, slit nostrils, canine tusks and inconspicuous ears. The hindquarters are powerfully muscled but the lower limbs are short and delicate in relation to the length and bulk of the body. The feet resemble miniature pig's trotters; they have naked, shiny black skin behind the hocks. The sleek, reddish brown coat is marked with longitudinal white stripes on the sides interspersed with bold dorsal spots. The throat and chin are covered in coarse hair boldly patterned in black and white. This coarse hair may act as a dispenser for scent secreted by chin glands unique to the chevrotains. When the tail is raised (or 'flashed') it reveals a vivid white underside.
Subspecies: Three named but not considered valid.
Distribution: From Guinea to W Uganda in well-watered equatorial lowlands.
Habitat: River valleys within lowland rainforest, the margins of swamps or streams. Never outside dense cover by day, they may forage in exposed clearings, floodplains, open riverbanks or sandy flats at night. It is reported to clamber into tangles of vegetation and up sloping tree trunks (perhaps to sun-bathe). Water is a major refuge from predators but only for brief periods. Animals can dive and progress under water but soon tire. Diving is a last resort after 'freezing', often in a shallow form or concealed refuge. Hollow trees or underground burrows may also be used during the day.
Food: Mainly fallen fruits, notably figs (*Ficus*), *Pseudospondias*, palm nuts (*Elaeis*) and breadfruit (*Treculia*); also the fruits of gingers, arrowroots and many others. Insects, crabs, scavenged meat and fish have also been recorded. The water chevrotain relies mainly on scent in order to find food.
Behaviour: The social system resembles that of a solitary carnivore. ♀♀ are spaced out in isolated home ranges with minimal overlap or contact. Related ♀♀ occasionally share a range but without much contact. ♂ ranges overlap those of at least two ♀♀. Young ♂♂ cluster around what are probably parental ranges but frequent wounding suggests that ♂ competition, enforced with long, sabre-sharp canines, helps space out fully mature ♂♂ so that they are up to several kilometres apart. Combatants rush forward with mouths wide open and make lateral swipes with their canines. ♂♂ are more aggressive and active than the larger ♀♀. When ♀♀ fight (they possess shorter, blunter canines), they utter a high, pulsing chatter. They scream when wounded and bark in alarm. Weak bleats may be rare contact calls.

When a ♀ is in oestrous the ♂ follows, calling through closed mouth. At each cry the ♀ stops, as if by reflex, whereupon the ♂ licks her rump. After many repetitions she permits copulation. One young is born after a 4-month gestation. ♀♀ are reputed to defend their offspring. The young lie up and are relatively inactive during the first 3 months, nourished almost entirely on milk suckled during periodic visits by the mother. Weaning coincides with dispersal at 9 months, about the time of sexual maturity, although full size and full dentition is only reached at 2 years. Although few survive 8 years, chevrotains are estimated to live for up to 13 years.
Adaptations: Both rump and throat are well protected in both sexes by a dense, thick skin or deep dermal muscles. These undoubtably mitigate the severe wounds inflicted by the ♂♂'s sharp canines.

Status: Naturally sparse and widely spaced, this species is known to suffer intensive hunting and has become rare in many parts of its range. It is also known to be susceptible to disturbance and animals leaving disturbed areas are unlikely to survive. Ghana has placed this species on Appendix 3 (CITES), a move that should be followed by other W African countries.

DEER CERVIDAE

Deer are a non-African line of ruminants that resembles antelopes very closely in body proportions and ecological niches. The most primitive species have sharp tusks like chevrotains. More advanced forms have tusks and small antlers which serve as defensive weapons against wounding by canines. In other species antlers have acquired elaborate branched structures and secondary uses in head-to-head clashes and 'wrestling'. Unlike the fixed horns of bovids, antlers are shed each year (their fast annual growth has physiological resemblances to forms of wound-healing processes, which suggests that antlers may have evolved from a type of scar-tissue). Species vary in the degree to which the side-toes have been reduced.

Deer digestive systems parallel those of bovids in having diverged in order to cope with different diets but differ in structural details. Both cervids and bovids are the most recently evolved of ungulates. The former are widely distributed over Eurasia and the Americas but are most diverse in South-East Asia and South America.

Red deer have been in North Africa no more than 1 million years and there is no evidence to suggest that other species colonised any other part of Africa.

Red deer *Cervus elaphus*

Other names: Fr. *Cerf élaphe*. Ger. *Hirsch*.
Measurements: HB 160–250cm. T 12–15cm. SH 90–140cm. W 100–150kg (♀), 150–225kg (♂).
Recognition: A large, long-legged antelope-like ungulate. ♀♀ are without head weapons. The larger ♂♂ also lack them, briefly in spring but grow prolonged bone-like 'antlers' over the summer months. Antler 'velvet' is shed in late summer and the horns are only used as weapons in the short autumn 'rut' or mating season. The winter coat is dark brown with longish hair. After the spring moult the shorter summer coat is lighter reddish with pale spots. The rump is yellowish. There are scent glands in front of the eyes, under the tail, between the hooves and behind the hocks.
Subspecies: *C. e. barbarus*.

Distribution: Known as fossils from Morocco to Tunisia for nearly 1 million years. Probable relicts of that population are now only found in the Medjerda Mts on the Algeria-Tunisia border. Their greatest resemblance appears to be to Corsican deer.

Habitat: Cork oak and wild olive forests growing on sandy mountain soils. Red deer remain in the woods during the day, only emerging into the open at night. The habitat is a mosaic of oak woodland, maquis and grassy meadows. Wallows are used in the summer, while moulting and during the rut (♂♂).

Food: Shoots of trees and shrubs, bark, young twigs, grasses, sedges and herbs; also fungi and cultivated crops. In spring and summer red deer enter fields and vineyards (at night or in the early morning). They are most active around dawn and dusk.

Behaviour: ♀♀ and ♂♂ live largely separate existences outside the rutting season. ♀♀ tend to be very residential. ♂ gatherings are strongly hierarchical, even for the period they are without horns. The rut, which is noisy and conspicuous in many parts of their range, tends to be more cryptic in N Africa, possibly as a response to hunting. All copulations are monopolised by dominant ♂♂. After a gestation of 235 days young are born in May and June. They tend to 'freeze' or hide when disturbed during the first 2 months. After moulting an infant coat they grow and develop rapidly, moult again into their winter coat and continue taking milk for about 7 months. They are sexually mature at 18 months (but ♂♂ can seldom win mates while still young). They live for about 15 years (rarely up to 25 years).

Adaptations: Long-term studies on red deer have shown that less than five surviving calves are the average lifetime offspring for each sex. However, ♂♂ that win more fights get more mates and have been found to sire up to 24 offspring (about twice the maximum for ♀♀). This massive success of the winning stags is the outcome of intense ♂ competition squeezed into the few weeks of the rut. It is antlers (backed by brawn and drive) that allow stags to win fights but outside the rut antlers have limited use. Were antlers permanent, frequent damage would eliminate otherwise healthy contestants. Each year's regrowth progressively enlarges and adds more branches to the antlers, thereby improving the chances of their owner winning fights and siring more offspring. It is therefore likely that large antlers were elaborated in the context of strongly seasonal breeding.

Status: Although deer have been introduced from Europe to both Morocco and South Africa, the Medjerda population is the only one thought to represent a stock that has occupied NW Africa uninterruptedly since the Pleistocene. They are protected on both sides of the border, in the El Kala National Park in Algeria and the Feijja National Park in Tunisia.

GIRAFFES GIRAFFIDAE

Giraffe	*Giraffa camelopardalis*
Okapi	*Okapia johnstoni*

Recognition: The two surviving giraffes are both tall, browsing animals whose long muscular tongue has been modified to serve as a plucking organ. They have 'horns' that begin as cartilaginous buds in the skin of the forehead. These become bony and eventually fuse to the skull below. Horns are covered throughout life with skin and fur. In ♂♂ bone continues to build up over the horns, orbits, nape and nose. Eventually the cap of rugose bone and thickened skin dwarfs the features below. Both the giraffe and the okapi have tall shoulders and sloping hindquarters.

Somali arid (camelopardalis and reticulata) Ca. Re.
Saharan (peralta) P.
N. savannah (cottoni) Co.
S. savannah (tippelskirchi, giraffa etc) T. G. A.
Cameroon (hybrids?)
Rothschild (hybrids?) R.
Galana hybrids X

The plate opposite suggests how giraffe diversity is the outcome of individual variation superimposed on regional pattern types.

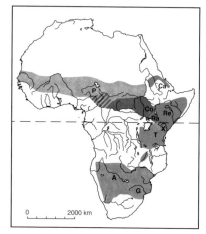

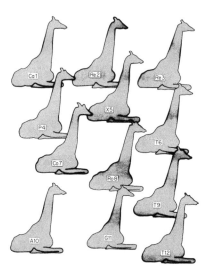

Giraffe distribution interpreted as four major types with mixed or intermediate populations in between.

Genealogy: Giraffes may represent one of the earliest artiodactyls to combine a shift out of the forest with enlarged body size. Thought to have derived from a chevrotain-like ancestor about 20 million years ago they diversified into many species, some becoming extinct quite recently. They included a grazing okapi (*Samotherium boissieri*), the giant-antlered *Sivatherium* and *Libytherium*, the tall, heavy *Giraffa jumae* and the lightly built *G. gracilis*.

Geography: Giraffes were widespread and diverse in Africa and S Eurasia between about 15 million and 1 million years ago. Their extinction was probably due to a combination of competition from bovids and predation by humans.

Ecology: Giraffes select very high-quality foliage and, in spite of being cud-chewing ruminants, rely less on mastication to release nutrients than on digestive efficiency. They have very large, tough, tongue-like papillae in the stomach which provide the largest absorptive surface area known in any ruminant. This very efficient stomach is half the size of that of a grass-eating buffalo. Long-necked giraffes flourish where there is abundant, year-long browse above 2m and below 5.5m. Not only are they clumsy at lower levels but competition from antelopes makes low-level herbage a mere emergency food for giraffes. The okapi exploits a lower, narrower browsing zone but its forest competitors are shorter still in stature and fewer in number.

Natural history: ♀ giraffes are both shorter and more lightly built than ♂♂ and feed from a narrower stratum. To compensate, they eat a wider variety of food species over a larger area. Further specialisations of this sort may explain how several giraffe species could co-exist in the past.

Adaptations: Apart from their long necks and legs, giraffes have unique gaits, a unique digestion and a unique circulatory system (with pressure-reducing valves). They also have unique shoulder-leaning modes of fighting in which the heavily reinforced, blunt-horned head is used somewhat like a club.

Giraffe *Giraffa camelopardalis*

Other names: Fr. *Girafe*. Ger. *Giraffe*. Swah. *Twiga*.

Measurements: HB 3.5–4.8m. T 76–110cm. Total height 3.5–4.7m (♀), 3.9–5.2m (♂). W 450–1,180kg (♀), 1,800–1,930kg (♂).

Recognition: The length of a giraffe's neck is only matched by that of its legs and its slow-motion lope covers ground at a great rate (its Arabic-derived name means 'fast walker'). The legs end in enlarged hocks and broad, rounded hooves. Giraffes can run at 60kph, at which rate the hoof may pivot forward so that the animal's weight is borne directly on the hock. Both young and old are able to outstrip most predators. The neck is fringed with a short, thick mane and both sexes develop three 'horns' above the eyes. Bony protuberances above the eyes preclude the giraffe from being able to see upward. The face is strongly tapered and a 45cm tongue is the principal means of gathering foliage in to the large, elastic mouth and lips. Colours vary greatly between individuals and occasional 'sports' have bizarre patterns, from uniform fawn or black to various blotchy permutations. In spite of this variation, four major populations can be recognised and, within these, further regional varieties or subspecies are commonly recognised.

♂ Masaigiraffe *G.c. tippelskirchi*.

Population	Taxa	Region
Somali arid	*G. c. camelopardalis*	Eritrea, Blue Nile
	G. c. reticulata	N Kenya, Somalia
Saharan	*G. c. peralta*	Sahara
Northern savannah	*G. c. congoensis*	Cameroon to Uganda
Southern savannah	*G. c. angolensis*	S Angola
	G. c. giraffa	S Africa
	G. c. thornicrofti	Luangwa valley
	G. c. tippelskirchi	E Africa

Intermediate populations occur in apparent 'overlap zones', notably in Cameroon, Uganda and SE Kenya and NE Tanzania.

Distribution: Formerly widespread throughout the drier savannahs of Africa (including the Sahara and Atlas Mts during the wetter conditions of about 7,000 years ago). They range up to 2000m but are rare in precipitous hilly country

Habitat: Savannahs, open woodlands and seasonal floodplains (with abundant termitary thickets). Commonest in areas where rainfall, soils, wind, fire, elephants or flooding favour scattered low and medium-height woody growth. They are especially associated with savannas where *Acacia*, *Commiphora* and *Terminalia* are abundant trees.

Food: Known to feed from over 100 species of plant but *Acacia*, *Commiphora* and *Terminalia* species are major staples. Feeding and movement patterns differ from wet to dry seasons. The wet season is a period of abundant, green deciduous growth, during which time the giraffes are widely dispersed. During the dry season they concentrate where evergreens survive. Sustained pruning of scattered bushes maintains a sort of acacia lawn. Irregular firing forces medium-term rotations by burning off light twig growth and removing browse for one or more years.

Giraffes, their extinct relatives and other browsers are thought to have shaped the biology of their food trees, including the evolution of thorns and galls, and the growth form of branches. Persistent and heavy browsing not only shapes the trees' form but often delays further growth.

The amount that giraffes eat in a day varies but is less than half the intake of typical grazers. It is the concentrated nutritional value of the foliage which they select and super-efficient digestion that makes modest feeding possible.

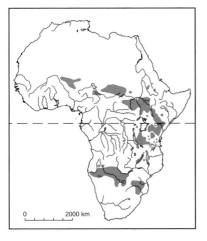

Giraffa camelopardalis

G. camelopardalis former range

Above: present and past
ranges of giraffe.
Right: neck sparring and
fighting in male giraffes.

Behaviour: All social units are temporary. Adult ♂ giraffes may be vestigially territorial because mature bulls monopolise all matings and tend to be intolerant of other large ♂♂ at the cores of their very variably sized home ranges (cores may be as large as 80km² but year-long movements are known to range from 5 to 654km² or more). ♀♀ have very unstable home ranges that may drift from year to year. These overlap those of very many other ♀♀ with which they may associate (in mixed sex groups of up to 50 animals). Such associations are temporary. The only stable associations of a ♀ giraffe's life are the year-long periods of motherhood and the traditional, highly localised, calving area to which she returns again and again to give birth.

Gestation lasts 14 months. An oestrous ♀ may attract close attention from many ♂♂ but the majority of matings are with one or other of a few very large ♂♂. These tend to be spaced out within her current range. Newborn calves rise to their feet within 5 minutes and after a week or so may join up to nine other very young calves also born in the vicinity. One or more mothers are often nearby, although they tend to leave the 'crêche' of youngsters on their own during the middle of the day (the time of day when they feed most intensively and when most predators are inactive). Lactation lasts from 6 to 12 months and the young remain close to the crêche for 3–4 months, after which they begin to accompany their mothers for gradually increasing periods of time. By 6 months a calf is moving independently with adults.

Between half and three-quarters of all giraffes fail to survive their first year. The main cause of death is predation from lions, hyaenas, leopards, crocodiles and humans. Their fearlessness and independence render them easy prey. ♂ calves are especially vulnerable because they remain in groups for 3–4 years before gradually becoming more solitary and localised. Their preoccupation with 'necking' may prejudice their survival still further.

Necking behaviour in young ♂♂ tends to result in some sort of hierarchy or *modus vivendi* being established among them. These contests of strength involve rival ♂♂ standing shoulder to shoulder, straining against each other, seeking to gain purchase in order to deliver and counter periodic arching blows of the head. The apparently languid pace is misleading – the necks and jaws of adult giraffes are occasionally broken in such contests and one blow has been seen to launch an adult eland into the air. By the time survivors are fully mature (at about 10 years) they are likely to have become more residential and narrowed their range. Ranges narrow especially in the dry season, the peak season for conceptions.

Adaptations: The long neck of the giraffe has involved a number of physiological and anatomical changes. The shoulders are deep and muscular, the thoracic vertebrae are exceptionally long in order to carry strong ligaments and the circulatory system has had to evolve very elastic vessels as well as valves to offset the sudden build-up of blood pressure whenever the head swings.

The exceptionally fast growth of giraffes (animals double their height in 1 year) probably represents an early evolutionary strategy whereby very large, but relatively defenceless, animals were able to mitigate predation by growing too large for predators to overpower. A vast and nutritious food supply and the ability to sustain high levels of predation from carnivores was probably shared with those other giraffe species that became extinct in relatively recent eras.

Status: Giraffes are now restricted to protected conservation areas and a few sparsely populated regions and their range continues to contract. Giraffe densities and biomass vary but, in optimal habitats, densities of up to 2 giraffes per km^2 (a biomass of 2,000kg per km^2) are sustainable without prejudicing the much higher densities of other grazers on the same land. This resource could be returned to many regions if more rational patterns of land-use were devised than those pursued by current pastoral and livestock interests.

While giraffes are not threatened as a species, local populations are vulnerable in many localities. The Nubian race *G. c. camelopardis*, is now the most restricted and endangered subspecies.

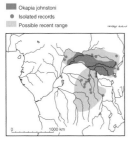

Okapi *Okapia johnstoni*

Other names: Fr. *Okapi*. Ger. *Okapi*.

Measurements: HB 190–215cm. T 30–42cm. Total height 150–180cm. W 210–250kg.

Recognition: A rotund, tall-shouldered ungulate with robust legs, a thick neck, large ears and exceptionally long, mobile tongue. The hornless ♀♀ are chocolate to chestnut brown with bold black and white markings on the legs and white stripes radiating out from the genital area across the rump. ♂♂ are similarly marked but smaller and darker, some almost purplish black. They have swept-back, skin-covered 'horns' above the eyes. A mane, prominent in juveniles, is reduced or absent in most adults.

Distribution: NE Zaïre and (formerly) Bwamba, Uganda. Mainly associated with minor tributaries of the NE Zaïre river basin at altitudes above 500m. It is absent from lower-lying parts of the basin and prefers firm ground. Fossils suggest that okapis or close relatives were formerly more widespread. The spread of fire, antelopes and prehistoric hunting may have combined to extirpate them.

Habitat: Dense, low undergrowth within the rainforest belt in river valleys, chablis and on higher ground in the wet season.

Food: Shade-loving plants in the undergrowth; also fruits, ferns and fungi. Violet-shrubs (*Rinorea*) and *Drypetes* (a common tree) are reported favourite foods. Single leaves or entire twigs are plucked with the long, muscular blue-black tongue. The okapi maintains a very consistent diet and browsing routine throughout the year.

Behaviour: Although of a restricted distribution and scarce over most of its range, the okapi is common in some localities, reaching 1–2.5 per km². ♀ home ranges average 5km². ♂♂ range over a much wider area and some ♂ territorial behaviour is suspected. They snort loudly when disturbed and make coughs and a piping sound. A ♀ remains in oestrus for as long as a month, during which time she is closely attended by a ♂. Both show frequent aggression interrupted by much rubbing, circling and head-tossing. There is an oestrus want call. Fighting ♂♂ wrestle with their necks but also charge and butt one another. One precocious young is born after a 427–457-day gestation. The calf maintains contact with the mother by coughs, bleats and whistles but remains hidden; the mother goes to suckle it when called. Calves are weaned by 6 months. ♂ horns develop at between 1 and 5 years. ♀♀ are sexually mature at 3 years. The okapi lives for 15–20 years.

Adaptations: The disposition of pattern differs fundamentally from that found in many bovids. The okapi has neutrally coloured ears and neck, dark fronts to the forelegs and is rather dull and inconspicuous from the front. In contrast the tail view is truly startling. Infancy and courtship (both involving close following) are the only major departures from a mainly solitary existence. Conditioning in infancy may serve to make the optical impression created by the stripes powerfully attractive, thus offsetting aggressive or anti-social behaviour.

Status: The okapi has enjoyed absolute protection since 1933. The emergence of a massive commercial bush-meat trade in Zaïre now threatens it in all parts of its range. Reintroduction to Uganda's now well protected National Parks should be considered.

BOVIDS, HORNED UNGULATES BOVIDAE

Bovines	Bovinae
Antelopes, goats and sheep	Antilopinae

Recognition: Horned ungulates are long-legged, hooved herbivores that range in size from the 2kg pygmy antelope to the 1,000kg eland. The ♂♂ of most species are horned with true keratinous horn sheaths over bony cores. In some species, ♀♀ are hornless; in others, ♀♀ also have horns (but never as heavy as in ♂♂). Most antelopes have a variety of scent glands. Most have horizontally oriented pupils. They come in a great variety of coat colours and patterns. All horned ungulates ruminate but food preferences vary widely: green-leaf-eating and dry-grass-eating are extremes (with fruit-eating duikers a specialised offshoot).

Genealogy: Likely to be of Eurasian origin, both conservative Asian and African spiral-horned bovines are less well adapted to very dry habitats than the more arid-adapted true antelopes, or Antilopinae, which are mainly African. A continental separation over 20 million years ago might have marked their first divergence. Antilopinae have evolved a highly efficient water-saving and cooling mechanism in the nose while the more conservative bovines rely on water-wasting sweat to cool down.

Geography: While Eurasia is home to the most primitive living bovids (called the boselaphines) and to the earliest fossils, bovids have entered Africa more than once. Thus neotragines are conservatives derived from the very earliest immigrants; spiral-horned bovines came next and buffaloes were still later immigrants from Eurasia. Sheep and goats are Asiatic 'mountain antelopes' that share common roots with proto-gazelles. The other antelope tribes are mostly African. The more arid-adapted groups have been better able to move between continents.

Ecology: Advanced rumination is the central adaptation of bovids. It could not have developed in very active animals forced to make frequent and varied demands on their metabolism. The more conservative species live solitarily in small well-known territories where they can pick food, swallow it and then retire to chew the cud. This ecological strategy would have typified the earliest bovids. Specialisation in grass-eating came much later and developed in parallel among several bovine and antilopine lineages.

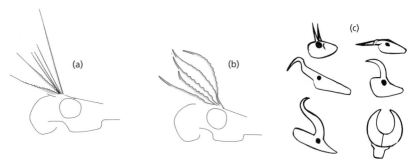

(a) Differing angles in simple, straight bovid horns. (b) Arching and recurving in simple, corrugated horns. (c) Bovid heads are transformed by the shape and orientation of their horns.

Natural history: The need for more efficient weapons helps to explain the development of horns. A most important difference between chevrotains and bovids is the loss of tusks in the latter, leaving the mouth wholly devoted to food-gathering. In the ♂ simple, short, sharp 'head spikes' replaced tusks as weapons and helped protect his exclusive access to one or more ♀♀. Subsequently horns have elaborated until they have totally transformed the architecture of bovid heads. Every type of horn is wielded according to appropriate fighting and defensive techniques. Most species are annual breeders with births tending to peak in the wet season. Bovids produce well-developed young which may remain hidden for a while or, in advanced species, are sufficiently strong to run after their mothers within hours of their birth.

ECOLOGICAL   NICHES OF BOVIDS

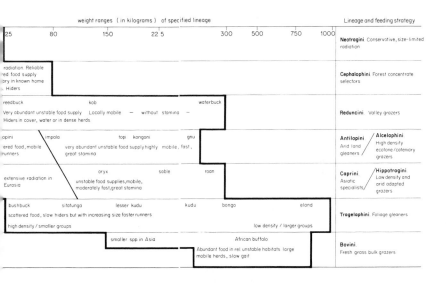

weight ranges (in kilograms) of specified lineage

25	80	150	22 5	300	500	750	1000	Lineage and feeding strategy

Neotragini. Conservative, size-limited radiation

radiation. Reliable ...ed food supply ...ary in known home ... Hiders

Cephalophini. Forest concentrate selectors

...reedbuck   kob   waterbuck
Very abundant unstable food supply   Locally mobile   —   without   stamina   — Hiders in cover, water or in dense herds

Reduncini. Valley grazers

...opini   impala   topi   kongoni   gnu
...ered food, mobile   very abundant unstable food supply highly   mobile, fast, ...runners   great stamina

Antilopini Arid land gleaners / **Alcelaphini** High density ecotone/catenary grazers

oryx   sable   roan
extensive radiation in   unstable food supplies, mobile,
Eurasia   moderately fast, great stamina

Caprini. Asiatic specialists / **Hippotragini** Low density and arid adapted grazers

bushbuck   sitatunga   lesser kudu   kudu   bongo   eland
scattered food, slow hiders but with increasing size faster runners
high density / smaller groups   low density / larger groups

Tragelaphini. Foliage gleaners

smaller spp. in Asia   African buffalo
Abundant food in rel unstable habitats. large mobile herds, slow gait

Bovini. Fresh grass bulk grazers

Adaptations: The grosser differences between bovines and antelopes concern thermoregulation, gland structures and horn types. The divergence probably began with a basal bovine stock in cooler Eurasia responding to unstable seasonal habitats by enlarging its body size and becoming nomadic. In Africa improved heat and drought resistance was linked at first with small body sizes. These features permitted stable home ranges and year-round territories.

Scent signals are augmented by a variety of loud barks, whistles, moos and trumpetings. Visual signals are also important, with heads, ears, legs and rumps marked with various contrasting patches which are flagged or flashed in appropriate contexts.

The development of hard cellulose digestion (grass-eating) from the universal 'nitrogen-metabolism' type of digestion (leaf-eating), has taken place independently in at least six of the ten main bovid tribes.

BOVINES BOVINAE

Oxen	Bovini
Spiral-horned bovines	Tragelaphini

These animals are distinguished from antelopes by their generally larger size, an absence of facial or pedal glands and smooth or keeled rather than annulated horns. Most are mobile and tend to form hierarchies in which ♂♂ generally avoid direct confrontation. Hierarchy encourages sexual selection in favour of larger ♂♂. ♀♀ are smaller, hornless or less heavily horned than ♂♂ in all bovines. The development or suppression of horns in ♀♀ is neither primitive nor advanced, rather both horns and hornlessness involve different mechanisms for getting at resources. Horned ♀♀ tend to resemble ♂♂ in establishing hierarchies. They are also more active in defending their young.

OXEN BOVINI

African buffalo	*Syncerus caffer*

Characterised by low, wide skulls with a short face and smooth horns which splay out sideways from the skull, oxen are large, heavy and short legged, needing long periods for rumination. Old ♂♂ tend to become slow and placid.

The living African buffalo has replaced a giant and very wide-horned type which was abundant and widespread from about 4 million years ago to a few thousand years ago.

Competition from cattle now threatens the existence of many wild animals. Rapidly accelerating exploitation of oxen and grasslands continues to raise major social, economic and political issues in Africa.

Above ♂ Cape buffalo. Opp. ♀ forest buffalo.

African buffalo *Syncerus caffer*

Other names: Fr. *Buffle d'Afrique*. Ger. *Büffel*. Swah. *Nyati, Mbogo*.

Measurements: HB 170–340cm. T 50–80cm. H 100–170cm. W 250–850kg.

Recognition: Large ox with thick, bossed horns and tasselled ears. The coat is short, often sparse and coloured from a rich red to black. The underside and chin of the buffalo is often pale (even creamy white) and patches of contrasting colour appear on the face and legs. The differences between forest and savannah buffaloes are very great but there are intermediate and mixed types.

Subspecies: Forest buffalo, *S. c. nanus*; western buffalo, *S. c. brachyceros*; Cape buffalo, *S. c. caffer*; plus the possible relict 'mountain buffalo', *S. c. mathewsi*.

Forest buffaloes are generally below 120cm in height and 320kg in weight while savannah forms tend to exceed these measures.

Distribution: Large savannah buffaloes are thought to represent recent expansion and evolution of the smaller and more conservative forest buffaloes. Until recently they ranged across all but the driest parts of sub-Saharan Africa, their local range being limited to about 20km from water. Greatly reduced by hunting and habitat loss, they may never have recovered from the 1890s' rinderpest epidemic in some southern localities.

Habitat: The forest buffalo depends on low-level browse and an undetermined minimum of grass in its diet, limiting it to grassy glades, watercourses and waterlogged basins. The humid climate ensures continuous plant growth which ensures that small areas will support buffaloes throughout the year. Heavy browsing and grazing in 'buffalo glades' helps to limit or delay plant growth. Savannah buffaloes also seek out forests and valley bottoms where possible but can stay in the open and resist overheating and desiccation by becoming immobile or by lying in wallows. Their need for water and dense cover, as well as grass, makes them favour mosaics and savannahs with patches of thicket, reeds or forest. They retain strong attachments to traditional ranges even when conditions change.

Food: Grazing, breaking and trampling by buffaloes favours rapid grass regrowth which encourages intense and repeated foraging. Particularly favoured grasses are *Cynodon*, *Sporobolus*, *Digitaria*, *Panicum*, *Heteropogon* and *Cenchrus* species but a wide choice of swamp vegetation is eaten. Grazing is quickly influenced by disturbance or human predation, with animals switching from continuous grazing to dawn, dusk and night-time grazing.

Behaviour: The forest buffalo forms small groups of up to 12 animals with related ♀♀ and their offspring as the core and one or more attendant ♂♂. Other ♂♂ are solitary or form small bachelor parties. Savannah buffaloes can assemble in much larger aggregations but similar 'family' clusters amplified into regular clan-like associations are also attended by

bulls. Within these clans adults of both sexes develop hierarchical rank orders. They have well-marked seasonal breeding peaks and the dry 'off-season' sees many ♂♂ breaking away from ♀ families or clans. Gatherings of as many as 2,000 animals are only possible during the rains or on major patches of rich pasture.

♀ receptivity is preceded by signs of oestrus that attract many bulls. Here the effects of ♂ rank come into play, with the top bull or bulls having priority. Nonetheless fights are common and collisions after head-to-head charges have ended in one bull cartwheeling into the air to land on his back. Gestation lasts about 11 months and birth intervals of 2 years are normal. The cow-calf bond is very strong and exclusive but the ♀♀ attachment to her herd is also close. Thus, all adults respond to distress calls and even bulls wounded by other bulls seek refuge in the herd. Blind or 3-legged buffaloes are known to be healthy members of their family or clan. Buffaloes have been known to live for 26 years.

Adaptations: The forest buffalo lives in habitats that do not suit large carnivores and offer easy retreat into cover. A heavy build, short legs and slow pace are therefore no disadvantage. Food is in limited, patchy but reliable supply, leading to scattered, small, resident herds. The small, back-swept horns of the forest buffalo reflect the infrequency of fighting and head-to-head weight-testing engagements. Increase in the frequency of fights and ever greater selection for larger ♂♂ has contributed to the rapid evolution of enormous horn bosses. When the field is free from obstruction to movement or vision, challenges are taken up from a distance and end in a full-tilt charge.

Savannah buffaloes betray recent forest origins in other ways. Vision, a dominant sense in most open-country animals is less important than sound. Quiet lowing is the preferred way of keeping in touch, especially in dark forests. This allows even blind buffaloes to remain safe in the herd.

Status: While this species as a whole is in no danger of extinction, its western and central African mountain forms are declining fast. Nonetheless it is well represented in numerous national parks and reserves. Not endangered.

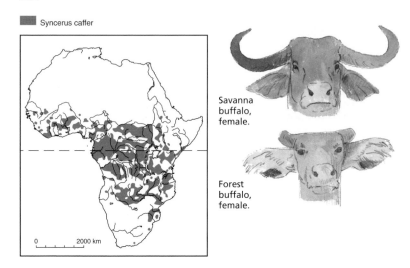

Syncerus caffer

Savanna buffalo, female.

Forest buffalo, female.

SPIRAL-HORNED BOVINES TRAGELAPHINI

| Nyalas, kudus and bushbucks | *Tragelaphus* (7 species) |
| Elands | *Taurotragus* (2 species) |

Recognition: Medium-sized to large bovines with a deep body and a narrow head with big ears and twisted or spiral horns in the ♂♂. Teeth are low-crowned and, like the digestion, adapted to a diet of young, nutritious vegetation. Glandular secretions are mostly diffuse (rather than from facial or pedal pockets). The hornless ♀♀ of most species have more of a generic resemblance than the larger ♂♂, which have distinctive horn shapes and darker, more contrasting coat patterns. The elands and bongo are 'giant' forms, with horned ♀♀.

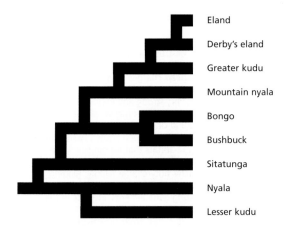

Eland

Derby's eland

Greater kudu

Mountain nyala

Bongo

Bushbuck

Sitatunga

Nyala

Lesser kudu

Tentative genealogy of the spiral-horned antelopes.

Genealogy: Some zoologists make no distinction between tragelaphines, oxen and an Asiatic animal that resembles both, the Indian nilghai (*Boselaphus*). Fossils suggest a common S Asian origin for all three bovine groups but their African branch has been distinct for at least 15 million years.

It seems possible that all African tragelaphines derive from a single immigrant ancestral type which subsequently branched into a larger and smaller lineage. The nyala, *T. angasi* (already recognised as fossils 6.5 million years ago) is a relict of the smaller or medium-sized type, which was once more widespread. The mountain nyala, *T. buxtoni*, is a relict of the larger type that was probably an immediate precursor of the kudu. A third form, resembling both nyalas, would have been a forest-adapted ancestor to both bongos ('giant' descendants) and bushbucks ('dwarf' morphs). The elands have almost certainly evolved from a giant form of kudu that was abundant about 1.3 million years ago.

Geography: The Asiatic ancestors of this now exclusively African group would have been relatively large and adapted to strong seasonal habitats. Forest species, such as the bongo or the swamp-dwelling sitatunga, are secondarily adapted. The lesser kudu, *T. imberbis*, living in dense, evergreen thickets within the Somali arid zone, has taken tolerance of aridity to an extreme. There is a strong E African bias in their distribution (typical of other organisms with 'immigrant' origins).

Ecology: All species are gleaners of green foliage in a wide variety of mostly unstable habitats. None tolerate true desert. Herding in the larger tragelaphines is not induced by the habitat (as it appears to be among the kobs, Reduncini) but is the defensive strategy of ♀♀ and young.

Natural history: Social structures are rudimentary. Vulnerability of the young is a major incentive for forming herds among the largest, most mobile species. ♀♀ are the more ready to associate, and the need to defend the young (as well as enforce rank) has influenced the development of horns in ♀ bongo and elands.

♂♂ also show rank orders and sometimes live at very high densities. Rank is assessed through size-enlarging displays and may be partly cyclical. Periodic testosterone 'surges' are signalled by aggression, or *ukali*. This deters confrontations. Rare instances of all-out fighting and death may result from confrontations between well-matched ♂♂ who are both in their *ukali* phase. ♂♂ of all species horn the soil, or vegetation. These are not territorial beacons but more general advertisement of status and presence.

Adaptations: In marked contrast to the buffaloes and other bovines, tragelaphines are alert and highly visual animals and visual signals are both subtle and highly structured. All species begin as striped and blotched infants that 'freeze' or hide to escape detection. They have conspicuous white flashes on ears, muzzle and lips. These function most obviously when mothers approach hidden young, at which time they bob or flag their heads up and down, sometimes calling very softly at the same time. Adult ♂♂ develop ritualised broadside displays to impose upon other animals. Manes, crests, black and white markings and rangy, flat-sided figures all serve to enhance ♂ displays during courtship but more especially in rank contests.

Another clue to rank is the loudness and timbre of the ♂ barks. Visual and vocal signals appear in different permutations in four closely related species. The flamboyant nyalas, living in mosaics of thickets laced with open corridors, valleys and glades, silently strut their frills and crests, occasionally uttering double barks. The lesser kudu, risking ambush in denser, drier bush, have subtle, close-contact patterns on legs, face and throat and bark sparingly. The sitatunga, submerged in thick gass, mud or water has vestigial or muted patterns but barks frequently, loudly and persistently. The bushbuck is the most versatile. Colourful and contrasty in the forested west, it is duller in the drier, more open and dangerous south and east. The volubility of both sexes is very variable. Its success as a species may well be assisted by greater flexibility in the ♂♂'s signalling systems.

Spiral horns have variable functions but are particularly well suited to defensive horn-wrestling. The differential growth mechanisms determining spirals are so simple that much variation is possible. Individual variations are common in some species but nonetheless the trajectory of spirals is highly species-specific.

Studies of tragelaphine brains have revealed that the nyala (*T. angasi*) and lesser kudu (*T. imberbis*) have much the smallest (and presumably primitive) brains, confirming their conservative status.

Bushbuck *Tragelaphus scriptus*

Other names: Fr. *Guib harnaché, Guib.* Ger. *Schirrantilope.* Swah. *Mbawala, Pongo.*
Measurements: HB 105–150cm. T 19–25cm. SH 61–100cm. W 24–60kg (♀); 30–80kg (♂).
Recognition: A small bovine, the bushbuck converges with many antelope and deer in having average proportions. ♀♀ and young are mainly red and ♂♂ become progressively darker with sexual maturity and age. Both sexes and all ages have a white underside to the broad, woolly tail, white flashes above black hooves and white markings on face and ears. Western forest forms are 'harnessed', with both vertical and horizontal white body stripes and numerous spots on the haunches. Eastern and southern 'sylvan' populations are sometimes plain and often sparsely marked with a few light spots or streaks on flanks or haunches. In central Africa there is a broad belt where the two types overlap or mix. The M's horns are 25–57cm long and vary from being very short, thick and nearly straight to longer and thinner with two marked kinks in the spiral. Montane and forest forms are blacker and/or redder while those from the driest areas are yellower. In between are intermediate tints. Pale dorsal crests are present in most populations. Necks and faces are short haired in most areas but hairy in some montane populations.

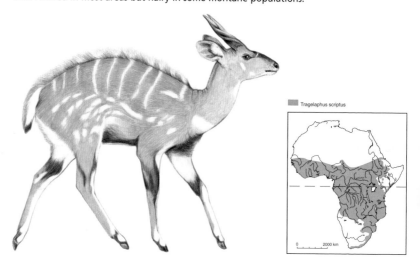

Tragelaphus scriptus

0   2000 km

Subspecies: Harnessed bushbucks: *T. scriptus scriptus*, W and central Africa. Sylvan bushbucks: *T. s. sylvaticus*, South Africa; *T. s. roualeyni*, SE Africa; *T. s. delameri*, E Africa; *T. s. meneliki*, S Ethiopia; *T. s. decula*, N Ethiopia. Intermediate types: *T. s. ornatus*, south-central Africa; *T. s. bor*, east-central Africa. Montane isolates: *T. s. barkeri*, NE Uganda; *T. s. heterochrous*, Mt Elgon. Individual variation has led to 27 races being listed.
Distribution: Sub-Saharan Africa but absent from the south-west, Kalahari and Somali arid regions. Locally absent in dry, open country, they are water-dependent. They range up to 3,000m on E African mountains.
Habitat: Essentially dependent on thick cover, even if this is no more than small thickets centring on termitaries. They need water but can subsist on dew. They sometimes live in reedbeds.
Food: Largely shrubs, leguminous herbs and growing grass (often a nocturnal preference); also pods, fruits of many species. Feeding patterns are strongly influenced by disturbance and predators. Frequently resting and ruminating, bushbucks are strictly solitary, even if they feed close to other bushbucks.
Behaviour: Living at very variable densities, the ♂♂ appear to maintain linear hierarchies where both colour-coded age grades and *ukali* (testosterone surges) may influence individual status. Although normally very residential they are not territorial, even at densities of up to 26 per km² (on a fertile bushy peninsula). Deaths, the incursion of immigrants, maturation of ♂♂ and coming into season of ♀♀ are potentially disruptive. ♀♀ form regular associations with other ♀♀ and a smaller number of ♂♂ that live in the same area (and are likely to be close relatives).

One young is born after a gestation of about 6 months. Infants keep well hidden for up to 4 months and mature by 1 year, although ♂ horns only reach adult size at about 3 years (at which time colouring and behaviour also change). They live for 12 years or more.

Adaptations: The survival of bushbucks in settled, agricultural areas and their very wide distribution imply that their smaller size and 'freezing' and crouching strategy helps conceal them from both humans and carnivores. A versatile diet and ability to subsist on both grass and browse also contributes to their success. ♂♂ have a very loud, deep, roaring bark which serves to mob or even intimidate predators, as well as to challenge or alert other bushbucks. ♀♀ also bark but less loudly and less frequently. When uttered repeatedly by a moving animal, barks indicate change and movement. Neighbouring bushbucks scarcely ever bark in response but usually change direction or seek shelter. ♂♂ utter a twittering call while courting.

Status: Isolated mountain morphs, such as the Mt Elgon and N Uganda bushbucks (*T. s. heterochrous* and *T. s. barkeri*), are locally vulnerable but overall bushbuck remain common and widespread. Not endangered.

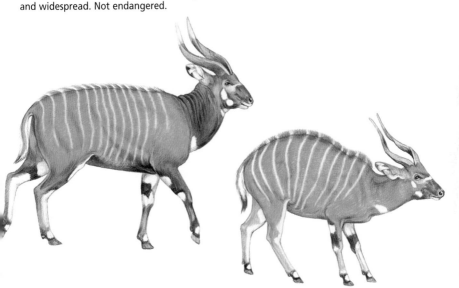

Bongo *Tragelaphus euryceros*

Other names: Fr. *Bongo*. Ger. *Bongo*. Swah. *Bongo, Ndongoro*.

Measurements: HB 170–250cm. T 24–65cm. SH 110–130cm. W 210–253kg (♀), 240–405kg (♂).

Recognition: Long-bodied, muscular bovine, coloured deep russet red, with 10–16 vivid white stripes on each side. Both sexes are spiral-horned and flat-sided. ♂♂ have a vestigial dorsal crest and bold, black and white markings on the extremities. ♂♂ continue to put on weight with age and slowly darken until they are nearly black. Body proportions vary, with W African lowland bongo consistently smaller and shorter legged. The Kenya mountain bongo is taller and much heavier. Glandular secretions appear to be dispersed over the body and are not restricted to discrete sacs or tracts.

Subspecies: Lowland bongo, *T. e. euryceros* (W and central African lowlands); mountain bongo, *T. e. isaaci* (Kenya highlands).

Distribution: Restricted to forest mosaics on or north of the equator. Bongos occur patchily from Sierra Leone to Mt Kenya. Like all tragelaphines they are adapted to unstable habitats. In Kenya they prefer slopes between 2,000 and 3,000m, ranging (in larger groups) above 2,500m up to 4,000m in the dry season and dispersing at mainly lower altitudes in the rains.

Habitat: Landslides, floods, fires, treefalls, heavy elephant-browsing, logging and fallow all favour regrowth of the low-level fresh greenery that they need and they only occur in such disturbed forest mosaics. In montane areas mass die-offs of bamboo suit them. They remain relatively inactive in dense cover during the day and tend to move at night but are always close to refuges in undergrowth or thickets.

Food: Over 80 food plants have been recorded from a single locality. These include the foliage of shrubs and young trees, herbs, young grass and especially vines that are dragged down off trees or pulled up from the ground. Occasionally particular species become favourites: young *Albizia* seedlings, the herbs *Acalypha* and *Rinorea*, balsam (*Impatiens*) and wild yam vines, (*Dioscorea*) have been noted.

Behaviour: Individuals (of both sexes) do not form permanent links with others beyond the mother-young bond. Nonetheless mothers suckling young after the latters concealment phase seek one another out. 3 months after the July–September birth peak in Kenya all lactating ♀♀ are in large nursery herds where their behaviour is more confident and relaxed than when single (and typically alert and timid). They range widely (possibly 120–300km²) and all classes have overlapping home ranges.

♂♂ do not herd ♀♀ nor coerce them, nor do they influence their movements or groupings. Typically scattered dispersal favours efficient tracking and testing of ♀♀ rather than direct competition for isolated, unpredictable mating opportunities. Body odours may assist this trailing process. Animals grunt and snort, ♀♀ have a weak mooing contact call and all classes bleat in distress. Like other tragelaphines, ♂♂ 'click' while courting the ♀. Gestation lasts about 284 days and the newborn young remains concealed until, with its mother, it joins a nursery group. Sexually mature after 2 years, ♂♂ are unlikely to mate successfully until they reach their prime at about 4 or 5 years. They live up to 20 years.

Adaptations: Bongos differ from elands in being shorter legged, shorter winded and water dependent but resemble them in having to range widely in search of concentrated nutritious herbage. They are vulnerable to predators and so stay in, or close to, thick cover where they can hide or defend themselves. ♂♂ resemble nyalas in parading their age and status in strutting displays but depend less upon visual illusion of mass than real mass. Displays are commonly performed at very close quarters at night.

Status: Still common in parts of Cameroon, Zaïre and central Africa, the bongo is in danger of extinction in Sierra Leone and Ghana. It has become rare or vulnerable in Ivory Coast, Gabon and Liberia. Conservation plans must take account of its need for unstable habitats. Being widespread in moderate numbers, IUCN classes the bongo's status as Satisfactory. Currently not endangered overall.

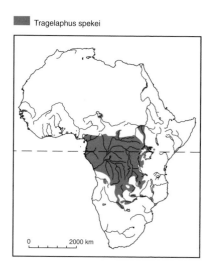

Tragelaphus spekei

0   2000 km

Sitatunga *Tragelaphus spekei*

Other names: Fr. *Sitatunga*. Ger. *Sumpfantilope*. Swah. *Nzohe*.

Measurements: HB 115–155cm (♀), 150–170cm (♂). T 18–30cm. SH 75–105cm (♀), 85–125cm (♂). W 40–85kg (♀), 80–130kg (♂).

Recognition: A shaggy, long-legged bovine distinguished by its long, splayed hooves and somewhat spread-eagled stance (both adaptations to living on boggy ground). The hornless ♀♀ resemble other tragelaphines and are rufous with eight or ten white dorsal stripes. ♂♂

are larger and darker, with heavy, sharply keeled horns measuring 45–92cm. They describe a shallow spiral with one and a half twists. Deep muscled cheeks contrast with a relatively short and slender muzzle.

Subspecies: Nile sitatunga – *T. spekei spekei* (Nile watershed); Zaïre sitatunga – *T. s. gratus* (W and central Africa); southern sitatunga – *T. s. selousi* (S Africa).

Distribution: The primary habitat and centre of sitatunga distribution is the Zaïre basin (where the ancestral population probably adapted to the shores and tributaries of the former L. Zaïre). Populations in the Niger and other river basins west of this region have been allocated to the same subspecies (*T. s. gratus*). Distinct populations inhabit swamps, lakeshores and valley bottoms centred on the R. Nile and R. Zambezi/R. Bangweulu drainage basins.

Habitat: Adaptation to a grassy diet and open swamps is secondary to inhabiting the more complex communities of shrubby growth, herbs, sedges, grasses and palms that border forest waterways. Eastern, southern and far western parts of their range are dominated by extensive beds of reeds (*Echinochloa*), bullrush (*Typha*) and sedge or papyrus (*Cyperus*).

Food: Shrubs, herbs and grasses with strong regional biases; *Monodora, Uvaria, Xylopia* and *Alchornia* species are favourite browse in Uganda, swamp grasses and sedges in Bangweulu, Okavango and the Sudd. Some flowering plants are especially favoured. Sitatungas often feed very intensively in a small area for some days or even weeks and then desert it. They are most active from 18.00–10.00h. but are less restricted in undisturbed swamps.

Behaviour: A rich, year-round supply of greenery permits exceptionally small home ranges and potentially high densities. On Nkosi, a small, wooded island in L. Victoria, densities once reached about 200 per km² and 55 per km² have been reported elsewhere. Temporary aggregations gather for a few hours on favourite pastures only to disperse. ♀♀ are especially prone to gather in high-density areas and may be accompanied by more than one generation of calves. They have a clumsy gait but are quiet and deliberate in their movements. They avoid attention by cautiously entering thick vegetation and sink down into water very slowly, leaving only the snout and part of the head above the surface.

Crescendos of barking are common at night in high-density areas, especially after a disturbance, and sometimes stimulate more than one barker. If listening ♂♂ can discern age and vigour from the timbre of a bark such calling could reduce the likelihood of lethal fights. Courtship resembles that of other tragelaphines. Gestation lasts over 7 months, with birth peaks noted in the dry season (July in E and SE Africa). One young is born on a trampled resting platform or in a 'form' in thick vegetation. It is then left on its own, except for quick visits by the mother. The ♀ keeps hiding and suckling places separate by leading the young into dense vegetation to nurse. The young are independent and playful from an early age.

Resting and ruminating are invariably solitary. Sitatunga mature by about 4 years and captive specimens have lived for up to 20 years.

Adaptations: The most striking adaptation is elongation of the hooves, which renders animals particularly clumsy on dry or broken terrain. Sitatungas emerge from swamps to wander more widely in the wet season. In the Sudd this represents a modest but discernible shift from deep permanent swamp onto the margins of a seasonal floodplain with different food plants.

Status: Hunting may threaten sitatungas in some marginal areas of their range. They are particularly vulnerable to persistent snaring, because they use paths and tunnels, and to wholesale burning or drainage of their habitat. However, they can withstand heavy and persistent hunting if the swamps remain intact. They are rare or endangered locally i.e. in Kenya, L. Chad, Zimbabwe, but substantial populations of all three subspecies remain. Possibly the best suited of all tragelaphines to domestication or semi-domestication. Not endangered.

Nyala *Tragelaphus angasi*

Other names: Fr. *Nyala*. Ger. *Tieflandnyala*.

Measurements: HB 135–145cm (♀), 150–195cm (♂). T 36–55cm. SH 80–105cm (♀), 100–121cm (♂). W 62–90kg (♀),100–140kg (♂).

Recognition: ♀♀ are slender and russet with up to 18 bold white stripes down their sides. ♂♂ begin with similar colouring but pass through a prolonged metamorphosis as they mature. First they turn sandy grey and grow tufts on the chin, throat and belly. As the horns lengthen the dorsal crest and continuous fringes of hair also grow in length. The colour darkens and the pale vertical stripes fade and may disappear altogether. The timing of all these developments varies individually and in some cases crests and colours remain relatively or absolutely undeveloped. The 'false' or side hooves are fringed with glands but nyala lack inguinal glands in the groin. ♂ horns range from 40 to 83.5cm in length. Chunky hooves leave a distinctive spoor, with a compact, rounded margin.

Distribution: The nyala occupies a highly anomalous region in SE Africa where Kalahari-type sands outcrop near the east coast. The low-lying Limpopo basin, with appreciably lower rainfall than its surroundings, forms the heart of its distribution but even outside this core area well-drained soils support a similar 'lowveld' vegetation unique to the region. It does not occur above 1,400m.

Habitat: A mosaic of dense mopane (*Colophospermum mopane*) thickets and more open woodlands, pans and scrub. Grass in the open areas tends to be ephemeral growth during the summer rains. Patchy fires help to maintain this very unstable mosaic. The nyala uses the thickets for browsing and shelter but emerges into more open areas at night, especially during the wet season. The denser areas of its habitat resemble those in NE Africa, with bush-willows (*Combretum*), shepherd's tree (*Boscia*), torchwood (*Balanites*), myrobalan (*Terminalia*) and baobabs (*Adansonia*), as well as acacias.

Food: Favoured browse species are *Acacia*, toothbrush trees (*Salvadora*), buffalo thorn (*Ziziphus*) and monkey apple (*Strychnos*). The nyala picks up fallen leaves, herbs, cucurbits and various small legumes. During the rains fresh green grass attracts it into open areas.

Behaviour: Up to 50 animals can gather on a flush of fresh growth while oestrous ♀♀ can attract much smaller aggregations. Essentially independent animals will readily meet and part with a frequency that depends on local nyala densities. Home ranges vary from 33 to 360ha, with an average of about 75ha. There are two slight breeding peaks but births can occur in any month. Gestation exceeds 7 months (about 220 days) and the young remain concealed for nearly 3 weeks before emerging to follow their mother and join other ♀♀ for variable periods. They are sexually mature by 18 months but ♂♂ are unlikely to breed until they have long horns, dark colouring and fully developed crests and tassels (at about 3 years). They live for at least 16 years.

Adaptations: Among bovids, nyala ♂♂ are the most extreme specialists in advertisement through visual display. Their fringes enlarge the body boundaries and dark colour increases the impression of weight and solidity. Strutting displays generally result in the subordinate ♂ lowering its head and crest as it quietly withdraws. Rare fights with the horns are all-out and can cause death or serious wounding.

Status: Currently satisfactory as it is represented in good numbers in many parks and reserves. The nyala is also a common zoo animal. Its habitat has rather low agricultural value although this could change with the provision of irrigation. Not endangered.

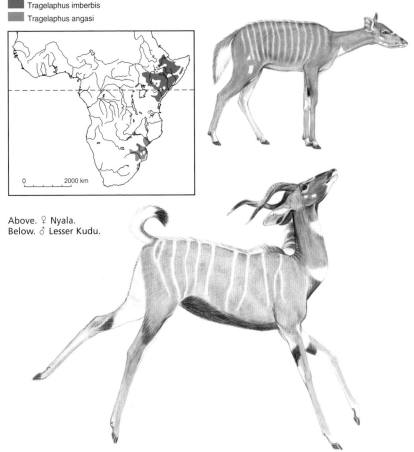

■ Tragelaphus imberbis
■ Tragelaphus angasi

0   2000 km

Above. ♀ Nyala.
Below. ♂ Lesser Kudu.

Lesser kudu *Tragelaphus imberbis*

Other names: Fr. *Petit koudou*. Ger. *Kleinkudu*. Swah. *Tandala ndogo*.
Measurements: HB 110–175cm. T 25–40cm. SH 90–110cm. W 56–70kg. (♀), 92–108kg (♂).
Recognition: ♀♀ and young are bright russet, with 11–15 vertical white stripes. They have a long, narrow head and resemble nyala very closely, except for slightly longer legs and

neck. Yearling ♂♂ acquire sandy-grey colouring that is almost identical to that of similarly aged nyala ♂♂. The black and white markings on face, tail, and tawny-orange legs are also extremely similar in both species, with the greatest contrast in ♂♂. Although the ♂♂ of both species darken with age, lesser kudu remain well-camouflaged by their colouring. The short and sparsely haired neck has geometric white markings on throat and chest. There are inguinal glands in the groin and secretions around the false hooves.

Subspecies: Two described: *T. i. imberbis* (Horn of Africa), *T i. australis* (E Africa), but apparently a continuum. A distinct form might have occurred in Arabia.

Distribution: Horn of Africa, E Ethiopia (up to 1,300m) and the drier, lower regions of Kenya and Tanzania. Formerly in S Arabia.

Habitat: Deciduous bushlands and thickets dominated by *Acacia and Commiphora*. Resident lesser kudus display some seasonal movement from the more deciduous upper slopes in the wet season to low-lying evergreen belts in the dry season.

Food: Browsers of foliage and herbage with a strong reliance on a few evergreen species during the dry season, notably the succulents (*Calyptrotheca* and *Euphorbia*) and the toothbrush tree (*Salvadora persica*). Nonetheless, over 100 species of plants have been recorded from a single locality, including sprouts (especially *Combretum* and *Cordia*), buds, leaves and pods of various *Acacia* species, flowers and fruits. Grasses are taken sparingly while green and fresh. Lesser kudus are able to extract sufficient moisture from their food but visit water-holes or rivers where they can.

Behaviour: Highly residential but non-territorial animals. ♀♀ tend to aggregate most (up to 24 in a group) and occasionally two or three ♀♀ (presumably close relatives) sustain long-term companionships. Hierarchies have not been observed and all classes meet and part casually. Older ♂♂ actively avoid each other except in the presence of oestrous ♀♀. ♀♀ are the most residential, with home ranges of about 60–500ha. Newly independent ♂♂ move over a larger area (up to 670ha) but gradually settle into a smaller home range.

The normal gait is a level walk but animals can leap 2 m when fleeing, throwing tail and hindquarters in the air and sometimes uttering a harsh bark as they go. Both sexes bark but this mainly serves avoidance and orientation rather than signalling alarm. There is no observable breeding peak. The ♂ courts the ♀ with a hicking, gasping call and whines, continually following her while rubbing and nibbling until she accepts copulation. A single young is born after about 222 days' gestation and remains concealed for about 2 weeks. Sexually mature between 18 months and 2 years, the ♂♂ have full length horns by 4 years. Lesser kudus live for 15 years.

Adaptations: ♂♂ strut and spar but their slender, tall proportions favour a form of see-sawing horn wrestling that is mainly powered by the neck and designed to bring opponents to their knees.

Status: Extreme alertness and shyness protect this species from predators (and conceal them from would-be assessors of their status). Animals are wholly dependent on their habitat remaining relatively closed and may even benefit from overgrazing that suppresses fire. As a widespread but patchily distributed species it is not endangered. Nonetheless it has disappeared from a large part of its former range in Somalia.

Mountain nyala (Gedemsa) *Tragelaphus buxtoni*

Other names: Fr. *Nyala de montagne*. Ger. *Bergnyala*.

Measurements: HB 190–200cm (♀),; 240–260cm (♂). T 20–25cm. SH 90–100cm (♀), 120–135cm (♂). W 150–200kg (♀),180–300kg (♂).

Recognition: In their general proportions and size the hornless ♀ mountain nyala resemble red deer hinds. They are of a pale liver-colour, with paler undersides and a scatter of vestigial spots and stripes. The horned adult ♂♂ can be nearly twice as heavy, with deep chests, a dorsal crest and body colour of sepia brown that slowly gets darker with age. This throws white markings on the ears, face, throat chest and forelegs into strong relief. They can be smooth and glossy or can become quite shaggy during the cold season. The tightness of the horns' spiral, and their thickness and length, vary; they can measure up to 118cm along the curve.

Distribution: Formerly ranging all over the SE highlands of Ethiopia from Ch'erch'er Mts to Sidamo; now limited to the Bale massif. Ranges from 3,000 up to 4,200m but stragglers occur as low as 1,800m.

Habitat: Currently flourishes best in a mosaic of high-altitude woodland, bush, heath, moorland and valley-bottom grassland. The woodlands (mostly juniper and *Hagenia*), heath and bush (dominated by sage brush, *Artemisia* and everlasting, *Helichrysum*) provide dry-season refuge. With the rains there is a greater choice of pasture at lower levels (a similar pattern found with the bongo in mountains). The sedgy grasslands tend to be waterlogged and animals have even been seen eating water-plants.

Food: Herbs and shrubs with occasional grass, lichens and ferns. The most frequent browse is plants of the tomato family (Solanaceae), St John's wort (*Hypericum*), lady's mantle (*Alchemilla*) and goosegrass (*Galium*). The mountain nyala eats fallen leaves of *Hagenia* during the dry season.

Behaviour: ♀♀ accompanied by one or two generations of young form very frequent but essentially impermanent associations with other mother-young groups. These are regularly joined or monitored by adult ♂♂. Numbering up to 13, such groupings tend to be smaller in the dry season when they range very widely. ♀♀ restrict their movements in the rains to about 5km². ♂♂, instead, range as widely as 20km². Young ♂♂ are more mobile and less solitary than the older ♂♂ and determine local hierarchies with frequent horn-wrestling contests. Older ♂♂ are more prone to slow, circling displays with raised crests. Once one ♂ begins to drop his head the engagement is broken off and the subordinate departs. There is a mating peak in about December and single young are born after an 8–9-month gestation, at the end of the wet season. The ochre-coloured young lie up for a couple of weeks and then stay closely attached to their mother for as long as 2 years, by which time ♀ calves are themselves pregnant and ♂♂ have long horns and join bachelor groups.

Adaptations: The lowlands surrounding the Bale massif are inhabited by greater kudu and it is very likely that this more arid-adapted and more agile species outcompetes the mountain nyala in these habitats. Adaptation to extreme temperature oscillations and a more limited diet of specialised montane vegetation is probably the product of their prior occupation (by some millions of years) in the region. While their ancestors had a wider span of habitats (before the evolution of greater kudu) they have now become montane specialists in their diet and physiology.

Status: Being so localised, this species is very vulnerable to both ecological and political upheavals. Nonetheless, a total of 2,000 to 4,000 animals was estimated in 1988, although at least half this population was restricted to a small part of Bale National Park (where they sometimes reach densities of over 20 animals per km²). The establishment of protected satellite populations in the Arssi and Harerghe Mts, and of captive breeding groups, may mitigate the vulnerability of the Bale nucleus. Listed as Threatened (IUCN).

Greater kudu *Tragelaphus strepsiceros*

Other names: Fr. *Grand koudou*. Ger. *Grosskudu*. Swah. *Tandala*.
Measurements: HB 185–235cm (♀), 195–245cm (♂). T 30–55cm. SH 100–140cm (♀),122–150cm (♂). W 120–215kg (♀); 190–315kg (♂).
Recognition: A tall dun-coloured bovine with 4–12 pale stripes on the body and spiral horns reaching a record length of 181cm (along the curve) in ♂♂. Both sexes have a crest down the middle of the back and a mane. ♂♂ have a tesselated dewlap. ♀♀ vary in colour from sandy yellowish grey to russet, ♂♂ tend to be greyer. ♀♀ are normally hornless. Both sexes have very large, rounded ears. All living forms are substantially smaller than pleistocene greater kudus.
Subspecies: *T. s. strepsiceros*, (South and E Africa), *T. s. chora* (NE Africa), *T. s. cottoni* (Chad to W Sudan).
Distribution: Originally from the mountains of SE Chad to Ethiopia and throughout the drier areas of E and S Africa, wherever there were thickets and dense woodlands to provide browse and shelter. Greater kudus are increasingly restricted to stony, hilly country by expanding settlement. They can survive without water if browse is sufficiently moist.
Habitat: Thickets and evergreen forests along watercourses and on cloudy heights provide dry-season refuges. In the wet season they disperse through deciduous woodlands and may emerge at night to graze off herbs and grass on open *Acacia/Commiphora* pans. Their long legs and necks allow them to browse to greater heights, exceeded only by the giraffe.
Food: A very wide range of foliage, herbs, vines, flowers, fruits, succulents and grass. There are striking seasonal changes in diet, with the trailing morning glory (*Ipomoea*), vines (*Vigna*), firebush (*Hymenodictyon*), lucky beans (*Abrus*) and bean trees (*Markhamia*) being typical wet-season browse. Choice is much more restricted in the dry season but Sodom apples (*Calotropis*), buffalo thorn (*Ziziphus*), *Acacia*, *Aloe*, *Cassia* and *Cadaba* are staples, while the slow leaf-fall of bush willows (*Combretum*) provides browse well into the dry season.

Behaviour: Wide dispersion during the rains tends to separate the sexes and there is a mating peak during the dry season when animals return to the core of their range in valley thickets. Groups of 2–25 typically include several adult ♀♀ with offspring of both sexes. Although parties mingle and separate frequently, some individuals form loose associations that last from one year to the next. ♂♂ also return to the same refuges every dry season. Here several clusters of ♀♀ regularly share the home range of a dominant bull (which averages about 10km²). Such ♂♂ are not territorial but they drive off any ♂♂ attempting to consort with their current ♀ companions.

Adults utter very loud and startling barks; ♂♂ grunt when fighting or during confrontations. A hooting bleat signifies distress and a courting ♂ makes a strangulated whimper as he persistently follows and nudges the ♀. Gestation lasts 9 months; the young lies up about 3 weeks and is weaned and fairly independent by 6 months but remains in touch for up to 2 years. ♀♀ are sexually mature by 3 years, ♂♂ by 5 years (their horns reach full length by 6 years). Greater kudus have lived for 23 years in captivity.

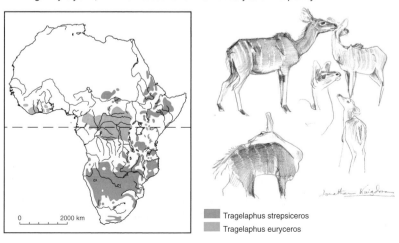

0   2000 km

▉ Tragelaphus strepsiceros
▉ Tragelaphus euryceros

Adaptations: There is a relationship between the kudu's height and the great length of its horns because they have to shield the body of a sparring ♂. Contestants engage their spirals in order to make a firm link-up before pushing and trying to throw one another off balance. The spiral structure relates to this wrestling technique but the horns are also visual symbols of rank which may influence ♀ preferences or choice for mating.

Status: Kudus are rare in some peripheral parts of their range. They are endangered in Somalia and Uganda and are thought to be vulnerable in Chad and Kenya. Their overall range in Tanzania continues to contract but they are still widespread and well represented in national parks and reserves. Not endangered.

Derby's eland *Taurotragus derbianus*

Other names: Fr. *Élan de Derby*. Ger. *Riesenelanantilope*.

Measurements: HB est. 210–240cm (♀), est. 240–320cm (♂). T 55–78cm. SH est. 140–160cm (♀), 150–176cm (♂). W est. 300–500kg (♀), 450–907kg (♂).

Recognition: A very large bovine with 8–12 vertical white stripes on a sandy grey or rufous body. Both sexes have horns; those of the ♂ are longer (up to 123cm), more widely splayed and have a looser spiral than in the common eland. Mature ♂♂ also have a black neck and pendulous dewlap from chin to chest. The ears are broad, rounded and prominently marked, as are the hocks.

Races: *T. d. derbianus* (west of R. Niger): rufous, average 15 stripes. *T. d. gigas* (east of R. Niger): sandy-grey, average 12 stripes.

Distribution: A narrow and increasingly fragmented belt of *Isoberlinia* woodland stretching from Senegal to the Nile and sandwiched between the dry but heavily cultivated wooded savannahs of the Sudanian zone and wetter mosaics of forests and grasslands to the south.

Habitat: Quite strictly confined to the *Isoberlinia doka* woodlands where herds (sometimes numbering up to 60) are highly mobile. Occasional vagrants into the wetter savannahs to the south of this region have given a misleading impression of the total range. They move long distances to drink but can do without water for some time.

Food: Browse consists of the dominant leguminous trees, notably *Isoberlinia*, *Julbernardia* and some young grasses and herbs early in the wet season. Derby's elands break branches with their horns to get at green leaves.

♂ eland.

Behaviour: Highly nomadic, with very large ranges and distinct seasonal movements. ♂♂ are often solitary and their contact with ♀♀ ranges from a few hours to several weeks. Large herds in both wet and dry seasons suggest that security of the young, or social rather than ecological factors, influence ♀ gregariousness. ♂♂ have been reported absent from some of these aggregations. Breeding patterns are likely to resemble those of eland or kudu with a 9-month gestation and a brief lying-up period.

Adaptations: Head carriage, horn and dewlap shape and neck colouring suggest that Derby's eland is intermediate between the 'horn exhibitionist' greater kudu and 'parade bull' eland (which displays its body and bulk as a single mass). Both kudu and Derby's eland emphasise height in their strutting displays. Markings serve to focus attention on the head, ears and neck. Of course large ears are more important for an animal living in thick woodland.

Status: Derby's elands have been totally or virtually exterminated over a large part of their former range. They remain common in parts of Senegal, Central African Republic, Cameroon and S Sudan, where they are nominally protected in national parks. Their wanderings render them vulnerable to hunting and they are exceptionally susceptible to rinderpest which hit them very hard in 1983. Listed as Threatened (IUCN). Niokola Koba National Park in Senegal now supports the only secure population of the western race.

Eland *Taurotragus oryx*

Other names: Fr. *Élan du Cap*. Ger. *Elanantilope*. Swah. *Pofu*.

Measurements: HB 200–280cm (♀), 240–345cm (♂). T 50–90cm. SH 125–160cm (♀), 135–178cm (♂). W 300–600kg (♀), 400–942kg (♂).

Recognition: A very large, tan bovine in which both sexes have horns and a dewlap, a long tail with a tufted tip and narrow, relatively small ears. ♂♂ tend to increase in weight throughout their life, neck and shoulders darken from tan to grey and the dewlap enlarges until it hangs like a curtain to below the level of the knees. Hair on the M's forehead also changes with time, becoming more and more bushy (but it can decline in size, suggesting hormonal control). The mouth and muzzle are small and pointed in comparison to those of buffaloes and cattle. Teeth, jaw muscles and stomach physiology are all adapted to a high-protein, low-fibre diet. The side, or 'false', hooves on the hindlegs are embedded in glandular patches which presumably leave scent trails.

364

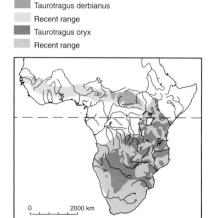

- Taurotragus derbianus
- Recent range
- Taurotragus oryx
- Recent range

Variations in frontal tuft colouring and horn shape.

Subspecies: Cape eland, *T o. oryx* (S and SW Africa): tawny, adults lose stripes. Livingstone's eland, *T. o. livingstonii* (central woodlands): brown, up to 12 stripes. East African eland, *T. o. pattersoni* (E Africa): rufous tinge, up to 12 stripes.

Distribution: Originally from the Cape to forest margins in the Zaïre basin, the R. Katonga, the Nile floodplain and arid N Kenya.

Habitat: Primarily animals of the woodlands and woodland-savannah. In South Africa they had extended their range into temperate Highveldt and the Karoo. Elands gather into larger herds during and after the rains and scatter into smaller groups in the dry season. For the ♀♀ this corresponds with a shift into more open country during the rains and into thickets and woodlands in the dry season. Mature ♂♂ move much less and venture less into the plains. In effect large ♀ groups form primarily as a defence and for protection of the young.

Food: Browse consists of foliage and herbs. Elands can tolerate tougher and more aromatic foods than other tragelaphines. In the dry season myrrh (*Commiphora*) and bush willows (*Combretum*) become the major foods in many localities. Marula fruit, *Acacia* seeds and reed syringa (*Burkea*) are other favoured dry-season foods; these are sometimes browsed in poor-quality scrub dominated by *Protea* or hemp (*Diplorhynchus*). Early flushes of grass and herbs attract elands (notably ♀♀ more than ♂♂). *Acacia* pods are eaten in quantities during the dry season.

Behaviour: Elands are gregarious but have a fluid and open system. Intense mutual attraction among calves leads to temporary isolated groups of up to 50 animals, all juvenile. These calf assemblies provide the nucleus for ♀ herds (in which mothers are to some extent interchangable). Hierarchies form within these juvenile herds and the principle of 'rank by age and size' remains typical of all ages of elands and both sexes. The expedient of defensive bunching in open habitats allows independent animals the benefits of herd life without forming ties. Thus no energy is expended seeking lost partners. On the other hand, every animal is alert to local events, such as fires, showers and thunderclouds, thereby causing temporary congregations of up to 1,000 head to form on flushes of green growth. Young animals, especially ♀♀, are highly nomadic, older animals, especially ♂♂, are more residential. Thus, home ranges have been found to vary from 1,400 to 1,500km². Neighbouring ♂♂ may be in one another's company with some frequency but seldom number more than six or seven. Larger ♂ assemblies are very temporary and tend to disperse rapidly. More matings have been recorded in the rains, leading to birth peaks nearly 9 months later at the end of the dry season. The young have a brief lying-out period before joining the 'crèches'. Growth rates are exceptionally fast, due in part to the extreme richness of eland milk. In spite of ♀ defence, mortality is high, with predators, disease and accidents all taking their toll. Animals are known to have lived for up to 25 years.

Adaptations: The huge size of ♂♂ is the most distinctive peculiarity of elands. Continuous enlargement of neck, shoulders, dewlap and facial brush ensures that most of the ♂♂ within a locality are strung out along a size gradient. This seems to be an extension of the

♀ eland.

hierarchy formed by very fast-growing calves. The only modification of this strictly linear rank order may be the outbursts of ♂ aggression, known as *ukali*, which may serve as a dispersal mechanism and is typical of most if not all tragelaphines.

Status: Elands are hunted over much of their range and have disappeared from most farmed areas. Nonetheless they are still widely distributed and well represented in national parks. They are semi-domesticated as exotics in several countries. Locally vulnerable or endangered (in Uganda and Rwanda) but overall not endangered.

ANTELOPES, GOATS AND SHEEP ANTILOPINAE

Duikers	Cephalophini
Dwarf antelopes	Neotragini
Rheboks	Peleini
Reduncines, kobs	Reduncini
Gazelline antelopes	Antilopini
Springbucks	Antidorcini
Alcelaphines, topi and allies	Alcelaphini
Horse-like antelopes	Hippotragini
Sheep and goats	Caprini

Coat patterns in Antelopinae. (a) Beira. (b) Springbok. (c) Bontebok.
(d) Signal diagram. (e) Gemsbok. (f) Goat.

Recognition: Ranging from less than 2 to over 400kg, the very diversity of antelopes typifies them. Horns, often of complex shape, are generally annulated on their forward surfaces, except for a smooth tip (small conservative species sometimes have short, smooth spikes). Their coat patterns are often idiosyncratic but many share a common format that focuses attention on the rump, flanks and head, suggesting a common origin or common mode of elaboration for their patterns. They have various permutations of skin and foot glands and one or two pairs of mammae. Antelopes have a water-saving and efficient method of 'nasal panting' to reduce temperature (bovines employ less economical sweating).

Genealogy: Antelopes probably parted from bovines some 25 million years ago, specialising initially in small size and drier habitats.

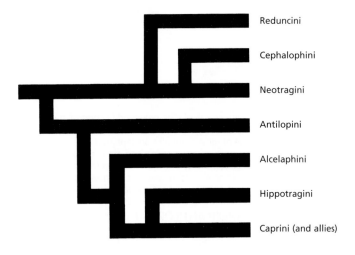

Reduncini

Cephalophini

Neotragini

Antilopini

Alcelaphini

Hippotragini

Caprini (and allies)

Tentative scheme of Antelopine relationships.

Geography: Antelopes probably began as the African branch of a common bovid stock. Later splits may then have separated tropical African from more arid-adapted lineages. The latter colonised drier and more difficult Asiatic habitats (giving rise to the goats and their allies).

Ecology: Improved temperature regulation in drier habitats, combined with small size, allowed early antelopes to live in stable permanent home ranges. This strategy is still evident in dikdiks and other dry-country dwarf antelopes.

Natural history: A long history of mainly solitary animals attached to defended territories is still evident in a strong bias towards territorial behaviour even among larger species which have become nomadic. Strong glandular and excretory scents are characteristic of all species. Some glands extrude solid secretions, others disperse aerosols.

Adaptations: Noisy gratings of the horns on branches or soil is closely associated with deposition of dung and glandular scents in territorial behaviour. Conspicuously bruised plants help to mark out territory and broadcast scents. Annulated horns assist this function, as well as being able to inflict damage on rivals and trespassers. The evolution of antelope horns has centred on the development of defensive sparring or wrestling and the elaboration of hooks, twists and rams, all of which features are linked with the irregular growth patterns typical of annulated horns.

DUIKERS CEPHALOPHINI

Bush duiker	*Sylvicapra grimmia*
Forest duikers	*Cephalophus*

Black-fronted duiker.

Bush duiker.

Recognition: Antelopes with a compact body and head. A short, wedge-shaped head with horns is normal for both sexes (except ♀ bush duikers). The mouth is large, with a wide maw. All species have 'smear-type' facial glands on the sides of their muzzle; some have glands in the groin, under tufts of hair on the legs or between the hooves. They range in size from 3.5 to 80kg. Legs vary in length from species to species but none can compare with open-country, running antelopes. Intensely territorial, the ♂♂ of most species can be called up by imitating the duiker's bleat.

Genealogy: Duikers follow a progression in which the smallest appear to be the more primitive while the largest are the more advanced. Dwarfing is one mechanism whereby leaf-eating herbivores can first adapt to the scarcity of herbage on the forest floor. Only after this initial adaptation could the ancestral duikers make a dietary reversal back to more frugivorous, even omnivorous, diets. Duikers are rare in the fossil record. However, their brain morphology is consistent with their being advanced derivatives of the dwarf antelopes. They are among the largest and most complex brains of all bovids.

Geography: Most duikers live only in forest but some have adapted to more open, swampy or montane environments. They are exclusively African and always have been. There are no fossils to suggest they ever crossed the Sahara.

Ecology: The ecological partitioning of forest duikers is summarised later (see page 369). The proliferation of 17 species involves both isolation, regional specialisation, partitioning of the habitat by food type, activity (diurnal, nocturnal) and, above all, size differences. All duikers are to a greater or lesser extent dependent upon monkeys, birds and fruit bats to dislodge the fruits, flowers and leaves on which they feed. Part of their alertness and 'strategic intelligence' is linked with this sensitivity to what is happening in the canopy. Some duikers can clamber up sloping trunks or dense tangles. One group have specialised in skilled concealment (mostly during the day), relying on a short fast dash to escape if found. These, the 'fibre duikers', *C. dorsalis*, *C. jentinki* and *C. ogilbyi*, have a different body build from other duikers (notably their powerfully muscled hindquarters). Explosive leaping is less typical of species with more continuous exposure but all can make prodigious leaps when pursued.

Natural history: All species are thought to be territorial and most form close associations between the sexes, each excluding others of their own sex. The size of territories and degree of exclusivity (particularly along margins) probably varies greatly. Well-trodden paths connect habitual feeding, ruminating, sleeping and refuge areas. All species use scents and vocalisations to regulate social contacts. Precocious young are born after a relatively long gestation. All are slow to reach full maturity, suggesting that prolonged learning may be necessary for successful exploitation of a difficult environment.

Adaptations: Duikers have thickened and enlarged frontal bones and their short, sometimes vestigial, horns grow from further back on the skull than in other antelopes. This can be correlated with hard head-butting in many species, directed at rivals and (less commonly) predators and hard fruits. Their reduced horns and other neotenous features are another indication of dwarfed origins.

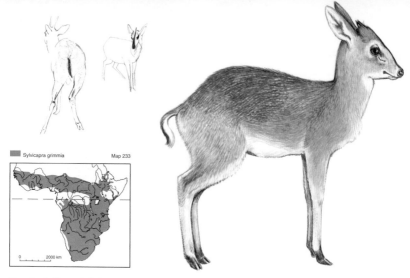

0   2000 km

Bush duiker *Sylvicapra grimmia*

Other names: Fr. *Céphalophe couronné*. Ger. *Knonenducker*. Swah. *Nsya*.

Measurements: HB 90–115cm (♀), 70–105cm (♂). T 7–19.5cm. H 45–70cm. W 12–25.5kg (♀), 11–21.5kg (♂).

Recognition: The long but typical duiker face has swollen face glands and a black midline down the nose, ending in a rounded, leathery black nose. The bush duiker is longer legged and larger eared than forest duikers. Colouring varies from region to region, with plain tawny animals in the far east and west and heavily grizzled, grey or brown animals in the central part of its range. The short tail is black above, white below. Straight, upright horns, only in the ♂ ♂, measure up to 18cm.

Subspecies: Over 40 listed but regional groupings are recognised. *S. g. grimmia* group (S Africa); *S. g. steinhardti* group (Kalahari region); *S. g. orbicularis* group (E Africa); *S. g. splendidula* group (S Zaïre basin); *S. g. rosevelti* group (Niger to Nile savannahs); *S. g. abyssinica* group (Uganda to Eritrea); *S. g. deserti* (Somali-Kenya littoral); *S. g. coronata* (Upper Guinea savannas). They are darker in moist habitats and lighter in drier habitats.

Distribution: Savannahs and woodlands of sub-Saharan Africa. They are absent from forests open plains, deserts and subdeserts but live in various mountain areas up to the coldest alpine zones.

Habitat: They flourish in a wide range of habitats where their need for shelter and suitable food can be met. They benefit from reduced predation and patches of low secondary growth in settled areas, including suburbia. They avoid the heat of the day and also rest up for a large part of the night.

Food: Leaves and shoots of numerous dominant bush plants, such as *Acacia*, bush willow *(Combretum)*, myrobalan *(Terminalia)* and morning glory *(Ipomoea)*. Fruits are also very important seasonally, notably the pods of leguminous trees and shrubs, figs and the fruit of the duiker tree *(Pseudolachnostylis)*. Flowers, bark, resin, roots, bulbs, tubers and fungi are also eaten; also traces of grass. Animal foods are rarer but not infrequent. Bush duikers do not need water.

Behaviour: ♂ ♂ defend territories with little or no overlap in range. ♀ home ranges are also discrete but may be based more on avoidance. ♂ territories can enclose more than one ♀ range. Lying up is solitary and ♀ ♀ prefer lower, denser refuges while ♂ ♂ select higher, more open vantage points at which to rest or ruminate. Both sexes are active during courtship, with much chasing and play. Gestation is thought to last about 6 months. The young lie up in dense cover for several weeks and mature very rapidly. Reaching near adult size in 6 months, some ♀ ♀ drop their first calf at 1 year of age. They live for at least 12 years.

Adaptations: In spite of being hornless, ♀ ♀ are larger than ♂ ♂ and capable of butting both other duikers and small predators approaching the young. Juveniles bleat very loudly if caught and both parents converge at once. This behaviour is exploited by hunters who imitate the bleat to call duikers within range.

Status: Still widespread and common. Not endangered.

Forest duikers *Cephalophus*

There are 17 species of forest duikers and one or more of them occupy virtually every type of forest in Africa. This enormous radiation can be divided into the following four adaptive lineages:

'Blue' duikers	Blue duiker	*C. monticola*
(conservative dwarfs)	Maxwell's duiker	*C. maxwelli*
'Red' duikers (broad	Ader's duiker	*C. adersi*
spectrum, main stem)	Natal duiker	*C. natalensis*
	Harvey's duiker	*C. harveyi*
	Ruwenzori duiker	*C. rubidus*
	Red-flanked duiker	*C. rufilatus*
	Black-fronted duiker	*C. nigrifrons*
	Zebra duiker	*C. zebra*
	White-bellied duiker	*C. leucogaster*
	Peter's duiker	*C. callipygus*
	Black duiker	*C. niger*
Giant duikers (enlarged 'reds')	Abbot's duiker	*C. spadix*
	Yellow-backed duiker	*C. silvicultor*
Fibre duikers (high-forest	Ogilby's duiker	*C. ogilbyi*
specialists)	Bay duiker	*C.dorsalis*
	Jentink's duiker	*C. jentinki*

Forest type	Lowland Forest closed, high canopy, thin undergrowth	Lowland and montane forest, broken canopy, dense undergrowth	Alpine and subalpine habitats	Swamp forest	Gallery, riverine and drier, low canopy forests	Forest edge and secondary growth
Main food resources for duikers in possible order of importance	Fruit, shoots and seedlings, leaves, flowers, bark and fungi	Fruit and herbaceous growth, leaves, shoots and seedlings, fungi	Herbaceous growth, leaves, fruit, moss, young grass	Fruit, herbaceous growth, fungi, bark, semi-aquatic vegetation	Fruit, leaves, seasonal shoots, seedlings and herbaceous growth	Fruit, herbaceous growth, shoots and seedlings
SPECIES						
C. silvicultor 68 (45 – 80) kg		mainly nocturnal (in Gabon 71% fruit 29% leaves)				
C. spadix 55 (52 – 60) kg		allopatric sibling sp. of above (montane only)				
C.dorsalis 22 (14·5 – 24) kg		Nocturnal. In Gabon 73% fruit 27% leaves				
C.callipygus 20 (16 – 23) kg	Diurnal. In Gabon 83% fruit 16% leaves					
C. nigrifrons 17 (13 – 18) kg			Diurnal. In Gabon 72% fruit 28% leaves			
C.harveyi 15 (13 – 16) kg		Diurnal. and nocturnal			Diurnal and nocturnal	
C. rubidus 15 kg			Diurnal			
C.leucogaster 13 (12 – 18) kg		In Gabon 73% fruit 27% leaves and flowers			Diurnal	
C.rufilatus 13 (12 – 14) kg					Diurnal and nocturnal	
C.natalensis 13 (12 – 14) kg					Diurnal and nocturnal	
C. adersi 8 (16·5 – 12) kg					Diurnal	
C. monticola 5 (3·5 – 9) kg	In Gabon 78% fruit 20% leaves				mainly Diurnal	

Food and habitats of duikers (dietary data from Gautier–Hion, Emmons and Dubost (1980).

The blue duikers are small greyish, brown, or fawn animals that have retained many of the original adaptive traits of the duiker tribe but clearly refined this niche at an early date. They have become a very successful and widely distributed type. The 'red' duikers are the most diverse group. The smaller ones are conservatives, occupying peripheries or islands that are marginal to their central habitat – equatorial forest. Thus Ader's duiker, *C. adersi*, is a relict 'dwarf red' confined to Zanzibar I. and a vestigial coastal forest in Kenya. The Natal duiker, *C. natalensis*, is another small, generalised duiker found in the degraded south-eastern margins of 'forest Africa'. The red flanked duiker, *C. rufilatus*, is a small, generalised 'red' found in more literally 'marginal' habitat along the northern edges of the rainforest belt.

Other red duikers have adapted to marginal environments <u>within</u> the forest. The black-fronted duiker, *C. nigrifrons*, is a swamp specialist while the Ruwenzori duiker, *C. rubidus*, lives at the highest altitudes on the very wet Ruwenzori Mts. (On drier peaks the bush duikers, *Sylvicapra*, have moved into this niche.) The white-bellied duiker, *C. leucogaster*, has a coarser diet than most other reds. This suggests that it could be close to the stock that gave rise to the 'fibre duikers'. Likewise the black duiker, *C. niger*, and Peter's duiker, *C. callipygus*, the largest 'reds', can be said to be 'proto-giants' because they share the smooth, short neck hair, robust, long skull and broad noses that typify the 'giant' black duikers.

The 'fibre duikers' probably originated in Upper Guinea. This lineage has retained its far western bias and is mainly confined to primary rainforest. The widely distributed bay duiker, *C. dorsalis*, is the most advanced in its adaption to hard, fibrous foods.

The giant duikers, more flexible in their diets and habitats, represent a continuation of the main trend in duiker evolution – enlargement from a miniature frugivorous ancestor.

The *Cephalophus* radiation has taken place over an unknown span of time and in response to repeated fragmentation of forest blocs as climates fluctuated. This mechanism helps to explain the survival of relict or specialised forms in marginal or isolated localities.

C. M. aequatorialis.

Blue duiker *Cephalophus monticola*

Other names: Fr. *Céphalophe bleu*. Ger. *Blauducker*. Swah. *Ndimba, Chesi*.
Measurements: HB 55–90cm. T 7–13cm. H 32–41cm. W 3.5–9kg.
Recognition: A small grey or brown antelope that has differentiated into a large number of regional and insular species. Populations living in very wet areas tend to be much darker than those in drier areas. They have large eyes, rather small ears and a very wide, flexible mouth. The tail has a narrow midline of black but the underside and fringe has white, crinkled hairs that reflect light so well that the flickering tail resembles a small flashlight going on and off along the dark forest floor.
Subspecies: 26 named. Seven main populations. Also montane and insular races.

C. m. monticola (S Africa, eastern littoral), *C. m. hecki* (east coast littoral), *C. m. defriesi* (central Africa), *C. m. anchietae* (Angola), *C. m. simpsoni* (S Zaïre basin), *C. m. aequatorialis* (R. Uelle to W Kenya), *C. m. schultzei* (R. Niger to R. Uelle).

Dark montane isolates: *C. m. lugens* (southern highlands, Tanzania), *C. m. schusteri* (eastern arc mountains, Tanzania), *C. m. fuscicolor* (Manica highlands).

Insular forms: *C. m. sundevalli* (Zanzibar I.), *C. m. pembae* (Pemba I.); *C. m. melanorheus* (Bioko I., formerly Fernando Po).

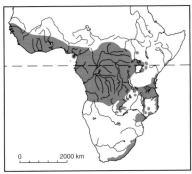

Maxwell's duiker.

Distribution: Forest and forest mosaics from the R. Niger to W Kenya, from Angola to the east coast (Cape to R. Tana).

Habitat: Lowland and montane rainforests, riverine and littoral forests and moist thickets. Patchily distributed and at variable densities because of its dependence upon a year-round supply of fruits. The animals normally rest all night, under cover from rain or beside tree trunks. In disturbed areas they may become more nocturnal.

Food: Where fruiting trees and shrubs are abundant, up to 80% of the diet may be fruits, otherwise foliage with traces of flowers, gum and animal matter is taken. Preferred fruits are the abundant small berries or seeds that are often typical of dominant trees in secondary or colonising forest. Dry fallen leaves are commonly eaten. Blue duikers have been seen to follow below monkeys and birds to pick up fallen fruits.

Behaviour: Bonded pairs are formed on a small and regularly traversed territory (as little as 2.5–4ha in rich W African forests). Such territories are saturated with scent clues emanating from a continuous flow from pedal glands (between the hooves), frequent rubbings from the face glands, and from faeces, urine and horn-gratings. Both sexes chase off intruding duikers but tolerate their own offspring for up to 18 months. Forays outside the territory are made to temporary food sources (and by the ♂ while the ♀ has her newborn lying-up). Gestation has been reported as 5 months but 4 months is a more likely estimate. The mother and young make contact through soft, groaning calls and both freeze at the slightest alarm, only running if encoutered unexpectedly. At such times a ♂ may utter a whistle or sneezing call that both signifies alarm and advertises movement and position to its mate and neighbours. Young mature slowly (i.e. 2 years) and are known to live for 10 years.

Adaptations: Densities of up to 62–78 per km^2 have been recorded in the fruit-rich forests of Gabon. This implies that this species is particularly efficient at picking up the ephemeral resources that fall from the trees above. It is very likely that such densities are only possible where there are very large numbers of monkeys and birds displacing and 'wasting' a super-abundant fruit supply. Close bonding of a pair may assist this strategy by reducing danger from predators and increasing the thoroughness with which the ground is covered.

Status: In spite of heavy hunting pressure all over its range, this duiker is still widespread and common. Felling of fruit trees and killing of monkeys may serve to degrade their habitat and food supply. Not endangered.

Maxwell's duiker *Cephalophus maxwelli*

Other names: Fr. *Céphalophe de Maxwell*.
Measurements: HB 63–76cm. T 12–15cm. H 35–42cm. W 6–10kg.
Recognition: The Upper Guinea counterpart of the blue duiker, distinguished by its strongly marked and more angular head, clearly demarcated facial glands and deeply pocketed pedal glands. It is grey-brown with paler neck, chest and undersides but without white markings. Both sexes are normally horned but some ♀♀ lack horns.
Subspecies: Six named (two from mid-river islands) but none generally recognised.
Distribution: Intermittently from Senegal to the R. Niger.

Habitat: Rainforest galleries and relicts, in moist or derived savannahs with abundant fruiting trees and shrubs.

Food: Fallen fruits, herbs, shrubs and new growth; probably some animal matter.

Behaviour: Generally resembles the blue duiker. i.e. pairs share a small common territory defended against others of the same sex. The territory is incidentally marked by the pedal glands, faeces and urine, more deliberately marked with facial glands. Gestation is reported to be 120 days. The young of captive specimens maintain tranquil relations with parents for over a year. They are fully mature by 2 years.

Adaptations: Face glands are used to mark not only surroundings but also companions within the territory. Both sexes mark and both also solicit and receive grooming in which face, ears and neck are licked vigorously. Gestures of appeasement are also linked with face-licking and suggest that close family bonds are continually maintained.

Status: Maxwell's duiker has lost much habitat and is hunted intensively, often excessively. In spite of this it is still widespread and common. Not endangered.

Ader's duiker *Cephalophus adersi*

Other names: Fr. *Céphalophe d'Aders*. Ger. *Adersducker*. Swah. *Paa nunga*.

Measurements: HB 66–72cm. T 9–12cm. H 30–32cm. W 6.5–12kg.

Recognition: A small duiker of a washed-out, tawny red ground colour with a bold white band across the buttocks and white freckling on the red legs. The neck is greyish and there is a red tufted crest. Fur is particularly soft and silky. The muzzle is pointed, with a rather flat front to the nose.

Habitat: In Zanzibar this species has become almost entirely restricted to tall thicket forest growing on waterless coral rag. Its survival is influenced by all the commonest trees and shrubs bearing prolific crops of flowers and berries. Dominant tree species are ebony (*Diospyros consolataei*), kudu berry (*Cassine aethiopica*) and bush guarri (*Euclea schimperi*), with an understorey of turkey berries (*Canthium* spp.) and *Polyspheria*.

Pairs live in territories and breed throughout the year. They feed from dawn to about 11.00h, after which they rest and ruminate before becoming active again from 15.00h to nightfall. Ader's duiker is extremely alert and sensitive to sound so that driving with nets and dogs or silent ambush at a feeding tree are the main methods of hunting it.

Food: Fallen flowers, fruits and leaves, often picked up beneath foraging monkeys and birds; also sprouts, buds and fresh growth.

Status: In danger of extinction in Kenya, the main hope for this duiker's survival lies in Zanzibar I. Unfortunately the island has no national park, in spite of a rich endemic fauna and flora. Regulation of hunting, formerly exerted by both central administration and by village elders, has been scrapped since the 1962 revolution and local hunters describe a reduction in their harvest of antelopes of 20–30% in recent years. This may be partly due to felling and charcoal-burning in the remaining areas of tall coral thicket. Hunters will travel as far as 30km on foot in order to obtain duikers from well-known 'hot spots', such as Michamvi and Mamboiya. At Mtende Ader's duiker has been estimated to form 70% of the hunters' antelope kills.

As its habitat becomes more fragmented, free-ranging or feral dogs become a major menace. Dogs are known to have eliminated the entire population of Ader's duiker on Funzi I. (where it had been introduced and flourished). Only the declaration and protection of national parks on Zanzibar offer any long-term hope for the survival of this species. Listed as Threatened (IUCN).

Natal duiker *Cephalophus natalensis*

Other names: Fr. *Céphalophe du Natal*. Ger. *Rotducker*. Swah. *Funo, Ngarombwi*.
Measurements: HB 75–87cm. T 9–14cm. H 40–43cm. W 12–14kg.
Recognition: A small duiker with red body, legs and frontal tuft. The neck may be red or pale grey. Margins of the ears, chin, throat and underside of the tail are white. The upperside of the tail, ears and muzzle are black.
Subspecies: Four named, probably all invalid.

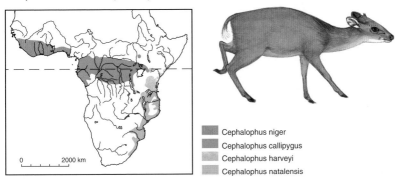

0   2000 km

Cephalophus niger
Cephalophus callipygus
Cephalophus harveyi
Cephalophus natalensis

Habitat: From central Natal to the R. Rufiji valley, inhabiting coastal forests and thickets, low-lying riverine growth, escarpment and montane forests east of L. Malawi and the R. Shire. A diversity of trees that may flower and fruit through most of the year are prerequisites for its presence.
Food: Opportunistic; fruits, flowers and foliage. All feeding is normally diurnal but the Natal duiker may become nocturnal in very disturbed areas.
Status: The Natal duiker is still widespread and common, but rarely seen, in spite of intensive hunting and trapping over most of its range. Conversion of its habitat for settlement and agriculture is proceeding rapidly in many parts of its extensive but already fragmented range. Not endangered.

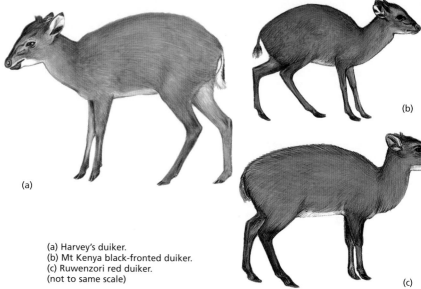

(a) Harvey's duiker.
(b) Mt Kenya black-fronted duiker.
(c) Ruwenzori red duiker.
(not to same scale)

Harvey's duiker *Cephalophus harveyi*

Other names: Fr. *Céphalophe de Harvey*. Ger. *Harveyducker*. Swah. *Funo*.
Measurements: HB 85–95cm. T 11–15cm. H 44–50cm. W 13–16kg.
Recognition: Rich red duiker with a black line down the centre of the face and nape. In most parts of its range it has dark legs and a black and white chin. The white, tufted ears are black-tipped.
Subspecies: This species appears to hybridise with *C. natalensis* in the region of Dar es Salaam and with *C. callipygus* in the Mau, central Kenya. *C. h. bottegoi* has been named from the coast in the Somali-Kenya border area.
Habitat: From coastal thickets to montane forests, riverine gallery and secondary forests wherever there is a variety of fruiting and flowering trees and shrubs. It ranges from the south Somali coast to the mainland opposite Zanzibar I. and across the mountains of E Kenya and Tanzania to Malawi and Nyika Mts.
Food: Fruits, flowers and foliage from the forest floor. Diurnal.
Status: Widespread and common but declining as its habitats become degraded or destroyed for charcoal or agricultural land. Not endangered.

Ruwenzori red duiker *Cephalophus rubidus*

Other names: Fr. *Céphalophe du Ruwenzori*. Ger. *Ruwezoriducker*. (Konjo dialect) *Isuku*.
Measurements: HB 75cm. T ave. 10cm. H ave. 45cm. W est. 15kg.
Recognition: A stocky duiker with a dense, glossy rufous coat with long, coarse hair on the neck, changing to dense, soft fur over the hindquarters. The belly is white, hindlegs are almost black and there are dark brown markings on the joints of the forelegs. A black or dark brown blaze stretches from the nose to crown. Down the midline of the back and neck there is a zone of dark grey underlying the uniform red tips of the fur. The underfur of the flanks is cream.
Subspecies: The lower slopes of the Ruwenzori Mts are inhabited by a race of the black-fronted duiker which has a thinner, harsher, grizzled coat. Nonetheless it is possible that the two are actively hybridising in a region of overlap at about 3,000m.
Habitat: Afro-alpine and subalpine zones, *Hagenia* woodland and bamboo zones of Ruwenzori.
Food: Browse in a rich and continuous pasture of herbs, notably wild parsleys, balsams, violets, sorrels and *Galium*, a scrambling herb much favoured by all high-altitude herbivores. The Ruwenzori red duiker is mainly diurnal but activity periods could be strongly influenced by rain.
Status: Heavily snared. Climbers have reported a substantial decline or disappearance along the Bujuku and Kitandara routes to the peaks. Vulnerable.

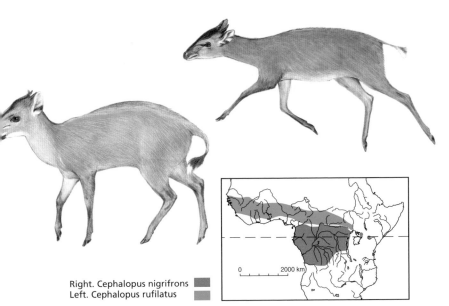

Right. Cephalopus nigrifrons
Left. Cephalopus rufilatus

Red-flanked duiker *Cephalophus rufilatus*

Other names: Fr. *Céphalophe à flancs roux.* Ger. *Rotflanken ducker.*

Measurements: HB 60–80cm. T 7–10cm. H 30–38cm. W 6–14kg.

Recognition: Prettily coloured with bright orange red on the face, neck and flanks, brown or blue-grey gauntlets on the limbs and a brown or grey dorsal patch which has pale grey underfur. The black nose and lower lip contrast strongly with white jaws and upper lip. The ears have black and white flashes. The nose is straight and the skull narrow. Relative to its size it has the largest preorbital glands of any duiker. This indicates exceptionally active marking behaviour.

Subspecies: *C. r. rufilatus* (Senegal to the Chari and Benue valleys), *C. r. rubidior* (Chari to Nile valleys).

Habitat: A resident, territorial species living in forest relicts and riverine thickets within the savannah along a broad band of country from Senegal to NW Uganda.

Food: Fruits, flowers and foliage from numerous riverine species of trees, shrubs and herbs.

Status: This species can withstand considerable hunting pressure as long as enough suitable habitat remains available. It is in decline in very heavily settled areas but is still widely distributed. Listed as Not Endangered (IUCN).

Black-fronted duiker *Cephalophus nigrifrons*

Other names: Fr. *Céphalophe à front noir.* Ger. *Schwarzstirnducker.*

Measurements: HB 80–107cm. T 7.5–15cm. H 45–58cm. W 14–18kg.

Recognition: A long-legged, long-hooved duiker with glossy red coat that is plain and thin in lowland forms and thicker, darker and more grizzled in montane forest forms. The legs, darker than the body, are almost black at the hocks and thinly haired. There is a distinct pale 'brow' below the black forehead blaze that gives it its name.

Subspecies: *C. n. nigrifrons* (lowland forest from Cameroon to E Zaïre), *C. n. kivuensis* (W Rift mountains and volcanoes), *C. n. fosteri* (Mt Elgon), *C. n. hooki* (Mt Kenya).

Habitat: From Cameroon to Mt Kenya where they are adapted to swamp forest and marshes at both low and high altitudes (up to 3,500m.). Like other duikers they have territories marked out with face glands and a loud whistling call. They also make a loud thumping sound in the chest (the vocal equivalent of a typical bovid foot-stamp?). They follow regular paths from night shelters to day-time feeding grounds in swamp.

Food: A variety of fruits and succulent vegetation, including balsam (*Impatiens*), wild coffee and other Rubiaceae. A ratio of 72% fruits to 28% foliage has been recorded in a fruit-rich Gabonese forest.

Status: Widely distributed but appears to have disappeared from Aberdares and might be vulnerable to intensive hunting, notably on Mt Elgon.

Zebra duiker *Cephalophus zebra*

Other names: Fr. *Céphalophe zébré*. Ger. *Zebraducker*.

Measurements: HB 70–90cm. T 10–15cm. H 40–50cm. W 15–20kg.

Recognition: As its name suggests this duiker has a panel of vertical, vivid black and cream stripes from behind the shoulder to the tail. The head, shoulders and lower legs are russet red, with hocks, muzzle and leg joints nearly black. Both sexes have robust, conical and very sharply pointed horns above a forehead and nasal area where the bone is massively thick and reinforced. They have prominent tufted glands just below the heels of the back legs and glandular pockets in the groin.

Subspecies: None. Alternative and now obsolete scientific names are: *C. zebrata*, *C. doria* and *C. doriae*.

Distribution: From Sierra Leone (R. Moa) to Ivory Coast (R. Niouniourou) within the primary forest zone. Commonest in east-central Liberia.

Habitat: Primary forests and along their margins and in clearings, extending into secondary growth and swidden cultivation. It favours lowland forest (notably the Sinoe and other river valleys in Liberia) but may also live in low montane and hill forests.

Food: Fruits and foliage. Details are unknown but the zebra duiker does not appear to have specialised teeth or diet. It may use its head to break open the shells of larger fruits.

Behaviour: Friendly relations between captive pairs involve mutual rubbing and licking, suggesting that breeding pairs are the normal social unit (as they are in most duikers). Because both sexes have horns and a thickened skull (which do not appear to correlate with a specialisation in ecology or diet), it seems likely that bonded pairs share defence of their home range against intruding duikers and their offspring against predators. Scarred heads suggest that the collisions which are normal in duiker confrontations are particularly vigorous and uninhibited in these exceptionally stocky and muscular antelopes.

Adaptations: Known to be a strong stimulus to the eye/brain sensory system, stripes may serve as a focus for social attraction (in which case the resemblance of these duikers to zebras may be more than superficial). An advantage of stripes in this species could be to inhibit goring of the soft abdomen during aggressive encounters. Thus, while other animals shield themselves from the worst effects of aggressive rivalry with thickened skin, bony plates, etc., these duikers may have a subtler strategy for reducing excessive aggression.

Status: Formerly widespread over much of Liberia and Sierra Leone, zebra duikers are declining fast as their habitat is being destroyed and commercial bush-meat hunting becomes more entrenched and comprehensive in its onslaughts. Listed as Threatened (IUCN) in Liberia but in danger of extinction in Sierra Leone and Ivory Coast.

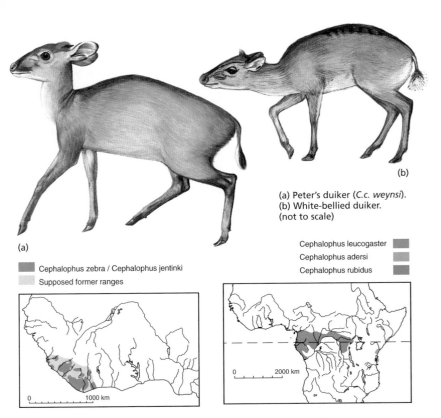

(a) Peter's duiker (*C.c. weynsi*).
(b) White-bellied duiker.
(not to scale)

Cephalophus leucogaster
Cephalophus adersi
Cephalophus rubidus

Cephalophus zebra / Cephalophus jentinki
Supposed former ranges

0   1000 km

0   2000 km

White-bellied duiker *Cephalophus leucogaster*

Other names: Fr. *Céphalophe à ventre blanc*. Ger. *Weissbauchducker*.
Measurements: HB 78–100cm. T 8–15cm. H 42–51cm. W 15–20kg.
Recognition: A pale, forest duiker with warm, sandy-brown forequarters, graduating towards grey near the black dorsal line. The rump has a rufous flush and the crest is orange. The front, heels and hocks are black. The underside is white. The nape is short-furred but the rest of the neck has long, coarse hair. The tail has a fluffy, black and white tip. It appears to have a deeper jaw, a wider gape and a stronger bite than other duikers with coarse neck fur.
Habitat: A very sparsely and intermittently distributed duiker ranging from the R. Sanaga to Ruwenzori and the W Rift, but only north of the R. Zaïre. It does not occur in extensively flooded forests and is only known to be common in a few highly localised places (notably N Gabon and Congo).
Food: A ratio of 73% fruits to 25% foliage (and a marked taste for flowers) has been recorded in Gabon. Hard-shelled fruits (among them mututu, *Klainedoxa*) in the diet implies that this duiker might smash them open (probably with the forehead).
Status: A sample of hunters' bags in Zaïre showed this species to be the least frequently caught duiker (thought to be a measure of low density and elusiveness). It is found in several reserves but is likely to be one of the earliest animals eliminated as the commercial bush-meat trade gathers momentum. Widespread but locally vulnerable. Currently not endangered overall.

Peter's duiker *Cephalophus callipygus*

Other names: Fr. *Céphalophe de Peters*. Ger. *Petersducker*.
Measurements: HB 80–115cm. T 8–16cm. H 45–60cm. W 16–23kg.
Recognition: A fairly large duiker of very variable colouring. The main body colouring can range from pale tawny to rich russet or dark brown. The dark brown may be confined only to the legs or tint the shoulders, neck and face. The frontal tuft is russet in all subspecies.

The forehead is among the most heavily reinforced of any duiker, with the dense bone of the frontal up to 13mm thick in some ♂♂.

Subspecies: *C. c. callipygus* (main forest bloc from between the R. Sanaga and R. Zaïre to the R. Ubangi), *C. c. weynsi* (R. Ubangi to Victoria Nile), *C. c. barbertoni* (E Uganda, W Kenya), *C. c. lestradei* (north end of L. Tanganyika). (Supposed hybrids with *C. harveyi* on Mau, Kenya.)

Habitat: Ranges through the moist equatorial forest zone from Cameroon to W Kenya in both lowland and montane areas. This diurnal and territorial species flourishes in regenerating patches after logging but is not found in outlying riverine strips and galleries. It prefers dense undergrowth.

Food: Recorded as taking 83% fruits and only 16% leaves (at Makoku, Gabon), this was the most completely frugivorous of all the duikers studied there.

Status: The dependence of this species on a year-round supply of fruits must render such large animals vulnerable to seasonal shortages but, in the absence of serious forest degradation, it can withstand regular hunting and is known to exist at densities of up to 20 per km² in Gabon. It is very vulnerable in Burundi, Rwanda, Kenya and Uganda but not endangered elsewhere.

Black duiker *Cephalophus niger*

Other names: Fr. *Céphalophe noir*. Ger. *Schwarzducker*.

Measurements: HB 80–100cm. T 7–14cm. H 45–55cm. W 16–24kg.

Recognition: A heavily built, long-bodied, long-headed, glossy black duiker with swollen nostrils and short, stocky legs. The coat pales to light grey around the throat and chin and the lining of the ears. The tail has a white underside. Short horns, normally present in both sexes, are largely hidden in a coronal tuft of dense reddish hair.

Habitat: Rainforest from Sierra Leone to SW Nigeria, also survives in some riverine galleries, isolated patches and semi-deciduous forests on the margins of its range. It can also survive in regeneration areas after logging. It is mainly diurnal and territorial and is thought to fill a similar niche in Upper Guinea to Peter's duiker, *C. callipygus*, in central Africa.

Food: Fallen fruits and flowers, leaves and herbs. The black duiker is presumed to be as dependent on year-round fruit fall as other largish duikers.

Status: This species suffers from overhunting throughout its range, except in some remote or better-protected localities in Liberia, Ivory Coast and Ghana. It is rare and endangered in Sierra Leone, Togo and Nigeria. Still widespread, its supposedly 'Satisfactory' IUCN status will change unless curbs are put on the ever more voracious bush-meat trade.

Right. Abbot's duiker.
Left. Black duiker.

Abbot's duiker *Cephalophus spadix*

Other names: Fr. *Cephalophe d'Abbott*. Ger. *Abbottducker*. Swah. *Minde*.

Measurements: HB 97–140cm. T 8–13cm. H 66–74cm. W 50–60kg.

Recognition: A large, glossy, nearly black duiker with a paler grey face, a very prominent russet tuft between the horns and a reddish tinge to the belly and lower flanks. The wedge-shaped head ends with a broad, flat-fronted nostril pad that overhangs the mouth (as with yellow-backed duikers). Overall, this is a stocky duiker with rather short, thick legs and a thick neck.

Habitat: Montane forest duiker restricted to the wetter (and therefore mainly eastern) sides of a few isolated massifs in E and S Tanzania. It is commonest in the Kilimanjaro National Park and Forest Reserve between 1,300 and 2,700m in forest and high-altitude swamps, but is said to range up to 4,000m and has been seen in high-altitude scrub and moorland. It formerly occurred above L. Manyara, in the Uluguru and Usambara Mts. It survives on Mt Rungwe and in the Uzungwa mountain range. Disturbance may drive this species into more nocturnal activity but its preference for dense cover and its alertness keep them from view.

Food: Fruits, flowers, green shoots and herbage; recorded browsing balsam (*Impatiens*).

Status: Although protected by law and in the Kilimanjaro National Park, this species is acutely threatened by poaching and the destruction of its habitat for charcoal, logs and potato fields. The proposed Mwanihana and Chita National Parks will be essential for the long-term survival of this and inumerable other forest endemics.

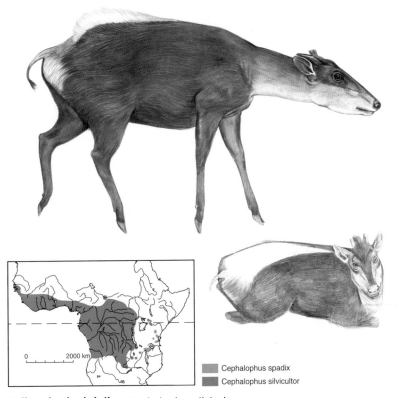

■ Cephalophus spadix
■ Cephalophus silvicultor

Yellow-backed duiker *Cephalophus silvicultor*

Other names: Fr. *Céphalophe à dos jaune.* Ger. *Riesenducker.* Swah. *Kipoke.*

Measurements: HB 125–190cm. T 11–20cm. H 65–87cm. W 45–80kg.

Recognition: A large, greyish brown duiker with a vivid cream-coloured patch on the back. The long, wedge-shaped head has a light grey muzzle and cheeks ending in a shiny black rhinarium. Eyes and ears are small. the horns can be as long as 21cm. Newborn calves are dark umber, with freckled sides and a deep reddish tinge all over the underparts. The centre of the back is all jet black and only changes to adult colouring by 9 months of age. Juveniles at intermediate stages of growth can be difficult to identify.

Subspecies: Nine described but all are likely to be within the normal range of variation.

Distribution: Senegal to SW Sudan and discontinuously to W Kenya. Angolan littoral to western shores of L. Tanganyika.

Habitat: Rainforest, montane forests and many permutations of forest-savannah mosaics, from narrow riverine strips to fragmented woods. It is often found close to deep swamps. It lies up singly in characteristic 'forms' at the base of large trees, under fallen trunks or in dense tangles. It likes to shelter from rain (and may even use the remnants of a pit-sawer's or hunter's lean-to). As many as six such resting places can be found within 1km². Throughout its range it lives only in pockets of suitable habitat where it can be quite numerous. It is attracted to salt-licks.

Food: Fallen seeds, fruits, berries and the bark of shrubs, fungi, ground moss and many herbs. In montane areas, waterberry (*Syzygium*), dog plum (*Ekebergia*) and yellow wood (*Podocarpus*) are favoured fruits. In lowland forests stem-fruit (*Chrysophyllum*), African mangosteen (*Garcinia*) and duiker tree (*Sapium*) have been recorded. Kudu berry (*Pseudolachnostylis*), raisin trees (*Canthium*), and snake beans (*Swartzia*) are savannah or forest-edge plants taken in the south of its range.

Behaviour: This duiker is mainly solitary and spaced out in territories (probably shared by a ♂ and ♀). Lying up on 'observation posts' on termite mounds suggests that surroundings are regularly monitored and broken ♀ horns could indicate active defence of territory by ♀♀.

One, rarely two, young are born after a 151-day gestation. The newborn lies tight for a week or more but starts to nibble vegetation almost at once. It grows rapidly and is weaned by 6 weeks. The horn buds appear after about a month when light hairs begin to show in the black back. Animals reach adult proportions and colouring by 9 months and are sexually mature by 1 year. Adults communicate with resonant grunts and a shrill bleat.

Adaptations: The yellow back is not as conspicuous in the field as one might suppose because the hair lies close, reducing the pale colour to no more than a streak. The hair can be erected in display but this has only been observed in captivity in response to disturbance. It is probable that the yellow back has a social function. It may cover glandular skin but this has not been verified.

Status: Widespread and common in many parts of its range, recent reports from Kenya suggest that it may have become endangered there, as it has in Gambia. Over much of the rest of its range, declining but not endangered.

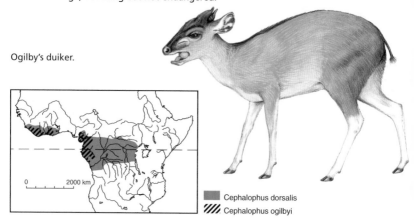

Ogilby's duiker.

Cephalophus dorsalis
/// Cephalophus ogilbyi

Ogilby's duiker *Cephalophus ogilbyi*

Other names: Fr. *Céphalophe d'Ogilby*. Ger. *Ogilbyducker*.

Measurements: HB 85–115cm. T 12–15cm. H 55–56cm. W 14–20kg.

Recognition: Orange to mahogany-coloured duiker with a very red rump, a paler underside, and a black dorsal line (of variable extent). The face has marked brows and short but peculiarly curved horns with strong corrugations (in both sexes). Legs vary in colour. The tail is short and tufted. In common with the bay duiker and Jentink's duiker, this species has massive hindquarters and a deep, slab-sided body but, unlike them, has long, slender legs.

Subspecies: *C. o. ogilby* (Bioko I., formerly Fernando Po), *C. o. brookei* (Sierra Leone to Cameroon), *C. o. crusalbum* (Gabon).

Habitat: Primarily forests close to the West African coast, where it is now rare and patchily distributed. On Bioko I., on the other hand, it is a common and dominant species, notably on the less disturbed upper slopes of the mountains. The absence of other large duikers (especially the bay duiker) is clearly a factor in this.

Food: Mainly fallen fruits, with the large, hard fruits of mututu (*Klainedoxa*) noted. The distribution of this species might be influenced by a super-abundance of fibrous fruits and numerous primates which contribute to the fruit-fall.

Status: Habitat destruction and degradation threatens *C. o. brookei* with extinction everywhere, except in the Korup National Park. *C. o. crusalbum* will only be secure if logging is stopped in the Lopé Reserve. *C. o. ogilby* is not currently endangered but requires the implementation of national park status for the Caldera de Luba on Bioko I. and control of the burgeoning urban bush-meat trade.

Bay duiker *Cephalophus dorsalis*

Other names: Fr. *Céphalophe bai*. Ger. *Schwarzruckenducker*.

Measurements: HB 70–100cm. T 8–15cm. H 40–56cm. W 15–24kg.

Recognition: Heavily built duiker with a red or yellowish brown coat, black or dark brown legs and a black midline along back and belly (definition varies individually). The fur is coarsely textured. The muzzle is extremely reduced and strongly tapered. The eyes are larger and higher in the head and the entire head is broader and flatter than in any other duiker, due to its enlarged cheek muscles (for lateral chewing action).

Subspecies: *C. d. dorsalis* (Senegal to Togo), *C. d. castaneus* (E Nigeria to E Zaïre).

Habitat: The entire equatorial lowland rainforest block from Senegal to L. Tanganyika, with a preference for high primary rainforest. Also patches within savannah mosaics (if undisturbed). Within the rainforest zone they may visit edges of clearings and prefer well-diversified zones with both dry and waterlogged areas. They shelter in hollow trees, between butresses, under fallen trunks and in dark, dense thickets, only emerging to feed at night. They live at a lower density than other duikers and even in the richest habitats it has been estimated that two or three animals inhabit 12–20ha.

Food: Hard or fibrous fruits, such as wild mango (*Irvingia*), mututu apples (*Klainedoxa*), African breadfruit (*Treculia*), and white star apple (*Chrysophyllum*), have been recorded; also less difficult fruits, such as monkey orange (*Strychnos*) and yellow mulberry (*Myrianthus*). Bay duikers are also known to stalk, kill and eat birds but fruits accounted for 73%, and foliage 27%, in a Gabon sample.

Status: A very widespread species but a popular quarry for hunters. Declining in many W African countries, this species is now rare in Nigeria and Sierra Leone and extinct in Uganda. Overall not endangered.

Jentink's duiker *Cephalophus jentinki*

Other names: Fr. *Céphalophe de Jentink*. Ger. *Jentinkducker*.

Measurements: HB est. 130–150cm. T est. 12–16cm. H est. 75–100cm. W est. 55–80kg.

Recognition: A long-horned (up to 17cm), very robust, short-legged duiker with a bold pattern of black, white and grey (its early name of 'forest goat' was not entirely inappropriate). The nearly black head and neck are offset by a vivid white halter over the shoulders and lower chest and a white border surrounds mouth and nose. This colouring involves both skin and fur, the latter being extremely short and fine. In contrast to the fore-end the hindquarters are grey agouti (their grizzled fur giving them a local name of 'squirrel-duiker').

Habitat: Only found in the high primary forest zone between Sierra Leone and the R. Niouniourou, a distribution that broadly coincides with many monkey populations and also that of the zebra duiker (see map, p. 377). Within this zone it enters secondary growth, scrub, farms, plantations and is even known to visit the sea-shore, presumably for salt. It is a 'hider', choosing hollow trees, fallen trunks and the buttress bays of kapok (*Ceiba*), *Bombax*, and mututu trees (*Klainedoxa*) for shelter. Unusually for duikers they sometimes lie up in pairs. Like the bay duiker it bolts from these day-time refuges with great speed if discovered, but has no stamina and does not go far. It is very residential and supposedly territorial but makes nocturnal forays out of thick forest, especially during periods when fruits is scarce. It is so secretive that it continued to survive less than 30km from Freetown, a city of half a million people, hiding on steep, densely forested slopes in the city's water catchment area. Its most basic requirements appear to be a diversity of fruiting trees and very dense shelter rather than a specific forest type.

Food: Known to enter plantations to eat palm nuts, mangoes and cocoa pods. The growing stems of tree seedlings are eaten (African teak, *Chlorophora*, has been identified). Hunters familiar with the duiker's habits have identified many fruits with hard seeds or shells, notably kola nuts, erimado (*Ricinodendron)*, cherry mahogany (*Tieghemella*), sand apples, (*Parinari*) and tallow tree (*Pentadesma*). Jentink's duiker has also been reported chewing roots after exposing them with its hooves.

Status: Reportedly common in Sierra Leone at the turn of the century (before commercial loggers stripped the forests), it is now only found in the few remaining areas of undisturbed forest where hunting is now intensifying. Likewise, in Liberia, a new generation of commercial bush-meat hunters are now entering formerly remote areas to take out meat (mostly smoked *in situ*). This form of asset-stripping is nominally prohibited in Sierra Leone and Ivory Coast but is legal in Liberia, the centre of the duiker's range and still its main stronghold. Listed as Endangered (IUCN) in Sierra Leone and Ivory Coast. It is vulnerable to new hunting practices in Liberia.

DWARF ANTELOPES NEOTRAGINI

Forest pigmy antelopes	*Neotragus*
Stem dwarf antelopes	*Raphicerus*
Oribi	*Ourebia ourebi*
Klipspringer	*Oreotragus oreotragus*
Beira	*Dorcatragus megalotis*
Dikdiks	*Madoqua* (4 species)

Recognition: Dwarf antelopes resemble one another in having slender legs, a longish neck, large eyes, a rounded head with a small mouth and muzzle, large preorbital glands and simple spike horns in ♂♂. Small variations in relative size and proportions of limbs, eyes, ears, and glands signify important (and long-established) differences in habits and habitat.
Genealogy: Of all living antelopes the Cape grysbok, *Raphicerus melanotis* provides the closest approximation to an ancestral type. It also resembles the earliest currently known antelope fossil, the 16-million-year-old *Eotragus* (from both Africa and Eurasia). Other dwarf antelopes are also very conservative but are more specialised.
Geography: Four adaptive lineages have different geographic foci. Dikdiks, *Madoqua*, are pygmies in the Horn of Africa. The beira, *Dorcatragus*, is a larger Somali endemic, with gazelle affinities. Other pygmies, *Neotragus*, are an equatorial forest group. A mainly southern and south-eastern group includes the 'stem dwarfs', *Raphicerus*, and oribi, *Ourebia*. The Klipspringers' origins may be Ethiopian.
Ecology: Habitats range from hot, dry and exposed to moist and dense. Size, centred between 8 and 12kg, declines to an absolute minimum of 1.5kg and ceilings at about 20kg. A modest but high-quality diet permits them to live in small territories without water.
Natural history: All neotragines have home ranges that are generally shared by a pair but marked and defended by the ♂ only. Secretions, notably those from preorbital face glands, are probably less important for land-labelling than for sustaining the cohesion of a pair (or a family). Each sex transmit signals that attract the other. The scents, calls and postures of adult ♀♀ generally provoke the close attention and interest of their ♂ partner several times a day. ♀♀ show less overt interest in ♂♂ but are exposed to almost continuous reminders of the ♂, either by his actual presence or through trails left by his pedal glands, landmarks demarcated by excreta or secretions, or whiffs of scent wafted from the M's sacs, brushes or patches.

Intimate and up-to-date knowledge of a small home range and its occupants ensures exclusive (and efficient) breeding for both partners. When their offspring are born and inducted into this universe of scents they too benefit from this shared security.
Adaptations: 'Nasal panting', a method of cooling blood in the nose with minimal water loss, is most likely to have begun in small, arid-adapted antelopes because small bodies in hot climates must conserve water and avoid overheating (they cannot afford to waste water through sweating). Being small is therefore functionally linked with this and other conservative habits, such as the possession and use of glands.

Antelopes that do not grow heavier than 16–20kg can survive in territories where exposure to danger is greatly reduced by familiarity with both its food resources and its refuges. They need not enlarge their range, lengthen their legs nor elaborate their horns. This very durable strategy for survival is common, in one form or another, to all small scale niches. They are also little modified descendants from the root stock of all antelopes and present a miniature model for the whole antelope radiation.

Right. Dwarf antelope.
Left. Royal antelope.

Royal antelope *Neotragus pygmaeus*

Other names: Fr. *Antilope royale*. Ger. *Kleinstbockchen*.

Measurements: HB 38–51cm. T 5–8cm. H 24–26cm. W 1.5–3kg.

Recognition: A tiny antelope with very thin, long legs, a small muzzle, large eyes, relatively small, flesh-coloured ears and a diminutive tail with a white underside. Body colour is reddish or golden brown, with a white belly, chin and chest and a rufous brown collar. Only ♂ ♂ have tiny, conical horns. Its gait is high-stepping under a bunched, compact body but it can slip away in a ground-hugging scamper or with fast, high jumps powered by disproportionately muscular upper hindlegs.

Habitat: Lives in spaced-out singles or pairs within very small territories, apparently sign-posted with dung. It prefers dense undergrowth at ground level along forest edges, in clearings, road verges and cultivation, both within the moist forest belt and in galleries in drier forest-savannah mosaics. It takes over a year to mature and can live for 6 years.

Food: Fresh greenery, buds, leaves, shoots and, less frequently, fruits and fungi. These are plucked with the very small mouth and long tongue. The royal antelope feeds during the day but is most often seen by torchlight when it visits verges or farms.

Status: Still widespread and abundant. Listed as Not Threatened Overall (IUCN) but its survival outside parks and reserves could become threatened. Not Endangered.

Dwarf antelope *Neotragus batesi*

Other names: Fr. *Antilope de Bates*. Ger. *Batesbockchen*.

Measurements: HB 50–57.5cm. T 4.5–8cm. H 24–33cm. W 2–5.5kg. (FF average 0.6kg. heavier).

Recognition: A small, extremely slender-legged, forest antelope with a short muzzle, large eyes and moderately small ears. The soft mahogany-brown fur has a shiny gloss. White markings in the ears and on the chin and throat are conspicuous. The belly is white and the short tail has a lighter underside. The smaller ♂ has very short conical horns.

Subspecies: *N. b. batesi* (very patchily distributed between R. Niger and R. Zaïre/R. Sangha), *N. b. harrisoni* (NE Zaïre, W Uganda). A third subspecies might exist in the S Ogooué basin.

Distribution: Found in discrete pockets in SE Nigeria, parts of SE Cameroon, Gabon and Congo to R. Sangha. A distinct and equally patchy population occurs in NE Zaïre and W Uganda. They are apparently poor colonists or recolonists and are dependent upon rainfall minima in the dry season (about 50mm per month).

Habitat: Dense, low undergrowth near water courses, roads, gardens, chablis (tree falls) or in areas regenerating after logging. They are especially common in cocoa plantations. Under favourable conditions they have been known to reach densities of between 35 and 75 per km².

Food: A browser of leaves and shoots, rather selective by species and for fresh growth. Recorded preferences are the acanthus (*Brilliantaisia*) and *Phaulopsis*, bitter cucumber (*Momordica*) and many cultivars, notably yams, sweet potatoes and peppers.

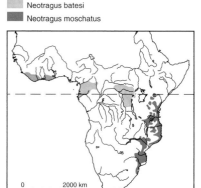

- Neotragus pygmaeus
- Neotragus batesi
- Neotragus moschatus

0   2000 km

♂ Suni.

Behaviour: ♂ ♂ mark their home ranges with the copious secretions of their facial glands and torn ears suggest that ♂ ♂ fight for territories. They do not seem to make middens, nor to ritualise defaecation. Panting raucous barks while fleeing may alert neighbours to a disturbance as well as to the runner's position. Nasal moans are a common contact call. Gestation is thought to be in the region of 6 months, possibly with biannual birth peaks at the end of the rains. Maturation times are not known.

Adaptations: Rapid closure of forest canopies may render this species very dependent on unpredictable tree-fall areas and make its home ranges less permanent. Periodic rotations of pastures have been observed and greater mobility might explain why overt territorial behaviour is not obvious in this species.

Status: In spite of its very sporadic occurrence over a vast range, it appears to be common where it is found. It is so marginal as to be very vulnerable in Uganda but is not endangered elsewhere.

Suni *Neotragus moschatus*

Other names: Fr. *Antilope musquée*. Ger. *Moschusbockchen*. Swah. *Suni, Paa mwekundu*.
Measurements: HB 57–62cm. T 8–13cm. H 30–41cm. W 4–6kg.
Recognition: A small antelope with long, slender legs, a typically compact stance and a disproportionately broad head on a short neck. ♂ ♂ have finely annulated horns that reach a maximum of 13cm. The facial glands are enormous, especially in ♂ ♂. The sleek, shiny fur is freckled dark brown with regional and individual differences in the tints of rufous or grey to body colour or legs. The underside is white or very pale grey. The tail has a white underside and is flashed from side to side (rather than flipped up and down, as is the case with the blue duiker).
Subspecies: *N. m. moschatus* (Zanzibar I.), *N. m. livingstonianus* (mainland). Note: If the island form can be shown to fall within the range of variation found on the mainland the 'Livingstone's' subspecies would be invalidated.
Distribution: A fragmented range from Somalia to Zululand east of the Great Rift Valley.
Habitat: Coastal forests and thickets wherever there is thick undergrowth and regenerating fallow. They are commonest in the broken forests skirting the foothills of large mountain massifs, especially along watercourses, margins and fertile pockets. They have favourite spots within tangles to lie up in. Both visible and invisible scented pathways are regularly followed. Individual and communal dung middens tend to be on the peripheries of a territory.
Food: Browsers with a varied diet of leaves, shoots and herbs and, more rarely, grass roots and mushrooms. Among the commonest food plants are Suni hemp (*Crotalaria*), *Commelina*, *Acacia*, brandybush (*Grewia*), which are all eaten off the plant. Sunis prefer false nettles (*Fleurya*) and morning glory (*Ipomoea*) that are wilted and pick up various dry fallen leaves. They gather under feeding colobus monkeys to pick up dropped leaves and shoots of brittlewood (*Nuxia*). They feed in short bursts interspersed with rests and are most active after rainstorms or spells of dense mist, especially between nightfall and 22.00h and after 04.00h. They rest during the heat of the day.

Behaviour: Mainly pairs on territories of approximately 3ha. Where larger numbers of ♀♀ (up to four) share a ♂♂ home range he associates more closely with just one ♀. Incursions into territories by other ♂♂ are met with energetic grating of the horns and chases in which the aggressor champs his jaws while trying to strike glancing blows or parry horn jabs. A higher ratio of ♀♀ in most populations is probably due to deaths following the fierce contests of territorial ♂♂. ♂♂ do not aquire full adult characteristics before 14 months of age but ♀♀ are thought able to breed by about 6 months. One, very rarely two, young are born after a gestation of 180 days. There is a birth peak just before the rains in February-March. Young keep hidden and make a soft, bird-like contact call that resembles grating marbles. They begin browsing within days of birth and the suckling period is very brief. Animals are known to live for at least 6 years.

Adaptations: Well named the 'musk antelope', it has a strong body odour (in addition to more specific preorbital and pedal gland scents). These smells demarcate territory and identify the sex and status of individuals but also appear to act as insect repellants.

Status: Although very localised in an environment subject to much depletion (for wood, charcoal and farmland), sunis remain common and widespread throughout their range. Not endangered.

(a) Cape grysbok.
(b) Sharpe's grysbok.

Cape grysbok *Raphicerus melanotis*

Other names: Fr. *Grysbok du Cap*. Ger. *Kaapgreisbock*.

Measurements: HB 65–80cm. T 4–8cm. H 45–55cm. W 8–12kg. (F 0.5kg. heavier).

Recognition: A thick-coated, chunky little antelope with russet brown fur densely interspersed with white hairs to give a 'strawberry roan' colour to the body. There is less white flecking on the head, neck and legs, which are yellower in tint. The ears are very large and lined with white hair. The short, blunt muzzle has a black bridge to the nose and a shiny black nostril pad and lips. ♂♂ have short, sharp and smooth horns (normally about 8cm long) which are widely spaced. Rump fur can be fluffed out to increase the impression of size. The tail is short and inconspicuous.

Habitat: A Cape relict species found between Albany and the Cedarberg Mts. It lives in scrub-covered sand dunes and thickets bordering rocky hills and steep gorges but also shelters in reed beds or along riverbeds along the southern margins of the Karoo. It is probably territorial and is usually seen singly. The young, born after a 6-month gestation, are hiders and grow fast. Most young are born between September and December (summer).

Food: Browser of thicket and shrubby growth. Although the Cape grysbok is active during the morning and late afternoon during winter, it is mainly nocturnal (possibly influenced by disturbance).

Status: As the closest approximation to the model of an antelope ancestor, the survival and study of this species is of great importance. In spite of greatly retracted habitats it is still common within its localised range and in numerous parks and reserves. Listed as Not Endangered (IUCN).

Raphicerus sharpei

Raphicerus melanotis

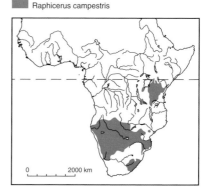 Raphicerus campestris

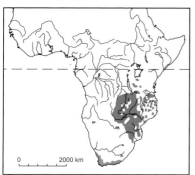

0 2000 km

0 2000 km

Sharpe's grysbok *Raphicerus sharpei*

Other names: Fr. *Grysbok de Sharpe.* Ger. *Sharpegreisbock.*

Measurements: HB 61–75cm. T 5–7cm. H 45–60cm. W 7–11.5kg.

Recognition: A small antelope with a 'skirt' of elongated fur over the hindquarters. The reddish fawn fur is densely interspersed with white hairs. The face, throat and underside are much paler, even off-white. Horns (present in ♂♂ only) and eyes are widely spaced and the muzzle is short but deep, with a large mouth and robust cheek teeth. The moderately large ears are mounted on a thick base (resembling the klipspringer in this respect). Their 'tipped-up' rump posture while grazing herbs results from a short neck and face on a relatively long-legged body.

Subspecies: Two subspecies have been named but are probably invalid.

Habitat: Ranging from L. Victoria to the Transvaal, the Zambezi valley bounds its western limits. Within this extensive area it is generally scarce and localised, preferring low thicket and secondary growth, stony outcrops and broken uplands, where it favours fertile zones on the lower foothills. It is predominantly nocturnal and lives in territories where pairs may form a loose association but are usually seen singly. Middens are found more easily than the animals themselves. At any disturbance the grysbok departs rapidly with short stamping hops (but otherwise silently). It has been reported hiding in aardvark burrows. In S Africa a birth peak during the summer rains has been suggested.

Food: Browses leaves, buds, herbs and fruits in a habitat where dry-season vegetation is generally tough. The teeth and jaw are well suited to such a diet and *Acacia*, raisin bush (*Grewia*), buffalo thorn (*Ziziphus*), ebony (*Diospyros*), and various fruits and berries have been recorded, along with grass (about 30%).

Status: Probably declining generally but impossible to assess accurately because of its extreme shyness. Not endangered overall but locally rare.

Steinbuck *Raphicerus campestris*

Other names: Fr. *Steenbok.* Ger. *Steinbockchen.* Swah. *Isha, Dondor.*

Measurements: HB 70–95cm. T 4–6cm. H 45–60cm. W 7–16kg.

Recognition: More slender than a bush duiker, less so than an oribi, the steinbuck can be mistaken for either but has characteristically rounded hauches without visible tail, very large, white-lined ears, a retroussé, black-bridged nose and big, black-rimmed eyes encircled by white. The ♂♂ have very upright, polished spike horns. Colour ranges from pale brown to fawn or bright rufous.

Subspecies: *R. c. campestris* (S Africa, 24 listed), *R. c. neumanni* (E Africa).

Distribution: All of S Africa from Angola to near the mouth of the R. Zambezi. E Africa on both the Kenya coast and open plateaus and savannahs inland up to 4,750m. Scarce or absent in most Miombo (*Brachystegia*) woodland areas.

Habitat: In S Africa they are mainly open-plains animals. In E Africa they are common in stony savannahs and among *Acacia*-grassland mosaics. Steinbucks favour transitional and unstable conditions, following bush-clearance by cultivation, roads or elephants, often under a very dry climate. In open plains they tend to focus on riverbeds or belts of thicket where they can find well-hidden, regularly used resting places or refuges.

Steinbuck.

Food: Browsers at or near ground level and adept at scraping up selected roots and tubers with hard, sharp hooves. Steinbucks favour shoots of dominant shrub and tree species, such as *Acacia*, leadwood (*Combretum*), buffalo thorn (*Ziziphus*), *Bridelia* and mopane (*Colophospermum*). They also take fruits and, during periods of early growth, may graze almost wholly on sprouting grass. They can survive without water and may live as far as 80km from water in the Kalahari subdesert.

Behaviour: Pairs are thought to live for long periods with the same partner on the same territory (4ha to 1km²). Members of such pairs appear to move and rest independently but observers have suggested that routines and scent cues could keep such pairs mutually aware of one anothers' movements and position much of the time. In the absence of territory-marking with face glands (which are very small in steinbuck) the principal scent beacons are dung middens. These are connected by trails laid by secretions that ooze from glands between the hooves. Middens are scraped following defaecation (by both sexes). It is possible that this associates individual 'signatures' in dung and urine with less specific hoof scents. The reception of such subtle clues is enhanced by the fact that most of the steinbuck's foraging is on or just above the soil surface.

A territorial ♂ becomes very aggressive during his ♀'s oestrus. Following a gestation of about 170 days a precocious fawn is born which remains well hidden for 2 weeks (in spite of being able to walk in 5 minutes) before joining its mother foraging. Lactation lasts 3 months and by 6–8 months ♀ offspring are fertile. Some ♀♀ are thought to breed twice a year, and this fecundity may explain their persistence in parts of South Africa in spite of sustained persecution. Animals live for at least 7 years.

Adaptations: As a first line of defence steinbuck resort to the infantile strategy of sinking to the ground and freezing, ears retracted while attentively watching any approaching danger. Their second strategy is to flee if the danger draws too close. Fast, zigzag flight alternates with repeated attempts at prostrate concealment. Both are compromise defences in a small conservative antelope that has invaded environments very different from those to which other *Raphicerus* are adapted.

Status: Although this species has been exterminated from many small localities, steinbuck are still common in suitable habitats. Overall status, not endangered.

Oribi *Ourebia ourebi*

Other names: Fr. *Ourébi*. Ger. *Bleichbockchen*. Swah. *Taya*.
Measurements: HB 92–140cm. T 6–15cm. H 50–67cm. W 12–22kg. (FF average 2kg. heavier).
Recognition: A tall, slender antelope of medium-small size and sandy body colour (yellowish or reddish tinted), with white undersides, upper throat, mouth and ear linings. The light-coloured muzzle deflects down sharply from the forehead (unlike the black-bridged retroussé nose of the steinbuck; nor are the eyes rimmed by intensely black lids as in the steinbuck). The ears are of moderate size. In addition to hoof (pedal) and groin (inguinal) glands, the oribi has scent brushes below the knees and ankles and black gland patches

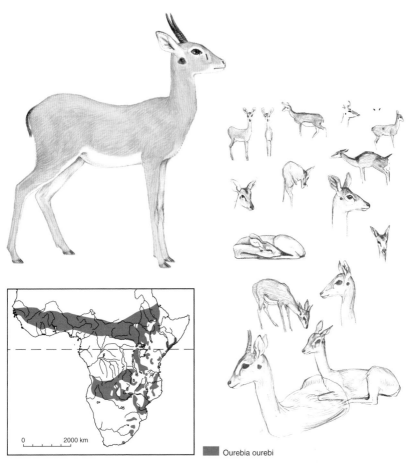

Ourebia ourebi

below the ears. The face glands (preorbital) are also exceptionally well developed. Alert and shy, the oribi's piercing whistle is frequently heard as it flees from the observer with a characteristic rocking-horse gait.

Subspecies: *O. o. ourebi* (S and SW Africa), *O. o. hastata* (SE Africa between R. Ruaha and R. Zambezi/R. Shire), *O. o. cottoni* (upland E Africa), *O. o. montana* (NE Africa east of the R. Nile), *O. o. haggardi* (coastal Kenya and Somalia), *O. o. goslingi* (northern savannahs, R. Chari/R. Nile), *O. o. quadriscopa* (Senegal to Chari, savannahs).

Distribution: Mainly Sudanic, E and SE Africa on fire-climax grasslands but under relatively reliable rainfall regimes.

Habitat: Grasslands maintained by fire or heavy grazing. They prefer flats or gentle slopes and are commonest on open lawns of grass kept short by compaction, termites, poor soils, fast drainage, trampling or heavy grazing by large herbivores. Such herds not only improve the oribis' range, but may also buffer them from predation; oribis tend to decline wherever such herds have been severely reduced or exterminated. On extensive floodplains oribis favour the less waterlogged areas where termitaries, herbs and woody growth provide cover and supplement the diet. In exceptional habitats densities of 45 per km^2 have been recorded.

Food: Mainly fresh green grass typical of fire-climax communities, i.e. *Themeda*, *Hyparrhenia*, *Loudetia* and *Eulalia*. However, many other grasses are taken, as well as various grassland herbs and the foliage of several shrub and tree species. Oribis cluster on scarce, short lawns within the sea of rainy-season long grass. Movements out of territories are typically oriented towards favourite mineral licks, which are visited regularly.

Behaviour: ♀♀ are larger than ♂♂ and are independent in their movements but, by becoming the object of continuous attention from a single ♂, each adult ♀ determines the area within which he is intolerant of other ♂♂. This area becomes a shared territory in which each partner repels others of the same sex (but ♀♀ tolerate adult ♀ offspring).

Pairings last for many years. Such territories adjoin supplementary pastures, refuges or salt-licks where other families may gather. Each territory is traversed daily by the ♂, who exchanges scents with ♀♀ and their young during elaborate, shared 'dung ceremonies'. Throughout the day he assiduously marks plants and soil with his own excreta and secretions.

Seasons, predators and reproduction all influence activity. Thus oribis rest longer on hot afternoons and may lie up during heavy rain. In exposed areas they prefer to graze at night, notably during full moons during the dry season. Their whistle may serve as both alarm and also to advertise shifting positions and movement. More breathy, puffing whistles keep friendly neighbours in touch. They bleat if pursued or captured. There is a mating peak in S Africa during April with births 7 months later. The precocious young is adept at concealment for 3–4 days. Thereafter it begins to follow the mother but still seeks shelter from time to time. Growth is very rapid and near adult height is reached, with weaning, by about 4 months. ♀♀ are fertile at 14 months. A preponderance of ♂♂ develops in some areas and territories may be dominated by older, even aged ♂♂. Animals are known to live for up to 14 years.

Adaptations: ♀ oribis are thought to excrete attractants that provoke continuous interest in ♂♂. ♂ alertness to ♀ excretory posture, urine and dung is relentless and stimulates him into non-stop glandular marking. On an adult ♂, there are 14 sites secreting odours and all likely to contribute to saturating the core of his territory with his individual scent signature.

Techniques for marking out small ♂ territories within dense thicket were evolved by ancestral dwarf antelopes. Their modification for use in much larger territories in open grassland has involved the specialisation of ♂ oribi into full-time factories and dispensers of odours. It is known that these odours are not only charged with information about their producers but have the potential of strongly influencing the behaviour of those smelling them. Because all inhabitants of a territory mix and exchange scents at daily 'dung ceremonies', dangerous, costly confrontations are avoided through repetitive habituation. More important, a ♀ is so frequently assailed with reminders of her partner's particular signature that she becomes habituated to his particular scent signature as an *essential* attribute of her environment. The ♂ gains an important reproductive advantage in that the ♀ stays within an area that he can control without physical coercion.

Status: Residential habits may make oribis poor colonists and this may influence the very patchy distribution of at least seven subspecies. Elimination from many localities has taken place this century. Nonetheless, the species is still widespread and not endangered overall.

Klipspringer *Oreotragus oreotragus*

Other names: Fr. *Oréotrague*. Ger. *Klippspringer*. Swah. *Ngurunguru, Mbuzi mawe*.
Measurements: HB 75–115cm. T 6.5–10.5cm. H 43–60cm. W 8–18kg. (average weights vary regionally 10–15kg.).
Recognition: A small, compact antelope, unique for walking on the tips of its hooves and for its dense cloak of light-weight fur, which is brittle, coarse and rustles when shaken or touched. This fur gives the illusion of greater size, especially when erect (when the animal is hot or sick). Widely spaced eyes behind a contracted and narrow muzzle give the animal a short, wedge-shaped face and binocular vision. There are strong regional differences in colouring but also much individual variation. Animals from the arid north-east are a creamy yellow, graduating into grey on the legs, with pale sepia hocks. Ethiopian populations are less bleached but similar. Bold colour contrasts and patches of softer fur are most apparent in animals from humid central and SE Africa. In E Africa boundaries between yellowish north-easterners and russet-shouldered central African animals become blurred and both colourings co-exist. The Zambezi marks the northern margin of the S African form. The klipspringer only signals from 'the front end' and displays none of the tail-wagging so typical of other small antelopes. Instead, its black-edged ears have tracts of white fur which readily catch the eye when flicked. The ♂♂ have short, upright horns and in some populations (Tanzania, Uganda, Ethiopia) there is a high incidence of horned ♀♀. Their horns are generally no more than 9cm long but ♂ horns of 16cm have been recorded.
Subspecies: *O. o. oreotragus* (South Africa), *O. o. aceratos* (SE Africa between R. Rufiji and R. Zambezi), *O. o. centralis* (south-central Africa), *O. o. schillingsi* (E Africa), *O. o. saltatrixoides* (Ethiopian highlands), *O. o. somalicus* (N Somalia), *O. o. porteousi* (Nigeria, Central African Republic).

Distribution: Mostly steep, rocky hillsides, escarpments or valleys or open screes of loose pebbles or cinders centred on Ethiopia (the most likely centre for their evolution). The Rift Valleys link this region with S Africa where prime habitats are also extensive. Numerous exchanges between W Eurasia and Ethiopia help explain the presence of fossil klipspringers outside Africa some 5 million years ago.

Animals can withstand day/night temperature fluctuations swinging from 42°C in the shade to freezing. This ability is clearly due to the insulating effect of their hollow shafted fur. Klipspringers occur up to 4,000m on Mount Kilimanjaro and on the summit of Mt Meru (4,500m) where frost and snow are frequent.

Habitat: The very varied habitats and latitudes in which klipspringers are found have two features in common: rocky, stony ground and abundant short vegetation. Food rather than cover is the crucial resource. Where drought or fire temporarily deprive them of food they tend to move down to escarpment or even valley bottoms. At such times klipspringers also abandon their territorial behaviour. Over most of their range they are greatly outnumbered by hyraxes, which are presumably their main competitors for food resources.

Food: Herbs and low foliage are the main items throughout the range, with green grasses mainly a wet-season food. In Ethiopia grass forms about 17% of the annual diet while herbs account for more than half, and bushes, shrubs, and creepers the rest. In some areas seeds, fruits, buds, twigs and bark are important seasonally; ephemerals such as *Vellozia* lilies can be temporary staples. Food distribution, temperature and disturbance all influence the duration and times of feeding. Klipspringers generally rest during the heat of the day and after midnight. Moonlight invites more activity than dark nights. Early morning sunning is important at high altitudes.

Behaviour: It is rare for klipspringers to remain solitary for very long. A ♀ is generally attended or followed by a ♂ and she commonly has a young one or an adult offspring with her or nearby. ♂♂ are much more vigilant than ♀♀. This may have benefits in spotting predators but appears to be primarily directed at keeping other ♂♂ away. Pairs are permanently resident in territories that range from 7.5 to 49ha. ♂♂ remain almost continually aware of their ♀'s whereabouts and 'duets' of whistling are a means of regaining contact after any disturbance. Mutual face-rubbing follows each reunion. Whistles also advertise territory and are an immediate response to predators. Conspicuous fluctuations in the size of facial glands have been observed to coincide with heightened sexual behaviour.

Mating peaks are recorded from several areas. After the lengthy gestation of several months a well-developed young is born and immediately hides. Only visited three or four times a day for suckling, the kid tends to remain a hider for up to 3 months. Over that period it gradually increases the time it spends with the mother. This prolonged hiding may be a response to heavy predation from the eagles that are very abundant in klipspringer country (which is also hyrax country). ♀♀ are sexually mature at 1 year, ♂♂ somewhat later, passing through a 'dispersal' phase during which they have no territory. Klipspringers are known to live for 15 years.

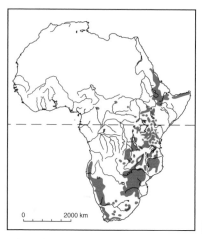

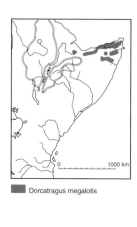

Dorcatragus megalotis

Oreotragus oreotragus

Adaptations: Moisture and nutrients on eroding hillsides and cliffs support a rich vegetation that is not accessible to herbivores without special skills in negotiating rocks and screes. The time required to evolve appropriate capabilities handicaps late-comers and favours pioneers. Conservative traits in klipspringer cranial anatomy suggest that their ancestors derived from the very earliest stock of African antelopes. Feet and hooves have gradually modified to the point at which no later bovids can compete. Even ibex, late colonists from Eurasia have not displaced klipspringers in Ethiopia.

Status: Many outlying populations are rare or endangered, notably those in Nigeria, the Central African Republic and agricultural regions. Nonetheless, they remain widespread and locally common. Not endangered.

Beira *Dorcatragus megalotis*

Other names: Fr. *Beira*. Ger. *Beira*.
Measurements: HB 76–87cm. T 5–8cm. H 50–76cm. W 9–12kg.
Recognition: A very long-legged, long-necked antelope with enormous ears, vertical, upright horns (9–13cm) in the ♂♂ only, and goat-like hooves which have rubbery centres

and are especially rounded on the hindlegs. The coarse, thick fur is grey on the back and neck, graduating into a broad, oblique stripe of very dark grey from elbow to thigh. The underparts, throat and inner limbs are cream while the outer limbs and cheeks are ochre yellow. The forehead and nose (with hairy, slit nostrils) are covered in short, bright russet fur. The lids of the eyes are intensely black, contrasting strongly with their surround of brilliant white fur. The ears are also made conspicuous by dense white hair tracts.

Distribution: Confined to hills and mountains in N Somalia, notably the Migiurtina, Warsengeli Xadeed, Buuraha and Marmar ranges where they favour loose rubble screes.

Habitat: Usually close to stony ridges, gorges and plateau margins (where the beira can make a quick get-away and break contact with potential predators). The extensive fields of finely fragmented stone in which it lives support scattered bushes but most plant growth is dwarfed or stunted and grows in the shelter of crevices, hugging very close to ground level. Some dominant plants in the preferred habitat are *Acokanthera*, *Buxus*, *Cadaba*, *Cadia*, *Carissa*, *Dodonaea* and various succulents, such as aloes, euphorbias and *Sansevieria*, are also abundant as are hemps (*Crotalaria*).

Food: Have been observed feeding on the very common shrimp plant, *Justicia*. The beira presumably browses the scattered shrubs while there is fresh growth on them but relies for its staple food on very small herbs growing among the pebbles. The raised rubbery cushions behind the hoof's margins are specifically adapted to walking and running on this very difficult terrain. Aloes and succulents probably contribute to its ability to survive without water.

Behaviour: Usually seen in pairs or parties with a single ♂. Larger groups, up to 12, are possibly temporary associations of two neighbouring families. Such aggregations are rarely seen and may include two adult ♂♂. Each group is known to be intensely attached to its own hillside or plateau. Gestation is estimated to last about 6 months and births have only been recorded in April (the peak of the rains).

Adaptations: Exposure to predators in an open environment demands speed. Stamina is less critical where any pursuer is less well adapted to the terrain than the pursued. Extensive home ranges and a scarcity of prominent landmarks helps to explain the beira's suppression of scent glands and overt marking behaviour. However, its ground-level foraging might have favoured the retention of pedal glands between the hooves. The beira's huge ears allow it to hear any approach across the loose stones, a capacity confirmed by its celebrated wariness and its survival in a region where many other species have become extinct.

Status: The beira's limited range, the absence of any protected areas within it, uncontrolled hunting, habitat degradation and competition from goats must all prejudice its long-term survival. It was thought to have made a slow recovery after dying in large numbers during the very severe 1975 drought. Nonetheless, its extreme specialisation for a very difficult and marginal habitat should continue to favour its survival for some time. The only viable captive breeding group is currently held in a private collection at Al Wabra (Qatar). Listed as Threatened with Extinction (IUCN).

Dikdiks *Madoqua*

Salt's dikdik	*Madoqua saltiana*
Silver dikdik	*Madoqua piacentinii*
Kirk's dikdik	*Madoqua kirkii*
Guenther's dikdik	*Madoqua guentheri*

Recognition: Very small, long-legged antelopes with a fine, soft, grizzled (sometimes colourful) coat. They have relatively large eyes and ears, a prominent crest and a fur-covered nose that is enlarged into a proboscis in at least two species. Prosboces are the visible sign of a technique of temperature control that is more developed in dikdiks than in any other antelope. The nose of each species shows a different degree of elaboration and specialisation. The tail is vestigial but the pale underfur of the buttocks can be fanned into discs that are more conspicuous than any tail signal.

Genealogy: Dikdik fossils are only known for some 4 million years (possibly 7 million years) but are likely to have begun as a distinct lineage (in the Horn of Africa) at a much earlier date. The distribution of living forms is some guide to the progress of evolution. Thus, the most conservative, least specialised forms, notably Salt's dikdik, remain confined to the evergreen thickets that fringe the Ethiopian plateau and the Somali coast. The most advanced and most heat-tolerant species lives in the driest deserts and subdeserts of the region. Intermediate types, of the *M. kirkii* complex, occupy a much broader range of habitats in E and SW Africa.

Geography: Essentially a group of small, arid-adapted antelopes endemic to the Horn of Africa, with a single outlying and isolated population in SW Africa. An arid corridor has clearly connected the two regions many times in the past, as is clear from other organisms with a similar pattern of distribution. Although Kirk's dikdik lives under a wide range of conditions in E Africa, its relative in Namibia is confined to warmer areas with less than 500mm annual rainfall.

Ecology: The more primitive species minimise the effects of high temperatures by being very largely nocturnal. The long-nosed Guenther's dikdik, with the greatest tolerance of heat, is more diurnal. All species depend upon low-level thickets and succulents growing on well-drained soils where there is little grass growth. If local changes allow patches of dense, tall grass to colonise their home ranges, animals shift to another area.

Natural history: Dung, urine and face-gland deposits are the boundaries, land-marks and focal centres for all social life. In the absence of scent marks (e.g. in a new area), all ages and sexes become alert and begin to seek or make them. While the ♂ is the principal marker and defender of an area, his movements are entirely subordinate to those of the ♀ – in a real sense *he* marks *her* territory. Territories may vary in size from 0.3 to 35ha. Densities range from 5 to 20 per km². Territories generally contain a mosaic of dense and more open ground with 6–13 stations where several dung and urine latrines are visited regularly. Where these are on a boundary two families may contribute, each sticking to its own side of the dung-marked border. ♀♀ and young contribute but ♂♂ always scratch and superimpose their own contribution.

While many disturbances evoke a crouching or a creeping departure, any sudden flight tends to elicit breathy whistles from both partners in a territory, sometimes in a duet. Reunions involve face-rubbing in which ♀♀ may lick the ♂♂'s preorbital glands (which flow in response to excitement). Flight is usually short but very swift (up to 42 kph has been recorded).

Adaptations: The flexible proboscis is lined with numerous blood vessels in the mucus membrane. These are cooled by increasing the normal breathing rate from one to nearly eight breaths per second. The cooled blood returns to the heart via a sinus where hot blood going to the brain is cooled in a form of 'radiator' or *rete mirabile*. Selective cooling allows general body temperature to rise without risking brain function.

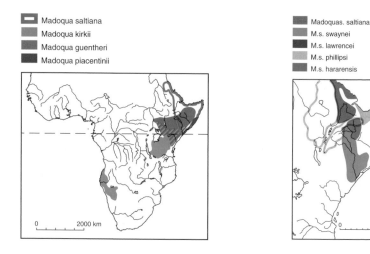

Madoqua saltiana
Madoqua kirkii
Madoqua guentheri
Madoqua piacentinii

Madoquas. saltiana
M.s. swaynei
M.s. lawrencei
M.s. phillipsi
M.s. hararensis

0   2000 km

0   1000 km

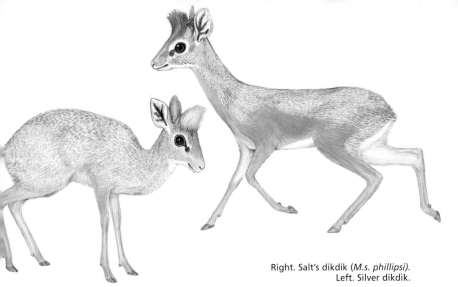

Right. Salt's dikdik (*M.s. phillipsi*).
Left. Silver dikdik.

Salt's dikdik *Madoqua saltiana*

Other names: Fr. *Dik-dik de Salt*. Ger. *Eritrea-Dikdik*.
Measurements: HB 52–67cm. T 3–4.5cm. H 33–40.5cm. W 2.5–4kg.
Recognition: A small antelope with a short, squared-off, furry nose. Short ♂ horns are up to 9cm. The coat is agouti freckled and the legs sandy or reddish. There are five regional forms; two are dull-coloured (Salt's and Swayne's), two are very brightly coloured (Phillip's and Lawrence's), and one (the Harar dikdik) is dark and somewhat intermediate. This is possibly best viewed as a superspecies but awaits further definition.
Subspecies: (some may be species) *M. s. saltiana* (Eritrea): reddish grey back, large. *M. s. swaynei* (Web-Juba valleys): brown-grey back. *M. s. hararensis* (Harerge): gingery back, dark red flanks. *M. s. phillipsi* (Gulf coast): grey back, orange flanks. *M. s. lawrencei* (Obbia coast): silver back, russet flanks.
Habitat: Evergreen and semi-deciduous bushlands and thickets in the Horn of Africa from Suakin and Hadendowa (SE Sudan) to the mouth of the R. Juba. Predominantly a nocturnal and crepuscular species, lying up in dense shade during the day. Predation must be the main factor suppressing bright colours in the western part of their range. Colours appear to correspond with colour-coding for aggressive and submissive gestures. Subordinates (of both sexes) lower their forequarters and expose their greyer backs. Dominant animals flare their red or yellow crests and strut in high-stepping, side-on displays of the red or yellow limbs and flanks.
Food: Herbs, foliage and shoots, especially *Acacia* browsed close to ground level.
Status: Numbers have decreased in densely settled areas but are otherwise probably little changed. Not endangered overall.

Silver dikdik *Madoqua piacentinii*

Other names: Fr. *Dik-dik argenté*. Ger. *Piacentini Dikdik*.
Measurements: HB 45–50cm. T est. 3–4cm. H 30–33cm. W est. 2–3kg.
Recognition: The smallest dikdik with very soft, fine fur and a distinctive black border to the ears. The back and sides are a uniform silvery grizzle, particularly fine on the neck and haunches. Limbs, ears and muzzle are sandy ochre, cheeks and crest are creamy yellow and the bridge of the nose is often a vivid russet.
Habitat: Shared with Lawrence's dikdik (an eastern representative of the *Madoqua saltiana* complex). This is possibly the most primitive and least arid-adapted of dikdiks. It inhabits very low, dense thickets growing along the Obbia coastal littoral on fertile, sandy soils under a powerful offshore wind. This specialised wind-shaped, sand-blasted community has year-long, low-level green growth, partly due to the sea's cooling and moisturising effect.
Food: Shoots and foliage of shrubs and herbs in undergrowth of the Obbia littoral thicket.
Status: The silver dikdik is hunted with nets and is without formal protection within its very restricted range. Its long-term survival (and that of many other endemics) must depend on conservation areas being established in this unique ecological zone.

Kirk's dikdik *Madoqua kirkii*

Other names: Fr. *Dik-dik de Kirk*. Ger. *Kirkdikdik*. Swah. *Suguya, Digidigi*.

Measurements: HB 55–72cm. T 4–6cm. H 35–45cm. W 3.8–7.2kg.

Recognition: A very slender, small-snouted antelope with grizzled or salt-and-pepper grey coat more or less suffused with yellowish ochre tints. Face, coronal crest and legs are tawny while the eye is bordered with white; ear lining, chin and belly are also white. Sharp, corrugated ♂ horns grow to 10cm. In spite of close external resemblances, similar-looking species are known to have different numbers of chromosomes and cannot produce fertile offspring.

Species/Subspecies: A preliminary breakdown suggests that there are four well-demarcated forms (all of which may be full species but await revision):

kirkii, syn. *minor*, *nyikae* (Somali/Kenya coast and lowlands to Pare and Usambara Mts): 47 chromosomes in males.

cavendishi, syn. *hindei* (uplands from E Uganda to Mbulu). 46 chromosomes.

thomasi (central Tanzania bushlands and thickets).

damarensis (SW Africa): specialised hooves without pedal glands.

Habitat: A very wide range of habitats but with distinct geographic and ecological subtypes. Superficial resemblances were formerly interpreted as a sign of relatively recent dispersal. Contemporary molecular studies indicate an older and subtler adaptation of these dikdiks over their very wide and scattered range.

In Namibia they favour very dense thickets on hard, stony ground and limestone pavements. In Tanzania thickets dominated by *Grewia*, *Baphia* and *Pseudopropsis* are typical habitat. In the E African highlands the commonest bush is an olive (*Olea*) while the main thicket shrubs are *Aspilaia*, *Tinnaea*, *Turraea* and *Psiadia*, with *Sansevieria* and aloes being favourite retreats. In the hot lowlands, north-east of these cooler uplands, the vegetation is again different, with many more acacias, *Indigofera*, *Duosperma* and *Boswellia*. Thus, these dikdiks inhabit regions that have few major physical barriers but which are very distinct in flora, soils, altitude, temperatures and rainfall pattern. In combination these may serve to keep adjacent populations genetically distinct (but much of this awaits study).

These dikdiks are both diurnal and nocturnal (especially active during full moon) and have similar habits to other dikdiks, including a tendency to add their dung to any new, strong-smelling intrusion into their territory. A tendency to sprinkle elephant dung with their own minuscule pellets has an amusing bite in one local folk tale. This tells that the dikdik, on stumbling over an elephant bolus, keeps piling up his own pellets in the hope that one day he will trip up the elephant.

♂♂ are also persistent whistlers. When whistling is initiated by the approach of a dog or leopard its immediate effects are to cause ♀♀ and young to hide. The whistles also serve to distract or 'mob' the predator and to broadcast an alarm. Another important, delayed effect is social cohesion. Once the danger has past ♀ and ♂ invariably join up, with much nuzzling and scent-marking.

Food: Browse evergreen shoots and foliage of the herbs, shrubs and succulents typical of the region.

Status: Although exterminated in many localities (as a result of agriculture, hunting and dogs) all types remain widespread and common. Not endangered.

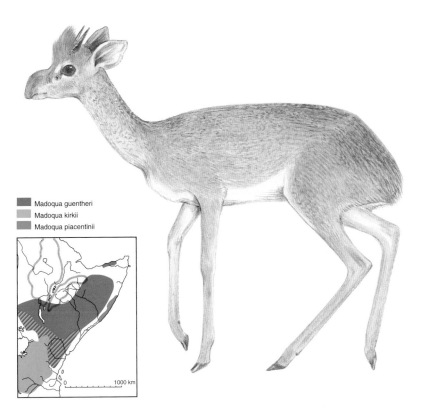

Madoqua guentheri
Madoqua kirkii
Madoqua piacentinii

0   1000 km

Guenther's dikdik *Madoqua guentheri*

Other names: Fr. *Dik-dik de Günther*. Ger. *Güntherdikdik*. Swah. *Digidigi ya pua murefu*.

Measurements: HB 55–65cm. T 3–5cm. H 34–38cm. W 3.7–5.5kg.

Recognition: A small, slender antelope, very similar in colour to Kirk's dikdik, i.e. grizzled grey with brown or reddish flushes on sides and neck, reddish fawn legs, nose and back of ears. Belly, chin, fur in the ear and around the eye are white. The nose is appreciably longer and more elastic than any other dikdik but a capacity to extend, shorten, 'empty' or inflate the probiscis makes it an unreliable characteristic for distinguishing *M. guentheri* from *M. kirkii* species in the field. In general the premaxilla and nasals are very reduced but even here intermediate skulls of both *kirkii* and *guentheri* sometimes make identification difficult. Hybrids have been bred in captivity (and might occur in the wild) but are known to be sterile. Intermediate forms and uncertain field identifications still make all documentation of Guenther's and Kirk's dikdiks very provisional. Molecular studies have revealed that this species can have 48 or 50 diploid chromosomes and that crosses produce offspring with 49 chromosomes which are themselves fully fertile.

Subspecies: (*M. g. wroughtoni, hodsoni, smithi*) Variation and confusion with *kirkii* types makes subdivision premature.

Habitat: Distribution centres on L. Turkana, reaching the Nile at Mongalla and possibly the Gulf of Aden at Maydh. South-eastern boundaries remain confused but are probably bounded by the R. Tana. Of all dikdiks they live in the driest, hottest desert and subdesert scrub, with aloes, *Euphorbia*, *Sansevieria*, *Cissus* and *Sarcostemma*, as well as *Acacia*, providing both shelter and food.

Food: Green (and wilted) foliage, buds, shoots and bark of dwarf shrubs and herbs.

Status: Large herds of livestock passing through are known to temporarily force dikdiks out of territories. These dikdiks survive well in dense, thorny thickets where livestock are less able to overbrowse. Very widespread and not endangered.

RHEBOKS PELEINI

Rhebok	*Pelea capreolus*

An enigmatic tribe represented by a uniquely South African species, the rhebok. Its scientific name, *Pelea*, latinises its Tswana name, *phele*, while *capreolus* means 'goat-like' or 'sheep-like', a reference to its chunky, mountaineering hooves and short, crinkled wool. Earlier names betrayed much uncertainty about its affinities. The archaic and obsolete *Cemas* embraced such diverse antelopes as klipspringers, oribis, springbucks and reedbucks. *Redunca villosa* and *Eleotragus villosus* (both meaning 'hairy reedbuck') put it firmly in the kob tribe while *Antilope lanata*, 'woolly antelope', was suitably generalised and descriptive.

Sustained adaptation to a unique herbivorous niche in the temperate mountains of S Africa has resulted in some convergence with sheep and disguised hints of possible common origins with oribis and the kob tribe. It may be distantly related to both but belongs to neither.

Pelea capreolus

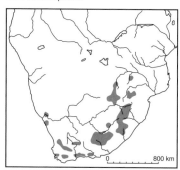

Rhebok *Pelea capreolus*

Other names: Fr. *Rhebuk, Péléa*. Ger. *Rehantilope*.
Measurements: HB 105–125cm. T 10–20cm. SH 70–80cm. W 18–30kg.
Recognition: A long-legged, long-necked antelope with a woolly, tawny grey coat rounding the body contours. The long, narrow muzzle ends with a small mouth below a blunt, swollen nose. The ears are very long and pointed, the forehead swollen and the black-lidded eyes are very prominent in a white surround. The tail is bushy and white below. Undersides are pale. The ♂♂ have very vertical spike horns that can be as long as 29cm. During ritualised postures, with erect neck and tucked-in chin, the unusually short back of the head becomes noticeable.
Distribution: Mainly upland South Africa but actually descends onto sand dunes in the Cape. Most numerous in strongly seasonal pastures above 1,000m, staying on the heights during the rains but descending to lower slopes when dry.
Habitat: Highveld, 'sourvelt' and secondary grasslands, mainly on plateaus and mountains. While some of its pastures are maintained by fire, most are on dry, deeply drained slopes where very severe frosts deter tree growth. These are patchy but extensive, well-established and ancient pastures that are peculiar to S Africa. The grasses tend not to grow very tall or rank so that the rhebok has a clear view. Unlike reedbucks it avoids very tall grass.
Food: Mainly a grazer. Some dominant grasses in the habitat are *Themeda, Eragrostis, Digitaria, Andropogon* and *Mermuellera*. Common herbs are morning glory (*Ipomoea*), everlastings (*Helichrysum*) and *Oxalis*, but the details of the diet await study. The rhebok is independent of water. Bouts of grazing and resting are irregular. In the dry season it tends to graze for longer (and at night) in valley bottoms. While the weather is hot it rests up during the heat of the day. Wet- and dry-season fodder differs radically in quality and quantity.

Behaviour: A ♀ and her ♀ offspring provide a basic social unit that can proliferate into a small herd (maximum 14). These live on home ranges of 15–80ha (smaller and higher in summer, larger and lower in winter). They are attended by an adult ♂ who spends much time patrolling and marking out their home area with urine (loaded with extra scents and melanin pigment from a preputial gland that is unique to the rhebok). He regularly surveys and postures from the top of mounds or ridges, or near rocks and trees where he also excretes (but not on a midden). If in sight of another ♂ he stamps, makes a sharp, clacking call and prances with various bouncy, rocking-horse gaits. Confrontations between ♂ ♂ are frequent along boundaries but charges nearly always stop about 1m apart, with heads down and horns lunging and stabbing without actual contact. Territorial defence and 'air-cushion fighting' are commonest during the summer mating season (January–April). After a 7-month gestation one, occasionally two, young are born in a secluded place. The young remain concealed for 6 weeks before joining the mother and her group. Sexual maturity is reached before 22 years, by which time young ♂ ♂ have taken up territories of their own. Short visits from ♀ ♀ still in their parental groups gradually get prolonged until they become permanent residents of the new territory. ♂ scent and ♂ behaviour appear to be actively attractive to ♀ rheboks and there are few signs of them being coerced by ♂ ♂.

Adaptations: Although it has been suggested that the rhebok could share a common ancestry with sheep, their similarities are certainly convergent. Cold South African winters on dry, stony uplands are miniatures copies of environments in the mountain chains of Eurasia where sheep evolved.

Status: The rhebok is well represented in numerous reserves, national parks and private farms where it is, for the most part, compatible with livestock. Although it has been exterminated over a large part of its former range, which is now very fragmented, it is common within these fragments. Not endangered.

REDUNCINES, KOBS REDUNCINI

Reedbucks	*Redunca* (3 species)
Kobs	*Kobus* (5 species)

Recognition: Medium-sized to large antelopes with slender to stocky legs, a long, well-muscled body and a relatively thick neck (especially in ♂ ♂). The largest species are shaggy; smaller ones are sleek or slightly fleecy. Most are tawny or tan but ♂ ♂ of the larger species can be dark brown or even black (usually with white or off-white markings). Horns, on ♂ ♂ only, are annulated and always curl forward at the tip (this corresponds with forward striking with the head, powered by muscles that help shape the bulging neck). Both preorbital and pedal glands are vestigial or absent but all have well-developed inguinal glands in the groin. All have a pungent overall odour that emanates from sebaceous glands and films the entire body. This provides a seal against water loss and possibly some insulation against temperature extremes but is also likely to carry socio-sexual signals (as must their musky urine). Reedbucks have black, glandular patches below the ears which, among other messages, advertise the ♀'s breeding condition. The smaller species make ritualised 'rocking-horse' displays which apparently signify subordination. These may be the long-grass equivalent of the 'stotting' or 'pronking' of antelopes in more open habitats.

Genealogy: Kobs probably began to evolve from neotragine grazers about 14 million years ago. The earliest fossils, about 11 million years old, come from E Africa but kobs were present in India by 5 million years ago.

Geography: Now restricted to well-watered areas of Africa, the reduncines' dispersal to India and N Africa implies long periods of moist conditions along the Nile valley, other rivers and along coastal forest zones. This is because they are poor dispersers, keeping a close attachment to their natal area.

Ecology: Sumplands are rich in food but are unstable because they dry out or catch fire. Antelopes find it difficult to cope with their fluctuating water levels, sticky soils and rapid growth of impenetrable grasses. Only the lechwe, with swamp-adapted hooves, can reside permanently in wetlands. For the rest, accommodation to radical seasonal changes inhibits extreme specialisation, making the kob tribe unusually homogeneous. The smallest species is the most conservative but it is secondarily adapted to coarse grazing and cool climates in upland pastures.

The instability of their enormously productive habitats encourages substantial fluctuations in numbers. This is exacerbated by their inability to disperse. Seasonal changes lead to short-distance movements that also cause crowding, sometimes of spectacular proportions (notably in kob).

Natural history: To accommodate both crowding and dispersal reduncines have very flexible relationships between the sexes. ♀♀ are usually independent and are the object of intense competition between ♂♂. Big differences in the size, morphology and behaviour of the sexes correspond to separate ♂ and ♀ strategies. The ♀♀ of reduncine species have more in common than the ♂♂ (which look and behave very differently from species to species).

Study of their social systems, which are largely mediated by invisible scent cues, have scarcely begun. However, it appears that fundamentally different social systems correspond with the particular kind of refuge sought by each species. Because reduncines lack stamina an animal facing danger has three possible sources of refuge: (a) thick cover (reedbuck, waterbuck); (b) water (most species but especially lechwe); (c) dense herds (kob). All species appear to track each other like bloodhounds and clearly broadcast much information through glandular scents.

Adaptations: Because they are the major bovid lineage adapted to valley grasslands reduncines have considerable potential for rational exploitation, having the fastest growth rates of any bovid, insignificant disease problems and very acceptable meat and hides. Large populations of the more social species are unlikely to survive unless their potential for sustained-yield cropping is realised because they occupy habitats with a high priority for agriculture or livestock development.

Mountain reedbuck *Redunca fulvorufula*

Other names: Fr. *Redunca de montagne*. Ger. *Bergriedbock*. Swah. *Tohe ya milima*.
Measurements: HB 110–136cm. T 17–26cm. SH 60–80cm. W 19–35kg. (♀); 22–38kg. (♂).
Recognition: A moderately-sized antelope with slender legs and a chunky body. The soft, fleecy fur is tawny grey, with white underparts and a bushy white underside to the tail. It is the smallest of the reedbucks and its eyes and their sockets are peculiarly prominent, as is the black gland patch below the ear and, in ♂♂, the short, forward-curved black horns.
Subspecies: R. f. fulvorufula (South Africa), R. f. chanleri (E and NE Africa), R. f. adamuae (N Cameroon).
Distribution: Widely separated mountains in S and NE Africa, with an outlying relict population on Mt Adamua in the Cameroon uplands. They live in cool, rather dry, mountainous regions mostly above 1,500m and up to 5,000m. These may be the vestiges of its range during more favourable glacial periods.
Habitat: They prefer grassy ridges in broken rocky country, on small outcrops and volcanic larva flows and cinder cones. In Kenya mountain reedbucks prefer the scrub-grass ecotone between slopes covered in camphor (*Tarchonanthus*) and open grassy valleys. They are often less nocturnal than other reedbucks.
Food: Almost wholly grazers, with *Themeda*, *Hyparrhenia* and *Cymbopogon* recorded as favourite food plants. Mountain reedbucks can live for a while without water but lose condition rapidly. Fluctuating food leads to fluctuating numbers.
Behaviour: ♀♀ with young form parties of two to eight but temporary aggregations of up to 50 can form. ♀ home ranges in S Africa are 36–76ha but ♂ territories average 28ha. ♀ ranges are unusual, therefore, in overlapping those of several ♂♂ which do not control their movements. Ranges cover a sample of the available habitats and run from hilltop to valley. 'Bachelor' groups are temporary and tenuous in where they can live and high mortality among ♂♂ tends to skew sex ratios. A single young is born after an 8-month gestation. It remains well hidden for up to 3 months before joining its mother's group. Prolonged hiding may reflect special risks from eagles, large cats, jackals and baboons in their habitat.
Adaptations: Intimate knowledge of their home ranges allows them to mitigate predation while the ubiquity of grass seldom makes them limited by food. However, strictly sedentary habits inhibit dispersal and render isolated populations vulnerable to extermination during prolonged droughts.

Status: An incapacity to escape local vicissitudes and very limited ability to disperse or recolonise lost ground suggests that the Cameroon model (steady shrinkage to vestigial proportions) will overtake other populations unless active reintroductions to suitable habitats are initiated. With careful management the survival of this species could not only be assured but improved. Listed as Endangered (IUCN) in Cameroon, Nigeria and Uganda but Not Endangered in other parts of their range.

Bohor reedbuck *Redunca redunca*

Other names: Fr. *Redunca*. Ger. *Gemeiner Riedbock*. Swah. *Forhi, Tohe*.
Measurements: HB 100–135cm. T 18–20cm. SH 65–89cm. W 35–45kg. (♀); 43–65kg. (♂).
Recognition: A medium-sized, sandy-coloured antelope in which the slender proportions of ♀♀ contrast markedly with the thick-necked, hook-horned ♂♂. It has deeply pocketed glands in the groin, black patches below the ears and is oily or greasy all over from sebaceous ducts at the roots of all hairs. Its loud whistles (mainly uttered at night) are the surest guide to its presence, especially in tall, wet-season grasslands where it is seldom seen. The size of horns appears to correspond to some extent with densities, i.e. stubby horns in E Africa at dispersed, lower densities and longer, splayed horns in the Nile valley with seasonally concentrated, high densities.
Subspecies: *R. r. redunca* (northern savannahs), *R. r. cottoni* (Sudd region), *R. r. bohor* (Ethiopia), *R. r. wardi* (E Africa).
Distribution: From Senegal to Ethiopia, south to L. Tanganyika and the Rovuma valley. Particularly wide shallow floodplains associated with major lake and river systems, i.e. R. Niger, R. Nile, R. Rufiji, L. Chad and L.Victoria.
Habitat: Mostly large-scale sump grasslands that are highly unstable, with extensive annual flooding, drought and fires. They are peculiarly well adapted to cope with these extremes and to changes in height and quality of the food supply and shelter grass. While they are dispersed, densities of about 5 animals per linear kilometre of valley bottom are common. During periods of concentration densities of over 100 per km^2 have been observed and they are not uncommonly found at distances of 25km from water during droughts on open floodplains.
Food: Exclusively grazers with a recorded preference for typically dominant species, i.e. *Hyparrhenia, Sporobolus, Heteropogon* and *Themeda*. Feeding mainly after dark, bohor reedbucks may make nightly forays to graze up to 8km from their day-time refuge. As the quality of the grazing declines during the dry season, nocturnal feeding alone becomes insufficient. Eventually some reedbucks may keep grazing both day and night.
Behaviour: ♀♀ disperse into discrete home ranges during the wet season (when most young are born). ♂♂ also appear to be very scattered at this time (in the absence of ♀♀ they can be quite tolerant of each other). Fires and drought (beginning in about October in the northern savannahs) drive the reedbucks into larger groupings. By the early dry season ♂♂ are intensely intolerant of each other and it is probably repeated fights and stand-offs with neighbours that define, perhaps temporarily, their 'territories'. In rare situations where home ranges are stable, 'territories' may be an appropriate term but their typically unstable habitat favours a system in which ♀♀ search out the best and safest remaining pastures while ♂♂ fight for mating rights over each ♀ or group of ♀♀.

The glandular ear patch is thought to play a part in advertising oestrus. In courtship ♂♂ circle ♀♀ making a bleat like a toy trumpet. After a gestation of 7 months one young is born and it remains well hidden (but with daily changes of retreat) for at least 2 months. Young ♂♂ sometimes form 'bachelor' groups before becoming fully mature at about 4 years. ♀♀ are fertile by 1 year. Animals live for at least 10 years.
Adaptations: Whistling and ritualised bounding are two conspicuous features of bohor reedbuck behaviour. Both are effective forms of communication in their dense, obstructed habitat. Leaps differ in amplitude, length and style. Likewise, whistles vary in number of blasts and in pitch. In the dry season choruses of whistling can be heard whenever animals change their positions, especially at night as they emerge to graze.
Status: Very common and widely distributed. This reedbuck continues to survive even in the face of agricultural expansion. Not endangered.

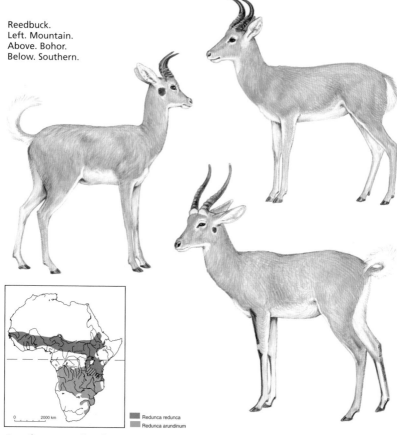

Reedbuck.
Left. Mountain.
Above. Bohor.
Below. Southern.

Reedunca redunca
Reedunca arundinum

Southern reedbuck *Redunca arundinum*

Other names: Fr. *Cobe des roseaux, Eléotrague.* Ger. *Grossriedbock.* Swah. *Tohe ya kusini.*

Measurements: HB 120–160cm. T 18–30cm. SH 65–105cm. W 50–85kg. (♀); 60–95kg. (♂).

Recognition: The largest reedbuck with a fine, almost woolly coat. Some are light buff, some dark brown, others are in between. The underside is paler, as is the chin and throat. Black and white markings on the front of the forelegs are prominent. The horns, only on ♂♂, grow up to 45cm long and resemble a diminished version of the waterbuck's, with a pale base. The tail is large and bushy, with white on the underside.

Subspecies: *R. a. arundinum* (south of the Zambezi), *R. a. occidentalis* (tropical Africa).

Distribution: SE and central Africa, with a substantial overlap in range with the bohor reedbuck in Tanzania (where it is rare).

Habitat: Widely distributed in the rank grass valleys and glades within Miombo (*Brachystegia*) woodlands where the greater part of their range is contained. Best adapted to mosaics of scrub and grass. They decline if denser, taller thicket replaces more open country but flourish in tall grass patches on the margins of more waterlogged swamps.

Food: Favourites are dominants in their habitat, i.e. *Hyparrhenia, Panicum* and *Leersia*, but southern reedbucks are not selective or specialised grazers. Much feeding is nocturnal and they are dependent on water.

Behaviour: Converging on water sources in the dry season, reedbucks only disperse widely when it is wet and the grass grows tall again. Home ranges get compressed to 5–35ha during the dry season but expand greatly during the rains. Births peak in the rains and both mothers and their young tend to remain well concealed in the long grass. As water gets scarcer and the fires begin ♀ attachment to ♂♂ becomes more obvious and frequent. Each ♂ actively keeps other ♂♂ away from one ♀ (more if he is able). Contact is maintained by means of whistles and leaping displays but it is thought that scent trails through the grass provide the main clue to each animal's whereabouts.

One young is born after a 31 week gestation. ♀ young are unusual in being the first to leave their mother as they become fertile at about 1 year. ♂♂ may remain with their mothers into their third year, by which time their horns are conspicuous and frequent appeasement of their mothers' 'consort' may be necessary.

Adaptations: Both ♀♀ and young ♂♂ make 'rocking-horse' displays towards adult ♂♂. Running around at speed they throw up their rumps and white tails in long, floating bounds. A popping sound is often made with the leaps, just as the hindlegs jerk back and out at the peak of each leap. The noise appears to result from a release of scented air from the inguinal pockets situated in each groin. Whistles are also commonly uttered with these jumps and the whole sequence would seem designed to appease the adult ♂♂.

Status: Although their total range is now very fragmented, southern reedbucks are well represented in reserves and parks. Not endangered.

Kob *Kobus kob*

Other names: Fr. *Cobe de Buffon*. Ger. *Grasantilope*. Swah. *Mraye*.

Measurements: HB 160–180cm. T 10–15cm. SH 82–92cm. (♀); 90–100cm. (♂). W 60–77kg. (♀); 85–121kg. (♂).

Recognition: A medium-sized antelope with a muscular, deep, rounded body and neck (especially in ♂♂) and robust limbs. The ♂♂ have thick, lyrate horns. ♀♀ are various shades of reddish or yellowish ochre, with a white underside and markings on the face, ears and hocks. ♂ colouring varies from rich cinnamon rufous, or pale yellowish brown, to black and white in the Sudd floodplain. Piebald colouring corresponds with fewer predators. Dark markings or tints occur on kobs from other large flood-plains and around the Sudd margins, blurring the boundaries between forms.

Subspecies: Western kob, *K. k. kob* (northern savannahs); Uganda kob, *K. k. thomasi* (E Africa and NE Zaïre); white-eared kob, *K. k. leucotis* (Sudd floodplain).

Distribution: Senegal to W Ethiopia to L. Victoria littoral.

Habitat: Low-lying flats or gently rolling country close to permanent water, without seasonal extremes. They favour short swards, cropped and trampled by concentrations of large ungulates or fire-induced grasslands. Where numerous enough they keep down limited areas of sward (kob fields) through the sheer weight of their own numbers. Totally dependent on regular drinking, kobs remain tied to areas within a short walk of water. They retain strong attachments to both grazing grounds and watering points, returning day after day and season after season.

Food: Grazers of the commonest grasses, notably *Hyparrhenia*, *Brachiaria*, *Setaria* and *Paspalum* species, among many others. Seasonal changes in diet (i.e. *Cenchrus* in the rains) emphasise the kobs' preference for a short sward.

Behaviour: Kob populations are prone to great fluctuations in numbers but these get compressed because attachment to locality and routine inhibits dispersal. Resident populations move daily between habitual grazing grounds and watering places. These grounds are parcelled out into ♂ territories of up to 50ha. The ♀ strategy of going to water *en masse* leads to ♀ aggregations which increase the stimulus that they present to ♂♂. The ♂♂ respond with more competition and fighting among themselves. Mating appears somewhat chaotic and would be more so without lengthy pauses at specific spots along the route from the grazing grounds to drinking places. Sexually active ♂♂ scramble for matings in these heavily contested 'assembly fields' where up to 40 ♂♂ may cluster in an area of about 1ha. Triangular territories radiate out from one or more 'hubs' within such areas, each 'hub' being signposted by a steady accumulation of dung and urine-soaked soil. Recent research has shown that the primary attractant which draws sexually active adults of both sexes to these heavily scented 'hot-spots' is the oestrogen-charged urine of oestrous ♀♀. Under the influence of the pervasive musk wafting from such centres, receptive ♀♀ allow themselves to be mounted by one or more of the associated territorial ♂♂. The considerable expenditure of energy required to defend their minuscule patches in the 'assembly fields' ensures that ♂♂ are quickly exhausted. Tenancies may only last a few hours so that ♂♂ are almost as transitory as ♀♀. By contrast territories on the grazing grounds may last a year or more.

Stereotyped, small-scale movements of a few kilometres are typical of populations resident in enclosed valley systems. Where the sump area is larger, as in the Sudd, kobs become migratory but their movement over many hundreds of kilometres are equally

(a) Uganda Kob.
(b) Puku.

bound by tradition. Here too, mass movement induces the formation of territorial 'slices' of ground arranged around beacons of ♀ urine. These radial slices of territory are fiercely contested by ♂♂.

In the S Sudan virtually all ♀♀ give birth along the south-eastern borders of the Sudd basin towards the end of the rains (September–December). After migrating 200km or more north, mating takes place along the eastern rim of the basin at a time when the plains are at their driest. After an 8-month gestation one young is born. Like reedbuck, their first 6 weeks are spent in hiding, after which they join their mothers and other kobs on the grazing grounds. ♀♀ are fertile at one year, ♂♂ become sexually active at 3 years.

Adaptations: If kobs evolved from a type of reedbuck their major innovation is the ability to congregate. Unlike some semi-social antelopes (such as oribis) they do not scatter when chased or attacked but often move as a single mass. This inhibits smaller predators while their open habitat protects them from some larger ones (lions are temporary, nomadic visitors to floodplains).

Status: In spite of having been eliminated from many areas (notably from all the shores of L. Victoria), kobs readily recover from near extermination. In terms of energetics, they assimilate poor-quality food, convert it to meat and grow faster than any other bovid. Kobs are potentially an exceptionally valuable resource. Fortunately they are still widely distributed and are not endangered.

Puku *Kobus vardoni*

Other names: Fr. *Puku*. Ger. *Puku*. Swah. *Puku*.

Measurements: HB 126–142cm. T 28–32cm. H 77–83cm. W 48–78kg. (♀); 67–91kg. (♂).

Recognition: This southern relative of the kob is sometimes treated as a mere subspecies. It has heavier proportions (particularly noticeable in the ♀♀), a coarser coat and shorter, less lyrate horns with less 'stem' than the kob.

Habitat: Upper basins of the R. Zambezi, R. Zaïre and R. Rufigi. It inhabits the margins of lakes, swamps, rivers and floodplains and is more tolerant of narrow grasslands and park-like woodlands than the kob. It lives on higher ground in the rainy season, descending in the dry season to graze the margins of lakes and rivers. It sometimes amalgamates into parties of 50 or more in the dry season (3–15 in the rains). Territories are spaced out and there is year-round breeding.

Food: Preferred grasses are *Brachiaria* (especially January–March), *Eragrostis* (July–August), and *Vossia* shoots (December). The puku will feed off lawns of many grass species.

Status: Exterminated from several parts of its range, the puku is locally endangered or very rare (Tanzania, Botswana, Namibia, Malawi). It is still common and widespread in parts of Zaïre and Zambia where it is listed as Not Endangered (IUCN).

(a) Male red lechwe
   K. l. leche.
(b) Female red lechwe.

Lechwe *Kobus leche*

Other names: Fr. *Cobe lechwe.* Ger. *Litschi.*

Measurements: HB 130–170cm. (♀); 160–180cm. (♂). T 30–45cm. SH 85–95cm. (♀); 85–110cm. (♂). W 60–95kg. (♀); 85–130kg. (♂).

Recognition: A heavily built antelope with elevated haunches, notable for its splayed, elongated hooves (generally hidden from view in water, mud or grass). It has large, widely spaced eyes, a rather short muzzle and, in ♂♂, long, slender but heavily annulated horns that sweep back (50–92cm). ♀♀ are red to tawny, graduating to white on the underside and throat, with white borders around the eyes and muzzle. ♂ red lechwe have similar colouring but black fronts to the white legs extend up onto the body in other subspecies. Here they spread with age. In one population, the black lechwe, this spread continues until fully mature. ♂ are boldly black and white. Normally phlegmatic, they rush through the shallows when disturbed, with clumsy, galloping bounds which sometimes begin with what David Livingstone described as a 'waddling trot'.

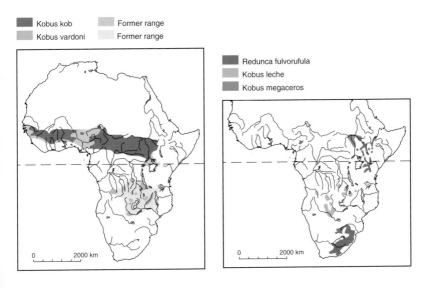

Kobus kob
Kobus vardoni
Former range
Former range

Redunca fulvorufula
Kobus leche
Kobus megaceros

0   2000 km

0   2000 km

Subspecies: Red lechwe, *K. l. leche* (NW Zambia, Zaïre, Angola, Botswana); Kafue lechwe, *K. l. kafuensis* (Kafue flats); black lechwe, *K. l. smithemani* (Bengweulu basin, R. Chambeshi).

Distribution: Restricted to the flat, silted-up river basins of the central African plateau (mainly the headwaters of the R. Zambezi and southern R. Zaïre tributaries) where they only occur in permanently waterlogged areas, being totally dependent on water to drink and in which to find food and shelter.

Habitat: Along the unstable margins between swamps and shallow floodplains. The larger and flatter the basin, the larger are the habitat and lechwe numbers. ♀♀ and young tend to stay on the wetter end of this zone, adult ♂♂ on the drier end. Keeping to the shallows/dry land margin involves continuous movement and distances of up to 80km may be travelled in very wet years (R. Chobe). Concentrations in favoured areas can reach temporary densities of 1,000 per km². In some areas herds may move inland to graze on short pastures following fires, mostly at night.

Food: Favoured grasses are *Echinochloa*, *Panicum*, *Brachiaria*, *Paspalium*, *Acroceras* and *Oryza*; also the fresh shoots of trampled reeds (*Phragmites*). Most feeding takes place for a few hours before dawn and after dusk.

Behaviour: ♀♀ seek out the best grazing, concentrating whenever it is localised, dispersing when it is widespread. They are unencumbered by any lasting bonds except with their young. The majority give birth during the late, hot dry season between July and October, but some breeding continues throughout the year. ♂♂ have a protracted rut during the early wet season (November–February) but sexual interest and the size of the testes decline throughout the late wet season and the dry season. All sexes tend to remain dispersed but sexually inactive ♂♂ are forced into peripheral 'bachelor' herds that can become quite large (50 or more members). This pattern changes with the rising flood levels during the early rains.

Before the grasses have regrown lechwe herds are at their densest and it is at this time that the rut begins. As ♀♀ come into oestrous, and are presumably drawn by the scents of other sexually active animals of both sexes, they gather at 'hot-spots'. Access to these is fiercely contested by ♂♂ who crowd around them. Those closest to the hot-spots occupy the smallest areas and achieve the highest number of copulations but are quickly exhausted. Further from the centres pressure is less continuous and intense. The ♂♂ here exclude each other from larger areas more effectively and hold much longer tenancies (but they presumably inseminate fewer ♀♀).

One young is born after a 225-day gestation. After lying up for some weeks the young emerge to join the ♀ herds. ♀♀ are fertile by 18 months, ♂♂ take more than 2 years and are not fully mature until 5 years. Animals live for up to 15 years.

Adaptations: Slow and clumsy on hard ground, lechwes are very strictly tied to swampy floodplains by their physiology and their soft hooves.

Status: Lechwes are known to have been exterminated in many peripheral areas, indeed one race (the Luena lechwe, *K. l. robertsi*) has already become extinct this century. They are very poor colonisers and recolonisers. The separation and subsequent speciation of central African and Nile lechwes implies a much wider distribution in the past. Both the Kafue and black lechwes are well represented in national parks. Elsewhere they are being progressively displaced by cattle.

Nile lechwe *Kobus megaceros*

Other names: Fr. *Cobe de Mrs. Gray*. Ger. *Weissnacken moorantilopen*. Dinka dialect *Abiok*.

Measurements: HB est. 130–170cm. (♀); est. 160–180cm. (♂). T 45–50cm. SH est. 80–85cm. (♀); est. 100–105cm. (♂). W est. 60–90kg. (♀); est. 90–120kg. (♂).

Recognition: A robust swamp antelope with longish hair, yellowish to russet in the hornless, smaller ♀♀. Like common lechwe it has a rather short face. The hooves are exceptionally elongated, the inner hoof much narrower than the outer. ♂♂ have double-curved, lyrate horns (50–87cm long) and slowly darken over several years, changing from tawny russet to a pale reddish grey that darkens until it is a deep chocolate black. The underside, tail, back of the neck and upper shoulder are creamy white, as are the muzzle and surround of the eyes.

Distribution: The Sudd region of the White Nile close to the various tributaries that converge near Malakal. This is a single, spidery swamp system flowing over an alluvial plain with surface gradients as shallow as 7cm per km.

Habitat: Mainly confined to the river-flooded grasslands that lie between deep swamp (dominated by *Cyperus papyrus* and Sudd grass, *Vossia*) and the drier rain-flooded grasslands (dominated by thatch grass, *Hyparrhenia rufa*). This river-flooded zone, or *toic*, is dominated by swamp antelope grass (*Echinochloa stagnina*), rice grass (*Leersia*) and wild rice (*Oryza*) and has numerous pools edged with bulrushes and water-lilies. Within the *toic* the lechwe follows the fluctuating margins between shallow floodwaters and drier ground. This involves continuous seasonal drifting up and down the flood tide lines. As floods deepen (about May) the lechwe moves further from the river and/or upstream, travelling as far as 30–40km between its high- and low-flood seasonal pastures. Because movement is now severely constrained by dense settlement and livestock herds all round the swamps, the lechwe tends to converge on levees and termitary complexes within the *toic* until the floods begin to subside in about October. By the time fires are burning the floodplain (January–March) the lechwe is occupying the patchy margins of the permanent swamp where it avoids papyrus but is commonly found in Sudd grass. At this time competition for grazing is keen and large herds of cattle tend to force it deeper into the swamps.

Food: Grazes on growing *Oryza* during the early flood season but mainly *Leersia*, *Echinochloa* and *Vossia* as the floods recede.

Behaviour: ♀♀ determine movements but spaced-out, fully adult, piebald ♂♂ drive competing ♂♂ away from ♀ groups. In the early dry season (November–December) single ♂♂ successfully exclude other piebalds from herds that can be in excess of 100. This is the period of peak births. By February calves have emerged from lying-up in the reeds and sometimes gather for playful chases, circling and jumping through the shallows. As ♀♀ move, gathering and fragmenting into larger and smaller groups in response to the state of the pasture or disturbances, they attract the attentions of piebald ♂♂. By March these ♂♂ are spaced out in a rather linear scatter along the swamp margins and there is much sexual activity that would seem to peak in about April. Piebald ♂♂ often tolerate the presence of several other well-horned ♂♂ in their vicinity but these can always be graded by colour and clearly represent hierarchically ordered age-classes. Dominant ♂♂ squirt urine onto their own throats, which may then get rubbed onto ♀♀. Because actual horn-to-horn engagements often submerge heads, ♂ fights in water tend to be brief tests of strength with very vigorous pushing and wheeling. Once the loser breaks away there is a token chase and the winner returns to the ♀♀ (if present). Exhausted ♂♂ seclude themselves in trampled arenas within the reedbeds. ♂♂ may utter squeaky grunts while fighting. ♀♀ are extremely vocal and there are choruses of toad-like croaking in herds that are actively on the move. Gestation has not been recorded but is probably about 8 months. Longevity is also not known but, given the slow, graduated maturation of ♂♂, probably resembles the common lechwe's 15 or more years.

Adaptations: The ♂♂'s bold black and white colouring is probably made possible by a scarcity of predators on very extensive floodplains. Crocodiles and pythons are known to take them but these predators do not hunt by sight. It may be significant that the one southern lechwe population in which the ♂♂ are black also lives on a very wide, flat floodplain with few resident predators. Colour-coding for age ranks assists hierarchies while marked differences between ♂♂ and ♀♀ would appear to allow each sex to pursue an independent life cycle. ♂♂ head-flag at the boundaries between their very ephemeral territories. Flagging involves sudden sweeping tosses of the head (as if to chase a fly off the flanks). This violent movement momentarily exposes the white ears, neck and shoulder patch and flourishes the horns. This intimidation display helps define temporary boundaries through repetitive stand-offs.

Status: About 16,000 Nile lechwes lived on the east bank of the Nile in 1983. A similar number has been estimated for the west bank. Nearly 1,000 have been estimated for the Machar marshes. Although constrained by competition from cattle, and subject to some hunting, numbers are probably stable. Plans to resuscitate the Jonglei canal, introduce irrigation or exploit oil could dramatically change this. Listed as Threatened (IUCN).

Waterbuck *Kobus ellipsiprymnus*

Other names: Fr. *Cobe defassa*. Ger. *Wasserbock*. Swah. *Kuru*.

Measurements: HB 177–235cm. T 33–40cm. SH 120–136cm. W 160–200kg (♀); 200–300kg (♂).

Recognition: A big, shaggy animal, rather variable in colour, with dark grey and rufous individuals sometimes occurring in mixed groups. ♂♂ tend to be darker and have long

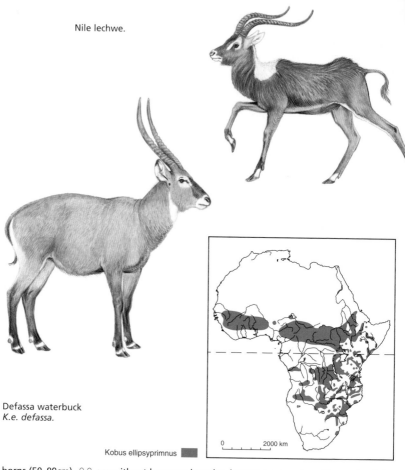

Nile lechwe.

Defassa waterbuck
K.e. defassa.

Kobus ellipsyprimnus

0   2000 km

horns (50–99cm). ♀♀ are without horns and tend to be warmer in colour. The angle of the chin, muzzle, ears and eye-surrounds are white, with black margins and tips to the ears. The dark legs also have short white spats.

Subspecies: *K. e. ellipsiprymnus* (SE Africa): rump crescent. *K. e. defassa* (NE, central and W Africa): white under tail.

Distribution: Well-watered valleys, mainly in tropical Africa and sandwiched between desert and forest. Absent from the dry north, north-eastern and south-western regions of Africa.

Habitat: Sedentary in savannahs, woodlands and forest/non-forest mosaics where there is permanent water. They favour woods or thickets where they inhabit the fringes of valley grasslands. They could be described as 'dry-land lechwe'.

Food: Many grass species, including reeds and rushes (*Phragmites* and *Typha*). Where green grass is scarce waterbucks may browse leaves or even fruits.

Behaviour: Both ♂♂ and ♀♀ remain for long periods (up to 8 years) on the same home range. ♀♀ travel over the larger areas (typically 200–600ha) but travel contracts with age. ♂♂ are most vigorous between 6 and 10 years of age when they hold the largest territories (ranging from 4–146ha), with continual change and readjustment as the relative status of neighbours waxes and wanes. Familiar ♂♂ that appease territory-holders are tolerated. ♀♀ travel at will over many territories, usually in ones and twos but sometimes assembling in temporary aggregations of up to 70. Young animals go through a stage of being chased and may emigrate to distances of up to 30km.

Gestation lasts over 8 months and the single young remains concealed for at least 2 weeks. Once it has joined its mother her raised tail serves as a signal to follow (the signal is emphasised by an elliptical ring or wholly white buttocks). Weaned at 6 months, ♀♀ generally mature at about 3 years while ♂♂ can scarcely compete before they are 5 years old. Animals are known to live for 18 years.

Adaptations: Scent is clearly of paramount importance for waterbucks and their own odour is so strong that it can sometimes be detected at a distance by the human nose. Partly or wholly uneaten kills by lions have led to the suggestion that they are distasteful but this is contradicted by the fact that lions, hyaenas and other large predators will kill waterbucks more frequently than their abundance would merit. It would appear that this is the price they pay for being easy to find by other waterbucks. The benefits of living both in herds and being able to come and go, assemble and dissolve, in response to an unstable environment appear to outweigh the extra risk from predators.

Status: Although waterbucks have been eliminated from many localities within their very extensive range they remain widespread and well represented in parks and reserves. Not endangered.

GAZELLINE ANTELOPES ANTILOPINI

Gazelles	*Gazella*
Dibatag	*Ammodorcas clarkei*
Gerenuk	*Litocranius walleri*

Recognition: Long-legged, long-necked antelopes with a light-coloured coat, large sensitive eyes and ears, a small mouth and, in the smaller species, preorbital glands. In dentition and skull structure they greatly resemble enlarged dwarf antelopes.

Genealogy: Fossils attributable to this group date back to between 12 million and 15 million years in both E and N Africa. In basic tooth structure they show surprisingly little change since that time.

Geography: One of the few antelope groups that have been outstandingly successful outside Africa, they are spread across an arc from N and NE Africa through Arabia to arid Asia.

Ecology: A major factor influencing their success in this region must have been their tolerance of heat and ability to extract adequate moisture from their diet. All rely on high-quality, protein-rich diets (and this limits how large they can get in very impoverished habitats).

Natural history: All are exceptionally alert to both sound and movement. In most species ♂♂ are territorial while ♀♀ and non-reproductive ♂♂ are mobile, with individuals coming and going, assembling and dispersing without difficulty. In richer environments they remain tied to a resident home range but for the most part they are nomadic over large areas.

Adaptations: The temperature regulation device typical of dry-country dwarfs (such as dikdiks and beira) has been taken still further in many gazellines. They too have increased the flexibility of their noses (to improve their performance as blood-cooling bellows) by freeing them from the constriction of a bony nasal tube.

The antilopine trend of lengthening limbs and necks has been carried to extremes in the giraffe-like gerenuk, *Litocranius*, and dibatag, *Ammodorcas*. What may have begun as an aid to greater mobility and speed in these species became a means of reaching more elevated sources of food. In spite of all these innovations, the diets, teeth, stomach structures and brains of antilopines have remained very conservative.

Gazelles *Gazella*

Dorcas group	Dorcas gazelle	*G. dorcas*
	Speke's gazelle	*G. spekei*
Rufous group	Red-fronted (Thomson's) gazelle	*G. rufifrons*
Palaearctic group	Rhim gazelle	*G. leptoceros*
	Cuvier's gazelle	*G. cuvieri*
Nanger group	Grant's gazelle	*G. granti*
	Soemmerring's gazelle	*G. soemmerringi*
	Dama gazelle	*G. dama*

Recognition: Very slender, fawn or rufous antelopes; often with a dark flank-mark separating the body colour from the white underparts. A pale brow streak runs from eye to nose, with a dark stripe below. Glands, sometimes vestigial, occur on the face, in the groin and between the toes. The tail is very short.

Genealogy: Very ancient antelopes (at least 10 million years) that partly owe their diversity to emigration back and forth between Africa and Eurasia. The Palaearctic branch, having adapted to much colder conditions in Asia, reinvaded Africa (probably during the Ice Ages) to colonise some marginally cooler niches in N Africa.

Geography: Restricted to N and NE Africa, Arabia and India, with the sand gazelles distributed as far as China.

Ecology: The four groups represent four adaptive trends. The Dorcas group are small desert gazelles. The rufous group are small gleaners adapted to less arid but very open steppes around the margins of the Sahara proper. The Palaearctic group are cold-adapted species. The Nanger gazelles are large, desert gazelles (in E Africa they have maintained occupation of benign habitats that were formerly drier).

Natural history: Horns and horn shapes are influenced by population density because frequent fighting selects for stronger weapons and more effective defence. Thus Grant's gazelle (more consistently numerous and densely distributed) has the longest and heaviest horns (up to 80cm.) The Saharan Dama gazelle normally lives at low densities and has horns half this length. Soemmering's gazelle, between the two extremes, has horn lengths of up to 58cm.

At an early stage in their evolution gazelles would have combined their ecological shift into more open habitats with a behavioural change towards visual rather than olfactory or vocal signals. As a result most species are highly conspicuous, with prominent signal patches (usually white) on head, rump, flanks and feet. All gazelles flag their head, posture, wag their tail, shudder their flanks, bounce, leap or race around. All are messages intended for other gazelles. Conspicuousness, in turn, has reinforced their dependence upon open country (where they normally have adequate warning of the approach of predators). Only as fawns do gazelles hide like the dwarf antelopes with which they share a common ancestry.

Adaptations: Heat tolerance in desert gazelles is achieved through a refinement of the nasal blood-cooling found in dikdiks. The less arid-adapted rufous gazelles are more wasteful of water, using conventional panting to cool down. Desert gazelles accumulate adequate moisture by feeding on dew-soaked vegetation late at night.

Gazella dorcas
Rare or absent

1000 km

Dorcas gazelle *Gazella dorcas*

Other names: Fr. *Gazelle dorcas*. Ger. *Dorkasgazelle*.

Measurements: HB 90–110cm. T 15–20cm. SH 55–65cm. W 15–20kg.

Recognition: The smallest gazelle but proportionally the longest limbed, with small, fine hooves. It is notable for its very long ears. Horns, on both sexes, are long (up to 38cm), with up to 25 annular rings, and lyre-shaped (out then in at the tips). Colour is light fawn with poorly differentiated flank stripes but light and dark streaks down the face.

Subspecies: *G. d. dorcas* (E Sahara), *G. d. massaesyla* (W Sahara), *G. d. isabella* (east of the R. Nile), *G. d. beccarii* (Eritrean uplands), *G. d. pelzelne* (N Somali coast).
Habitat: N and NE Africa in driest subdeserts, mainly on stony or compacted soils with very sparse vegetation. Resident animals tend to disperse in small parties but converge on localised resources in larger numbers. When nomadic, they may aggregate in herds of up to 100. They are fecund, with a 6-month gestation. Sexually mature in 18 months, they live for over 12 years.
Food: Herbs (notably *Chrozophora*), succulents and, especially during the driest periods, shoots of shrubs such as *Acacia*, *Maerua* and *Leptadenia*. Dorcas gazelles are mainly active at night and around dawn and dusk.
Status: Endangered or exterminated in many localities but still widespread over much of its range. Not endangered overall.

Speke's gazelle *Gazella spekei*

Other names: Fr. *Gazelle de Speke*. Ger. *Spekegazelle*.
Measurements: HB 95–105cm. T 15–20cm. SH 50–60cm. W 15–25kg.
Recognition: A rather small gazelle with an inflatable nasal region just behind the nostrils. It is fawn with a crisp black flank stripe (and paler band above it), white buttocks with dark margins, a pale face and undulating horns with broad annulations.
Habitat: The Indian Ocean littoral of Somalia in stony semi-desert dominated by stunted succulents, aloes, shrubs and sparse desert grasses (*Panicum* and *Eragrostis*). The centre of its range is the Nogal Valley where small groups, occasionally numbering up to 20, gather or disperse in response to the sparse vegetation. It is notable for a loud sneeze, said to be an alarm call (probably as much an advertisement of status), that is made by inflating and emptying the nasal sac. Muscular spasms also dispense scent from preorbital glands.
Food: Grass, herbs, shrubs and succulents.
Status: Still widespread, although intense competition from livestock may have reduced numbers in some areas. Not endangered.

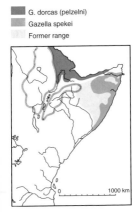

Speke's gazelle.

Red-fronted (Thomson's) gazelle *Gazella rufifrons*

Other names: Fr. *Gazelle de Thomson*, *Gazelle à front roux*. Ger. *Thomsongazelle*, *Rotstirngazelle*. Swah. *Swala tomi*.
Measurements: HB 80–120cm. T 15–27cm. H 55–82cm. W 15–25kg. (♀); 20–35kg. (♂).
Recognition: A compact little gazelle with a warm reddish back and white underparts separated by a black flank band. The white buttocks have black marginal stripes and the colour on the back extends to the root of the all-black tail. The face is boldly striped (with much individual variation) and the ears are of moderate length and narrow. The mildly undulating horns have numerous sharp annulations.

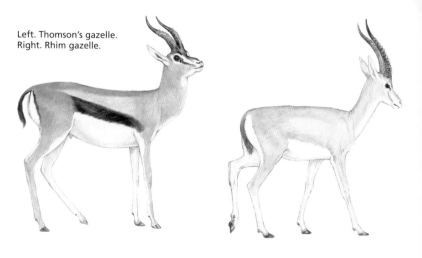

Left. Thomson's gazelle.
Right. Rhim gazelle.

Subspecies: Red-fronted gazelle – *G. r. rufifrons* (W Sahel), *G. r. laevipes* (E Sahel), *G. r. kanuri* (South of L. Chad); Eritrean gazelle – *G. r. tilonura* (Eritrea); Mongalla gazelle – *G. r. albonotata* (Sudd, east of the Nile); Thomson's gazelle – *G. r. thomsoni* (East of Rift Valley), *G. r. nasalis* (West of Rift Valley); Red gazelle – *G. r. rufina* (Algeria (extinct?)).

Habitat: The dry grasslands and shrubby steppes of the Sahel and similar (but moister) habitats in E Africa. They prefer heavily grazed, trampled or burnt grasslands or naturally open steppe (and stay on pastures long deserted by larger herbivores as long as some miniature growth remains). Socially they are exceptionally flexible. They are migratory animals, without lasting ties between individuals, spread out in a loose mosaic of overlapping ♀ herds. Each individual shares with many others a particular home range within which activities such as going to water (treks of 15km are not unusual), resting and moving to fresh pasture are often co-ordinated. Such temporary associations among a large number (up to 100 or more) form, fragment and reform, suggesting that, in spite of their individual independence, each gazelle knows and remembers a large number of 'friends', 'clan' members or other relatives. ♂♂ are less flexible and mature individuals fight to hold and defend territories within the ♀♀'s favourite pastures. When resources are exhausted only thirst or hunger drives them away. Solitary territorial ♂♂ in an empty landscape are a common sight.

This species retains active preorbital glands and ♂♂ mark grass stems and twigs at preferred spots (often hillocks or compacted bare patches). They also drop dung at these places. Frequent fights and stand-offs help maintain boundaries between neighbours. ♂♂ attempt a mild, ineffectual 'herding' of ♀♀ in order to delay their departure but their primary interest is in finding oestrous ♀♀ to mate with.

Food: Mainly growing green grass in the rains but switches to herbs, the foliage of shrubs and seeds (of *Acacia*, *Balanites*, *Boscia*, *Sida* and *Solanum*) in the dry season. *Themeda*, *Cynodon* and *Harpachne* are preferred grasses in Kenya.

Status: Once widespread throughout their range, red-fronted gazelles now occur in fragmented and declining patches but are still locally common at reduced densities. In some areas their status is unchanged (i.e. Mongalla and Thomson's gazelle's in national parks). Not endangered overall.

Rhim gazelle *Gazella leptoceros*

Other names: Fr. *Rhim*. Ger. *Dünengazelle*.

Measurements: HB 100–110cm. T 15–20cm. SH 65–72cm. W est. 14–18kg.

Recognition: A medium-sized gazelle of very pale yellowish grey colour, only faintly marked with face and flank stripes. The ears are long and narrow. Horns (appreciably thicker and longer in ♂♂) are long and nearly straight, with 20–25 well-defined annulated rings. Outer hooves are broader than the inner ones.

Habitat: Strictly confined to the great sand deserts, or *ergs*, of the E Sahara from Algeria to Egypt. Here it lives among the dunes in very small parties, usually a ♂ with one or more ♀♀ and their young.

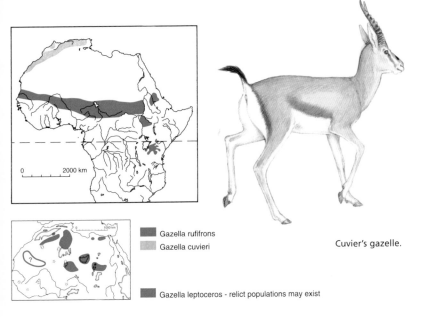

Gazella rufifrons
Gazella cuvieri

Cuvier's gazelle.

Gazella leptoceros - relict populations may exist

Food: Main grass reported to be a feather grass (*Aristida pungens*, or 'drinn'); also succulents, herbs and foliage of scarce shrubs. The Rhim gazelle feeds at night and in the early morning. Water requirements are drawn solely from moisture in its food.
Status: In spite of its remoteness, the Rhim gazelle has been a traditional quarry for mounted (and now motorised) hunters and its horns used to be sold as ornaments in N African markets and shops. Known to be rare, possibly endangered. Exact status not known.

Cuvier's gazelle *Gazella cuvieri*

Other names: Fr. *Edmi*. Ger. *Echtgazelle*.
Measurements: HB 95–105cm. T 15–20cm. SH 60–69cm. W 15–20kg. (♀); 20–35kg. (♂).
Recognition: A tallish grey-brown gazelle with broad, lighter and darker bands across the flanks, a white belly and buttocks, and a black tail. The top of the nose has a prominent black spot. The face is well striped and the ears are pale, long and narrow. Horns are long (25–37cm) and well formed in both sexes; strongly annulated, they rise vertically before diverging out and back; the smooth tips curving in and forwards.
Habitat: From Morocco to Algeria (formerly to Tunisia) in *maquis* scrub mosaics, open parkland of pines (*Pinus halappensis*) evergreen oak thickets and patches of rushes (*Juncus*). It favours both stony and sandy ground on hills and plateaus. Here it lives in widely spaced territories where ♂♂ attend one or more ♀♀ and their young. It is rarely seen in groups of more than eight. Mating takes place in early winter with births in the spring (April–May).
Food: Grass, herbs and shrubs; often visits cultivated fields.
Status: Rare and now scattered in a decreasing number of localities, Cuvier's gazelle is protected in a few reserves. Because it is heavily poached and suffers continuing habitat degradation, mainly from overgrazing by livestock, it is in danger of extinction.

Grant's gazelle *Gazella granti*

Other names: Fr. *Gazelle de Grant*. Ger. *Grantgazelle*. Swah. *Swala granti*.
Measurements: HB 140–166cm. T 20–28cm. SH 78–83cm. (♀); 85–91cm. (♂). W 38–67kg. (♀); 60–81.5kg. (♂).
Recognition: A large pale gazelle with upright stems to the long horns above relatively small eyes, which are set in characteristic, leaf-shaped eye patches, or 'masks', of jet-black skin and hair incorporating vestigial preorbital glands. Above the nostrils there is a slightly inflatable nasal sac and the mouth is proportionately large for a gazelle. The tail is markedly tapered and carries a wispy fringe. There are hoof and knee glands. The root of the tail is white, extending the buttock patch into a bold white configuration (the rectangularity of

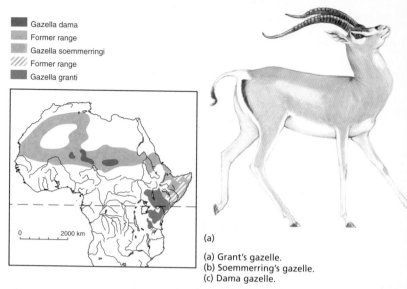

Gazella dama
Former range
Gazella soemmerringi
Former range
Gazella granti

0   2000 km

(a)

(a) Grant's gazelle.
(b) Soemmerring's gazelle.
(c) Dama gazelle.

which is emphasised by a dark vertical stripe down each thigh). Colour varies individually, especially on the flanks, but with distinct regional trends. Thus, ♀♀ often have dark flank stripes, but less often in the north-east, while the flanks of ♂♂ are also dark only around L. Turkana. Horns also vary individually and regionally (50–80cm). ♂ horns west of L. Eyassi and L. Natron tend to splay at a sharp angle, with downward curls at the tip. North of Mt Kenya horns tend to be more parallel.

Combinations of variation, both within and between gazelles from neighbouring regions, suggests substantial gene flow in the past and may invalidate the 'subspecies' tentatively listed below. Some ten forms have been described; one is the very distinctive Tana, or 'Peter's, gazelle, *G. petersi* which has a back that is fawn brown from neck to tail, with a white buttock patch reaching only to the anus. The limbs and overall proportions are smaller. Facial stripes are faded, with an almost white band above the eye and a brown spot on the lower nose. The horns are among the least elaborated and most conservative in shape, being almost straight.

Subspecies: Grant's gazelle, *G. g. granti* (Mt Kenya to Ruaha valley); 'Robert's' gazelle, *G. g. robertsi* (west of L. Eyassi and L. Natron); 'Bright's gazelle', *G. g. notata* (north of Mt Kenya); Tana gazelle, *G. g. petersi* (lower Tana valley).

Habitat: This could be called the 'Rift Valley gazelle' because its distribution spills over from the central axis or 'spine' of the E Rift. This upland distribution coincides with rain-shadows and with an arid corridor of unstable climate across the E African plateau that is known to have been very much more arid in the past. The Tana subspecies lives in the lower Tana valley, Lorian swamp, Wajir and the Dheere-Madheeri depressions (west of the R. Juba in Somalia). Here the gazelles live on very flat plains that are briefly flooded during occasional and unpredictable rains (when they do flood it tends to be in April or December). Where their range becomes dense bush the gazelles are restricted to glades or open, scrubby valleys. However, in the 1950s, elephants became so numerous in Tsavo that they cleared large areas of woody growth (a clearance extended recently by charcoal-burners) and the Tana gazelles expanded west and south, meeting up with Grant's gazelles across a broad front in the Galana valley. Where conditions suit them all year, both sexes are resident, the ♂♂ on midden-marked territories of 8ha to 10km², the ♀♀ circulating over still larger areas. Elsewhere, seasonal movements take them from higher, well-drained areas during the rains out onto flat, grassy valleys in the dry season. They do not tolerate soft soils but will live in bush and tall grass more readily than any other gazelle (but only seasonally). Fighting and territorial displays, characterised by flicking of the raised head on the bulging neck and slow, stiff circling, increase during biannual mating peaks (December and May north of the equator). Births follow a 6-month gestation. Rainy-season births appear to take place in denser cover. The fawn remains hidden for several weeks. At this time mothers may actively attack small predators.

(b)　　　　　　　　　　　　(c)

Food: Herbs and shrub foliage are preferred during the later wet and dry seasons; grass is grazed only while it is young and green. The fruits of *Balanites* and *Solanum* have also been recorded. Intense grazing by other species removes grass, thereby favouring herbs and the gazelles which feed on them. Grant's gazelle is typically found in herbivore concentration areas, such as the Serengeti plains, and are commonly seen in mixed groups. Herds of these gazelles may number up to 500 at such times.

Status: Although eliminated in some agricultural regions and areas where poaching is uncontrolled, these gazelles are still widespread and common both within and outside national parks and reserves. Not endangered.

Soemmerring's gazelle *Gazella soemmerringi*

Other names: Fr. *Gazelle de Soemmerring*. Ger. *Sömmerring-gazelle*.

Measurements: HB 125–150cm. T 18–23cm. SH 81–90cm. W 38–46kg.

Recognition: A large, generally pale gazelle with extensive white on the rump, strongly marked facial blazes, a large head and heavy, short, backwardly swept horns that form a lyrate shape with in-pointed hooked tips. It is long in the leg, with big hooves and a relatively short neck. The tail, like that of other Nanger gazelles, is short and tapered, with a mainly white fringe of short hairs.

Subspecies: *G. s. soemmerringi* (Sudan): brown face, shorter horns. *G. s. berberana* (Somalia): black face, longer horns. *G. s. butteri* (S. Ethiopia): dark flank, thigh stripes. An unnamed dwarf from Kebir I. in the Dahlac archipelago has differently curled horns and could be a distinct species.

Habitat: Endemic to the Horn of Africa where they once inhabited most of Somalia and the last, lowest foothills of the Ethiopian massif on its northern and eastern faces. Here they once gathered in hundreds on open plains and made substantial seasonal migrations (notably down from the upper Atbara valley to spend the wet season on the exposed plains below Kasala). They favour rough, hilly country with scattered evergreen thickets and *Acacia/Commiphora* steppe, as well as open, short-grass plains. Today they are seldom seen in herds larger than about 15. These are often groups of ♀♀ and their young herded by a single ♂ on his midden-marked territory. Like Grant's gazelle, ♂♂ flick their heads during confrontations. They yank their hooked horns sideways during fights in efforts to destabilise the opponent. When tending or herding ♀♀, ♂♂ make a nasal croak. A mating peak has been recorded between September and November. Gestation lasts 198 days and the young lie up for a month. They are weaned by 6 months and reach sexual maturity by 18 months. Animals live for 14 years.

Status: Exterminated over the greater part of their range these gazelles now exist in numerous small pockets. Although hunting may have played a significant part in this decline, overgrazing and habitat degradation by domestic stock is probably the main cause. Listed as Threatened (IUCN).

Dama gazelle *Gazella dama*

Other names: Fr. *Gazelle dama*. Ger. *Damagazelle*.
Measurements: HB 140–165cm. T 25–35cm. SH 90–120cm. W 40–75kg.
Recognition: The largest of all gazelles, with long legs and neck, a big head and short, compact, double-curved horns. The face and underparts are white in all forms; the most westerly resemble Soemmerring's gazelle in pattern but are a vivid rufous rather than fawn. The most easterly populations are very variable but have many individuals where the rufous element is confined to the neck and upper shoulders but are otherwise white. The tail is short and white, with a sparse fringe.
Subspecies: Mhorr gazelle, *G. d. dama* (W Sahara); Nubian gazelle, *G. d. ruficollis* (Sahara west of the Nile). There was formerly a wide zone of very variable integration between these two.
Habitat: Until recently one of the most widespread and common of Sahara gazelles, making mass movements between its wet-season pastures deep in the Sahara and dry-season range in the semi-deserts and open bushlands of the Sahel. Herds of many hundreds used to be seen on the move before dispersing into smaller groups numbering up to about 15. The principal mating peak in the Sahara was between March and June, the wettest months. Births would peak in about December, by which time the gazelles had moved well to the south so that the newborn could find shelter in the light scrub and grassland of the Sahel. Similar movements between moister and drier parts of their range took place in Morocco and Algeria. Here they travelled south into the Sahara, returning north where they preferred *reg* and *hammada* pastures. The last animals here were seen in the 1950s.
Food: Mainly herbs, succulents and shrubs (notably *Acacia*, which the gazelles could browse above 2m by standing up on the hindlegs like a gerenuk). These gazelles were also reported to eat coarse desert grasses. Their seasonal movements were symptomatic of their need for moisture (albeit moisture contained in browse).
Status: Dependence on movement into the Sahel was fatal for Dama gazelles. Large, very conspicuous antelopes, they came into contact with ever-increasing numbers of livestock and people along almost the entire length of their range and declined very rapidly between the 1950s and 1970s. They are now extinct in Algeria, Mauritania, Senegal and Burkina Faso, nearly so in Mali, Niger and Sudan. The principal authority on wildlife in this region, J. E. Newby, wrote in 1990, 'the problems for these animals and for the people trying to conserve them have been exacerbated by a new wave of hunters invading the Sahelian countries in search of new hunting grounds'. Wealthy and irresponsible foreigners are purchasing a part in the extermination of Sahelian wildlife. Less accessible parts of this vast region may allow survival for a while but only in Chad do Dama gazelles have a realistic hope of recovery once fighting ceases. Listed as Threatened with Extinction (IUCN).

Dibatag *Ammodorcas clarkei*

Other names: Fr. *Dibatag*. Ger. *Lamagazelle*.
Measurements: HB 152–168cm. T 30–36cm. SH 80–88cm. W 22–29kg.
Recognition: A very tall, slender antelope with large eyes, long, black-tipped ears and a face with typical gazelline markings down an elongated but sharply tapered muzzle. The mouth, teeth and jaws are minuscule. The ♂ ♂ have shortish horns with heavy, annulated bases and tips that are sharply angled forward. Its name means 'erect tail' in Somali and the heavily furred black tail, carried like a waggling baton, is indeed its most conspicuous feature. During flight the tail and head are carried erect which distinguishes this species from the gerenuk, which adopts a more horizontal posture. The body colour is a uniform fawn grey, with ochre-coloured legs and a red forehead. The undersides and brow stripe are white and the long buttock hair can be flared out into a brilliant white signal. There are preorbital glands and glandular 'brushes' below the knees.
Distribution: Restricted to a single vegetation type in central Somalia and the Ogaden (Ethiopia). Here it prefers areas of well-drained, sandy soils. It avoids dense thickets and very stony ground.
Habitat: A plant community called camel-brush or 'gedguwa'. This is an *Acacia/Commiphora* deciduous bushland and thicket in which important evergreens are *Boscia*, *Dobera*, *Salvadora*, *Grewia* and *Cadaba*. During and immediately after the rains it visits more open glades and in general prefers a mosaic of thickets and grassland with scattered trees.

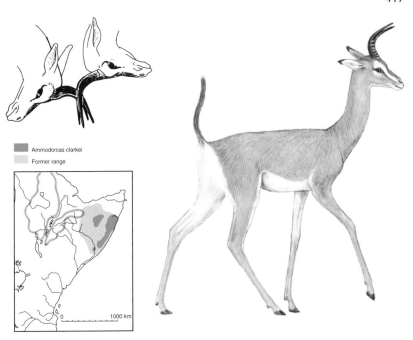

Ammodorcas clarkei
Former range

0   1000 km

Food: Mainly the foliage of *Acacia* (at least six species noted), *Commiphora* and other evergreen trees and shrubs, but probably less dependent on woody growth than the gerenuk. It has been reported to graze on herbs and new grass during the rains. Sodom apples (*Solanum*) have also been recorded in its diet. The small, mobile, very pointed but muscular lips assist the plucking of minute items, such as buds and shoots, from within dense barricades of thorns. The dibatag can reach up into small trees and bushes by balancing on its hindlegs, keeping balance with lightly propped forelegs but this mode of feeding is thought to occur less frequently than in the gerenuk.

Behaviour: ♂♂ are territorial, visiting their latrines daily to renew the piles of small, dark, oblong pellets but they are also reported to make periodic small-scale shifts in range. Up to five ♀♀ and their young have been seen with single adult ♂♂ but singles or twos are commoner. Captive ♂♂ rub their facial glands on the ♀'s rump and both sexes have been seen to nibble or lick one another's glands. ♂♂ dowse their muzzles in ♀ urine and lip-curl like all other bovids. There is a mating peak during the heavy rains in April and May. After 6 months' gestation a single fawn is born during the short rains (October–November) and lies up in thick bush. Young remain concealed for 2 weeks and reach sexual maturity at between 12 and 18 months. The dibatag is thought to live for 10–12 years.

Adaptations: The contrast between great height, substantial weight and extreme delicacy of mouth parts poses special problems for fighting ♂♂. Not only must they avoid injury to the muzzle, they also risk toppling because tall, heavy animals are easily thrown off balance. ♂♂ squaring up for a fight therefore tuck their vulnerable noses between their forefeet. Their horns are sufficiently long to force them into a standing contest. Their thick, heavy napes and upper necks engage and the horns clash along their curved back surfaces. From this position, pushing hard and wrestling from the pivot of their broad napes, each animal seeks to hook his opponent off balance. This technique of fighting ensures that there is little risk to their fragile muzzles and it is the rumps of fleeing losers that are more likely to get stabbed by sharp horn tips.

Status: This species has lost at least half of its known recent range and probably occupies a much smaller fraction of its original area of distribution. There are two or three remaining pockets where it remains fairly common but poaching and displacement by domestic stock makes continued decline likely. Proposed conservation areas at Hobyo (Obbia), Haradere-Awale Rugno in Somalia and E Ogaden in Ethiopia must await more peaceful times to be implemented. Listed as Vulnerable (IUCN).

Male.

Female.

Gerenuk *Litocranius walleri*

Other names: Fr. *Gazelle de Waller*. Ger. *Giraffengazelle*. Swah. *Swala twiga, Njonga*.
Measurements: HB 140–160cm. T 22–35cm. SH 80–105cm. W 28–45kg. (♀); 31–52kg. (♂).
Recognition: A very tall, long-necked, long-eared antelope with a two-toned chestnut back, light fawn sides and white underparts. Like the dibitag it has extremely small mouth parts for a large antelope. The contrast is greatest in the very heavily horned ♂♂ where the upper neck is thicker than its lower part and the dainty little muzzle protrudes from a heavily reinforced brain-case. The horns have thick, diverging shafts, rising in a bold arc and then curling forward in a tight hook towards the tip. It has preorbital face glands, scented brushes below the knees and glands between the hooves.
Subspecies: Two listed but ill-defined.
Distribution: The Horn of Africa extending into NE Tanzania. Mainly semi-arid bushland below 1,200m. Known to have been more widely spread in the more distant past (up the Red Sea littoral).
Habitat: Dependent on an abundance of bushes and small trees, including evergreens. It avoids true, dense thickets and is commonest on flats where *Acacia*, *Commiphora* and other bushland species are well spaced or in small clumps. It has a wider tolerance of bushland types than the dibitag.
Food: Almost exclusively a tree-foliage browser (creepers and vines being the main exception). Acacias, with their very small, nutritious leaflets, are the major staple but seasonal and regional variations follow what plants are in leaf or in bud at the time. Skunk bush, *Premna resinosa*, is a favourite in Kenya but 87 different trees and shrubs have been recorded in the diet. The gerenuk habitually rises on its hindlegs to reach a zone over 2m high (where giraffes are the only, partial,competitors). Its minute, pointed muzzle can extract leaves from very thorny tangles.
Behaviour: The gerenuk is normally very residential, living in well-spaced home ranges of 3–6km². Here single adult ♂♂ exclude other adult ♂♂ but regularly associate with ♀♀ and their offspring. In some cases ♂♂ share exactly the same range as one or more ♀♀, regularly visiting or following them. Shifts of range are known but are probably rarer with age. ♂♂ in particular become more strictly residential with age. ♂♂ mark out their territories by inserting twigs into their preorbital glands. Unlike the dibitag they do not make dung middens (which in other antelope species tend to abut the ranges of other ♂♂ and are often contributed to by both neighbours). It is therefore interesting that gerenuk facial gland deposits are distributed along the borders of very small domains which do *not* abut on those of neighbours, suggesting that ♂♂ live in such large home ranges that they can only mark core areas. It is possible that some kind of no-man's-land lies between ♂ gerenuk territories. Among ♀♀ overlaps in range and sporadic associations (sometimes larger aggregations) hint at the existence of local 'clans' of related animals that know one another. The contact call is a frog-like humming grunt.

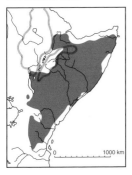

Litocranius walleri

Like dibatag, gerenuk ♂♂ rub their face glands on ♀♀. Occasionally they threaten them, making a low rumble (apart from a buzz of alarm they are otherwise rather silent animals). Young are born after a 7-month gestation and most births occur during the rains. The newborn is well hidden and only emerges to join its mother after several weeks. A mother may be accompanied by more than one offspring (F young become independent at about 12 months, ♂♂ parting later, at up to 18 months). Animals are thought to live for 10–12 years.

Adaptations: In spite of many similarities, gerenuk and dibitag ♂♂ differ most in the shape of their horns. The gerenuk's fighting technique differs fundamentally as its much heavier horns, which curve in the opposite direction, are clashed together with violent downward nods of the head. Backward extension of the very hard brain-case (*litocranius* means 'stone-skull') provides the immediate leverage for the hammer-like blows exchanged by fighting ♂♂.

Status: Although eliminated from parts of its range in E Africa, the gerenuk is still widespread both within and outside national parks and reserves. Not endangered.

Springbucks *Antidorcini*

Springbuck	*Antidorcas marsupialis*

Recognition: In size and general proportions the springbuck superficially resembles impala, oribi (even pampas deer) and gazelles. Gazelle-like, they share striped faces and bands on thighs and flanks with goats, impala, oryx and young blesbok. Their behaviour, horns and general body build are so like gazelles that they are generally assumed to be a sort of 'southern gazelle.' However, there are several differences that clearly distinguish them.

Genealogy: One difference concerns the internal structure of the horns. Gazelles, in common with dwarf antelopes, duikers and kobs, have solid horn cores. Springbucks have hollow cores, in common with the Eurasian tribe of goats or chamois and the impala and its allies. The fossil record (replete with horn cores) suggests that this difference is much more fundamental than it might seem because it is one that goes back many millions of years. Gazelles were already distinct from springbucks 15 million years ago and the two lineages probably parted before then. Each has given rise to later offshoots that scarcely resemble either of them. There are probably two reasons for the close resemblance between springbucks and gazelles. One is that their ancient common ancestor had much the same size and form as its living descendants. The other reason relates to the fact that both have pursued parallel ecological strategies in very dry habitats. Refinements have been relatively minor and have not affected their ancient, generalised, gazelle-like body plans.

Geography: The original split between springbucks and gazelles could have been between continental populations, with the earliest gazelle ancestors remaining in Africa while the ancestral springbuck and its putative cousins, the chamois and goats, developed in Eurasia (some early springbuck fossils are known from Eurasia).

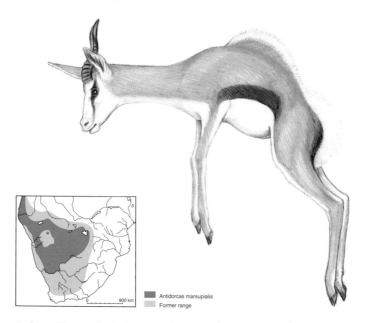

Antidorcas marsupialis
Former range

800 km

Ecology: Pliocene fossils from the Atlas Mts show that springbucks (of the living genus, *Antidorcas*) were already adapted to cool Eurasian-type habitats some 4 million years ago. Today's springbucks survive in SW Africa, the main region of the continent that has remained both dry and (periodically) cool. This region has been connected with N and NE Africa by arid corridors with every major Ice Age.

Natural history: It is not only in their horns that the two lineages differ. Springbuck teeth are more like those of a coarse-grass grazer than the narrower teeth of herb- and leaf-eating gazelles. A more abundant food supply permits bigger, denser herds to form and more competition among springbuck ♂♂ during the rut.

Adaptations: Several adaptive traits distinguish this antelope and its numerous fossil antecedents. One of the most important is modification of the teeth for coping with coarse plants on dry winter pastures. Another is accommodation to permanent, large herds (as opposed to scattered groups on territories) involving increased competition, expressed in more frequent and severe head-butting. Severe buffetings of the head favoured the development of hollow, backward-swept horns which are better able to absorb the force of heavy blows and so better insulate the brain.

Springbuck *Antidorcas marsupialis*

Other names: Fr. *Antidorcas*. Ger. *Springbock*.

Measurements: HB 120–150cm. T 14–28cm. SH 68–90cm. W 20–43kg. (♀); 30–59kg. (♂).

Recognition: A gazelle-like antelope with white underparts extending well up the sides, rump and dorsal midline. The head is also white but marked from crown to mouth with brown streaks (which conceal the very protuberant eyes). The white ears are exceptionally long and narrow. Upperparts are cinnamon fawn above an arc of black or brown on the flanks. The springbuck differs from gazelles in having a longer, broader and less flexible bridge to the nose, deeper, more muscular cheeks, and horns that sweep backwards and hook inwards from peculiarly swollen bases above the eyes. The white dorsal crest is normally hidden beneath two long folds of scent-secreting skin that run along the lower spine but it can be erected (as can the white hair on the buttocks) to create an eye-catching, and presumably odoriferous, signal.

Subspecies: Smaller south-western populations grade into larger north-eastern ones. Individual variation has led to 11 subspecies being named (from a single population in a continuous range). None are now considered valid.

Distribution: SW Africa, the Namib, Kalahari and Karoo deserts. This species or its immediate antecedents was once sufficiently common in E Africa to become the most frequently fossilised of all antelopes (three species found over a period of more than 2 million years).

Habitat: Dry, open plains with a marked preference for flat drainage lines and the fringes of pans where soil conditions or overgrazing keep grasses and herbs low. It lives in dry *Acacia* savannahs in the Kalahari, bushy shrubland in Namibia, dwarf and grassy shrublands in the Karoo. It is exceptionally mobile, moving long distances to find scarce pastures during droughts but instantly returning to traditional and well-known localities when the rains break. Vast herds of migrating springbucks earned the Afrikaner name of *treckbokken*. It avoids tall grass, thick woodland and broken ground.

Food: Broadly a summer grazer and winter browser, the springbuck can survive on the residual moisture in plants. In the absence of any surface water it seeks out succulents, cucurbits and even paws out shallow roots. It feeds most intensively around dawn and dusk. The staple in some areas consists of 9 species of grasses and 11 species of shrubs but it has varied tastes. Some of the grasses favoured are coarse- or hard-stemmed species, such as bristle grass (*Aristida*), love grass (*Eragrostis*), stargrass (*Cynodon*), buffalo grass (*Panicum*) and rush grass (*Sporobolus*).

Behaviour: ♀♀ are highly mobile, moving quite independently of one another (but with current offspring). Because they form no close attachment to others or to territory less is known of them than ♂♂ which comprise three main classes: immatures; unattached, non-breeding 'bachelors'; and territorial, breeding ♂♂. Breeding ♂♂ normally ignore subordinate 'bachelors' but periodically enter a rut in which they become fiercely intolerant of all other ♂♂ and seek to detain passing ♀♀ within their 25–70ha territory. The rut can occur at any time and lasts 5–21 days; ♀♀ that are not already pregnant may come into oestrus within a day or so of the ♂♂'s rut. Large numbers of young are therefore born about 6 months later in a synchronised but unpredictable birth peak. However, births tend to peak in summer within the summer rainfall area of the Cape. Newborns lie up for a few days and run with their mother's group within 3 or 4 weeks. ♀♀ are sexually mature at 7 months but ♂♂ are seldom sexually active until they have full-sized horns and have won a territory. They are known to live for at least 10 years (probably a lot more).

Adaptations: The name 'springbuck' comes from the mainly juvenile and subadult habit of leaping up in a series of 'pronks', or hunch-backed bounces, that appear somewhat haphazard or playful at a superficial glance. In fact the pronking animal is extremely alert and watchful as it circles round or casts about from left to right. By slowing down the speed while maximising the height of its jump the young animal can take a series of bearings, not only on its physical surroundings but also on the position of predators and other springbucks. It was formerly assumed that pronking was a warning or, more recently, a 'flaunting of fitness' in the face of disturbance by humans or other predators. Both explanations could be incidental benefits but a primary function of pronking is orientation in inexperienced animals; adults seldom pronk, presumably because they already know their surroundings and neighbours..

There is also a social dimension to pronking. The white hairs that flare up into view with each jump are saturated with scent from the glands that line the spinal pouch or marsupium. As a result jumps broadcast both visual and olfactory messages to other springbucks. A static version of the pronk suggests a meaning for the message and a possible precursor for the evolution of both pouch and pronk. Young animals appease threatening adults by lowering their heads and presenting their rear ends for an olfactory inspection. 'Presenting' during a soaring and eye-catching jump may represent a fast and efficient way of broadcasting an appeasing message. All ages and sexes tend to pronk more frequently immediately after rain, when evaporation and drying-out fills the air with strong soil and plant scents. The release of dorsal scent by all or most members of a group superimposes the springbuck's signature on its surroundings. The scent may be both generally attractive to all springbucks, as well as containing specific indications about the status of an individual. If this social ritual is combined with scanning and memorising the landscape and its signposts, pronking evidently contributes to survival in at least two important ways.

Just how well the springbuck remembers geography is revealed by its phenomenal capacity to 'home' back to small territories after months of travelling. Its return journey can begin at a moment's notice when the rains return.

Status: Most springbucks in South Africa are now effectively a form of livestock that lives on fenced farmland. A completely chocolate-coloured variety has been bred and selection for larger animals has begun. In parts of Namibia and in the Kalahari nomadic movements continue but are increasingly constrained by steady expansion of the livestock industry.

ALCELAPHINES, TOPI AND ALLIES ALCELAPHINI

Impala	*Aepyceros melampus*
Hirola	*Beatragus hunteri*
Bontebok and topi	*Damaliscus*
Kongoni	*Alcelaphus buselaphus (inc. lichtensteinii)*
Gnus (Wildebeest)	*Connochaetes*

Recognition: Alcelaphines have a long face and legs, double-curved, hollow horns, fast gaits and a part or wholly grass diet in common. They separate either side of the 40kg mark into medium-sized and large species. The impala and hirola resemble many other antelopes (and even deer) in their dimensions. The larger topi, kongoni and gnus have diversified into more distinctive types. The gazelle-like impala is often placed in a tribe or family of its own but the fossil record suggests it is a specialised offshoot of the earliest alcelaphines. This and its resemblances to the hirola serve as a reminder that the larger species have evolved relatively recently from much smaller ancestors.

Geneology: Most of the alcelaphine peculiarities were already present, albeit in a less marked form, in both fossil ancestors and in their modern descendants, namely the relict hirola and highly successful impala. Evolving from impala or springbuck-like ancestors, alcelaphines emerged late (less than 8 million years ago) and their fossil remains demonstrate very rapid change. Their hollow horns and forehead permit remodelling of the skull so that closely related forms can easily acquire very different horn shapes. The hammer-shaped head of the kongoni is due to a bending of axes, the muzzle tipping downwards while the horns twisted round (as is revealed by a good fossil series) until their hooked tips were literally 'back to front'.

Geography: Alcelaphines evolved in Africa and were very successful. Some early forms spread out to India but later became extinct there. Advanced, water-dependent grazers, they have always been most abundant and diverse on the eastern side of Africa. Nonetheless, their recent range included the N African littoral, the W African savannahs and the Horn, where they lived in immense numbers on a variety of pastures. Most of these populations belonged to the kongoni group, *Alcelaphus*.

Ecology: Alcelaphines are grazers adapted to live at high density on a very abundant but unstable food supply. They tolerate substantial seasonal fluctuations but few do well in really arid habitats. Exposure on open plains has selected for great speed and stamina.

Natural history: As high-density grazers living in close proximity, alcelaphines have evolved advanced, but somewhat unusual, social systems dependent on scent-marking of bodies rather than sites in the environment. All have retained very active pedal scent glands and most species kick, stamp or cavort to disperse scent during social displays. The combination of an intensely competitive social life and a capacity for great speed means that a number of displays are performed on the run, such as ritualised gaits and postures as well as fast gestural signals (such as the impala's tongue-flash).

Adaptations: The usual effect on limbs of increasing body weight is for them to become proportionately shorter and thicker. However, the larger alcelaphine species have retained fast gaits, long legs and a heavy, muscular body, but without elongating the neck in proportion. This disproportion has therefore led to a long face that is able to reach the ground. The short, muscular neck is an essential adjunct to the frequent horn-fighting necessary in a high density, competitive society.

Impala *Aepyceros melampus*

Other names: Fr. *Impala*. Ger. *Schwarz Fersen Antilope*. Swah. *Swala pala*.
Measurements: HB 120–160cm. T 30–45cm. H 75–95cm. W 40–60cm (♀): 45–80cm (♂).
Recognition: A medium-sized gazelle-like antelope with a brown or yellowish brown back that becomes lighter on haunches, shoulder, neck and head, and sharply lighter on the flanks. Underside, chin, mouth and ear linings are white. Ear tips, thigh stripes, midline of tail and back, and bushy fetlock glands are black (there are bold black eye stripes and a black bridge to the nose in an isolated Namib population). Adult ♂♂ have long, narrow horns, with shallow, well-spaced annulations, that arch up and out then back and up.

During rutting the necks of ♂♂ thicken, their coats become darker from the grease of sebaceous secretions and they acquire a musky scent. There are no preorbital glands but the entire forehead is glandular and fossils reveal preorbital pits in ancestral forms.

Subspecies: Common impala, *A. m. melampus* (SE Africa). Black-faced impala, *A. m. petersi* (SW Africa): a relict population with several conservative features – sometimes treated as a species.

Distribution: A patchy scattering from Kenya south to the Transvaal, Botswana and E Angola. The black-faced impala is an isolated population in SW Angola and a small area of Namibia.

Habitat: 'Edges' between grassland and denser woodlands, notably *Acacia*, are preferred. They require high-quality fodder (whether grass or leaves), moisture, shade and cover. This unstable mosaic is characteristic of SE Africa, where impalas are known to have been present for at least 4 million years. In favourable localities numbers can reach over 200 per km^2. Grassland is occupied during the rains, woodland more in the dry season. Adult ♂♂ have a greater tendency to remain in denser vegetation than ♀♀. In all areas impalas are highly residential, seldom moving more than 10km and even then only temporarily.

Food: Almost wholly grazers during the rains. The amount of grass in the diet drops to about 30% in the dry season when impalas are mostly in the woodlands, browsing on shrubs, herbs, pods, and seeds. *Acacia*, *Combretum* and *Grewia* are important in most areas. Feeding usually takes place in two major bouts (around dawn and dusk) and two minor bouts (midnight and early afternoon), with shading and ruminating in between.

Behaviour: Recent research has shown that ♀♀ form 'clans' of 30–120 animals with home ranges radiating out from fairly stable centres but extensively overlapping the ranges of neighbouring ♀ clans. From such centres year-round movements may extend for about a kilometre but core ranges have been estimated at 80–180ha. Although gregarious, neither ♀♀ nor ♂♂ form any lasting associations (not even with their young).

M offspring share their mother's home range but begin to wander more widely as they mature (shifting their focus up to 4km away from the mother's range). Full horn and neck development is reached by ♂♂ at about 4 years but the intolerance of other ♂♂ restricts their movements and forces them to defend themselves within an area much smaller than their parental home range. Their attachment to this area becomes more marked with age. The nature of their 'tenure' changes or cycles with their own hormonal condition and with that of other ♂♂ that share part or all of their home range. Most healthy adult ♂♂ become intensely intolerant of other ♂♂ when in the presence of oestrous ♀♀. This intolerance is expressed in direct challenges and fights during the rut. In S Africa the rut only lasts a few weeks and, since ♂♂ are almost continually inspecting, herding and copulating with ♀♀, confronting other ♂♂ or rushing around roaring and chasing, they are soon exhausted and capitulate to fitter ♂♂. At the highest densities any single M's tenure of a 'territory' is ephemeral, lasting only 3–13 days.

If both the boundaries and the tenure of ♂ territories appear unstable this is because being excluded or becoming an excluder depends almost entirely on the presence and sexual condition of ♀♀. Mating peaks coincide with the rains in both S and tropical Africa, but in the latter region two seasonal peaks are very much less sharply defined. One young is born after a gestation of about 200 days in a secluded spot. The mother remains nearby and visits only to suckle it. After some days the young begins to follow but seeks shelter at the least alarm. About half of all young are lost to predators within the first few weeks. ♀♀ are sexually mature in 18 months and animals live for up to 15 years.

Adaptations: Fetlock glands, unique to impalas, assist the laying of trails, presumably by helping temporarily detached or 'lost' individuals to find company. This function relates not only to trails left while walking; high kicks (another impala peculiarity) send out puffs of scent that may help dispersed animals to regroup after a scare. Roaring of ♂♂ allows them to space themselves acoustically, to intimidate potential rivals and assess risks with respect to other ♂♂ within a wooded environment. This and other peculiarities reinforce the supposition that impalas derive from open-country antelopes that made a secondary shift back into more wooded country.

Status: Widely distributed, fecund and well represented in numerous national parks, impalas are only vulnerable or endangered on the outer margins of their range, as in Uganda and Rwanda. Not endangered overall.

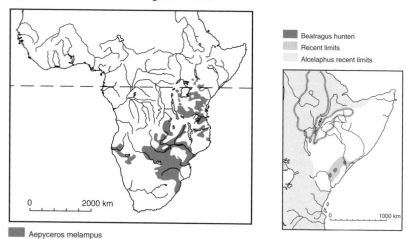

Beatragus hunteri
Recent limits
Alcelaphus recent limits

0   2000 km

0   1000 km

Aepyceros melampus

Hirola *Beatragus hunteri*

Other names: Fr. *Antilope hirola*. Ger. *Hirola*. Swah. *Hirola*.

Measurements: HB 120–200cm. T 30–45cm. SH 100–125cm. W est 80–118kg.

Recognition: An antelope with unusual proportions and colouring, of medium weight, with long legs and a long body but a relatively short neck and a long face. The lyrate horns are not unlike those of the impala but have less flare and much heavier bases with pronounced annulations. The uniform sandy colouring gives way to a slaty grey in older ♂♂. The long tail and black-tipped ears are startlingly white, as are the 'spectacles' around the eyes (patterns that emphasise the eyes are typical of some kob types but most antelopes have a dark 'mask' which conceals the eyes). The structure of its large pre-orbital gland and muzzle differs from that of topi and kongoni.

Distribution: Since the mid-Pleistocene, less than 1 million years ago, the emergence of more advanced, high density grazers, kongonis, might have contributed to the hirola's steady decline. Whatever its history it is now confined to a rapidly shrinking corner of SE Kenya (it possibly also survives in Somalia).

Habitat: A narrow strip of seasonally arid, grassy plains sandwiched between the waterless *Acacia* bush of the hinterland and forest-savannah mosaic on the coast (desert and thicket barriers might have served to exclude kongonis from this area). The northern margins of its range coincide with a type of very dry *Acacia* scrub where the grass cover becomes very much sparcer. Richer pastures used to be shared with moderate numbers of other grazers.

Food: Strictly a grazer, feeding on the dominant grasses, notably species of *Chloris*, *Cenchrus* and *Digitaria*. The large molars are well suited to chewing such coarse grasses. It feeds most intensively in the early morning and evening. Able to go without drinking, it also survives drought by laying down fat and avoiding energetic activity.

♂ Hirola.

Behaviour: ♀♀ with young formed groups numbering between 5 and 40, often attended by a single territorial ♂. All ♂ groups were common, occasionally associated with topi ♂♂. Herds were thought to be relatively sedentary and solitary ♂♂ particularly so. Such ♂♂ posture on habitual stamping grounds, which they scrape with the feet and mark with accumulations of dung. They also mark grass stems and other vegetation with their preorbital glands. Posturing includes head-flagging in which the white ears and spectacles are conspicuous. Most calves were born at the beginning of the short rains in October–November, suggesting a mating peak at the start of the main rains in March–April. Calves pass through a very vulnerable stage in which jackals and dogs, as well as hyaenas, the larger cats and eagles, may all be significant predators. The hirola's life-span is not known but capture experiments revealed that it was subject to muscular dystrophy. Delicacy during capture may be due to a lowered metabolism in the dry season.

Adaptations: A peculiarity of the ♂♂ is the very thick skin of the nape (a necessary protection against the sharp horns of rivals during fights), which folds up behind the horns when the ears are pricked. They apparently fight on their knees when in earnest and in a standing position when sparring.

Status: Although IUCN has classed this very unusual species as Threatened, the facts of its decline suggest that it is in danger of imminent extinction. Censuses in the 1970s estimated 10,000 to 13,000 hirola and a growing population of about 200,000 cattle in Kenya. By the end of that decade cattle numbers stood at about half a million (supported by more and more bore-holes) and I predicted that, if nothing was done, extinction was imminent. By 1983 hirolas were estimated to number 7,000 animals, by 1985 less than 1,000. By 1995 numbers were down to 300. Survival within its original range now depends upon protection and exclusion of the vast livestock holdings of the region from the 533km² Arawale Reserve. Outside, in Tsavo National Park, a small herd introduced in the 1960s and another in 1996 are still managing to sustain their numbers.

Bontebok, Blesbok *Damaliscus dorcas*

Other names: Fr. *Bontebok, Blesbok*. Ger. *Buntbock, Blessbock*.

Measurements: HB 140–160cm. T 30–45cm. SH 85–100cm. W 55–70kg (♀); 65–80kg (♂). Bontebok an average 8kg lighter.

Recognition: Smaller southern cousins of the topi, with very strong contrasts of colour in adults but fawn young with completely different, gazelle-like colouring. They have a compact body, short neck and a long nose with an expanded muzzle. Their horns resemble enlarged gazelle horns. The tail is short with a black, tufted tip. The differences between subspecies are given below.

Subspecies: Bontebok, *D. d. dorcas* (W Cape): glossy dark purplish brown with white buttocks and 'stockings'; very dark horns. Blesbok, *D. d. phillipsi* (Highveld): dull reddish brown with ill-defined off-white buttocks and off-white lower legs; paler horns.

Distribution: South African isolates sharing a geologically recent common ancestry with topi. The blesbok formerly inhabited the plateau grasslands known as the Highveld. This is the watershed for innumerable smaller rivers between the larger valleys of the R. Limpopo and R. Sundays. 'Sweepstake' colonisation of the Cape (probably across the Nieuwveld range and within the last few thousands of years) led to physical and genetic isolation of the bontebok. Derived from a small number of founders, it was unlikely to have been widespread, even before the arrival of humans with livestock.

Habitat: The blesbok originally ranged over the entire Highveld, grazing the fire-climax grassland dominated by red oat grass, *Themeda*. The bontebok inhabited a different Cape fynbos habitat where grassy areas were scarcer. In both parts of their range animals had regular access to water.

Food: Red oat grass, *Themeda* (at various stages of growth), *Eragrostis* and *Chloromelas* form the main part of the blesbok's diet. A species of *Setaria* is only taken in winter and there are seasonal changes of pasture. The bontebok also feeds on *Eragrostis* species but local dominants, *Bromus* and *Danthonia*, are the preferred grasses.

Behaviour: The blesbok formerly tended to migrate between seasonal pastures, forming huge mixed herds in the autumn and winter. Where the pastures in modern enclosures are sufficiently extensive to support them blesboks still gather in semi-nomadic herds. Even in smaller groups within still smaller enclosures both subspecies retain the habit of circulating around their available range in loose herds. The membership and numbers of these mobile aggregations are unstable but include sexually inactive ♂♂ and younger, but independent ♀♀ less than 2 years old. Adult ♀♀ with offspring tend to move over much smaller areas, a restriction reinforced by the territorial ♂♂ living there. These ♂♂ have focal centres to their territories which are marked with dung and urine on middens. Although the spacing between ♂♂ varies greatly, their inner core of 'markable' and 'defendable' territory is always less than 5ha. ♀ bontebok seldom gather in groups of more than ten (including their young) and they circulate over two or three ♂ territories during the February rut. Blesbok ♀ groups number up to 25 and mating peaks in April. Pregnant ♀♀ do not leave the herd to give birth. Both subspecies have an 8-month gestation and their young are up and mobile within an hour or two of birth. They mature in about 2 years and can live for up to 17 years.

Adaptations: The young of blesbok and topi are apparently identical at birth except for the former's smaller size. Both begin as pale, sandy-fawn animals with creamy undersides. First the bridge of the nose darkens, then dark leg and flank stripes (like those of springboks or gazelles) begin to extend over the sides and limbs. This darkening proceeds until there are more or less separate black patches in tropical topi. Pale undersides become ochre-coloured in topi, white in bontebok. The pale root to the tail is very similar in some topi and blesbok. As the bontebok matures this cream-coloured area turns white and forms a sharply defined genital beacon. In both blesbok and bontebok the bridge of the nose becomes the badge of maturity. As their horns lengthen it turns white with crisp black borders against the sides of the face. Most topi keep a black nose but rare individuals switch colours as they mature and have white blazes as conspicuous and of the same shape as that of the bontebok. These transformations during the development of individuals and the variation evident even in today's impoverished herds illustrate the potential for rapid differentiation in isolated populations.

That blesbok and topi have diverged very recently is shown by a perfect intermediate form, a supposed common ancestor, being very common in both S and E African fossil deposits that are less than 1 million years old. *Damaliscus agelaius* was similar in size to the blesbok, suggesting that this lineage has become more than twice as heavy in the rich sumplands of the tropics while their southern counterparts on the leached Highveld have remained more conservative. One reason for their divergence may have been the emergence of a new competitor, the kongoni, taking over as dominant grazer in dry savannah grasslands.

Status: The blesbok is now commercially ranched livestock and very few occur in formal conservation areas. The bontebok is also kept on farms (one having been made into a national park). Although both are now extinct as wild animals their survival is now more secure. Not endangered.

R. Bontebok.
L. Blesbok.

L. Tsessebe.
R. Topi.

Topi, Tiang, Tsessebe *Damaliscus lunatus*

Other names: Fr. *Damalisque*. Ger. *Leierantilope*. Swah. *Nyamera, Topi*.

Measurements: HB 150–230cm. T 36–42cm. W 75–150kg (♀); 120–160kg (♂).

Recognition: A large, compact antelope with a deep chest, prominently ridged shoulders, a rather short neck and a long face. The tail is narrow and fringed. Horns vary from one region to another in their splay and arching but all have backward-curving stems and forward- or inward-curving tips. The body colour varies from rather yellowish bleached brown to red or even purplish brown. There are black patches on the hindquarters and forelegs above ochre-coloured 'stockings'. The bridge of the nose is black (very occasionally turning white with maturity). The coat of healthy animals is always tight and very glossy. The hooves are narrow and splay out on soft ground.

Subspecies: Tsessebe, *D. l. lunatus* (S Africa); korrigum, *D. l. korrigum* (Senegal to W Nigeria); tiang, *D. l. tiang* (NE Nigeria to W Ethiopia); nyamera, *D. l. jimela* (Great Lakes region); topi, *D. l. topi* (E African coast).

Distribution: Sumplands and floodplains in otherwise relatively dry regions south of the Sahara, E and central Africa. All populations centre on large-scale ecosystems and they are absent from the many small, isolated floodplains that are scattered throughout tropical Africa. Although there must have been continuous connections in the past, small isolated groups appear to be vulnerable to vicissitudes of climate (and possibly competition and predation).

Habitat: These antelopes live in seasonally flooded grasslands where they follow receding waters in the dry season and retreat onto higher ground in the rains or flood season. Two of their local names are synonymous with 'mud'.

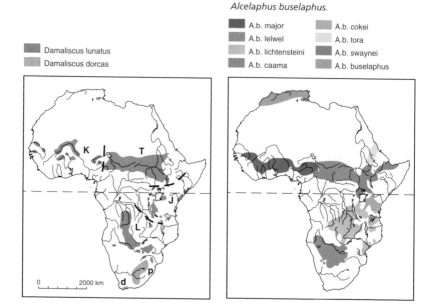

Alcelaphus buselaphus.

A.b. major
A.b. lelwel
A.b. lichtensteini
A.b. caama
A.b. cokei
A.b. tora
A.b. swaynei
A.b. buselaphus

Damaliscus lunatus
Damaliscus dorcas

0   2000 km

They favour naturally short or medium-height pastures (such as alkaline pans), regrowth after burns or else concentrate in large herds in tall grass (commonly on wet-season higher ground retreats). Here heavy trampling soon opens up large glades and stimulates continuous regrowth. These annual cycles of movement can involve huge herds of tens of thousands in round journeys of nearly 1,000km, small circuits within closed valleys, or sustained residence on 'permanent' pockets of suitable grassland. The instability and unpredictability of floodplain pastures renders the last group peculiarly vulnerable. The advantages of living in very large, mobile herds include reduced predation, and optimum grazing, partly due to their own trampling. Younger animals benefit from older animals' knowledge of the region's pastures.

Food: Most valley grasses are taken. Longer rather than very short leaves are stripped from the stems with a nodding action that finely balances raking wrenches with clipping bites.

Behaviour: Although many topi live in large migratory herds, they may be neighbours to (or co-exist with) small clusters of residential animals. The residential animals are probably offshoots of the larger aggregations but display different behaviour in that they occupy territories defended by ♂♂ (and sometimes also by ♀♀). Scattered residents tend to be less seasonal in their breeding. Large groups instead tend to have very intense periods of rutting while herds are at their most concentrated. In some areas mating may take place 'on the hoof' but in most instances it tends to focus on territorial clusters. Close proximity may stimulate hormones in both sexes and the build-up of scent in particular 'hot-spots'. ♂♂ fight for access to oestrous ♀♀, who are probably drawn in by the scent. Competition among ♂♂ results in ever smaller territories (down to 0.05ha) where all the elaborate preliminaries of prolonged courtship are abbreviated and intensified. Young are born after an 8-month gestation. The sandy-fawn calf lies up for a few days before joining its mother. Young often gather spontaneously and ♀♀ may form a defensive ring around them. The age of sexual maturity varies (12–28 months in ♀♀, ♂♂ up to 42 months). Loss of teeth after about 15 years results in death. ♀♀ are fertile to the end and bear young even as the last roots of their teeth fall from their jaws.

Adaptations: Adaptation to living on floodplains appears to be relatively recent in topi as their feet are only slightly modified for walking in soft soils. It is possible that ancestral topi ceded the greater part of a formerly more extensive grass-eating niche to the larger kongoni which is a more recently evolved, more advanced grazer. Greater speed, stamina, mobility and versatility enable the topi to compete with the kob, lechwe and waterbuck.

Status: Topi have been eliminated from the greater part of their range but can still reach very high densities in their remaining refuges. Currently well represented in reserves and national parks. Not endangered.

♂ Korkay.

Kongoni (Hartebeest) *Alcelaphus buselaphus* (inc. *lichtensteinii*)

Other names: Fr. *Bubale*. Ger. *Kuhantilope*. Swah. *Kongoni*.
Measurements: HB 160–215cm. T 30–70cm. H 107–150cm. W 116–185kg. (♀); 125–218kg. (♂).
Recognition: A large, high-shouldered, deep-chested antelope with long legs, a short neck and a very long, narrow face. The horns are carried on hollow bases, or 'pedicels', and show considerable variation (45–83cm) from individual to individual and from region to region. Coloration also shows considerable regional variation (red and black in the Kalahari, tan in E Africa, golden brown in W Africa) and also individual variation, especially in the korkay from Ethiopia (*A. b. swaynei*) in which the overall body colour ranges from silvery purplish to red or dark brown and the blotches of black on shoulders and knees vary in shape and extent. The kongoni has preorbital and pedal (hoof) glands.
Subspecies: Bubal, *A. b. buselaphus* (N Africa), extinct 1925; tora, *A. b. tora* (E Sudan and N Ethiopia); korkay, *A. b. swaynei* (Ethiopia); kongoni, *A. b. cokei* (S Kenya and N Tanzania); khama, *A. b. caama* (Cape, Kalahari); kanki, *A. b. major* (W Africa); lelwel, *A. b. lelwel* (L. Chad to L. Turkana); nkonzi, *A. b. lichtensteinii* (central and SE Africa).
 Note: The eight subspecies listed above have been generally recognised since 1894. Among some 50 named forms are many collected from interzones between the ranges of these eight subspecies. Most of these appear to be unstable hybrids rather than graduated intermediate forms, suggesting that former isolation has broken down as two forms, the lelwel and nkonzi, expanded their ranges.
Distribution: Formerly all African grasslands and savannahs (except for a very narrow strip between the R. Juba and R. Tana and the South African Highveld). The short-pedicelled, more conservative subspecies (tora, korkay, kongoni) live in NE Africa. The khama in the Kalahari and kanki in W Africa have high pedicels and are more advanced. The lelwel, with the highest pedicels, appears to have intruded into the former ranges of all its neighbours in each case creating hybrid zones. The nkonzi, of the same stock as the kanki, has also colonised a vast territory wedged between the ranges of the kongoni and khama, apparently hybridising with both (how extensively remains to be determined).
Habitat: Although regional differences are substantial, kongonis are consistent everywhere in being grazers that live on boundaries between open grassy plains or glades and parkland, woodland or scrub (often on shallow slopes). They go to water regularly (but territorial ♂♂ go without for quite long periods). They move down drainage lines for grass and water in the dry season and up onto better drained, thinly grassed woodlands during the rains.
Food: Grazers, selective of neither species nor component parts of the grass. However, certain species are avoided, notably *Cynodon*, a grass that is readily grazed by other herbivores. All studies have shown that broad-leaf foliage accounts for less than 5% of the diet.

Kanki.

Lelwel.

Nkonzi.

Khama.

Behaviour: ♀ kongonis are gregarious and to variable degrees move up and down shallow grassy valleys in pursuit of the best grass. ♂♂ become dispersed along the margins of each drainage line and establish dung-marked territories that embrace all the vegetation types from top to bottom of the slope. Where there is pressure from neighbours, territories may get narrowed but nearly always from the sides and not from above or below. ♂♂ waylay ♀ groups as they pass through their territories. In some areas breeding is compressed into a short period during the rains (May in Uganda) and most ♂♂ only become territorial at this time. In other areas some breeding continues throughout the year and territories are held more or less continuously. ♂♂ mark their territories with dung and posture with the head held upright and the legs placed well back. This is a gesture that suggests ritualised defaecation and may serve to deter neighbouring ♂♂ and attract passing ♀♀. ♂♂ fight most intensely in the presence of oestrous ♀♀ and are especially aggressive towards attendant ♂ offspring. At high densities ♂♂ are sometimes killed in fights. ♀♀ defend their young vigorously and also form temporary all-F hierarchies in which threatening gestures with horns are noticable. A single young is born after an 8-month gestation and growth rates are strongly influenced by nutrition. Sexual maturity is reached in 1 year in some and not until the fourth year in others. Animals live for up to 19 years.

Adaptations: With the exception of the nkonzi, *A. b. lichtensteinii* (which could be regarded as an incipient species) all subspecies have been recorded in very large dense herds at various times (the same was true of the bubal in the 1830s and 1840s in Souf, Algeria).

Tora.

Kongoni.

Populations crash to very low levels during droughts, disease epidemics or under sustained competitive pressure from cattle. However, they recover quite rapidly when conditions improve. This capacity to build up their numbers is fuelled by subsistence on a normally super-abundant resource. They are also socially versatile with ♀♀ finding the best pastures at all density levels and the ♂♂ adjusting the size and distribution of their territories accordingly.

Status: Extinction of the bubal should serve as a warning about the vulnerability of this species. At present the tora, korkay and kanki are all at very low levels. The korkay is now extinct in Somalia where it was once present in vast herds. Apart from being easy to hunt and possessing very tasty meat, this antelope declines wherever there is competition from intensive cattle-keeping. The tora is listed as Endangered (IUCN) and the korkay as Threatened. Other subspecies are Not Endangered at present.

Brindled gnu, or wildebeest *Connochaetes taurinus*

Other names: Fr. *Gnou bleu.* Ger. *Streifengnu.* Swah. *Nyumbu.*
Measurements: HB 170–240cm. T 60–100cm. SH 115–145cm. W 140–260kg. (♀); 165–290kg. (♂).
Recognition: A dumpy, thick-necked, long-faced antelope with horns that flare out sideways and then upwards (rather like a cow's). The flat, rather square nasal plate (with hair-lined, flap-edged nostrils) is bounded by an even broader, grass-nibbling mouth. Dense tufts of hair on the long, convex muzzle conceal very active preorbital glands and help to diffuse scent from them. The muzzle is black in all subspecies, as is the shaggy mane and tail. The body colours of the four or five different subspecies varies from dark grey-brown to slate blue to pale greyish fawn, with variable degrees of brindling. This strongly textured streaking of the neck, shoulders and flanks mimics the visual effect of a long, lank mane very closely. The neck and chin are bearded in long, black, brown, cream or white hair. The short legs are brown or ochre, with pedal glands between the large true hooves (there are prominent false lateral hooves).
Subspecies: Brindled gnu, *C. t. taurinus* (south of the R. Zambezi, Kalahari); Nyassa gnu, *C. t. cooksoni* (Luangwa valley); Mozambique gnu, *C. t. johnstoni* (SE Africa); White-bearded gnu, *C. t. albojubatus* (S Kenya, N Tanzania).
  Note: some authorities subdivide the last subspecies, with the Rift Valley walls west of L. Natron and L. Manyara as a natural barrier between them. If accepted these western white-bearded gnus would be 'Dr Heck's gnu', *C. t. hecki*.
Distribution: Open bushland and grassy plains in relatively dry areas of E, SE and south-central Africa. The gnus' dependence on water limits their extension into drier regions but they persisted on the North African littoral into prehistoric and possibly historic times.
Habitat: Short grasslands (maintained by fire, shade, rainfall, water table, drainage, soil chemistry, herbivore grazing and trampling) always within about 20km of permanent water. Migration permits gnus to rotate pastures where these requirements are seasonal.

♂ Brindled gnu.

Food: A wide variety of nutritious grasses that form short swards. At times brindled gnus may be forced to strip leaves from tall stems but this is a temporary and inefficient expedient. They are unable to graze persistent rank growth, which helps to explain their absence from many areas of equatorial Africa and their inability to survive (as reintroductions) into long-grass areas.

Behaviour: Social grazers that congregate in response to the local distribution of short grass pastures and water. Where these are adequate throughout the year, ♀♀ and their young can remain permanently on home ranges of a few hectares. Other similar ♀ groups may share some of their range without friction but external intruders can be severely harrassed.

Where their food and water dry out, resident gnus tend to move on to more extensive seasonal pastures. Here they join other gnus, soon losing their local identities in the amalgam of herds. These seasonal aggregations are sometimes quite temporary.

Permanent large herds are more continuously nomadic, with ♀♀ joining up to lead mass movement from one major pasture to another. The celebrated Serengeti migration is just such a circuit in which the dry season is spent on the grasslands of the L. Victoria littoral and the rainy season on ashy volcanic plains closer to the Rift Valley. During this annual cycle ♀♀ initiate movement off the open plains as surface water and herbage begins to dry out. Both sexes are in peak condition after several months on the fertile volcanic pastures.

As with kob, topi and many other mammals, enforced collectivisation triggers the hormonal changes in both sexes that are known as the rut. Rutting ♂♂ attempt to exclude each other from access to oestrous ♀♀. Because movement along the route is jerky (the mega-herd moving on after exhausting each pasture), ♂♂ tend to win 'territories' that are simply marked out by their own behaviour. They 'broadcast' sound, scent and eye-catching visual displays in the form of belching grunts and snorts, flurries of scent (transferred from the face to everywhere they can reach) and frantic leaping, cavorting and head-shaking. Such territories can be no more than a fraction of a hectare. Depending on the pace of movement the ♂ can remain in one place for many days or a few hours as herds continue their relentless movement. A scatter of ♂♂ remains in the wake of the herds, exhausting their energies in fruitless posturings and stand-offs with a fast-diminishing audience of other left-over territorial ♂♂.

One calf is born to each ♀ in the following wet season, 8 months later. While some large carnivores can keep up with or waylay the herds, one of the benefits of nomadism is outmarching the predators. Synchronised calving also helps to reduce the toll from predators. Births take place on exposed pastures, almost all in the space of a few weeks and calves born outside this period seldom survive. The newborn begins walking within minutes.

♂ White-tailed gnu.

It is tan at first but acquires the distinctive gnu colouring by stages, beginning within 1 or 2 months of birth. Rates of maturity vary, with ♀♀ becoming fertile by about 16 months. ♂♂ do not normally take up territories until they are 4 or 5 years old. Gnus are known to live for up to 20 years.

Adaptations: Isolated individuals and scattered small groups are seldom found very far from the annual range of a much larger regional population. Attrition is generally quite swift in such vulnerable outliers. Although gnus have stamina and a fast turn of speed, adults can be outrun and killed by at least six major carnivore species. Their calves are vulnerable to many more. Gnus are therefore adapted to living in large, dense herds. As grass ruminants a large part of their body mass is given over to the digestive tract. Since their security depends more in belonging to a herd than in outrunning predators (as kongoni can do) gnus do not need such long legs, heads and necks. This is a special advantage for ♂♂ because they can specialise in becoming efficient fighters and horn-wrestlers with their heavy necks, heads and horns. ♀♀ must also be sufficiently robust in order to defend their offspring from the ♂♂.

Status: Land settlement, livestock, their diseases, fences and easy poaching with modern weapons all represent threats. More than most species it is dependent on deliberate conservation policies for its survival because its year-round requirements of water and pasture must be met and each local population must remain sufficiently numerous to be viable. Each subspecies is well represented in conservation areas and national parks but both protection and land areas are often inadequate. They continue to decline and are unlikely to survive outside such areas. Overall, the brindled gnu is rated as Not Endangered (IUCN) but that status will be tested in future years.

White-tailed gnu (Black wildebeest) *Connochaetes gnou*

Other names: Fr. *Gnou à queue blanche*. Ger. *Weisschwanz Gnu*.
Measurements: HB 170–220cm. T 80–100cm. SH 90–121cm. W 110–160kg (♀); 140–180kg (♂).
Recognition: A stocky, thick-coated antelope with heavily bossed horns that swing down, forward and upwards in tight angular hooks. The long muzzle is very broad, flat-fronted and covered in dense black fur. The flapped nostrils are set above a wide rectangular mouth. The body colour is dark brown, with a black beard and chest tassels. The upright mane hairs are off-white with intensely black tips. The long, flowing tail is wholly white.

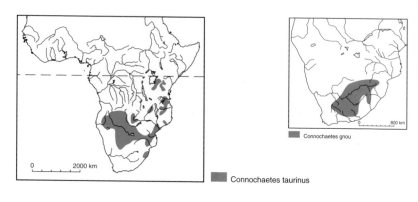

Connochaetes gnou

Connochaetes taurinus

The pelvis is peculiarly prominent. The large hooves of the forelegs have interdigital glands. Preorbital glands are also very active, especially in adult ♂♂ (scenting not only the face but, by transfer, also the body and tail).

Subspecies: None (four obsolete names).

Distribution: Originally migratory over a large part of the Karoo and Highveld. Overall range from the valley of the R. Vaal in the north to the R. Salt in the south, and from the Orange R. valley in the west to the Drakensberg Mts in the east. Now extinct as a wild animal.

Habitat: Temperate grasslands and Karoo shrub lands where it migrated between summer pastures in the Karoo and eastwards to grasslands of the Highveld during the winter. These large-scale movements ceased when European settlement moved into the interior where, by the mid-nineteenth century, this gnu had been brought close to extinction.

Food: Grazes but supplements grasses with succulents and shrubs (such as *Pentzia*, *Salsola*, *Nenax* and *Osteospermum*), which permits grazing of the arid Karoo without regular water. The white-tailed gnu is more continuously active in cool weather but lies up for the heat of the day in summer.

Behaviour: Unknown as a wild animal but some reconstruction has been possible on the basis of studies of small groups on fenced farms or reserves. ♀♀ wander in groups of up to 60 over home ranges of about 100ha. As they pass through ♂ territories they are inspected and the ♂ attempts to deter them from passing on into the territory of his neighbours. This herding is most intense during the period of ♀ oestrus. Because most ♀♀ only mate at the end of the hot wet summer (March–April) it would appear that mating used to coincide with a massed eastward shift towards the Highveld winter pastures. Births over 8 months later (250 days' gestation) would have been on their summer range in the Karoo. In confinement ♀♀ form hierarchies and fight ♀♀ not already known to them. By contrast ♂ bachelor groups generally show few signs of aggression and some animals in the group have been observed to come to the rescue of bullied, bawling subordinates. This species has evolved particularly dangerous horns and with them elaborate appeasement gestures (including prostration). Yearling offspring are generally driven off by their mothers after the birth of a new calf. For the 6–9 months before weaning mother and young remain very closely bonded. Young ♂♂ do not normally take up territories until they are 4 years old, at which time they posture, fight challengers and mark the centre of their ranges with dung and urine in which the ♂ paws and rolls. The thick coat is well suited to hold this scent (and that from the preorbital glands) and rutting ♂♂ have a pervasive rank odour. They are also very vocal with a metallic snort, a two part 'ge-nu' (hence the Khoi name) and a very resonant, single 'hick' which is uttered with a violent spasm of the head and neck.

Adaptations: The front-facing horns are extremely dangerous when hooked forwards and upwards from below. The gnu's kneeling position while fighting greatly mitigates this danger with hefty bosses on the top of the head serve both as shields and battering rams during ritualised fights between rivals. However, in any normal frontal encounters with their environment (including other gnus) close contact is debarred not by spikes but by the rounded midshafts of the sharply angled horns. This barrier protects the muzzle and especially the preorbital glands from all such direct contacts. As a consequence these gnus are unusual in hardly ever rubbing one another face to face, nor do they normally rub their face glands on the ground or vegetation. Instead liquid secretion flows along hair tracts down into the beard and up into the bizarre tuft of long hair on the muzzle (found in both sexes). Beard and tuft therefore act as scent-dispensers as well as 'enlargers', extending, together with the mane and haired chest, the silhouette of the forequarters. In the intensely competitive context of migrating, mating herds, such characteristics would appear to have magnified the impression of physical power (further enhanced by dark colour which emphasises mass). Their cavorting, head-tossing and kicking would appear to exaggerate the energetics of movement while their amplified voices and behaviour such as rolling and pawing augment the social signals transmitted by strong scent. Their arched crests and long white tails served to make their large repertoire of displays highly conspicuous.

Status: Private initiatives in the face of reluctant, indifferent or hostile policies have saved many species from extinction in South Africa, of which the white-tailed gnu is one. Even now many small farms are replacing livestock with indigenous herbivores. Vested interests in pastoral agriculture will probably not allow gnus sufficient space to begin behaving as wild animals again. Nevertheless, from a nadir estimated as low as 300 to 600 animals, present populations have risen to about 10,000 (however, inbreeding presents some problems). Currently rated as Rare, but Not Endangered.

HORSE-LIKE ANTELOPES HIPPOTRAGINI

Roan and sable antelopes	*Hippotragus*
Oryxes	*Oryx*
Addax	*Addax nasomaculatus*

Recognition: Large, barrel-bodied antelopes with long, slender and well-annulated horns, long ears and broad, heavy hooves (with well-developed pedal glands). False hooves are particularly well developed in the oryxes and addax. The coat is sleek, in various shades of tan, white and black, and the face is striped rather like a goat or gazelle. The thick, tapering necks and mane earned these antelopes their Latin name, Hippotragini, which means 'horse-goat'. Sexes are similar but ♂♂ are heavier and have thicker horns. Some species have vestigial preorbital glands.

Genealogy: Horse-like antelopes share a common ancestry with goats or gazelles. Like them they are arid adapted and represent an early, grass-eating 'giant' branch. By 4 or 5 million years ago oryxes (in more or less modern form) were already abundant in N Africa. The fact that no other bovid has been able to challenge them for the larger-scale desert niche implies that they have had a long head-start in adapting to heat, drought and unpredictable desert pastures. The roan and sable antelopes occupy isolated positions in the spectrum of tropical antelopes and the teeth of fossils confirm their common origins with oryxes, suggesting that they moved south from drier, more northern habitats.

Geography: Although now exclusively African there are fossils from India and Europe which suggest that the ancestral lineage of these antelopes was once more widespread and might have penetrated tropical Africa from a Eurasian source.

Ecology: All species are grazers with molar teeth well suited to grinding hard grasses (roan antelopes possess particularly broad teeth). They have specialised in exploiting zones with an impoverished fauna and flora. Their narrowed choice (even within the tropics) is due to their attachment to particular localities in which they build up intimate knowledge of large home ranges (which may include systematic avoidance of areas with numerous predators and competitors).

Natural history: Anatomy, ecological dispersal patterns, modes of communication and social structures have probably been influenced by an ancestral 'desert ordeal.' Young animals are exceptionally social and active. They spend much of their time playing or rushing around, with stylised gaits, horning objects or mock-fighting.

Adaptations: Horse-like antelopes are unusual in that the ♀♀ have horns as long as those of the ♂♂. ♀ social units tend to have closed membership. Horns provide them with the means of excluding outsiders from scarce resources and resisting any attempt by ♂♂ to limit their movement or threaten their offspring.

Roan antelope.

Sable antelope.

Roan antelope *Hippotragus equinus*

Other names: Fr. *Rouanne, Hippotrague.* Ger. *Pferdeantilope.* Swah. *Korongo.*
Measurements: HB 190–240cm. T 37–48cm. H 126–145cm. W 223–280kg (♀); 242–300kg. (♂).
Recognition: A tall, powerful antelope with a thick neck, robust muzzle, long, droop-tipped ears, and massive, arched horns (50–100cm in ♂♂). The hooves are large (with pungent interdigital glands) and the false hooves are prominent. The coat is very coarse, becoming shaggy on the throat; hairs on the upright mane are dark tipped. The face pattern varies individually but also regionally (the dark markings are more extensive in the north, the light ones in the south). Body colour is also subject to both individual and regional variation (from greyish in the south, more tawny in the north, to reddish in the moister parts of its range). Tail lashes, earflips and the penis of the ♂ are all made more conspicuous by dark tips.
Subspecies: Two main populations (provisional subdivision below):
  Northern savannahs: *H. equinus koba* (Senegal to Nigeria). *H. equinus bakeri* (Chad to Ethiopia): reddish in south, i.e. *sharicus* type.
  Southern savannahs: *H. equinus equinus* (S Africa), *H. equinus langheldi* (E Africa), *H. equinus cottoni* (central Africa).
Distribution: Formerly very widespread in northern savannahs and woodlands and in the more westerly parts of the southern savannahs. Largely absent from the eastern seaboard and its hinterland. They range from Sahelian steppe (but only within reach of water) and flat floodplains through various woodland and savannah types to montane and plateau grasslands up to 2,400m.
Habitat: Roan habitats are definable less by the exact composition of plants than by the scarcity of other herbivores. Even within very diverse communities of herbivores, roan prefer localities in which there are few competitors and carnivores. In many areas they have distinct wet- and dry-season ranges, dispersing in the former and concentrating in the latter. Areas of a few square kilometres are grazed intensively for weeks or even months but overall ranges in South Africa have been estimated at 60–120km². In Tanzania a herd of 14 animals was seen to inhabit an area of 12km² over a period of 17 years. Roan prefer thinly treed grasslands, park-like savannahs and mosaics where there are clumps of trees or woodland margins in which shade and quiet resting places can easily be found. Although predators might be an ultimate factor detering roan from certain areas, they are not entirely passive and have been seen to face-off and threaten approaching lions on a number of occasions.
Food: Grazers of medium to short grasses belonging to dominant species, such as red oat grass (*Themeda*), thatch grass (*Hyparrhenia*) and couch grass (*Digitaria*). Roan occasionally browse shrubs or herbs and pick up *Acacia* pods in the dry season. They drink regularly.

Hippotragus equinus

Hippotragus niger

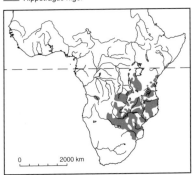

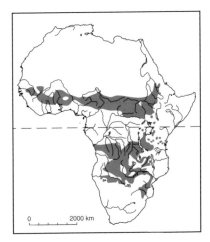

0   2000 km

Behaviour: Herds totalling 5–35 animals (average about 10) are made up of ♀♀ and their young attended by a single adult ♂ who excludes other ♂♂. Such groups circulate through a well-known and mainly exclusive home range but may converge temporarily on a pasture which is shared with other roan while grazing. Such aggregations are rare and both individuals within herds and separate herds maintain a distance between one another. When adult ♂♂ meet they strut in 'proud' lateral circuits before bounding forward, dropping on their knees as they clash their horns violently together. Submission is signalled by lowered head, concealed tail and mute, open mouth. Extreme submission may lead to crouching flat on the ground. Young animals within a herd associate very closely (and are sometimes left on their own).

Breeding takes place throughout the year but births are rare in the dry season. The gestation period is about 280 days. Births take place in seclusion and the mother returns to the herd within a week. Once the young can keep up it also emerges from hiding and joins the herd. Young roan are a focus of attention and attraction not only from the mother but also from all other immature animals. Suckling lasts 4–6 months. Sexual maturity is reached by 2 years in ♀♀ while ♂♂ are expelled from their maternal group at about 3 years, spending the next 3 years in a peripheral 'bachelor' group (of up to ten young ♂♂) before winning an apparently permanent or semi-permanent association with a ♀ herd. Roan are known to live for up to 17 years.

Adaptations: The roan derives from a giant species that is widespread in E and S African fossil deposits. Although latterly both existed contemporaneously, the giant form has a longer history (going back at least 2 million years). The roan's behaviour and ecological niche (e.g. a slow gait of less than 60 kph, water dependence and occupation of extensive home ranges) may be conservative characteristics appropriate to very large antelopes.

Status: In spite of their very extensive distribution roan have seen a substantial contraction in range and numbers during this century. The main threat has come from an expanding livestock economy. Their close attachment to localities and routines is linked with a very poor ability to colonise or recolonise. Their absence down the eastern littoral could be due to past depredations of disease and/or large human populations (before historic records). Although roan are close to extinction in Mauritania, Niger, Uganda and Kenya, their overall status is Not Endangered (IUCN).

Sable antelope *Hippotragus niger*

Other names: Fr. *Hippotrague noir*. Ger. *Rappervantilope*. Swah. *Mbarapi, Palahala*.
Measurements: HB 190–255cm. T 40–75cm. SH 117–143cm. W 190–230kg (♀); 200–270kg (♂).
Recognition: A large, strongly built antelope with a thick neck, long, narrow muzzle, pointed ears, vestigial face glands, large, compact hooves and a longish, tufted tail. The

sable antelope is celebrated for its magnificent, arched horns, which commonly exceed 1m in length and reach over 160cm in the Angolan giant sable. The upright mane reaches to behind the shoulders. The coat is short and glossy in the tropics but grows longer in the south (and during the winter in captivity). Infants are dun-coloured and almost without markings. Older juveniles and young adults are rich russet, with white-striped muzzle and ears, belly and inner surfaces of the hindlegs. As ♂♂ mature black tints on the face, flanks and shoulders begin to suffuse the red until, by 5 years (but for the white face pattern and underparts), they are black. ♀♀ of the southern most population also turn black. In other populations ♀♀ blacken more slowly and less completely.

Subspecies: Black sable, *H. n. niger* (south of the R. Zambezi); common sable, *H. n. kirkii* (R. Zambezi to R. Galana); giant sable, *H. n. variani* (Angolan isolate).

Note: The isolated Kenya coastal population (with somewhat smaller horns) is recognised by some authorities as the 'Shimba sable, *H. n. roosevelti*'.

Distribution: Scattered through the central and eastern parts of the Miombo (*Brachystegia*) woodlands, with two isolated populations in Angola and Kenya.

Habitat: Miombo (*Brachystegia*) woodland. In fact they are not wholly confined to the woods, living there from about October–May and shifting out as these well-drained and seasonally burnt woodlands begin to dry out. They gather closer to permanent water, in valley-bottom grasslands, or mbugas, for the dry season. Here they have firm ground under foot and can exploit seasonal grassy mosaics (many created by local fires) but still remain close to the woodland-grassland edges. Such shifts may involve a few kilometres in richer more dissected landscapes or a wholesale seasonal shift in more impoverished ones. Estimates of the extent of home ranges exceed 300km^2 in the latter situation and only 10–25km^2 in the former.

Food: New grass growth or grasses of medium height belonging to locally dominant types are preferred. Well before the rains begin sable antelopes leave the valley bottoms (like horses they avoid deep mud if they can) and greatly increase the normally small proportion of woody foliage in their diet. Arrival of the rains and regrowth of the thin woodland grasses follow the temporary flush of leaves. This is a time of maximum dispersal in which small groups constantly rotate their pastures.

Behaviour: ♀♀ form regional 'clans' of less than 100 animals which readily divide up into subgroups of unstable membership. The fission of these subgroups (about 10–30 animals) may range from a few hours up to a month or more. Longer periods apart eventually lead to the formation of separate clans. In spite of overlaps in their home ranges ♀♀ from different clans are hostile to one another when they meet. Adult ♂♂ sometimes follow these herds during their movements (a pattern typical of roan and oryx) but the majority disperse themselves over the available pastures and control territories with boundaries that tend to coincide with rivers, forest margins, banks (or even roads). Here the ♂ makes very vigorous attempts to detain any herd that passes through, persistently and very fiercely driving them back towards the centre of his territory. During the period they are kept there all adult ♀♀ are inspected and oestrous ♀♀ are mounted. Copulation is achieved in a matter of seconds, with a sudden bipedal lunge after long-drawn-out preliminaries, including much chasing, testing, nudging and kicking. Breeding peaks occur but seem to have more to do with poorly understood social dynamics than with seasons. Gestation lasts 240–280 days. The sandy-coloured calf stays concealed for some 3 weeks and then joins the other youngsters in the mother's group. It only seeks out its mother for milk but will call her with a high, piping call when lost. ♂♂ are driven out into 'bachelor' groups at about 3 years, joining 2–20 other young ♂♂. ♀♀ usually have their first calf after they reach 3 years old. Sable are known to live for 17 years.

Adaptations: Sable are secondarily territorial. One indication of their nomadic, open-country origins is the ♂♂'s reliance on visual self-advertisement. Unlike other woodland and forest antelopes scent-marks are strictly subordinate to the ♂ sable's posturings and direct herding of the ♀♀. Black colouring is both the mark of super-seniority in the colour-coded hierarchy of the ♀ herd and also the central beacon of a defended territory. Battered bushes, dung piles and foot-scrapes in the centre of a 3 or 4km^2 territory may help deter other ♂♂ but it is the imposition of ♂ physical presence that dominates both hierarchy and territory.

Status: The giant sable is rated as Vulnerable. The Shimba population is rated Endangered and in South Africa it is rated Rare (IUCN). Elsewhere expansion of the livestock industry is forcing sable into steep decline but they are not endangered (yet).

Scimitar-horned oryx *Oryx dammah*

Other names: Fr. *Oryx algazelle*. Ger. *Sabelantilope*.
Measurements: HB 190–220cm. T 45–60cm. SH 110–125cm. W 135–140kg.
Recognition: A large, rotund antelope with a deep chest and relatively short, sturdy legs with broad hooves and prominent false-hooves. The face is long with medium-sized ears and, unlike other oryx, it has vestigial preorbital glands. Its horns are very long, slender and arched (100–115cm), with many fine annulations. The tail is long and bushy. The vestiges of a structured pattern show up as pale apricot-brown tints on a predominantly white animal. Faint facial stripes run down the nose, cheeks and 'through' the eyes. The flanks and rump are also faintly striped or tinted while neck and shoulders look as though they are deeply stained.
Distribution: Formerly from Morocco to Egypt and from Mauritania to Sudan along the interface between true desert and less arid Sahelian or Mediterranean habitats under an annual rainfall of between 75 and 150mm. Having originally ranged over more than 4 million km^2 it is now almost extinct.
Habitat: Semi-desert grasslands of the Sahel and their N Saharan equivalent. *Acacia*, *Commiphora* and heglig (*Balanites*) growing in moisture-retaining troughs between dunes and outcroppings provided some woody cover and thin shade but it was flushes of grass that drew the nomadic oryxes back and forth across unknown distances. How far they travelled in order to take advantage of desert flushes was indicated by a single aggregation of 10,000 animals seen in Chad in 1936. An authoritative estimate of typical density suggests one oryx for every 40km^2 of desert habitat. At such a density the reservoir for this gathering was 400,000km^2, with the most distant animals coming in from about 300km away. This suggests that the potential range of an oryx group under every extremity might be in the order of 100,000km^2. The implications for their ability to orient as well as their stamina in a waterless desert are obvious.
Food: Mostly grasses but herbs, shrubs, pods and fruits have been reported.
Behaviour: The scimitar-horned oryx is nearly always seen in herds of ten or more and it is capable of aggregating and dispersing in response to its very ephemeral pastures. Its reluctance to remain solitary was evident in the observed attachment of old ♂♂ to parties of Dama gazelles. While known to be opportunistic breeders the oryxes were reported to have extended birth peaks around March and October. With a gestation of 242–256 days matings would have peaked at the end of winter and during the first rains. Birthing mothers seek a brief seclusion but both mother and baby rejoin the group within hours (some indication of the imperative to keep mobile at all times). Captive animals have lived for 17 years.
Adaptations: The almost white colouring of the scimitar-horned oryx is highly visible from a great distance. If its behaviour resembles that of the even whiter Arabian oryx, then this colouring can be assumed to have helped 'lost' individuals to regain contact with the group. By standing on the top of a dune an individual would be able to see and be seen by other oryxes from a long way off.
Status: One aspect in the decline of this species is the fact that it presents an easy standing target. However, given that the N Saharan populations became extinct hundreds of years ago, it seems likely that its decline has mainly ecological causes. The most obvious is disruption and competition from expanding populations of domestic stock. It is now thought to be extinct in all Saharan nations except Chad but has been reintroduced to a fenced park in Tunisia. Conservation remains a low priority for all other Saharan nations. This species is rated as Gravely Endangered (IUCN).

Beisa oryx *Oryx beisa*

Other names: Fr. *Oryx beisa*. Ger. *Beisa spiessbock*. Swah. *Choroa, Bara bara*.
Measurements: HB 153–170cm. T 45–50cm. SH 110–120cm. W 116–188kg (♀); 167–209kg (♂).
Recognition: A large, compact, muscular antelope with a thick neck, long face, long straight horns and distinctively shaped and patterned ears. The longish tail terminates in a black brush. Strong but slender legs terminate in large, very black hooves (and false hooves that are given extra visual emphasis by emerging from black tufts of hair). The brownish grey coat is demarcated from black and white facial, flank and foreleg patterns. The line of the back-swept straight horns (60–110cm) continues right across the face in the form of a black stripe. There is very little difference between ♂♂ and ♀♀.

Subspecies: Beisa oryx, *O. b. beisa* (north of the R. Tana); fringe-eared oryx, *O. b. callotis* (south of R. Tana).

Distribution: The Horn of Africa from the Red Sea littoral (Haddendowa) to Somalia and south to arid central Tanzania. Their most westerly limit is Jebel Lafon in S Sudan and Karamoja in NE Uganda. Some parts of their range have up to 250mm annual rainfall, more humid than for any other oryx. The southern oryx, or gemsbok, of the Kalahari is a close relative, often classed as the same species.

Habitat: These oryxes inhabit arid grasslands and bushland but avoid tall grass in the rains (and thick bush in the dry season). Both grazing and the condition of the ground underfoot influence seasonal movements. They move out of waterlogged or soft-soiled depressions during the rains up onto higher ground but may return in regular cycles of movement. In the driest parts of their range movement is less regular and large numbers gather or disperse unpredictably. Densities vary greatly, with up to 1.4 per km^2 in the choicest localities. Home ranges of 200–300km^2 have been recorded for ♀♀ and 150–200km^2 for adult ♂♂.

Food: Grasses, but will browse *Acacia* and other shrubs in the absence of grass, especially during the dry season. During droughts they dig out tubers and roots with their hooves for moisture. Where water is available they drink regularly but can do without, having a lower rate of water turnover than a camel.

Behaviour: Mixed herds are formed in which the sexes are sometimes equally balanced in numbers (but usually more ♀♀). Both sexes establish hierarchies, possibly at a 'clan' level in which subunits can join up or disperse in different permutations. The upper limit of such local population units is not known but typical groupings can reach 60 (with aggregations of up to 200 on rare occasions). Groups probably have more or less closed membership and are constantly testing or asserting status with a great variety of subtle gestures and signals. Where herds remain relatively stable there is always a dominant, sexually active ♂ (usually a second-ranker as well) but senior ♀♀ initiate and lead movement. As a class ♂♂ are less permanently attached to a group and are the only animals to remain solitary for any period of time. Of several estimates 265 days appears the most likely gestation period. Breeding is not normally seasonal but occasional crops of synchronised births have been reported. Calves lie up for very variable periods (between 2 and 6 weeks). They join other young to form peer groups and may stay together up to a year. They become fertile by 18–24 months and have survived for 22 years in captivity.

Adaptations: Beisa oryxes indulge in ritualised 'tournaments' the function of which appears to be the testing and reinforcement of rank order. Commonly seen at dawn or during a shower these start with one or more animals running in broad circles. A galloping spurt

Black and white signals flagged during tournament display.

builds up the momentum to permit a long, high-stepping, 'floating' pace in which the neck is bunched, chin raised and the head swung from side to side in rhythm with the pace. The black and white head flashes in time with the high-stepping knees and flying hooves. Because the most frequent and active participants are juvenile or young animals, this performance may be a primary way of learning and exploring social position. It is also possible that there is a spatial dimension and that the runner is learning to 'take a fix' that reinforces its memory of the home range.

Status: This species is known to have declined, especially in its marginal ranges in Sudan, Uganda, Tanzania and most especially in Somalia and Uganda, where its formerly extensive range is reduced to fragments and it is in imminent danger of extinction. Its range is being progressively usurped by livestock. Elsewhere it is in decline but not endangered.

Scimitar-horned oryx.

Beisa oryx.

Southern oryx.

Southern oryx (Gemsbok) *Oryx gazella*

Other names: Fr. *Gemsbok*. Ger. *Südafrikanischer Spiessbock*.
Measurements: HB 180–195cm. T 40–47cm. SH 117–138cm. W 180–225kg (♀); 180–240kg (♂).
Recognition: A large, very thick-necked antelope with long, straight horns (60–120cm) aligned with the muzzle, large, rounded ears and a long, bushy black tail. White muzzle, face stripes, belly and 'stockings' contrast in every instance with bold black markings on the face, flanks, upper legs, midline and rump. Like other oryx, the neck and shoulders are enveloped in exceptionally thick, inelastic and dense skin. This gives adult bulls a rather 'jacketed' appearance.
Subspecies: Nine listed, none valid, but Angolan animals have narrower black markings.
Distribution: A Kalahari desert species that formerly ranged from the Karoo to near Benguela and from the Atlantic littoral to the upper Zambezi valley and W Transvaal. Exterminated from most of its South African range. It lives under an annual rainfall of 50–250mm.
Habitat: Wooded grasslands and *Acacia* bush of the central Kalahari and Karoo shrublands, entering wetter grasslands and bush along the margins of its main range. Its extensive distribution includes areas of very variable fertility and rainfall, with pastures permanent in some places, ephemeral in others. As a result, home ranges vary from about 4 to 400km². ♀ ranges, shared with other travelling companions, are always much larger than those of single ♂♂, which may centre on a particular locality for a long period. Animals are known to follow regular circuits between favourite localities where they may spend many weeks on small pastures. Their presence in such places may be marked by regularly used 'scoops' (for resting or ruminating in), pathways and neat little piles of excreta carefully placed by squatting ♂♂ on bare pans or prominences. Seasonal and regional differences in the quality of their range are reflected in thick fat deposits under the skin and visible changes in their physical condition.

Food: A grazer that will turn to browse or herbs in the absence of grass. It digs up tubers and roots for moisture and, in spite of being able to go without water, will go on long treks in order to find it and will dig deeply in dry riverbeds. ♂♂ will fight for access to water as well as to ♀♀. It regularly visits salt-licks.

Behaviour: Although most ♀ groups are nomadic and many ♂♂ remain attached or in attendance, other, mostly old, ♂♂ become much more sedentary. In Etosha National Park, where year-round grass-growth can support them, a scatter of resident ♂♂ may be less than 1km apart (behaving rather like sable antelopes in taking an interest in passing ♀♀). ♀ groups number up to 50 but occasionally aggregations of 400 or so have been seen. Breeding is not seasonal and one young is born after a 264-day gestation. Hiding places change frequently but newborn young remain concealed for 3–6 weeks. Animals mature at about 2 years and young ♂♂ may remain in their mother's group for at least a year. They live for about 20 years.

Adaptations: An observer with experience of all oryx species has noted that low-level aggressive behaviour is more sustained and continuous in this species than in other oryx populations. Such interactions involve threat displays, horn gestures, butting, circling and parallel-walking as well as outright fighting. Corresponding appeasement gestures are equally common; head-bowing, chin-lifting, head-throwing and bent-leg creeping are all directed at dominant individuals. Its very strong markings may enhance the semaphore of the southern oryx's intense social life.

Status: In spite of great contraction of range, the southern oryx is well represented in major national parks as well as being tolerated in some of the large enclosures that now subdivide its former range. Not Endangered.

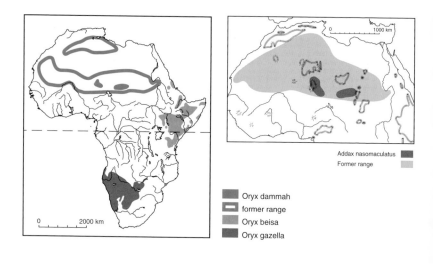

Oryx dammah
former range
Oryx beisa
Oryx gazella

Addax nasomaculatus
Former range

0 2000 km

0 1000 km

Addax *Addax nasomaculatus*

Other names: Fr. *Addax*. Ger. *Mendesantilope*.

Measurements: HB 120–175cm. T 27–35cm. SH 95–115cm. W 60–90kg (♀); 100–135kg (♂).

Recognition: A stocky, almost white antelope with long, annulated horns following loose spirals. The blunt, narrow head has a chocolate-brown tuft on the forehead, a paler brown muzzle and eye patches, a white face mask, narrow ears, and a short brownish fringe of hair down the throat. The broad, spatulate hooves have protruding false hooves and interdigital glands. Sexes differ very little in size and morphology.

Distribution: Formerly from the Atlantic to the Nile in the central Saharan desert; now extinct except for small pockets in Niger and (possibly) Chad. Migrations in pursuit of seasonal flushes once brought addaxes together in herds in excess of 1,000 animals.

Habitat: Sand-dune deserts (*erg*) and, formerly, clay-gravel plains (*reg*) and stony plateaus (*hammada*). The addax is principally active at night and at dawn and dusk, resting up during the heat of the day.

Food: Coarse desert grasses, but with distinct seasonal preferences. *Stipagrostis vulnerans*, *Panicum*, *Tribulus* and drinn (*Aristida pungens*) were known staples. When grasses were absent the addax browsed *Acacia* foliage and leguminous herbs, such as *Indigofera*. It was able to extract moisture from its food plants so effectively that one of the incentives for Saharan nomads to kill the addax was to extract the copious water in its rumen.

Behaviour: Formerly the addax tended to travel in groups of 2–20 animals, sometimes aggregating in larger groups, very occasionally in hordes of many hundreds. Its movements within the Sahara tended to be longitudinal (oryx reputedly made more latitudinal shifts). Groups were usually mixed but ♂♂ would leave small piles of pellets (like oryx) while ♀♀ scattered their dung. Two birth peaks (autumn and late winter) were reported, suggesting that mating took place 8 months earlier during the coldest and hottest months of the year (but in each case at a time when there might have been movement and aggregations). ♀♀ mature at 18 months, ♂♂ before they are 3 years old. Captive specimens have lived for 19 years.

Status: It is some measure of human penetration of the Sahara that this animal has been exterminated from a range of some 8 million km². At about the turn of this century, in Ouargla (the main Algerian city beside the great Eastern Sand Desert), fresh addax meat was sold every week in the market. In less than a century mounted or motorised hunters with modern firearms, together with expanding pastoral agriculture, have almost wiped out a species that has survived the vicissitudes of a desert environment for more than a million years. Endangered in Mali and Chad; extinct elsewhere.

SHEEP AND GOATS CAPRINI

Barbary sheep (Aoudad)	*Ammotragus lervia*
Nubian ibex	*Capra ibex*

Recognition: Mostly medium-sized, thick-legged, compact antelopes with limbs and hooves modified for climbing and leaping over rough or stony ground. Both sexes are horned but ♂♂ have enormous arched or spiral horns. Scent glands are well developed and vary in site from species to species. Both African species have them between their hooves and on the underside of the tail.

Genealogy: As a distinctive Eurasian offshoot of the mainly African antelopes, the caprines may have diverged some 18 million years ago (while still resembling gazelles). In dentition and diet they have mostly remained adaptable and generalised but they have a modified physiology, limbs and social behaviour in order to cope with extreme climates and difficult terrain. Sheep and goats are thought to have split about 6 million years ago (the Barbary sheep is an offshoot from the intermediate sheep/goat stage). By contrast the ibex is an advanced type of goat and a very recent coloniser of Africa.

Geography: Evolving in Eurasia, caprines were restricted by the prior occupation of most richer habitats by deer. Their own exclusion of deer from extreme habitats in mountains may have derived from an early superiority under extremes of temperature and from their agility on broken ground.

Ecology: The N African mountains are a minor extension of the great mountain chains of Eurasia in which goat-antelopes evolved. Here they exploit unstable, seasonally variable pastures in relatively inaccessible terrain.

Natural history: Within their restricted fastnesses caprines are the most successful herbivores. Reaching high densities (especially in Asia) intense competition for mates among ♂♂ has led to the evolution of very large horns in all the more advanced forms. Less specialised, small-horned species live in tropical Asian forests.

Adaptations: While the Barbary sheep shows some sheep-like adaptations, the ibex is a typical goat in relying on the rapid escape of individuals up into rocky hills. True sheep, instead, rely on clumping and fleeing *en masse*. Wild sheep have wider pastures and a dispersed society. Wild goats are more confined and have a condensed, more stable social system. Domestic species derive from non-African populations.

Male.   Female.

Barbary sheep (Aoudad) *Ammotragus lervia*

Other names: Fr. *Mouflon à manchettes*. Ger. *Mähnenschaf*.

Measurements: HB 130–165cm. T 15–25cm. SH 75–90cm (♀); 90–100cm (♂). W 40–55kg. (♀); 100–140kg. (♂).

Recognition: A heavily built, thick, short-legged animal that is intermediate between a sheep and a goat. It has outward-arching horns which are slender and rounded in ♀♀, thick, ridged and much longer in ♂♂ (which have twice the body weight of ♀♀). The face is long and tapered, ears small and the white mouth parts contrast with the pale tawny-brown coat colour. The fleece is woolly in winter, with a harsh texture, but moults to a sleek summer coat. Both sexes have tufts of hair on the upper foreleg and a hanging fringe down the throat but those of the ♂♂ are denser and longer (almost reaching the ground). The short tail, naked below, like a goat's, has scent glands that are especially well developed in the ♂.

Subspecies: *A. l. lervia* (Morocco to Tunisia), *A. l. fasini* (Hamra plateau, Libya), *A. l. ornata* (Egypt east of the Nile), *A. l. sahariensis* (Hoggar-Tassili massif), *A. l. angusi* (NW Mali to Tibesti), *A. l. blainei* (Darfur and Libya-Egypt border region).

Distribution: Sahara massifs and plateaus, originally from central Mauritania to the Hamra plateau in Libya and from the Algeria/Niger border area to Darfur in W Sudan. An isolated population occupied the Red Sea hills in Egypt and was reputed to have once ranged through Sinai.

Habitat: Desert hills and mountains, stony plateaus (*hammada*) and the slopes of valleys (*wadis*) well away from mountains. They avoid the sand deserts (*ergs*), which seem to have acted as barriers between regional populations. They prefer habitats with a choice of shady day time retreats, either caves, rock overhangs or under trees, but at night will graze plains that are at some distance from any cover.

Food: Grass and herbs; also browse shrubs and trees and will even get up onto their hindlegs in order to reach foliage. Barbary sheep prefer to feed at dusk, dawn and during the night. They will drink water but can go without, extracting it from plants that become temporarily moister or are dewed at night.

Behaviour: Barbary sheep form small family parties in which a single adult ♂ attends several ♀♀ and their offspring. These tend to remain scattered but have been reported to gather into larger parties (i.e. 30 members) late in the dry season (July). A rut is thought to take place after the autumn rains (October) and births follow a gestation of 150–165 days. One or two young are born in a secluded site where mother and young lie up for a few days before rejoining their group. ♀♀ mature in about 18 months and captive specimens have been known to live for 24 years.

Adaptations: Magnificent tassels on the forequarters of ♂♂ are part of their intimidatory displays when competing for access to ♀♀. Unlike goats (that occupy relatively small home ranges and know neighbouring ♂♂ well) the more dispersed Barbary sheep must assess less well-known and less frequently seen competitors before risking a clash. In this they resemble sheep more than goats and molecular studies confirm their affinity with sheep, in spite of several goat-like features. They are likely to have entered Africa well after the sheep/goat divergence and are only known from fairly recent fossil deposits.

Status: It has taken centuries of expanding settlement and uncontrolled hunting to eliminate Barbary sheep from most of their N African range. Competition and disturbance from livestock are probably the major causes of decline but hunting (with dogs and rifles) may have tipped the balance in some areas. Their meat has been reported to be a routine commodity on market stalls in Algerian and Moroccan towns and villages for nearly 100 years. In recent times military and oil-field personnel have used helicopters to reach their more remote haunts. The Barbary sheep is now doing well on many ranches and reserves in the southern USA. In Africa it is extinct, endangered or vulnerable over all parts of its former range.

Nubian ibex *Capra ibex*

Other names: Fr. *Bouquetin*. Ger. *Steinbock*.

Measurements: HB 140–170cm. T 15–25cm. SH 65–100cm (♀), 75–110cm (♂). W 50–100kg. (♀), 60–125kg. (♂).

Note: Nubian ibex average 8cm shorter and about 22kg lighter than Walia.

Recognition: A close relative of the domestic goat, the ibex has gone furthest in developing short, muscular limbs and chunky, rubbery hooves. Of all goats, ♂ ibex have developed the longest and most heavily reinforced horns (100–119cm). They have short ears, a beard on the chin and a mane from nape to tail. The tail is short and secretes scent from glands on its lower surface. There are vestigial stripes on the face, flanks and thighs. The underside and inner limbs are white or cream, with white hock and knee patches. The Nubian ibex is various shades of slaty brown. The Walia ibex has greyish sides and haunches below a rich russet neck and back. Its horns tend to have fewer knobs on their forward surfaces and average a few centimetres less in length.

Subspecies: Nubian ibex, *C. i. nubiana* (east of the Nile, formerly from Suez to Massawa); Walia ibex, *C. i. walie* (Simen Mts, Ethiopia).

Distribution: A Eurasian species (or superspecies) with various forms in Europe and the Middle East. The Nubian ibex formerly ranged throughout the more hilly parts of Arabia and found its way down the Red Sea littoral into Africa. The Ethiopian population has become distinct but this is likely to combine a recent 'genetic bottle-neck' or 'founder effect' with local adaptation.

Habitat: Rocky mountains, gorges, outcrops and loose stony screes in areas with a sparse cover of trees, scrub and grass. The Walia ibex has moved into a higher, wetter zone (between 2,500 and 4,500m). Here there were juniper and other montane forests, subalpine grasslands and scrub, a year-round supply of water and bake/freeze contrasts in day/night temperatures.

Food: Grass is grazed but main food plants are herbs, shrubs and trees. Leaves, buds, fruits and, in some cases, bark and flowers are eaten from a wide range of desert and montane plants. A special liking for the foliage of *Cadaba* and *Pluchea* has been noted in the Nubian ibex.

♂ Nubian ibex.

Behaviour: Ibex live in confined ranges of a few km², or less. ♀♀ may be briefly on their own to give birth but normally have a loose association with other well-known ♀♀ sharing the home range. ♀♀ defend their young and fight strange ♀ ibex. ♂♂ lead an independent existence until the rut (between September and November) when dominant ♂♂ seek to exclude all other ♂♂ from oestrous ♀♀. At this time they eat little, fight and chase much, and suffer a marked deterioration in condition. Courtship involves a crouching approach, tongue-flicking, much wagging of the scented tail, urine-squirting onto chest and chin (the main function of the beard being scent-dispensing). The ♂ also hisses, grunts and kicks; the combined impact of a barrage of sounds, scents and touches may both speed up oestrus and improve the ♀'s receptivity. After a gestation of 150–165 days one, occasionally two, kids are born. They remain concealed a few days before joining their mother (also, sometimes, siblings of up to 3 years). Sexually mature at about 1 year; they are thought to live for about 12 years (probably more).

Adaptations: The huge, knobbly, arched horns are designed to batter rivals in fights and to catch and absorb the blows of opponents. Contestants vie for more elevated points from which to leap up and accelerate down onto the defender. These contests begin from standing positions no more than a couple of metres apart but they generate enormous forces and must give each fighter an accurate, if sometimes stunning, measure of his opponent's strength.

Status: Now extinct in Egypt and endangered in Sudan and Ethiopia. Protected in the small Simen National Park but vulnerable both to expanding settlement, livestock and hunting.

	Capra ibex		A.l. angusi
	Ammotragus l. lervia		A.l. fasini
	A.l. blainei		A.l. ornata

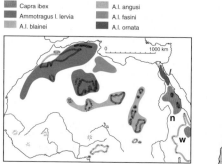

THE AFRICAN ENVIRONMENT

PHYSICAL

Africa is the largest and, in terms of its global position, the least mobile fragment left over from the break-up, between 270 million and 200 million years ago, of the super-continent Gondwanaland. Its other fragments, South America, Australia, India, the Middle East, South-East Asia and Antarctica, are now scattered across the southern hemisphere.

Distribution of rivers and lakes in Africa.

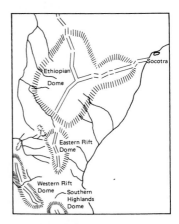

North-east Africa over 10 million years ago showing formation of domes which split open to form rifts, valleys and lakes.

The continent's major aspect is of vast alluvial basins and plains textured by branching streams (see above). Down the eastern side is the great Rift Valley system derived from several phases of uplift, the most recent upheavals being 22 million, 6 million and 2.5 million years ago. The brittle crust bulged up in domes, the largest in Ethiopia being 400km wide. Aligned over thousands of kilometres in a jagged course from north to south the uplifted face has split along its axes to form rift valleys that average about 40km in width. Plateaux have been lifted and associated volcanics have spewed out lava over extensive areas and thrown up volcanoes such as Kilimanjaro, which is 5,895m high. Earlier volcanoes have eroded away and deposited deep sediments. Cycles of erosion and deposition have created dramatic landscapes of mountains, deep valleys and gorges. Recent volcanics and the tipping of land surfaces have changed the direction of rivers and diverted waters from one basin to another. Among the most dramatic and consequential of developments is the filling of the Rift Valley and other basins with lakes. Some of these have been ephemeral. L. Chad in the Sahara has expanded and contracted more than once.

L. Victoria began as a result of the blockage of two large tributaries of the R. Zaïre. Due to uplift in what is now Rwanda and Burundi the waters of these rivers ponded back creating the present very shallow lake about 1 million years ago. All these lakes have been important as barriers to the spread or mixture of mammal populations. In Zaïre a very large lake persisted for several million years until the late Pliocene. Then, cut-back by a small Atlantic river created a new drainage line, emptying the Zaïre basin of its huge lake. This relatively recent event has left a pattern of distribution that makes the R. Zaïre one of the most consistent and major biogeographic boundaries in Africa (in spite of the vegetation north and south of the river being superficially indistinguishable). Overspill from the former L. Zaïre was north of its present drainage. Its most likely course was down the Ogooué valley, which is disproportionately deep and wide for its contemporary catchment area.

Another major biogeographic boundary, along the R. Cross in E Nigeria, may also find its explanation in the re-routing of a major river. The R. Niger is thought, formerly, to have emptied east of its present delta, at the mouth of the R. Cross.

Other geological events may have shaped recent distributions. In the Virunga volcanoes area, major eruptions about 22,000 years ago blocked and deepened L. Kivu. Subsequent eruptions, one as recent as 9,000 years ago, are thought to have depleted fish and reptile fauna and it is possible that release of vast accumulations of methane gas in L. Kivu combined with tremors and eruptions to send a poisoned fireball down over the slopes west of L. Kivu. In any event this area has many unusual anomalies of mammalian distribution which require research and explanation.

In contrast with these areas of recent volcanic activity are rarer old Gondwana surfaces. Here and there blocks of ancient rocks have been thrust up and cut back. Among these are the Saharan massifs, rift-edge mountains between Ruwenzori and L. Malawi and the crystalline mountains of E Tanzania. Chains of ancient mountains run on southwards, reaching over 3,480m in the Drakensberg and ending up in the eroded landscapes of the Karoo and Cape. These undisturbed, geologically ancient landscapes support ancient or conservative mammal types, such as insectivores, golden moles, blesmols and galagos.

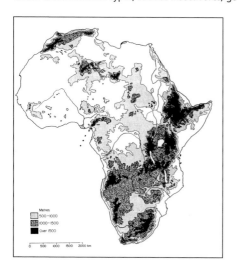

Metres
500–1000
1000–1500
Over 1500

0 500 1000 1500 2000 km

Surface relief

Note separation into distinct north-west, north east, east, south, south-west, Cameroon and Saharan uplands. These represent discrete centres of endemism or refuges for numerous organisms. Some mammals that are adapted to cool or montane conditions have speciated or subspeciated following this pattern.

For other species the separation of river basins and river banks has influenced their distribution and evolution.

Africa's links with Eurasia have pivoted on periods of connection with Arabia. Sometimes the land masses touched at the south end of the Red Sea but mostly it has been in the north at Suez. The land bridges between Morocco and Spain, across the Straits of Gibraltar and between Tunisia and Italy over the Straits of Sicily, might have been more tenuous and appear to have been less influential for mammals.

The most important period of connection, during which there was a significant exchange of fauna and flora, was about 30 million years ago (following many millions of years of isolation). The better-known emigrants were African apes and elephants, while early ungulates, hares, some Eurasian rodents and carnivores were immigrants.

At a more local and contemporary level, altitude, latitude, natural barriers and soils all influence mammals in ways that are touched upon in the profiles of species.

CLIMATE

Africa is a relatively dry continent and its rain derives from evaporation off seas that warm and cool with the seasons. As a result the equatorial belt is the only region that enjoys two wet seasons.

Because cooler conditions bring less evaporation, Africa is dry north of the equator during the northern winter and dry to the south in the southern winter. In the tropics this means 'summer' rains; in the subtropics conditions are more generally hot and dry. The mountains have their own climatic pattern, with marked temperature extremes between day and night, heavy rainfall, especially in the equatorial and tropical belts and generally cooler temperatures overall. The Cape and Mediterranean littorals have a different pattern of dry summers and wet winters.

Excluding the equator, coastal strips and mountains are the main beneficiaries of rain coming in off the Atlantic and Indian Oceans and heavy rains in all tropical uplands create long river systems that often flow across otherwise arid lands. The archetypal river of this sort is the Nile but many less well-known rivers show a similar pattern (in SW Tanzania foreign technocrats are impounding waters in the upper reaches of the Ruaha for rice-growing schemes, thus drying out lower reaches of the river where large populations of mammals are declining as their pastures and water disappear).

Rainfall and Vegetation

Diagram below correlates the duration of humidity (in months) with vegetation zones. A fall exceeding 5cm indicates a humid month.

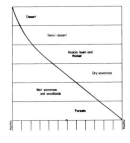

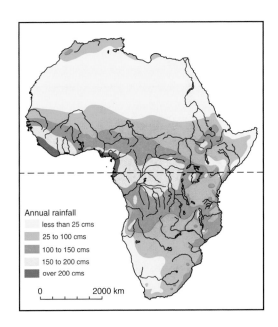

Annual rainfall
less than 25 cms
25 to 100 cms
100 to 150 cms
150 to 200 cms
over 200 cms

0   2000 km

The irregularity of seasons, especially in the subtropics and in the dry belt that runs from NE to SW Africa, often cause floods followed by droughts. In shallow basins, such as the Rukwa depression and L. Chad, massive evaporation and empty feeder-streams cause periodic drying up of these lakes with attendant die-offs of large antelope and hippopotamus populations. Very arid hinterlands often have narrow coastal strips where nocturnal fogs are sufficient to support some vegetation. On the Namibian foreshore, the Somali coast, up the Red Sea and along the Mediterranean and Atlantic coasts these dew thickets or fog-fed grasses support uniquely adapted plant and animal communities that survive on 'islands' bounded by sea on one side and desert on the other (mammal examples are the silver dikdik in Somalia, Grant's golden mole and a hairy-footed gerbil in Namibia).

The Sahara and Somali desert areas are part of a much larger zone, stretching to the Himalayas, where dry air subsides and clouds rarely form. Throughout Africa it is drought that inhibits plant growth not absence of light nor low temperatures. Snow and frost are regular features only on the very highest mountains and at the temperate extremities of Africa. Surface drinking-water is the single most limiting climatic influence for the majority of mammals. Those species that can extract sufficient moisture from their food alone are the classic desert rodents, antelopes and carnivores.

Mountain & Cape vegetation

Lowland forest

Forest mosaics

Moist woodlands &
woodland mosaics

Acacia savannas & Mediterranean

sub-desert, semi-desert,
& dry bushlands

Deserts

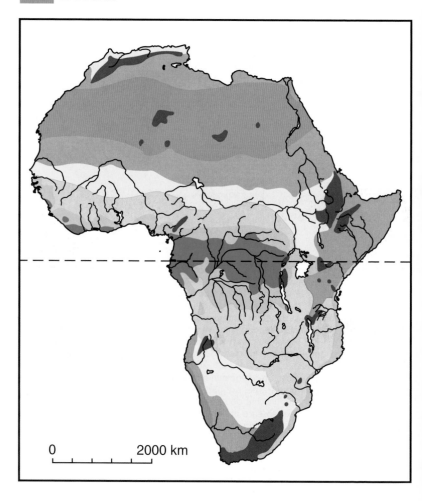

0   2000 km

VEGETATION

African vegetation is dominated by an equatorial belt of rain-fed forest and three principle desert areas: the Sahara, the Horn (Somalia) and SW Africa (Namibia). Between these extremes are moist forest-savannah mosaics, woodlands (dominated by leguminous trees, called Miombo in the south-east and Doka in the north-west), various wooded grasslands or savannahs, often dominated by *Acacia* bush or scrub, and verging on subdesert or semidesert in places. The desert graduates from bare sand dunes (*erg*) and rocky pavements or screes (*hammada*) through various conditions in which ephemeral grasses or herbs, scattered shrubs and small trees modify the desert sufficiently to permit various mammals to survive.

Montane areas also range from nearly bare screes on the top of Mt Kilimanjaro through various Afro-alpine habitats to montane grasslands, moorlands and forests. In the Cape and Karoo there are unique shrublands, moors, grasslands and semi-deserts subject to frequent summer fires and sustained by winter rains. There are few places where these vegetation communities have not been affected by human settlement, felling, frequent fires and large herds of livestock. Nonetheless national parks have often succeeded in maintaining relatively healthy and representative communities of indigenous animals and plants.

The gross vegetation zones listed above break down into subtypes that often define the habitats of particular mammal species. Some major types and categories are:

Diagram of forest profile, showing changes in ground cover.

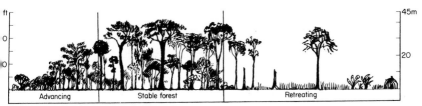

Swamp forest, Phoenix, Marantocloa, Pseudospondias, Elaeis, Mitragyna, Calamus

Montane Forest, Podocarpus, Cyathea, Ocotea, Aningeria.

A. FOREST
1. Lowland rainforests (wetter and drier types)
2. Dry evergreen forests
3. Swamp forests (palms, mangroves, etc.)
4. Montane forests (Afro-montane, Mediterranean, etc.)
5. Mediterranean oak and conifer forests
6. Various mosaics and transitions

452

Woodland, Brachystegia, Terminalia spp.

B. WOODLANDS
1. Miombo (*Brachystegia/Julbernardia* dominant)
2. Sudanian Doka (*Isoberlinia* dominant)
3. Mopane (*Colophospermum* dominant)
4. Various mosaics

Acacia Savanna, Acacia spp.

Thicket, Commiphora, Combretum, Acacia, Teclea, Maba.

Savanna, Combretum, Acacia, Borassus.

C. SAVANNAHS, BUSHLANDS AND THICKETS
1. Various *Acacia* dominant (evergreen to very dry)
2. Bushlands and thickets (often *Commiphora* dominant)
3. Mosaics (from moist to very dry)

Swamp, Pistia, Nymphaea, Phragmites, Papyrus, Miscanthidium, Phoenix.

D. GRASSLANDS AND MARSHES
1. Fire-induced grasslands (*Themeda*, etc.)
2. Valley bottom grasslands (some semi-aquatic)
3. Montane grasslands
4. Various mosaics and secondary types

4m

Alpine zone, Lobelia,Carex,Senecio.

12m

Subalpine or Ericaceous zone, Erica arborea.

18m

Bamboo, Arundinaria.

E. MONTANE AND AFRO-ALPINE
1. High-altitude alpine types
2. Bamboo (plus forest/grassland mosaics)
3. Undifferentiated (from arid to humid)

4m

Semi Desert, Aloe,Calotropis,Sansevieria,Commiphora,Balanites,Euphorbia.

F. SHRUB, SCRUB, MOOR AND SEMI-DESERT
1. Semi-arid shrublands
2. Succulent Karoo types
3. Cape fynbos
4. Desert margins scrub and mosaics

G. DESERTIC
1. Absolute desert
2. Sand deserts (*ergs*)
3. Stone deserts (*hammada*, reg)
4. Sub-deserts (graded or mosaic)
5. Semi-deserts (graded or mosaics)

454

Former Great Lakes, Zaire (centre) & Mega Chad (S. Sahar

"Hot-spots" (dry) in Sahara, NE & SW Africa

"Wet-spots" Equatorial scatter

Mountains & plateaus

N.S. excursions during dry periods

E.W. excursions during wet periods

Possible volcanic catastrophes

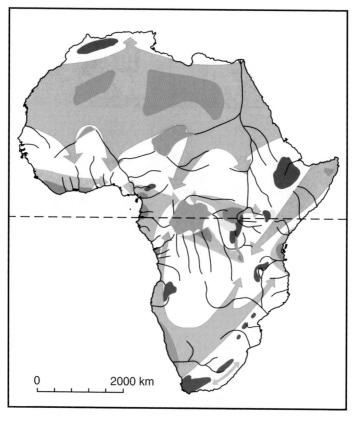

The Dynamics of Change

A more extensive exploration of the dynamics of faura and flora is available in J. Kingdon's 'Island Africa', Princton University Press, 1990.

THE PAST

HABITATS

The broad outlines of modern habitats, deserts, forests and various intermediates, were already well developed many millions of years ago. However, their relative importance has fluctuated widely, following huge swings in global climate that go back more than 15 million years but are best known for the last 1 million years.

Today's extensive rainforests and warm savannahs are exceptional and we live in a period close to the wettest and warmest end of the scale.

The last major spell of cold, dry weather peaked in Africa about 19,000 years ago, coinciding with the last global Ice Age. This was the most recent of more than 20 Ice Ages, each of which brought dry weather to most of Africa.

At such times lowland rainforests would have retreated to especially favoured spots in Liberia, Cameroon, E Zaïre and Tanzania, all close to the equator. The communities of animals and plants that are now restricted to cool, relatively dry belts on African mountains would then have spread over very extensive areas and mammals that are now restricted to temperate or cool areas (like springbuck in S Africa or gelada in Ethiopia) are known from fossils to have once been abundant in tropical areas.

The gross pattern of climatic change is a simple one. Dry habitats have tended to expand or contract from north to south and vice versa. Warm wet periods on the other hand cause forests to pulse on an equatorial east-west axis. The result has been repeated fragmentation of both wet and dry habitats and, with that fragmentation, populations of animals and plants have suffered repeated bouts of isolation. While relatively stable species have simply pulsed with their habitats, many others have made local adaptations and speciated or subspeciated. This mechanism helps to explain the extraordinary diversity of species and subspecies, especially among equatorial mammals. A glance at the distribution patterns of many primates, squirrels and small carnivores suggests that climatic changes must have been very important because many of these species only live in restricted regions, often identifiable as refuges, within much more extensive forests.

Amid all the changes there have been identifiable areas of stable climates. Somalia has always been a hot, dry spot, Namibia a cool one, Cameroon consistently warm and wet, Ethiopia high and dry, and Ruwenzori high and wet. The coast and mountains of equatorial E Africa have always caught rain from the Indian Ocean while Liberia and Cameroon have caught it from the Atlantic. At the centre, the Ruwenzori mountains are moistened from both east and west.

Where major variables meet along consistent boundaries a great variety of biological niches becomes possible. Wet meets dry, high meets low, cold meets warm. Faces of hills, mountains or escarpments tilt towards rain or rain-shadow, towards moist or desiccating winds. Many localised species survive in these narrow zones, which are found on mountain slopes in S and SW, NE, E and central Africa.

These narrow corridors and the stable foci, both wet and dry, are 'centres of endemism' and they give a special interest to areas such as the Cape, the equatorial coasts and mountains, Ethiopia and Somalia as natural 'reserves' for rare and conservative species.

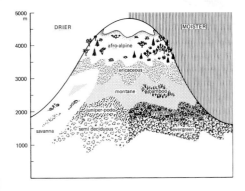

Montane and forest vegetation in relation to altitude and moisture.

SPECIES

The roots of Africa's mammalian diversity must be traced back in time. To illustrate how deep those roots are there is at least one mammal with very ancient antecedents that are known as fossils.

Phenacodus (fossil proto-ungulate).   Aardvark.

The aardvark's basic anatomy, stripped of its specialisations (spade-like claws, massive shoulders and ant-eater's muzzle), closely resembles that of 60-million-year-old proto-ungulate fossils. By about 30 million years ago fossils of aardvarks were different from the living species but were recognisably aardvarks, not proto-ungulates. Although many other 'orders' of mammals derived from proto-ungulates they have been more thoroughly transformed by further specialisation to become rhinoceroses and hippopotamuses, etc. The aardvark, with some justification, can be called a 'living fossil' because, at a general level, it retains features from 60 million years ago and, at a more specific level, from 30 million years ago. Such observations are only made possible with the help of fossils. Dutch settlers in the Cape called the animal 'earth-pig' yet the aardvark is the sole member of a unique family and a unique order. It differs more from any other living animal than the pig does from, say, the giraffe.

By contrast the long-faced, short-necked kongoni antelope, with its bizarre horns, is known to have appeared within the last million years. Fossils not only tell us that the kongoni is a relative new-comer but they reveal that these large, oddly proportioned antelopes derive from much smaller, gazelle-like ancestors and are in an actively speciating phase today.

The recent evolution and graceful ancestry of kongonis could never be inferred from the living animals alone, nor could superficial scanning reveal the unique conservatism and long ancestry of the aardvark. These examples show that fossils constitute an essential data source in reconstructing the diversification of mammals in Africa.

A catalogue of ancient bones remains just that until each extinct animal's place has been found on the tree of mammalian evolution. Kongonis are more numerous and *appear* to have more impact than the aardvark on the landscape but, when it comes to evolutionary trees, their status is very different. Kongonis are represented by tiny, outermost twigs while the aardvark is represented by a long, thin branch that comes straight from the trunk. The tree on page 6 summarises current thinking about relationships between the major groups of mammals.

Mammal groups divide into those that were present in Africa during the Oligocene (some 30 million years ago) and those that crossed more recent land bridges from Eurasia. Among the former are apes and monkeys, bats, insectivores and elephant shrews, miacids (possibly precursors of mongooses) elephants, hyraxes and the aardvark. Among the supposed colonists from Eurasia are hares, squirrels and rat-like rodents, most carnivores and the odd-and even-toed ungulates. Of these, true horses (i.e. zebras) are among the most recent arrivals.

It is surprising to learn that the stock for many groups that now typify African fauna came from Eurasia but it must be remembered that the Oriental region too owes its elephants, some primates (and many more recent immigrants) to Africa. Understanding all these ancient comings and goings depends on the interpretation of fossil data.

In Africa the fossils of countless extinct species await excavation and, doubtless, many surprising finds await discovery. Few students of mammalian biology will escape the fascination of these new discoveries but it is as well to remember that a great many living species, including so-called 'living fossils', are heading for extinction. The rate of extinctions caused by human activities now threatens to take on apocalyptic proportions unless urgent action is taken on a global scale.

CONSERVATION

Zoo-dealers who advertise animals in their catalogues place high prices on every specimen. The species listed in this guide have no price on them but those countries with the richest variety and greatest numbers are, in a real sense, 'biological millionaires'. A quick flick through the maps will reveal that some countries are particularly rich while others, such as Algeria, South Africa and Togo, have already spent much of their biological inheritance. Their large mammal populations have gone, are very small or have become extinct. Distribution maps are like balance sheets in that they show which species have been lost, stolen or mislaid. Those who see today's resources as something we borrow from our descendants would condemn the destroyers of once-flourishing mammal populations as thieves. If we imagine today's disappearing habitats as the subject of future criminal court cases and their destroyers on trial, those in the dock would be the logging companies, their accomplices, commercial bush-meat traders and the livestock industry. However, the real blame lies with world appetites for hardwoods and beef that bear no responsibility for environmental costs so long a such goods remain cheap. Putting curbs on such appetites is one dimension of conservation. Alerting people to what they are losing is another.

Some of yesterday's 'biological millionaires' are today's destitutes. So, are today's 'biological millionaires' in danger of becoming tomorrow's paupers? Take Tanzania, for example. It has Kilimanjaro with its unique alpine environments, as well as an extraordinary spectrum of habitats, ranging from forests and swamps to semi-desert. The country's status as one of the most important conservation regions of the world depends upon formal protection for viable and representative samples of every one of these habitats (this a primary target for all national conservation programmes). One of these unique areas is its only 'Somali-arid' sample, a small reserve called Mkomazi. The livestock interests that are trying to wrest this area away from the nation's conservation estate threaten a vital asset – the range and depth of Tanzania's biological wealth. They seek to impoverish one of the world's most fortunate nations. This is a struggle that is being played out all over Africa and it began early this century when formal conservation began, with reserves and parks for large mammals. Even then it was appreciated that disappearing mammal populations were the first indications of wider ecological collapse.

Since then conservation has passed through many stages. Today there is more respect for and understanding of the ecological and evolutionary processes that govern all life on earth. Environmental bodies seek to maintain biological diversity, monitor quality and study natural processes. Indeed comprehending how the planet's ecosystems work is not just a technical challenge; caring for Nature in the light of its own rules has become an urgent new moral imperative, imposed on us by our own power over global environments. In Africa there is the added dimension that these were the ecological communities that nurtured the entire course of human evolution. The need to know more about our own prehistory and pre-prehistory adds practical self-interest to the many other justifications for conservation in Africa.

Our self interest derives from entirely new insights coming from contemporary science. The language of genes, hidden in our eggs and semen, reveals an unbroken thread of ancestry going back to the beginnings of life on earth. Of that immensely long lineage the mammalian part is relatively small but most of it was spent in Africa. The human part was smaller still but it was wholly shaped in communities of African mammals such as we see today.

Science is not only retrieving our history from fossils and flints, it is re-examining our physiology, our anatomy, our susceptibility to diseases and our behaviour in order to project our past into the future. A picture of the most interesting and complex of all mammals is emerging and there is ever more evidence that the human animal is almost wholly African. Before any of our direct ancestors left Africa we were essentially modern humans. Long before there was agriculture, livestock or industrialisation we possessed qualities we still admire – technical and athletic skills, artistic and musical talents, eloquence, charisma, vivacity and physical beauty.

We became human in a very specific setting — within rich communities of African animals and plants. To destroy those communities is to detach ourselves, irrevocably, from our biological past. To drift, senseless of our origins, is to impoverish science and medicine, to mythologise and trivialise our culture and to diminish us as descendants of countless generations of intelligent African mammals.

There is no other continent where the large mammal communities known to our ancestors can still be seen and studied. Eurasia, the Americas and Australia have been emptied of their large mammals and our collective history of vandalising the earth can only be redeemed by conserving the full spectrum of surviving habitats in our mother continent. In Africa there is still hope for many such ecosystems, if the vision and political will can be found to fend off the rapacity of cattle-men, loggers and land-grabbers before it is too late. Those who founded the great national parks and reserves fought real battles with bureaucracies and vested interests. In every case the heroes were nameable individuals. Today battles must continue to be fought and, although conservation societies have grown in importance, visionary individuals are still crucial.

Anyone seriously interested in conservation in Africa should become an active member of a conservation society (e.g. the Uganda wildlife clubs, the Ethiopian Natural History Society, etc.). It is vital that regional pressure groups have support from both within and outside their countries. There are also international conservation societies, each with its own special interests and emphasis. Among them are organisations trying to regulate the powerful outlaw cowboys and wildcat loggers. Others, among them the largest and most influential, pursue confusing and contradictory policies which should be subject to constant re-appraisal and criticism. More voices are always required to help put across the case for conserving Africa's animals and their habitats. Above all, new ideas are required on how to achieve conservation aims. Among many encouraging initiatives have been community efforts to save the last natural habitats in the Cape, the creation of island sanctuaries in Lake Victoria (and elsewhere) and reintroductions of 'lost' species to vandalised habitats.

Conservation is not simply about saving mammals and nor do arguments from science, history, ethics, aesthetics and ecology provide the only rationales in support of it. The tourist industry in Africa is heavily dependent on large mammals as a major attraction. Tourism has generated many ancillary industries and there is still much scope for investments in conservation, both small and large scale.

The short history of industrial urbanisation in Africa means that national parks have made a late start on cashing in on the recreational needs of citydwellers. The world's first national park was described as a 'pleasuring ground' by its founders, who saw it as a sort of zoo-park. For the majority of the citizens of the first industrial societies, city parks, circuses, zoos and playgrounds served as the main places of recreation and escape from the constraints of city life. This is still true but there is more to our environment than a place in which to play.

The users of an early field guide could read without surprise that the mammals of Africa inhabited a 'unique, giant zoo'. When they are not reduced to trophies, meat and leather, African mammals are still often regarded as zoo specimens, now to be gathered up and their genes stored ahead of ecological collapse. Parks are increasingly manipulated by professional managers and the danger of mammals being domesticated in human minds is perhaps greater than their domestication in man-made enclosures.

We do need samples of nature in all its diversity and, yes, we should conserve future gene banks. We can portray mammals as characters on screens or in books, and certainly national parks should be managed for the delight and distraction of the work-weary but, if we are not prepared to preserve viable natural habitats for their own sakes, to give animals spaces of their own, then, in a real sense, we will have lost sight of our place in this world. Parks in Africa will have failed if they do not encourage people to wonder at the natural order of life on earth and to reflect upon the world beyond civilisation and its physical and mental boundaries, a world beyond grasping human hands where eyes, minds and memories alone can be touched by its eternal mystery and grace.

FURTHER READING

Information on mammals is mostly published in scientific papers. Several of the works mentioned below have extensive bibliographies of such papers which are beyond the scope of this list.

1 GENERAL ACCOUNTS AND LISTS OF MAMMALS

Grzimek, B. (ed) (1972) *Animal Life Encyclopaedia*, Vol. 13, *Mammals*. New York: Von Nostrand Reinhold.
Macdonald, D. W. (ed) (1984.) *The Encyclopaedia of Mammals*. 2 vols. London: George, Allen & Unwin.
Nowak, R. M. & Paradiso, J. L. (eds) (1983) *Walker's Mammals of the World*. 2 vols. Baltimore: Johns Hopkins University Press.
Wilson, D. E., & Reeder, D. M. (1992) *Mammal Species of the World*. Washington: Smithsonian Institution Press.

2 BOOKS ON AFRICAN MAMMALS THAT ARE CONTINENTAL IN SCOPE

Allen, G. M. (1939) *A Checklist of African Mammals*. Boston (Mass.): Museum of Comparative Zoology, Harvard.
Dorst, J. & Dandelot, P. (1970) *A Field Guide to the Larger Mammals of Africa*. London: Collins.
Estes, R. D. & Otte, D. (1990) *The Behaviour Guide to African Mammals*. Berkeley: University of California Press.
Haltenorth, T. & Diller, H. (1980) *A Field Guide to the Mammals of Africa*. London: Collins.
Lydekker, R. (1908) *The Game Animals of Africa*. London: Rowland Ward.
Selous, F. C. (1899) *Great and Small Game of Africa*. London: Rowland Ward.

3 REGIONAL MAMMAL BOOKS

Ansell, W. F. H. (1978) *The Mammals of Zambia*. Chilanga: N.P.W.S.
Ansell, W. F. H. & Dowsett, R. J. (1988) *Mammals of Malawi*. Zennor: Trendrine Press.
Bere, R. M. (1962) *The Wild Mammals of Uganda*. London: Longmans.
Dekeyser, P. L. (1955) *Les Mammifères de L'Afrique Noire Française*. Paris: Inst. Fr. Afr. Noire.
Drake Brockman, R. E. (1910). *The Mammals of Somaliland*. London: Hurst and Blackett.
Happold, D. C. D. (1987) *The Mammals of Nigeria*. Oxford: Clarendon Press.
Hill, J. E. & Carter. T. D. (1941) *The Mammals of Angola*. New York: American Museum of Natural History.
Kingdon, J. S. (1971–1982) *East African Mammals: An Atlas of Evolution in Africa*. 7 parts.London: Academic Press.
Kowalski, K. and Rzebik-Kowalska, B. (1991) *Mammals of Algeria*. Warsaw: Ossolineum.
Malbrant, R., & Maclatchy, A. (1949) *Faune de L'Equateur Africain Français*. Paris: Le Chevalier.
Roberts, A (1951) *The Mammals of South Africa*. Johannesburg: Central News Agency.
Schouteden, H. (1948) *Faune du Congo Belge*. Tervuren: Mus. Roy. Congo Belge.
Setzer, H. W. (1956) *Mammals of the Anglo-Egyptian Sudan*. New York: USA National Museum.
Shortridge, G. C. (1934) *The Mammals of South-West Africa*. London: Heinemann.
Smithers, R. H. N. 1966. *The Mammals of Rhodesia, Zambia and Malawi*. London: Collins.
—— (1971) *The Mammals of Botswana*. Bulawayo: Mus. Mon. Rod.
—— (1983) *The Mammals of the Southern African Subregion*. Pretoria: Pretoria University.
Stuart, C. & Stuart, T. (1988) *Field Guide to the Mammals of Southern Africa*. London: New Holland.

There are many important monographs on individual species, families and orders. Books on evolution that are relevant to an understanding of the importance of mammals (especially African mammals) to humanity and the future of humanity include Charles Darwin's *Origin of Species*; Richard Dawkins's *The Blind Watchmaker* and *River Out of Eden*; Steven Jones's *The Language of the Genes*; Jonathan Kingdon's *Self-Made Man*; Richard Leakey & Roger Lewins' *Origins Reconsidered*; Christopher Stringer's *African Exodus*; Edward Wilson's *The Diversity of Life*.

GLOSSARY

Adult. A physically and reproductively mature individual.

Agouti. Grizzled appearance of the coat resulting from alternating light and dark banding of individual hairs.

Allopatry. Condition in which populations of different species are geographically separated.

Amphibious. Able to live on both land and water.

Anal gland or sac. A gland opening either just inside the anus or on either side of it.

Apocrine glands. Cutaneous scent glands which produce complex and chemically variable secretions.

Aquatic. Applied to animals that live in fresh water. All aquatic mammals move readily on land.

Arboreal. Referring to animals that live in trees.

Arthropod. The largest phylum in the animal kingdom, including insects, spiders, crabs etc.

Artiodactyl. A member of the order Artiodactyla, the even-toed ungulates.

Biome. A major type of ecological community such as savanna or desert.

Biotic community. A naturally occurring group of plants and animals in the same environment.

Bipedal. Two-footed stance or locomotion of four-footed animals.

Bovid. A member of the cow-like artiodactyl family, Bovidae.

Brachydont. Low crowned molars of browsers.

Brindled. Having dark streaks or flecks on a grey or tawny background.

Browser. A herbivore which feeds on shoots and leaves of trees, shrubs and forbs.

Bullae (auditory). Globular, bony capsules housing the middle and inner ear structures. Built onto the underside of the skull.

Callosities. Patches of thickened skin and tissue (as on the hind quarters of monkeys or knees of some ungulates).

Canine teeth. The usually long pointed teeth, one in each quarter of the jaws that are used by animal-eating mammals for killing their prey.

Carnassial teeth. In carnivores, the fourth upper premolar and first lower molar are specialized for shearing meat and sinew.

Carnivore. Any meat-eating organism but also a member of the mammal order Carnivora.

Caudal gland. An enlarged skin gland associated with the root of the tail. (subcaudal: below the root: supracaudal: above the root.)

Cecum. A blind sac situated at the junction of the small and large intestine, in which digestion of cellulose by bacteria occurs.

Cellulose. Main constituent of the cell walls of plants. Very tough and fibrous, and can be digested only by the intestinal flora in mammalian guts.

Cervid. A member of the deer family (Cervidae), of the Artiodactyla.

Chablis. Tree-fall opening in the forest.

Cheek pouches. A pair of deep pouches extending from the cheeks into the neck skin, present in non-colobid monkeys and some rodents and used for the temporary storage of food.

Cheek teeth. The row of premolars and molars used for chewing food.

Class. A taxonomic category – the mammals, Mammalia, are a class.

Colonial. Living together in colonies. Notably bats and rodents.

Concentrate selector. A herbivore which feeds on those plant parts such as shoots and fruits which are rich in nutrients.

Conspecific. A member of the same species.

Convergence. The evolution of similarities between unrelated species occupying similar ecological niches.

Crepuscular. Active in twilight.

Crustaceans. Members of a class within the phylum Arthropoda typified by crayfish, crabs and shrimps.

Cryptic. Concealing, inconspicuous. Usually referring to colouration and markings.

Cud. Partially digested vegetation that ruminant regurgitates, chews, insalivates and swallows again.

Cursorial. Being adapted for running.

Cusp. A prominence on a cheek-tooth (premolars or molar).

Dental formula. A convention for summarizing the dental arrangement whereby the numbers of each type of tooth in each half of the upper and lower jaw are given: the numbers are always presented in the order; incisor (I), canine (C), premolar (P), molar (M). The final figure is the total number of teeth to be found in the skull. A typical example for Carnivora would be 3 / 3. I / I. 4 / 4. 3 / 3 = 44.

Dentition. The arrangement of teeth characteristic of particular species.

Dicot. Short for dicotyledon.

Dicotyledon. A plant with two seed leaves; the subclass of angiosperms containing most higher plants.

Digit. Latin for finger or toe.

Digitigrade. Animals that walk on their digits rather than the whole foot.

Dimorphism. Two forms, typically the morphological differences between males and females (sexual dimorphism).

Dispersal. The movements of animals, often as they reach maturity, away from their previous home range (equivalent to emigration).

Display. Any relatively conspicuous pattern of behaviour that conveys specific information to others, usually to members of the same species: can involve visual and or vocal elements, as in threat, courtship or 'greeting' displays. A behaviour pattern that has been modified (ritualized) by evolution to transmit information by a sender to a receiver.

Diurnal. Referring to species that are primarily day-active.

Dorsal. The back or upper surface (opposite of ventral).

Dung midden. Pile of droppings that accumulate through regular deposits, typically in connection with scent-marking (see also latrine).

Ecological niche. The particular combination of adaptations that fits each species to a place different from that filled by any other species within a community of organisms.

Ecology. The scientific study of the interaction of organisms with their environment including both the physical environment and the other organisms that share it.

Ecosystem. A community of organisms together with the physical environment in which they live.

Emigration. Departure of animal(s) usually at or about the time of reaching adulthood, from the group or place of birth. Also of biogoegraphic exchange between continents or regions.

Endemic. Native plants and animals.

Eocene. Geological epoch 54–38 million years ago.

Epidermis. The outer layer of the skin or surface tissue of a plant.

Equatorial. Geographical region bordering the equator.

Estrogen. Hormone produced by ovaries and responsible for expression of many female characteristics.

Estrus. Behaviour associated with ovulation, being in most mammals the only time when females are sexually receptive ('in heat').

False hooves. Vestigal nails (digits 2 and 5) which persist in many ruminants as paired hooves or bumps on the fetlock.

Family. A taxonomic division subordinate to an order and superior to a genus.

Feral. Living in the wild (of domesticated animals, e.g. cat, dog).

Fetlock. Joint above the hooves.

Folivore. An animal whose diet consists mostly of leaves and other foliage.

Forbs. Herbs other than grass which are abundant in grassland, especially during the rains.

Fossorial. Adapted for digging.

Frugivore. An animal that feeds mainly on fruit.

Gallery forest. Trees and other vegetation lining watercourses, thereby extending forested habitat into more open zones.

Generalist. An animal that is not highly specialized. For example, feeding on a variety of foods which require various foraging techniques.

Genotype. The genetic constitution of an organism, determining all aspects of its appearance, structure and function.

Genus. (plural Genera) A taxonomic division superior to species and subordinate to family.

Gestation. The period of development between conception and birth.

Glands. Specialized glandular areas of the skin.

Grazer. A herbivore which feeds upon grasses.

Guard hairs. The outer coat that overlies the shorter, softer hairs of the underfur (underfur is sparse or absent in many tropical mammals, e.g. most ungulates and primates).

Gumivorous. Feeding on gums (plant exudates).

Harem group. A social group consisting of a single adult male, at least two adult females and immature animals.

Herbivore. An animal whose diet consists of plant food.

Herd. A social group, generally applied to gregarious ungulates.

Heirarchy. As applied to social groups, a usually linear rank order in which members dominate all those of lower rank and are dominated by all individuals of higher rank.

Hindgut fermentation. Process by which breakdown of cellulose occurs in the cecum and large intestine.

Home range. The area occupied by an individual or group (usually determined by points where the individual(s) is seen over a period of time and plotting the perimeter).

Hysodont. High crowned characteristic of the molars of grazing mammals (opposite to brachydont).

Hybrid. The offspring of parents of different species.

Inguinal. Pertaining to the groin.

Insectivore. An animal eating mainly arthropods (insects, spiders).

Interdigital. Between the digits; e.g. the interdigital (hoof) glands of many antelopes.

Intestinal flora. Simple plants (e.g. bacteria) which live in the intestines of mammals. They produce enzymes which break down the cellulose in the leaves and stems of green plants and convert it to digestible sugars.

Invertebrate. Animal which lacks backbone (e.g. insects, spiders, crustaceans).

Juvenile. Stage between infant and adult.

Karroo. Arid part of the interior plateau in temperate southern Africa. Dominated by dwarf shrubs and adjoined by Highveld grassland.

Keratin. Tough fibrous substance of which horns, claws, hooves and nails are composed.

Lactation. The secretion of milk from mammory glands.

Larynx. Dilated region of upper part of windpipe,

containing vocal chords. Vibration of chords produces vocal sounds.

Latrine. A place where animals regularly deposit their excrement.

Liana, liane. A vine climbing woody plants; major constituents of rain forest.

Mandible. The lower jaw.

Maquis. Dense secondary scrub dominated by heathers and strawberry trees (Mediterranean).

Masseter. A powerful muscle, subdivided into parts, joining the lower and upper jaws, used to bring jaws together when chewing.

Melanism. Darkness of colour due to presence of the black pigment melanin.

Metabolism. The chemical processes occurring within an organism, including the production of protein from amino acids, the exchange of gases in respiration and liberation of energy.

Microhabitat. The particular parts of the habitat that are encountered by an individual in the course of its activities.

Midden. A dunghill or latrine for the regular deposition of faeces by mammals.

Migration. Movement, usually seasonal, from one region or climate to another for purposes of feeding or breeding.

Miocene. A geographical epoch 26–7 million years ago.

Montane. Referring to African mountain habitats, including forest, grassland, bamboo zone, moorland etc.

Morphology. Referring to an animal's form and structure.

Mucosa. Mucous membrane; a membrane rich in mucous glands such as the lining of the mouth and nasal passageways.

Mutation. A structural change in a gene which can thus give rise to a new heritable characteristic.

Natural selection. Process whereby the fittest genotypes in a population survive to reproduce; a determinant process in evolution.

Niche. The role of a species within the community, defined in terms of all aspects of its life history from food, competitors and predators to all its resource requirements.

Nocturnal. Active at night-time.

Nomadic. The wondering habit. Among mammals, species that have no clearly defined residence most of the time; distinct from migratory species, which may be resident except when migrating.

Nose-leaf. Characteristically shaped flaps of skin surrounding the nasal passages of nose-leaf bats. Ultrasonic cries are uttered through the nostrils, with the nose leaves serving to direct the echo-locating pulses forward.

Occipital. Pertaining to the occiput at back of head.

Olfaction, olfactory. The olfactory sense is the sense of smell, depending on receptors located in the epithelium, or membrane lining the nasal cavity.

Oligocene. A geological epoch 38–26 million years ago.

Omnivorous. A mixed diet including both animal and vegetable food.

Opportunistic. Referring to animals which capitalize on opportunities to gain food with the least expenditure of energy.

Order. A taxonomic division subordinate to class and superior to family.

Ovulation. The process of shedding mature ova (eggs) from the ovaries where they are produced.

Paleocene. Geological epoch.

Parturition. The process of giving birth.

Perineal glands. Glandular tissue occurring between the anus and genitalia.

Perissodactyl. Odd-toed ungulate.

Pheromone. Secretions whose odours act as chemical messengers in animal communication.

Phylogenetic. (Of classification or relationship) based on the closeness of evolutionary descent.

Phylogeny. A classification or relationship based on the closeness of evolutionary descent. Often portrayed graphically by a branching tree.

Phylum. A taxonomic division comprising a number of classes.

Physiology. Study of the processes which go on in living organisms.

Pinna. The projecting cartilaginous portion of the external ear (especially in bats).

Placenta. Structure that connects the fetus and the mother's womb to ensure a supply of nutrients to the fetus and removal of its waste products.

Pleistocene. Geological epoch 2–0.01 million years ago.

Pliocene. Geological epoch 7–2 million years ago.

Polymorphism. Occurrence of more than one morphological form of individual in a population.

Population. Members of the same species that are within an area at the same time.

Post-partum estrus. Renewed ovulation and mating within days or weeks after giving birth.

Predation. The killing and eating of living animal prey.

Predator. Any animal that subsists mainly by eating live animals, usually vertebrates.

Preorbital. In front of the eye (where a gland occurs in many ungulates).

Presenting. The act of directing the hind-quarters toward another individual, either in a sexual context or as a gesture of appeasement derived from sexual presenting.

Protein. A complex organic compound made of amino acids. Many different kinds of proteins are present in the muscles and tissues of all mammals.

Proximal. Near to the point of attachment or origin.

Quadrupedal. Walking on all fours.

Race. A subspecies.

Radiation. Speciation by a group of related organisms in the process of adapting to different ecological roles.

Rain forest. Tropical and subtropical forest with abundant and year-round rainfall. Typically species rich and diverse.

Range. (Geographical) area over which an organism is distributed.

Rank order. A hierarchial arrangement of the individuals in a group.

Relict. A persistent remnant population.

Resident. Living within a definite, limited home range, as opposed to being migratory or nomadic.

Reticulum. Second chamber of the ruminant artiodactyl stomach.

Rinderpest. A lethal artiodactyl disease.

Ritualization. Evolutionary modification of a behaviour pattern into a display or other signal, through selection for improved communication.

Ritualized. Referring to behaviour that has been transformed through the process of ritualization.

Rodent. A member of the order Rodentia, the largest mammalian order, which includes rats and mice, squirrels, anomalures and porcupines.

Rumen. First chamber of the ruminant artiodactyl stomach. In the rumen the food is liquefied, kneaded by muscular walls and subjected to fermentation by bacteria.

Ruminant. A mammal with a specialized digestive system typified by the behaviour of chewing the cud. Their stomach is modified so that vegetation is stored, regurgitated for further maceration, then broken down by symbiotic bacteria. The process of rumination is an adaptation to digesting the cellulose walls of plant cells.

Rut. Period of concentrated sexual activity, the mating season.

Savannah. Vegetation characteristic of tropical regions with extended wet and dry seasons. Dominated by grasses and scattered (predominantly leguminous) trees. The trees vary in type and density from broad-leafed, deciduous woodland in the wetter savannah to grassland with scattered thorn trees and acacia bush grading into subdesert.

Scent gland. Area of skin packed with specialized cells that secrete complex chemical compounds which communicate.

Sebaceous glands. The commonest type of cutaneous scent glands, consisting of localized concentrations of flask-shaped follicles that produce volatile fatty acids manufactured by symbiotic bacteria.

Sedentary. Pertaining to mammals which occupy relatively small home ranges.

Selection. Any feature of the environment that results in natural selection, through differential survival and reproductive success of individuals of differing genetic types.

Sexual dimorphism. A condition in which males and females of a species differ consistently in form, size and shape.

Sexual selection. Selection of genotypes through competition between members of the same sex (usually males) and mating preferences by members of the opposite sex (usually female).

Sinus. A cavity in bone or tissue.

Solitary. Unsocial, referring to animals that do not live in social groups.

Speciation. The process by which new species arise in evolution. Typically occurs when a single species population is divided by some geographical barrier.

Species. Population(s) of closely related and similar organisms which are capable of interbreeding freely with one another, and cannot or normally do not interbreed with members of other species.

Species-specific. Characters that serve to distinguish a species such as its shape, markings or habits.

Spoor. Footprints.

Subadult. No longer an infant or juvenile but not yet fully adult physically and/or socially.

Subdesert. Regions that receive less rainfall than arid zones, but more than true desert.

Subspecies. Population(s) that has been isolated from other populations of the same species long enough to develop genetic differences sufficiently distinctive to be considered a separate race.

Superspecies. A grouping of closely related species.

Swidden. Rotational agriculture in rain forest.

Symbiotic. A mutually dependent relationship between unrelated organisms that are intimately associated, e.g. the symbiosis between a ruminant and the microorganisms that live in its rumen.

Sympatric. Overlapping geographic distribution; applies to related species that coexist without interbreeding (reverse of allopatric).

Systematics. The classification of organisms in an ordered system based on their supposed or known natural relationships.

Tarsal. Pertaining to the tarsus bones in the ankle, articulating between the tibia and fibia of the leg and the metatarsals of the foot (pes).

Termitary. Termite-hill.

Terrestrial. Living on land.

Territoriality. A system of spacing wherein home ranges do not overlap randomly – that is, the location of one individual's or group's home range influences those of others.

Territory. An area defended from intruders by an individual or group.

Testosterone. A male hormone normally synthesised in the testes and responsible for the expression of many male characteristics.

Thermoregulation. The regulation and maintenance of a constant internal body temperature in mammals.

Thoracic. Pertaining to the thorax or chest.

Tooth-comb. A dental modification in which the incisor teeth form a comb-like structure.

Tropical. The climate, flora and fauna of the geograhic region between 23½ degrees N and S of the equator. The latitudes reached by the sun at its maximum declination known respectively as the Tropics of Cancer and Capricorn.

Tsetse fly. Two-winged blood-sucking flies, which transmit 'sleeping sickness' (trypanosomiasis) to man and domestic livestock. The flies' presence in the woodlands of African south of the Sahara slowed the pace of settlements and thereby preserved habitats for wild animals which have a natural immunity to tsetse-borne diseases.

Undercoat. The soft insulating underfur beneath the longer, coarser guard hairs of the outer coat.

Ungulate. A member of the orders Artiodactyla (even-toed ungulates), Perissodactyla (odd-toed ungulates), Proboscidea (elephants), Hyracoidea (hyraxes), and Tubulidentata (aardvark), all of which have their feet modified as hooves of various types.

Ventral. The underside, lower surface of an animal, opposite to dorsal.

Vertebrate. An animal with a spinal column and skeleton of bone, including amphibians, reptiles, birds and mammals.

Vestigial. A characteristic with little or no contemporary use, but derived from one which was useful and well developed in an ancestral form.

Vibrissae. Stiff, coarse hairs richly supplied with nerves, found especially around the snout and with a sensory (tactile) function.

Vocalization. Calls or sounds produced by the vocal chords of a mammal, and uttered through the mouth. Vocalizations differ with the age and sex of mammals but are usually similar within a species.

Yearling. A young animal between one and two years of age (referring to species that take at least two years to mature).

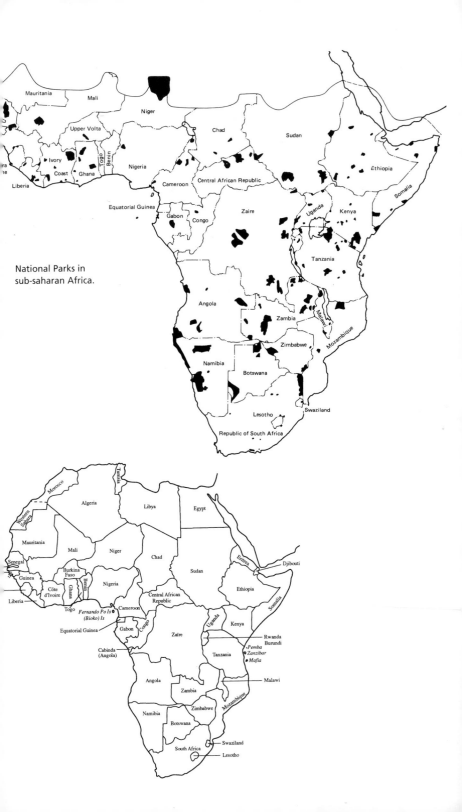

National Parks in
sub-saharan Africa.

ADDENDUM

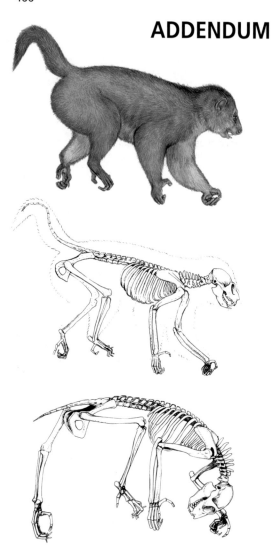

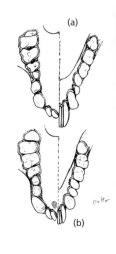

Above, left: reconstruction of Martin's potto.
Middle: skeleton of Martin's potto.
Below: skeleton of common potto.
Above, right: upper and lower tooth rows of
(a) Martin's potto
(b) Common potto.

Martin's Potto *Psuedopotto martini*

Measurements: HB est 27–30cm. T est 8–12cm. W est400–650g.

Recognition: Currently only known from one skeleton and two skulls and some undocumented sightings around Mt. Kupe, Cameroon. The skeleton came from a specimen that died in Zurich Zoo. The skin of this animal was not preserved and the illustration above has been based on a reconstruction of the animals proportions and anatomy, as deduced from the skeleton and the general impression of observers that the animal resembles a long-tailed common potto. Externally this species seems to differ from the potto in its smaller size, less prominent muzzle and relatively long, tapered tail. It is said to be of a darkish, nondescript brown colour. Distinctive proportions in the teeth have been the main justification for creating a new generic name for this species. The cusps of the cheek teeth are more pronounced, with sharper points and blades than those of the common potto. The lower end of the ulna is also less hooked than in the common species so that the wrist might be even more flexible. [In spite of widespread acceptance the validity of both genus and species is still contested on the argument that the specimens are aberrant individuals of the common potto.]

ADDENDUM

Distribution: The Zurich Zoo specimen was labelled 'Equatorial Africa'. The second, subadult skull came from Cameroon and animals supposed to belong to this species have been reported from between 820–940m altitude on Mt Kupe, a locality that until recently sheltered many unique endemic species of animals and plants.

Habitat: Uncertain. If the sightings around Mt. Kupe are indeed of this species, it is possible that it is restricted to montane forests on the Cameroon highlands and, perhaps, to lower lying forests in the immediate vicinity.

Food: Among prosimians, tall sharp-cusped cheek teeth are 'primitive' but also imply an insectivorous diet. The common potto consumes a lot of gum, especially during the dry season, and has broader, blunter molars. It is possible that the larger species' ability to buffer its diet with gum constitutes one of its major competitive advantages over Martins potto and that the latter represents the relict of an early form of potto that is more primitive in its diet.

Behaviour: Unknown but the supposed Mt. Kupe sightings suggest many resemblances with the potto. Normally seen singly, two adults have been sighted together on one occasion. According to C. Wild, the principal observer of the Kupe animals, they tend to climb vertically when disturbed, sometimes fleeing at quite a fast pace, in bursts of action. When travelling on horizontal twigs they tend to carry the tail straight out behind.

Adaptations: Martin's potto has similar but less prominent spines on the back of the neck. This implies that the species may share scenting rituals that also involve stimulating the flow of glandular secretions through friction with the neuchal spines.

Status: If the Kupe area represents the only locality in which this species can be found Martin's potto, in common with many other unique species, can be predicted to become extinct very soon. In recent years all restraints on the exploitation of resources, including timber, have broken down in this locality. However, the total range of this species is unknown and while undoubtedly very rare and critically endangered, little can be done to protect any species in the absence of real knowledge of its biology and in the face of scepticism over its status as a new species. The most immediate priority is to study the ecology and behaviour of living animals in the wild.

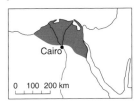

Cairo

0   100 200 km

Short-tailed bandicoot rat *Nesokia indica*

Measurements: HB18.4 (14–21) cm. T 12 (8.8–12.7). W 130–250g.

Recognition: A coarse-coated rat of variable colour, ranging from grey or reddish brown to fawn. Underside paler grey to off-white. Well-clawed feet are short , broad and well clawed. Tail naked. Muzzle short and deep with protruding nostrils

Habitat: An Asiatic species only found in Africa in Egypt and NE Sudan in fallows and cultivated ground in sub-desert and on irrigated land. Lives in deep, self-excavated burrows.

Food: Grain, grass and roots.

Status: A common species, colloquially known as 'Pest Rats'. Originally excluded from this field guide as a presumed human introduction but its presence in late Pleistocene sites show that its invasion of Africa must have been natural and predated agriculture.

ENGLISH NAME INDEX

SCIENTIFIC NAME INDEX

476